THE GEORGETOWN SET

THE
GEORGETOWN SET

FRIENDS AND RIVALS
IN COLD WAR WASHINGTON

GREGG HERKEN

ALFRED A. KNOPF · NEW YORK · 2015

THIS IS A BORZOI BOOK
PUBLISHED BY ALFRED A. KNOPF

Copyright © 2014 by Gregg Herken

www.aaknopf.com

Library of Congress Cataloging-in-Publication Data
Herken, Gregg, [date]
The Georgetown set : friends and rivals in Cold War Washington / by Gregg Herken.
—First edition.
pages cm
Includes bibliographical references and index.
ISBN 978-0-307-27118-1 (hardcover)   ISBN 978-0-385-35304-5 (eBook)
1. Georgetown (Washington, D.C.)—History—20th century.   2. Washington (D.C.)—
History—20th century.   3. Political culture—Washington (D.C.)—History—20th
century.   4. Cold War.   5. Upper class—Washington (D.C.)—History—20th
century.   6. Washington (D.C.)—Social life and customs—20th century.   7. Georgetown
(Washington, D.C.)—Biography.   8. Washington (D.C.)—Biography.   I. Title.
F202.G3H47 2014
975.3—dc23   2013047033

Map illustration by Robert Bull

Front-of-jacket photograph: Joseph and Stewart Alsop © Henri Cartier-Bresson/Magnum Photos
Jacket design by Carol Devine Carson

Manufactured in the United States of America
Published October 31, 2014
Reprinted One Time
Third Printing, January 2015

In memory of

Marguerite M. Herken

1911–2013

The hand that mixes the Georgetown martini

is time and again the hand that

guides the destiny of the Western world.

—HENRY KISSINGER

CONTENTS

PART III

DÉGRINGOLADE

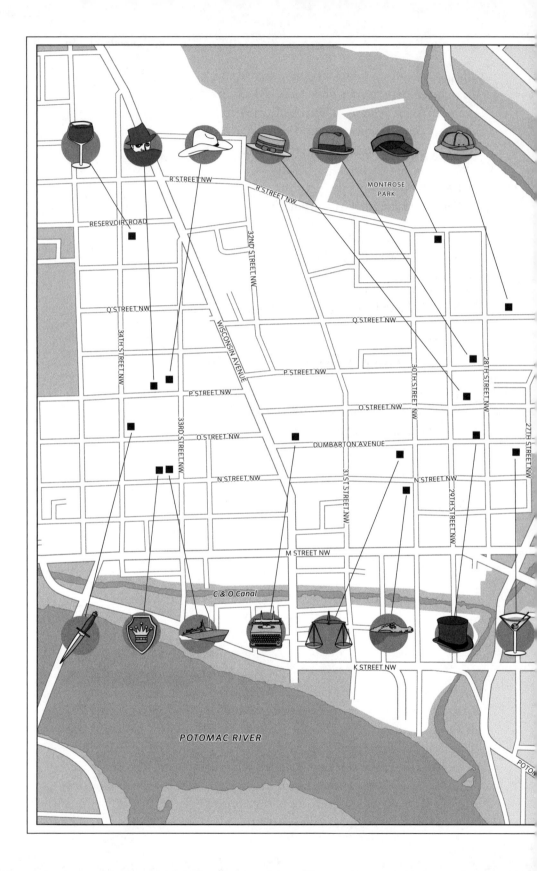

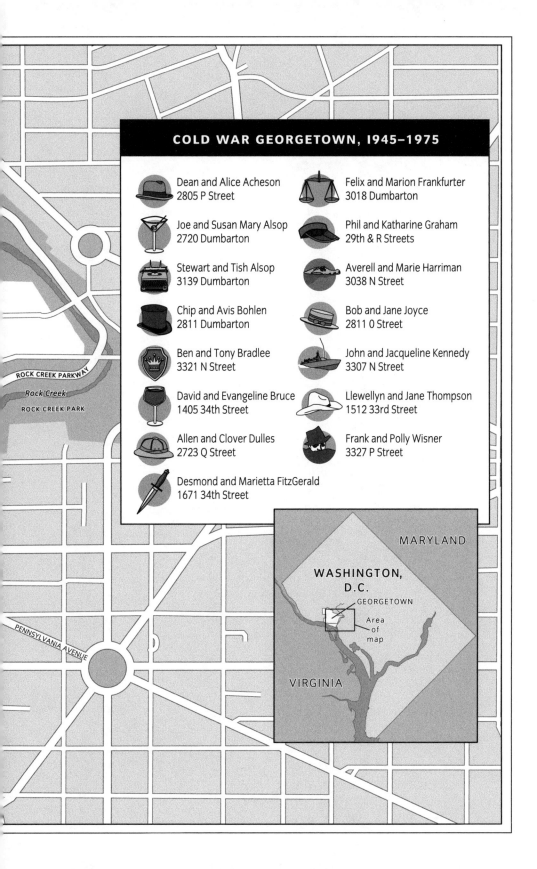

COLD WAR GEORGETOWN, 1945–1975

Dean and Alice Acheson
2805 P Street

Joe and Susan Mary Alsop
2720 Dumbarton

Stewart and Tish Alsop
3139 Dumbarton

Chip and Avis Bohlen
2811 Dumbarton

Ben and Tony Bradlee
3321 N Street

David and Evangeline Bruce
1405 34th Street

Allen and Clover Dulles
2723 Q Street

Desmond and Marietta FitzGerald
1671 34th Street

Felix and Marion Frankfurter
3018 Dumbarton

Phil and Katharine Graham
29th & R Streets

Averell and Marie Harriman
3038 N Street

Bob and Jane Joyce
2811 O Street

John and Jacqueline Kennedy
3307 N Street

Llewellyn and Jane Thompson
1512 33rd Street

Frank and Polly Wisner
3327 P Street

ROCK CREEK PARKWAY

Rock Creek

ROCK CREEK PARK

PENNSYLVANIA AVENUE

MARYLAND

WASHINGTON,
D.C.

GEORGETOWN

Area
of
map

VIRGINIA

THE GEORGETOWN SET

Prologue
"Salonisma": When Washington Worked

ON A SUNDAY EVENING in June 1961, President John F. Kennedy was looking for advice, and some help. Less than two weeks earlier, he had met in Vienna with the leader of the Soviet Union, Nikita Khrushchev. For Kennedy, the meeting had been a disaster. Khrushchev had played up the young president's inexperience and could point to a number of recent setbacks for America in the Cold War. Two months earlier, the Soviet Union had sent the first man into space. Kennedy, at the same time, had had to shoulder the blame for a bloody fiasco—a CIA-sponsored invasion that tried, and failed, to overthrow Fidel Castro, the Kremlin's client in Cuba. More ominously, Khrushchev had warned Kennedy at Vienna that there would soon be a showdown over the future of Berlin, the Western enclave inside Communist East Germany that was a center-piece of the Soviet-American confrontation.

The previous Friday, June 16, the White House had announced that the president would spend the weekend at Glen Ora, the nineteenth-century farmhouse in the Virginia hunt country that Kennedy used as a retreat. The official explanation was that the president needed to recuperate from a strained back. Kennedy's back problems had indeed grown worse in Vienna, but that was not the reason for his absence from Washington. The president had decided that he would not retreat from Berlin. But Kennedy was worried about how Khrushchev would respond to the administration's new hard line—and, even more important, whether a tough stand on Berlin would have the support of the American people.

To help ensure that it would, Kennedy had summoned, in secret, a few of those whose support he judged crucial to the success of his plan.

Charles "Chip" Bohlen was a former U.S. ambassador to the U.S.S.R. who had since become a senior adviser to the State Department on the Russians. Philip Graham was publisher of *The Washington Post,* the capital's most influential newspaper, and had also recently acquired *Newsweek* magazine. Joseph Alsop was one of America's best-known political journalists. Since 1946, Joe and his brother Stewart had written a widely read column, Matter of Fact, that appeared in the *Post* and more than two hundred other newspapers around the country.

Phil Graham and Joe Alsop were also among the president's oldest friends in Washington. During the 1960 Democratic convention, the two had helped persuade Kennedy to pick the Texan Lyndon Johnson as his running mate. Johnson had captured the critical southern vote for Kennedy, in what turned out to be the century's closest presidential election. Along with Joe and Susan Mary Alsop, Phil and his wife, Katharine, were Jack and Jackie's guests at the first private dinner held in the Kennedy White House.

At Glen Ora, the president's guests gathered in the living room while the president, seated in a rocking chair, read portions from the transcript of his tense meeting with Khrushchev. "He read and reread the sections on Berlin," Bohlen remembered. Kennedy ended with the grim prediction that he had made in response to one of Khrushchev's threats as the summit concluded: "It's going to be a cold winter."

Later, during dinner, discussion ranged from Kennedy's options in Berlin to the Russians' likely response. Since Khrushchev's ultimatum requiring the United States to abandon West Berlin might well result in a Soviet-American military confrontation, the topic of nuclear war also came up. The president had been informed of possible casualties resulting from such a conflict shortly after assuming office. Classified studies estimated that more than 200 million people—Americans, Russians, and Chinese—might be killed, with additional millions around the world doomed to a lingering death from radioactive fallout.

Despite that terrifying prospect, all of Kennedy's guests agreed that he was right in rejecting Khrushchev's ultimatum. Joe Alsop was perhaps most vehement in urging the president to stand firm on Berlin.

There was an unspoken element to the near-fanatical enmity that Joe held for the Russians. On a visit to Moscow four years earlier, Alsop had been ensnared and photographed in a homosexual tryst orchestrated by the KGB. Frank Wisner, Joe's friend and neighbor—and the former head of covert operations for the Central Intelligence Agency—had persuaded Alsop to alert the CIA and the FBI to the Moscow incident, thereby drawing the sting from the KGB's blackmail threat. But the threat nonetheless continued to hang over the journalist, and years later the incriminating pictures would mysteriously begin showing up in the mailboxes of Alsop's enemies in Washington.

Phil Graham, too, had become increasingly critical of the Russians: an attitude evident both in his personal views and in the editorial policy of his newspaper. On June 19, the Monday evening after the meeting at Glen Ora, the *Post* publisher met with the two Soviet experts who had advised Kennedy at Vienna, Chip Bohlen and Llewellyn "Tommy" Thompson, America's ambassador to Moscow. Each had told Kennedy that Khrushchev might try to bully him at the summit and had warned the young president against engaging the veteran Communist in a political debate. Both believed that if Kennedy stood up to Khrushchev, the Russian would back down.

Joe Alsop, Frank Wisner, Chip Bohlen, and Tommy Thompson were all Phil Graham's good friends. They were also Graham's neighbors in the exclusive Washington, D.C., enclave of Georgetown, where the men and their wives often gathered on Sunday nights for supper and animated, martini-fueled discussions of world affairs. The meeting on the nineteenth took place at Bohlen's house and went late into the night.

On Tuesday morning, Phil Graham called *Newsweek*'s Washington bureau chief, Ben Bradlee, into his office at the *Post,* along with his newspaper's editors and top reporters. Graham let it be known that he, and his publishing empire, would be on the president's side in the coming showdown with the Russians. "We knew he was actually asking us to write something to promote Kennedy's policies, which was a legitimate news story, but it made us uncomfortable," recalled Chalmers Roberts, the *Post*'s diplomatic correspondent.

Over the next several weeks, a multipart series on the "beleaguered bastion" of Berlin appeared on the paper's front page. Shortly after the former vice president Richard Nixon publicly criticized Kennedy for timidity—"never in American history has a man talked so big and acted so little"—*Newsweek* leaked word that the Pentagon was evacuating U.S. military dependents from West Germany and increasing nuclear readiness. The president himself was suspected of authorizing the leak. The *Post*'s syndicated cartoonist, Herblock, likewise joined in the anti-Khrushchev campaign.

Alsop, too, beat the drum for Kennedy, without ever mentioning the evening spent at Glen Ora. By mid-July, Joe had devoted no fewer than nine columns to Berlin, one of which compared Khrushchev to Hitler; another argued that a successful outcome to the crisis was even worth the risk of nuclear war. Alsop also sent Kennedy a personal note with this assurance: "I'm ready to follow your lead."

Even though tensions ratcheted up again in mid-August, when the East German government erected a wall physically dividing Berlin, with Soviet and American tanks advancing to either side of the barrier, their guns facing muzzle to muzzle, *Post* editorials and the Alsop column never once wavered. As Bohlen and Thompson had predicted, Khrushchev failed to act on his threat to force the United States and its allies out of Berlin. By late fall, the danger had passed. The crisis was over.

On a crisp October evening the following year, Kennedy was once again in the company of the Grahams, the Alsops, and the Bohlens. The occasion was a dinner at Joe and Susan Mary's house to celebrate Chip's new posting as U.S. ambassador to France. Before cocktails were served, Kennedy took Bohlen aside and out along the path that led into the ornate back garden, where they could speak privately. Just that morning the president had learned that the Soviet Union, contrary to assurances, had installed offensive nuclear missiles in Cuba.

Once again, the Georgetown set—the diplomats, pundits, and spies of Washington, D.C.'s exclusive enclave—was destined to play an important role in history.

"What," the president asked Bohlen, "have the Soviets done historically when their backs are to the wall?"

THIRTY-FIVE YEARS before the election of Ronald Reagan—while George H. W. Bush was still a college student—the American strategy that would lead to victory in the Cold War was already taking shape. It was a strategy not only to contain but to defeat our adversary the Soviet Union. It originated in the firm belief—as Secretary of State John Foster Dulles once proclaimed—that if Americans were able and willing to "run the full mile," they would leave the Soviets in the dust: economically, psychologically, and ideologically.

The United States did indeed leave the Soviet Union in the dust. But it was an inordinately long race: eight American presidents and seven Russian leaders would come and go before the outcome was no longer in doubt. In the process, moreover, this country, too, was transformed. Nor was the conflict without its casualties, including some of the very ones who had made the victory possible.

Those who inspired, promoted, and—in some cases—personally executed America's winning Cold War strategy were not generals at the Pentagon but a coterie of affluent, well-educated, and well-connected civilians living in a fashionable Washington, D.C., neighborhood.

Named for the close-knit village of narrow, leaf-strewn cobblestoned streets and tidy redbrick mansions next to the Potomac River, "the Georgetown set," according to the author Robert Merry, was "a group of government officials and journalists who combined brains, ambition, style, and a thoroughly modern view of America's role as world power." The Georgetown set would also be described as "one of the most extraordinary clubs the world has known, a natural aristocracy." Yet Georgetown was as well "a place of public power and deep secrets—personal and state."[1]

The Georgetown set included the husband-and-wife publishers of the most influential newspaper in the capital; a pair of odd-couple brothers who were among the country's premier political pundits; a driven, manic-depressive lawyer in charge of covert operations at the CIA; and two lifelong ideological rivals: a notoriously cranky diplomat and a canny former investment banker who, together, would define the U.S. approach to the Soviet Union followed by every president from Truman to Reagan. In the history of the Cold War, the Georgetown set was not only present at the creation; its members had raised the curtain on the opening scene. And the survivors would play a final role in bringing that curtain down.

Their battles were planned and directed not from the Pentagon's war room or the mahogany-paneled cloisters of Foggy Bottom but from Georgetown's cozy salons, where high policy was sometimes made between cocktails and dinner, in what was both a ritual and an institution in Washington: the Sunday night supper. There was even a word—"salonisma"—coined to describe the power that the Georgetown set wielded in Washington. It was, observed one of the set, "a form of government by invitation."[2]

Those who belonged to the Georgetown set were not only close in years but also, for the most part, close friends. They had gone to the same schools—Groton, Harvard, Yale—had their lives changed by the same war, and, perhaps most important, shared many of the same values. Perhaps foremost among those was the conviction that the United States had the power—and the moral obligation—to oppose tyranny and stand up for the world's underdogs. For it was not geographical proximity but personal and political identity that really defined the Georgetown set. Theirs was a sense of duty that went beyond mere noblesse oblige and held to an unswerving belief in the rightness of the country and its causes—which were, more often than not, their own. Thus, the mock-innocent question that a member of the set posed at one supper—"What are we going to do about the Italian election?"—betrayed not only a frank acknowledgment of power but an unspoken sense of entitlement.

The Georgetown set included not only those who would later be known as "the best and the brightest," "the old boys," "the imperial brotherhood," and "the wise men" but also a woman who became one of the most powerful people in the capital, if not the country. The set was celebrated as the "WASP ascendancy" and derided as the "eastern establishment," and its influence reached into every aspect of the government and helped shape public opinion on the major issues confronting Cold War America.

Yet, for that very reason, the Georgetown set also bears no slight responsibility for the miscalculations and disasters of that era: the danger, profligacy, and waste of a runaway nuclear arms race; reckless and costly clandestine adventures overseas; complacency in the face of political reaction at home; and, not least of all, the protracted debacle of Vietnam.

Like the Cliveden set—British aristocrats identified with England's disastrous appeasement of Hitler—or the Bloomsbury group—the handful of upper-class artists, writers, and intellectuals who dominated London society between the world wars—the Georgetown set left its mark on history. Its members were the iconic representatives of what would be called the American Century—an abridged era that actually lasted a bare thirty years, from the Japanese surrender in World War II to the evacuation of Saigon's U.S. embassy in 1975. And its fate would likewise mirror that of American liberalism in the aftermath of Vietnam.

This is a book about an extraordinary—and extraordinarily colorful—collection of individuals, living at a remarkable time, in a city aptly described as "the capital of the Cold War."[3]

A HISTORY OF Washington, D.C.'s political insiders during the Cold War may seem a curious choice for a native Californian, educated, for the most part, at that state's public schools in the 1950s and 1960s. To be sure, my chosen field of study in graduate school—modern American diplomatic history, at Princeton—had impressed me with the extraordinary influence on U.S. foreign policy of this small, elite coterie of individuals living in the nation's capital. A faded photograph of Princeton grads in the prewar Foreign Service was on prominent display in the graduate student lounge, and I imagined similar photographs adorning the walls of other Ivy League schools. A subsequent summer internship spent on the Soviet internal affairs desk of the Central Intelligence Agency similarly introduced me to the close ties that existed, at the time, between the CIA, the press, and academe. I realized then that a history of the Cold War—a subject I would subsequently teach at several universities—could be told through the lives of those Americans who not only lived through it but had a disproportionate effect on the outcome.

While the tidy mansions of Georgetown still stand, the uniquely influential assemblage of newspaper journalists, diplomats, and spies who inhabited them in the immediate postwar years—the "set"—has long since passed into history, along with the conflict to which they devoted their energies, their careers, and even their lives. For my generation, as for theirs, the Cold War was ever present, usually in the background, but sometimes scarily the focus of our daily concerns. It was difficult to imagine the world without it, or even how it might end—at least peacefully.

Few today long for a return to those days or would claim that those times were necessarily better than the present. Those who feign nostalgia for the Cold War have forgotten duck-and-cover drills, fallout shelters, and McCarthyism. Nor do many (except perhaps some of its modern-day descendants) mourn the passing of the so-called WASP ascendancy—the dominance of white Anglo-Saxon Protestant males in America's social and political life—and its replacement by a kind of rough egalitarianism, in an earnest (if flawed) meritocracy.

But it would be equally false, and wrong, to deny that much has been lost in the transition from that long-ago era in Washington, D.C.—the "coziest capital in the world," as one Georgetown denizen described it—to the hyper-partisan atmosphere of the present day. "Washington," the columnist Meg Greenfield observed, shortly before her death in 1999, "has gradually become more and more a colony of political independent contractors, loners, and freelancers." Indeed, the famed postwar bipartisan consensus of Republicans and Democrats—which, in just three short years, crafted the Marshall Plan, the Truman Doctrine, and the North Atlantic Treaty Organization—seems today a memory not only distant but foreign.[4]

Finally, it would also be shortsighted to ignore the lessons to be learned from that earlier "long, twilight struggle." Thus, the Georgetown set's success in coping with—and ultimately triumphing over—a determined enemy imbued with a fanatical ideology seems a tale with some salience for the present.

But all this would become evident only in retrospect.

Remarkably, the policies and stratagems that ultimately brought down the Soviet Union, and helped bring about the world we live in today, began with a simple invitation to cocktails and dinner.

PART I

THE WASP ASCENDANCY

The WASP ascendancy . . . was a much narrower group. I don't know quite how to define it without sounding a fool, except to say that it really was an ascendancy—in fact an inner group that was recognizable as a group, on the one hand, because its members tended to resemble one another in several ways, frequently knew one another as friends or at least acquaintances, and might even be related to one another by blood.

—JOSEPH WRIGHT ALSOP V

CHAPTER ONE

"A Political Village"

THE WAR WAS OVER, and those who had been away for so long finally began to come home.

A thirty-four-year-old journalist, Joseph Alsop, was one of the first to arrive back in Washington. Joe returned in September 1945 to the small brick town house on Georgetown's Dumbarton Avenue where he had lived before the war. A U.S. Navy lieutenant, Alsop had been in Hong Kong when Pearl Harbor was attacked by the Japanese. Sent to an internment camp, he was repatriated to the States in a June 1942 prisoner exchange. But Alsop had quickly gone back to China, becoming an aide and adviser to General Claire Chennault, commander of the American Volunteer Group—the famed "Flying Tigers." There, Joe had deliberately inserted himself into the labyrinthine complexities of Sino-American affairs. "He was literate, excitable and persuasive with just enough superficial acquaintance with the situation to be opinionated and to appear knowledgeable," the historian Barbara Tuchman, a noted China expert and Alsop critic, later wrote.[1]

Joe had sided with Chennault in the latter's protracted feud with the U.S. Army general Joseph "Vinegar Joe" Stilwell over America's strategy in China. Chennault trusted in air power and in Nationalist Chinese leader Chiang Kai-shek, a U.S. ally, to defeat the Japanese. Stilwell believed Chiang—whom he derisively called "the Peanut"—to be hopelessly corrupt, and planned to beat the enemy in a traditional ground offensive, using Chinese troops bolstered by American lend-lease aid. Alsop's lobbying on behalf of Chennault ultimately played a role in President Franklin D. Roosevelt's 1944 decision to recall Stilwell. Alsop returned from the war in Asia with a strong anti-Communist bias, an enduring belief that it was America's duty to stand up for the underdog, and an impressive collection of Ming dynasty ceramics.

On his way home from China, Alsop had stopped off in Paris to visit his longtime friend and Harvard classmate Bill Patten. Bill's wife, Susan Mary, recalled that Joe's luggage contained "lots of emeralds . . . and rare old Chinese bronzes for the Alsop collection."[2]

The emeralds were for the wife of Joe's younger brother Stewart, who had been kept out of the U.S. Army after Pearl Harbor by asthma and high blood pressure. Stew had instead joined Britain's King's Royal Rifle Corps, transferring in 1944 to America's Office of Strategic Services, where he became a member of the legendary OSS Jedburghs, three-man commando teams who had parachuted into Nazi-occupied France to aid the Resistance. At war's end, he was awarded the Croix de Guerre with Palm by the French government for his work with the partisans. Stewart was preparing for similar Jedburgh missions in Thailand when Japan surrendered.[3]

Uninterested in the prospect of returning to his prewar desk job as an editor at Doubleday after his derring-do with the OSS, Stew had filled out an application for the Foreign Service before deciding to throw in his lot with Joe, as co-author of a syndicated political column for the *New York Herald Tribune*. The man who would be described as "the kinder, gentler Alsop," and "a more human version of his older brother," added a needed perspective and more moderate temperament to the column they dubbed Matter of Fact. Their four-times-a-week column, Stewart boasted, would be "essential reading for those who want, not only the news-behind-the news but the news-before-the news." Both Alsops would also write longer pieces for *The Saturday Evening Post,* with which Joe had a long-standing relationship.[4]

Stewart and his British-born wife, Patricia Hankey—Tish— temporarily moved in with relatives but later bought a house on Dumbarton, just down the block from Joe. The first installment of the brothers' newspaper column would appear on the last day of 1945.[5]

LIKE STEWART ALSOP, the attorney Frank Gardiner Wisner, thirty-six, had spent the war overseas in the OSS and had just as little interest in returning to his prewar job. Enlisting in the navy six months before Pearl Harbor, Wisner had transferred into the country's fledgling intelligence service shortly after fighting began. Stationed first in Egypt, then in Turkey, he later became the OSS station chief in Bucharest, Romania. In 1944, Wisner's official task had been to help rescue downed American fliers. But his "first priority" was keeping tabs on the Soviets in the Romanian capital, as the Red Army pushed the German Wehrmacht out of Eastern Europe.[6]

Wisner's apprehensions about Soviet intentions had grown in step with the Russian advance. The final shock had come in early winter 1945, when Frank watched helplessly as the Russians filled more than two dozen unheated boxcars with thousands of ethnic Germans—men, women, and children—and shipped the families to an uncertain fate as slave laborers in the east. (Like a modern-day Paul Revere, Wisner had driven frantically around the Romanian capital in his jeep, trying to warn the *Volksdeutsche*—but he was too late.) Until then, Wisner wrote in his final OSS report from Bucharest, the Soviets had been "fairly careful to avoid giving the appearance of taking over the country." Frank finished out the war in U.S.-occupied Germany, keeping an eye on the Russians just across the border. With characteristic impatience, Wisner secretly sent three OSS operatives through Soviet lines to recruit new agents for a postwar spy network; the ink had barely dried on the German surrender document when Frank had his first report on life in Russian-occupied Berlin.[7]

Temporarily at a loss as to what to do in a world at peace, Wisner reluctantly went back to his prewar job at the Wall Street law firm of Carter Ledyard in early 1946. But he had recently told his wife, Polly, that he was bored with being an attorney and tired of living in New York City. Wisner had discovered that his time as a wartime spy chief—quartered in the requisitioned thirty-room mansion of a Bucharest beer magnate, with a fleet of captured Mercedes in the courtyard and a young Romanian princess serving as his self-described "hostess"—still held a siren-like appeal. Anticipating a move to Washington in the near future, Frank purchased a three-hundred-acre farm in rural Maryland.[8]

THIRTY-YEAR-OLD Philip Graham returned to a Washington very much changed by the war. The parochial town said to have a reputation for northern charm and southern efficiency had suddenly become the capital of the Free World. A magna cum laude graduate of Harvard Law, class of 1939, Graham had clerked for the Supreme Court justice Felix

Frankfurter following law school. But the brilliant political career that most assumed lay ahead of Phil was first postponed, and then forgotten, after he married his future boss's daughter, Katharine Meyer, in 1940.

As only his wife and close friends at the time knew, Graham's confident and charming demeanor masked a carefully hidden secret. Beginning with his undergraduate years at the University of Florida, Phil had shown signs of the sudden and radical mood swings that would characterize his later life: periods of almost-maniacal and "incandescent" energy alternated with bouts of deep, incapacitating depression.

Shortly before Pearl Harbor, Phil had joined the Office of Emergency Management, which was readying the country for the coming conflict. In 1942, he enlisted in the Army Air Forces as a private, ending the war as a major on the AAF intelligence staff in the Philippines. He had originally signed up with the more prestigious OSS but after two weeks decided that he had had enough of what he called the "white-shoe boys" and requested reassignment to a "bombardment squadron, or similar duties."[9]

By April 1945, Katharine Graham—Kay—had given birth to the couple's second child and moved the family into a new home at Georgetown's Thirty-Third and O Streets. A dozen years earlier, Kay's father, Eugene Meyer, had bought a struggling newspaper, *The Washington Post*, at a bankruptcy sale. Meyer had extracted a promise from Phil that the son-in-law would take over the paper when he returned from the war.[10]

Having previously worked as a reporter on a San Francisco newspaper, Kay gave up her job on the *Washington Post* circulation desk to devote her full time to the children and Phil, who became the new associate publisher of the paper on January 1, 1946. Along with the *Herald Tribune*, the *Post* was one of the major urban dailies subscribing to the syndicate that would publish Matter of Fact. The previous day, in small type at the bottom of the front page, the *Post* had announced, "Joseph Alsop and his brother Stewart begin their new column today on page 9."

For the Alsops, the Wisners, and the Grahams, it was the beginning of a long, tumultuous, and consequential friendship.

JOE ALSOP'S NEIGHBORHOOD, Georgetown, was the oldest part of Washington—originally the site of a peaceful village known as Tahoga to the Nacotchanke Indians, until the British displaced the natives in 1696. With the arrival of white settlers early in the eighteenth century, the locale was dubbed the Rock of Dunbarton by a Scottish soldier who had picked the wrong side in England's civil war and fled to the New World. Incorporated as the city of Georgetown in 1751, it had then been part of Maryland, a British colony. Roughly a square mile in area, bounded by Rock Creek on the east and the Potomac River to the south, Georgetown was a thriving slave-and-tobacco port during the early nineteenth century and the home of freed blacks after the Civil War. Gentrification had begun in the 1930s, when arriving New Dealers were drawn to the relatively affordable houses within walking distance of their jobs in the first Roosevelt administration. That process was still under way when Joe moved to the capital from New York City in the midst of the Great Depression. Alsop's rent was $125 a month, and he claimed to be among the first white people on the block. His neighbors at that time included a funeral parlor, a brothel, two churches, and a senator's former mistress.[11]

In 1933, two years before Joe's arrival in Georgetown, a writer for *Vanity Fair* had described Washington as "a political village which has become a world capital, without becoming a metropolis . . . conspicuously lacking in what might be described as intelligentsia":

> There is a small group composed chiefly of newspaper correspondents, who live in Georgetown and aspire to create a sort of Greenwich Village or synthetic *rive gauche* on the right bank of Rock Creek, but hitherto they have failed to produce anything but malicious gossip and political muckracketeering . . . They scamper around, weighted down with mimeographed hand-outs, burdened with personal friendships, cramped by editorial policies, and they grind out, day by day, year by year, the mass of dull and misleading information, facts and opinions, which has made Washington journalism conspicuous for its irresponsible and stupefying inertia.[12]

The Alsop brothers would be among the reporters to transform both Georgetown and Washington journalism after World War II. But when Joe arrived in the District of Columbia—shortly after Christmas 1935, as the Washington correspondent for the *New York Herald Tribune*—he thought it "a step back into the American past." One hoary old tradition in the nation's capital was the formal dinner party. In a city where the sole industry was politics, and where elections made impermanence a fact of life, there was a long-established tradition of entertaining at table. For elected officials, dinner was an occasion for enlisting and cultivating political allies; for journalists like Joe Alsop, it would become a necessary part of reporting, an opportunity to find out what was really going on in town. (Joe simply ignored the proffered advice of a rival reporter, the *New York Times*'s Arthur Krock: "You know, Alsop, the first thing you have to realize is that in Washington newspapermen have no place at the table.") As Joe's brother Stewart would later observe, "For most denizens of Political Washington dining out is part of the job."[13]

The twenty-five-year-old Joe's initial encounter with what he called "Dining-Out Washington" had been a narrow brush with disaster. Unfamiliar with the custom of dropping off a calling card with the hostess the day after a formal dinner, Joe apologized that he had neither the cards nor the time to spare, since he was covering news of the Senate. The young Joe found equally quaint the Washington custom requiring that female guests be "taken in" to the dining room by a male companion: "like the animals going into the ark—two by two." Arriving ten minutes late to his first affair, wearing an ill-fitting evening coat with white tie and tails that he had rented, Alsop was "met with looks of blackest hatred from the rest of the assembled party." In his memoirs, Joe recalled that what the hostess had described as the evening's "simple dinner"

> consisted of a consommé that must have cost the lives of innumerable chickens and perhaps some animals, too, followed by two impressively large salmon, accompanied by a generous vat of hollandaise sauce, and a cucumber-and-tomato salad on the side. These delights, in turn, were followed by roast guinea hens with fried bread crumbs and bread sauce, served with hot vegetables. Then came two mousses of foie gras with green salad, and, at long last, an ice-cream bombe wreathed in the peculiar spun-sugar hay that I remembered from children's parties. This plus three wines were enough to send one away comfortably full.

"I myself ended the evening feeling giddy and somewhat dazed, happy to have witnessed such an archaic gathering but glad, all the same, to have survived the event without precipitating some sort of social disaster." His uncomfortable initiation notwithstanding, Joe later judged that his introduction to the Washington dinner party had a profound impact on his later life and career: "The old prewar Washington was the backdrop of everything that happened to me in my young professional life and had its influence on my every idea as it developed . . . This noble, congenial, curious old world became a kind of personal benchmark for all that came after it."[14]

WORLD WAR II brought a temporary, unceremonious end to the tradition of the formal Washington dinner party. The autumn of 1945 would be the first time in almost four years that the country had known peace. With no more mandatory blackouts or wartime rationing, entertaining returned to Georgetown. Kay Graham recalled those coming back from the conflict encountering a "craze for giving entertainments of special colors—a pink tea, an orange reception, blue and purple affairs"—that offered a dramatic contrast to the drab and dark hues of the wartime capital. One society matron, hosting a dinner party with a Grecian theme, hired a local fortune-teller to be the Oracle of Delphi. Another asked those she invited to a costume party to come dressed as the political problems of the day. (The hostess went as the White House balcony, which was then undergoing a controversial renovation under the new Truman administration. Her guests' costumes included the recently devalued British pound and the nationwide coal strike—"black satin dress, bituminous coal necklace.")[15]

But the most sought-after and exclusive invitation was to one of Joe Alsop's Sunday night suppers, a cocktails-and-dinner ritual that began during the Great Depression but would become a tradition and a fixture of life in postwar Georgetown. Less formal than the capital's prewar soirees, the suppers were an occasion for a close coterie of those Joe called his "tribal friends" and assorted guests to get together when their maids and cooks had the night off. Alsop called them "zoo parties," since the invitation list typically included a brace of prominent senators and foreign ambassadors, a Supreme Court justice or two, some young rising star in the current administration, and, of course, Joe's own well-connected friends and neighbors. As Katharine Graham later wrote, the invitation list was strictly independent of partisan affiliation: "Within Washington there's a nucleus of people who know each other and enjoy each other's company and see each other no matter what's happening politically or who is in or out of power." It was said that the devil himself would be welcome at Joe Alsop's dinner parties—so long as Beelzebub wore patent leather shoes and kept his tail discreetly hidden under the table.

Their relative informality notwithstanding, Joe's Sunday night suppers adhered to the same strict protocol dictated by prewar etiquette. Anne Squire's *Social Washington,* published in 1923, was a veritable *Robert's Rules of Order* for entertaining in the capital city. (During the Nixon administration, when Henry Kissinger broke one of Squire's cardinal rules—he had an assistant telephone regrets for a dinner invitation at the Grahams', rather than call Kay in person—Kissinger was sharply admonished by Joe Alsop. The secretary of state contritely promised Joe that it would not happen again.)[16]

Dinner parties in Georgetown also stuck to what was called the "eleven o'clock rule"—the time at which all remaining guests must depart—"a curious, un-American custom imposed by the fact that Washington is filled with diplomats and other protocol-conscious persons," as described by Stewart Alsop. The chronic "extra-man problem"—unavoidable in a city known to be "a haven for rich widows protecting their investments"— was solved by enlisting the aid of a limited crop of available bachelors, some of whom found the repetitive social whirl "exhausting" as well as fattening. (President John Kennedy would be the "extra man" for at least one Georgetown dinner party, when Jackie was out of town.) In another decades-old Washington custom, following dessert, the sexes were separated—the men retiring to the library to discuss politics over brandy and cigars, while the women dutifully trooped upstairs. Joe Alsop's niece Corinne "Teeny" Zimmermann recalls that attractive single women were also routinely invited to the Alsop salons—and seated next to the male guests, who, she noted, generally leaned over their dinner partners to talk to their fellow "lions": "There were a lot of women whose faces were almost pushed into the soup."[17]

Joe Alsop actively encouraged spirited political debate among his guests—goading "a lion or two to roar away at the head of the table"— although, if one failed to appear, the host himself was always glad to assume the role. And, while Joe routinely flattered those guests he used as sources for his column—"It was," he noted dryly, "also useful to a reporter to feed the lions"—Joe did not suffer bores. At one zoo party after the war, where Stewart had politely listened to the perennial presidential candidate Harold Stassen drone on for some long minutes, Joe finally burst out with a laconic "Harold, would you cut out all this bullshit."[18]

The liberal pouring of cocktails, usually dry martinis, preceded Joe's signature dishes of leek pie and terrapin soup. Preparation of the soup was itself a ritual, involving hours of boiling turtle parts in a buttery broth flavored with sherry and cayenne pepper. The result was "an unctuous, even gelatinous stewlike dish," Alsop recalled, adding, "Although its aroma reminded one a bit of the way feet sometimes smell, it was absolutely delicious." The soup was, in any event, an acquired taste.[19]

After drinks, guests gathered in the dining room for what Joe called gen con—general conversation. There was always a sharp political edge to the gen con, and it was understood that the Alsops routinely used the information gleaned from these occasions in their reporting. During dinner, his chin cupped in both hands, peering over the tops of tortoise-shell glasses from his permanent seat at the head of the table, Joe would stare fixedly at a guest and ask archly, "So . . . what do you think of *this?*" Before the startled victim could respond, Joe himself would usually hold forth, at length, on what all should believe about the issue at hand. Making what one dinner guest described as "learned catarrhal noises"—Joe deliberately interjected a droning "ahum . . . ahum . . . ahum" between each of his sentences to make sure that he held the floor—the elder Alsop put an unambiguous end to any discussion with a final and plosive "Bah!" But any lingering ill feelings were usually dispelled by the host's good-natured banter, culminating in Joe's favorite toast: "Here's to all of us!" Despite his gruff exterior, Joe could be both generous and surprisingly sentimental. One friend called him an "emotional hemophiliac."[20]

From the outside, Joe's own little house at 2709 Dumbarton was almost lost among the bigger Federal-era brick edifices that made up historic Georgetown. Inside, however, strategically placed family portraits in the parlor and on living room walls covered in bloodred Chinese silk were subtle reminders of the Alsops' distinguished lineage, as well as Joe's extensive travels in Asia. A gilt-framed painting of his great-uncle Teddy Roosevelt was in prominent view from the dining room table. ("It was Teddy on a bad day," Joe explained of the ex-president's glowering visage.) One visitor vividly remembered the "small, seawater-cold eyes" of Alsop ancestors staring down at him throughout supper. "The place just exuded significance," observed another.[21]

There was, Joe Alsop later noted, a "peculiar trait" that accounted for what was broadly known as "Georgetown charm . . . Its chief ingredients are the old houses' ancient brick, handsome doorways and fine, severe windows, making an agreeable pattern along the tree-lined streets." ("The houses were as pretty and meticulously appointed as yawls, the front doors fire engine red or lacquered ebony, glittering brass knockers catching the eye," wrote the Georgetowner Ward Just in his novel of Washington, *In the City of Fear*.) Not all who lived in Georgetown, of course, were sold on its celebrated "charm." In her memoir, Joe Alsop's friend and fellow columnist Meg Greenfield recalled how "better-bred, country-house English remains the stylistic model, the affectation of choice . . . The essence is impersonation: the appropriation of someone else's heritage, the donning of another identity."[22]

Newcomers found Joe Alsop's Georgetown salons either "exhilarating" or "terrifying." Dinnertime discussions at the suppers, always animated and alcohol fueled, sometimes came to an abrupt halt as the host ordered one of his guests out of the house for some offending remark. (At one supper, Phil Graham was halfway out the door before he realized that the house he was being kicked out of was *his*.) Joe told friends that it was not really considered an argument in the Alsop family until someone had left the table and stormed out of the dining room at least twice. "He roared so that his ancestral portraits shook on the walls," recalled Joe's niece.

Veterans became inured to what was known as "the Alsop method"— bold assertions made on the basis of little or no knowledge, yet in hope that a denial or a contradiction would elicit real information. Joe verbally nudged reticent sources with a leering "That's right, eh?" Silence was interpreted as confirmation. Unwary newcomers were shocked to discover presumably innocent comments made the night before transformed into the headline of the next morning's column in the *Post* and the *Herald Tribune*. Savvy Washington politicians, on the other hand, found Matter of Fact an invaluable springboard for big ideas and matching ambitions—as well as a convenient venue for news leaks and a surefire way of settling scores with their enemies.[23]

The brothers claimed to adhere to two journalistic rules in their column: never express an opinion not supported by reporting, and always include at least one new item of hard information appearing nowhere else. Another "almost rule," which led to Joe and Stewart's frequent globe hopping, was "go and see it for yourself." (Joe wrote that he traveled like a "moulting vulture slow on wing but sharp for bodies.") The Alsops tried to do at least three interviews for each column they wrote, with some of those "interviews" actually being conducted over cocktails in Joe's house. Believers of *in vino veritas,* Joe and Stewart looked upon alcohol as a lubricant vital to the success of the weekend suppers. Among friends, Joe called the dinners the "Sunday Night Drunk." On one memorable evening, the country's ranking expert on the Soviet Union, standing atop a kitchen chair and wearing a mop on his head, led Joe and other guests in a lusty rendition of the Communist "Internationale."[24]

As one of Joe's fellow journalists observed, the brothers' brand of reporting was intended "not to enlighten but to *effect,* to move the principal players on decisions." The elder Alsop, it was said, wrote more for the president than for the public. Joe was the "most imperial and imperious of American journalists," noted a critic.[25]

In contrast to reporters like Walter Winchell, Joe Alsop showed little interest in sharing his views with a larger audience through the medium of radio. (On the one occasion when he agreed to join Stewart in a broadcast, Joe later wrote to Susan Mary, "The trouble is that the medium absolutely prevents you from saying anything . . . And you find that you don't understand what you are talking about when you listen to the recording of your own words.") When Alsop and his colleague Robert Kintner were writing for the *New York Herald Tribune* in the late 1930s, Joe had stubbornly refused to listen to news broadcasts. Kintner boasted that he only tuned in to *The March of Time* on Sunday evenings. Although Joe would eventually acknowledge what he called "the curious power of the voice," he also claimed that his own peculiar pattern of speech was probably "too aloof" to attract many listeners. Indeed, Alsop's diction, a combination of clipped consonants and stretched vowels, would be described by others as "Groton lockjaw," an "upper-class blend of Connecticut Yankee and Harvard Yard," and even "Charles Laughton playing Oscar Wilde." (A friend of Joe's observed, more generously, that the older Alsop had "a characteristic Churchillian impediment of speech—a thickening of all the sibilants.") In any event, Joe decided to stick to print.[26]

Skeptical, if not openly contemptuous, of "objective" journalism, Joe Alsop was never reluctant to embrace causes—whether popular or lost. In 1940, shortly before the German invasion of France, when he worked for the *Herald Tribune,* Joe published a small booklet, *American White Paper,* which had made an impassioned argument against isolationism. President Franklin Roosevelt, an Alsop relative—Joe and Stewart were FDR's fifth cousins—reportedly suggested some of the sources used for the piece.[27]

Before Pearl Harbor, the talk at Georgetown dinner parties had been of Roosevelt's efforts to pull the country out of the Depression and the coming confrontation with fascism. The Alsops' family connections had greatly facilitated their reporting on the New Deal: the brothers would occasionally celebrate Christmas or New Year's at the White House with "Uncle Franklin" and "Cousin Eleanor." Washington's grande dame, Alice Roosevelt Longworth, Teddy Roosevelt's oldest child, was both an Alsop relation and an important social connection for Joe and Stewart. In his memoirs, Joe Alsop would attribute his early success in Washington to the intervention of "Mrs. L." But the notoriously crusty doyenne of D.C.—who described herself as "Washington's *other* monument"—remembered Joe less fondly as "a fat, sullen, sour little boy." Asked to come up with a "nice" story about him in a reporter's interview, Alice could only recall the time that young Joe had played the role of a horse in a humorous skit that he and Stewart performed at Yale. It had been, of course, a nonspeaking part.[28]

CHAPTER TWO

─────────

"Some Higher Realm of Intellect and Power"

W ITH THE END of World War II, a new and younger generation
had come to Washington. Ambitious, idealistic, and shaped—or
scarred—by their experience in the recent conflict, the newcomers congregated in Georgetown. In contrast to the so-called cave dwellers, the
affluent society matrons whose families had lived in the stately mansions of nearby Kalorama for generations, many of Georgetown's new
residents would be linked to the federal bureaucracy that had burgeoned
in Washington during the New Deal and grown even larger because of
the war. Like Kipling's loyal civil servants of the British Crown, they
filled the expanding ranks of the diplomatic and military satrapies that
administered the lands newly liberated from tyranny. What united them
was neither wealth nor ancestry but the experience of the war, a crucible
that had created in most a belief in the worth of public service and a
common bond of trust.

At the conflict's end, the country also had a new and untested president. "To those who have returned after four years' absence, the most
conspicuous single fact in Washington is Harry S. Truman," the Alsops
began their inaugural column, on New Year's Eve 1945. Joe dismissed the
president as "an average man in a neat grey suit" whose cronies filled the
White House with the "odor of ten-cent cigars." It was the beginning of
a mutual enmity. President Truman would refer to Joe as "Mr. All Sop."[1]

The death of the charismatic FDR had put a sudden end to the easy
access that Joe and Stewart had previously enjoyed to Washington's corridors of power. Soon there was a different set of faces around Joe's dinner table and a different kind of guest at the zoo parties. Among their

number were, for the first time, atomic scientists, as well as earnest academics and youthful members of the postwar diplomatic corps, fresh
from overseas adventures and privy to important secrets of state.

One such guest was the OSS veteran and newly minted Harvard historian Arthur Schlesinger Jr., who had recently moved with his family
into a rented house "within easy striking distance" of Georgetown, in
order to try his luck as a freelance writer until classes began in Cambridge. Schlesinger later remembered a "heady evening" spent with Joe
and some of the administration's top policy makers, and Washington as
"a city filled with couples our age happily reunited after the war . . . now
mingling carefree postwar gaiety with purposeful postwar ambitions . . . [As] a young historian back from the war, I felt transported to
some higher realm of intellect and power."[2]

Indeed, in the six months following his return to Washington, Alsop
would preside over more than a score of zoo parties, each with at least a
dozen invited guests.

Susan Mary Jay, the wife of Joe's Harvard classmate Bill Patten, was
another Alsop confidante—she was his trusted source on the changing
political situation in postwar Europe—and likewise a frequent dinner
guest at Dumbarton Avenue during her visits home from Paris. (Susan
Mary's mother lived at a house on Twenty-Ninth Street, just around the
corner from Joe). At age nineteen, when she and her girlfriends were
asked to imagine what lives they saw for themselves in the future, most
focused on marriage and children, but Susan Mary wrote, "Parties,
People and Politics." "There's no future in being an ordinary person,
leading an ordinary life," she once told a reporter. Petite and rail thin,
Susan Mary became a *mannequin du monde* for Balenciaga and Balmain
gowns—which the designers offered to her at a discounted price—while
she and Bill lived in Paris, where her husband was an economic analyst
at the U.S. embassy. "If you put her stark naked in the middle of the
Gobi Desert, she would still be elegant," recalled Joe Alsop's admiring
young niece.

A descendant of the country's first chief justice, "Soozle" readily
deflated the pretensions of snobby guests at Washington dinner parties
with a curt reminder: "My forebearers helped get this show on the road."[3]

From her perch at the Paris embassy, Susan Mary was also a pen pal
with one of Joe's Georgetown neighbors, Marietta Peabody FitzGerald,
the granddaughter of the notoriously strict founder and rector of Groton School, Endicott Peabody. Like another mutual friend, the British

novelist Nancy Mitford, Susan Mary and Marietta prided themselves on being present at "history on the boil." (In Mitford's 1951 novel, *The Blessing,* Susan Mary appears as the character Mildred Jungfleisch, a pretty American woman living in Paris and "deeply concerned about the present state of the world." But Mitford's portrait was not always flattering: she wrote that Mildred only talked "about conferences, vetos, and what Joe Alsop had told her when she saw him in Washington.")[4]

Soozle was both "courageous" and "witty," Marietta wrote, while also possessing a rare talent for recalling "stories, statistics, or slips" by cabinet ministers and ambassadors at embassy dinner parties: "She would have made an excellent Mata Hari." (Marietta was not the first to recognize her friend's potential. In 1939, when Susan Mary quit her job as a researcher at *Vogue* to marry Bill, the magazine's editor wrote, "I will miss you more than others because of your fine spy work. I shall recommend you to a friend in Washington in case the espionage runs short of undercover agents!")[5]

WITH THE WAR against fascism finally won, a different set of concerns fueled the gen con at Joe's dinner parties. Two topics in particular dominated the conversation as 1945 came to a close: the Russians and the bomb.

Since the dissolution of the country's wartime alliance with Russia, relations had quickly soured between Joseph Stalin and Harry Truman. Joe Alsop learned firsthand of the difficulties from one of his sources in the Truman administration, Secretary of State James Byrnes. In September 1945, Byrnes had returned from the first postwar meeting with his counterpart, the Soviet foreign minister Vyacheslav Molotov, chastened and warning that the Russians were "stubborn, obstinate, and they don't scare." "The great question remains," Joe wrote to a friend that November: "How are Britain and the United States to deal with the Soviet Union?"[6]

Joe's own fears for the future bordered on the panicky. "Everything is awful here," he wrote to his former boss Chennault that winter. "The Administration is weak and seems to grow weaker by the day. The world situation is already appalling, yet appears to be deteriorating further with great rapidity. The Russians seem to me very likely to win the ball game, and no one here has any remedy in mind but further appeasement. God help us all."[7]

As early as their third column, on January 4, 1946, the brothers had made the growing trouble with Russia a focus of Matter of Fact. "I admire [the Russians] deeply, and fear them not a little," Joe confided to his fellow columnist and sometimes rival Walter Lippmann.[8]

As it was for many Americans at that time, the other source of Joe Alsop's angst was the atomic bomb. A letter from Susan Mary to Marietta, reflecting upon Truman's announcement of the destruction of Hiroshima, captured the mood: "One felt that such news should come with a clash of cymbals and the vocabulary of the three witches from *Macbeth*. Truman looks like my dentist in Washington, and the tone was the same as Dr. Osborne's 'Open just a little wider, please' . . . But rending garments will get us nowhere."[9]

The bomb was also the subject of the Alsops' first real scoop. In late January 1946, the brothers published the details of a classified report by the Pentagon's Operations and Plans Division on the strategic significance of the awful new weapon. Their principal source was the physicist Louis Ridenour, one of the report's authors. Ridenour's was another of the fresh faces that had recently appeared around Joe's dining room table.[10]

The perilous nuclear age was likewise the subject of a lengthier article by the brothers in *The Saturday Evening Post* a few months later. "Your Flesh *Should* Creep" described the aftermath of a prospective nuclear war in stark and unsparing detail: "In brief, expert opinion holds that a single fusillade of atomic bombs will be capable of killing a third or a half of the people of a great nation, and demolishing an even higher percentage of its productive capacity." The brothers explained the concept of deterrence, painting a prophetic vision of a future world locked in an enduring nuclear stalemate, where missile-bearing submarines silently prowled the world's oceans, and cities were held hostage by fearsomely destructive weapons kept on hair-trigger alert. "The only sure defense of this country is now the political defense," they concluded.

In what would become a familiar pattern, Joe and Stewart promoted the *Post* article in their syndicated column, which, by the following summer, was running in more than fifty newspapers around the country. The piece was also reprinted in *Reader's Digest*.

The twinned subject of the Russians and the bomb was one that the brothers would return to and, in effect, make their own in columns and articles appearing over the months—and years—to come. Their pessimistic take on the Cold War promptly earned them the nicknames

"Doom and Gloom" and "the Brothers Cassandra," while the elder Alsop was branded "old black Joe." One critic joked that Matter of Fact should really be called "For Whom the Bell Tolls." But when the *Herald Tribune*'s own editor complained about the Alsop column's seeming obsession with the Russian threat, Joe promptly retorted, "The first job is to arouse people to the fact that a crisis is in progress."[11]

Their *Post* magazine article also demonstrated just how well connected the brothers had become during their short time back in Washington. Among the other unnamed sources on the nuclear danger was the physicist Robert Oppenheimer, the man soon to be heralded as the father of the atomic bomb. Two days before the State Department's plan for the international control of atomic energy was leaked to the press, the Alsop brothers summarized the contents of the document—which was largely Oppenheimer's work—in a Matter of Fact column.[12]

Just as Ridenour and Oppenheimer were the Alsops' sources on the bomb, concerning Russia, Joe and Stewart listened to two men. One was a longtime friend; the other a stranger, but a rising star in Washington's foreign policy firmament.

LIKE JOE ALSOP, forty-one-year-old Charles "Chip" Bohlen had gone to Harvard, where both belonged to the prestigious Porcellian Club, the unofficial "undergraduate citadel" of the eastern establishment. Handsome, articulate, and supremely self-confident, Bohlen was described by his Foreign Service examiner as a "thoroughbred" possessing "great charm" and "extraordinary intelligence"—even though Chip had been drunk on bathtub gin when he took the orals. (Bohlen seemed to consider alcohol not so much a beverage as a food group, his doctor warned him.) Chip had been one of the first diplomats sent to the American embassy in Moscow, after the United States extended diplomatic recognition to the Soviet Union in 1933. He was so often Joe's houseguest upon returning from missions overseas that Alsop dubbed his spare bedroom at Dumbarton Avenue "Bohlensnest."[13]

Later posted to the U.S. embassy in Tokyo, Bohlen wound up being sent to the same internment camp as Joe Alsop following the attack on Pearl Harbor. In 1942, the pair returned to the United States on the same ship, the *Gripsholm,* where "Joe was his usual urbane self and frequently gave cocktail parties on the deck," Chip recalled. After serving as a translator and adviser for Roosevelt at Yalta and Truman at Potsdam, Bohlen moved back to the home that he and his wife, Avis, owned at 2811 Dumbarton Avenue, just a block down from Joe Alsop. (Like Joe's house, the Bohlens' was furnished in what Chip's son irreverently called "the Episcopal manner"—with books, Oriental rugs, paintings of hunting scenes, and gilt-framed portraits of famous relatives.) Chip's new job at Foggy Bottom was as special assistant to the secretary of state and counselor on matters pertaining to the Soviet Union. In that role, Bohlen would witness firsthand the deteriorating relations between Washington and Moscow.[14]

The Alsops' other source on the Russians was Bohlen's close friend and fellow Kremlin expert, George Frost Kennan.

The forty-two-year-old Kennan was late in returning to the capital, not arriving until mid-May 1946. Little more than three months earlier, in February, Kennan had risen to sudden prominence in diplomatic circles when his 5,518-word response to a routine State Department inquiry about Soviet intentions touched a nerve in official Washington. Known, appropriately enough, as the "long telegram," Kennan's prescription for the future of postwar Soviet-American relations had earned him a countrywide lecture tour and the title of deputy commandant for foreign affairs at the newly established National War College. George and his wife, Annelise, moved into a house previously occupied by an army general on the grounds of Fort McNair in southwest Washington.[15]

Bohlen and Kennan had gotten to know each other when the two were assigned to the fledgling Moscow embassy together. In contrast to the outgoing and unflappable Bohlen, Kennan was introspective, brooding, and mercurial. By 1938, he had been recalled to Washington to head the State Department's Russian desk. After postings in Prague and Berlin—including five months of internment in Nazi Germany, following America's entry into the war—Kennan was shuffled next to Lisbon, then London. In May 1944, he became the deputy chief of mission and minister-counselor at the American embassy in Moscow, the second-highest-ranking position there, upon the request of the U.S. ambassador, William Averell Harriman.[16]

On the day after the Nazi surrender, as the embassy's chargé d'affaires in Harriman's absence, Kennan ordered a Soviet flag unfurled next to the Stars and Stripes. Balanced precariously on a ledge in front of the chancellery, Kennan had given a brief but uncharacteristically impassioned speech praising the victory of America's Soviet ally before an enthusiastic crowd of Muscovites in Red Square.[17]

Privately, however, Kennan was pessimistic about the future of Soviet-American relations. A few weeks later, sitting on his suitcase in the back of a lend-lease C-47 flying over the fields and forests of the Russian hinterland, Kennan entered this bleak assessment in his diary: "But the fact is: there is no way of helping the Russian people. When a people places itself in the hands of a ruthless authoritarian regime which will stop at nothing, it places itself beyond the power of others to help."[18]

From the Soviet capital, near the end of the war, Kennan had sent a series of reports to Washington notable for a common theme: American expectations that the wartime era of good feelings between the United States and the U.S.S.R. would continue into the peace were misplaced and grossly unrealistic. But in the euphoria of victory, Kennan's pessimistic assessments were simply ignored: he later estimated that his warnings were read by, at most, five people in the entire government. It was, he wrote, "like talking to a stone." Feeling very much the dishonored prophet, Kennan had twice threatened to resign from the Foreign Service by that fall, immodestly suggesting that the State Department might wish to send "two successors" to replace him. Not for the last time, Kennan's friend Bohlen talked him out of leaving.[19]

For Kennan, the breakthrough had come that winter, when, racked by a nagging cold, he used what he confessed was an "outrageous encumberment of the telegraphic process" to give vent to long-pent-up frustrations. "They had asked for it," Kennan wrote in his memoirs. "Now, by God, they would have it."[20]

This time, Kennan's views found a ready and receptive audience. While the timing was right—a recent speech by Stalin had dispelled any lingering doubt that the bloom was finally off the rose of Soviet-American friendship—the response was not entirely unexpected. Harriman would later take credit for inciting Kennan's long telegram. But it was really Bohlen who had done the "prodding." While he was not as pessimistic as Kennan, Bohlen generally shared his friend's skepticism regarding the future of Soviet-American relations.[21]

Moscow embassy telegram 511 combined analysis with argument, and the two were sometimes hard to separate. Kennan's message was that the disintegration of U.S. relations with the U.S.S.R. was not America's fault but the inevitable consequence of a Soviet leadership that promoted the image of a hostile outside world to justify its own autocratic rule. The United States, Kennan argued, should confront the threat of Soviet expansionism calmly and confidently and, by its own example of a successful society, offer an alternative more attractive than Communism to the Soviet and the non-Soviet world alike. In the end, Kennan predicted, Russian Communism would either collapse of its own weight or be so transformed by its internal contradictions as to cease to be a threat to the West.[22]

Kennan banged the tocsin of alarm throughout a nationwide lecture tour before taking up his post at the National War College. But his message to the public, remembered one listener at Stanford University, had "fallen on stony ground." Returning to Washington, Kennan made a better impression on the man whom Truman had chosen to head the new U.S. Atomic Energy Commission. After attending one of Kennan's lectures at the National War College, David Lilienthal wrote this description in his diary: "Bald, slight, not impressive except for his eyes which are most unusual: large, intense, wide-set. Perceptive man [but] . . . rather full up with Russia."[23]

The individual responsible for spreading Kennan's gospel in Washington's inner circles was James Forrestal, a fellow Princetonian. Coincidentally, Forrestal was also, with Jimmy Byrnes, another holdover from the Roosevelt administration and a friend as well as a news source for Joe Alsop. Appointed secretary of the navy by President Roosevelt in 1944, Forrestal had long been suspicious of the Russians. As such, his had been a lonely voice in the capital until Truman became president.[24]

With all the zeal of an acolyte preaching to the newly converted, Forrestal sent copies of Kennan's long telegram to high-ranking colleagues in the Pentagon, to Truman's cabinet secretaries, to the president himself, and to anyone else he felt might listen.[25]

The long telegram had also brought Kennan to the attention of the next secretary of state, George Marshall, who replaced Byrnes in early 1947. Returning that January from yet another failed summit meeting with the Russians, Marshall picked Kennan to head a new think tank in the State Department. Marshall's instructions to Kennan were characteristically, and famously, succinct: "Avoid trivia." The new secretary of state would come to rely on Kennan's Policy Planning Staff as a kind of intellectual incubator for bold ideas on how to run the postwar American imperium.[26]

Those whom the press dubbed "Marshall's brain trust" included an emeritus professor of history from Williams College, an army colonel, an economist, a Foreign Service officer, and a former assistant to FDR's secretary of state Cordell Hull. But the dominant figure on the planning staff was Kennan himself. After a discussion with its other members, Kennan would typically retreat into solitude, eventually emerging with a finished paper notable for its polish and erudition, if not its pragmatism. (Nor was the author receptive to editing. Kennan "looked upon each report he prepared as etched in steel," wrote Paul Nitze, a subsequent PPS colleague. Chip Bohlen concurred: "Once he got on paper, George couldn't be moved.") State Department colleagues joked that for a first-rate analysis of a problem, one needed Kennan; but for a practical solution, Bohlen.[27]

In early May 1947, Kennan and his staff moved into a single cramped office on the fifth floor of the State Department's new quarters, a sprawling but nondescript building at Twenty-First Street and Virginia Avenue with rambling, mazelike corridors. Marshall's office was next door. Critics described the building as looking like "an up-to-date hospital" and having "about as much character as a chewing gum factory in Los Angeles." But at least it had that relatively new marvel: air-conditioning. Previous occupants of the building that would become known as New State had included General Leslie Groves and the staff of the wartime Manhattan Project.[28]

Despite his native reticence, Kennan was not content to remain merely an observer on the sidelines of the titanic struggle shaping up between East and West. He was also not shy about cultivating relations with the ranking members of the Washington press corps, including the Alsops—a trait that rankled the famously closemouthed Marshall.[29]

While Forrestal and Marshall would be responsible for introducing Kennan's ideas on Russia to official Washington, it was Joe and Stewart Alsop who first made them known to a broader public, on May 23, 1947, with a column titled "The Kennan Dispatch." The fact that Kennan's long telegram remained a classified document, and had only circulated thus far in the rarefied upper echelons of the national security bureaucracy, was no impediment to Joe Alsop. Indeed, as the brothers knew well, secrets leaked from the State Department or the Pentagon not only gave a story greater authority but had the added frisson of alerting readers to information that their government did not want them to know.[30]

Describing the long telegram as "the most important single state paper on the Soviet Union to be written since the Soviet problem began to dominate international relations," the Alsops reduced Kennan's lengthy recommendations for America's policy toward Russia to a few brief sentences. The United States, they wrote, should aim to "bring about a situation in which the rulers of the Kremlin, inspecting the world even through their distorting glasses, must admit the error of their previous analysis. When that time comes they must formulate a new analysis and new policy." Kennan's prescription, the brothers concluded, "is one which can be accepted with confidence by all men of good will."

THERE IS A CERTAIN IRONY in the fact that Joseph Wright Alsop V would become George Kennan's friend and promoter. It was an unlikely pairing, both politically and socially. Indeed, the two men were, in many ways, exact opposites: a blue-blooded descendant of the eastern establishment who championed democracy versus a middle-class midwesterner with aristocratic sympathies and sensitivities.[31]

Their first encounter had been years earlier, before the war, when Alsop and Kennan were seated next to each other during a dinner party at the Bohlens'. The evening did not go well. Kennan had impressed him, Alsop later wrote, as a "cautious, ineffectual, all-too-cerebral diplomat." For his part, Kennan made things worse by complaining to Joe that the country was doomed "because it was no longer run by its 'aristocracy' and had ceased to be responsive to 'aristocratic' suggestions"—a comment that Alsop judged "as about as silly a remark as I had heard at any a dinner table . . . I was very nearly sick."[32]

Kennan would never feel entirely comfortable at Joe's Sunday night suppers, although he attended many. Stewart's wife recalled one evening where, while Joe and Chip Bohlen argued loudly about politics in the dining room, Kennan sat forlornly on the living room couch, telling Tish about his troubled childhood. ("While I knew all these people, and some of them quite well, I was never properly a member of what was called the Georgetown set," Kennan wrote late in life. "I was for much of the time too poor, and too little urban . . . But it was more than that. While some of these friends knew me quite well, professionally if not personally, they, I thought, looked at me slightly askance . . . For these, and for all the others, I hovered uncertainly on the horizon, a strange occasional social phenomenon, over-intense, seldom relaxed, to be fitted into no known category, to be approached with a certain respect but also with a certain wariness. You never knew, they thought, when I would fall out of the proper tone, or in some other way violate the rules. And they were not wrong, I never knew it, myself.") "To the extent that I was accepted among those in the Establishment," Kennan would observe, "it was in the role they decided to cast for me, rather than because of who I really was." Thus, although Kennan believed that Joe Alsop respected his talent as a fellow writer, he concluded that Alsop actually "knew little about me, and what he thought he knew was mostly wrong."[33]

The Alsop brothers professed to be men with and for—but not actually *from*—the people. During his student days at Yale, Stewart had considered himself a "Marxist liberal." Joe, temperamentally and politically more conservative, had nonetheless outraged their staunchly Republican father by his support of the New Deal. ("Joe was the kind of liberal who thought it was a good idea for men of property—who wanted to remain men of property—to keep an eye on the social problems of the masses," observed a fellow reporter.) Both brothers were quintessential representatives of what Joe called "the WASP ascendancy": the rise of white Anglo-Saxon Protestant men to the positions of highest power in America. One of Joe's closest friends dubbed him an "American Aristocrat"—a characterization that Alsop rejected, ironically, as "common."[34]

The Alsops could trace their roots back to mid-seventeenth-century England. Immigrating to America before the Revolution, one of the brothers' ancestors inaugurated the family tradition of backing unpopular—and ultimately doomed—political causes. John Alsop— New York's delegate to the Continental Congress in 1774—had, like Georgetown's founder, picked the losing side in a fight, aligning himself with the loyalist Tories. For refusing to affix his name to the Declaration of Independence, he famously became known as "John the Non-signer" in family lore. (One Alsop descendant claimed that it was not political sentiment but economic self-interest that motivated John's stand: he simply believed that the Revolution would be bad for business.) Another Alsop ancestor was an antiwar Copperhead who backed General George McClellan against Abraham Lincoln in the 1864 election.[35]

Despite such fraught beginnings, the Alsops' American branch eventually produced ship captains and banking magnates who became important figures in the West Indies rum trade and, Stewart speculated, in the Chinese opium market. The family also married into the Oyster Bay branch of the Roosevelts, the closest thing this country had at the time to a royal dynasty. "Our father used to say a little sourly that our mother's family ran for office as instinctively as lemmings run into the sea," Joe later wrote.[36]

By the early twentieth century, Joseph Wright Alsop IV, the future columnist's father, was a gentleman farmer presiding over a seven-hundred-acre estate outside the rural village of Avon, Connecticut. A visitor to the Alsops' Wood Ford Farm compared the family to "one of those sturdy British dynasties that we were accustomed to encountering in novels, which possessed over many generations a family seat, tucked away among rooky elms, in a water-meadow in some green country-side . . . From a literary point of view, only the rooks were missing." Joe number V was born in 1910; brother Stewart followed four years later.[37]

Known simply as "the boys" in the Alsop clan, Joe and Stewart were influenced most by their mother, Corinne Robinson, a dominant figure in local Republican politics and a commanding presence at the twenty-eight-room farmhouse where they, John, the youngest Alsop brother, and their sister, Corinne, grew up. But it was the example of his maternal grandmother, Corinne Roosevelt Robinson, Teddy Roosevelt's sister, that Joe would most closely emulate. Two things determined success in life, Grandmother Corinne had instructed the boys: "climbing the top of your tree, whatever tree you pick, and becoming part of the larger world." Her spirit likewise infused Joe's Sunday night suppers. After one of Grandmother Corinne's notoriously large and animated dinner parties, one guest advised a prospective future attendee, "Talk as loudly as you possibly can and answer your own questions." "The Alsop family gatherings went beyond raucous," confirmed a relative.[38]

Growing up in a life of privilege, Joe and Stewart would later write about the childhood idylls they had spent each summer at Henderson House, the mansion in upstate New York owned by the Robinson clan. Following the farewell dinner on the last Sunday of the season—after the hymn "God Be with You till We Meet Again" was sung—the boys' aunt would signal an end to the vacation with a time-honored family ritual: "The conch shell had been acquired by Aunt Harriet, heaven knows where, and she had established the custom of blowing it at all departing guests . . . We would all be in the big old Pierce Arrow before we heard this otherworldly sound. Grandmother would be standing on the steps, waving wildly and calling out, 'Good-by, good-by! Come back, come back!' We would be waving, too, when the car would be put in gear, the conch shell would ululate mournfully, and so another Henderson summer would end."[39]

Joe's membership in Harvard's hallowed Porcellian Club—the Porc—also gave him an entrée to the wealthy and powerful who would become, in later years, both his friends and his sources as a reporter. Hired by the *Herald Tribune* right out of college—Grandmother Corinne intervened with her "tribal" friends the *Tribune* owners Ogden and Helen Reid to get him the job—Joe arrived at work wearing a bespoke suit, silk shirt, and hand-sewn shoes from Peal in London, even though it was the depths of the Great Depression and his salary a mere eighteen dollars a week. "A perfect example of Republican inbreeding," muttered the city editor when Alsop walked into the newsroom. Despite that dubious initiation, Joe and his *Trib* colleague the White House correspondent Robert Kintner collaborated on two books and wrote a well-respected political column—the Capital Parade—during the next four years, until the outbreak of World War II.[40]

IN CONTRAST to Joe Alsop, George Kennan was born to a Milwaukee couple of modest means and raised mostly by relatives following the death of his mother, Florence, when he was just two months old. The family's single claim to notoriety was Kennan's great-uncle and namesake, who had traveled extensively in Russia during the late nineteenth century and written a well-received book on political exiles in Siberia. The young George felt a special identity with his distant relative.[41]

Kennan went to a public school across the street from the Schlitz brewery until the ninth grade, when his father sent him to St. John's, a nearby military academy. If the intent of Kennan père had been to toughen up his quiet, bookish son, the cure did not take. George would be plagued throughout his adult life by an assortment of recurrent ailments. Beyond any limitations caused by physical illnesses, however, Kennan's own introspective nature, bordering on neurosis, seemed his most notable and enduring character trait. He was, George himself freely acknowledged, "a queer duck."[42]

Admitted to Princeton on a scholarship, Kennan spent his college years, as he later wrote, "an innocent, always at the end of every line, always uninitiated, knowing few, known by few . . . an oddball on campus, not eccentric, not ridiculed or disliked, just imperfectly visible to the naked eye."[43]

Despite his plebeian origins, Kennan had, early on, demonstrated an elitist disdain for those he judged less intelligent or less worthy, as well as a reactionary longing for an imagined America of the past—a lost Eden. Returning in 1936 to the country of his birth after most of a decade spent abroad, Kennan was horrified by the extent to which automobiles had replaced the railroads and, in the process, transformed American life. (In a telling exchange, Joe Alsop once told Kennan, "You know, George, the problem with you is that you're a nineteenth-century man." "No," Kennan riposted, "I'm an *eighteenth*-century man.")[44]

Yet the egalitarian spirit and progressive politics of the New Deal bothered Kennan even more. "I hate democracy; I hate the press . . . I hate the 'peepul'; I have become clearly un-American," George had unburdened himself to his sister and confidante Jeanette the year before. ("He is a man who understood Russia but didn't understand the United States," Kennan's boss in Moscow, Averell Harriman, would perceptively observe of him some years later.) In the summer of 1938, Kennan began writing a lengthy essay, "The Prerequisites," which envisioned a country run by a male Anglo-Saxon meritocracy—an "enlightened elite"—where recent immigrants, women, and African-Americans would be simply disenfranchised. Kennan never finished his intemperate screed, which might have been more the product of a hot Washington season and his own chronic distemper than any deeply held conviction. But it would later surface and come back to haunt him.[45]

Kennan, in fact, suffered a recurrent melancholy, which he kept secret from the outside world but confided, sometimes cryptically, to the personal diary he kept for more than fifty years as an adult. ("When I was happy and busy, I wasn't writing," Kennan once admitted.) These dark moods were also reflected, frequently, in his private correspondence.[46]

In 1942, while at the internment camp in Nazi Germany, Kennan had begun writing a letter to his children, to be read in the event that he did not survive the war. While the letter—unfinished and never delivered—was ostensibly about the history of the Kennan clan, it actually revealed much more, unintentionally, about its author. There were, George warned, "certain uniform qualities in the Kennans. They are not all admirable ones. They fail to include some very important ones: among others, gaiety, phantasy, humor, the courage to be honest with yourself, and the self-discipline to learn to sin gracefully and with dignity, rather than to try unsuccessfully not to sin at all."[47]

There was, as well, an occasional mystical streak revealed in Kennan's unpublished writings. In a journal that he kept independent of his personal diary, he tried to decipher the meaning of his most vivid dreams. When he experienced a powerful sense of déjà vu during a wartime visit to Leningrad, Kennan wondered whether he had been to the city in a previous life. Kennan was "an impressionist, a poet, not an earthling," observed one of his longtime critics.[48]

Despite their awkward first encounter at the Bohlens', Joe Alsop would eventually come to have a more positive view of George Kennan, who became his lifelong friend. If not temperament and outlook, the two men surely had ambition in common.

But Kennan was, at least for the interim, content to maintain a lower profile, using Forrestal as his proxy for self-promotion. In a letter to his boss, Undersecretary of State Dean Acheson, Kennan reacted to Alsop's public disclosure of the long telegram with mock horror: "Lest there be any misunderstanding about Joe Alsop's column this morning in the Post, I should like to say the following: I did not show this dispatch to Alsop, nor have I ever discussed it with him."[49]

Acheson was another of the new and promising additions to the Truman administration whom Joe had lured to the dinner table at Dumbarton and tried, unsuccessfully in this case, to turn into a confidential source. Dean and his wife, Alice, were also Joe's Georgetown neighbors, living at a house on nearby P Street that they had bought in 1922 without ever having glimpsed the inside. The son of Connecticut's Episcopal bishop, a Yale and Harvard Law grad, the dapper and mustachioed Acheson had a well-deserved reputation for gravitas, if not priggishness. (With his neatly trimmed Guardsman mustache, Acheson was said to look like central casting's idea of a nineteenth-century British diplomat. But, among friends at least, he also had a mordant sense of humor. Voted "wittiest" and "sportiest" when a Yale undergraduate, Acheson told his State Department colleagues, "All that I know I learned at my mother's knee and other low joints.") "He was a little shorter than the Washington Monument: erect, elegant, dogmatic, and ironically witty . . . Dean was not the sort of man you'd hand your hat to by mistake," the *New York Times* reporter James "Scotty" Reston would recall. Acheson's influence with Truman was such, wrote Reston in a 1946 *Times* article, that many considered him the "No. 1 No. 2 Man in Washington." Yet Acheson had responded to Joe Alsop's usual flattery and old-school-tie bonhomie with a flinty indifference. Privately, Acheson considered Joe a "pest."[50]

Despite his protestations to Acheson, George Kennan actually reveled in the newly acquired attention he was receiving in Washington. Having labored long in obscurity, the quiet diplomat rejoiced that what he called his "official loneliness" was finally at an end. "My voice now carried," Kennan exulted.[51]

Indeed, just three days before Joe's column on the long telegram appeared, Kennan had submitted the galley proofs of an essay that would cement his reputation as the country's foremost expert on the Soviet Union. "The Sources of Soviet Conduct" had its origins in a speech that Kennan gave before the Council on Foreign Relations in New York the previous January. Published in the July 1947 issue of *Foreign Affairs,* the semiofficial organ of the diplomatic establishment, Kennan's article repeated some of the long telegram's familiar themes: Soviet foreign policy was expansionist and ideology-driven at a strategic level, but tactically opportunistic, and hence dangerous only when confronted by weakness. Kennan compared Soviet expansionism to a "fluid stream," a "toy automobile," and even a dying plant that "bears within it the seeds of its own decay."[52]

But in one memorable phrase Kennan had inadvertently coined the term that would henceforth be used to describe the country's new approach to the Soviet Union: "It is clear that the main element of any United States policy toward the Soviet Union must be that of a long-term, patient but firm and vigilant containment of Russian expansive tendencies."

Since Kennan was conscious of the need to distinguish his notion of "containment" from official State Department policy, he had signed the article simply "X." However, its origins did not remain a secret for long. On July 8, 1947, the *New York Times* columnist Arthur Krock identified Kennan as author of the "X article." Henceforth, the shy diplomat would be recognized as the principal architect of America's postwar policy toward the Soviet Union.[53]

KENNAN WOULD MOVE out of the shadows and into the limelight even sooner than he expected. The Policy Planning Staff and its director had quickly come to agreement that the most important question facing the United States was how to bring about the revival and reconstruction of war-devastated Europe. But the pressure of deadlines imposed by Acheson and Marshall had already begun to take a toll. One day that spring, Scotty Reston discovered Kennan walking trancelike around the State Department building, uncontrollably weeping.[54]

On May 23, 1947—coincidentally, the same day that his name was in Alsop's column for the long telegram—Kennan had sent Marshall the first product of the State Department's "deep thinkers." PPS-1, "Policy with Respect to American Aid to Western Europe," was a sixteen-page plea that the United States take immediate and dramatic action to halt the economic disintegration of Europe. But the paper also argued that the rescue of Europe required a long-term, continuing commitment of American financial aid and other assistance. A speech that Acheson gave two weeks earlier had been intended to be a "reveille" awakening Americans to the danger of a Soviet takeover of Western Europe. Instead, Acheson's clarion call had fallen flat. Delivered before an overheated and inattentive audience in a steamy gymnasium at a Mississippi teachers college, it received little attention from the press.[55]

Acheson's speech and Kennan's paper would nonetheless become major inspirations for the commencement address that Secretary of State Marshall gave at Harvard on June 5, 1947. The text had been written mainly by Chip Bohlen, who lifted some phrases from Acheson and borrowed others from Kennan. But Bohlen's awkward wordsmithery and Marshall's understated delivery combined to mute the importance of the speech.[56]

Sitting on the dais that day alongside the secretary of state was Joe Alsop, resplendent in academic regalia as honorary overseer of the graduation ceremony at his alma mater. As Joe later wrote, his reporter's instincts on this occasion failed him—possibly because he was hungover from celebrating with friends at the Porc the night before: "I confess that the wording of the speech was so vague and its delivery so lacking in vigor that I had not the dimmest notion of what the secretary of state was saying, let alone that he was making a proposal that would change the world."[57]

Yet the significance of the Marshall Plan was evident soon enough, and the Alsops, like other journalists, highlighted its importance in articles and columns during the weeks that followed the Harvard speech. Indeed, Washington's press corps had been specifically targeted by the administration, which was already engaged in a public relations campaign aimed at "selling" the idea of sending economic aid to Europe. Forrestal had sent Kennan to see Walter Lippmann, the man whom most Americans considered the dean of Washington's journalists, the previous April. Lippmann's twice-weekly syndicated column, Today and Tomorrow, alternated with the Alsops' Matter of Fact on the editorial pages of the *Herald Tribune* and *The Washington Post*. Spurred on by Acheson, the *Times*'s Scotty Reston likewise took up the cause of European recovery in that paper throughout the spring and summer. For his part, Forrestal lobbied Arthur Krock—who, like the defense secretary, had gone to Princeton but left before graduating.[58]

By 1947, the Alsop brothers—and especially Joe—had established a reputation among readers that set them apart from the other leading lights of the Washington press corps. "Joe Alsop was more flamboyant and outrageous than the impersonal Lippmann and the responsible Reston," noted Joe's friend Arthur Schlesinger Jr. The Scottish-born Reston was, in fact, relatively new to Washington, having been a *Times* correspondent in London just before the war. While as well connected politically and socially as Joe and Stewart, Reston wrote of Washington policymakers with a reserve that contrasted with the impetuous, opinionated Alsops.[59]

Equally in contrast to the brothers' unvarnished brand of journalism was the celebrated hauteur of Walter Lippmann. Joe Alsop's relations with Lippmann were complex. Although he had asked his rival on the opinion page to welcome Stewart and Tish home from the war in his absence, Joe was ever mindful that the fifty-six-year-old Lippmann was a better-known and more respected commentator on the national scene: a silver-haired sage who had actually assisted President Woodrow Wilson in crafting the latter's famous Fourteen Points and was a founding editor of *The New Republic* journal. "Lippmann was in a world of his own, and it was a world that Joe envied," noted a *Washington Post* reporter who knew both men.[60]

The New York Times's Arthur Krock had been a journalist even longer than Lippmann—as the Washington correspondent for the Louisville *Courier-Journal* as early as 1911. In 1932, Krock was made head of the *Times*'s Washington bureau and in less than a decade had won two Pulitzers for his coverage of politics in the capital city with his thrice-weekly column, In the Nation. But Krock's conservative critique of the New Deal—he accused FDR of creating "a neosocialist welfare state"—and his early endorsement of the isolationist views of Joseph P. Kennedy, the U.S. ambassador to London before the war, undermined his credibility in the eyes of many Americans, the Alsops among them.[61]

Unlike the Alsop brothers, Arthur Krock, Scotty Reston, and Walter Lippmann would each receive Pulitzer Prizes for their reporting. But Joe and Stewart had arguably been even quicker than their journalist rivals to focus attention on the critical importance of resurrecting post-war Europe to save it from Soviet aggression. As early as April 1946, the brothers had promoted a Marshall-type recovery plan in their column. Throughout the spring and summer of 1947, the Alsops would use Matter of Fact, as well as longer articles they wrote for *The Saturday Evening*

Post, to beat the drum for the cause. By the end of the year, the brothers had devoted more than two dozen columns to the critical importance of getting Europe back on its feet. But, as the Alsops also made clear, it was neither altruism nor humanitarian concern so much as unbridled fear of Russian expansionism that provided their motivation. A typical piece by them in the *Post* magazine, titled "If Russia Grabs Europe," began, "If Italy and France fall to the communists, where does that leave us, and what are we going to do about it?"[62]

CHAPTER THREE

"Is War Inevitable?"

B Y TEMPERAMENT as well as training, Stewart Johonnot Oliver Alsop was less excitable than his older brother—arguably a result of Stew's service with the British and American armies during World War II. (When researching the family history, Stewart was surprised to discover that he was the first Alsop to have been in the military in any capacity.) The two brothers were dissimilar in other ways, including personal traits. Whereas Joe was always fastidious in manner and dress, Stewart opted for casual comfort: his habitual uniform on summer weekends consisted of open-collar shirts with rolled sleeves and khaki shorts. On one formal occasion, Stew shocked his older brother by wearing an ascot as a cummerbund. Joe wrote Susan Mary that when his brother was a bachelor in New York City before the war, Stewart's simple apartment had been "furnished only with a bed and a passé motor-cycle." Stewart's daughter, Elizabeth, would later describe weekly trips from her parents' home to Joe's house as akin to "traveling between two continents . . . Ours was a shelter for a messy, unruly pack of children, while his served as a monument to a single man's personal tastes, his desire for order and his passion for beautiful objects . . . In Uncle Joe's house, tabletops gleamed, floors were waxed, books were shelved in proper order so that you could in fact find something you were looking for. Leather was oiled, brass was polished and the crystal glasses sparkled."[1]

By contrast, Elizabeth wrote, "Our house was shabby and comfortable . . . Chair legs came unglued, light bulbs wobbled dangerously on the tops of lamps where the wiring had loosened, the paint on some of the antique portraits was flaking off here and there because of dry heat.

There was always a new leak starting in the living room ceiling, the little crenelated molding at the top of the living-room walls was gray with dust, books were shelved in a haphazard and indiscriminate manner, drawers stuck. Our house, filled as it was with children, looked lived in."

"I hardly ever go there without wanting to tidy everything up at once," Joe confided to Susan Mary after a visit to his brother's house.

In contrast to Joe, who was profligate in his spending habits, Stewart would spend evenings painstakingly sewing up the holes that Susan Mary's high heels routinely poked in his prized antique Aubusson rugs. (Eventually, Stew simply glued the rugs to the living room floor.) When the younger brother bought a mail-order product meant to cover up fingerprints on gilt picture frames, Joe took one look at the stuff and sniffed, "Oh God. Radiator paint." Whereas Joe's manicured garden was a point of pride, Stewart left his own backyard untended, cheerfully declaring, "God is the best gardener."[2]

Regarding the mortal danger that the Soviet Union posed to the United States and its allies, however, Joe and Stewart Alsop saw eye to eye.

Eager to gauge the Russian threat on his own, Stewart Alsop in the winter of 1946–1947 embarked on a three-month trip to Turkey, Greece, and the Middle East. In Athens, Stew scored a journalistic coup upon learning from sources at the American embassy that Britain was planning to withdraw its forces from the eastern Mediterranean, despite a growing Communist-led insurgency in Greece.

Two Matter of Fact columns in February 1947 carried Stewart's scoop about the "panic" in the Truman administration over the situation in Greece, along with news that the president was considering a "politico-economic fire brigade" to deal with the crisis. Joe's friend Susan Mary wrote to Marietta from Paris of the anxious atmosphere there: "The Greeks are going straight into the Russian sphere, politically, unless they get help fast, and the English look like being too poor to help them . . . My feeling is that Truman and Marshall and Acheson will fill the gap and sell it to Congress somehow."[3]

In fact, less than a month later the president announced in an address to Congress what would become known as the Truman Doctrine, promising $400 million in military and economic aid to Greece and Turkey and declaring that henceforth it would be U.S. policy "to support free peoples who are resisting attempted subjugation by armed minorities or by outside pressures."[4]

While the Truman Doctrine faced relatively little organized opposition in Congress, the same would not be true of the Marshall Plan—where, as even its backers conceded, the ultimate cost to the U.S. taxpayer was unknowable. Acheson had told Reston that at least sixteen billion dollars would be necessary over the next four years. And, unlike the threat posed by Greece's armed guerrillas, the danger facing Western Europe was more subtly that of subversion and revolution, rather than imminent physical attack. The difference was starkly reflected in the popular mood. A month after Marshall's Harvard speech, public opinion polls indicated that while 90 percent of Americans were aware of recent purported flying saucer sightings, only 49 percent had heard of the Marshall Plan, and of that number fewer than half said they would be willing to support higher taxes to pay for it. Indeed, one State Department skeptic compared the plan itself to a flying saucer—in that "nobody knows what it looks like, how big it is, in what direction it is moving, or whether it really exists."[5]

In contrast to most journalists in the capital, Joe and Stewart did not hesitate to take on congressional critics of the Marshall Plan. When a key Republican, Michigan's Arthur Vandenberg, chairman of the Senate Foreign Relations Committee, threw his support behind the plan, the brothers praised Vandenberg as a farsighted statesman. But after another important Republican and aspiring presidential candidate—the Ohio senator Robert Taft—refused to take a position on the bill to fund European recovery, the Alsops attacked Taft and his party's isolationists as "the Republican economizers." Throughout the rest of the year, the Alsops kept up the attack on Taft and other partisan opponents of European aid. Matter of Fact on June 15, 1947, was headlined "Isolationist Republicans Imperil Carrying Out of New U.S. Policy." The following month, the Alsops gave an unambiguous response to what they felt was the crucial question behind aid to Europe, headlining their column "The Answer Is Yes; Subject: Can We Afford the Marshall Plan?"[6]

THE COUNTRY's newspaper publishers would likewise play a major role in selling the Marshall Plan. Prominent among that number was Joe Alsop's friend and Georgetown neighbor Phil Graham.

Although much would later be made of Graham's supposedly humble origins—including by Phil himself—he was actually the son of a relatively prosperous dairy farmer who had also made money in real estate.

Following several failed business ventures, Ernest Graham had settled his family in the Florida Everglades in the early 1920s and benefited from the explosive growth of Miami, some fifty miles away. Even as an adolescent, Phil Graham could be ebulliently "up" on some days but silent and brooding the next morning. He was, in any case, noted Joe Alsop, "a man in whose company it was impossible to be bored."[7]

Those close to Phil Graham observed that his need to prove himself, to be his own man, seemed an increasingly salient part of his personality following his marriage to Kay, the boss's daughter. A longtime colleague, Joe Rauh, thought Graham's demons were born of that fact: "He felt he hadn't succeeded because he had inherited it all. He became unhappy because it was all given to him." When Phil was still a student at Harvard, editor of the law review, and later, as a clerk for Justice Frankfurter, Graham's friends assumed his ambitions included a possible political career—or a federal judgeship. Few, if any, imagined Phil at a newspaper. Those unfulfilled expectations sometimes haunted him. "I might be in the Senate today," Phil bitterly reminded those who talked of his good fortune in marrying Katharine Meyer. Having grown up amid affluence but with a domineering mother and a remote, if loving, father, Kay Graham had her own share of demons.

Although Eugene Meyer remained chairman of the board of the Washington Post Company in 1946, he gradually began shifting more responsibility to his son-in-law, the associate publisher. Prior to Meyer's taking it over, the *Post*—run by an alcoholic playboy—had become something of a joke in the capital city. (In 1911, a notorious *Post* article on the recent theft of the *Mona Lisa* had been illustrated with a picture of the wrong painting.) Since then, Meyer had not hesitated to use the paper as a pulpit to crusade for causes he believed in. In August 1940, with Paris under the Nazi banner, Meyer fired the newspaper's editor, a Quaker and an isolationist, replacing him with a spirited advocate of American intervention in the war. A subsequent, similar campaign by Meyer and the *Post* helped push lend-lease aid to embattled Britain through Congress. Beginning in the spring of 1947, the cause that he and his son-in-law would embrace was Europe's economic recovery.[8]

That summer, at Phil Graham's urging, Eugene Meyer and the *Post* reporter Alfred Friendly went on an inspection tour of Europe, gathering material in preparation for Meyer's testimony in support of the Marshall Plan at congressional hearings scheduled for early 1948. The duo's dispatches from war-scarred France, Italy, and Germany were published as news features on the front page of *The Washington Post.* "We were Marshall Plan even before Marshall," Friendly later boasted. In a *Post* editorial that Meyer wrote, he urged Congress to meet in special session, if necessary, to approve Marshall Plan funding.[9]

By the end of the year, the efforts of Eugene Meyer, Al Friendly, Phil Graham, and others had begun to show results. Polls showed that two-thirds of Americans were at least aware of the Marshall Plan, and a bare majority supported it. As the debate began in Congress over the legislation, the drumbeat by the plan's supporters, including the Alsops and the *Post*'s publisher, increased, *Boléro*-like, in both urgency and intensity.[10]

The selling of European aid by the national press was abetted by the Truman administration's own public relations blitz. Foremost among the several government organizations promoting European recovery that fall was the President's Committee on Foreign Aid, otherwise known as the Harriman Committee. Its chairman, William Averell Harriman, the son of the railroad tycoon E. H. Harriman, was Kennan's former boss at the Moscow embassy and Joe Alsop's Georgetown neighbor. During the war, FDR had sent Averell Harriman to England as his special envoy. In 1946, Truman had called on him to serve as secretary of commerce. At fifty-six, Harriman, the multimillionaire owner of a shipping line and a Wall Street investment bank, was considerably older and more experienced than most Marshall planners—Averell's first visit to Russia had been in 1899, when he was seven, in the company of his father. Moreover, Harriman had earned a reputation for persistence and shrewdness as a result of his wartime dealings with Stalin. But Harriman told Truman that he would only serve as a "pitchman" for the European aid effort.[11]

Seemingly somnolent at State Department briefings, Harriman had a habit of suddenly stirring to life to eviscerate the briefer with a pointed comment that earned him the nickname the Crocodile. (Harriman was "quiescent looking . . . until the dictates of common sense or the great interests of the United States are attacked," wrote Joe Alsop in one column. "Whereupon the great jaws open and another fool finds that he is figuratively missing a leg.")[12]

During the war, Harriman had loaned the family homestead, Arden House—a 100,000-square-foot mansion located on a twenty-thousand-acre estate outside the eponymously named town of Harriman, New York—to the U.S. Navy for use as a temporary convalescent hospital. As a substitute, Averell and his wife, Marie, remodeled their nine-bedroom

Georgetown pied-à-terre at 3038 N Street into a permanent residence. Just two blocks down, on P Street, lived Harriman's friend and State Department colleague Dean Acheson—whom Harriman had taught to row as coach of Yale's freshman crew.[13]

While Harriman buttonholed business leaders in Washington and embarked on a speaking tour to women's clubs around the nation, the real work of his twenty-member committee would be done by another man, its executive secretary: Richard Bissell.[14]

A Connecticut blue blood—the family had emigrated from England in 1636—Bissell was nonetheless an iconoclastic figure, born in Mark Twain's old house in Hartford, fittingly enough. Bissell was an economist by training, having received both graduate and undergraduate degrees from Yale, where he had, early on, demonstrated an independent streak by turning down an invitation to join Skull and Bones, the college's prestigious secret society. Stubbornness was equally a Bissell trait. After nearly breaking his back in a fall while free-climbing Connecticut's Pinnacle Rock, the young Bissell, following weeks in the hospital, returned to the site and finished the climb, unheralded, alone, and unroped.[15]

Dick Bissell had been Joe Alsop's classmate and only friend at Groton, where the two managed to duck the athletic contests that were mandatory for the other boys. "I was shy, I wasn't a good athlete, and I was scared of them," Bissell recalled in a memoir. Instead, the pair took long walks around the bucolic Massachusetts campus. (Another famous "Grottie," Averell Harriman, believed that, like sports at Eton, unhappiness at Groton was a prerequisite for later success among WASP families.) But their friendship was tested when Bissell set off a stink bomb in Alsop's study, which drove the furious Joe out into the February snow. While the duo eventually reconciled, a certain good-natured combativeness remained. Bissell, acting as prosecutor, bested Alsop in the school's mock-trial debate—"Resolved: Napoleon Bonaparte was a war criminal"—by stealing Joe's notes, making copies, and returning only fragments of the originals to the defense. Joe would later claim that he chose to go to Harvard instead of Yale because he didn't want Dickie running his life. Nonetheless, it was to Bissell that Alsop turned for help in balancing the checkbook Joe was required to regularly submit to his father for inspection during his college years. Despite heroic feats of financial legerdemain by Bissell, the father quickly saw through the pair's fraudulent accounting.[16]

Bissell would have better luck with figures when he became a planner, in 1942, for the War Shipping Administration. He and his wife, Ann, rented a house on Georgetown's Q Street for the duration of the war. Using only three-by-five-inch index cards and a hand-cranked calculator, Bissell invented a logistics database that matched the cargo capacity of Allied ships with military demands for war matériel. He later boasted that his system operated with a margin of error of less than 5 percent. Frustrated by the bureaucratic obstacles and personal rivalries he encountered in a subsequent job for the Truman administration, however, Bissell returned to Cambridge and a professorship at MIT shortly after V-J day. He would remain in the groves of academe barely a year.[17]

Moving back to Washington in September 1947, Richard and Ann rented a house in the District, anticipating a quick retreat to MIT when his work for the Harriman Committee was finished. Given only two months to write a report to the president and Congress, detailing the amount of Marshall Plan aid that was needed and outlining how it might be distributed in Europe, Bissell turned to the titans of American industry, the nation's labor leaders, and a few of his own academic cronies at MIT and Yale for help. Finishing their work in the early morning of November 7, Bissell and his colleagues sent their three-inch-thick report to the White House mere hours prior to releasing it to reporters—and before some members of the Harriman Committee had even read the final draft. (A fellow staffer subsequently praised Bissell's briefing to the committee as "more boring than he had ever heard, and more long-winded . . . By the time you were through, the committee would have been ready to agree to almost any numbers you wanted to put in the report, just to get through that part of the discussion.") Their report nonetheless received "magnificent press," Bissell recalled, including paeans of praise from the Alsop brothers and glowing editorials in *The Washington Post*.[18]

Shortly thereafter, Phil Graham rounded up some of his newspaper's top reporters for a special sixteen-page supplement promoting the Marshall Plan. "This Generation's Chance for Peace" appeared as an insert in *The Washington Post* on November 23, 1947, and was reprinted widely in other papers throughout the country, eventually winning the *Post* a public service award.[19]

Although the majority of Washington's press corps and newspaper publishers remained solidly in favor of the Marshall Plan, members of Congress and citizens alike balked at the projected twelve- to sixteen-billion-dollar cost of the program laid out in Bissell's report. With Republicans a majority in Congress for the first time in two decades, opponents like Senator Taft felt emboldened to denounce the plan as a "European TVA" and a "giveaway program." The real task for Marshall Plan supporters, it had become clear by early 1948, would be persuading recalcitrant members of Congress to approve funding for what was officially called the European Recovery Plan.[20]

The logical man for that job was George Kennan, who had privately lobbied Walter Lippmann, Scotty Reston, and the Alsop brothers on behalf of the Marshall Plan for more than a year. But the shy and temperamental Kennan balked at the idea of public testimony, as he confided to his diary following a tempestuous encounter with Joe Alsop: "I argued with him at length about the extent of our responsibility for the education of Congress in these matters. I pointed out that personally . . . my specialty was the defense of U.S. interests against others, not against our own representatives."[21]

Consequently, the task of selling the Marshall Plan on Capitol Hill fell to one of Kennan's State Department colleagues, Paul Henry Nitze.

KENNAN HAD FIRST MET NITZE by chance during the war, on a train traveling between New York and Washington. The two hit it off immediately, Nitze remembered, and saw eye to eye on a topic that would come to dominate both their lives: "We got into a discussion about the USSR in the war and the postwar world. I found he was interesting, brilliant, charming. I was very fond of him right away. I thought everything he was saying made very good sense."[22]

It was perhaps the last time the two men would agree on the subject of Russia.

Although Nitze and Kennan were close in age—and had even, in different years, attended the same midwestern summer camp as children—the two inhabited different worlds. Born into privilege—Paul's grandfather, a German immigrant, was a successful banker in Baltimore—Nitze had skated through his classes at Harvard in a haze of alcohol and partying with Porc Club mates like Chip Bohlen. At Princeton, by contrast, the penurious Kennan had been a virtual social outcast. During a 1929 holiday in Germany, Nitze had met and befriended the sculptor Alexander Calder, with whom he bicycled around Europe in a "traveling circus" of artists and self-styled intellectuals. In Paris, Nitze had even briefly considered becoming an art dealer, until the realization dawned, he later said, that "the whole profession was a bunch of crooks."[23]

Nitze remembered Berlin as "full of life." At nearly the same time as Nitze's visit to the German capital, George Kennan was toiling away at the University of Berlin, learning Russian. Kennan found the city gloomy and depressing, writing in his diary of old imperial buildings with "weather-streaked, unpainted walls and their peeling facades."[24]

But the difference in their temperaments was perhaps most evident in the response that the two men had to the raucous rallies of the Communist Party, which was then vying with the Nazis for control of Germany. After witnessing one such rally, which ended in violence, Kennan wrote in his diary, "For all my contempt for the falseness and hatefulness and demagoguery of communism, I had a strange desire to cry." Nitze's reaction to the rallies, on the other hand, was characteristically less emotional, and the lesson he took away more pragmatic: when the police arrived to break up a demonstration, he observed, it was better to run toward them than away.[25]

Despite their disparate personalities, one thing that Kennan and Nitze had in common was a surprising psychological insecurity. In the case of the shy, soft-spoken Kennan, it was evident for all to see. Nitze's vulnerability was better hidden and likely had its source in the fact that his father was a well-known academic, a professor of Romance languages at the University of Chicago. No matter how successful the son would become in the worlds of banking and business, the father's disappointment that Paul was a mere "money-lender" lay behind the latter's insistent need to prove himself intellectually equal, or superior, to any challenger. Defensively, the son dismissed the scholar's life as unpragmatic: "The whole essence of academia is novel ideas, not wisdom."[26]

Nitze's up-front arrogance armored him against being labeled a dilettante: during his life, he would discuss and debate art with Calder, literature with the novelist Marguerite Yourcenar, historical determinism with the Oxford philosopher Isaiah Berlin, and nuclear weapons design with the physicist Edward Teller. Calm, confident, and seemingly serenely self-assured, Nitze fancied himself an intellectual and possessed the rare ability of persuading his audience—and himself—that he was an expert on subjects about which he, in fact, often knew comparatively little.[27]

Their respective demons made Kennan and Nitze alike in yet another way: they were equally driven.

Nitze had made his first million by the age of thirty as a Wall Street investment banker, before turning his talents as a self-professed "problem solver" to the cause of public service. Brought to Washington in 1940 by Forrestal, Nitze had been assigned to work on Latin American issues for the navy. He was staying at a small hotel in Asunción, Paraguay, part of a three-man delegation visiting U.S. embassies, when the group received news of Pearl Harbor. Nitze spent the first months after the Japanese attack in Washington, as head of the metals and minerals branch of the Board of Economic Warfare. Put in charge of procuring vital matériel for the war effort, he cornered the market on such esoterica as Mexican prairie dog bones, used in making glue, and dried cuttlefish, for grinding bombsight lenses.[28]

Nitze found his next assignment better suited to both his interests and his abilities. Although he had graduated from Harvard cum laude with a degree in economics, he considered himself foremost a logician, able to "put calipers" on a problem in order to solve it. (Nitze enjoyed telling the story of the palm reader he had gone to in college. She had stared at his palm in silence for fully five minutes before issuing her verdict: "I can say nothing about this man; he has a purely practical hand.") For Nitze, pragmatism was not only a noble goal but a matter of personal pride.[29]

As vice-chairman of the U.S. Strategic Bombing Survey in 1945, Nitze had traveled with his staff throughout the devastated cities of Germany and Japan, interviewing survivors and even measuring the depth of bomb craters, in an effort to gauge—precisely—the effectiveness of the Allies' aerial assault. "We tried to put quantitative numbers on something that was considered immeasurable," he later explained.[30]

Indeed, he believed he had done exactly that. Disregarding radiation effects, Nitze calculated that the damage caused by the nuclear weapon dropped on Hiroshima was equivalent to the conventional high-explosive bombs and incendiaries from 210 B-29 bombers. For Nagasaki, the comparable figure was 150 B-29s. More controversial still was the survey's conclusion that Japan would likely have surrendered before the planned U.S. invasion of the home islands "even if the atomic bomb had not been used." His critics would later charge that Nitze, in typical fashion, had come to this conclusion before he set foot in Japan and had simply concocted the numbers to give seeming weight to his argument.[31]

In fact, Nitze's outspokenness and willingness to promote a contrarian view would subsequently stand in the way of his own considerable ambition—preventing him from achieving any of the top posts in government that he so plainly desired. But that did not make the stubborn "problem solver" any less outspoken or determined.

After the bombing survey was completed, Nitze had originally planned to join a start-up venture capital firm in New York with one of his Harvard friends. But Potomac fever and his family's wishes intervened. As the new deputy director of the Office of International Trade Policy, Nitze could walk from his home on Woodley Road, near the National Cathedral, to his State Department office downtown in Foggy Bottom.[32]

In late spring 1947, Nitze was given the task of assessing the cost of restoring Europe's economies by his superior at the State Department, Will Clayton. After Nitze told Joe Alsop at dinner one night of how his boss was playing a key role in Europe's economic recovery, Alsop highlighted Clayton's work in his column the following day. Nitze grew worried when Acheson began the next morning's staff meeting by asking who had read the Alsop column. But before anyone could reply, Acheson said that "it was the most helpful thing that could have happened."[33]

To better coordinate their separate and often disparate efforts, Nitze convened a weekly luncheon meeting of Marshall planners, including Richard Bissell, at the capital's Metropolitan Club. That summer, the group began shuttling between their Washington offices and the Hôtel de Talleyrand in Paris, the temporary European headquarters of the nascent recovery program, located across the street from the U.S. embassy. Despite tight deadlines and cramped quarters—secretaries had to work in the hotel's lavatories, typewriters balanced precariously on bidets—Nitze and Bissell shared a sense of optimism and excitement characteristic of the time. "The Marshall planners thrill me," Susan Mary wrote to Marietta from Paris, where Soozle and Bill were hosting the visitors, many of them close friends, in their own salons. "They are working in the Grand Palais, one of the hottest buildings in town because of the immense amounts of glass. Of course no air conditioning, but I don't think the planners notice it much, for the sense of urgency is great and they don't even seem to mind their hours, 9 a.m. to midnight."[34]

Compared with Bissell's more public effort on the Harriman Committee, Nitze and his experts at the State Department labored in relative obscurity. "We had done a hell of a lot more work than anybody working for Harriman, but they were getting a hell of a lot more publicity," Nitze later complained. Nonetheless, the two prospective rivals, Nitze and Bissell, became friends and allies instead. Their studies, carried out independently but in parallel, arrived at essentially the same conclusion:

a program to revive Europe's war-shattered economies was feasible but would likely take a minimum of five years to accomplish and require an initial commitment from American taxpayers of at least five billion dollars.[35]

While achieved at some personal cost—two of Nitze's economists suffered nervous collapses, and the State Department assigned drivers for the rest after a pair of auto accidents following all-night sessions—the work done by Nitze and his team would prove to be invaluable in the test coming up with Congress. Their so-called Brown Books cataloged, country by country, the health of each European nation's economy, immediate and long-term needs, and the type and amount of U.S. aid required.[36]

In January 1948, Nitze, the Brown Books at his side, began testifying before the Senate and also defending the Marshall Plan at press conferences. But it was not until after Truman signed the plan into law in early April, creating the European Cooperation Administration, that Nitze faced his first real challenge. At the head of the House Appropriations Committee, whose approval was necessary to obtain Marshall funding, was Congressman John Taber, a Republican from upstate New York with "beetling eyebrows and a perpetual scowl." First elected to the House in 1922, the sixty-eight-year-old Taber had demonstrated an enthusiasm for budget cutting that inspired the nickname Saber Taber. Nitze would appear before Taber's committee more than forty times, losing fifteen pounds in the process. At the opening session of his Marshall Plan hearings, Taber let Nitze know that any testimony based on the Brown Books would be disregarded.[37]

Stripped of the detailed charts and tables that were both the symbol and the substance of his expertise, Nitze found himself unexpectedly on the defensive before Taber, who grilled him on such minutiae as whether it was cheaper to grow pulse beans on Austrian farms rather than grow and ship them from the United States. Almost single-handedly, Taber held up progress on the Marshall Plan for weeks, all the while garnering headlines for himself. The witness was eventually rescued by the intervention of Undersecretary of State Robert Lovett, Averell Harriman's former banking partner and a fellow Yale Bonesman, who had taken over for Acheson while the latter went back to his law firm to make some money. But, for Nitze, the experience with Taber had been an unforgettable lesson—about the limits to logic and precision in the face of political theater and the surprising efficacy of polemic.[38]

———————

EVEN AS APPROVAL for funding the European recovery moved forward in Congress, the mood in Washington and overseas was darkening by early 1948. That winter, a Communist coup in Czechoslovakia overthrew the only democratic government in Eastern Europe to survive the war. In both Italy and France, Communist and pro-Soviet parties continued to make election gains, while the Red Army still occupied Austria and seemed poised to strike at Turkey and Iran. The civil conflict in Greece raged on.

Less than three years after Japan's surrender, it seemed the world was once again about to be plunged into a conflagration. The war scare had the positive effect, at least, of pushing the Marshall Plan through Congress. It was no longer necessary, in the words of Dean Acheson, to make the Soviet threat "clearer than the truth" to persuade the nation's legislators of the danger. Even that chief Republican economizer and consummate isolationist, Bob Taft, had voted for the European Recovery Plan in the end. Bohlen and Kennan correctly predicted that Stalin would coerce the Soviet Union's satellites to reject Western aid, thereby removing a lingering fear of Marshall planners. Truman made Averell Harriman the European overseer of the European Cooperation Administration, and the Crocodile picked the former head of Studebaker automobiles, Paul Hoffman, as its Washington director. Hoffman promptly chose Richard Bissell to be his deputy.[39]

"Serious people take the possibility of a Russian offensive seriously," Susan Mary had written from Paris the previous winter. While personally discounting that risk, she thought that the future, as viewed from Europe, looked grim enough: "I see a dreary slow return to the Dark Ages, hungry peasants tearing Poussins out of the Louvre in order to use the frames for firewood, wolves chewing away at rich bindings in the Bibliothèque Nationale."[40]

The tone of the Alsops' column likewise mirrored the brothers' growing pessimism. "The atmosphere of Washington today is no longer postwar. It is a prewar atmosphere," they wrote in Matter of Fact. For Joe particularly, a sense prevailed that time was running out on the Western democracies in their struggle against what he called "the slave world of the East." Using one of his favorite analogies, the elder Alsop warned that Russia's Sparta was beating America's Athens. "The world seems to be coming apart at the seams relentlessly at a constantly accelerating rate," he wrote to his fellow journalist Vincent Sheean. "The process is, of course, not inevitable, since the United States could halt it overnight by determined action, but I see no sign of the requisite determination in this country, and I fear the worst."[41]

Increasingly, the Alsops viewed Kennan's proffered response to the Soviet threat—containment—as a meager and temporary expedient at best and prospectively a tragic failure. Nor did Joe believe that the author of containment was of much use in describing how his elegant theory might work in practice. As Walter Lippmann had pointed out in a series of fourteen consecutive Today and Tomorrow columns during the summer of 1947, the distressing truth was that Kennan had never explained—in his long telegram, the "X article," or subsequently—exactly *how* or *where* Soviet expansionism was to be stopped. Containment, Lippmann had argued, was a "strategic monstrosity" that called for the "military encirclement" of the Soviet Union and would compel the United States to support corrupt puppet regimes around the world, so long as they professed to be anti-Communist. The cost of the conflict that Lippmann dubbed the "Cold War"—in lives, treasure, and reputation—would be "incalculable," he predicted.[42]

Like Nitze and Kennan, the difference between Joe Alsop and Walter Lippmann was partly a matter of temperament. Unlike the no-holds-barred verbal jousting of Joe's zoo parties, dinners at the Lippmanns' house in Cathedral Heights near Woodley Park "were meditative, cerebral, choreographed, blending philosophy with politics . . . If tempers flared, [Walter] or his wife, Helen, changed topics to avoid a full-blown conflagration," wrote a Lippmann biographer. Walter and Helen were also occasional guests at Joe's Sunday night suppers, where the contrast with the Lippmanns' "meditative" soirees could not have been more stark. After one unusually tempestuous dinner, Alsop wrote to Lippmann to apologize "for becoming both garrulous and heated the other evening. In my family, no argument really *was* an argument unless everyone left the room at least twice, and this was bad training for the future."[43]

Privately, Joe disdained Lippmann's Olympian detachment, which contrasted with his own "shoe leather" approach to reporting and was a sign, he felt, of the latter's intellectual arrogance. ("His role models were not journalists but the great figures of the Harvard Philosophy Department," the fellow reporter David Halberstam would write of Lippmann.) While conceding that his rival was indeed a "very brilliant man," Joe told

Arthur Schlesinger Jr. that "Walter's column was saved from constant repetition only by the simple fact that he changed his views roughly once every eight months." Worse, Alsop felt, was the fact that Lippmann had little knowledge of—or affection for—Asia, which Joe claimed as his own area of expertise. Instead, Lippmann spent summers at his Mount Desert Island retreat in Maine and focused his overseas columns almost exclusively on Europe. ("Walter was a very hard-working reporter in his way but his sources have never been American, or at least American officials," Alsop told an interviewer years later. "His own government he always regarded with suspicion and even contempt.")[44]

Yet on one issue—containment—the two pundits agreed. Both believed that Kennan's prescription for how to deal with the Soviet Union was fatally flawed, albeit for different reasons. Whereas Lippmann considered that containment went too far—condemning the United States to the role of a harried fireman, putting out conflagrations around the globe—Joe believed Kennan's doctrine failed to go far enough. As Alsop later wrote to Lippmann, at the heart of their divergent views lay the question of how to respond to the Soviet threat: "I begin to realize that our basic difference probably lies in different assumptions concerning Russian intentions . . . I, on the contrary, am convinced that the Russians, being a peculiar combination of a tyrannic, imperialist despotism and a crusading religious organization, will not be stopped anywhere except by the hard counter-balance of superior force."[45]

In his memoirs, Alsop would compare Kennan to "the priestess on the tripod at the Greek oracle at Delphi who inhaled the sacred smoke and then held forth. For part of the time, the God spoke truth through her mouth; for part of the time, her speech was sheer gabble. The trouble was you never knew which element in what she said came from the God."[46]

Kennan's gauzy explanation of how containment would actually work—the need for the United States to maintain "small mobile forces" and to improve the "self-confidence, discipline, morale and community spirit of our own people"—was, in Joe's view, sheer gabble. Thus, while Kennan's advice in the "X article," that "we must have courage and self-confidence to cling to our own methods and conceptions of human society," was a laudatory sentiment to be sure, it hardly presented an effective counter to Stalin's armed legions. Paul Nitze would later claim that Kennan told him in the summer of 1949 that two mobile marine divisions were probably sufficient to keep the Red Army in its barracks—a comment that Nitze thought "ridiculous," and one that Kennan subsequently denied making.[*47]

Joe Alsop's friend Isaiah Berlin, a Russian expert in his own right, and one close to Kennan, likewise expressed doubts about the prospects for containment. "Are moral forces alone sufficient to bury the Soviet grave diggers? I doubt it," Berlin wrote to Kennan. Berlin believed that it would require more than just the mere threat of physical force to thwart Russian expansionism. But on that point, Kennan demurred. The author of containment had even objected to the blunt language that the president used in announcing the Truman Doctrine, appending to the planning staff's paper on the subject a section "clarifying" its recommendations to make them sound less confrontational.[48]

Moreover, Kennan's critics worried about the prospective military, financial, and even emotional requirements of containment. In discreet conversations with trusted friends, Joe Alsop had begun to explore the possibility of a radical alternative: a nuclear attack on the Soviet Union. Alsop argued that as morally reprehensible as it seemed, preventive war might be the only alternative to a world ruled by Moscow. "The theory that the world can be permanently divided into two gigantic armed camps, each bristling with weapons and glaring at the other with wild hostility, yet that in these conditions peace can be long preserved, seems to me absolutely bloody nonsense," Joe wrote to the *New York Times* columnist Cy Sulzberger.[49]

Indeed, the potential *human* cost of containment—of a protracted, indecisive conflict of uncertain duration—was already becoming evident. By early 1948, James Forrestal, Joe's friend and Kennan's earliest promoter, was psychologically obsessed with the Russian threat and on the verge of a nervous breakdown. Elevated to the post of secretary of defense the previous September, Forrestal felt trapped between Truman's edict to reduce military spending and his own responsibility to

---

* In a January 1947 speech before the U.S. Chamber of Commerce, Kennan had emphasized the need, in peacetime, for "the maintenance of small, compact, alert forces, capable of delivering at short notice effective blows on limited theaters of operation far from our own shores." A decade later, in a series of public lectures, Kennan suggested that Western Europe might look for its own defense to "a territorial-militia . . . somewhat on the Swiss example, rather than regular military units on the World War II pattern"—and could, in any case, count on indigenous resistance movements to eventually oust any Soviet invaders.

protect America and its allies from Soviet aggression. Finding little relief at home—his wife, Jo, the former editor of a fashion magazine, was emotionally unstable and an alcoholic—Forrestal had taken to sleeping nights on a cot in his office. At meetings, when the subject of Russia came up, Pentagon colleagues noted that the defense secretary was strangely silent and seemingly distracted, with a new and disconcerting nervous habit: Forrestal repeatedly and absentmindedly wet his dry, chapped lips with an index finger dipped in his water glass. Worried friends urged Forrestal to join them on trips out of the capital, believing that leaving the pressures of Washington behind would allow him to relax. But their efforts were unavailing, and Truman's defense secretary remained in the grip of paranoid fears. Forrestal believed—quite literally—that the Russians were coming.[50]

THAT TENSE WINTER, the Harvard Law School Forum asked Joe Alsop to give a speech on the future of U.S. foreign policy. For his topic, Joe chose the theme "the United States and Russia—is war inevitable?" Ruling out, at least for the moment, a surprise nuclear attack on the U.S.S.R. as an option, Joe looked to America's atomic arsenal to hold the Soviet Union in check. But the U.S. nuclear monopoly was, as he acknowledged in his talk, at best only a fleeting advantage, a wasting asset, while the Marshall Plan—even if successful—would still take years to resurrect Europe's economies and instill political order there. The answer that Joe gave to his own rhetorical question was carefully framed and equivocal: if not inevitable, war with Russia seemed nonetheless increasingly probable.[51]

At the same time, as was becoming increasingly obvious to Alsop and others, including even George Kennan, there was a limit to what Congress and the American people could and would tolerate in responding to the Russian threat. Forrestal's psychological disintegration graphically underscored the point. The partisan opposition to the Truman Doctrine and the Marshall Plan, Congress's recent rejection of universal military service, and the strictures that Truman himself had put on increases in the defense budget all pointed to a single inescapable conclusion: in order to work, any long-term strategy to contain, much less defeat, the Soviet Union would need to have elements that were deliberately kept out of the public eye—and hidden in the shadows.

CHAPTER FOUR

"Would He Go into the Woods?"

As THE COUNTRY and its capital mobilized for the Cold War, there was a new and more splendid venue for the Georgetown salons than Joe Alsop's cramped town house. Phil and Katharine Graham had abandoned what Kay called their "very odd house" on O Street—the kitchen and dining room were located in the basement—for a sprawling cream-colored Georgian mansion with a green mansard roof and manicured grounds just a few blocks away, at R and Twenty-Ninth Streets. The house had belonged to the U.S. Army major general William "Wild Bill" Donovan, head of the Office of Strategic Services, America's wartime intelligence agency.

Once elegant, the house bore the marks of having been used as Donovan's unofficial headquarters: a front room just off the entry had been occupied by the general's OSS staff, while the floor of the adjoining living room was marred and scratched from constant foot traffic and carelessly moved filing cabinets. Since Kay ate breakfast there every morning with the children—three-year-old Elizabeth and Donald, one—Phil dubbed it the "Shredded Wheat Room." The parents temporarily camped in the library while Katharine set about doing an extensive makeover of the house interior: painting the drab dun-colored walls eggshell white and installing blue velvet curtains in the dining room.[1]

When Kay had finished decorating the house, the Grahams would hold a black-tie party to celebrate the two hundredth anniversary of the founding of Georgetown. Among the score of invited guests that night were George Kennan, Dean Acheson, and Felix Frankfurter. The Supreme Court justice and his wife, Marion, lived nearby at

3018 Dumbarton Avenue. In the highlight of the evening, Phil delivered a champagne-fueled toast to the place where most of them lived. "Georgetown was an entity unto itself," he began, "home to the great, the near great and the once great in government and in journalism . . . In other cities, people go to parties primarily to have fun. In Georgetown, people who have fun at parties probably aren't getting much work done. That's because parties in Georgetown aren't really parties in the true sense of the word. They're business after hours, a form of government by invitation . . . It's fair to say," he concluded on an expansive note, "that more political decisions get made at Georgetown suppers than anywhere else in the nation's capital, including the Oval Office."[2]

The party's self-congratulatory mood was dampened, however, by after-dinner discussions of the day's political news. And the spell was broken altogether when Phil, deep in his cups, confronted the French ambassador, the guest of honor, over France's policies in Indochina. Kay intentionally knocked over a tea service to avoid flying fists, and the remaining guests left quickly. Phil's wife attributed the outburst, as usual, to her husband's heavy drinking. But it was a harbinger of the trouble to come.

THE R STREET HOUSE had gone on the market because Donovan was moving back to New York to resume his law practice, having lost his Washington job when the OSS was abruptly abolished by President Truman in mid-September 1945. Wild Bill had fallen victim to fears that he planned to establish an American-style Gestapo after the war. Donovan was the particular target of the FBI director, J. Edgar Hoover, who saw the OSS as a potential rival to the bureau. Although it was not the reason behind his firing, Donovan had also been slow to awaken to the Soviet threat. Indeed, his view of the Russians was exactly the sort of wishful naïveté that Kennan had rebelled against in his long telegram and the "X article." Late in 1943, Donovan had proposed a remarkable series of joint initiatives with his Soviet counterpart, Colonel Pavel Fitin, the head of the Committee for State Security, or KGB, in hopes of ensuring that Soviet cooperation with U.S. intelligence would continue after the war.[*3]

---

* Historically, the Soviet foreign intelligence service went by many names—Cheka, GPU, OGPU, NKVD, NKGB, and MGB—before becoming the Committee for State Security (Komitet Gosudarstvennoy Bezopasnosti), or KGB, in 1954. However, KGB is used here for consistency.

The full details of Donovan's dealings with the Russians would not become known for another half century, with the declassification of U.S. intercepts of Soviet wartime cables and the release of KGB documents following the collapse of the Soviet Union. Those sources show how Donovan pledged to help Fitin deploy KGB agents in postwar France and Germany and readily turned over to the Soviets an illustrated catalog of special weapons and spy gear developed by the OSS, as well as a list of members of the so-called Hoettl chain: captured German experts on the U.S.S.R. who had hoped, in vain, that they might bargain their specialized knowledge in exchange for protection by the United States.[4]

Donovan's efforts to woo Fitin and other senior KGB officers included a meeting at America's Moscow embassy in early 1944, which concluded with a screening of the James Cagney movie *Yankee Doodle Dandy*. (Showing the patriotic film had been Ambassador Harriman's idea.) What Fitin and his comrades thought of the evening was not recorded. But an inside account of the OSS chief's Moscow visit was later sent to Fitin by Duncan Lee, a former member of Donovan's Wall Street law firm who was on Wild Bill's senior staff at the OSS but who had been secretly recruited as a spy by the Soviets. As the KGB agent code-named Koch, Lee wrote to Fitin, "The Soviet govt. made a tremendous impression on Donovan, and he is enthralled by it. He regards Stalin as the smartest person heading any govt. today. He said that Americans have no reason to be afraid of the line—communist domination of the world."[5]

Among Donovan's other gifts to the Soviets were some fifteen hundred pages of material "purporting to contain the key to certain Russian codes, both military and [KGB]," which the OSS had obtained from friendly foreign intelligence services.[6] ("The codes are for 1941–43. They have been completely replaced," a subordinate informed Fitin.) Likewise handed over, according to a KGB report, were OSS lists of its own operatives "in territory occupied by the Sov. Army."[7] In December 1944, Donovan also gave Fitin information on an anti-Soviet plot being hatched by members of the Romanian military, who were promptly arrested when the Red Army occupied that country.[8] Wild Bill's efforts toward a personal rapprochement with the Russians only ended, in fact, when he was removed from his post and the OSS—code-named Cabin in the secret cables sent from the KGB's Moscow Center headquarters—was abolished. "As a result of the termination of contact, the disbanding of the OSS and D[onovan]'s retirement, the case was closed," a final report to Fitin advised. Reportedly among Wild Bill's last gifts to the KGB was Hitler's dental chart, to help in identifying the charred corpse that the Russians had found in the ruins of Berlin's Reich Chancellery.[9]

Donovan's largesse went unrewarded, and a Soviet agent later delivered his own candid verdict about the KGB's erstwhile rival and would-be collaborator: "The main principle of the entire OSS is the principle of amateurishness."[10]

The extent to which the KGB had successfully penetrated the OSS, and indeed virtually all of official Washington, would remain a secret well after the end of World War II. But recently declassified documents reveal how the Georgetown set, too, was inadvertently caught up in the Russians' spy network. Thus, defense secrets that Phil Graham learned working for the Office of Emergency Management before Pearl Harbor, such as the production rate for U.S. heavy bombers, were likely passed along to the Soviets by Graham's OEM colleague Lauchlin Currie, who operated under the KGB code name Page. While serving as an economic adviser to FDR in 1941–42, Currie was sent to China, where he became an occasional source for Joe Alsop's reporting.[11]

Among the guests at Kay Graham's first dinner party as a single hostess during the war was the British diplomat Donald Maclean, who threw the gathering into disarray by verbally attacking another guest. Maclean accused his countryman Isaiah Berlin of consorting with Americans who were "fascist and right-wing." (Seven years later, when he was about to be exposed as the Soviet agent Homer, Maclean would defect to the U.S.S.R.) While he worked for the Foreign Economic Administration—which Lauchlin Currie headed in 1943—Paul Nitze saved rationed gasoline by carpooling to the office with two other State Department colleagues subsequently identified as Russian spies: Laurence Duggan/Prince, chief of the Latin America desk at State, and Alger Hiss/Ales, who would be part of the U.S. delegation at the Yalta meeting of FDR, Churchill, and Stalin. (Duggan committed suicide in December 1948, ten days after being questioned by the FBI about his ties to Soviet intelligence. Hiss continued to insist on his innocence up to his death in 1996.)[12]

Even the dean of the capital's press corps, Walter Lippmann—assigned the KGB cryptonym Hub—was unknowingly ensnared in the Soviet dragnet. Lippmann employed a secretary, Mary Price/Dir, who routinely reported to Moscow on the journalist's activities and contacts during the early years of the war.[13] Not surprisingly, Soviet agents had a special interest in the Washington press corps, especially its most left-leaning members. Although the Russians succeeded in recruiting Michael Straight, later the editor of *The New Republic,* they evidently had less luck with the journalist I. F. Stone. Both Straight and Stone ignored KGB overtures after the tide of battle turned against the Axis. But Soviet intelligence also paid keen attention to American journalists who were implacably hostile to the Soviet Union—as Joe Alsop would subsequently discover.

A FAR MORE POSITIVE IMAGE of Wild Bill Donovan and the Office of Strategic Services would emerge from the book that Stewart Alsop and Tom Braden published in 1946 about their exploits with the OSS. (Critics joked that the initials stood for "oh-so-social" and that the OSS was "the last refuge of the well-connected," given Donovan's success at recruiting the rich and influential to spy for their country.) The publication of *Sub Rosa: The OSS and American Espionage* might actually have been encouraged by Donovan, who had not yet abandoned hopes of resurrecting his old spy agency in the new climate created by the confrontation with Russia.[14]

The Alsop-Braden book, in any case, promptly became a best seller, describing the wartime exploits of the legendary OSS Jedburghs, who had parachuted into Nazi-occupied France to bring money and supplies to the embattled French Resistance, the maquis. Its romantic image of the fearless, knife-clenched-between-the-teeth commando derived from the real-life missions of the Jeds.[15]

Although Braden's Jedburgh team never saw action—his parachute jump into northern Italy was scrubbed because of bad weather, just before the war ended—in August 1944, Jed team Alexander, which included Captain Stewart Alsop, had helped the maquis liberate the French city of Angoulême from the Germans. In *Sub Rosa,* Stew gave an understated and self-deprecating account of his actions under fire. Joe's brother claimed that the closest he had come to being killed was shortly after he transferred from the British army to the OSS, when a U.S. Army colonel noticed that the infantry insignia on Stewart's uniform was upside down and his silver bars pinned in the wrong place. Unable to produce proper military identification, Stew was almost shot as a German spy.[16]

For Alsop and Braden, their time in the Jedburghs had been a formative experience. It also gave them a standard by which they would, as they wrote, judge others in the future: "The men in the maquis left their homes and property, their jobs, their children—and went to the woods . . . In the years that followed the war the authors of this book have often amused themselves by classifying acquaintances according to the question: 'Would he go into the woods?' "[17]

Given the Alsops' interest in and personal connection with espionage, it was hardly surprising that the brothers would devote a substantial number of their early columns to the ongoing feud in Washington over creation of a postwar U.S. intelligence agency, a successor to Donovan's OSS. Like Stewart, John, the youngest Alsop brother, had signed up for Wild Bill's outfit, serving in Europe and China before returning to his peacetime career as a Wall Street attorney with periodic involvement in Connecticut politics. While Joe, during his time in China with Chennault, had not been directly engaged in spying, Kermit "Kim" Roosevelt Jr., subsequently a high-ranking CIA operative—and, as Teddy Roosevelt's grandson, a distant Alsop relative—would later boast that *his* introduction to espionage had been through Joe's kindly intervention with "friend" Donovan.[18]

From the outset, the real question behind the creation of a new spy agency was whether its primary emphasis would be on gathering intelligence on current and future foes or on performing cloak-and-dagger covert operations intended to disrupt and defeat the enemy—such as sabotage, assassinations, and other so-called dirty tricks.

But the Alsops' most immediate concern was that President Truman would let control over foreign intelligence fall into J. Edgar Hoover's grasping hands. During the war, the FBI director had warned President Roosevelt that Donovan's dalliance with the KGB was "a highly dangerous and most undesirable procedure." Jealously protective of his turf, Hoover took Wild Bill's subsequent comeuppance as both a vindication and an opportunity to extend the bureau's purview into new realms. The FBI director was also notoriously vindictive. (Stewart's source for a 1946 Matter of Fact column on Hoover's efforts at empire building was a bureau agent. When Hoover learned of the leak, he summarily fired the hapless gumshoe.) Another early Alsop column told of how the FBI had spent much time and money in South America during the war, following up tips given them by a spy who turned out to be fabricating his information for the money. "The moral of this little tale is obvious," the brothers wrote. "Secret intelligence is not a job for amateurs, however zealous and well intentioned."[19]

After a surviving wartime remnant of the OSS, the Strategic Services

Unit, had been allowed to wither away, the victim of active opposition from both Hoover and Army G-2, military intelligence, the Alsop brothers joined the call for a separate and independent intelligence agency, run by civilians and modeled after Britain's Secret Intelligence Service. The need for such a service was urgent, they argued, and its creation long overdue.[20]

In January 1946, the president had authorized formation of the Central Intelligence Group, belatedly recognizing the need for a new national entity to report on and counter the growing Soviet threat. But the men chosen to head the nascent CIG had neither the temperament nor the authority to follow in the footsteps of Wild Bill Donovan, and the organization was—in the words of a future CIA director—"completely dependent upon the kindness of others." Thus, the CIG's first head, Rear Admiral Sidney Souers, was a Truman crony who had previously been director of naval intelligence and had little heart for his new job. (When Souers was asked at his swearing in what his plans were for the spy agency, he reportedly replied, "I want to go home.") Truman himself seemed not to know what to make of the successor to the OSS and was plainly worried that it might turn into a secret police force on American soil. At the investiture ceremony for Souers, the president presented the latter with a black hat and cloak, a wooden dagger, and a certificate bearing the title "Director of Centralized Snooping."[21]

Souers lasted in the post only a few months and was actually grateful to be replaced by the U.S. Army lieutenant general Hoyt Vandenberg, who tentatively expanded his mandate to create the Office of Special Operations. In theory, the fledgling OSO would run covert missions in so-called denied territory, behind the Iron Curtain. Yet Vandenberg, too, soon recognized that he and the CIG were, in effect, only placeholders until legislation could be passed creating a permanent spy agency.

The Alsops thus applauded the passage by Congress in the summer of 1947 of the National Security Act, which created the cabinet-level National Security Council to advise the president, along with the civilian Central Intelligence Agency. However, unlike the British example—which split foreign intelligence and domestic counterintelligence into two separate entities, MI6 and MI5—the CIA combined operations, analysis, and counterintelligence in a single organization. It would prove to be a choice with fateful consequences.[22]

On September 18, 1947, the CIA moved into its new headquarters—a collection of rickety, World War II–era temporary buildings on the grounds of the navy's Bureau of Medicine and Surgery in northwest Washington's Foggy Bottom. The State Department, a local brewery, a dilapidated roller rink, and an abandoned gasworks were the spies' closest neighbors. Truman appointed Rear Admiral Roscoe Hillenkoetter—"Hilly"—the first director of Central Intelligence.[23]

Barely had the agency opened its doors when the question of whether the CIA was to be a secret newspaper for the president or a dirty tricks factory was forced on it. Ultimately, the decision to emphasize covert action was arrived at neither by thoughtful reflection nor by official decree but by default.[24]

In the weeks that followed creation of the CIA, pressure from both Secretary of Defense Forrestal and Truman's National Security Council to do something about the deteriorating political situation in Western Europe overcame the ethical qualms of the agency's novice director and the CIA's own general counsel about conducting secret operations overseas. What most worried Forrestal and the NSC were the upcoming elections in France and Italy, where polls showed Communist Party–backed candidates steadily gaining support. If that trend continued, it seemed possible—even likely—that one or more of the European democracies might soon have a government overtly sympathetic to the Soviet Union.[25]

Hillenkoetter assigned thirty-year-old James Angleton, a lanky, chain-smoking Yale graduate—and former editor of the college's poetry journal—to carry out the agency's first dirty tricks on foreign soil. (Angleton's favorite poem was T. S. Eliot's "Gerontion": "History has many cunning passages, contrived corridors . . . / In a wilderness of mirrors. What will the spider do?")[26] Operating under the code name Artifice, Angleton had been a wartime operative in Italy for X-2, a supersecret branch of the OSS, and simply elected to stay in Rome when the CIA replaced his old employer. Headquartered at the OSO's storefront office on the Via Archimede, Angleton was given ten million dollars, with which he bought newsprint—and, allegedly, the newspapers that used it—to advertise for anti-Communist candidates. Angleton also cajoled Hollywood stars into making radio announcements and writing hand-wringing letters about purported left-wing atrocities in Italy. For good measure, Artifice hired local thugs to tear down the posters of rival candidates. In its unorthodox election campaign, the CIA not only enlisted the aid of the Vatican but—in the event that the worst happened, and the Communists actually won—was prepared to supply the Italian army with guns.[27]

It was only logical that OSS veterans like Angleton would be among the CIA's first recruits and a growing presence in the top ranks of the agency. But the tight bond formed among Donovan's men during the war likewise translated into valuable access in peacetime for ex-Jeds like Stewart Alsop. The declassified minutes of the CIA director's weekly staff meetings reveal that Hillenkoetter met personally with the younger Alsop "re Italy" in early March 1948. The following month, during what Joe described as "one of our regular trips of inquiry," Stewart visited Angleton in Rome, bearing a letter of introduction from his older brother, who had stayed with the erudite spy in the Italian capital the previous summer. Joe had cryptically written to Angleton, "Stew has all sorts of messages from me to you . . . [but] I can tell you one thing: the powers that be here are delighted with what you are accomplishing—they have told me so rather boastfully, and I think I have noticed some of the reasons for their approval in the papers."[28]

Ten days later, Italy's center-right party, the Christian Democrats, won 307 out of 574 seats, thereby excluding the Communists from any significant role in the government. Within the CIA, Angleton's Italian operation was hailed as the agency's first real success and both a model and a precedent for dirty tricks to come.

CHAPTER FIVE

"To Fight Fire with Fire"

Freeing himself at last from the drudgery of the law, Frank Gardiner Wisner, along with his wife, Polly, had arrived in Washington in the autumn of 1947. The man responsible, during the war, for finding recruits who would go into the woods to fight America's enemies had finally had enough of peacetime contracts and debentures on Wall Street. His wartime service with the OSS in Bucharest, where he witnessed the forced relocation of Romania's *Volksdeutsche*, had convinced Frank that democracy's new enemy was the Russians and that Washington had been dangerously slow in recognizing the mortal peril posed by the Soviet Union. After spending vacations and occasional weekends at his Locust Hill Farm near Galena, Maryland, Frank and his family moved into a rented house on Georgetown's Thirty-Fourth Street, a few blocks west of Joe Alsop and the Grahams.

Wisner was the scion of a prominent Mississippi clan whose patriarch had made his fortune as a lumber baron and banker. Frank would sometimes make much of his southern roots—boasting of how, as a child, he had had to get up early "to sweep the raccoon farts out of the kitchen." But Ellis, one of Frank's four children, believed his father simply exploited "all that hard-bitten southern crap" as a kind of disguise; both of Frank's parents had, in fact, been born in the Midwest. Raw ambition and unbridled energy lay close behind and belied Wisner's soft-spoken drawl and courtly southern manners, as did a combative spirit. A gifted sketch artist even as a child, Frank had drawn a mural of the Romans battling the Gauls that hung on his bedroom wall when he was growing up.[1]

Wisner had become an Olympic-class track star at the University of Virginia by simply powering past his competition, in a characteristic demonstration of will and determination: "cool yet coiled, a low hurdler from Mississippi constrained by a vest," was how one friend described him. On campus, Wisner had belonged to a multitude of service organizations and three secret societies. (Frank's own children would not learn of their father's membership in the university's Seven Society until after his death—when a wreath of black magnolias in the shape of a 7 appeared mysteriously overnight at the Arlington grave site.)[2]

Wisner's friends and classmates used words like "aggressive," "zeal," and "intensity" to describe him. "Frank Wisner was the key to a great many things," the *New York Times* reporter Harrison Salisbury would later write, "a brilliant, compulsive man, a talker . . . a man of enormous charm, imagination, conviction that anything, *anything* could be achieved and that he could achieve it." But, like Phil Graham, there was also a hidden, brittle side to Frank's persona. Psychologists today would likely classify him as manic-depressive, or bipolar.[3]

Initially, what Frank had experienced in Bucharest was what veterans would call "a good war." Photographs from the time show Wisner in a snappy uniform of his own eclectic design: an army-issue Eisenhower jacket, navy khaki trousers, and a navy officer's cap. Upon getting settled in the Romanian capital, in late summer of 1944, Frank's team had promptly cabled back to Washington, "This place is wild with information and Wisner is in his element. We have a beautiful entrée to the government and a place to use it fast while it is available and hot stuff." Early on, Frank and his OSS agents had enjoyed cordial relations with the generals of the advancing Red Army. "We feasted on caviar from the Delta Danube, sliced salami, smoked sturgeon, chicken roasts and cakes dripping with cream," recalled a colleague.[4]

Yet Wisner's warnings of a grasping, expansionist U.S.S.R. with postwar plans to occupy the Balkans, and territorial ambitions that extended as far as Turkey, were simply ignored at Donovan's headquarters. Twice the OSS chief personally warned Wisner not to antagonize the Russians "by speech or action." Frank tried in earnest to make peace with the occupiers—even scurrying around the ballroom at Soviet diplomatic functions, urging terrified Romanian aristocrats to dance with Red Army officers. Later, he would be awarded the Legion of Merit for his wartime service in Bucharest—for "establishing, developing, and maintaining good working relations with the Russians." But the forced deportation of ethnic Germans by the Soviets that he witnessed in early 1945 remained, for Wisner, a bitter, indelible, and rankling memory.[5]

Sent to Wiesbaden in occupied Germany shortly after the Nazi surrender and put in charge of intelligence collection there, Frank had sought permission to purchase some two hundred bicycles so that his agents and their handlers in the American sector of Berlin might ride through the Soviet-occupied parts of the city and report on Russian troop deployments. The bikes might also provide an emergency means of escape, if and when the Red Army moved west, as Wisner fully expected. When his request was denied, Frank abruptly resigned his commission in disgust and returned to lawyering.[6]

By October 1947, however, he was itching to get back to the work that he had known and loved during the war—spying. Wisner joined the Office of Occupied Territories, an obscure and recently established branch of the State Department that was growing in importance. One of his first contributions was a paper outlining the tactics that the Soviets had used in gaining control of Romania. Still antsy, however, Frank did not remain deskbound for long.[7]

In a profession already grown accustomed to telephone wiretaps, electronic bugs, and cipher locks, Wisner put an old-fashioned emphasis on the human element of espionage. Like most other OSS veterans, he was more interested in action than gathering intelligence, contemptuously dismissing the analysts at the agency's Office of Special Operations as "a bunch of old washerwomen, exchanging gossip while they rinse through the dirty linen."[8]

Frank Wisner's anti-Russian bias would surely have received support and reinforcement at the Sunday night suppers that he and Polly soon began attending in Georgetown. Encouragement would have come not only from his hosts, the Alsops and the Grahams, but also from a trio of frequent dinner guests that a British historian has dubbed "the Dumbarton Avenue sceptics"—Washington-based Russian experts who shared a common concern about the Soviet Union's postwar intentions.[9]

Among the skeptics was Isaiah Berlin, the Oxford philosopher and historian who had been hounded from Kay Graham's inaugural dinner party by Donald Maclean. Berlin was an information officer at the British embassy in Washington during the war, when he had regularly reported to London's Whitehall on the ups and downs of Anglo-American relations. "Our work was not secret: it resembled that of any foreign correspondent worth his salt, save that the reports, some of them in code, went to a far smaller and more carefully selected group of readers," Berlin later wrote of his missives. Indeed, Isaiah's weekly news summaries from Washington—reportedly a reading favorite of Winston Churchill's—were a textbook example of how gossip, careful observation, and analysis could combine to make intelligence.[10]

During his stint in wartime Washington, the Latvian-born Englishman was often the dinner companion of Joe Alsop and another skeptic, Chip Bohlen. In a 1941 letter to his parents, Berlin described Alsop as "a fanatical Anglophile, intelligent, young, snobbish, a little pompous, and my permanent host in Washington."*[11] Berlin was likewise a good friend of the fellow Soviet expert George Kennan, who had hosted the former during his visit to Russia in December 1945—praising Berlin on that occasion as "undoubtedly the best informed and most intelligent foreigner in Moscow."[12]

By early 1946, Isaiah Berlin was back in Washington and in his old role of intelligence gathering. Although the city had meanwhile been "turned topsy-turvy" by the Cold War, Isaiah wrote to Susan Mary, he was trying not to be infected by a friend's chronic pessimism: "It does not need Joe to come daily and say doom, doom, doom—like the old gentleman in one of Peacock's novels, who used to come in through the garden window saying, 'The devil is amongst us; have great wrath,' and then drift out again . . . If it were not for my beloved hosts the Bohlens, I should go about spreading gloom and discontent among His Majesty's subjects abroad."[13]

Yet it was neither Berlin nor Bohlen but Kennan, perhaps the greatest skeptic, who had the most influence on Frank Wisner. George and Annelise had moved from their temporary quarters at the National War College to a rented house in Foxhall Village, a government employees' enclave on the western fringes of Georgetown. Soon after Wisner's arrival in Washington, and possibly during one of the Sunday suppers at the Alsops', the Bohlens', or the Grahams', Kennan and Wisner discovered how much they had in common.

In his time with the Office of Occupied Territories, Wisner had come

---

* Since housing in the wartime capital was notoriously scarce, Berlin and another friend of the Grahams moved into a recently vacated residence on Georgetown's Thirty-Fifth Street that had been the scene of a grisly murder-suicide involving two OSS employees. The house was said to be haunted. Ever the pragmatic philosopher, Berlin simply plastered over the bullet holes in the ceiling and placed a dark-colored rug on top of the bloodstained carpet.

to believe that Nazi Germany's former soldiers and diplomats, since displaced by the war, might be invaluable assets in America's struggle with the Soviet Union. Frank was also aware that the OSO was still struggling to breach the Iron Curtain. A recent attempt to smuggle anti-Communist resistance leaders into Romania had ended in ignominious failure: Wisner's top wartime agent, whom he had recruited in 1945, was captured and imprisoned; as well, Frank's former personal secretary committed suicide rather than betray his comrades. But Wisner was not yet ready to abandon efforts to penetrate so-called denied territory. Indeed, he believed that renewed and expanded covert operations in Russian-occupied Eastern Europe might be the key to unraveling the Soviet empire.[14]

To that end, Frank Wisner found an unlikely ally in George Kennan. The day after the Nazi surrender, Kennan had written a secret letter to a colleague at the American embassy in Paris, asking that the State Department locate and rescue a friend of his, Helmuth von Moltke, a German diplomat whom Kennan had gotten to know during his prewar posting in Berlin. Kennan envisioned von Moltke, the relative of a national hero, as the prospective leader of a reborn, democratic Germany. What Kennan did not know was that his friend had belonged to a wartime resistance group known as the Kreisau Circle, whose members masterminded the failed attempt to assassinate Hitler in July 1944. Von Moltke and his colleagues had been executed by the Gestapo early in 1945.[15]

Disappointed in the failure of his first humanitarian effort, Kennan tried again, shortly after taking the reins of the Policy Planning Staff. His target this time was Gustav Hilger, whom Kennan had befriended in Moscow and whom he now wished to bring to the United States. Hilger had been the economic counselor at the German embassy before the war and was, as Kennan wrote to a State Department official, "one of the few outstanding experts on Soviet economy and Soviet politics." But Hilger had also been the interpreter for the German foreign minister, Joachim von Ribbentrop, at the signing of the Nazi-Soviet nonaggression pact in 1939. Probably unknown to Kennan in 1947 was that Hilger's signature appeared on several SS "activity reports" from the eastern front, indicating that his friend was at least aware of, if not actually complicit in, Nazi war crimes. For that reason, the Soviet government had demanded Hilger's extradition to the U.S.S.R.[16] But the Americans, including Kennan and Wisner, flatly refused to give up their prize. Hilger was living at the time in U.S.-occupied Germany, assisting Frank and the army in a secret project known as Operation Rusty, which interrogated Soviet occupation troops who had defected to the American zone. Officially, the army claimed that Hilger was too sick to travel.[17]

Kennan's efforts at sheltering wayward Germans like Hilger dovetailed precisely with Wisner's growing interest in exploiting anti-Soviet ex-Nazis in the Cold War conflict with Russia. Indeed, Wisner had already demonstrated that he was not excessively worried about the background of those he brought to the cause. At the end of the war, he and his army colleagues had recruited the Wehrmacht's intelligence chief on the Russian front, Major General Reinhard Gehlen. Anticipating that his knowledge might soon be in demand by the latest conquerors, Gehlen brought with him footlockers full of captured Soviet documents on the Red Army's order of battle and other valuable secrets. Wisner came to look upon Germans like Hilger and Gehlen as a kind of Rosetta stone for understanding—and ultimately destroying—America's new enemy.[18]

IN THE YEARS TO COME, George Kennan would go to extraordinary lengths to deny, or at least discount, the important role that he played in the origins of U.S. covert operations. But declassified documents reveal a little-known and carefully hidden side of the quiet, introspective Kennan: a Walter Mitty–like fascination with spies and spying.[19]

Kennan's first real exposure to espionage had been at the Lisbon consulate in 1942, where his job was to coordinate American intelligence in Portugal, a haven for wartime spies. Later, at Moscow's U.S. embassy, the sole OSS operative there, Thomas Whitney, a former Associated Press correspondent, became Kennan's "trusted colleague."[20]

In June 1946, before he took up his responsibilities at the National War College, Kennan had signed a secret contract to become a "special consultant" on Russia to the Central Intelligence Group; he would continue in that role after the CIA was formed. Despite his natural reticence and unpredictable mood swings, it was actually Kennan who had spurred Forrestal to pressure the CIA into undertaking its first covert action, in Italy. Likewise, it was Kennan who had argued, late in 1947, that the United States should give "very careful consideration to the idea of sending American combat troops to Greece" to counter the insurgency there.[*21]

This unseen side of the bookish scholar's persona had surfaced again in September 1947, barely a week after the CIA was created, when Kennan sent the secretary of defense a report urging that the United States establish a secret "guerrilla warfare corps" to operate in countries under Communist domination. In an accompanying memo, Kennan argued that it was important to keep U.S. involvement in this and other paramilitary operations hidden from the American people, who would probably not support such actions if undertaken in their name. Nonetheless, he concluded, "it might be essential to our security to fight fire with fire."[22]

How far Kennan was prepared to go in that direction became evident in a paper that he sent to Marshall in mid-March 1948. In it, Kennan proposed that the United States use the chaos expected to break out in Italy following a Communist election victory as a pretext for sending American forces to reoccupy military bases and other strategic sites on the Italian mainland. Acknowledging that such a step might provoke a civil war—and even lead to the political breakup of Italy—Kennan judged the latter preferable "to a bloodless election victory, unopposed by ourselves, which would give the Communists the entire peninsula at one coup and send waves of panic to all surrounding areas."[23]

The outcome of the Italian election removed the need for any such drastic action. But as Kennan and other CIA insiders surely knew, the agency's success in Italy was not going to be repeatable on a routine basis. The funding for Angleton's dirty tricks had only become available as the result of a last-minute ad hoc arrangement involving private bank accounts and captured Nazi gold, secretly laundered through the U.S. government's Exchange Stabilization Fund. To be effective, Kennan's guerrilla army would need to be regularly provided with money, weapons, and supplies on a mammoth scale—yet all the while kept secret from American taxpayers.[24]

Nor was that the only obstacle.

---

[*] In July 1949, Kennan proposed that the United States move with "resolution, speed, ruthlessness, and self-assurance" to physically evict—in "the way that Theodore Roosevelt might have done it"—Chiang Kai-shek's 300,000-man army from the island of Taiwan, where America's erstwhile client had retreated following his defeat by Mao's Communist forces. "Most people have mood swings . . . few, however, turn theirs into prophetically impractical policy memoranda," wrote Kennan's authorized biographer.

Angleton's relatively modest operation in Italy had been carried out despite the reservations of the CIA director and the agency's general counsel, Lawrence Houston, who were hesitant about entering into the shadowy world of covert operations. Houston had warned Hilly that the agency had no legal authority to conduct "commando type functions" overseas. It had taken the direct and spirited intervention of Forrestal to overcome such opposition and to make the Italian operation possible.[25]

Kennan and Forrestal both recognized that the main barrier to carrying out secret paramilitary operations was likely to be the CIA's own Hillenkoetter, who, like his predecessor Souers, came from a military background and was plainly uncomfortable in the role of spymaster. Kennan, however, already had a ready solution to that problem in mind. After failing to replace Hillenkoetter with someone known to have more enthusiasm for covert affairs, Kennan proposed putting dirty tricks under the purview of the State Department—at least until the CIA had a director more receptive to cloak-and-dagger derring-do. As Kennan later informed Marshall, he and the planning staff "decided to let the CIA sleeping dog lie and recommend a separate organization which might at a later date be incorporated in CIA."[26]

Exactly what Kennan had in mind he spelled out in a remarkable proposal that he labeled "The Inauguration of Organized Political Warfare" and personally presented to the National Security Council on May 4, 1948. "It would seem that the time is now fully ripe for the creation of a covert political warfare operations directorate within the Government," Kennan began. He went on to propose a variety of new activities by the United States, ranging from overt measures similar to the Marshall Plan—"'white' propaganda"—to covert or "'black' psychological warfare," including the "encouragement of underground resistance in hostile states." Two weeks later, Kennan urgently reminded the secretary of state that "time is running out on us. If we are to engage effectively in intelligent, organized covert activities, appropriations must be obtained from the Congress."[27]

Marshall, the NSC, and Congress could hardly challenge Kennan's assertion of timeliness. That winter, the democratically elected government of Czechoslovakia had been replaced with a pro-Soviet regime. A few weeks later, Russian forces in Berlin had begun harassing traffic headed to the city's western occupation zones—a precursor to the total blockade that would be in place by the summer.

The cumulative effect of these setbacks was enough to spur the

Truman administration to action. On June 18, the National Security Council—"taking cognizance of the vicious covert activities of the USSR"—agreed with Forrestal and Kennan that "the overt foreign activities of the US Government must be supplemented by covert operations." NSC 10/2 created the Office of Special Projects, which, in a reflection of continued bureaucratic infighting, would be nominally located in the CIA but would receive its guidance from the State Department in peacetime and the Pentagon in the event of war. Almost immediately, the name of the new entity was changed to the Office of Policy Coordination—a term of art intended to confuse Russian spies.[28]

There was, however, no disguising OPC's actual mission, which encompassed, according to its charter, obvious measures like propaganda and economic warfare but also added, more ambiguously—and ominously—"preventive direct action." The latter subsumed a long list that included but was not limited to "sabotage, anti-sabotage, demolition and evacuation measures; subversion against hostile states, including assistance to underground resistance movements, guerrillas and refugee liberation groups, and support of indigenous anti-communist elements in threatened countries of the free world."[29]

Only a week after the creation of OPC, as if to emphasize the importance and urgency of America's bold venture into the back alleys of Cold War politics, the Soviet Union cut off all land and water access to the western zones in Berlin. At the end of June 1948, Kennan forwarded six possible candidates to head the new dirty tricks directorate. The first name on Kennan's list was Frank Wisner's.

The alliance of Kennan and Wisner would prove as fateful as it was unlikely, given their disparate personalities. Kennan wrote at the time that he had put Wisner above the other candidates "on the recommendations of people who know him. I personally have no knowledge of his ability, but his qualifications seem reasonably good, and I should think that it would be relatively easy to spare him for this purpose." The disclaimer was somewhat disingenuous, however, since Kennan already knew Wisner socially from the dinners in Georgetown and from Wisner's own parallel efforts to bring Hilger to America.[30]

Secret CIA histories of the Office of Policy Coordination, since declassified, describe Wisner obliquely as "a man of intense application" and "a singular choice to create a covert organization"—seeming code words for a loose cannon. (Indeed, a State Department official predicted, prophetically, that Kennan's choice to head OPC, together with the organization's only notional place in the CIA, had "the real makings of a jumble, because it is obviously impossible to get a man big enough to be over Wisner and small enough to be under Hilly.") How well the director of the Policy Planning Staff actually knew the man he wished to head OPC is questionable, given the glib assurance that Kennan passed along to his immediate superior, Undersecretary of State Bob Lovett: "A cardinal consideration in the establishment of Wisner's office . . . was that, while this Department should take no responsibility for his operations, we should nevertheless maintain a firm guiding hand." In an earlier memorandum of understanding with Kennan, however, Wisner had insisted on, and gotten, a promise of "broad latitude in selecting his methods of operations."[31]

Kennan's boss was in no position to question his subordinate's choice. As Lovett had previously advised Kennan, regarding preparations for Project Umpire—an inaugural clandestine scheme to beam propaganda broadcasts to Eastern Europe and the U.S.S.R. from radio transmitters in U.S.-occupied Germany—"he wanted to know very little about our project but in principle he had no objection." Already accustomed to the rules of the covert world, Kennan had written the memo authorizing Umpire on plain paper rather than official State Department stationery so that Lovett and his boss, Marshall, would have that sine qua non of every Cold War bureaucracy: plausible deniability.[32]

KENNAN ALSO APPOINTED a trusted subordinate on the Policy Planning Staff, John Paton Davies Jr., to head a committee that would oversee and approve the missions to be carried out by Wisner's OPC. Davies was one of the State Department's foremost so-called China hands, having been born to Baptist missionaries and raised in Sichuan Province. Subsequently joining the Foreign Service, Davies had been sent back to his birthplace, where, during successive diplomatic postings, he witnessed the advance of Japan's army into China and Japanese atrocities against Chinese civilians. Following the attack on Pearl Harbor, Davies volunteered to serve as aide, adviser, and interpreter to the U.S. commander in the China-Burma-India theater, the army general Joseph "Vinegar Joe" Stilwell.[33]

Kennan's choice had already demonstrated impressive sangfroid under fire. In August 1943, when the army transport in which he was flying developed engine trouble over Burma, Davies first helped the other passengers with their parachutes before jumping from the plane and later led the group through dense jungle to safety—a feat for which he would be awarded the Medal of Freedom after the war. (Ironically, one of those whom Davies rescued was none other than Duncan Lee, the spy known to the KGB as Koch, who served on Wild Bill Donovan's personal staff.)[34]

Kennan had first gotten to know Davies when the two were posted to the Moscow embassy in 1934 and considered him "a man of broad, sophisticated, and skeptical political understanding." (Indeed, Davies was one of the first to predict the subsequent Sino-Soviet split and to warn, as early as September 1949, concerning Vietnam, that "Ho Chi Minh is going to be, in all probability, a headache for us for a long time to come . . . I feel that it is essential that we establish immediately channels into Viet territory.")[35]

Davies had since become Kennan's close confederate. When Kennan had given his impromptu victory speech outside the embassy chancellery on the occasion of the Nazi surrender, it was Davies who had stood beside him, tearing up calendar pages and tossing them to the crowd below as celebratory confetti. (His confidant shared Kennan's own doubts about the durability of the Soviet-American alliance, however. "The next morning people walked by the Embassy as if we did not exist, heads down-turned or staring straight ahead. The hours of spontaneous, undisguised Russian friendship with Americans were over," wrote Davies in a memoir.)[36]

For the liaison contact between the Policy Planning Staff and OPC, Kennan and Wisner chose another mutual friend and OSS veteran. Robert Joyce had resigned from the Foreign Service in 1943 to join the OSS and was a confirmed believer in covert operations who knew Frank from Joyce's time during the war as a control officer in the Balkans. Early in the conflict, when he served as consul at the American embassy in Havana, Joyce had tried—and failed—to interest the OSS and Donovan in recruiting the novelist Ernest Hemingway to spy on the Nazis. (Ironically, the KGB evidently had the same idea, at the same time, and even optimistically assigned Hemingway a code name: Argo. But both intelligence services came away disappointed, each independently concluding that "Papa" was simply too "individualistic" to be a reliable agent.)[37]

Along with John Davies, Bob Joyce had recently been recruited by Kennan to State's Policy Planning Staff. The Joyces moved to Georgetown and were soon hosting their own Sunday night suppers. Like Frank and Polly's rented residence, the town house that Bob and his wife, Jane, owned at 2811 O Street became another informal and unofficial venue for the making of postwar American foreign policy.[38]

DESPITE KENNAN'S TALK of exercising a "firm guiding hand" over the State Department's new spy shop, Frank Wisner did not await further orders before recruiting the other senior members of the Office of Policy Coordination. Not surprisingly, they, too, would be mostly OSS veterans and Frank's longtime associates. (Some State Department insiders would jokingly refer to OPC as "FOW"—"Friends of Wisner.")[39]

Knowing of Stewart Alsop's background with the Jedburghs, Frank first asked Joe's brother to be his deputy at OPC. When Stewart turned down the job, Wisner next approached Franklin Lindsay, a Stanford graduate who had spent most of World War II as the OSS liaison to Tito's partisans in Yugoslavia and was an explosives expert. Upon returning home from the war, Lindsay, like other veterans, quickly discovered that academe paled in comparison to jumping out of airplanes and smuggling guns to guerrilla fighters. He and Wisner, in turn, approached another colleague of theirs from the Balkan wars, Charles Thayer, to join them in the coming crusade.[40]

Thayer was arguably the embodiment of the OPC ideal. An OSS veteran and Foreign Service officer who had come to diplomacy by unconventional means—via West Point, where he reportedly racked up a record number of demerits—Thayer had helped establish the prewar U.S. embassy in Moscow with Bohlen and Kennan. The latter took credit for having discovered Charlie hanging out at the city's Hotel National as "a tourist of sorts." At the embassy, Thayer became Kennan's man Friday and general factotum, celebrated for his charm as well as his resourcefulness. Careening around the wintry Soviet capital on a borrowed motorcycle, his tattered fur cap flapping in the wind, Thayer had performed a legendary feat: quickly and efficiently shepherding forty carloads of furniture for the embassy chancellery through Russian customs. (Charlie's luster dimmed later that year, however, when he hired a troupe of trained seals from the Moscow Circus to perform at the ambassador's Christmas party. After balancing champagne glasses on their noses, the animals drank the bubbly libation, becoming extravagantly sick on the ballroom floor.)[41]

Having joined the diplomatic corps at Kennan's urging, and following postings in Germany and Russia—where he introduced the Red Army to polo—Thayer earned a reputation as a kind of American Lawrence of Arabia in the Balkans and the Near East.*[42]

In the Balkans, where he preceded Franklin Lindsay as an OSS training officer for Tito's guerrillas, reporting to Bob Joyce, Thayer had learned the difference between Washington's rear-echelon war and the one being fought on the front lines by the partisans. When Thayer demonstrated the "panic creator"—an OSS spy device designed to make a loud noise when the enemy leader was making a speech—guerrilla fighters were unimpressed. "You mean after all that it wouldn't even hurt Hitler?" one asked incredulously.[43]

It probably helped Thayer's postwar Foreign Service career that he was Chip Bohlen's brother-in-law and a regular at the Georgetown salons. Moreover, Lindsay and Thayer were already enthusiastic supporters of Wisner's and OPC's covert mission. As consultants to the State Department, they had authored the study that inspired Kennan to write to Forrestal, urging that the United States arm anti-Soviet émigrés to create a guerrilla army and "fight fire with fire."[44]

Helping Wisner recruit new members for OPC was Allen Welsh Dulles, Frank's old OSS boss in Germany. Dulles had joined the Foreign Service just before America's entry into World War I and, following a peacetime legal career at the Wall Street firm of Sullivan & Cromwell, returned overseas in 1942 to direct OSS operations in Switzerland. In Operation Sunrise, Dulles established his reputation as a spymaster—secretly negotiating with an SS general to arrange the surrender of German forces in Italy. Returning to his old law firm after the war, Dulles, like Wisner, discovered that it was "an appalling thing to come back, after heading a spy network, to handling corporate indentures." "Most of my time is spent reliving those exciting days," Dulles wrote to his former OSS colleagues. Since the Truman administration

---

* Thayer would become known as "the court jester of the Foreign Service." In a memoir, Charlie related how, having joined a falconry club when he was stationed in prewar Hamburg, he looked forward to continuing the sport after he was sent to Afghanistan: "And again I picture the final scene luring me on: that day when Yang would hoist me onto my rearing mare while the Indian *sice* held her down with two strong hands on her bridle. Abdulla would place the falcon, *my* falcon, on my wrist. The stableboy would loose the dogs from the kennel. The gardener would swing open the gates, and with a shower of gravel, feathers, horses and dogs I would burst out into the unsuspecting streets of Kabul on my way to the quail fields."

offered him no job he had been willing to accept, Dulles instead soldiered on, always in the background. In 1947, as president of the Council on Foreign Relations—an organization he and his brother John had helped to create a generation earlier—Dulles accompanied a congressional delegation on a European inspection trip for the Marshall Plan.[45]

Later moving to Washington, Dulles assumed the role of a Republican in exile, patiently awaiting his party's return to power. Until that day arrived, he remained a passionate but behind-the-scenes promoter of the country's growing intelligence establishment, including OPC and its covert war against the Soviet Union. Dulles had helped Wisner secure his original job with State's Office of Occupied Territories and later appointed him to a task force looking into the efficiency of the CIA. Dulles and Wisner had also been among the first to urge that Reinhard Gehlen, the former Wehrmacht general, be recruited by the OSS. In another early collaboration, Dulles and Wisner used an OPC front organization, the American Committee to Aid Survivors of the German Resistance, as a conduit for bringing to the United States other anti-Soviet Germans, including some ex-Nazis—America's new allies in the postwar campaign against foreign Communism.[46]

By late 1948, that campaign was well under way and making some progress. Kennan's long telegram and his "X article" provided both the intellectual rationale and the strategy for containing Soviet expansionism, while the Marshall Plan and the Truman Doctrine would supply the funding and, if necessary, the military means to accomplish that end. Meanwhile, Wisner and his recruits were poised to carry the fight to the enemy.

In Washington, however, Wisner suddenly encountered an obstacle to his plans—a former wartime ally who had meanwhile become Frank's chief rival in building America's intelligence establishment.

RICHARD HELMS HAD BEEN a wire service reporter in Berlin before the war and listed among his most memorable encounters a 1936 interview with Adolf Hitler. Like Frank Wisner and Allen Dulles, Helms had been "hooked on intelligence" as a result of his wartime experience with Donovan's OSS. (Helms recalled how another OSS veteran—a "soft-spoken, internationally known ornithologist specializing in Africa"—had reacted upon learning that Donovan's organization was to be abolished: "Thrusting both arms toward Heaven, he shouted, 'Jesus H. Christ, I suppose this means that it's back to those goddamned birds,' and stumbled from the room." Like Helms, the ornithologist joined the CIA instead.)[47]

Shortly after the end of the war, Dick Helms, Bob Joyce, and Frank Wisner had served together under Allen Dulles at the OSS spy station in Germany, which was headquartered in a former champagne winery outside Wiesbaden. Billeted nearby at a luxurious villa, the group founded what they called the Horned Rabbit Club, named for the mounted hare's head hanging in the study, to which a mischievous taxidermist had affixed a miniature set of antlers. (Another member of the club, Arthur Schlesinger Jr., left Germany and returned to the London OSS station in July 1945. He reached his decision in part, Schlesinger later claimed, because he was "disturbed by the alacrity with which Frank Wisner seemed to be preparing for the Third World War.") When Dulles returned to Washington that fall to pursue loftier goals, he left the thirty-two-year-old Helms in charge of the OSS station in West Berlin.[48]

The son of an Alcoa executive and grandson of a prominent international banker, Helms was tall, handsome, debonair, and multilingual—he had spent two years at a private high school in Switzerland—and thus fit the Hollywood image of a spy far better than the growing-portly, rapidly balding Wisner and the rumpled ranks forming behind him at OPC.

But the differences between Dick Helms and Frank Wisner went beyond mere appearances. Helms had gone directly from the navy and OSS to a career with the fledgling CIA, where he was put in charge of the Central Europe desk at the Office of Special Operations—the intelligence-gathering "washerwomen" whom Wisner dismissed. Wisner had insisted that OPC have complete independence from OSO, its bureaucratic rival in the intelligence business. He had also extracted a promise that the State Department would let him recruit OPC's field operatives by matching their peacetime salaries, significantly higher than the civil-service scale received by OSO's analysts, who were, for the most part, penurious academics. Noted one disillusioned analyst, "It was not uncommon for OSO officers to reject a candidate for employment, only to discover later that he had walked to an adjacent building and been hired by OPC for a higher position . . . These personnel practices produced considerable acrimony." In some cases, OPC's recruits jumped two or three grades over their civil-service counterparts. (The inequalities were soon apparent in the parking lots of OPC's and CIA's respective headquarters on E Street. While Wisner's "cowboys" drove late-model MGs and Jaguars, Helms's men came to work behind the steering wheels of Fords and Chevrolets. The wives of OPC operatives recalled their husbands spending weekends just trying to get the temperamental foreign cars started.)[49]

Likewise fundamental to the rivalry between OPC and the OSO was a difference in attitude toward the covert operations that would become the centerpiece of Wisner's operation. Helms was fond of pointing out a fact usually ignored or glossed over in the heroic tales that Stewart Alsop and others told of the wartime Jedburghs—namely, that many such daring operations had failed, in the process costing the lives of the Jeds as well as the maquis they were trying to help. The jaundiced eye that Helms cast upon such exploits was a result of his own wartime experience of having sent spies into enemy territory, as he recounted in a memoir:

> After a handshake and final word with his case officer, the agent was guided to the plane. He turned, waved a token salute, and pulled himself up the narrow ladder into the belly of the aircraft. Six of us watched as the plane lurched across the field toward the takeoff area . . . The aircraft was to maintain strict radio silence. It would be hours before it returned to base and could report that the drop had been made on target, and a great many more hours before the agent could set up his radio and signal a safe landing.[50]

As Helms wrote, many of those he sent off on missions to so-called hard targets in enemy territory were never heard from again.

Although Wisner had been his boss in the OSS, Helms believed that Frank was making the classic mistake of preparing to fight the last war all over again—but this time against a very different enemy. Unlike Hitler's Germany, Stalin's Russia had a seasoned and top-notch foreign intelligence service in the KGB, which was equally skilled in rooting out spies. Moreover, in contrast to the Wehrmacht, the Soviet Red Army was militarily unchallenged in the countries it occupied throughout Eastern Europe. The principal lesson that Helms had taken away from his time in the OSS was that wars were won by carefully collecting and analyzing intelligence on the enemy and then exploiting his weaknesses—not by jumping out of airplanes. The conflict between Helms's "washerwomen" and Wisner's "cowboys" would be the cause of a simmering intelligence war within the CIA itself—one that proved enduring at the agency and had consequences for the broader Cold War.

CHAPTER SIX

"Some Brave New Approach"

By 1948, JOE AND STEWART ALSOP were busy celebrating the country's new activism on the international scene in newspaper columns and magazine articles. Their *Saturday Evening Post* essay that January, titled "Must America Save the World?," began, "The biggest story on Earth—a straight news story, deserving all the eight column heads and outsize type in all the newspaper offices of this continent—is the story of the new world role of the United States." Bluntly acknowledging that "we are already in the business of making and breaking foreign governments," the brothers gave the rhetorical question posed by their title an unequivocally affirmative answer.[1]

The brothers' insider status also gave them a privileged perspective on the Truman administration's increasingly combative attitude toward the Russians. Stewart had likely learned of OPC when Frank Wisner tried to recruit Stew as his deputy at the State Department's dirty tricks factory. Joe borrowed one of his favorite metaphors for Soviet expansionism, the so-called dictum of the bayonet, from Chip Bohlen, who, in turn, attributed it to Lenin: "Probe with the bayonet. If you meet steel, stop. If you meet mush, push." Bohlen had let Joe know the classified details of how the Kremlin had actually been behind the Czech coup but asked that Alsop refrain from telling the story until the State Department's secret evidence could be released. Even earlier, Bohlen had tipped the brothers off to the fact that Greece was likely to be the next country in Moscow's gun sights. On a chill fall evening, Bohlen joined Marshall and Forrestal at Phil and Kay Graham's house to give the Alsop brothers and other reporters a confidential briefing on the crisis likewise developing over Berlin.[2]

Lest their readers underrate the seriousness of the coming showdown with Russia, Joe and Stewart had just published a piece in the *Post* magazine with the ominous title "If War Comes . . ." The article contained startlingly accurate details on U.S. war plans, for which Forrestal was the likely source. So upset by the Alsops' scoop was *The New York Times*'s Arthur Krock, Forrestal's usual outlet for such news, that the brothers' jealous rival publicly upbraided the defense secretary for leaking vital military secrets.[3]

By that summer, most in Washington needed no further convincing that the Russian bear was at the door. Beginning in late June, shortly after the creation of OPC, Stalin had cut off all road, rail, and water access by the Western Allies to Berlin, preventing food and fuel from reaching the encircled city, located deep in Soviet-occupied eastern Germany. Rather than confront Red Army troops directly, the Truman administration decided to keep the city supplied with necessities via the only means of transport still available—by air. The mercurial Kennan had been particularly rattled by the Russians' move. "G. Kennan wants to call up the National Guard," Joe Alsop wrote to a friend.

The brothers' heightened concern about the Cold War's new and dangerous direction was likewise reflected in the increasingly breathless tone of their Matter of Fact columns. Joe and Stewart had doubtless heard about the advice that Michigan's senator Arthur Vandenberg, chairman of the powerful Foreign Relations Committee, had reputedly given Truman the previous winter, when aid to Greece and Turkey was being debated before Congress. At a climactic meeting of the president with congressional leaders, after Acheson had spoken eloquently about how the fate of Western civilization hung in the balance, Vandenberg had stated what was instantly clear to everyone in the room—namely, that the president personally needed to go before Congress and "scare hell out of the country." Two weeks later, the Truman Doctrine was born. The Alsop brothers in the fall and winter of 1948 were likewise prepared to scare hell out of the country, in order to awaken the American people to the dimensions of the growing Soviet threat.[4]

The Berlin crisis allowed Joe to indulge his flair for the literary and dramatic. "In Wiesbaden this morning, a steely haze hung very low over the steel-grey ground," began his eyewitness account of an American airlift of relief supplies to Berlin two days before Christmas. Joe's column described the flight of an air force transport, *Big Easy 103,* carrying a cargo of canned applesauce, dried apricots, cement, and roofing supplies to the "beleaguered city": "We were above the clouds now, between the pale sunny blue of the winter sky above and the serrated, brilliantly lit expanse of white wool below. Ten miles away and a thousand feet below us there was a speck which was another C-54 carrying another ten-ton load to Berlin. And ten miles behind and a thousand feet below us, the chatter on the radio announced the presence of still another." In subsequent columns, Joe and Stewart wrote that the United States had to face the fact that Operation Vittles, the Berlin airlift, might need to be made "semi-permanent."[5]

Yet as even the gloomy Alsops were forced to concede, some glimmers of hope had recently appeared on the horizon—including a possible crack in the Iron Curtain.

In June 1948, Stalin had expelled Yugoslavia's Marshal Tito from the international organization of the Communist Party, the Comintern, for challenging Moscow's hegemony in Eastern Europe. At the Policy Planning Staff, the "Tito heresy" would be the subject of a hurried paper prepared two days later—the same day that George Kennan advanced Frank Wisner's name as his candidate to head OPC. While couched in cautions, the PPS paper celebrated the fact that "for the first time in the history of the movement, a servant of the international communist movement . . . has defied, with at least temporary success, the authority of the Kremlin."[6]

Joe Alsop happened to be in Kennan's office at the State Department when the communiqué arrived announcing Moscow's break with Tito. A suddenly ebullient Kennan told Alsop that it was the first firm evidence confirming his "X article" prediction that Communism contained the seeds of its own destruction—a point that Joe would echo in his column the following morning. The normally dour Kennan was so cheered by news of the split that he took down a ceremonial balalaika he had hung on the wall and strummed a Russian folk tune for his guest.[7]

Even Joe's own chronic melancholy seemed to lift, at least briefly, near year's end, when Matter of Fact proclaimed the ongoing Soviet-American conflict a "stalemate"—comparatively good news, in view of Alsop's usual prediction of imminent Russian victory. But Joe's upbeat mood was destined not to last. At a postelection dinner with Truman's aide Clark Clifford, Joe attacked the president's recent decision to cut the defense budget, prompting Clifford to leave the table in a huff. The next morning, Alsop sent his offended guest a letter of abject apology.[8]

Joe had never been shy about allowing his political views to color his reporting. On the eve of the 1948 presidential contest, Alsop had described a Dewey campaign rally as "opulent," whereas a similar event for Truman was "threadbare and visibly unsuccessful." ("A reporter who was responding to political nuance out in the field might have sensed something was up, but Alsop did not," snipped the critic David Halberstam.) Less than three weeks before the election, the brothers had written a *Saturday Evening Post* article titled "What Kind of President Will Dewey Make?"[9]

Despite such missteps, there were increasing signs that the Alsops and their writings were having an impact—in this country and abroad. Notwithstanding the scarifying tone of their column—or perhaps because of it—the brothers' popularity continued to grow. Recently, Joe and Stewart had been paid perhaps the ultimate compliment: the "notorious" Alsops were singled out for attack as "warmongers and militarists" by Moscow's official Communist Party newspaper, *Pravda*.[10]

By the end of 1948, Matter of Fact was appearing in more than a hundred newspapers around the United States. Their "provocative column," wrote one admirer, "blended erudite background, calculated opinion, and yeasty gossip." The Alsops "earned reader loyalty through a combination of Lippmannian hauteur, Restonian legwork, and virulent anti-Communism," noted another.[11] But even as it attracted more readers, Matter of Fact had also drawn detractors. One critic carped that Joe's columns "sometimes sounded as if they had been written in Latin and then lost a little zing in the translation." Another protested that Alsop's writing was "without an ember of warmth." The one notable exception, most critics agreed, was the so-called garden column that Alsop wrote every spring and fall, usually focused on his own sometimes-despairing efforts to keep the flowers and plants around his house in a healthy state. In one typical mid-March column, Alsop wrote, "As any experienced pruner knows, you need boldness to prune plants well. It may be less well known, but it is a fact that a good time to prune is after a jolly, boldness-inducing Sunday lunch, with good wine in the sun among friends. It was after such a lunch that the wretched little myrtle plant was ruthlessly attacked, on the rule that desperate remedies are in order when all hope is probably lost." Joe's biannual garden column was the one place where the controversial journalist avoided politics.[12]

With the brothers' increasing fame, their income had also grown accordingly. Stewart and Tish had recently acquired a dilapidated farmhouse with spring-fed plumbing on 160 acres in rural Maryland, thirty miles outside Washington, as a weekend retreat. Stew named it Polecat Park upon discovering a family of seven skunks living in the basement. While Joe visited occasionally on weekends, he found the accommodations too primitive to spend the night. ("The pool is a pond; the house is a shambles; and life there is a perpetual rather messy picnic. But it's curiously relaxing," the older brother wrote to a friend.) Joe himself had purchased a vacant lot across the street from his house at 2709 Dumbarton and was talking to architects about building a bigger, more modern home.[13]

JOE ALSOP RETURNED from a European trip early in 1949 to find the house for which he had decided to be "amateur architect" in the disarray of construction. A roofless structure of bare cinder block, with "staring gaps instead of windows," confronted him as he got out of the taxi. Tired of what he called "Georgetown fakery" and its "charming, if somewhat insipid, Federal architecture," Joe had resolved to strike out in a new and unconventional direction. Rather than copy the dominant Regency style—"three flights of stairs and a maid's room behind the coal hole, in a house just big enough for a couple with one child and a poodle"—his new home would be wide and shallow and unmistakably contemporary.[14]

In a radical break with Georgetown tradition, the entrance was on the second floor, the front door at the summit of a tall and winding staircase. But the most arresting feature of the new house was its color: a bilious yellow. "Ocher," sniffed Joe, when a delegation of townswomen arrived to inspect the house and left with mouths agape at the steel casement windows and stucco exterior.

In an article that he wrote for *The Saturday Evening Post*—"I'm Guilty! I Built a Modern House"—Alsop cheerfully admitted that his creation was "a heinous outrage against 'Georgetown charm.'" Joe's neighbors were quick to agree. One described the house as looking from the outside like "a converted garage"; another, as "something you'd expect to find in Sioux City, Iowa." Susan Mary—back in Georgetown to see her mother at the house on Twenty-Ninth Street—confided to her Paris friends that Joe's new home was "ugly as sin." Alsop himself jokingly suggested a new architectural style: "Garage Palladian."[15]

Within weeks, the Citizens Association of Georgetown had voted a municipal ordinance that would prevent another cinder-block house from being built in the neighborhood. In less than a year, Congress, under intense lobbying from the locals, would pass the Old Georgetown Act, which officially set the boundaries of the historic district and point-edly gave the U.S. Commission of Fine Arts "advisory powers over all exterior construction and building alterations within that area."[16]

Joe, however, remained unapologetic. The result of his foray into do-it-yourself house design was, he wrote, "a green, cool, private place," with high ceilings and sliding glass doors that opened onto what he considered the most important feature and the centerpiece of the new house: an interior courtyard garden that included lush tropical plants, nine varieties of boxwoods, white azaleas, and a wisteria-covered loggia. (Alsop told friends that he so hated the multicolored azalea popular with suburbanites that he tried not to leave town when the flowers were in bloom.) With a jeweler's eye for detail, Joe had consulted the U.S. Naval Observatory's astronomer regarding optimum sun angles for Washing-ton's latitude before planting the wisteria. "For all these things, a high stoop and a certain sense of criminality seem to me a small price to pay," his *Post* article concluded.[17]

Moreover, the interior of Joe's new house was more sumptuous than ever: the portraits of famous ancestors still peered down at visitors, but from peacock-green walls in a book-lined living room. The host's signa-ture terrapin soup and leek pie would henceforth be served in a spacious dining room, able to comfortably seat a dozen guests around the table. Downstairs, facing the street, was an office where the brothers—hunched over identical Underwood typewriters—could collaborate on their col-umn. There also was a bedroom for José and Maria, the couple who were Joe's butler and cook. Mornings Joe spent, kimono clad, drinking coffee and reading newspapers in the south-facing "garden room," his favorite, which had a skylight ceiling and a breakfast nook surrounded by more junglelike foliage. (One of Alsop's first overnight guests in the new house, Arthur Schlesinger Jr., later sent Joe a note of thanks, add-ing, "I cannot escape, however, certain H. G. Wellsian anxieties over the picture of yourself, watering those somewhat sinister plants day after day, until eventually they seize and strangle you."[18])

By the time Joe moved into his new house—"like a wounded beast taking refuge in a disordered lair"—creeping ivy and clematis had already begun to soften the stark facade, and a kind of wary truce between the owner and the citizens' association prevailed. But for years to come, longtime Georgetowners were said to cross the street and avert their eyes when walking past 2720 Dumbarton.[19]

SUSAN MARY was another frequent guest at the Sunday night suppers that spring. It was, she wrote to a friend in England, "thrilling" to be back home again: "Washington is the coziest capital in the world, and it's nice to feel the optimism and the sense of controlled power."[20]

Across town at the State Department, George Kennan, far from feeling optimistic or powerful, was once again in a glum mood. Despite the brief glimmer of hope that followed Tito's break with Moscow, there had been no further sign of the impending collapse of the Soviet empire. On the contrary, the Kremlin had since tightened its control over the puppet governments in Eastern Europe and cracked down even harder on dissent. That winter, the Russians had also begun jamming radio broadcasts of the Voice of America, closing one of the few remaining gaps in the Iron Curtain. Kennan and Chip Bohlen were part of a State Department committee that reviewed the weekly VOA scripts. In a rambling nine-page letter to Dean Acheson, who had replaced George Marshall as secretary of state at the beginning of the year, Kennan was yet again threatening to resign from the Foreign Service. "I am afraid that we are not really getting anywhere," he protested.[21]

Acheson persuaded Kennan to opt instead for a change of scenery and a temporary leave of absence; that spring, the latter embarked on an inspection trip to Germany. "Last full day in the office. A hard and unfriendly day," Kennan wrote in his diary on March 2, 1949. Before leaving town, he attended a final round of dinners with the Wisners, the Joyces, and the Bohlens.

Kennan's depression followed him across the Atlantic. Strolling by a fog-enshrouded cemetery in Germany, he was suddenly seized by a visceral sense of his own mortality. A visit to Hamburg, where he witnessed the devastation wrought by Allied bombing, provoked this unusually strong response in his diary: "And here, for the first time, I felt an unshakable conviction that no momentary military advantage—even if such could have been calculated to exist—could have justified this stupendous, careless destruction of civilian life and of material values, built up laboriously by human hands over the course of centuries for purposes having nothing to do with this war." The West, Kennan wrote, "had to learn to fight its wars morally as well as militarily, or not fight them at all; for moral principles were a part of its strength." At the same time, he believed that the Western world also had "the obligation to be militarily stronger than its adversaries by a margin sufficient to enable it to dispense with those means which can stave off defeat only at the cost of undermining victory."[22]

In Berlin, the sight of children walking their dog through light snow falling on the bomb-shattered city, oblivious to the destruction that surrounded them, prompted this musing upon the children's future—and Europe's: "The answer will depend partly on you, since none of us is without will and responsibility who is not completely a prisoner. But it will depend more on us Americans. For we have won great wars and assumed to ourselves great powers. And we have thus become the least free of all peoples. We have placed upon ourselves the obligation to have the answers . . . And I'd watch that one, if I were you, come to think of it; because we aren't too sure about all things ourselves."[23]

Back again in Washington, Kennan's spirits lifted enough for him to summon his confidant on the Policy Planning Staff, John Davies, to receive fresh instructions. Kennan asked Davies to come up with "some brave new approach on the question of what to do with Eastern Europe." Augmented by a panel of Soviet experts, Davies and Bob Joyce duly called together the rest of the planning staff. Paul Nitze had only recently joined the group, as Kennan's deputy. Kennan had actually wanted to recruit Nitze at the staff's inception, but Acheson had "blackballed" him, Nitze said—protesting that Kennan's choice was too much "a Wall Streeter" and "not a deep thinker." (The opportunity to appoint Nitze had arisen when Acheson temporarily left the State Department to return to his law practice. Nitze returned the slight by naming a particularly stubborn horse at his Maryland farm for the secretary of state.)[24]

Together, Nitze and Kennan had quickly devised a bold new idea of their own, which they planned to present at a forthcoming meeting of foreign ministers in Paris: the reunification of Germany, conditional upon the mutual withdrawal of Soviet and Allied occupying forces. The duo dubbed their so-called disengagement proposal "Program A." The idea not only was radical and ahead of its time but ran directly counter to the Truman administration's goal of European and American collective security, which had already culminated, by mid-1949, in the creation of the North Atlantic Treaty Organization. As it turned out, NATO was another idea that Kennan had opposed—probably because he did not invent it, joked State Department colleagues. Instead, Kennan favored a more limited Western alliance, consisting of the United States, Britain, and Canada.[25]

Program A never made it beyond the drawing board, after a column by the *Times*'s Scotty Reston leaked the Kennan-Nitze plan on the eve of the Paris foreign ministers meeting, and Acheson publicly disavowed it. When an Alsop column outlined Kennan's notion of an exclusive Anglo-American alliance as an alternative to NATO, more howls of outrage were heard from Foggy Bottom. Kennan's proposal had upset not only the French and Acheson but also Bohlen, who chided his friend for his predictably contrarian views. As before, Kennan, in mock horror, assured Acheson that he had nothing to do with the leak. The secretary of state, already wary of talking to the Alsops, reassured Kennan in a handwritten note, "Don't worry about it . . . This is life in a disordered democracy."[26]

But the incident served to emphasize Kennan's growing isolation at State and showed, once again, that the temperamental diplomat was "more comfortable speaking from his own pulpit than joining a chorus," as one critic observed. ("His becoming modesty is at times overlain by an appalling, nanny-like intellectual arrogance, and even self-pity—a sort of God-like, above-it-all stance," Bob Joyce wrote of Kennan, whom he knew well.) Kennan informed Chip Bohlen that he planned to return to private life in the near future: "I find my estimate of my potential usefulness here shaken by the depth of this disagreement."[27]

The confrontation with the Soviet Union was also exacting a human toll. While both Kennan and Nitze were still at the foreign ministers meeting in Paris, word came from Washington of Jim Forrestal's suicide. That spring, the abyss into which the secretary of defense had been staring for the past two years stared back. Caught in a tug-of-war between the Joint Chiefs of Staff, who argued for increased military spending to counter the Soviet threat, and the president, who hoped to economize by reducing conventional forces, Forrestal sided with the chiefs. Dismissed from his Pentagon post by Truman in March for his intransigence on the defense budget debate, Forrestal suffered a nervous breakdown weeks later and was confined to a secure wing of the navy's hospital in Bethesda, Maryland. During the early morning hours of May 22, 1949, after a restless night spent copying lines from the chorus of Sophocles's play *Ajax,* Forrestal fell to his death from the window of his room on the hospital's sixteenth floor.

He would be the first senior-ranking American casualty of the Cold War.[28]

NEAR THE END OF 1949, John Paton Davies Jr.—Kennan's colleague on the Policy Planning Staff and the primary author of the recent staff paper on Eastern Europe—unexpectedly found himself at the center of a feud between Kennan and Joe Alsop over U.S. policy toward China. As Chiang Kai-shek's Nationalist armies fell back in disarray before Mao's Communist forces, Joe traced the roots of the debacle to America's wartime China experts, among whom was John Davies. Thus, Davies had been among those State Department advisers who warned Roosevelt and Truman, in vain, against making the corrupt and unpopular Chiang America's client in China. Worse still, as Vinegar Joe Stilwell's political officer, Davies had been Joe Alsop's opposite number—and rival—in the bitter wartime feuding between Chennault and Stilwell. By the time Mao seized power in October 1949, Joe had already written half a dozen columns blaming the setback on the so-called China hands and, specifically, on experts like Davies, who, Alsop claimed, had mistakenly dismissed the Communists as mere "democratic agrarian reformers."[29]

When Acheson and the State Department issued a 1,054-page white paper blaming the Nationalist failure not on American experts but on Chiang's own incompetence and venality, Joe wrote a lengthy and combative rebuttal—a three-part series for *The Saturday Evening Post* that bore the provocative title "Why We Lost China." Alsop's opening broadside began, "Throughout the fateful years in China, the American representatives there actively favored the Chinese communists. They also contributed to the weakness, both political and military, of the National Government. And in the end they came close to offering China up to the communists, like a trussed bird on a platter, over four years before the eventual communist triumph."[30]

Joe's articles provoked a firestorm—becoming fodder for other columnists and inspiring partisan speeches in Congress. But they also revived a running dispute between Alsop and George Kennan. During a lunch with Stewart, Kennan complained bitterly about "the campaign of vilification which his brother Joe had carried on for years against John Davies." After word of the criticism got back to him, Joe promptly telephoned Kennan "in white heat about this and talked for three-quarters of an hour straight on the subject," Kennan wrote in his diary. That same evening, Kennan and Joe Alsop once again found themselves in uncomfortable proximity as guests at a Georgetown dinner party. "However, we all avoided the subject," remembered Kennan.[31]

Knowing of Kennan's close friendship with Davies, Joe had warned the former of what was to come and even offered to show both men a draft of his articles before they were published. He was, Joe assured Kennan, "anxious to avoid the faintest appearance of personal animus or persecution." But Kennan remained unimpressed. "I would be happy to let the past bury its dead," he wrote to Alsop.[32]

The controversy was very far from dead, however. On January 23, 1950, just two days after the last of his *Saturday Evening Post* articles appeared, Alsop—perhaps realizing he had gone too far—dedicated a Matter of Fact column to *defending* Davies. In "Oh, What a Tangled Tale," Joe decried the "attempt, now going on in Congress and on the radio, to prove that there was some sort of pro-Communist plot in the State Department. There was no such plot." (And, in a belated act of contrition, Joe had his personal secretary send a gift in his name to each of the Davies children at Christmastime.)[33]

But it was too late for Alsop to summon back the demons he had conjured. In a speech barely two weeks later, on February 9, the Wisconsin senator Joseph McCarthy told the Women's Republican Club of Wheeling, West Virginia, that he possessed a list of State Department employees who were "members of the Communist Party and members of a spy ring." While McCarthy never produced the actual list, and his tally of alleged Communists and spies constantly fluctuated, among the four suspects he named in his Wheeling speech was John Stewart Service, one of the China experts whom Alsop had written about in the *Post* articles, as well as John Davies's close friend and Foreign Service colleague.[34]

The Alsops had addressed the question of internal security in their column many times before. Joe and Stewart were vocal critics of the Truman administration's domestic loyalty program, initiated in 1947, for "putting a premium on ignorance," "carrying 'guilt by association' too far," and creating a "government of drones and toadies." In March 1948, the brothers had also characterized as "gross incompetence" the attack by the House Committee on Un-American Activities on the physicist Edward Condon, director of the National Bureau of Standards, for supposed ties to the Communist Party. Later that same year, when allegations of Communist sympathies held up Arthur Schlesinger Jr.'s clearance for a job with the European Recovery Program in Paris, the Alsop brothers had castigated the bureau's informants in the case as "singularly ignorant and stupid." Another of Schlesinger's friends, Phil Graham, personally intervened with the FBI's Hoover on his behalf. Shortly thereafter the clearance came through.[35]

Additionally, after Secretary of State Acheson had come to the defense of Alger Hiss, the former State Department aide accused of being a Soviet spy, Joe reminded his readers that "no conclusive case has been built" against Hiss. Alsop was prepared to go even further and argue for Hiss's innocence but had been warned away by Acheson himself. ("It is always a mistake to write about anything that is *sub judice*," Dean reportedly told Joe.) The Alsops sympathized with Hiss, since, as they noted in one column, their younger brother, John, had previously been denied a security clearance, and Joe himself had been wrongly detained by U.S. authorities following his release from the Japanese prison camp—both being cases of mistaken identity. Uncertain, however, on how far he should go in championing the accused, Alsop instead secretly advised Hiss's defense team on how they might undermine the credibility of the prosecution's chief witness, Whittaker Chambers, by pointing out "homoerotic themes in Chambers' poetry and in his translation of German texts."[36]

Because Joe was in Europe when McCarthy made his speech at the women's club, it fell to Stewart to respond to the Wisconsin senator's charges. On March 5, 1950, three days before hearings began in the special Senate subcommittee that had been created to investigate McCarthy's claims, Stew wrote in a Matter of Fact column,

> It is possible that Senator Joseph McCarthy, the big, raw-boned pride and joy of the real estate lobby, has rendered the country a major service. Senator McCarthy has charged that there are fifty-seven (or eighty-one, or more than 200) Communists in the State Department. If so, and if he can prove it, he will of course deserve a vote of thanks for demonstrating that the State Department is riddled with potential spies. The available evidence suggests, however, that Senator McCarthy's service will be of a different sort. Responsible officials in the State Department are confident that

in the forthcoming Senate investigation of his charges McCarthy will get his head so thoroughly washed that neither he nor any of his like-minded colleagues will soon again use this particular vote-catching technique.[37]

It was the opening salvo in what proved to be a long and bitter war.

CHAPTER SEVEN

"A Land of Conspiracy, Run by Conspirators"

I N A SIGN of their expanding importance as part of the nation's burgeoning intelligence establishment, Frank Wisner and his Office
of Policy Coordination had moved to larger quarters—to temporary
buildings located on the National Mall. Ironically, Frank's next-door
neighbor was his archrival: Dick Helms and the CIA's Office of Special
Operations, which had meanwhile outgrown its own cramped warren
on E Street. Wisner's operatives worked in Buildings I and J; Helms's
analysts were in adjacent Buildings K and L. Helms remembered the
tin-roofed, un-air-conditioned "tempos" as "cold in winter, wet in rain,
soggy and stifling in summer." Because of the chronic dampness, he
noted, OSO's analysts often had to peel apart the stuck-together pages
of their classified reports, "like the Dead Sea Scrolls." Wisner philo-
sophically dubbed his own ramshackle, rodent-infested quarters near the
Reflecting Pool the "Rat Palace." To cover up peeling paint on the walls,
and for martial inspiration, Frank hung lithographs of the British navy
destroying the French fleet at the Battle of the Nile.[1]

Their unglamorous surroundings notwithstanding, Wisner and
his recruits pitched into their work with enthusiasm. William Colby,
another of the wartime OSS veterans who had rallied to Frank's cause,
compared the early mood at Wisner's headquarters to "the atmosphere of
an order of Knights Templar, to save Western freedom from Communist
darkness—and from war." Using Kennan's memo on the inauguration of
political warfare as his guide, Wisner had drawn up an extensive organization chart for OPC, consisting of four sections and sixteen programs,
along with an ambitious array of covert operations. The latter included

the creation of so-called freedom committees, composed of émigrés in the United States and Europe; unspecified "underground activities behind the Iron Curtain"; and "support of indigenous anti-Communist elements" whenever and wherever they might be found.[2]

One of OPC's earliest projects, code-named Bloodstone, was actually a carryover from Wisner's previous job at the State Department and aimed at using "native anti-communist elements" within the Soviet Union's satellites in Eastern Europe as a kind of fifth column, to undermine and subvert Communist rule from within. The key to understanding Wisner's long-term strategy was contained in the language he used to promote projects like Bloodstone: Soviet Communism was routinely described as an infection, for which the politically disaffected were "natural antidotes." It was no accident that Wisner was partial to picking agent code names from among various infectious diseases—his own secret wartime OSS moniker had been Typhus—since his goal was to plant the fatal germ of rebellion in the Soviet Union's body politic.[3]

Another OPC emphasis, under the heading of "psychological warfare," was propaganda. As early as March 1948, Kennan had instructed Davies to explore the possibility "of penetrating the iron curtain . . . via clandestine radio situated in . . . our occupied zone." With a go-ahead from the State Department, Wisner had begun looking for suitable locations in western Germany from which to begin beaming OPC's message of hope and rebellion to the captive populations of the Soviet bloc.[4]

While the permanent mechanism for funding OPC's covert operations was deliberately left somewhat vague in its charter, here, too, Kennan and Wisner had some helpful ideas. In his presentation to the NSC on the inauguration of political warfare, Kennan proposed using a "public American organization" as a front to sponsor and support anti-Communist refugees and émigrés. Ostensibly funded by private U.S. citizens, the freedom committees would provide a useful cover for the psychological warfare operations that Wisner planned to carry out in Soviet-occupied Eastern Europe. Ideally, Wisner hoped that the freedom committees might even provide the shock troops for the nation's secret guerrilla army. "This is primarily an overt operation which, however, should receive covert guidance and possibly assistance from the Government," Kennan had explained. He asked John Davies to help set up an institute overseas as a clearinghouse for émigrés who would serve as the front men on the committees.[5]

Wisner, in turn, went to his own longtime ally Allen Dulles for assistance in approaching prominent Americans, including members of the prestigious Council on Foreign Relations, to serve on the boards of the freedom committees. The National Committee for a Free Europe, incorporated under the laws of the State of New York on June 1, 1949, was the first fruit of Kennan and Wisner's initiative. NCFE's plush suite of offices on the third floor of the Empire State Building was theoretically paid for by the money collected through the Crusade for Freedom, a public fund-raising effort headed by a former OSS officer who had become, in peacetime, a publicist for General Mills, the cereal company. But in fact the committee's principal funding came from Wisner's Office of Policy Coordination, in a weekly check laundered through the Wall Street investment bank owned by Henry Sears, Wisner's close friend and a nearby neighbor to Locust Hill Farm.[6] (The paternity of the freedom committees would later be disputed. When a former NCFE board member wrote to Kennan in 1954, inquiring where the idea had come from, Kennan replied, "It is, I think, correct that the initial impulse to this undertaking came from myself." Wisner, who also saw the letter, wrote to Kennan's secretary with a correction: "I feel sure that Mr. Kennan's statements in this regard were intended for a good purpose . . . but for the actual record I should like to observe that there were, after all, just a few others involved in the real work.")*[7]

For OPC's operations on foreign soil, Wisner and Kennan turned to a little-known provision in the Marshall Plan legislation, which specified that up to 5 percent of the local currency that participating countries contributed to the European Recovery Program would go directly to the U.S. government, for "administrative" costs. The responsibility for these so-called counterpart funds was put in the hands of the program's deputy administrator, Richard Bissell. Unknown to the public—and to all but a handful in Congress—approval of the Marshall Plan had thereby also given the green light to the covert warfare campaign proposed by Kennan, Wisner, and OPC.[8]

Dick Bissell would later recall how he had first learned about the

---

* "We took the germ of George Kennan's idea and literally built the house ourselves. I know this was so because I was one of the architects and carpenters," Wisner subsequently wrote. In the thousand-plus pages of his two-volume memoirs, Kennan would make no mention of Frank Wisner, OPC, or the National Committee for a Free Europe. Of OPC and his own role in the genesis of U.S. covert operations during the Cold War, Kennan told the Church Committee investigating the CIA in October 1975 only "It did not work out at all the way I had conceived it."

existence of the Office of Policy Coordination on a foggy evening in Paris near the end of 1948. Bissell's informant was his friend and fellow Marshall planner Franklin Lindsay. Bissell was nonetheless "somewhat baffled" when Frank Wisner called on him shortly thereafter in Washington with a request that Marshall Plan counterpart funds be released to OPC. When Bissell inquired of Wisner how the money would be used, the latter flatly replied that "he could not be told" but that the arrangement had already been approved by the program's top administrator, Averell Harriman. Bissell promised Wisner the money, and OPC became, in effect, the shadowy silent partner of the Marshall Plan.[9]

BY EARLY 1949, Wisner was throwing out "ideas for rolling back the Soviet empire—some good, others wildly impractical—like a human pinwheel." He envisioned carrying out a simultaneous, multipronged offensive against the Soviet Union, using psychological, political, and economic weapons for as long as there was no shooting war and "preventive direct action"—mainly sabotage, small-scale military operations behind front lines, and even assassination—in the event that the Cold War suddenly turned hot. The soldiers in Frank's war would be recruited from among the swollen ranks of those who had fled the Communist takeover of their countries and filled the refugee camps of Western Europe, as well as those lucky émigrés who had succeeded in coming to America but were eagerly awaiting the day when they could return home.[10]

To prepare for the coming battle and to soften up the enemy in advance, Wisner decided to focus first on radioing messages of hope and reassurance to the "captive people" of Eastern Europe while at the same time confusing their Communist masters with false rumors and disinformation. In a later stage of his campaign, weather balloons would be used to drop leaflets, urging the native population to rise up against its Soviet oppressors. The freedom committees that Kennan and Wisner had established and funded through OPC would provide the necessary cover for these operations. Wisner affectionately dubbed his secret propaganda machine "the mighty Wurlitzer."[11]

Nor did he intend that the Wurlitzer would necessarily be heard only overseas. Early on, Wisner had shown that he looked upon the Washington press corps as a prospective cheering section for the freedom committees, as well as an enthusiastic—albeit unwitting—promoter of OPC's secret operations behind the Iron Curtain. Stewart Alsop claimed that Wisner suffered from "the Chip Bohlen Syndrome—the notion that the press should be an instrument of American foreign policy." But if journalists proved reluctant or too slow to rally to the cause, Frank himself was ready and eager to provide the stories that they *should* report. One of those who worked for OPC in those days remembered Wisner keeping a bank of wire service tickers across the hall from his office: "A story would come over and he'd get on the phone. Get something out! The Mighty Wurlitzer! He was compulsive about answering everything."[12]

Overseeing Wisner and his busy spy shop from the State Department, Kennan had as yet betrayed no sign of a faint heart. Indeed, quite the opposite. By late 1948, he was meeting weekly with Wisner—and might even have had a hand in planning some of the covert operations behind the Iron Curtain. (Ironically, Kennan would later claim—regarding OPC—"I scarcely paid any attention to it.")[13]

When Frank expressed anxiety about the army's willingness to support OPC's clandestine training bases in Germany, Kennan and Bob Lovett had promptly gone to the Pentagon and gotten Forrestal to smooth the way. Early in 1949, when Wisner submitted OPC's budget for 1950, Kennan had deemed it "the minimum of what is required from the foreign policy standpoint in the way of covert operations during the coming year," adding, "As the international situation develops, every day makes more evident the importance of the role which will have to be played by covert operations if our national interests are to be adequately protected." Kennan advised Frank that "in one or two instances . . . we will have to ask you to add to the list of functions."[14]

By then, George Kennan had an additional, personal reason to be grateful to Frank Wisner. The previous October, in the culmination of a lengthy campaign, OPC had finally succeeded in bringing Gustav Hilger to the United States. Kennan expressed his gratitude in a private note, congratulating Wisner for "having done the right thing" in bringing not only Hilger but also the diplomat's family to freedom. Shortly after his arrival in this country, Hilger spent the weekend as a guest at his benefactor's Pennsylvania farm. The German expert on the Soviet Union was also made a paid CIA consultant at Kennan's instigation.[15]

Kennan could hardly have been unaware that there was a certain irony in his enthusiasm for covert operations as a way of fighting "fire with fire," given the closing admonition—and valedictory—of his famous long telegram, which warned, "After all, the greatest danger that can befall us in coping with this problem of Soviet communism, is that we shall allow ourselves to become like those with whom we are coping." Indeed, there were—had Kennan wished to heed them—early warning signs that the "firm guiding hand" he promised to wield over Wisner and OPC might already be losing its grip. Thus, even before the first bass notes of the mighty Wurlitzer had been heard, in the United States or overseas, the Wiz was already thinking beyond clandestine transmitters and weather balloons.

For it was not only leaflets and radio broadcasts but men that Frank Wisner planned to send behind the Iron Curtain.

BY MID-1949, Frank Wisner, Bob Joyce, Franklin Lindsay, and Charles Thayer were busy working the pedals and stops of OPC's mighty Wurlitzer, practicing themes both large and small. Their plots ranged from the merely madcap—replacing the toilet paper on trains leaving Vienna for Budapest with tissue bearing the visage of Hungary's Communist leader—to the wildly ambitious and even bizarre: A scheme to assassinate Stalin was abandoned early in the planning stage. Kennan personally vetoed another proposal, for a kind of oceangoing Potemkin village, meant to promote the benefits of the American lifestyle to envious would-be consumers overseas. Operation Flattop envisioned sending "a U.S.A. Main Street abroad on a Navy carrier" and had originally been suggested by an article in *Collier's* magazine.[16]

A sign of Wisner's growing reach, and likewise his attention to detail, was his directive instructing the U.S. embassy in Paris to end the rationing of newsprint so that France's anti-Communist press might resume publication. Another OPC scheme, to spread "the story of the Tito heresy," involved distributing a recent *Atlantic Monthly* article on Yugoslavia throughout the Soviet bloc by balloon. Because of its American origins, however, Wisner suggested that it "be caused to appear in disguised forms."

In addition to helping Davies think up bold new ventures in Eastern Europe, Bob Joyce spent most of his time at the State Department clearing obstacles to Wisner's plans. After a brief stint at the helm of the Voice of America, Charlie Thayer had taken over direction of Radio Free Europe, whose OPC-subsidized broadcasts were the product of the National Committee for a Free Europe, the first of the freedom committees proposed by Kennan. The Institute for the Study of the U.S.S.R., established in Munich, was another Franklin Lindsay project that had originated with Kennan and received funding from Wisner—as was the American Committee for Liberation, a front organization operating out of offices in Munich and several other European cities. Among the targets of AMCOMLIB were "defectors, deserters and escapees" from the Soviet bloc. The German-based Russian institute, on the other hand, sprang from Kennan's conviction that Europe's displaced intelligentsia could be enlisted in the fight against Communism.[17]

Frank Wisner was equally unwilling to concede the battle to the enemy at home. After nearly a thousand left-leaning artists and writers—including Lillian Hellman, Arthur Miller, and Norman Mailer—denounced "US warmongering" in a rally at New York's Waldorf-Astoria hotel in March 1949, Wisner obtained sixteen thousand dollars in Marshall Plan funds to stage a pro-American counterdemonstration the following month in Paris. Organizers were horrified, however, when a noisy band of anarchists hijacked the event, turning it, an agency operative observed, "into a nuts folly of miscellaneous goats and monkeys whose antics [discredited] the work and statements of the serious and responsible liberals."[18]

Wisner's colleagues would call these efforts to woo European and American intellectuals "the battle for Picasso's mind." But Frank himself was happy to aim lower. Until the intellectuals and revolutionaries appeared, the head of the Office of Policy Coordination was willing to settle for the kinds of people who lurked in alleyways and carried knives.

Since its creation the year before, OPC had grown at an astonishing rate. By late 1949, it employed more than three hundred people and had an annual budget of nearly five million dollars, not including the Marshall Plan counterpart funds acquired overseas. In addition to those who labored at the "tempos" in the shadow of the Washington Monument, Wisner hired case officers and foreign operatives to staff OPC's far-flung field offices, located throughout Western Europe and along the Mediterranean. These were the men and women who would go into the woods—or send others there.[19]

One of the first, and easily the most colorful of that number, was Carmel Offie. Having grown up in Pennsylvania coal country, the son of an Italian immigrant railroad worker, Offie seemed a classic American success story: a Horatio Alger–like figure who, although only a lowly State Department clerk, had, by his mid-thirties, befriended the likes of Kennan, Bohlen, Thayer, and Joyce, all of whom became Carmel's passionate defenders. A 1946 letter by Kennan for Offie's dossier remarked on the latter's "unbounded energy, enthusiasm, a highly sociable nature and a great loyalty and helpfulness with respect to those who take a personal interest in him." But Kennan also noted, tellingly, another Offie characteristic: "a certain lack of measure and discretion in his speech." The CIA's Jim Angleton would later describe Offie as "a world-class sophisticate who could put a stiletto in an opponent and offer him a treatise on the cognac he was serving him at the same time."[20]

In reality, Offie was a Dickensian figure, a real-life Uriah Heep who alternated between oily obsequiousness in the presence of his superiors and jaw-dropping rudeness to those he felt he could insult with impunity. (Sometimes Offie showed both sides simultaneously. In the summer of 1939, he hosted John and Joseph Kennedy during the brothers' visit to Paris. Offie later wrote, "I remember Jack sitting in my office and listening to telegrams being read or even reading various things which actually were none of his business, but since he was who he was we didn't throw him out." Although the young Kennedy initially claimed that he and Carmel were "the greatest of pals," the relationship quickly soured. "Offie has just rung for me, so I guess I have to get the old paper ready and go in and wipe his arse," Jack wrote to a friend near the end of his visit.)[21]

It was Bohlen who recommended Offie to Wisner, since the diminutive clerk had been a troubleshooter and general factotum at the Moscow embassy for the first ambassador, William Bullitt. Offie had arrived at Wisner's spy shop after being dismissed from the Foreign Service for being too good at his job as procurer—reportedly using the embassy's diplomatic pouch for illegal currency transfers and to smuggle not only precious jewels but, in one improbable shipment, three hundred Finnish lobsters. (One associate's indelible memory was of Offie's rushing to catch a flight at the Rome airport with an enormous ornate candelabra tucked under each arm. A joke told at OPC has a newly damned soul discovering himself in hell, neck-deep in a sea of stinking offal. When he observes to his neighbor, Dean Acheson, that their fates could hardly be any worse, the unflappable Acheson tells him, "Just wait till Carmel Offie comes by in his speedboat.") Subsequently described as "one of Frank Wisner's occasional blind spots," an "utterly shameless wrangler," the "royal dwarf," and even a "wild man," Offie nonetheless also lived up to his reputation as a "wily operator" at OPC—finding a cook for the Wisners, household servants for the Kennans, and a surplus army radio transmitter for Thayer's Radio Free Europe. "He had more lines out than the phone company," noted one impressed observer, who predicted that either Offie would be secretary of state one day or his body would be found floating in the Potomac.[22]

Not least important for Offie's future career, he had finally managed to bring Gustav Hilger into the country, thereby securing the lingering gratitude of both Kennan and Wisner. In what was surely a kind of inside joke, Wisner's headquarters assigned Carmel the code name Monk.[23]

Another loyal soldier brought to the colors by Franklin Lindsay at this time was Michael Burke. Burke had been a football star at the University of Pennsylvania and was reportedly being scouted by the Philadelphia Eagles when Pearl Harbor was attacked. Having first joined the navy, Burke was, by 1944, an OSS agent in occupied France. Tall, slim, and handsome, he not only looked the part of the secret agent in a Hollywood film but actually played the role in a 1946 movie, *Cloak and Dagger,* starring Gary Cooper. Three years later, Wisner sent Burke to Rome as the representative in Italy of Imperial Films, a fictitious company with no assets apart from official-looking stationery and a post office box in New York City, both paid for by OPC.[24]

In April 1948, while working for the Marshall Plan administrator, Averell Harriman, at the American embassy in Paris, Howard Hunt was personally recruited by Wisner over the Easter holiday. Hunt recalled the head of OPC promising him that the job would go well beyond simple intelligence gathering. "We'll be what America needs in this Cold War, an action arm," Frank had boasted. Wisner sent Hunt to Mexico with a prefatory warning that since the head of the FBI was "dead set" against OPC's extending its fiat into that country, he should keep a low profile.[25]

Wisner had good reason to be cautious. The bureau's director, J. Edgar Hoover, viewed his initiatives with growing alarm and was particularly upset that OPC's influence had spread into Mexico and Latin America, traditionally the FBI's bailiwick. Having previously disposed of Donovan and the OSS, Hoover saw Wisner and OPC as his latest potential rivals. Hoover ordered his G-men to launch an investigation of Frank and those known around the bureau as "Wisner's weirdos."[26]

Not surprisingly, Offie was first on Hoover's list. Openly and unabashedly homosexual, Carmel had the disconcerting habit of rubbing his own nipples when engaged in conversation with other men. (Arrested in 1943 by an undercover cop for lewd behavior in Lafayette Park, across from the White House, Offie had been rescued by none other than Secretary of State Cordell Hull, who told the authorities that Offie was on a secret wartime mission to rendezvous with an informant.) Likewise, it surely had not escaped the attention of bureau agents that Offie lived in an imposing brick manse on Cathedral Heights' fashionable Woodley Road. His next-door neighbors included Paul Nitze, Scotty Reston, and Walter Lippmann. How Offie could afford such a house—in addition to a sizable farm outside Markham, Virginia—on a government clerk's salary was the subject of much speculation and several contending theories. Offie's FBI file would eventually run to more than three hundred pages.[27]

But the fact that Offie did nothing to hide his sexual preferences, and that no incriminating paper trail could be found to shed light on his extensive real estate holdings, protected him from exposure and prosecution, at least for a time. Moreover, Wisner, not Offie, was Hoover's real target. And to bring down that prize, the FBI director was willing to be patient.[28]

DESPITE ALL THE TREASURE, talent, and effort that Wisner had put into his mighty Wurlitzer, the impetus for OPC's first major operation came from outside—from the British.

Early in 1949, Wisner learned that King Zog, Albania's exiled monarch, had plans for returning to his native land behind a five-hundred-man invading army. The force was to be recruited from among Zog's countrymen, who had flooded into displaced-persons camps in Italy and Greece when Albania slipped into the Soviet orbit. With the help of MI6 and the CIA, Zog and his supporters hoped to overthrow Enver Hoxha, the ruthless, doctrinaire Stalinist who had ruled Albania since 1944. Frank promptly sent Carmel Offie to Alexandria, Egypt—Zog's temporary place of refuge—to consult with the king and his fellow exile and ally the Albanian diplomat Midhat Frashëri. Offie discovered that the would-be royalists turned revolutionaries had already contacted the British about their plans.[29]

That spring, while Kennan was still on his moody hegira to Germany, Wisner, Offie, and Joyce received a visiting delegation from Britain's Secret Intelligence Service, MI6. Like Kennan and his planning staff, England's spies had concluded that the Soviet satellites in Eastern Europe were the Communist empire's weak link, and Albania's government was deemed the weakest. The British planned to send anti-Communist Albanian émigrés back to their native land to perform an initial reconnaissance and, eventually, to lay the seeds of a resistance movement that might overthrow the Hoxha regime. Recognizing, however, that Wisner and OPC possessed resources far in excess of their own, the British had decided to bring their U.S. allies into the plot. "Church mice do not start wars," one Foreign Office toff sternly reminded his spy colleagues.[30]

Wisner was instantly seized by the idea; indeed, OPC's intervention in Albania would be similar to Britain's, but on a much larger and more ambitious scale. Frank's plan, as outlined to MI6, was "to detach Albania from the Soviet orbit." Davies and Joyce, still in search of Kennan's brave new venture, had conveniently provided the rationale for just such an undertaking in a recent Policy Planning Staff paper, which declared, "The time is now ripe for us to place greater emphasis on the offensive to consider whether we cannot do more to cause the elimination or at least a reduction of predominant Soviet influence in the satellite states of Eastern Europe." In a draft PPS paper, Davies wrote boldly of "taking the war to the enemy."[31]

Offie returned from his meeting with Zog and Frashëri full of enthusiasm for the Albania project. Hoping to overcome the objections of skeptics—which evidently included Wisner's own chief of operations, James McCargar—Carmel wrote to Frank, concerning Albania, "It is a land of conspiracy, run by conspirators. And we are now engaged in a tough, dangerous conspiracy. We must act accordingly." After receiving tentative approval from State's deputy assistant secretary for European affairs, Llewellyn "Tommy" Thompson, Wisner instructed Offie, "Expedite, through Mr. Kennan, a written concurrence from the Department of State in the Albanian plan as presented and revised."[32]

Wisner put Offie in charge of organizing training camps in Germany and Italy for the Albanian émigrés who would become the vanguard of Zog's army. Frank called them "ethnic agent teams," but the British more colorfully dubbed their volunteers "pixies." Michael Burke was made responsible for finding recruits among the approximately fifteen hundred Albanian exiles, many of whom had flocked to Rome the way anti-Communist Russians had congregated in Paris after the Bolshevik Revolution. The British called their plan Operation Valuable. Wisner, true to form, chose a more stirring name for OPC's enterprise: Project Fiend.[33]

ON FRIDAY MORNING, June 10, 1949, Project Fiend became Frank Wisner's new front in his personal covert war on the Soviet Union. "Gentlemen, I have come before you today to describe a projected OPC operation against Albania," Frank began, speaking to a handpicked group gathered in his Rat Palace by the Reflecting Pool. "This operation is not a large one by modern standards and even with complete success it will not be decisive in the cold war," Wisner conceded. But there were three reasons, he argued, why it deserved support: it would be OPC's first major undertaking; it had "obvious military implications"; and its success would vindicate the decision to put clandestine operations in OPC's—and, specifically, Wisner's—hands.[34]

Frank's plan was to parachute as many as fifty OPC-trained Albanian exiles, assembled in four- to five-man teams, into their native country over the next nine to eighteen months. Equipped with submachine guns, hand grenades, and a foot-operated wireless transmitter, the infiltrators, once on the ground, would organize a resistance movement, conduct acts of sabotage, and prepare the way for an eventual armed insurrection against the Hoxha regime. "All that is necessary is leadership, subsidy money and eventually some arms," Wisner promised—not needing to add, before this audience, that OPC had all three in abundance.

Since it was vital to disguise the fact that "the United States was directly and overtly fomenting rebellion in Albania," however, an additional part of the plan was to be the creation of another of Kennan's freedom committees, consisting of exiled leaders of the various Albanian émigré groups. The National Committee for a Free Albania would be established under the auspices of the National Committee for a Free Europe, with offices in New York and overseas. Yet Wisner left no doubt as to who would really be in charge: "In actual fact, the Committee will be our agent. It will be able to operate only through facilities which we control. The words said over the radio will be prepared by us and the people sent into Albania will be selected and trained by us."

Wisner intended to launch the first mission by September and to make a decision within two months whether "armed revolt is feasible." As a preparatory step, OPC would destabilize the Hoxha government by flooding the country with counterfeit currency. Any Soviet-bloc ships bearing logistical support for the Albanian military would be interdicted en route.[35]

Wisner ended his presentation by emphasizing what he called the plan's two most "salient characteristics—caution and flexibility. In

undertaking it we have nothing to lose except our immediate investments in time, personnel, and money." A positive outcome, on the other
hand, would give the nation a much-needed victory in the Cold War: "If
we have great success we shall have eliminated a pocket of communist
imperialism and dealt the Soviet Empire a blow that will resound behind
the iron curtain."*[36]

Fiend was officially approved by the State Department twelve days
later. Even though Wisner already worried about Offie's profligate
spending habits, he authorized the shipment of ten thousand gold coins
to Burke in Rome to pay for the project. The National Committee for
a Free Albania opened its inaugural storefront office, in Paris, on July 1,
1949.[37]

Coordination of the parallel British and American operations in Albania was discussed at the highest levels that fall, during a visit to Washington by the foreign secretary, Ernest Bevin. A joint campaign of denial
and disinformation was already under way. At Britain's urging, Acheson
cabled the U.S. ambassador in Rome with instructions to "deny that
formation of Free Albanian Comm. portends any active measures by us
against Albanian Gov't."[38]

Ironically, the explicit goal of Project Fiend—an internal revolt against
the Hoxha regime—was an outcome dismissed as unlikely at best by a
secret CIA report completed just days after Bevin's visit. It concluded
that "a purely Albanian uprising at this time is not indicated, and, if
undertaken, would have little chance of success." The agency's analysts,
however, had probably not yet been informed of Fiend at the time they
wrote their report.[39]

Indeed, OSO's despised "washerwomen," including Richard Helms,
continued to cast a gimlet eye upon Wisner's ethnic agent teams and
remained skeptical as well of OPC's psychological warfare campaign
against the Communist regimes in Eastern Europe. As Helms patiently

---

* Wisner's prolixity and his weakness for high-flown phrases were notorious. In his memoirs, Kim Philby, a former MI6 operative—and Soviet spy—who worked with him on the
Albanian project for the British, wrote that Wisner "favoured an orotund style of conversation which was disconcerting." Philby cited a meeting in London where Wisner spoke of
the need to camouflage the source of secret funds going to the freedom committees. When
Frank had said, "It is essential to secure the overt cooperation of people with conspicuous
access to wealth in their own right," the note taker simply wrote, "rich people." An aide to
the subsequent CIA director Walter Bedell Smith was more blunt. "Why can't you write
in plain English?" he challenged Wisner.

pointed out, regarding Wisner's enthusiasm for leafleting from balloons, it hardly seemed likely that even "the most news-starved citizen would risk a stiff jail sentence by rushing to pluck pamphlets from a nearby bush." And how, Helms asked rhetorically, could 1.5 million Albanians be expected to listen to the broadcasts of Radio Free Europe when many in that country did not even have electricity, much less a radio? (The story circulated in the CIA that when agency analysts tried to obtain a telephone book for the Albanian capital, Tirana, they discovered there were only five telephones in the entire city and that everybody already knew those numbers by heart.)[40]

In contrast to Wisner, Helms was the personal embodiment of CIA caution: one of those timid souls whom Stewart Alsop would jauntily dismiss as the "Prudent Professionals."[41]

Meanwhile, undeterred by Helms's skepticism, Wisner and his crusade only picked up speed. In a blatant violation of spy tradecraft, Michael Burke had begun keeping a personal diary, where, in a cramped and barely legible scrawl, he recorded the progress of OPC's Albanian operation. Burke dubbed it his "Fiend File."

An early entry in the file, dated October 27, 1949, documented how Britain's first incursion into Albania had met with disaster.[42]

Trained in Malta and landed by boat on Albania's rocky Karaburun Peninsula, the first two teams of British pixies had been ambushed almost at once by a force of Hoxha's militia, the Sigurimi. Five of the group, including its leader, had been killed or captured. The four survivors, after failing to find help among relatives in a nearby village, had spent the following weeks frantically evading patrols, hiding in caves during the day and hiking through the mountainous terrain at night, until they finally reached sanctuary in Greece. Burke's Fiend File recorded the frantic wireless messages sent by the men under their code names during the ordeal—as well as their ultimate fate: "*Bribe:* killed . . . *Bogus:* (nothing heard) . . . *Bale:* (report regularly) . . . *Bean:* (reported in danger . . . heading Greek border)."[43]

A few months later, on March 27, 1950, a brief account of the disastrous British raid appeared in *The New York Times.* The story by C. L. Sulzberger, a *Times* correspondent with close ties to U.S. intelligence—Frank and Polly Wisner were occasional guests at the villa that Cy maintained on the Greek island of Spetsai—was said to have angered the CIA as well as MI6. But Sulzberger's scoop claimed that Washington and London were content "to see the Communist regime continue in office" and that this was likely "the last attempt to upset the Hoxha regime by violence." In reality, the first ethnic agent teams of Project Fiend would be parachuted into Albania that fall.[44]

Wisner's mighty Wurlitzer was hard at work.

CHAPTER EIGHT

"Why Has Washington Gone Crazy?"

BEDLAM . . . BY 11:13 the news was on the radio. For the rest of the day I was busy talking with newspaper men," George Kennan began his diary entry for September 23, 1949. The "news" was the revelation that the Soviet Union had exploded its first atomic bomb, years ahead of General Groves's cocky estimate that it might take the Russians a generation or more to break the American nuclear monopoly. Kennan had actually learned about the Russian bomb—dubbed Joe-1 by the United States, in Stalin's honor—more than a week earlier, and only shortly after Western scientists had concluded that the airborne radioactive debris which betrayed the blast came from an actual weapon and not a runaway nuclear reactor. A few days later, Kennan had met with Paul Nitze over dinner to discuss whether the shocking development should be publicly announced by the administration or simply leaked to reporters. Ultimately, Truman's press conference on the twenty-third had unleashed the banner headlines and outraged commentary that Kennan feared.[1]

The three Matter of Fact columns that Joe and Stewart Alsop published over the following week only helped to fuel the frenzy caused by what the brothers called "the Beria bomb"—for Lavrentii Beria, head of the Soviet secret police, who had overseen the Russian atomic project. The Alsops coupled their ire over the U.S. intelligence failure with an attack on the administration for its "trance-like reception of the news" and the recent announcement by Truman and his new secretary of defense, Louis Johnson, of major cuts in the Pentagon budget.[2]

A few days after the last of the Beria bomb columns appeared, Kennan visited Alsop at his new home, where Joe was recuperating from the flu. The two were careful to avoid the subject of China and John Davies—"for that reason our discussion, while violent, was not acrimonious," Kennan later wrote in his diary. The purpose of the visit was instead "addressed to our military problems and consisted mostly of my effort to make Alsop understand that it was primarily a political, and not a military, problem which we face at this time."[3]

Joe plainly disagreed. Indeed, Kennan likely realized that his own complacency about Joe-1 was a minority view not only in the State Department but even within the Policy Planning Staff. A week after the revelation of the Soviet bomb, the staff's morning discussion had been dominated, Kennan noted, "by new claims staked out for time and energy in the coming period. Nitze and [Undersecretary of State James] Webb both think that we must work on a reappraisal of U.S. policy in the light of the Russian progress in atomic energy."[4]

To be sure, few were willing to go as far as Davies, who argued in the weeks after Joe-1 that the time might be right for a "nuclear showdown" with the Soviet Union. (Such was the "horror" Davies's paper inspired in Kennan that the latter "insisted not just in collecting all the original copies, but all the carbons on which the copies were made," Joe Alsop remembered. Kennan "even examined with suspicion the platen of the erring typewriter in case the rubber might have retained some dreadful trace of the words recorded on it.") Kennan believed, with Germany's Bismarck, that the advocates of preventive war were like the man who, fearing death, commits suicide.[5]

But Kennan also recognized that the Soviet bomb could not go unanswered. Having resolved in earnest to leave the Foreign Service by the coming summer, he shrank at the prospect of the tasks that needed to be accomplished before his departure: "Reflecting on this development, I realized that I face the work of these remaining months with neither enthusiasm nor with hope for achievement."[6]

About to replace Kennan as head of the planning staff, Nitze felt no such dread or compunction. Indeed, Nitze exulted in his new importance, writing in a letter to his mother, "Congress is in a mean and discouraged mood, the world rocks and creaks, the Russians gloat over our problems and cleverly spread dissension amongst us and I am supposed to come up with good and workable ideas on all problems what-so-ever." When Acheson, as expected, ordered a reassessment of American defense policy in light of the Soviet bomb, Nitze was ready.[7]

AT THE CENTERPIECE of the ensuing policy debate was the question of whether the United States should proceed with development of the so-called hydrogen superbomb, the "Super." After Kennan drafted a series of nine questions for Acheson, to help frame the issues around the H-bomb, Nitze added a tenth to the list, the answer to which, he felt, was crucial to determining what the United States did next: "Would we know if the Soviets were making [an H-bomb] too?"[8]

Kennan followed up his questions with a seventy-nine-page *tour d'horizon* of postwar Soviet-American relations that, drawing on quotations that ranged from Shakespeare to the Bible, argued that the United States should forswear development of the bomb, which several top U.S. scientists, including Robert Oppenheimer, had recently condemned as "a weapon of genocide." In a rare—and unwarranted—fit of optimism, Kennan had even prepared the draft of a speech for Truman to deliver to the American people, announcing "that it is not in the national interest that we should proceed at this time to the development of this type of explosive."[9]

Nitze, for his part, would use the shock of Joe-1 to make a very different case in his own tendentious policy paper, which received input as well from John Davies and C. B. "Burt" Marshall, another self-professed "planning staff Indian." Like Kennan's case, much of Nitze's argument was abstract and philosophical—focusing, for example, on the fundamental differences between a free society and a totalitarian state. But, in contrast to the vision in the "X article" of a cautious yet opportunistic Soviet leadership, Nitze described a Kremlin that was "inescapably militant" and "animated by a peculiarly virulent blend of hatred and fear." The Cold War of Nitze's treatise was a Manichaean struggle between good and evil where "a defeat of free institutions anywhere is a defeat everywhere" and where "the survival of the free world is at stake." While rejecting on the one hand the extreme step of preventive war, Nitze was equally dismissive of continuing with the status quo: "A democracy can compensate for its natural vulnerability only if it maintains clearly superior overall power in its most inclusive sense." Without military superiority, he wrote pointedly, "a policy of 'containment' . . . is no more than a bluff."[10]

On the specific question of the H-bomb, Kennan had been influenced by Oppenheimer, a skeptic concerning both the need for the Super and its military utility. Nitze, on the other hand, chose to listen to the physicist Edward Teller, an unabashed enthusiast for the hydrogen bomb. In his paper, Kennan had urged that the United States formally promise to never again initiate the use of nuclear weapons in a conflict. Nitze rejected outright the notion of such a no-first-use pledge.[11]

Given the passions aroused by the H-bomb debate, the outcome was anticlimactic. Truman took only seven minutes at the end of January 1950 to side with Nitze and Teller over Kennan and Oppenheimer. Brushing aside the ethical objections raised by superbomb opponents, the president ordered that work on the weapon proceed. The question that Nitze raised at the outset had indeed been decisive, and the logic unassailable: if the United States could build the weapon, so could the Russians.[12]

Truman was doubtless also feeling pressure to act because news of the H-bomb debate within his administration had already surfaced in the press. After the Colorado senator Edwin Johnson inadvertently leaked word of the superbomb on a television news show in early January, speculation was rife about the weapon and its possible impact on defense planning. By mid-month, the *Washington Post* reporter Al Friendly had pieced together an accurate account of the stakes in the debate, including the split within the State Department's own planning staff. But Friendly, at Phil Graham's urging, had held back from publishing the piece. As a result, it was the Alsops who broke the H-bomb story in three Matter of Fact columns.[13]

Titling the series "Pandora's Box," the brothers reprised their earlier, 1946 *Saturday Evening Post* article to describe how ocean-spanning, H-bomb-tipped missiles would revolutionize modern warfare. The last column, headlined "Truman Can't Seem to Make the Decision to Build the Hydrogen Bomb," had appeared on January 27, 1950, just three days before the White House meeting that settled the issue. Their fellow journalist Richard Rovere would later credit the "Alsop brothers, in one of the most remarkable journalistic performances of recent years," with forcing "the hydrogen bomb story into the open." Their series on the H-bomb burnished the brothers' growing reputation for reporting what Stewart had called "not only the news-behind-the news but the news-before-the news."[14]

DISAPPOINTED BY Truman's rejection of his advice on the Super, Kennan went into another deep funk. Recently, he had told Joe Alsop that the foreign policy recommendations of an expert such as himself should be received with the same seriousness as the prescriptions of a learned physician. Instead—as Kennan silently complained again to his diary—he was being treated like a "court jester . . . valued as an intellectual gadfly on the hides of slower colleagues, but not to be taken fully seriously when it came to the final, responsible decisions of policy."[15]

In truth, Kennan's views on nuclear weapons, like his attitude toward covert operations, were never as consistent as he would later try to make them appear. But, following the superbomb decision, his opposition to so-called weapons of mass destruction would be unwavering.[16]

In the aftermath of the H-bomb debate, Kennan was also facing his own decision about the future. Richard Bissell, teaching at MIT, proposed that Kennan join the faculty there. Instead, Kennan accepted an invitation from another friend and fellow combatant in the superbomb wars: Robert Oppenheimer. Oppie offered Kennan a research position at Princeton's Institute for Advanced Study, which the famous physicist headed.

For as long as he remained at the State Department, Kennan's dark mood persisted and was again confided to his diary: "Pondering today the frustrations of the past week, it occurred to me that it is time I recognized that my planning staff, started nearly three years ago, has simply been a failure . . . All this impels me to the thought that if I am ever to do any good in this work, having the courage of my convictions, it must be outside the walls of this institution and not inside them." Kennan had earlier announced that he would be taking an extended leave of absence, starting that summer. He deliberately kept the date of his return uncertain.[17]

Even before he learned of Joe-1, Kennan had complained of "an uneasy feeling that we were traveling down the atomic road rather too fast." In the wake of the president's decision to proceed with the H-bomb, he feared that progress down that road would henceforth be heedless and pell-mell. Before leaving his interim post as counselor to Acheson, Kennan decided on one last act that he hoped might at least slow the juggernaut.[18]

At the core of his differences with Nitze was Kennan's belief that the country's almost single-minded focus on the military potential of the Soviet adversary was misplaced. "I cannot overcome the conviction that thinking in these terms reflects a vast over-estimation of Russian capabilities and a misunderstanding of Russian intentions," Kennan wrote, following a briefing on U.S. war plans. "But I cannot prove this conviction, and the matters in question are too important for anyone to dare act on a hunch."[19]

Since he was unable to respond publicly to critics like Nitze—whose policy paper, like his own, was classified top secret—Kennan instead poured out his frustration in the March 1950 issue of *Reader's Digest*. Choosing as his topic the same question that Joe Alsop had addressed at Harvard two years earlier—"Is war with Russia inevitable?"—Kennan offered a more upbeat answer. In the article, he virtually dismissed the military threat from the Soviet Union, which, he argued, had already "bit off more than it could comfortably chew" in Eastern Europe, as shown by Tito's recent defection. Kennan also questioned whether the advent of the Russian bomb significantly increased the danger to the United States, decrying the country's—and, by inference, Nitze's—"morbid preoccupation with what *could possibly happen if.*"[20]

The response to Kennan's cri de coeur was immediate and almost universally hostile. Stewart Alsop branded it "The Kennan Swan Song" and attacked the author in a Matter of Fact column for leaving "the impression that no special extra effort is now required to win the cold war." (Joe had meanwhile decamped to London, where he was busy "exhausting us by melancholy monologues," wrote his long-suffering host, Isaiah Berlin.)[21]

The H-bomb debate had Kennan likewise rethinking the wisdom of his earlier recommendation that Nitze take his place as head of the Policy Planning Staff. Nitze's views on the Soviet threat were gaining traction in the Truman administration, while Kennan's star had correspondingly slipped. The previous fall, Kennan had written to Bohlen suggesting that unless Chip himself felt inclined to fill the top policy planning post, perhaps "they should leave it vacant for a while."[22]

But the reality was that world events and the State Department had already moved on, and the decision was not Kennan's to make. While Acheson was not unsympathetic to Kennan's views, especially on the H-bomb, the secretary of state had grown impatient with his counselor's unpredictable mood swings and navel-gazing introspection and had simply stopped reading the latter's lengthy memos. (Kennan's missives were "long-winded and so blatantly seeking to be literary rather than to provide information," similarly complained David Bruce, then U.S. ambassador to France.) When Kennan came to him to complain about the president's H-bomb decision, Acheson testily replied that, had Truman chosen otherwise, Kennan should don "a monk's robe and [carry] a tin can and announce that the end of the world is nigh."[23]

On January 1, 1950, Paul Nitze had become the new director of the Policy Planning Staff. The transition portended a change not only of style but of substance. As Nitze later observed, "There was no point in producing a marvelous piece of paper if it didn't get read." Nitze's policy paper—submitted to the National Security Council in mid-April 1950—defined the Soviet threat in terms of Russian capabilities, not intentions. Christened NSC 68, the paper dictated that containment of the U.S.S.R. would henceforth be achieved by the threat of clearly superior military force and not by moral example or diplomatic suasion.[24]

IN A FIT of high dudgeon that spring, Kennan was even suggesting that the State Department put a stake through the heart of the creature that he and Frank Wisner had created: the Office of Policy Coordination. Shortly after his *Reader's Digest* article appeared, Kennan wrote to Undersecretary of State Webb, requesting that he be relieved of responsibility for overseeing OPC's covert activities, adding, "However, I do not think that any successor to me should be appointed in present circumstances."[25]

To be sure, the "firm guiding hand" that Kennan originally promised to wield over OPC had, early on, lost its grip to the impetuous Wisner. Even the "Hilger project," as Kennan called it, had led to disappointment. "We seldom get from him precise answers to precise questions," noted a candid assessment of the German's work as a CIA consultant on the U.S.S.R. that spring.[26] (The agency also had a more practical concern: since Hilger, a foreign national, was routinely having lunch in the CIA cafeteria, he risked blowing the cover of the American spies eating there.)[27]

Likewise, in the so-called battle for Picasso's mind—OPC's political warfare initiatives, including the National Committee for a Free Europe—results had thus far fallen well short of expectations. Wisner's would-be liberators among the various exiles and refugees had proven to be a decidedly fractious lot, riven by personality clashes and long-standing ethnic rivalries.[28]

Yet, ironically, just as Kennan seemed inclined to extinguish Wisner's operation, Nitze's NSC 68 had breathed new life into it. As Bob

Joyce vigorously reminded his colleagues at an OPC briefing in April, their new marching orders were to *"take dynamic steps* to reduce the power and influence of the Kremlin *inside* the Soviet Union and other areas under its control. The objective would be the establishment of friendly regimes not under Kremlin domination." Joyce did not need to add the obvious—that Britain's Operation Valuable and OPC's Project Fiend were the only ongoing, aggressive efforts aimed at achieving that objective.[29]

Since the first abortive landing more than a year earlier, MI6 had sent several additional pixie teams into Albania, with similarly disappointing—indeed, disastrous—results. Most infiltrators had been quickly apprehended by Hoxha's Sigurimi and either sent to prison or shot outright. (In his Fiend File, Michael Burke continued to chronicle the problems and setbacks that OPC encountered with its own Albanians: "Two Pixies on island must be disposed of if camp closes down. We need Pixie speaker here for recruiting . . . Must tell XXXX that invasion is off, as many Pixies are refusing to emigrate, and we will be stuck with them, will be our responsibility . . . Frank: how does one get a stateless passport in Italy?")[30]

Meanwhile, the optimistic deadline that Wisner had originally set for the insertion of OPC's first ethnic agent team into Albania had been repeatedly moved back, as difficulties were encountered in recruiting and training the pixies, as well as with the expatriate Polish pilots who would fly the dangerous missions over the Iron Curtain. And, in the interim, Midhat Frashëri, the sixty-nine-year-old leader of the National Committee for a Free Albania, who was to form the nucleus of a post-Hoxha government, had dropped dead in a Manhattan hotel, presumably of a heart attack. No replacement had yet been named, because of an ongoing feud among Frashëri's would-be successors.[31]

Undaunted, on May 10, 1950, Wisner assembled the OPC faithful once more to brief them on what he described as a "reevaluation" of his pet project.

The news, Frank acknowledged, was not good. The eighty agents provocateurs that the British had originally hoped to send to Albania had since been pared down to the thirty who had actually landed; of that number, half had fled to Greece, barely escaping with their lives, while only one group of five was still in touch by wireless transmitter. "The rest are either known to be or presumed to be dead," Wisner glumly reported.

As a result, the British were shutting down their training base in Malta and scaling back Operation Valuable. If necessary, Frank announced, he—and OPC—were prepared to soldier on alone.[32]

Similar misfortune had afflicted the American side. Fewer than half of the planned fifty U.S.-trained pixies had actually been recruited from the displaced-persons camps in Italy and Greece—where the host governments were eager to evict them. With the loss of Malta, a substitute covert training base for America's Albanians had meanwhile been established in the Bavarian Alps. But staffers there complained to Wisner that their charges "were spoiled by good living conditions [in Germany] and expected everything to be done for them here, including all the . . . cigarettes and beer they could consume. They become temperamental when their various whims were not fulfilled."[33]

Accordingly, Wisner conceded, it was "necessary that a new approach be considered." Judging "the present conception of the reconnaissance phase . . . inadequate," the father of Fiend, having lost the opening bet, decided to double down: "A considerable amount of outside aid, namely, arms and ammunitions, must be provided or the ultimate results of the joint British-U.S. venture will be negligible." Yet the goal, Wisner emphasized, remained the same: "Successful overthrow of the Hoxha regime would be the first instance of the 'rollback' of Soviet power in the satellites."[34]

WHILE OPC and Wisner remained fixated on Albania, attention in Congress had shifted to threats at home. On March 8, 1950, in the midst of lurid newspaper headlines about "Red atom-spies" among the nation's top scientists, the Senate's Tydings Committee had begun hearings on Joseph McCarthy's charge that scores of Communist agents were hiding in the State Department. To the Alsops' surprise, far from the "first-round knockout" that Stewart had predicted, McCarthy dominated the proceedings, even adding new names to the list of those he had previously accused of treason. Seated in the Senate press gallery, Stew and his wife watched in fascination as an older and well-respected senator approached McCarthy—who had promised to let any of his colleagues examine the "evidence" behind his charges—only to be dismissed by McCarthy with a contemptuous remark. When none of the others in the chamber rose to the fellow's defense, Stewart muttered to Tish, "There goes the end of the Republic."[35]

By month's end, *The Washington Post*'s political cartoonist had coined a new term for the phenomenon. On March 29, Herblock's drawing showed a reluctant elephant being pushed toward a wobbly tower of dripping tar pots by a gaggle of Republican senators. The biggest tar pot at the top was labeled "McCarthyism."[36]

Joe and Stewart's hatred of the Wisconsin senator was profound and visceral. Although the brothers were careful not to raise the issue of class in their column, the aristocratic, patrician Alsops were the virtual antithesis of the populist, lowborn McCarthy. The son of Irish immigrant farmers, Joe McCarthy had demonstrated, early on, an unparalleled—and unprincipled—talent for seizing the main chance. His rapid political ascent, begun with a fraudulently misrepresented war record, had reached its apotheosis with his recent, opportunistic embrace of an anti-Communist crusade. "It seemed to me the sewers of our public life had burst and the accumulated filth was flowing in the streets," Joe later wrote of the political climate that McCarthy had engendered in the nation's capital.[37]

Beyond their personal revulsion, of course, the Alsops had a larger concern. In the first of four Matter of Fact columns that they devoted to McCarthy between March and June, the brothers protested that Washington's obsession with internal security was distracting attention from the real threat—the Cold War with Russia. ("The Alsops regarded communism as a danger *to* America but not a danger *in* America," Arthur Schlesinger Jr. told friends.) As McCarthy's allegations focused more on the State Department's China experts whom Joe had featured in his *Saturday Evening Post* articles, however, the Alsops' attention also shifted. In comments to friends, Joe worried that McCarthy's popularity might presage the rise of "something like a native fascist party." From Europe, he cabled Stewart the text of a letter he had just sent to Tydings. At his brother's urging, Stew arranged for the letter to appear prominently in both the *Herald Tribune* and *The Washington Post* on May 8, 1950. In it, Joe offered to testify before the Tydings Committee on behalf of those McCarthy had attacked. With regard to the China hands, Alsop had written, "I think it is my duty to say that while I disputed their judgment, I never had the faintest doubt of the loyalty of any of the American officials or others whom McCarthy has attacked . . . I still believe the loss of China was unnecessary. But I think it far more important that we should not destroy the decent traditions of American political life. These now seem to be endangered."[38]

A few days earlier, George Kennan had returned to Milwaukee, his hometown, to deliver his own verdict on McCarthy. Like many others, Kennan had initially underestimated the controversial senator. Speaking before what he remembered as a "rather apathetic audience," Kennan lamented the ongoing assault on the country's diplomatic corps that McCarthyism represented. Although he had already announced his pending leave from the Foreign Service, Kennan's speech contained what seemed a veiled threat: "I must tell you that the atmosphere of public life in Washington does not have to deteriorate much further to produce a situation in which very few of our more quiet and sensitive and gifted people will be able to continue in the Government."[39]

Others, too, were beginning to share the Alsops' and Kennan's concern. Once again back in Paris, Susan Mary wrote to her friend Marietta of the reaction overseas: "We thought that Senator McCarthy (of whom by the way I have never heard, who is he?) must be mad with his crusading speech last month against Communists in the State Department and that no one would pay any attention to his ranting generalizations, instead of which there is now the Tydings Committee to give him a platform and the press coverage he must long for . . . One of the French papers yesterday said of him that he was a demagogue without support and would soon disappear from sight, I do hope that you can reassure me that this is true."[40]

Later that spring, Stewart Alsop went to McCarthy's office for an interview, part of the research for a *Saturday Evening Post* article that Stew was writing on the capital's political phenom. The piece—which appeared in the magazine on July 29, 1950—was titled "Why Has Washington Gone Crazy?" and began,

> One must know by now that something has gone wrong, very wrong, in the capital of the United States . . . A visit to the McCarthy lair on Capitol Hill is rather like being transported to the set of one of Hollywood's minor thrillers. The anteroom is generally full of furtive-looking characters who look as though they might be suborned State Department men. McCarthy himself, despite a creeping baldness and a continual tremor which makes his head shake in a disconcerting fashion, is reasonably well cast as the Hollywood version of a strong-jawed private eye. A visitor is likely to find him with his heavy shoulders hunched forward, a telephone in

his huge hands, shouting cryptic instructions to some mysterious ally.[41]

Shortly before the article appeared in the *Post,* Stewart had joined George Kennan for a Sunday supper at the Joyces' house on O Street. Preparing to leave for Princeton's institute, Kennan was in the process of saying good-bye to his Georgetown friends. Yet the dinner conversation that night was not about Kennan's impending departure but about McCarthy's rising star. Stewart let Kennan know that he intended to use parts of the latter's Milwaukee speech in his forthcoming essay—confessing surprise "that the *Post* had consented to take an article so strongly anti-McCarthy."[42]

The conversation then turned to another topic: Kennan's legacy as he left Washington.

Kennan had recently met with Frank Wisner to discuss a report the two men had just received from Joyce. It concerned Operation Rusty, the CIA's project to encourage Red Army defections, which had used Gustav Hilger as a consultant. Joyce based his report on the interrogation of ten Russian soldiers who had recently escaped to the West after listening to a VOA broadcast promising that defectors would not be returned to Soviet authorities. Kennan wrote in his diary of how he had been cheered by the news. However, the author of containment no longer showed much enthusiasm for fighting fire with fire. Disillusioned with the political warfare he had inaugurated—or at least with the way that it had turned out—Kennan even seemed pessimistic about a previous favorite of his, the freedom committees: "Met this afternoon with a group of officials to consider the problem of using our influence among the Russian émigrés in Europe to create happier conditions and a better atmosphere and attitude . . . Given the U.S. Government as it is, I have deep misgivings about it, but we will see what we can do."[43]

After emptying his desk, clearing out his State Department office, and announcing at a press conference that he did not believe that Russia wanted war, Kennan confided his parting thoughts—as usual—to his diary: "I left . . . with a feeling of one who has succeeded in pushing a large boulder off the cliff, who is sure that something is going to happen but does not know just what; and who knows that it is now too late to do anything about it."[44]

Shortly afterward, on a warm summer afternoon, Kennan dropped by Joe Alsop's house to explain why he was leaving the government. Alsop had returned from Europe earlier than planned in order to confront McCarthy's latest charges concerning the China hands. For two hours, Joe listened politely to what he called Kennan's "long, gloomy monologue on the perishable nature of democracy and the hopelessness of coherent policy making in the face of the country's confused and conflicting political demands." ("When George broods, he becomes a little silly," Alsop noted.) Kennan's painful disquisition was a litany of regrets—not least among which was the fact that Frank Wisner and OPC had transformed the policy of containment into Project Fiend's covert assault on the Soviet empire.[45]

Joe finally cut Kennan's complaints short with an invitation to dinner at Dumbarton the coming Saturday. Eager to right earlier wrongs, Joe had also invited his old adversary and Kennan's good friend, John Davies. Like Stewart's recent magazine piece on McCarthy, the supper was part of the brothers' rueful and belated attempt to repair some of the damage done by the *Saturday Evening Post* series on the "loss" of China. Thus, as Joe now realized, he had unwittingly given McCarthy much of the ammunition for the senator's latest attacks and, in the process, had loosed forces beyond Alsop's—or anyone's—ability to predict or control.

CHAPTER NINE

"A Rather Serious Border Incident"

THE DINNER PARTY that Joe Alsop hosted on Saturday, June 24, 1950, featured the usual eclectic roster of official Washington, the powerful in addition to the merely well connected. Among the guests were the secretary of the army and the assistant secretary of the air force, a *New York Times* reporter and his wife, and the Supreme Court justice Felix Frankfurter. In addition to John Davies, Alsop had invited another China expert, Dean Rusk, the assistant secretary of state for Far Eastern affairs. George Kennan had politely declined Joe's offer; he and Annelise fled the city to spend the weekend at their Pennsylvania farm.

As it was a typical balmy early summer evening, the men had retired to the terrace to smoke cigars and sip brandy under the wisteria-covered loggia when Joe's butler, José, interrupted to say that there was a telephone call for "Mr. Rush." Dean Rusk returned to the party "white as a sheet," Joe remembered, and announced that there had been "a rather serious border incident" in Korea that required him to go immediately to the State Department. Subsequent calls in quick succession summoned the Pentagon officials, who, in turn, also left the party in a hurry. As the house emptied out, Alsop and his remaining guests, including Davies, spent the remainder of the night discussing whether "this was *it*"—the beginning of the war with Russia that Joe had long been predicting.[1]

North Korea's invasion of the south had come as a complete surprise to U.S. intelligence and was a failure on a par with Pearl Harbor or the shock of Joe-1. President Truman was told of the attack while vacationing at his home in Independence, Missouri. Secretary of State Dean Acheson and his wife were spending the weekend at Harewood, their country estate in Sandy Spring, Maryland. Kennan only learned of the invasion from newspaper headlines when he and Annelise drove home from their farm on Sunday afternoon. Paul Nitze, salmon fishing on a remote river in Canada, heard the news on his guide's radio. At dawn the next morning, Nitze paddled a canoe back to where he had left his car and "drove at breakneck speed to the nearest town with an airport."[2]

One unanticipated result of the North Korean invasion was to delay Kennan's departure from Washington. In Nitze's absence, Kennan was once again head of the Policy Planning Staff. Miffed at being nonetheless excluded from an urgent Sunday night meeting on the crisis with the secretary of state and the president, Kennan warned Acheson against taking any action that might cause America "to 'back into' an all-out conflict with the Soviet Union." "This was generally agreed to. Thus I was instrumental in establishing the Department position on this point," Kennan wrote with satisfaction in his diary. Two days later, on June 27, after Truman announced that America would be coming to the rescue of South Korea under the banner of the United Nations, Kennan also urged that the administration issue a press release affirming that the United States had no intention of occupying North Korea.[3]

When Joe Alsop ran into Kennan that evening, on their way to the same dinner party, Joe was struck by the change in his friend's mood since the latter's grim monologue at his house barely a week before. "Well, Joe, what do you think of the democracies now?" Kennan enthused. Alsop responded—"quite crossly," Kennan thought—"I think about democracy exactly what I always have, but not what you thought when you came to see me."[4]

Yet Kennan's triumphant mood was not to last. When he arrived at the State Department on Monday morning, July 3, Kennan encountered Paul Nitze, back from Canada. Kennan was also nonplussed to discover the Policy Planning Staff engaged in a debate over the paper that he had written, at Acheson's request, detailing possible U.S. responses to further Soviet-sponsored aggression: "As far as I could determine, [the discussion] seemed to be devoted principally to criticism of the paper, although it had been cleared word by word with the Staff on Friday afternoon. It was agreed that Nitze would represent the Department on the further work in the NSC in connection with the paper."[5]

In fact, Nitze had returned in time to take over from Kennan, his temporary surrogate, who silently complained that evening in his diary of wounded amour propre:

I felt somewhat uneasy about this after the discussion of the morning, because I could see that my whole framework of thought . . . was strange to Nitze, and that he would be apt to act on concepts of his own which differ from those I had put forward. I don't mind this from my own standpoint, but I think it unfortunate that the Department should be represented by two points of view in the NSC on the same matter, and I have just enough confidence in my own experience and instinct to be concerned when I see a tendency to sweep it aside in a moment as important as this.

Kennan's paper wound up in a filing cabinet with a handwritten notation at the top: "Not used—overtaken by events."[6]

THE UN VOTE condemning North Korea's aggression resolved the Truman administration's dilemma of whether to wage an exclusively "American" war. But the surprise attack overseas also had unanticipated consequences at home. Following the initial near disaster of the U.S. military intervention, where ill-trained and poorly equipped troops were forced into a protracted retreat, critical attention was focused on recent cuts in the Pentagon budget. Even well before the outbreak of the war, the Alsops had condemned the reductions imposed by the president and the defense secretary, Louis Johnson, as responsible for the country's "armed feebleness." The previous winter, in a series of four Matter of Fact columns, Joe and Stewart had, in effect, demanded Johnson's resignation. The brothers kept up their attack throughout the summer and fall, as the news from the front worsened. In September 1950, their campaign reached a successful culmination when Truman fired Johnson, replacing him with George Marshall.[7]

The Korean War also meant the end of the president's austerity drive. Shortly after the North Korean invasion, the administration's thirteen-billion-dollar annual defense budget request was nearly doubled, to twenty-four billion dollars. Only a brief time earlier, Paul Nitze had been reluctant to let Truman know the true cost of NSC 68, which envisioned spending up to fifty billion dollars a year on defense and would have sacrificed the production of consumer electronics, including television sets, in order to meet military needs. (Nitze also briefly considered levying an additional tax on any new automobile having more than one hundred horsepower, to save both fuel and matériel for rearmament. But the idea found few supporters and was abandoned.) At Acheson's suggestion, Nitze had deliberately submitted NSC 68 to the president without a budget. When Nitze tried to brief Louis Johnson on the new and expensive military buildup, the defense secretary had simply stormed out of his office.[8]

In the wake of Korea, and for the duration of the war, Pentagon spending soared, to nearly fifty-two billion dollars for fiscal year 1952—more even than what Acheson and Nitze had dared hoped for. The Alsop brothers celebrated their victory over Johnson—and, by inference, their increased clout in the capital city—with an unabashedly I-told-you-so article in *The Saturday Evening Post* titled "The Lessons of Korea."[9]

Louis Johnson was not the administration's only casualty of the war. The CIA director, Roscoe Hillenkoetter, lasted barely a week longer than the doomed defense secretary before he, too, was thrown over the side by the president for the agency's failure to predict the Korea invasion. Like Johnson, Hilly was replaced by a military figure with a reputation for getting results: the U.S. Army general Walter Bedell Smith. "Beetle" had turned down the job of CIA director twice before finally giving in. "I expect the worse and I am sure I won't be disappointed," he reportedly told Truman, who hoped the no-nonsense general would run the CIA with a firm hand.[10]

As soon became evident, the substitution of Marshall and Smith for Johnson and Hillenkoetter was, for the Alsops, something of a mixed blessing. Marshall had neither forgotten nor forgiven Joe's support for Chiang Kai-shek, whom the general blamed for the failure of his earlier effort to mediate China's civil war. Likewise, Beetle Smith demonstrated, early on, a flinty indifference to Joe's flattering and blandishments, in contrast to the cozy relationship that Alsop had enjoyed with Hilly. Joe had recently written to Hillenkoetter protesting that the CIA's analysts were wrong in their estimate of Soviet uranium resources and helpfully suggesting where else they might look for evidence of Russian progress in building bombs. Hilly promptly wrote back with assurances that Alsop's information was already "familiar to us . . . together with a great deal more from other sources."[11]

But the Alsops' real fear was that the wartime atmosphere which had suddenly descended on Washington—along with the imminent departure of some of their tried-and-true sources, like Kennan and Hillenkoetter—threatened their brand of so-called access or elite journalism, which was almost wholly dependent on news leaks and privileged entrée to Washington's policy makers.

Shortly after Kennan announced his plans to leave the State Department, Joe had paid tribute to his friend in a personal letter that contained a seemingly heartfelt valedictory: "I hardly know how things will go on without you." And, some months later, in what turned out to be a premature send-off, the brothers praised Kennan in a column titled "An Unsung Hero's Exodus." In a characteristic bit of hyperbole, Joe credited his friend with having "helped to save the country and the world," comparing Kennan to "a flawless piece of Soong eggshell ware."[12]

But, in reality, Joe and Stewart were already cultivating, and counting on, other sources for their reporting. Acheson—under fresh attack by Senate Republicans for being "soft on Communism"—remained more wary than ever of talking to the brothers, despite their repeated entreaties. Whereas Joe respected the secretary of state—"the only sober man on a raft of drunken lumberjacks"—he also believed that Acheson's usefulness to Truman had been undermined by partisan attacks on the man derided by conservatives as "the red dean of the cowardly college of containment." (Acheson, for his part, would later describe his relationship with the press as "baiting them and making up: I thought they were spoiled; they thought I was irritable; we're both probably right.")[13]

Instead, the brothers turned by default to Nitze, who once more headed State's Policy Planning Staff. Yet Nitze, too, balked at embarking on what Joe termed variously, in a long and tendentious letter to his friend, "the two way street," the "special relationship," and the "partnership" that, Alsop argued, *should* exist between the journalist and any high government official.[14]

Feeling shunned and shut out in Washington, the brothers were, as well, increasingly agitated by the military setbacks in Korea. "The situation here is too ghastly to be described and I shall not attempt to describe it," Joe wrote to Bohlen, at the U.S. embassy in Paris. "All our friends hold up under the strain surprisingly well, although Paul Nitze has aged five years in the past five months." As a veteran and the father of three small children, Stewart was not enthusiastic about rushing to the front to cover the war. For Joe, on the other hand, the crisis in Asia had stirred his reportorial instincts—or at least his urge to travel. At the end of July 1950, with luggage consisting of two suitcases containing pressed khakis, assorted blankets, a folding bed, and a bulging "apothecary case"—

as well as a copy of Thucydides's *Peloponnesian War* stuffed in his back pocket—Joe flew to Tokyo, the start of his new career as a combat correspondent.[15]

"MY FIRST DAY at the Institute," wrote Kennan in his diary, in Princeton, on September 10, 1950. "Gentle rain fell all day—an English sort of rain—as though by deference to all the Gothic towers and battlements and all the quiet green of the place. I installed myself in my new office, with windows looking out over the field to the woods, and had a sense of peace and happiness such as I have not had for a long, long time."[16]

Having given up the lease on their house in Cleveland Park, in anticipation of the move to Princeton, George and Annelise had been staying with the Joyces in Georgetown. When Joe Alsop left for Korea, the Kennans temporarily moved into 2720 Dumbarton (where George absentmindedly left behind his checkbook). At a farewell dinner for Joe, Kennan and Chip Bohlen had gotten into an argument with another Alsop guest, Averell Harriman. The Crocodile was recently returned from his Marshall Plan assignment in Paris. "Chip and I were partly amazed and partly amused," recorded Kennan in his diary that evening, "to hear Averell Harriman, when I spoke about the McCarthy business, say 'you fellows in the State Department' had to learn the necessity of coming clean with the public about your own mistakes; that 'you' could not go on putting out white papers as 'you' did in the case of China, whitewashing the mistakes 'you' had made . . . Neither of us accepted the challenge," Kennan wrote, "for we saw no point in arguing the question of responsibility for China policy with another government official in the presence of the Alsop brothers." Kennan and Bohlen likewise diplomatically refrained from pointing out that Harriman had been FDR's adviser at the Yalta Conference, where the shape of the postwar world was decided.[17]

Kennan had bidden a lingering good-bye to friends and well-wishers, including Nitze, who he thought looked "tired, harried, and worried." (For good reason. Earlier that day, the head of the planning staff had met with an army general "to discuss the question of possible use of the atomic bomb in Korea.") In a letter offering some parting advice to the new secretary of state, George Marshall, Kennan rather high-handedly suggested that "the element most lacking in our government work is a certain reflectiveness and repose of the spirit which it is hard to find in the pressures of Washington."[18]

To his colleagues at the State Department, Kennan dedicated a melancholy and somewhat wistful poem, "Their Peculiar Fate":

> Let not the foggy harshness of the air,
>   the season late,
> The counsels of despair,
> The prospect of the sword, unsheathed,
> Deter you from persistence in this task.
> Do not, as I did, importune the skies . . .
> The bureaucratic heavens do not ask . . .
> To tell you where the reasons lie
> Why you . . . why no one else . . . should
>   bear this weight.*[19]

But subsequent diary entries reveal that Kennan's academic idyll at Princeton was soon interrupted by the return of self-doubt and worry—as well as the growing realization that his self-imposed exile had isolated him from events in Washington, which was now a capital at war. An invitation to update his seminal "X article" from the editor of *Foreign Affairs*—who observed that containment had spread from Europe to Asia, as a result of Korea—initially awakened little interest in its author. "I am afraid that there has been a general misinterpretation of the term 'containment,' as I first used it," Kennan wrote to a defense analyst at the Rand Corporation think tank that fall. "It was never meant as exclusively, or even primarily, a military concept." Like the retired draft horse that stirs at the familiar sound of the fire bell, Kennan missed the excitement of his old job. Nitze recalled that Kennan, on a return visit to Washington for a nostalgic lunch with his former colleagues, greeted Nitze and Dean Acheson with a rueful gibe that contained more than

---

* Burt Marshall, Nitze's ally and a frequent Kennan critic on the Policy Planning Staff, penned his own verse in response, including this passage:

> Meanwhile to duller bees we'll give our heed;
> The myriad busy insects of routine
> Buzzing in our collective bonnet need
> Our care. Not every bee can be a queen.

a kernel of truth: "When I left the department, it never occurred to me that you two would make foreign policy without having first consulted me."[20]

In mid-November 1950, barely two months into his stint at the institute, Kennan sent Nitze a copy of the letter he had written to a newspaper reporter, in response to what Kennan felt was a particularly ill-informed column on the situation in Korea. There was a plaintive, almost pleading quality to Kennan's addendum: "And if it can be of any use to the Department, I shall be only too glad. Perhaps Barrett would be interested in it, and anyone else who is concerned at present (if anyone is) with briefing the columnists on such policy matters." The letter received no reply.[21]

IN LATE OCTOBER 1950, George Kennan welcomed Joe Alsop back from Korea with a paean of praise. "Your accounts were the best I have seen in our press," Kennan enthused—adding, perhaps a bit too generously, "They were like Tolstoy's passages in 'War and Peace.'" Joe had arrived in Korea just in time to witness one of the darkest moments of the war, as American soldiers were pushed back into the southern tip of the country—the "panicky pocket" of Pusan. But he stayed long enough to see the tide of battle change dramatically, following the U.S. amphibious landing at Inchon in mid-September. The North Korean army fled back across the 38th parallel, with American troops in hot pursuit.[22]

Joe Alsop's critics had always made fun of his snobbism and dandified manners. Famously, Alsop refused to eat in some Parisian restaurants, claiming that vibrations from the nearby Metro disturbed the sediment and bruised the vintage wines in their cellars. Joe had likewise recoiled in mock horror when a well-meaning friend suggested that he consider adding some of the newly fashionable drip-dry shirts to his traveling wardrobe: "Dear boy, nothing but silk ever touches my skin!"[23]

Yet, appearances and eccentricities aside, Joe's reporting from Korea was, as Kennan implied, not only literate and colorful but done from the fighting front. (Matter of Fact would win the Overseas Press Club Award in 1951, and again in 1953, for Best Interpretation of Foreign Affairs.) After he quickly attached himself to a marine regimental combat team that was also newly arrived in the country, Alsop and the jarheads had spent an uncomfortable night pinned down on a hillside by enemy mortar and sniper fire. Later reporting on a battle with a main force North

Korean unit, Joe was described as "fearless" by the marines and his fellow journalists. Alsop had also volunteered to cover General Douglas MacArthur's daring Inchon assault. Joe and an accompanying marine officer were first puzzled and then disappointed by the lack of enemy resistance—until the realization slowly dawned that they had been landed on the wrong beach. Caught up in the fervor that followed the U.S. advance above the 38th parallel, Joe urged the "liberation" of North Korea in a parting column.[24]

Ironically, Alsop's triumphant homecoming occurred just weeks before China's unanticipated entry into the conflict turned the apparent U.S. victory into a near rout. In a letter to Britain's air marshal, Sir John Slessor, Joe reacted to news of the unfolding disaster in his usual manner: "Never before has this horrible hopelessness overtaken me . . . But now I see no future, I do not know anything that can be done, and what I do therefore seems meaningless . . . God help us all."[25]

On a somewhat calmer note, Alsop's letter also raised, once more, the possibility of launching an all-out nuclear attack on the Soviets while the United States still maintained a relative strategic advantage over its adversary. Not surprisingly, Slessor demurred. But Joe told a friend soon thereafter that he was thinking about making a quick trip to Yugoslavia so that he might witness firsthand the Russian tanks coming over the border and the outbreak of the third world war.[26]

For George Kennan, conversely, the changing military fortunes in Korea meant the possibility of a reprieve, one that would rescue him from the boredom and ennui of his semiretirement at Princeton's institute. Just prior to his accepting a job offer from Richard Bissell to join the Ford Foundation—which was being used as a secret conduit to fund OPC's front organizations in Western Europe—Kennan received an urgent telephone call from Chip Bohlen, then minister at the American embassy in Paris.[27]

A transcript of their conversation suggests that Kennan was hurt the summons had not come sooner and from higher up:

BOHLEN: Why aren't you in Washington?
KENNAN: I have not been asked to come.
BOHLEN: . . . I am on the phone to implore you, for God's sake, to get on the train, go to Washington, and see Dean [Acheson] and Marshall . . . I swear to God I think it is vital.
KENNAN: I was down there about three weeks ago . . . but I was

quite aware that I was not being put into possession of all of the
facts . . .

BOHLEN: . . . Jump on a train and at least let them have your
views . . .

KENNAN: I have told them that I would be willing to give all the
help I can.

BOHLEN: . . . I implore you to get down there. You can't lose and
it will do no harm.

KENNAN: I'll think seriously about it. Thanks for calling.[28]

Kennan did not need to think about it for long. The following afternoon he received a call from John Davies, who confirmed that Acheson
and Nitze did indeed seek his counsel. By that evening, Kennan was
in Washington, staying at Davies's house, and the next morning back
in his old office at the State Department. Over the days and weeks to
come, Kennan and Nitze together would prove to be a force for modera-
tion. Nitze, notably, put a damper on talk of using nuclear weapons in
Korea by asking proponents two simple questions: What if the United
States used the bomb on the battlefield and the results were not decisive?
What credibility would America's atomic arsenal have then in deterring
an attack on the U.S. homeland by the Soviet Union? Kennan likewise
pointed out that the use of nuclear weapons in Korea, even if militarily
advantageous in the short term, ran the risk of drawing China into the
conflict. When intelligence revealed that Russian pilots were actually at
the controls of Chinese and North Korean MiGs shooting down U.S.
warplanes, Nitze conspired to suppress the information, lest outraged
public opinion beat the drums for war with the U.S.S.R.[29]

The conflict in Korea had also briefly reawakened Kennan's interest
in and support for Soviet émigrés. In mid-May 1951, the Free Russia
Fund was created—"to increase the usefulness to free society of exiles
from Soviet power." Kennan was its president, and the fund received a
$200,000 annual budget channeled through the Ford Foundation from
the CIA.[30]

Some time later, after the immediate danger had passed and the war
in Korea was settling into a military stalemate, Kennan returned to his
academic haven at Princeton. But to the bleak pessimism he already felt
about the American political scene was now added a personal crisis. Fearing that "McCarthyism has already won, in the sense of making impos-

sible the conduct of an intelligent foreign policy," Kennan's melancholy gave way to remorse and self-pity:

> The result is that there is no place in public life for an honest and moderate man. I was wrong to do the things I have done. I should not have signed up for the Ford Foundation. I do not share their basic assumptions. I should not have started the enterprise to help Soviet fugitives. Some day we will have to give it up out of sheer embarrassment and humiliation over the conduct of our country . . . Except for the little boy [Kennan's son, Christopher], the best thing that could happen would be that I should go with the services and get myself killed.[31]

As before, Kennan's agitated mental state turned out to be only a passing storm, which became clear a few weeks later. After he overcame a case of writer's block, joined the Century Club, and received an honorary degree from Princeton, which also appointed him an alumni trustee, Kennan's self-confidence returned. "Now—most of the pressure is over," he wrote in late June.[32]

Yet no sooner had this latest emotional turmoil ended than Kennan was facing another crisis, this one involving a close friend. That spring, Kennan received word that John Davies, his erstwhile colleague on the planning staff and comrade since their days in wartime Moscow, was to be investigated by the State Department for disloyalty.

GEORGE KENNAN was not the only one having trouble adjusting to changed circumstances. Frank Wisner found Beetle Smith, his new boss at the CIA, anything but an "amiable lightweight," as Frank had once described Hillenkoetter. With Hilly's pliable hand at the helm, Wisner had early on mastered the technique, highly regarded in Washington's bureaucratic circles, of using secrecy to thwart oversight and hide questionable deeds from his superiors. For Wisner, need-to-know was less a burden than a tool, which he used to exercise control over his domain—in some cases, assigning the same operation to different agents without their knowledge. Making a fetish of security, Frank insisted that even those who were cleared to read NSC 10/2—the secret directive that had established the Office of Policy Coordination—did so in his presence, before returning the document with a flourish to his private safe. One such initiate remained unimpressed: "All it said was, they do it, and therefore we have to do it too."[33]

For his part, Beetle Smith was stunned to discover the extent to which intelligence gathering had been subordinated to covert operations. Fearful that the "operational tail will wag the intelligence dog," Smith predicted that it would soon be necessary "to decide whether CIA will remain an intelligence agency or become a 'cold war department.'" Intent upon avoiding the latter, the new CIA director within days of occupying his office ordered Wisner to look into amending NSC 10/2. Smith's goal was to fold OPC into the CIA and subordinate the maestro of the mighty Wurlitzer to the will of the agency's director. When Frank requested a table of organization from his boss, Smith's tart reply—"Wisner, you work for me"—was also a warning. Nonetheless, foot-dragging by Frank, as well as competing wartime demands, delayed the change from fully taking place for almost two years.[34]

Smith had taken the CIA job intending to clean house, even sending a spy to the Sunday night suppers to finger "dubious security risks and dilettantes." He reportedly instructed his agent, "I don't care whether they were blabbing secrets or not. Just give me the names of the people at Georgetown cocktail parties." Smith also dispatched a trusted army colleague, General Lucian Truscott, to check out Wisner's operations overseas. "I'm going to go out there and find out what those weirdoes are up to," Truscott confidently declared before embarking. The stunned emissary reported back that he had discovered Ivy League–educated dilettantes playing at being spies—and "a world out of an F. Scott Fitzgerald novel."[35]

For the interim, however, Wisner and OPC would remain in control of the country's dirty tricks.

Even Frank's nominal allies, the British, were taken aback by Wisner's audacity. After MI6 spies accidently "stumbled" across a rogue OPC operation to overthrow Tito—using anti-Communist Serbs dressed, bizarrely, in U.S. Air Force uniforms—they sputtered to their superiors at Whitehall about such "inconceivably stupid . . . [and] idiotic American behavior."[36]

Because of Korea, however, Wisner's organization continued to grow virtually unconstrained. Between 1949 and 1952, OPC's personnel roster increased almost tenfold, from 302 to 2,812, not counting more than

3,000 foreign contractors. During the same period, its annual budget ballooned from under $5 million to more than $80 million. Incredibly, Wisner's request for covert operations in the coming fiscal year reportedly exceeded $400 million—three times the previous year's budget for the entire CIA.*[37] Originally sent to seven countries, by the end of the Korean War, Frank's agents would be operating out of forty-seven overseas stations in six geographical divisions scattered around the world. By 1952, Wisner's mighty Wurlitzer was being used to promote up to three dozen different covert operations in one central European country alone. OPC's propaganda organ was also being heard much closer to home. The previous year, filming had begun of a movie based on George Orwell's novel *Animal Farm,* secretly funded by the CIA. An adaptation of *1984* was soon to follow—with both films bearing a strong cautionary message about the creeping danger of Communist totalitarian rule.[38]

As the editor of *Foreign Affairs* noted, the spread of Kennan's containment doctrine to Asia had created an entirely new theater for U.S. covert operations. It was a gap into which Wisner's men jumped with enthusiasm. While remnants of Chiang Kai-shek's Nationalist army were mobilized for secret missions in Communist China, other venues—including Bangkok, Thailand, as well as Saipan and Taiwan—became major staging points for OPC operations throughout the Far East.[39] In Europe, meanwhile, new front organizations and freedom committees continued to spring up like toadstools after a heavy rain.[40] Watching these developments with fascination yet growing concern from afar in mid-1951, the head of Britain's office of naval intelligence predicted darkly, "It is doubtful whether, in a year's time, the US will be able to control the Frankenstein monster which they are creating."[41]

Indeed, as might be expected from such metastatic-like growth, not all of the activities that Wisner and OPC sponsored went smoothly or according to plan. On July 4, 1950, under the auspices of the National Committee for a Free Europe, Kennan's inaugural freedom committee, Radio Free Europe had begun beaming propaganda to Soviet satellites in Eastern Europe from its headquarters in Munich's Englischer Garten,

---

* The exact budget and personnel figures for OPC remain something of a mystery even today. While $82 million was the amount quoted in the 1976 Church Committee's investigation of the CIA, subsequent figures suggest that the covert operations budget might have been as much as four times higher. Detailed CIA budgets, past and current, remain classified as of this writing.

via "Barbara," the army surplus radio transmitter that Carmel Offie had procured. Shortly afterward, RFE's head, Charlie Thayer, was puzzled to receive letters from Russian émigrés living in Peru, thanking him for the inspiring broadcasts. Thayer subsequently ordered the station's antennas reoriented, to face in the right direction. Similarly, little more than a year later, when the CIA-funded Crusade for Freedom sent three million leaflets aloft in weather balloons from a German hillside, initial results seemed to belie the crusade's motto: "The winds of freedom blow from west to east." Organizers were relieved to see the balloons, after they gained altitude, head toward their intended target—Czechoslovakia. (The balloons carried open boxes of propaganda leaflets, wedged in place by blocks of dry ice. As the ice melted, the leaflets would spill from the sky. Dick Helms remembered the confusion resulting when a pair of errant balloons—silvery objects enshrouded in smoky vapor—landed upright in the market square of a small town: "It took the local priest to convince a clutch of village grandmothers that the odd couple were neither Heaven sent nor invading Martians.")[42]

In Wisner's defense, not all of OPC's expansion was a result of his unbridled ambition. The fact that the Pentagon would assume control of covert operations in the event of war meant that Frank and his men were also besieged by requests from the military services to prepare for prospective missions, ranging from the rescue of air crews forced down in enemy territory to logistical support for so-called stay-behind units—local partisans who would conduct acts of sabotage and harassment meant to slow the Red Army's advance. Wisner put the stay-behind project in the hands of Franklin Lindsay, who, in turn, passed it along to OPC sword carriers like Michael Burke and Carmel Offie.[43]

A pair of clandestine operations intended, in part, to prepare the ground for armed resistance to a Soviet occupation of Western Europe were run by Wisner himself. Red Cap was the code name assigned to a 1951 project aimed at inducing defections among KGB agents serving overseas. Red Sox was the name given an even more ambitious secret program to infiltrate OPC agents into the Soviet Union itself.[44]

Wisner had told friends that he would never succumb to Potomac fever, which was why he and his wife, Polly, had always rented since arriving in the capital four years earlier. But as Frank's responsibilities grew, along with the size of his family, that attitude changed. In addition to their teenager, Frank George Wisner—Frank II—the couple now had two other sons, Ellis and Graham, as well as a daughter, Elizabeth, nicknamed Wendy. Early in 1952, Frank and Polly purchased a four-story white brick mansion at 3327 P Street in Georgetown, a few blocks west of the Alsops, the Bohlens, and the Grahams. After extensive remodeling, the Wisner home became another venue for the Sunday night suppers, as well as the scene of elaborate cocktail parties where Frank pumped his important and inebriated guests for information. The CIA reportedly underwrote the cost of the parties with a generous stipend. But Frank made sure the deed for the P Street house remained in Polly's name. On his State Department employment form, Wisner listed Locust Hill Farm in Galena, Maryland, as his permanent address.[45]

Another reason why Wisner had decided to put down roots, and fiercely resisted turning OPC over to Beetle Smith, was that Frank's own pet project—Fiend—had finally taken flight.

ON THE MOONLESS NIGHT of November 11, 1950, after the navigator had failed to find the designated drop zone, the first three of OPC's Albanian volunteers decided to parachute from their C-54 anyway, landing in a forest some twenty-five miles northeast of the capital, Tirana. A fourth infiltrator, tardy in jumping, landed separate from the others and immediately became lost. All of the team's equipment had inadvertently been left behind on the plane. Nonetheless, a second, five-man team was dropped only minutes later, setting up temporary camp a dozen miles outside the village of Zarrisht. The heavy packs containing most of their weapons, their radios, food, spare ammunition—even the toilet paper—came down in a different town altogether and had to be abandoned. After his crew kicked out some bundles of anti-Hoxha leaflets, the Polish pilot, in a final act of bravado, flew at treetop level down the length of Tirana's main street before turning west over the Adriatic, toward Athens and home.[46]

Within days of landing, most members of Wisner's ethnic agent teams had been either shot or captured by the Sigurimi. Only a handful succeeded in making the tortuous six-week trek overland to sanctuary in Greece or Yugoslavia. As had been the case previously with Britain's pixies, survivors of the ordeal reported that Hoxha's militia was waiting for them—and had even called some by name when challenging them to surrender.

As contact was lost with the infiltrators, OPC's clandestine broadcasts to "PIXIELAND"—Albania—took on an increasingly urgent, even frantic, tone:

> Dear Children: Remain at all costs where you are. Everything is being done to send you what you need to the original fixed point . . . Rest assured that we will get in touch with you and that everything is being done to contact and help you. Again we insist you remain where you are, keep your spirits high and aid will soon reach you.[47]

Ominously, there was no reply.

Despite these setbacks, Wisner and OPC's Albanians remained undaunted. Indeed, similar teams were already being trained for insertion into the other captive nations of the Soviet bloc, including Ukraine, Poland, and Romania. In late July 1951, Wisner and Joyce met with State Department representatives to urge that Fiend be extended to Asia with creation of an anti-Communist "Third Force" in Thailand and southern China.[48]

At OPC's secret training base in Germany, meanwhile, additional émigré volunteers were being trained, with five more pixie teams sent into Albania that fall and winter—all yielding similar results. (Two OPC agents would be dropped into a mountainous region of Romania in mid-1951. By October, both had been apprehended and summarily executed.) In his briefing to the faithful two years earlier, Wisner had promised of Fiend, "It is so conceived that it can be interrupted at any time if we think we have reached a point of diminishing returns or that success is compromised." Instead, with the first blood having been shed, the project seemed to take on a life of its own.[49]

Wisner gamely tried to rally his troops. "F.W. said our activity still based on 'Cold War' concept . . . and will not until decreed by DCI [Smith], change emphasis," Michael Burke, Wisner's loyal foot-soldier, wrote in his Fiend File the previous winter. But while Frank remained stoic, others had begun to have doubts. And Burke's cryptic shorthand notes suggest that the first to develop cold feet were not the Albanians: "XXXX very much disheartened; feel we have no confidence, waning outcome . . . [Edgar] Applewhite completely cynical his morale is shot his interest in his work is almost nil." Burke had even stayed up all night trying, without success, to buck up the doubting Applewhite before finally concluding, "At this time I feel he is *not* psychologically ready to participate in our nefarious activities."*[50] Burke's notebook also revealed that a third OPC operative, one of Fiend's original boosters, wanted to cut the project's losses—at least in matériel. "We should not use valuable aircraft," Franklin Lindsay advised.[51]

To be sure, Burke's own enthusiam for Fiend was likewise fading. Early in 1951, he was reassigned, becoming OPC's liaison at the U.S. consulate in Frankfurt, Germany. In a brand-new notebook, Burke wrote about his success in recruiting a former SS general and persuading colleagues of "the necessity of exploring operational possibilities among even the most unsavory group."[52]

Another of Burke's jobs in Frankfurt was to assist Lindsay in preparing the stay-behind forces, if and when a shooting war broke out in Europe. Burke wrote that he had been instructed to prepare "two sets of assets: one to be used at once and the other to be committed six months to a year later. Former is expendable." Indeed, because of the deteriorating military situation in Korea, Burke, like Wisner before him, had begun preparing for the worst. His checklist for the end of April 1951 began, "Evacuation: Buy bicycles for everyone . . . Should password be given our infiltrees?"[53]

Only three days later, however, Burke was once again back in Rome, being feted at a farewell luncheon by the Sons of the Eagle, an Albanian fraternal organization to which many of OPC's pixies belonged. The latter toasted their case officer for "your many acts of kindness, your devotion to our cause and your continuing efforts on our behalf." As guest of honor, Burke rose, in turn, to salute the group's leader, Abaz Kupi, and to pay tribute to those who had already sacrificed their lives or their freedom on the altar of Project Fiend:

It is with deep regret that I relinquish my place beside you in our common fight, but I remain emotionally bound and constantly

---

* Edgar Applewhite—Jim Angleton's roommate at Yale, class of 1941—eventually overcame his ethical qualms and had a distinguished career at the CIA. During his more than twenty years with the agency, he supervised the 1955 Berlin tunnel operation that intercepted Soviet military communications, later served as Beirut station chief, and retired in 1970 as the CIA's deputy inspector general. In 1967, Applewhite was assigned the task of discrediting the editors of *Ramparts* magazine, which was about to publish an exposé on the agency. "I had all sorts of dirty tricks to hurt their circulation and financing," he admitted.

devoted to the cause in which we dedicated ourselves and so long worked for together in basic harmony. As we separate momentarily, I carry with me something of the splendid spirit of the Sons of the Eagle and an indelible memory of each one whom I have grown to know so well and love; I hope that some part of me rests with them. My dear Abaz Aga, I salute you as a great soldier of Albania and look for the day when we will be joined again in final victory.[54]

Burke wrote in his journal that evening of the luncheon "laid on with care and effort by Pixies" and their "touching goodbye." Meanwhile, like the Frankenstein monster of the British spy's warning, Wisner's Fiend lumbered on.

BACK IN WASHINGTON, the CIA's Beetle Smith had finally succeeded in gaining some control over Frank Wisner and the OPC. Early in 1951, Smith had put Allen Dulles, an experienced intelligence professional—and Wisner's former boss at the OSS—in charge of the agency's covert operations. Frank was made Allen's deputy. A few months later, when Beetle promoted Dulles to his second-in-command at the CIA, Wisner took over the latter's previous spot. The result was scarcely harmony, and Wisner continued to chafe at the unaccustomed oversight, even though Dulles ultimately proved to be as much a covert ops enthusiast as Wisner. Agency wags dubbed Dulles, their new deputy director, "the Great White Case Officer."[55]

Allen Dulles soon showed himself to be as adept as Wisner at working the pedals and stops of the mighty Wurlitzer. A few weeks before the 1952 presidential election, Dulles asked Phil Graham if the two could get together in order to discuss "various problems with our present relations." Meeting at the Grahams' house on R Street, Phil advised the spymaster henceforth to check with him or the *Post*'s managing editor, Al Friendly, directly anytime a contentious issue arose about the paper's coverage of the CIA.[56]

By then, Beetle Smith had also achieved his long-deferred and oft-frustrated goal of streamlining the CIA's spy bureaucracy, finally merging the Office of Policy Coordination with its perennial rival, the Office of Special Operations, into a single clandestine entity, the Directorate of Plans. (The position of deputy director of plans, or DDP, would be aptly described, in a subsequent CIA report, as the spawn of

"The houses were as pretty and meticulously appointed as yawls, the front doors fire engine red or lacquered ebony, glittering brass knockers catching the eye." But Georgetown was also "a place of public power and deep secrets—personal and state."

The Alsop brothers, Joseph and Stewart (right), were among the premier political pundits of the Cold War. Their Matter of Fact column appeared four times a week in two hundred newspapers in this country and overseas during the 1950s.

Frank Gardiner Wisner at his Locust Hill Farm in the 1950s. A classified CIA history would describe "the Wiz," who headed the CIA's Plans Directorate, as "a man of intense application" and "a singular choice to create a covert organization."

The Georgetown set gathers at Glen Welby, the Grahams' Virginia estate, during the Berlin crisis, June 1961. Left to right: Charles Bohlen, Frank Wisner, Llewellyn Thompson, Philip Graham, Joseph Alsop (foot).

Washington Post publisher Philip Graham in 1954. He was "a man in whose company it was impossible to be bored," observed Joe Alsop. But Graham's bipolar disorder eventually led to his suicide in 1963.

Washington Post publisher Katharine Graham in 1973. She was called the "Queen Bee of Washington," "Our Lady of the Potomac," and the "Valkyrie of American Journalism" for the *Post*'s coverage of the Watergate scandal. Joked Art Buchwald at Graham's seventieth birthday, in 1987: "If there is one thing that brings us all together here tonight, it is fear."

Joe Alsop called his "Garage Palladian" house at 2720 Dumbarton Avenue "a heinous outrage against 'Georgetown charm.'" The neighbors agreed—persuading Congress to pass a law forbidding any more cinder-block houses in Georgetown.

The garden room at Dumbarton Avenue, Joe Alsop's "green, cool, private place." A houseguest, Arthur Schlesinger Jr., warned Alsop that "those somewhat sinister plants" would one day "seize and strangle you."

Joseph Wright Alsop, the columnist's namesake. One visitor to Dumbarton Avenue remembered the "small, seawater-cold eyes" of Alsop ancestors staring down at him throughout supper. "The place just exuded significance," observed another guest.

During dinner, his chin cupped in both hands, peering over the tops of tortoiseshell glasses from his permanent seat at the head of the table, Joe Alsop would stare fixedly at a guest and ask archly, "So . . . what do you think of *this*?" Guests found the dinners either "exhilarating" or "terrifying."

Susan Mary Alsop at Heron Bay, Marietta Peabody's Barbados estate, 1965. "If you put her stark naked in the middle of the Gobi Desert, she would still be elegant," recalled Joe Alsop's admiring young niece of "Soozle."

МИНИСТЕРСТВО СВЯЗИ СССР

МЕЖДУНАРОДНАЯ
ТЕЛЕГРАММА

П Р И Ё М: ПЕРЕДАЧА: Адрес: Ленинград
Бл. № 858 90 Гостиница
Принял: Передал: У/О. Астория
Из № сл. го ч. м. Хозоер Алсоп
Служебные отметки:

№ 120

M42

PRAVITELSTVENNAIA   MOSCOU   05/21 33 21 1100Z-
JOSEPH ALSOP C/O ASTORIA HOTEL OR EVROPEISKYA LENINGRAD-
HAVE URGENT PERSONAL MESSAGE FOR YOU WHICH AMBASSADOR SAW
BEFORE DEPARTURE. HE SUGGESTS YOU RETURN IMMEDIATELY MOSCOW.
PLEASE CALL ME ON RETURN

DAVIS, AMEMBASSY"

In February 1957, U.S. ambassador to the Soviet Union Charles Bohlen sent this telegram, urgently summoning Joe Alsop back to Moscow, where he was persuaded by Frank Wisner to write an account of his recent entrapment in a homosexual affair filmed by the KGB. Alsop's "confession" went to the CIA and FBI, and was later used by Joe's enemies at home in a failed attempt to silence him.

Frank Gardiner Wisner (front row, fifth from left) is captain of the University of Virginia track team in this 1931 photograph. Tom Braden, later Wisner's colleague at the CIA, described him as "cool yet coiled, a low hurdler from Mississippi constrained by a vest."

Frank Wisner (right) headed the Office of Strategic Services in Romania during 1944–1945. OSS chief William "Wild Bill" Donovan twice warned him not to antagonize the Russians "by speech or action."

Wisner's Locust Hill Farm on Maryland's Eastern Shore became a frequent refuge during his bouts with depression. He spent summers at the farm with his teenage son Ellis, harvesting hay, planting vegetables, and weeding the garden plot.

TOP, LEFT The Wisners and Joyces posed for a novelty photograph at the Alhambra fortress on a 1964 visit to Spain. When Frank Wisner canceled plans for their annual hunting expedition there the following spring, Charles Bohlen became concerned. Wisner killed himself a few months later.

BELOW The bronze plaque cast by the CIA to honor Frank Gardiner Wisner following his suicide in 1965. At a 1971 dedication ceremony, CIA director Richard Helms spoke of Wisner's struggle with the "night of dark intent."

In Memory of
FRANK GARDINER WISNER
1909 —— 1965
Sprinkling System

LEFT Frank Wisner's widow, Polly, paid for the sprinkler system at the National Cathedral's Bishop's Garden, dedicating it to her husband—who took special pride in his vegetable garden at the Locust Hill Farm.

"a shot-gun marriage.") Wisner was made DDP in August 1951. Frank's old friend and former competitor, Dick Helms, became his deputy and chief of operations.[57]

For the CIA's director, Smith, the final straw had come that spring, when it had been necessary for the agency's inspector general, Lyman Kirkpatrick, to resolve a dispute at the agency's Bangkok station. An attempt by OPC "cowboys" to recruit an OSO source—a high-level official in the Thai government—had escalated to the point of drawn revolvers. The local OPC chief subsequently kidnapped the station's radio operator in an unsuccessful effort to keep Beetle Smith from finding out about the incident. His intervention had been necessary to keep the two rival sides from "shooting live bullets at each other," the incredulous Kirkpatrick reported back to the CIA director.[58]

In the meantime, not only did Project Fiend continue unabated in Albania, but other ethnic agent teams were still being parachuted into Poland and Ukraine, in hopes of sparking anti-Communist uprisings there.[59]

Yet the agency thus far had little to show for Fiend—as even Wisner himself was ruefully forced to admit. Few weeks went by without word being received at the CIA of the "annihilation" of another ethnic agent team in an ambush. And, not surprisingly, morale among the Albanian recruits at the secret training base in Germany was beginning to be "a serious problem," their handlers acknowledged. That summer, for the first time, several graduates of the CIA school refused to go on a mission and had to be "disposed" of; they were put in an agency safe house under guard and eventually sent back to Greece.

Meanwhile, in Albania, some of those few infiltrators who had succeeded in contacting their CIA handlers were sending the required all-clear signal in an unfamiliar "fist"—the pattern of Morse code unique to each individual—raising concerns that the sender was either under control of the "roaches," the Sigurimi, or actually an enemy agent posing as a pixie. (Challenged to explain why his transmissions had suddenly changed, the wireless operator for Team APPLE claimed that his right hand had been broken in the parachute jump, so he was sending with his left. The CIA's credulous case officers recommended that henceforth tape recordings be made of all operator trainees using both right and left hands.)[*60]

---

* At least some around Wisner guessed what might be behind the Albanian project's failures. Scrawled in the margin of a May 1951 CIA report on "Valuable-Fiend relations" was

Even Allen Dulles, Frank's longtime ally, had begun to question whether Fiend was worth the cost in lives and treasure. After Dulles told the British that the CIA was reevaluating the Albanian operation, Wisner wrote an angry memo to his boss, asking why he had not been included in Dulles's briefing of MI6. Allen's aide fired back: "Dulles has made no commitment to 'wipe out' Fiend, he merely said Fiend is on trial. Mr. Dulles believes, therefore, there is no reason to be excited over his statement to the British." Beetle Smith, on the other hand, did not mince words in a memo to Wisner following the latter's progress report on Fiend: "He could not understand what we are accomplishing or, more important, what we are trying to accomplish." To avoid further scrutiny, Frank ordered that the gruesome transcripts of the transmissions from Albania, as well as the pixies' own dire after-action reports, "be withheld from State where possible." (Wisner's reluctance was understandable. Read one such report: "The destruction of the BGFIEND OLIVE party . . . on 27 July, three days after its infiltration, was reported by the Jayhawk TIGER team upon its exfiltration on 7 August . . . Surrounded, the OLIVE team suffered this fate: Identity (3) was captured; (4) killed himself together with (5) who had agreed to a double suicide with a grenade. One died with a grenade but the other lived to kill himself with his pistol.")[61]

The CIA's analysts, the so-called washerwomen much despised by OPC's operatives, had, in the interim, washed their hands of Fiend. As the analysts informed Wisner, one of the original justifications for the Albanian operation—the use of that country as a supply base for anti-Communist fighters elsewhere in the region—had vanished in 1949, when the Greek civil war ended with a victory for the Western-backed government. Ironically, the agency's new fear was that Albania, far from serving as a model for future insurrections against Soviet control, might be used instead as a casus belli by the Russians to invade the one country in Eastern Europe that had thus far successfully defied the Kremlin: Tito's Yugoslavia. Moreover, far from removing Albania from the Soviet orbit, Fiend had actually solidified Hoxha's control. The dictator's brutal

---

this handwritten notation: "Did I make a slip when we informed Philby of the approach to [Abaz] Kupi?" Five days earlier, Kim Philby—the SIS liaison to Fiend—had been implicated in the defection to the Soviet Union of the British diplomats Guy Burgess and Donald Maclean.

efficiency in rounding up and eliminating Fiend's infiltrators had terrified the native population. Pixies who escaped Albania revealed that those who had assisted them in their homeland, including whole families, were routinely tortured and executed by the Sigurimi.[62]

EARLY IN 1952, the Wiz found himself under attack on yet another front. In his continuing campaign to discredit Wisner, FBI director Hoover had sent Beetle Smith a "personal and confidential" report, based on information from an unidentified informant, who claimed that Wisner's "girl friend" in wartime Bucharest, Princess Tanda Caradja, was actually a Soviet spy. According to the FBI, the twenty-four-year-old Tanda—a red-haired, green-eyed beauty, who was reportedly a distant relative of a more famous Transylvanian, Vlad the Impaler, the inspiration for Dracula—had "adopted" Wisner and his OSS team in wartime Bucharest. Tanda supposedly later boasted to a cousin that she had been spying for the Russians at the same time. Although Smith discounted this and subsequent reports he received from Hoover, it was nonetheless further evidence that Wisner had powerful enemies in the Washington bureaucracy and could soon become a liability to the CIA.[63] (When Beetle first took control of the agency, he had asked for a personal meeting with Hoover, naïvely believing that he could remove the "misunderstandings" between the CIA and the bureau since "a large number of them were the result of personalities rather than any question in policy." Hoover would have none of it.[64])

Frustrated at his inability to get at Wisner directly, the FBI director instead took aim at a more vulnerable target: Carmel Offie. Never one to pass up an opportunity to undermine those he took to be potential rivals, Hoover met with Beetle Smith at Washington's Mayflower hotel to warn of sexual deviants inside the CIA. "The case of Carmel Offie represents a typical example," read an internal FBI memo prepared for Hoover's meeting with Smith. But after the swarthy Monk made an ill-advised pass at an army counterintelligence agent—who promptly reported the contact to his superiors—even some of those around Wisner had finally had enough, and Offie's dossier was brought to the attention of Senator McCarthy. Challenged by the Tydings Committee on April 25, 1950, to provide evidence of "subversive activities" by federal employees, the Wisconsin senator had alluded darkly to an unnamed former State Department employee "now assigned to the Central Intelligence Agency . . . a homosexual . . . who spent his time hanging around the men's room in Lafayette Park."[65]

Perhaps anticipating what was to come, Frank Wisner spirited his devoted acolyte away and out of sight just five days after McCarthy's testimony, assigning Offie to serve as liaison to the CIA-funded Free Trade Union Committee headed by Jay Lovestone, a former Communist turned labor activist. The FTUC's offices were in Washington's Dupont Circle. "The usual 'brush off' all around," grumbled Hoover to an aide.[66]

Beetle Smith's remarks at an all-hands meeting of the CIA in October 1952 gave Wisner additional reason to squirm. Pointedly blaming the agency's repeated failures on "the use of improperly trained or inferior personnel," Smith "stated that until CIA could build a reserve of well-trained people, it would have to hold its activities to a limited number of operations that it could do well rather than to attempt to cover a broad field with poor performance. He reminded the meeting that the Agency's primary mission was intelligence and that he would do nothing that militated against accomplishing this objective."[67]

The exasperated CIA director was even more outspoken in private concerning Wisner. "For Christ's sake, can't I get people who don't hire people who bugger cows?" Smith erupted to an aide, upon learning that OPC's personnel director had been committed to a psychiatric hospital for bestiality. Smith himself quashed one of Frank's longtime favorite projects, telling one of Wisner's men, "Kindly do not bring in here any more of those goddamned *balloon* projects of yours."[68]

The halcyon days of the Wiz and OPC's mighty Wurlitzer were plainly in the past; and, for Frank, more trouble lay just ahead.

CHAPTER TEN

"Venomous, Exciting and Pretty Frightening"

GEORGE KENNAN had earlier railed against what he called "the sinister stupidities of the [State] Department's loyalty investigators," who had, nonetheless, been newly empowered by a recent Truman executive order to seek out suspected traitors hiding in government ranks. But the case of John Davies hit particularly close to home. "I cannot stand by and consider myself unaffected by things that happened to a junior officer by virtue of his official activity under my authority," Kennan wrote to Paul Nitze.[1]

Ironically, Davies had come under suspicion because of a secret program he proposed in response to Kennan's 1949 adjuring of "some brave new approach" to counter Communism overseas. In the wake of Mao's accession to power and Tito's split with the Kremlin, Davies had been given the task of coming up with specific ideas for how to apply a so-called wedge strategy to China.[2]

As the term implies, the aim was to create mistrust and suspicion between the two Communist giants, driving them apart. To that end, Davies had met with a handful of OPC operatives to discuss some promising schemes. Intent, he said, upon "injecting a discordant element into the other camp," Davies laid out a plan whereby half a dozen Asian scholars in the United States would be recruited to write anti-Mao propaganda leaflets. The leaflets would be dropped by balloon across China, in hopes of fomenting dissent and even, ideally, resistance leading to another revolution. In his presentation to OPC, Davies had mentioned several such experts by name, most of them his personal friends. Since the authors of the leaflets would not know that they were actually working for U.S. intelligence, and to make their message more persuasive, Davies had added a couple of "fellow travelers," or suspected Communist sympathizers, to his list. His secret ploy, doubly deceptive, was given the code name Tawny Pipit—a small bird renowned for singing loudly in flight.[3]

Unbeknownst to Davies, two of those at his briefing—Lyle Munson and Ed Hunter—were security specialists who had recently been hired by OPC in accordance with Truman's executive order aimed at ferreting out disloyal government employees. Without even waiting for Davies to finish, Munson and Hunter had left the room and gone directly to the CIA's director, Hillenkoetter, reporting that the State Department was proposing to "hire communists." Hilly, in turn, promptly passed this information on to J. Edgar Hoover and the FBI, Munson's former employer. In short order, word of Tawny Pipit had leaked out to the archconservative China lobby, thence to McCarthy, and finally to the press.[4]

Summoned before the State Department's own loyalty board that summer, Davies was flummoxed by the eleven charges leveled against him, most of which dealt with the time he had spent in wartime China, centering on the claim that he was "bitterly anti–Chiang Kai Shek . . . [and] in sympathy with the Chinese Communists." While only a single allegation related to Tawny Pipit, Davies felt constrained by security rules from giving details on his ill-fated propaganda gambit, which remained classified and hence unmentioned by name in the State Department letter of charges. Davies later compared his situation to that of "a rabbit being shot at in an open field." The perplexed and embattled diplomat turned to his friends—and to those who had gotten him into this mess—for help.[5]

For one of those friends, the Davies case presented a quandary. Kennan was certainly sympathetic to his plight and quickly sent off a letter of support to the head of State's loyalty board, the U.S. Army brigadier general Conrad Snow. Perhaps because of the strictures of secrecy, however, Kennan's missive seemed more a stock character reference than the ringing defense of a longtime comrade. Most important, the letter said nothing about Kennan's own role in the events that had led to the investigation of Davies.[6]

Joe Alsop, for his part, promptly wrote to Snow that he, too, was choosing to intervene in the Davies case "out of the blue, as it were," and explained why:

First, I played a leading part in the events in China which have now caused Mr. John Paton Davies, Jr. to be called before the Loyalty Board. Since I knew Mr. Davies very well, and at that time bitterly opposed the policy which he advocated, I feel that my judgment of his motives and loyalty may be of some value . . . I wish, therefore, to volunteer to appear before your Board, if you so desire. Second, I am much puzzled, and indeed much concerned, by the operations of our loyalty review system. I have been told that you are willing to explain how it works. May I therefore come to call on you in my capacity as a reporter, for the purpose of being enlightened on this point?[7]

As promised, Alsop appeared before the loyalty board five days later, on July 23, 1951. Breaking his own rule against writing columns in the first person, Joe gave an account of his testimony in Matter of Fact later that week. Describing Davies as a sacrificial "burnt offering" to the Red-baiters in Congress—specifically, McCarthy and his chief political ally, the Nevada senator Pat McCarran—Alsop even conceded that Davies's "judgment of the Chinese scene had stood the test of time rather better than my own." In conclusion, Joe suggested that instead of Davies the government should investigate "the politicians who are now working all-out to destroy the last vestiges of decency and fair play in our public life."[8]

That autumn, Davies was informed by the State Department that he would be temporarily posted to Berlin, until the question of his loyalty could be resolved. Anticipating the move to Germany, he and his wife, Patricia, had already sold their home in Washington; she and their four children moved in with relatives. In the interim, McCarran's Senate Internal Security Subcommittee announced that it, too, would be investigating the Tawny Pipit affair. McCarran threatened to charge Davies with perjury for lying to Congress, if his testimony contradicted Munson's.[9]

Flying back from a Norwegian vacation at his own expense, Kennan would also testify before Snow's loyalty board on Davies's behalf—appearing on the same day as Alsop but in closed session. While Kennan was in Washington, Acheson inquired whether the temperamental diplomat would agree to end his self-imposed exile and serve as the U.S. ambassador to the Soviet Union. Later writing to Arthur Schlesinger Jr.,

Kennan noted that he was finishing up his work at the institute and looked forward to the Moscow assignment: "One can never quite tell what the responsibilities of that post will be, but it would be wrong to expect that they would include much drama. The probabilities are that the main qualifications for the job, which I will do my best to meet, will be patience, taciturnity, and inner fortitude." Still hopeful of influencing policy at home, Kennan boxed up and sent to Nitze and State's planning staff some three hundred pages of notes from the essays he had written while at Princeton's institute.[10]

Arriving in the Russian capital as U.S. ambassador in early May 1952, Kennan wrote back to the State Department that his reception by Soviet authorities had been "one hundred percent 'deadpan.' If it reflected any special orders or directives from the top, they could only have been a rigid injunction to avoid anything that might give me a clue as to the feelings of the Kremlin about my appointment and presence in this city." Had he listened to Radio Warsaw's announcement of his arrival, Kennan would have had such a clue. Describing the new American ambassador as "the enemy of the Soviet Union and all peace-loving Nations," whose "whole career has been devoted to preparing for a new war and to dealing with spies and diversionists," the broadcast added, ominously, that the Kremlin would be keeping a sharp eye on "so-called American diplomats who exploit diplomatic privileges to disguise their espionage activities."[11]

THE ALSOP BROTHERS, having already received considerable attention—both positive and negative—for Stewart's article on McCarthy in *The Saturday Evening Post,* were busy planning another volley aimed at the Wisconsin senator and his allies. The previous spring, when one of those allies, the Ohio senator Robert Taft, complained about a recent column Stewart had written—"The Sinister Alliance Between McCarthy and Taft"—Stew did not hesitate before firing back at his accuser: "I believe that McCarthy is thus a disgrace to the Republican Party. Yet I am convinced that certain Republicans have concluded that he is a political asset, a conclusion which seems to me dangerous both to the Republican Party and the country."[12]

Since Matter of Fact was published under both Alsops' byline, it had likely escaped the attention of most readers that Joe himself had yet to enter the fray against McCarthy. The Wisconsin senator's outraged response to Stewart's July 1950 *Post* magazine article hinted at a reason. In the piece, Stew had branded as a "vulgar folly" the efforts of politicians like McCarthy "to elevate the subject of homosexuality to the level of a serious political issue." In a letter to the editor of *The Saturday Evening Post,* McCarthy protested that the "task of removing perverts from our government" could hardly be considered vulgar—except perhaps to someone like Joe Alsop.[13]

Although he estimated that more than a quarter of *Post* readers agreed with McCarthy, Joe vowed that he would not be intimidated by the senator's implicit blackmail threat. The older brother had always been careful to conceal his homosexuality, recognizing that it would be a serious impediment to his job as a journalist were it to become generally known and, given the temper of the times, might even be career ending. Joe himself spoke dismissively of "fairies" and of men who were "light on their feet." But homosexuality was rarely a topic for public discussion in Washington and virtually never mentioned in the press. (This did not mean that Joe's sexual preferences went unremarked in the capital. Back in March 1951, the FBI had sent Truman's aide Matthew Connelly a report alleging that the bureau had evidence Alsop was gay.[14])

Stewart had bristled at McCarthy's sly innuendo in his own letter to Ben Hibbs, the brothers' longtime editor at *The Saturday Evening Post,* and was disappointed by Hibbs's tepid response. Brandishing his own anti-Communist credentials before McCarthy, Hibbs pointed to the times that the *Post* had actually supported the senator—a flaccid defense that did not prevent another attack by McCarthy, this time on the magazine and its editor for paying insufficient attention to the Red menace in the past.[15]

The two brothers had good reason to feel besieged. Several of Joe's friends from his China days had since deserted him because of his support for Davies. That included Alfred Kohlberg, the conservative businessman who headed the China lobby and supplied Joe with his beloved silk shirts. There was, Alsop explained to another of his former allies, the U.S. Army general Albert Wedemeyer, an effort to "re-write the whole China story around a dark, imaginary plot, which has forced me back into the controversy."[16]

Nor had the brothers thus far found much support from fellow journalists for their stand against McCarthy. With the exception of Joe's Georgetown neighbor Drew Pearson—who, in his own syndicated column, Washington Merry-Go-Round, had drawn attention to irregularities in the senator's tax returns as early as March 1950—no one else in the nation's press corps had been willing to take on McCarthy. In a letter to Henry Luce, the owner and editor in chief of *Time,* Joe complained about the "almost tolerant, almost amiable note" in the magazine's coverage of "McCarthy, McCarran and company." "I agree with all you say against 'McCarthyism,'" Luce wrote back, "but, if I may say so, you don't deal with all the facts: you do not, for example, deal with the fact that millions of your reasonably decent fellow-citizens condone or approve of most, if not all of [McCarthy's] doings."[17]

The Alsops were no less chagrined to discover the sources that they had long relied on for news—and leaks—suddenly drying up. Beyond their feud with McCarthy, another likely reason was that a recent scoop of theirs had, for the first time, drawn the unwanted attention of President Truman and the FBI. Months earlier, shortly after Louis Johnson had publicly expressed doubts that the Soviet Union actually possessed nuclear weapons, the brothers had written a column containing classified details of how U.S. detection techniques had confirmed the existence of the Russian A-bomb. Although an extensive inquiry by the bureau failed to identify the source of the Alsops' information, just the appearance of snap-brimmed FBI agents on one's doorstep was, for most citizens, an intimidating experience.[18]

As he had previously, in the case of John Davies's loyalty hearing, Joe made the occasion—a visit to his home by a pair of the FBI's "young gentlemen"—into an opportunity to hold forth in Matter of Fact on how Hoover's tactics were being used as "a weapon to muzzle the press . . . The point here is very simple indeed. In a free society, secrecy is not security . . . And this 'security investigation' caused by the publication of information most vital to the national future shows how great is the confusion and the danger."[19]

To be sure, the brothers had a lengthy history with the bureau, going back to the early days of their column. The FBI's own thick files on Joe and Stewart confirm that Hoover and his G-men had an equally long memory. "Joseph Alsop has made ridiculous, vehement attacks against the Director and the FBI since May, 1940," noted one internal bureau report. Following the brothers' 1946 column on Hoover's efforts to expand his intelligence empire, the FBI chief had contacted Truman's attorney general for the purpose of "pointing out these falsehoods." A subsequent column by the brothers was derided by the bureau as the "usual Alsop smear of our efforts." In August 1947, Hoover himself had written to the editor of the *New York Herald Tribune,* protesting a Matter of Fact column on the FBI's role in the recent firing of ten State Department employees for alleged disloyalty. ("I am feeling pretty pure today and I am therefore not very alarmed, but my rectitude might not last, so please, if possible, keep me out of [Hoover's] black books," the *Trib* editor wrote to Joe.) Hoover also sent a copy of his letter to Joe and Stewart—"in protest of the fabrications and untruth in [the] Alsops' column and in an effort to correct the record."[20]

But it was all to no avail, so far as Hoover and the bureau were concerned. Although questioned once more by the FBI in February 1951, and again the following month, Joe and Stewart refused to reveal their sources for the A-bomb story. (Stewart later divulged that the supposedly top secret information was actually an informed guess by the head of Georgetown University's Physics Department.)[21]

The FBI's inquiries nonetheless had the intended effect, in that they put a temporary chill on the brothers' journalistic efforts. One of the Washington insiders whom Joe Alsop had come to rely on for information was Paul Nitze. The two men had long enjoyed a cordial, albeit occasionally combative, relationship. (Paul described Joe as a "joyous person"; Alsop jokingly chided Nitze for being "a bureaucrat.") But at a lunch that winter, Joe was distressed to find Nitze unusually tight-lipped in his presence. Subsequent attempts to draw out Beetle Smith's right-hand man, the CIA's deputy director William Harding Jackson, were similarly rebuffed; as was Alsop's approach to Jackson's close friend and fellow southerner Gordon Gray. Jackson had reportedly told Gray that the Alsop brothers, because they published military secrets, were "worth ten divisions to the enemy."[22]

Formerly Truman's secretary of the army, Gray had recently been appointed by the president to head a new organization, the Psychological Strategy Board. The PSB was the latest vain attempt by Beetle Smith to rein in Frank Wisner, by keeping track of and coordinating the many disparate and competing political warfare projects being run by OPC and the agency. Gray had taken the job with trepidation and lasted in it less than a year. One reason for his exceptionally brief tenure might have been the constant importuning of the Alsops. (Years later, Gray's son Boyden vividly recalled Joe Alsop's failed attempt to cultivate his father as a news source: "Now, Gordon . . . Baaah . . . I think we've got to collaborate here . . . Baaah . . . Old-school tie and all." But Alsop's appeal had fallen flat. "Joe, I didn't go to Groton," Gray reminded him.)[23]

Yet it was not only the unwelcome attention of the FBI nor the sudden reticence of their usual sources that inhibited the Alsops' reporting on the Washington scene. Indeed, Joe and Stewart were surprised to discover their own editor and publisher the main obstacle to taking on McCarthy. For as long as the Wisconsin senator remained in power, *The Saturday Evening Post* would not publish another Alsop article on McCarthy, although Joe and Stewart proposed several to Hibbs.[24]

Perhaps less surprising was the resistance the brothers encountered from Whitelaw "Whitey" Reid, publisher of the conservative *New York Herald Tribune,* to a series of three columns they planned to write in the fall of 1951 on the work of McCarran's Internal Security Subcommittee. Following Joe's testimony before the State Department loyalty board in support of Davies, McCarran had subpoenaed Alsop to appear before his Senate subcommittee as well. Joe requested that he be allowed to testify in open session so that he might again write about the experience of being at a loyalty hearing. McCarran flatly refused.[25]

On September 15, 1951, the day after Matter of Fact accused McCarran's chief counsel, Robert Morris, of conducting sloppy investigations, the *Herald Tribune* ran an editorial by Reid disavowing the Alsop column. The *Trib* editorial followed Reid's decisions to delay release of the first column in the series to other papers in the syndicate, citing "legal difficulties," and to print the last column as a news item, rather than on the editorial page. Joe Alsop was outraged. "You have the right to use our stuff as you please," he wrote to Reid. "But I think when you in effect indicate your own lack of confidence in us to our clients, and thus undermine their confidence in us as well, you are going very far indeed."[26]

Joe's friend Arthur Schlesinger Jr. sent a protest letter of his own to Reid on the latter's handling of the Alsop columns on McCarran. "Two years ago the Herald Tribune would have been proud to print them," Schlesinger wrote. "Today, it disowns Joe, its own columnist, defends Pat McCarran and Robert Morris and even goes to the wild extreme of calling the members of the McCarran subcommittee 'six distinguished lawyers.'"[27]

Privately, Joe and Stew discussed the possibility of breaking their contract with the *Herald Tribune* or even abandoning Matter of Fact outright. "The fight really is not going too well, since I have not as yet succeeded in getting my columns followed by the national press," Joe admitted to Schlesinger.[28]

The brothers were cheered, however, when one paper in the syndicate—

The Washington Post—decided to defy Reid and print the controversial column on Morris and McCarran anyway. As an exultant Joe informed Reid, "The more timid spirits on the [*Post*] staff took alarm, and there was a discussion, which was of course settled by Philip Graham in favor of printing the column as written, without qualification or remark."[29]

Much relieved, Joe Alsop notified Stew that they had a new and much-needed ally in their fight with McCarthy: the *Washington Post's* publisher, Phil Graham. "You really need not, I think, be excessively alarmed about the crisis with the *Tribune*," Joe reassured his brother that November, adding, somewhat cryptically, "I have become a secret State Department and White House adviser on how to go after McCarthy, for example."[30]

FOR THE BROTHERS, it was a welcome, if unexpected, reprieve.

What Phil Graham knew about Joe Alsop came mostly from his wife, Katharine, who had met Joe in 1935, when she was eighteen and he twenty-four, at a "coming-out" party arranged by Kay's mother. It had been an inauspicious first encounter. At the time, Joe, a cub reporter for the *Herald Tribune*, weighed nearly 250 pounds. Kay found both Alsop's physical presence and his intellect overpowering: "I was appalled by his appearance and unable to cope with his mature mind." Since then, however, the Alsops and the Grahams had become close friends, as hosts of the rotating Sunday night suppers. But Phil's relationship with Joe remained on professional grounds, that of publisher to reporter.[31]

Despite his combative nature, Phil Graham had thus far been uncharacteristically cautious in his newspaper's approach to political controversy. "And even in stories like the McCarthy story, I confess that I am fearful of our using our power unfairly when we try to print the 'whole truth' instead of merely being 'objective,'" he wrote to a sympathetic reporter. It was not until mid-1948 that Eugene Meyer had put the *Post* firmly in the hands of his son-in-law, and Phil still worried that a principled stand on his part might leave the paper in financial jeopardy. While Phil's support for the Marshall Plan was relatively noncontroversial, he and the paper had come under attack from both sides for the *Post's* coverage of the Alger Hiss case and had lost advertisers over articles critical of the House Un-American Activities Committee.[32]

During a vacation in the spring of 1950, Phil Graham had learned of a *Post* editorial praising Earl Browder, the former head of the American

Communist Party, for refusing to name names before a Senate investigating committee. Phil ordered a disclaimer printed in subsequent editions and was only talked out of firing the man in charge of the editorial page by his friend and former boss, Justice Felix Frankfurter. On other occasions, Phil had upbraided Herblock for what Graham felt was a politically insensitive or unfair caricature.[33]

Like many others in the newspaper business, the *Post* publisher had initially dismissed McCarthyism as a fleeting political phenomenon. "McCarthy is causing a lot of noise here and doing a lot of harm, but I am hopeful that he will eventually end up on his backside," Phil told friends shortly after the senator's Wheeling, West Virginia, speech. By June 1951, however—when McCarthy, in a three-hour tirade on the Senate floor, accused Secretary of Defense George Marshall of aiding the Communists, and after the titular leader of the Republican Party, Robert Taft, refused to distance himself from McCarthy's remarks—Graham felt that the danger could no longer be ignored. Still, Phil's criticism remained muted and, for the most part, confided privately to friends—as in the speech he made later that year to members of his old fraternity chapter at the University of Florida: "We are adopting some strange habits for a people who have grown great in the pursuit of reason and the search for truth. We are now wondering whether self-preservation does not demand restrictions on thinking and limitations on ideas." But Graham did not mention McCarthy by name.[34]

Early on, Joe Alsop had joined Phil's critics, believing Graham to be both too tentative and too late in confronting McCarthy. "Even the Washington *Post*, after promising to run a series of editorials, published not a line," Joe wrote to Schlesinger in disgust that fall. But Phil's willingness to print the controversial Alsop columns on McCarran, defying Reid, increased Joe's respect for Graham—even as the two disagreed on what motivated McCarthy. When Isaiah Berlin, in a lunch at Joe's house, accused McCarthy of deliberately promoting anti-Semitism, Alsop was furious that Phil objected. A shouting match ensued, and Graham eventually walked out in a huff.[35]

But Joe Alsop and Phil Graham *did* see eye to eye on what it would take to discredit and unseat the Wisconsin senator.[36] It had been clear to both men, early on, that neither Truman nor Taft was likely to stand up to McCarthy. And, while temperamentally and intellectually sympathetic to an up-and-coming contender for the Democratic Party's nomination for president—Adlai Stevenson—neither Joe nor Phil felt that the cerebral Stevenson had the back-alley instincts necessary to deal with a man like McCarthy. (In a September 1952 Matter of Fact column, Stewart would refer to Stevenson and his supporters as "egg-heads." The image stuck, and the term helped to brand Stevenson as an ineffectual, dithering nerd.)[37]

Phil Graham had already broken with his father-in-law's long-standing tradition of avoiding political endorsements in the *Post*. The previous March, Phil announced that he and his paper would be supporting a former war hero, Dwight Eisenhower, for the presidency. Kay and Stewart, on the other hand, both backed Stevenson—as did Marietta and most of the Georgetown set.[38]

With the election season in full swing by that summer, Joe decided to abandon Washington for the hustings, crisscrossing the country by train for nearly two months in order to cover the rival campaigns of Stevenson and Eisenhower. Writing to a friend, Alsop described the political atmosphere in the country as "venomous, exciting and pretty frightening." (In an era before scientific polling, Joe's shoe-leather approach made for some highly subjective—and personal—reportage. A colleague at the *Post*, who accompanied Joe on these rounds, remembered the latter searching out farmers in Minnesota. Sporting a green tweed jacket, tailored gray slacks, and highly polished, handmade shoes, Joe would nudge the interview subject with his walking stick and inquire, "So, what do you make of it, old boy? Eh?")[39]

Phil Graham, abandoning any pretense of impartiality, served as the master of ceremonies at an Eisenhower campaign rally that October. And the *Post* drew mostly praise from readers later in the month, when it ran a strong anti-McCarthy editorial following a televised speech by the senator, who accused the Democratic presidential nominee of being a Communist sympathizer. But Graham still observed limits. When Herblock penned a drawing that criticized Eisenhower and his running mate, Richard Nixon, for refusing to condemn McCarthy's mudslinging tactics, Phil refused to let the cartoon run in the *Post*. Two weeks before the election, Graham stopped publishing Herblock altogether when the subject was Ike, believing that Eisenhower represented the last, best chance of stopping McCarthy.[40]

WATCHING THE DEPREDATIONS of McCarthyism from the vantage point of the CIA, Frank Wisner found himself powerless to intervene in the Davies case—caught between a desire to prevent an injustice from being done to the hapless diplomat and the security restrictions that kept Tawny Pipit in the agency's top secret file. Thus, McCarran's efforts to get Frank Wisner to testify about Davies's role in the work of OPC were rebuffed by the CIA's lawyers—on the grounds of national security. "I am most anxious for you to know certain things about this matter which are by no means what they appeared to be in the newspaper accounts which you have presumably seen," Wisner cryptically wrote to Kennan, shortly before the latter left for Russia. Because of Tawny Pipit and the Davies affair, Kennan had recommended that State Department employees henceforth have nothing to do with OPC.[41]

At the U.S. embassy in Moscow, meanwhile, Ambassador Kennan drafted a long letter to Acheson containing a vague threat of resignation if "this matter [Tawny Pipit] should have any unfortunate consequences for Davies." Kennan urged the secretary of state to let Truman, the attorney general, and McCarran himself know "that the future handling of this matter may affect not only Davies' position but also my own usefulness to the Government at this time." However, Kennan's letter remained unsent.[42]

In fact, Kennan's resignation threat became moot only a few weeks later, when his prediction that the ambassador job would be lacking in drama was proved spectacularly wrong. On September 19, 1952, during a plane-side press conference at Berlin's Tempelhof Airport, Kennan, in response to a reporter's routine inquiry about conditions for diplomats in Moscow, gave vent to long-pent-up frustrations. Perhaps mindful of a recent incident at Spaso House, the ambassadorial residence, where Soviet guards had prevented Russian children from playing with his two-year-old son, Christopher, Kennan compared the Moscow posting to his wartime internment in Nazi Germany. The Kremlin, furious, declared Kennan persona non grata and refused to let him back into the country.[43]

Ironically, Acheson suggested, via Bohlen, that it might be equally impolitic for Kennan to return home, so close to the presidential election, lest his presence remind voters of the country's rocky relations with the Soviet Union. Condemned to wander Flying Dutchman–like around Europe for the interim, Kennan wrote to the embassy's chargé d'affaires, his temporary replacement, that his "one personal regret about leaving Moscow lies in feeling that I am leaving the rest of you in the lurch and enjoying a life of soft western indulgence that I do not deserve. But there is nothing that I can do about it now."[44]

Kennan finally returned to Washington on November 11, 1952, exactly a week after the country elected Dwight Eisenhower its next president. Since George and Annelise had rented out their Princeton home for the duration of what they assumed would be a lengthy stay in Moscow, the couple, their children, and a nanny moved into the rustic farmhouse on the Kennans' property in Pennsylvania. A quick visit to the capital to see Truman and Acheson yielded no hints, Kennan recalled, as to his own future. Instead, Kennan found that they, too, were preoccupied with the increasingly vicious and partisan attacks on men like Davies, who, until recently, had been their friends and colleagues in the government: the outgoing secretary of state and the lame-duck president "had in their eyes the faraway look of men who know that they are about to be relieved of heavy responsibilities and who derive a malicious pleasure in reserving their most bitter problems for those who are about to displace them."[45]

PART II

BOLD EASTERNERS

In the Dulles-Wisner-Bissell period, which was also the period of the agency's greatest power, the CIA was dominated by . . . the Bold Easterners. The men of this sort came, for the most part, from the East; had gone to private schools in the East and to Ivy League colleges; had some money of their own; and brought to their jobs with the agency a certain spirit of derring-do, a willingness to take risks.

—STEWART ALSOP, *The Center*

CHAPTER ELEVEN

"Stray and Gusty Winds"

T HE FIRST REPUBLICAN PRESIDENT to occupy the White House
in nearly a generation meant a sea change for Washington and for
Georgetown. Joe Alsop was among those who awaited the arrival of the
Eisenhower administration with eager anticipation—and no little anxiety. "Evangeline is a great source of news," Alsop wrote to Susan Mary in
Paris, "since every rich man who thinks he's coming to Washington—and
as far as I can see no one is coming to Washington without a million
dollars a year—begins by calling the Bruces to see if they can buy their
house. I am thinking of selling my tiny home for 200% profit, since the
market in palaces is so very good."[1]

But the boom in Georgetown real estate that Alsop had predicted
simply failed to occur. Most of those appointed to cabinet-level posts in
the Republican administration chose to live elsewhere, moving to the
Virginia suburbs or settling in Spring Valley, an upscale development
in northwest Washington near American University. Rumor spread that
Ike had specifically forbidden Republican appointees from even setting foot in Georgetown, which—as the abode of the Alsops, Bohlens,
Bruces, Harrimans, and Grahams—had gained such a reputation as a
liberal bastion that some spoke of a "P and Q Street Axis," and even a
"P Street Mafia."[2]

There were, of course, exceptions.

Allen Dulles, the man whom Ike chose to head the CIA, lived at 2723
Q Street with his wife, Clover. The couple, through their connection
with the Wisners—Allen was Frank's boss—were already frequent guests
at the Sunday night suppers and had once rented Joe Alsop's house while

he was away on a world tour. But to Joe's frustration, Allen Dulles demonstrated more interest in acquiring secrets than dispensing them at the dinner table. In a favorite ploy, the veteran spymaster would launch into a long and rambling story about some classified derring-do. Just before getting to the punch line, and the secret, Allen would halt in mid-sentence, consult his watch, and, quickly rising, announce that—goodness!—he and Clover had stayed too long and must get home forthwith.[3]

Allen's older brother, John Foster, also a Wall Street attorney and Eisenhower's choice for secretary of state, had already joined the general Republican exodus to Spring Valley. (But John Foster, too, eventually put down Georgetown roots—moving to 3107 Dumbarton, a few blocks south of his brother's house.) The Alsops were quick to cultivate the Dulles brothers, as well as George Humphrey, Ike's secretary of the Treasury, plying them with dinner invitations and, in Humphrey's case, a flattering profile in *The Saturday Evening Post*. Whatever good effect this had, however, was probably undone by a dinner at the Grahams', where the Treasury secretary's wife lamented the financial sacrifice that her husband had made by leaving his Cleveland firm to take a government job. "Mrs. Humphrey," observed Phil dryly, "making that kind of remark down here in Washington is like belching in Shaker Heights." The target of Graham's barb "turned all the colors of a dying dolphin," Joe remembered, and "seemed to gasp for air during the rest of the dinner."[4]

Privately, Joe was circumspect about the new arrivals, writing to a friend with the prediction "Eisenhower's Washington will, I think, be unbearably boring, although rich." Stewart shared Joe's jaundiced view, describing the Republicans in a memo to the *Post* editor as "dull fellows who work late and go to bed early." ("Dull, Duller, Dulles" was how another critic described the new administration—a gibe directed at Ike's secretary of state, a stern and self-righteous figure whose attitude and values reflected his upbringing as the son of a Presbyterian minister. Stewart Alsop would later write a *Saturday Evening Post* article, "Why Are Republicans So Boring?" But he later thought better of the title. It was published as "Just What Is Modern Republicanism?") While politically more sympathetic to Stevenson, both Joe and Stewart considered Adlai too "genteel" to be president. (The elder Alsop later claimed that he had decided not to vote in the 1952 election.) The brothers' first column of 1953, which laid out the challenges facing Eisenhower—ending the war in Korea, countering "the Soviet rearmament program"—gave

Ike the benefit of the doubt and concluded on a hopeful note: "The signs are that Eisenhower will succeed." The column made no mention of McCarthy.[5]

But the honeymoon barely survived the inauguration. "The Alsops are writing about the administration in very impatient tones, as if Ike had personally let them down," Arthur Schlesinger Jr. wrote in late January. A lingering case of jaundice did little to improve Joe's mood. By February, the brothers were describing the Eisenhower cabinet as "eight millionaires and a plumber." (Secretary of Labor Martin Durkin had formerly been head of Chicago's plumbers' union.)[6] For Joe, an early and unpleasant encounter with Ike's national security adviser, Robert Cutler, had been a portent of the trouble to come. Believing—wrongly—that Cutler's status as a fellow Harvard and Porcellian Club alum made Bobbie susceptible to his old-school-tie approach, Alsop met with Cutler in his office early in the New Year. Cutler would describe the encounter in his memoirs:

> [Alsop] spoke of "confidants" in the press whom former Presidents had used to create a favorable background and of the benefit derived from that relationship. Such a person, trusted by a President, could provide an anonymous channel to help shape public opinion . . . Joe said in "our" case there could be a much closer "relation of confidence" . . . Naturally, he did not contemplate that I would reveal anything of a secret nature. But by periodically outlining background material I could provide enough orientation to make his column an authoritative, but of course anonymous, spokesman for the President. In this way, a helpful channel would be open to the President without the world being aware of the source of the background. While there was no mention of "exclusive," I sensed that Joe anticipated such a sensible arrangement.[7]

Cutler let Alsop know that he had no intention of becoming the reporter's "confidant." Instead, he urged Joe to go for news to the president's press secretary, James Hagerty, who already had a reputation among journalists for a lack of forthrightness. The next day, Alsop sent Cutler a letter. Joe's tone, this time, was more threatening than chummy: "I cannot refrain from writing to give you my opinion, as a friend and not as a newspaperman, that you are making a very great mistake," adding, pointedly, that a lot of the difficulties encountered by the previous administration's officials, like Dean Acheson, had been due to their "refusal to have anything to do with reporters." Cutler gave Joe's letter to Eisenhower, along with assurances that he had told Alsop he would not talk to him about government business. "That goes for me, too," Ike responded sharply. The brothers soon realized that whatever advantage their Roosevelt lineage had given them in Democratic administrations, it was an outright liability in newly Republican Washington. For the next eight years, his standing with the Eisenhower White House would be "lower than a snake's belly," Joe complained.[8]

Not surprisingly, the first issue on which the brothers cudgeled Ike and the Republicans concerned the country's defense. The Alsops had constantly berated President Truman for an unwillingness to spend enough on the Pentagon. Now the advent of a fearsomely destructive new weapon, coinciding with the start of Eisenhower's term, focused Joe and Stewart's anxieties anew.

In January 1953, the brothers had written a series of columns on the test of the world's first hydrogen bomb by the United States the previous fall. The explosion of the device code-named Mike had been equivalent to more than ten million tons of TNT and dug a crater some two miles wide out of the Pacific seabed, casting a pall of radioactive debris into the upper atmosphere. The Alsops had grimly described the likely result if hundreds or even thousands of such weapons were to be used in a future war, perhaps leaving the Earth habitable only by insects. Their Matter of Fact columns—the first to accurately describe the phenomenon of nuclear fallout—drew the attention of newspapers around the world (and also of the U.S. Congress, where the chairman of the powerful Joint Committee on Atomic Energy demanded that the FBI identify the Alsops' sources).[9]

The inspiration for their frightening story was not only the H-bomb but a discovery that the brothers did not share with their readers: Eisenhower had been so shaken by the briefing on Mike he had received shortly after the election that he was considering an unprecedented speech to the American people, laying out in full and frightening detail the possible consequences of an all-out nuclear war. Within the administration, the prospective speech was given the title "Operation Candor."[10]

"Candor" also dovetailed neatly with another cause the brothers had recently decided to promote in their column and magazine articles: defense against air attack. In a secret study carried out over the previous summer, dubbed Project Lincoln, U.S. scientists and strategists had concluded that it would be feasible to protect the country from a Soviet nuclear attack with a nationwide system of radar-guided jet interceptors, built at a cost of perhaps twenty billion dollars. In March 1953, Stewart lobbied for a Lincoln-style air defense network in a *Saturday Evening Post* piece titled "We Can Smash the Red A-Bombers." That spring, Joe devoted half a dozen columns to the subject.[11]

Both brothers were stunned at the hostile response their articles received. Detractors ranged from Luce's *Time* magazine—which dismissed Project Lincoln as a "Maginot Line of the Air"—to Secretary of the Air Force Thomas Finletter, who, along with the air force chief of staff, General Hoyt Vandenberg, hinted darkly that the Alsops' enthusiasm for air defense might even be Communist inspired.[12]

In fact, the brothers, knowingly or not, had stepped into a major controversy raging behind closed doors in Washington. At its center was one of their most trusted sources, the physicist Robert Oppenheimer, a vocal proponent of both Operation Candor and Project Lincoln. Arrayed on the other side of the debate were veterans of the so-called H-bomb lobby: the air force's Strategic Air Command; the physicist Edward Teller, the self-professed father of the hydrogen bomb; and the soon-to-be-confirmed chairman of the U.S. Atomic Energy Commission, the former New York investment banker Lewis Strauss. At issue was whether a major emphasis of America's nuclear strategy—and of the Pentagon's budget—should be defense, as proposed by Project Lincoln, or offense, relying on an expanding arsenal of hydrogen bombs and a phalanx of intercontinental-range bombers to carry them to targets in Russia, should war break out.[13]

Evidently hoping to bring Alsop to his side in the debate, Strauss invited Joe to his quarters in the Old Executive Office Building on May 20, 1953. Promoted to the temporary rank of rear admiral in the naval reserve during the war, Strauss used the title for the rest of his life and insisted that his last name be pronounced "Straws." An exceptionally vain and vindictive man, Strauss was notorious for using flattery or bribery to win over adversaries, but if that approach failed to work, he resorted to threats and blackmail.[14]

After sitting through a half hour of patronizing remarks by Strauss about the good work that he and his brother were doing in Washington, Joe interrupted to ask a question about the AEC's stand on the H-bomb and air defense. "Surely, Mr. Alsop, you can't expect me to talk about that sort of thing now, especially as you're a member of the press,"

Strauss answered. Responding heatedly that the AEC chairman had just wasted thirty minutes of his time, Alsop stormed out of Strauss's office. (Joe would have been even more upset had he known that Strauss was the source for an anonymous anti-Oppenheimer article appearing that month in *Fortune* magazine. The author of "The Hidden Struggle for the H-Bomb" was Charles Murphy, a reserve air force officer who had once worked for Secretary of the Air Force Finletter.) Strauss would later use the story of Alsop's visit as an example of Joe's legendary arrogance. Alsop, for his part, complained that Strauss had treated him as a "boob." "If there is one thing I dislike," Joe wrote to a friend, "it is being treated as a boob." Alsop's run-in with Strauss was, in fact, only the start of a long-simmering mutual enmity.[15]

TWO OTHER PROMINENT Washingtonians were also feeling left out in the cold at the dawn of the Eisenhower years, and likewise for partisan reasons.

After licking his wounds at his Pennsylvania farm, George Kennan had grown concerned that there was no word from the new administration summoning him back to Foggy Bottom. "I have as yet heard nothing from the Republicans about the capacity in which they expect to use me," Kennan wrote to Acheson in late December. As more time passed, Kennan's anxiety—and boredom—grew. In January 1953, he complained to another Truman administration veteran, Bedell Smith, who had meanwhile left the CIA to become undersecretary of state: "I am residing here in the country because I do not know what else to do." Kennan had recently given a speech before the Pennsylvania Bar Association that dismissed the notion of rolling back the Iron Curtain—a central tenet of John Foster Dulles's foreign policy—as both unrealistic and ill-advised. "Dulles Policy 'Dangerous,' Kennan Says," headlined a front-page *Washington Post* story the following morning.[16]

Not surprisingly, when the secretary of state finally met with Kennan in mid-March, it was to inform him that there was "no niche" for him in the Republican administration. Writing to Robert Oppenheimer, Kennan confided that Dulles had told him that it was unlikely he could be confirmed in any major diplomatic post—"tainted as I am with 'containment.'" "I know of no other example in recent years in which a career officer of my age and status has failed to be offered an appointment," sniffed Kennan in another letter, to Robert Cutler. After cleaning out his desk and bidding farewell to his secretary—there were, he noted, few familiar faces left, the rest "guarded, impassive, at best coldly polite, faintly menacing"—Kennan vacated his office at the State Department on July 29, 1953, for what he imagined would be the last time.[17]

Separated from the Foreign Service after twenty-seven years, Kennan was forced to consider a new career. He had already sounded Oppenheimer out about returning to the institute at Princeton. But there was also a wealth of other options. Frank Wisner offered Kennan a long-term job as a Russian analyst at the CIA. Phil Graham hoped Kennan would consider writing some articles for *The Washington Post.* Joe and Stewart Alsop dedicated a second valedictory Matter of Fact column to their friend—describing Kennan's retirement as a "real loss" to the country. After some hesitation, and more prodding by Wisner, Kennan finally accepted both Oppie's renewed invitation to Princeton and Frank's offer of a CIA consultancy. Four days after he had been shown the door by Dulles, Kennan signed a two-year personal service contract with the agency. Under Contract P-468–53, Kennan's identity would henceforth be shrouded in CIA memorandums under an anonymous rubric—"the expert."[18]

George and Annelise temporarily moved back to Washington that spring, renting a house on Cleveland Park's Quebec Street. The author of the long telegram and the "X article" got his revenge on Eisenhower's secretary of state shortly afterward, when Cutler invited Kennan to present the case for containment in a classified assessment of foreign policy alternatives known as the Solarium study. During his presentation at a briefing in the White House basement later that summer, Kennan observed, with satisfaction, his erstwhile nemesis in the audience: "At my feet, in the front row, silent and humble but outwardly respectful, sat Foster Dulles, and allowed himself to be thus instructed." Despite the Republicans' preelection talk of "liberation" and "rollback," there would be no dramatic deviation from containment and the status quo during Eisenhower's presidency.[19]

Like Kennan, Paul Nitze had reason to believe that he might occupy a top post in the new administration. As the major contributor to NSC 68, Nitze by rights should have been included in the Solarium study. But his name had reportedly been stricken from the roster personally by the president—who was intending to lower, not raise, defense spending. Foster Dulles informed Nitze that he, like Kennan, was too closely identified with the previous administration to remain as head of the Policy Planning Staff. Instead, Nitze was offered a job in the Pentagon. Within days of that announcement, however, a pro-McCarthy newspaper in the capital, the Washington *Times Herald*, attacked Eisenhower's appointment of another "Truman-Acheson lieutenant." Subsequently, Ike's defense secretary, Charles Wilson, asked Nitze to withdraw his name for the Pentagon post. Outraged, the Alsop brothers published a column on Nitze's ouster—"Another Surrender"—warning that "in making war on Nitze, the right-wing Republicans are making war on the President himself."[20]

"So ended my official government service for the duration of the Eisenhower administration," Nitze later wrote.[21]

Both Kennan and Nitze would spend an inordinate amount of their time out of government defending the decisions they had made while working for Truman. The *Times Herald* article intimated that Nitze had benefited financially from "pouring billions into Europe" through the Marshall Plan. In Kennan's case, it was the ghost of the bird Tawny Pipit that came back to haunt him.

In early January 1953, Kennan had been subpoenaed by McCarran's subcommittee to testify in its ongoing investigation of John Paton Davies. For Kennan, the Davies affair was a constant reminder of how the figurative boulder that he had loosed from the cliff, with the creation of OPC, continued to claim real victims as it careened out of control, leaving chaos and destruction in its wake. Kennan himself now seemed directly in its path. Ominously, the focus of the McCarran hearings had meanwhile shifted from Davies to the latter's defenders. Writing to his sister Jeanette, Kennan warned that "meanwhile the McCarran committee has stumbled over me in its pursuit of Davies, and there is plenty of trouble ahead for me there." Kennan was so shaken by the grilling he received at the hearing—and its implied threat of a perjury indictment—that upon returning home, he wrote to the FBI, requesting that it "make at once a complete and exhaustive re-check of my own loyalty and fitness for office" so that he might officially clear his name. Kennan also asked for a personal meeting with Eisenhower's attorney general, Herbert Brownell, to discuss the Davies case. Brownell flatly refused. That fall, when McCarthy added Davies's name to the list of Foreign Service officers he was accusing of treason, Kennan had finally had enough, sending Davies a telegram: "In view McCarthy statement have decided throw myself publicly into your case beginning with major statement to [*The New York*] *Times* Sunday accompanied nationwide publicity designed make national issue of case. Feel strongly this is right course but will refrain if you disapprove . . . You and Patricia can depend on our full support."[22]

Kennan also appealed to Averell Harriman, who, he hoped, might be willing to extend financial help to the cash-strapped Davies family. But when the Crocodile turned him down, Kennan informed Nitze, "For the moment I shall just carry on myself."[23]

Still under a dark cloud of suspicion, Davies had meanwhile been relieved of his post in Germany and sent to a relative diplomatic backwater, becoming chargé d'affaires of the U.S. embassy in Lima, Peru. ("My friends were falling away like autumn leaves," he later wrote.) On December 29, 1953, the State Department notified Davies that it was reopening its investigation of him and Tawny Pipit—the ninth one so far. Following drinks with Joe Alsop and dinner with the Nitzes, the accused wrote to his wife that he was considering new careers, including the possibility of running a restaurant: "I shall see what else flies about in these stray and gusty winds."[24]

AT THE CIA'S PLANS DIRECTORATE—which remained insulated, for now, against the political storms roiling the State Department— the Eisenhower administration was viewed as a welcome change. Indeed, Ike would prove even more receptive than Truman to covert operations—possibly because he had seen how disinformation and deceptions had saved lives in the European war. For Wisner, this favorable reversal of fortunes came none too soon. The covert crusade that he had launched against the Soviet Union seemed to be suddenly collapsing all around him.

Late in December 1952, Radio Warsaw described how Poland's security apparatus had uncovered a Western plot that would have unleashed a foreign puppet army, loyal only to the CIA. That secret army, known by its acronym, WIN—*Wolność i Niepodlegtość,* "Freedom and Independence"—had been one of Wisner's early inspirations and was part of Franklin Lindsay's plan for stay-behind forces in Europe. Over the past four years, the CIA had parachuted some five million dollars in gold bars, as well as radios and automatic weapons, to a handful of supposed guerrilla leaders, the vanguard of shock troop battalions intended to slow the Red Army's advance to the English Channel in the event of war. In fact, WIN had been a Soviet provocation from the outset. Confronted with evidence of their collusion with the CIA, Wisner's Poles had promptly sold out the operation to their Communist masters, who continued the charade in order to learn more about OPC's capabilities and its strategy for post-invasion partisan warfare.[25]

Beyond the human and material cost of the debacle—some of the CIA's bullion was reportedly used to fund Italy's Communist Party—the exposure of Wisner's phantom Polish army was a personal blow for Frank, who had assured Beetle Smith just six months earlier that his operation was "riding high." Thus, not only was the fiasco a setback on the agency's psychological warfare front, but Radio Warsaw's propaganda coup showed that the Soviets, too, had a mighty Wurlitzer and were even beating Wisner at his own game—in effect, winning the so-called war of the black heavens.[26]

Another of Wisner's ambitious plans—to convert a cadre of young, disaffected East Berlin lawyers into an armed anti-Communist underground—foundered when one of their number was captured and gave up his comrades' names under torture. A second operation in Germany, to recruit former SS officers as a stay-behind force, occasioned a scandal in that country when reporters learned that the Nazi veterans planned instead to kill leading Social Democrats if war broke out.[27]

By then, as well, Kennan's freedom committees in Europe had become so riven by ethnic factionalism that their CIA handlers joked the splinter groups were becoming sawdust. "At times the writer is stunned by the cross currents, or forces of discord, which pervade the [headquarters of the National Committee for a Free Albania]," wrote the agent in charge of NCFA's Rome office. In his "status report," the fed-up CIA operative summed up two years of constant frustration: "It seems that, no matter what the magnitude of any given problem (or activity), some pressure group, impelled by some unworthy purpose invariably arises." (One faction, vying for control, had even threatened to take its case to Congress and Joe McCarthy. This "potential embarrassment . . . would almost certainly reveal our direct operational support," the head of the CIA's Southern Europe desk warned Wisner.)[28]

Meanwhile, Project Fiend still showed no greater prospects for success, and the agency's own analysts had declared the enterprise both futile and counterproductive. (The only thing the parachute landings accomplished, observed Dick Helms wryly, was to prove that gravity was the same in Eastern Europe as at the training camp in Germany.) The CIA and the State Department had repeatedly imposed temporary bans on Wisner's leafleting campaign. Frank's foreign allies had likewise all but abandoned any idea of further cooperation with their American cousins in the Albanian enterprise. (The British "did not give evidence of particular enthusiasm," observed Wisner, with admirable understatement, after meeting with representatives from MI6.) And Fiend's inspiration and original patron, the exiled Albanian king Zog, was now facing criminal charges of tax evasion in two countries, the United States and Egypt.[29]

Wisner himself admitted that the "series of disasters" which had befallen his pet project "raises serious doubts as to the overall-advisability of the undertaking." Nonetheless, Frank soldiered on, the only visible evidence of increased strain being a new nervous habit. During CIA briefings on Fiend, Wisner would silently flex the muscles in his forearms, a distracting tic that prompted worried aides to recall Forrestal's final days. (Frustrated by the agency's failures, Wisner and Allen Dulles swung ever more wildly in an effort to connect with the enemy, as evidenced by the CIA's Project Artichoke—a scheme inspired by reports of brainwashing in Korea, which proposed using mind-altering drugs to "improve" the interrogation of suspected spies. The program resulted in at least one suicide before it was abandoned.)[30]

Yet, just as Fiend seemed moribund, it received a new lease on life from the Eisenhower administration. Following a secret briefing on the Albanian project in early April, C. D. Jackson—the former Time-Life publicist and speechwriter who had meanwhile replaced Gordon Gray on the Psychological Strategy Board—enthusiastically endorsed "a program of action leading up to a decisive result during the calendar year 1953." Jackson also urged that "serious consideration" be given to a "very substantial" expansion of Wisner's program for disseminating propaganda behind the Iron Curtain, including a whole new enterprise that surely would have excited Frank: a balloon-delivered "weekly newsletter of the air." By August 1953, the CIA's "Country Plan—Albania" observed that Fiend "continues today in substantially its original form."[31]

With the exception of the Wiz, however, OPC's veterans of Fiend had finally had enough. Among the first to go was one of the earliest advocates for sending the ethnic agent teams behind the Iron Curtain. Before taking up his new post as counselor at the U.S. embassy in Paris, Bob Joyce reflected upon four years of covert operations in a January 1953 swan song—and dazzling mix of metaphors—that he sent to the State Department and Allen Dulles. "The CIA," Joyce wrote, "has tried to take on too much in too little time . . . It is being realized that an intelligence bull is misplaced in the world china shop of 1953 and that a cat and later a soft-treading leopard is a more suitable and effective animal."[32]

Franklin Lindsay was likewise departing, having written his own nine-page valedictory, at Allen Dulles's request, even before Joyce. With Wisner's permission, Lindsay had set up a "murder board" to weed out questionable or hopeless operations in the CIA's Directorate of Plans. The board had terminated perhaps half of the schemes inherited from OPC, many of which, Lindsay noted, had "taken on a life of their own." In another exercise, Lindsay and Dick Bissell conducted an independent secret study, aimed at estimating the chances that any single covert op might be compromised. They concluded that the odds approached certainty as the operation grew to include more and more émigrés. (Britain's MI6 had come to the same conclusion a few years earlier.)[33] On a fall Saturday morning at Allen Dulles's house on Q Street, Lindsay had explained to the disbelieving head of covert operations why the agency's efforts to overthrow Communist regimes in the Balkans were doomed to failure from the start. "Frank, you can't say that," Dulles responded; he told Lindsay that if nothing else, Fiend had at least given the United States "good experience for the next war."[34]

Even that stalwart soldier Michael Burke had finally given notice. After a farewell luncheon at Wisner's house with Allen Dulles, the former football star left the CIA to join the big top. Through connections he had made while in the OSS, Burke was offered the job of general manager of Ringling Bros. and Barnum & Bailey Circus.[35]

Taking the place of these disillusioned veterans was a fresh batch of recruits who would carry the CIA's banner into other countries, other climes, and other crusades.

Tom Braden, former Jedburgh and Stewart Alsop's close friend and co-author, had joined the agency in 1950 as a patriotic response to the Korean War. Braden was made head of the CIA's International Organizations Division, which secretly funneled money to trade unions and freedom committees overseas. Another Jed veteran, and Frank Wisner's former law partner, was Tracy Barnes. Wisner put Barnes in charge of psychological and paramilitary warfare. Shortly after Korea, the ex-marine Phil Geyelin also joined Wisner in OPC's sweltering "tempos" on the Mall. (Geyelin lasted less than a year, however, before embarking on a journalism career that took him to *The Wall Street Journal* and eventually *The Washington Post*.) Another recruit, Desmond FitzGerald, was the former husband of Susan Mary's longtime friend and pen pal, Marietta Peabody. (The couple divorced in 1947. "This business of being loved really for your bosum [*sic*], but ostensibly for your high ideals, is on the whole deluding," Joe wrote to Susan Mary upon hearing the news.) FitzGerald's Harvard roommate, Paul Nitze, had introduced "Desie" to Frank Wisner. An army veteran with wartime experience in China and Burma, FitzGerald was put in charge of the Far East division of the Plans Directorate.[36]

Even bookish Richard Bissell, having meanwhile grown bored of pushing paper at the Ford Foundation, allowed himself to be lured into the clandestine world. Allen Dulles had approached Bissell about joining the agency at one of Stewart Alsop's dinner parties in the autumn of 1953. Bissell had turned Dulles down on that occasion but later changed his mind. (As Dickie noted prominently in his memoirs, espionage was in his blood. An ancestor—Sergeant Daniel Bissel—had spied for George Washington during the Revolution. Sent behind enemy lines, Bissel had enlisted in the British army, serving in the same regiment as Benedict Arnold, where Bissel continued to spy for the rebels.) By early 1954, Richard Bissell would be known at the agency as "Dulles's apprentice."[37]

What united Braden, Barnes, FitzGerald, and Bissell—Stewart Alsop's "Bold Easterners"—was a penchant for action. "We are not here to monitor communism," FitzGerald once famously told a friend, "we are here to destroy it."[38]

WHEREAS WISNER and the CIA's mighty Wurlitzer thus far showed mixed results overseas, they had found a willing audience at home.

As far back as 1946, the *New York Times* publisher, Arthur Hays Sulzberger, had assured General Hoyt Vandenberg, head of the Central Intelligence Group, "You and your representatives will always meet with the fullest cooperation from all of us here." Since then, the *Times's* connection with the CIA remained based, in part, on personal ties. Cy Sulzberger, Arthur's nephew and the paper's long-serving foreign affairs columnist, was a good friend of Frank Wisner's. Sulzberger instructed Wisner to mark any letters for him sent to the *Times* "personal" and "confidential," so that they would be forwarded unopened.[39]

Similarly, Frank considered *Fortune* magazine's Charles Murphy— author of the 1953 article attacking Robert Oppenheimer—an ally as well as a friend, and Murphy frequently turned to Wisner as a source for his reporting. ("Frank Wisner had me for lunch at the Vendome with one of his colleagues. On this occasion he spelled out in more detail what he wanted me to do, and I agreed to help him," reads an entry in Murphy's private diary.[40])

For their part, the Alsop brothers, like most reporters, were acutely sensitive to claims that they willingly did the agency's bidding. One of those attending a dinner party at Joe's house remembered the fracas that broke out after another guest accused the host of showing favoritism toward the CIA in his column. Joe had taken violent exception to the charge, and the two men were "soon rolling around on the floor, kicking and flailing."[41]

But Joe Alsop was, in fact, a willing co-conspirator with Wisner when it came to the mighty Wurlitzer—and on more than one occasion helped Frank give the CIA's slant on a news story. At Wisner's request, Joe had traveled to the Philippines in September 1953 to report on the upcoming presidential election, where the CIA-favored candidate, Ramon Magsaysay, was challenging the liberal incumbent, Elpidio Quirino. Allen Dulles had earlier informed Eisenhower and Wisner that "Magsaysay's position is considerably weaker than we had previously been led to believe." In columns that he filed from Manila, Joe's description of Quirino—"aged, crafty and insatiable"—contrasted with that of Magsaysay—"dark, vigorous, burning"—and left no doubt as to which one was, from Alsop's and the agency's perspective, the favored son. Wisner would later boast to confidants that he had "orchestrated" the press coverage of the Philippine elections and Magsaysay's victory.[42]

Joe also spread CIA disinformation, wittingly or not. Scotty Reston claimed that Joe's columns about the July 1954 "kidnapping" by Soviet agents of Dr. Otto John, the head of West German counterintelligence, was actually a story planted by Allen Dulles. In reality, Dr. John had defected to East Germany—something the CIA knew.[43]

Naturally, cooperation between the press and the CIA worked both ways. Many of Stewart Alsop's wartime OSS comrades, like Tom Braden, had continued or resumed clandestine lives with peacetime careers in the agency. When a Soviet publication, *The Literary Gazette,* invited Stewart to write an essay on peaceful coexistence for a forthcoming issue, Stew had turned to the CIA for assistance, writing to his friend Dick Bissell, "As I also told you, if I could get such expert help, perhaps in the form of a rough draft of the kind of contribution I might make . . . it would certainly be both in your interest and in mine that such help should be kept wholly confidential . . . I'd particularly like to have Frank Wisner's reaction also."[44]

Nor did the brothers hesitate to ask the spies they knew for other favors. Before embarking on a reporting trip to Germany in 1951, Joe had written to Nicolas Nabokov, a White Russian émigré who headed the CIA-funded Congress for Cultural Freedom in Paris, asking Nabokov to put him "in touch with the right people in the two intelligence nets reaching into the East Zone that you mentioned to me."[45]

Following the defection to the Soviet Union of the British spies Guy Burgess and Donald Maclean, some at the CIA concluded that the agency's relationship with the Georgetown set might be *too* close. The counterintelligence chief Jim Angleton's discovery of a reference in Burgess's journal to "an interesting binge the night before at Joe Alsop's house" had particularly raised eyebrows. In September 1953, the CIA's head of security, Sheffield Edwards, conducted an investigation into the Wisners' "close social" relationship with the Alsop brothers. Polly Wisner acknowledged in an interview with Edwards that she and her husband were "very active socially" but defiantly proclaimed that she "feels she has every right to continue these friendships so that as a result the Wisners do entertain and see the Alsop brothers quite frequently," wrote Edwards in his report. Frank likewise freely admitted to often getting telephone calls at the office from Joe Alsop. "These calls are innocuous but they are embarrassing to Mr. Wisner," Edwards noted.[46]

In the paranoid atmosphere created by Joe McCarthy, even Washington's spies feared being spied upon. Tom Braden told friends that he was convinced Jim Angleton had planted a microphone in the bedroom of his home and was sending Allen Dulles transcripts of intimate conversations Tom had with his wife, Joan. (Braden would quit the CIA in 1954, move to Southern California, and become publisher of a small-town newspaper, the *Oceanside Blade-Tribune*.) A rumor spread in Georgetown that J. Edgar Hoover had planted bureau agents as cooks and butlers in the more prominent families, in order to spy upon the residents. (One P Street matron reportedly complained that she lost the best cook she ever had when her FBI man was reassigned.) Nor were Hoover's gumshoes the only ones spying on the Georgetown set. Agents for Israel's intelligence service, the Mossad, based at the embassy on nearby Connecticut Avenue, were said to never pass up an invitation to cocktails at the Alsops', the Wisners', or the Grahams'.[47]

The Alsop brothers were understandably careful to conceal their reliance on the CIA as a news source and an ally—since it was a practice one of them had publicly condemned. In their 1946 book on the OSS, *Sub Rosa,* Stewart Alsop and Tom Braden wrote about the inevitable conflict of interest that existed between journalists and spies: "Our own view is that the conflict is inevitable, that in a democracy there must be perpetual war between the intelligence service and the press, and that on the whole this is a good thing." Since then, however, Stewart, like Joe, had come to rely on the agency's spooks for information in his reporting. Not surprisingly, the suspicion persisted among their fellow reporters that the Alsop brothers had, in this particular war, made a separate peace.[48]

CHAPTER TWELVE

"The Wild Pigs of Capitol Hill"

A FTER THE REPUBLICANS retook control of the Senate in the 1952 elections, Joe McCarthy's power had grown substantially. As chairman of the Government Operations Committee and its Subcommittee on Investigations, the Wisconsin senator and his loyal chief counsel, Roy Cohn, had been given subpoena authority in their purported campaign to "root out traitors" in the U.S. government. Together, the team of McCarthy and Cohn contributed to a climate of fear in Washington that would be difficult to imagine in the years to come.

Among the constant, gnawing frustrations of Frank Wisner's job at the CIA was being unable to protect his friends from McCarthy. One reason Bob Joyce had left the agency, and would soon leave the government, was a fear that he and his colleagues might be the senator's next targets. As Joyce warned in a letter to a friend, "If the present process continues . . . we will acquire a Foreign Service designed to serve a hagridden totalitarian state rather than a liberal and self-confident democracy."[1]

At the State Department, John Foster Dulles had done little to resist McCarthy's onslaught on the diplomatic corps. Instead, the secretary of state had given a chilling speech to State's employees about the need for "positive loyalty" shortly after being sworn in. And, in a transparent attempt at appeasement, Dulles had even put the State Department's loyalty investigations in the hands of a notorious McCarthy henchman, Scott McLeod. ("Dulles' people," observed Dean Acheson, "seem to me like Cossacks quartered in a grand city hall, burning the paneling to cook with.")[2]

By contrast, Allen Dulles, Wisner's boss, had, to his credit, fought a kind of rearguard action against McCarthy. Allen defended Cord Meyer, a decorated war hero and Tom Braden's deputy, against charges that Meyer was a security risk and refused to bow to McCarthy's demands that a senior agency analyst, William Bundy, appear before the senator's investigative subcommittee. In a Matter of Fact column, Joe Alsop celebrated Dulles's stand as McCarthy's "first total, unmitigated, unqualified defeat" and a potential "turning of the tide." (The CIA director himself was likely Joe's unidentified source.) Nonetheless, the victory was more apparent than real. By the summer of 1953, the CIA itself was under assault by McCarthy—who accused the agency of being a "sink-hole" of Communist subversion.[3]

Like many others who had voted for Eisenhower in 1952, Phil Graham believed that the wartime supreme commander of Allied forces in Europe would be the kind of president to take on McCarthy and end his reign of terror by tribunal. As Graham wrote to his friend Arthur Schlesinger Jr., he believed that "the surer way to control McCarthy lies in the election of Eisenhower." Phil had even drafted a simple declaration for the president to make right after his inauguration—"I feel impelled to make clear that the tactics of Senator McCarthy are in direct opposition to my fundamental beliefs"—but Ike ignored him. On election night, Phil told Murrey Marder, the *Post* journalist who had been covering McCarthy, that Marder would soon have to find a new subject to write about, since the Wisconsin senator was finished. Marder disagreed, predicting, correctly, that the *Post* would instead need to assign a second reporter to the McCarthy beat.[4]

While Phil and Joe Alsop agreed over the need to rid the nation of McCarthy, a stormy encounter between the two friends, during a dinner party at Alsop's house, had Joe wondering if there was not something deeper behind their quarrel. The dispute had been over witnesses who pleaded the Fifth Amendment in response to McCarthy's grilling. Joe believed that invoking the Fifth to avoid self-incrimination would inevitably be interpreted as an admission of guilt. Phil countered that it was simply the exercise of a constitutional right. This time, before Graham could walk out, Alsop ordered him to leave. When tempers had cooled, Joe sent his friend a note of apology: "As nearly as I can disentangle our discussion, you may perhaps have thought I was teasing you because you are now a successful man."[5]

Even though Graham and his newspaper were prospering financially, Phil remained haunted by his demons. His sudden and irrepressible enthusiasms masked a manic personality that could, just as quickly and easily, plunge into deep depression. Phil had endured such a bout the previous fall, around the time of Eisenhower's election. To provide a haven and a retreat for him on those occasions, the Grahams bought a farmhouse on three hundred acres in the Virginia horse country outside the village of Middleburg. It was to Glen Welby that Phil would repair when a black mood seized him, sometimes spending much of the day in bed, virtually incapacitated, his usual garrulousness gone and long sullen silences or jags of uncontrolled weeping in its place. In the grip of these fits, Phil would also lash out at his wife, ridiculing Katharine for gaining weight or crudely mocking her Jewish heritage. Kay's friends worried that Phil's tirades, fueled by alcohol, sometimes went beyond just verbal abuse.[6]

Phil Graham's psychological storms could last for weeks or even months. But when they ended, the sun returned, shining with renewed brilliance. By the spring of 1953, Phil's characteristic energy was back and found focus in a new cause. Graham himself had begun writing some of the *Post*'s anti-McCarthy editorials. While previously reluctant to attack the Wisconsin senator by name, Phil gave a speech before the National Council of Jewish Women in May that likened McCarthy to the "big lie" approach of the Nazi propaganda minister, Joseph Goebbels—who, Graham contended, was "an amateur" compared with McCarthy. A response was quick in coming. McCarthy began calling the *Post* the "Washington *Daily Worker*," a Communist Party newspaper.[7]

Because McCarthy and Cohn had declared the previous Democratic administrations guilty of "twenty years of treason," it was hardly surprising that their next targets would be holdovers from the Truman years. That March, the senator set his sights on Chip Bohlen, whom Eisenhower had nominated to replace Kennan as the next ambassador to Moscow. After he attacked Bohlen for what he claimed had been a "sellout" to the Russians in 1945 at Yalta—where Chip's job had been as a translator—and for a too-close association with Alger Hiss—who had previously worked for John Foster Dulles, not Bohlen—McCarthy's final charge was based on allegations made to the FBI by an anonymous State Department clerk who, claiming to have a "sixth sense for moral terpitude [*sic*]," had deduced that the ambassador designate was homosexual.[8]

OPC's notorious fixer might also have secretly testified against Bohlen. Carmel Offie had previously performed the same service for his boss at the Moscow embassy, Ambassador William Bullitt, who used Offie to spread word of a homosexual affair involving Bullitt's longtime rival, Undersecretary of State Sumner Welles. Facing a threatened Senate investigation of Welles, FDR had reluctantly accepted the latter's resignation in 1943. Bullitt apparently felt equal enmity toward Bohlen, who he believed had overshadowed him at the prewar embassy. Ironically, Chip had been the one to originally recommend that Wisner hire Offie, after Carmel had been dismissed from the Foreign Service. "He obviously did it at Bullitt's insistence," Chip's daughter Avis observed of Offie's betrayal of her father. "He really didn't feel comfortable doing this. But here he was turning on him." (Offie proved equally ungrateful and spiteful toward Wisner, who, after Carmel's CIA contract expired in 1952, found him a new job working for a prestigious K Street law firm. But when Frank ignored a dinner invitation from Bullitt, Offie showed up at Wisner's P Street home the next day and fired the cook that he had found for Polly.)[9]

The Alsops promptly came to Bohlen's defense in their column, reminding readers that "the existing security system is not foolproof." The dramatic high point of Bohlen's confirmation hearings occurred when the ranking senators from each party, Bob Taft and John Sparkman, agreed to read the raw FBI files on the nominee, later returning with the verdict that Bohlen was "a completely good security risk in every respect." On March 27, 1953, Chip was confirmed by the Senate in a 74–13 vote. The Alsop brothers were among the reporters who toasted Bohlen during a celebratory luncheon the following day at Washington's Metropolitan Club.[10]

The victory, however, was not without its casualties. Even before targeting Bohlen, McCarthy had launched an investigation into the Voice of America, which he accused of harboring Communist sympathizers. (A VOA producer who wished to play Rimsky-Korsakov's "Song of India" was reportedly told, "We're not supposed to use anything by Russians.") The VOA's first director had been Charlie Thayer, Bohlen's brother-in-law and Georgetown neighbor. McCarthy investigators discovered that Thayer had fathered a child out of wedlock with a Russian woman who had once been his secretary. Incredibly, Thayer was nonetheless branded with the same bête noire of that day as Bohlen—that he was gay. Rather than publicly contest the charges against him, and subject his sister and brother-in-law to another ordeal under the klieg lights, Charlie quit the Foreign Service that spring, while the Bohlen hearings were still in progress. Thayer's early retirement was perceived by some in Chip's family as a necessary sacrifice to ensure Bohlen's confirmation. Curiously, Chip himself had actively discouraged Joe Alsop from coming to Charlie's defense—"lest it provoke McCarthy to new slanders."[11]

An internal FBI document sheds light on Thayer's predicament and may also explain the mystery of Carmel Offie's repeated, catlike escape from the bureau's clutches. The March 4, 1950, memo advised J. Edgar Hoover of "an anonymous letter making certain allegations against Charles W. Thayer of the State Department, which letter indicates that one Carmel Offie, if contacted, could furnish further derogatory information concerning Thayer."[*][12]

The latest of McCarthy's victims, Thayer and his wife moved to the Spanish island of Mallorca, where he became an itinerant writer. (Thayer wryly joked that "under Stalin you went to Siberia, under Hitler to Dachau or Buchenwald but under McCarthy to Mallorca, which counts as progress.") On the way to his island exile, Charlie stopped off in Germany to warn his friend John Davies. Prophetically, Davies predicted that he "might well be [the] next casualty" of Washington's witch hunt. Another recent retiree from the Foreign Service—George Kennan—wrote to Thayer with words of encouragement and sympathy: "It will not be easy for either of us, for the government has been our home in a much more serious degree than we sometimes realized. But we will have to accustom ourselves to this situation and learn to live with it."[13]

Stewart Alsop invited Thayer to write about his ordeal in *The Saturday Evening Post*—"with the thought that you might possibly be angry enough to want to slam about a bit." Joe seconded Stew's suggestion in his own letter to Charlie: "I feel very confident that you can make a real ten-strike as a magazine reporter." But the proffered job of defense correspondent failed to pan out—Thayer blamed the lingering effects of McCarthy's VOA hearings—and the budding novelist's career stalled when his books failed to sell. A year into his exile, Thayer was toying with the idea of returning to Washington to personally confront McCar-

---

* Offie's furtive wheeling and dealing ultimately contributed to his undoing. Paul Nitze thought Carmel might be a Soviet agent; the FBI suspected Wisner's Monk of spying for Israel. Although Offie successfully eluded Hoover's gumshoes, his luck finally ran out on June 18, 1972, when the British European Airways jet on which he was a passenger crashed shortly after takeoff from London's Heathrow Airport. Investigators found no evidence of foul play.

thy and answer the charges against himself. In a book he meant as a guide for future diplomats, Thayer told the story of the senator who had asked his opinion of a congressional investigation involving another Foreign Service officer. Charlie answered that it reminded him of German game laws, which dictated the season, the time of day, and even the caliber of weapons that could be used in hunting—with one exception: wild pigs were fair game in any season, at any hour, with any weapon. "The foreign service," Thayer wrote, "are the wild pigs of Capitol Hill."[14]

FRANK WISNER PROFESSED to see in the Bohlen case a hopeful turning point. "There are some encouraging signs beginning to appear that people in Washington and elsewhere are gradually awakening to a realization of the deeper issues which are involved in this matter," he wrote to Kennan. Wisner was in a good position to know about Bohlen's ordeal, since Chip and Avis were Frank and Polly's houseguests during the painful confirmation hearings.[15]

Kennan was particularly sensitive to the damage that McCarthy's rampage and Eisenhower's seeming paralysis were causing American diplomacy. When Stalin died suddenly on March 5, 1953, Kennan and the CIA's other Russian experts had been alerted to the possibility of a succession crisis in the Kremlin. Less than two weeks later—after Dulles had given Kennan his walking papers—when the secretary of state asked the latter for a candid assessment of the situation, Kennan was nonplussed. As he told Annelise that evening, it was as if he had said to her, "You know, I'm divorcing you as of today, and you are to leave my bed and board at once. But I love the way you cook scrambled eggs, and I wonder if you'd mind fixing me a batch of them right now, before you go."[16]

Paul Nitze felt that the end of Stalin's rule presented a critical opportunity to bring about a thaw in the Cold War. Before leaving the Policy Planning Staff, Nitze had written a paper, "Exploitation of Stalin's Death," arguing that "a real possibility may arise in the next few months." Nitze proposed sending Bohlen to Moscow to initiate negotiations aimed at a permanent settlement for the divided Korean peninsula. But Chip was ensnared by that time in the ugly business of his confirmation hearings, and the U.S. embassy in Moscow had been without an ambassador since Kennan's expulsion the previous fall. As Bohlen would later wonder aloud, perhaps a precious opportunity had been missed.[17]

Nitze's proposal went nowhere, and weeks later Nitze himself would be out of the government and devoting his energies to a new venture—an educational foundation for the Foreign Service affiliated with Johns Hopkins University. Kennan, too, had meanwhile returned to the world of academe, working at Princeton's institute on a two-volume history of Russian-American relations. Nitze spent weekends at his Maryland farm, while Kennan joined his wife's family in Norway that summer for a long sailing vacation.

THE SUNDAY NIGHT SUPPERS and other social rituals continued uninterrupted at Georgetown, even as the political mood darkened in the nation's capital. Phil Graham jokingly dubbed the three-way telephone conversation that took place each morning between his wife, Polly Wisner, and Evangeline "Vangie" Bruce the "nine o'clock network"; he told Kay that he would like to buy time on it. On most Monday afternoons, Polly, Kay, and Vangie joined Avis Bohlen, Janet Barnes, Jane Joyce, and Annie Bissell at the Olive Street home of their friend, the former OSS clerk Julia Child, for a gathering known as the Cooking Class. The husbands and Joe Alsop would show up in the evening for a dinner based on one of the complicated creations in Child's cookbook, where the recipe for lobster thermidor ran to twenty-six pages. No criticism of the meal, or the chefs, was allowed. (Frank Wisner would be banished after complaining that a juniper-berry-stuffed chicken was too dry, and Chip Bohlen was exiled to the parlor when he insisted on smoking during the meal.)[18]

A more formal occasion was the thrice-yearly Dancing Class, established decades earlier by the doyenne of Kalorama's cave dwellers, Ma Williams, the mother of Kay's friend Oatsie Leiter. The class was held at the posh Sulgrave Club—a Beaux Arts mansion located on Massachusetts Avenue, just off Washington's Dupont Circle. Dancers were serenaded by the Meyer Davis Orchestra, which played from a suspended music gallery at one end of the mirrored ballroom, where "amusing crystal tassels" hung from the ceiling. Since admission to the Dancing Class was strictly controlled—and politicians were generally excluded—an invitation to join was widely perceived as a sign of having arrived in Washington society. (Truman's vice president, Alben Barkley, and Barkley's wife, Jane, took it as a personal snub when they were refused membership.) Both Alsop brothers belonged, as did the Wisners, who received an invitation shortly after moving to Georgetown. Even Phil Graham, notoriously disdainful of snobbery, eventually bowed to Kay's entreaties and joined the Dancing Class—largely because of the important connections it allowed him to make for his newspaper.[19]

In an effort to raise morale during the spring of 1954, at what seemed a particularly grim time in the capital, the Wisners, the Alsops, and the Grahams joined the Nitzes and the Bissells in organizing a new festive tradition. Dubbed the Bankruptcy Ball—the bill for alcohol, arriving "by the truckload," came to over four hundred dollars for each couple, Paul Nitze remembered—the party was held at the home of Tom and Joan Braden. Located on a dead-end road in rural Virginia, the Braden house featured a huge living room with a stone fireplace and a picture window overlooking the Potomac. Local legend held that the place had been a gambler's hideout during Prohibition. The hosts and more than 150 guests danced away the night to a hired orchestra. But the sun rose the next morning on a tableau of remorse. Phil Graham, drunk and belligerent, had feuded with Kay when they left the party, at one point getting out of the car and walking alongside as she drove home. The Bradens had also fought afterward, over Tom's objection to the social pressure, cost, and ostentation of being part of the Washington scene. "We really don't belong here," he told Joan. An account of the ball, appearing on *The Washington Post*'s society page, was included in the intelligence reports given to Allen Dulles and the CIA's deputy directors the next morning. (One CIA operative joked to another that if he ever wanted to know what Dulles was up to, all he had to do was read the gossip column in the *Post*.)[20]

Those attending the Bankruptcy Ball doubtless felt the need for some levity, given the corrosive atmosphere created by McCarthyism—where even the true and the just were afflicted with paranoia. When *The New York Times* reported, of a lecture by Isaiah Berlin at Mount Holyoke College, that the speaker "had been urging American universities to take up Marxist studies," a panicked Berlin quickly wrote to the *Times* editor, explaining that he had been misunderstood and had instead spoken "of the errors and distortions in which Marxism abounds." Berlin, teaching at Harvard, also wrote to the university provost with assurances that he was not a Communist and asked Kennan to pass the same message to the FBI's liaison at the State Department. (Berlin later confessed sheepishly to Kennan that he regretted his request: "I am indeed anti-communist,

but perhaps when heretics are being burnt right and left it is not the bravest thing in the world to declare one's loyalty to the burners, particularly
when one disapproves of the Inquisition.")[21]

Spending the summer in Wellfleet, on Cape Cod, Arthur Schlesinger Jr. wrote to Joe Alsop that "the local American Legion struck a
grim note in the otherwise frolicsome July 4 parade with a float consisting of a man hanging in effigy, marked 'The Only Good Communist.'
No reactions from the crowd." For years, Schlesinger's critics had accused
him of being a secret member of the American Communist Party.[22]

From Alsop's perspective, Schlesinger was in good company. For Joe,
too, had recently been branded a Communist—by the *Chicago Tribune*.
When Alsop threatened to sue Robert McCormick, the *Tribune*'s publisher, for libel, the paper printed a retraction. Under the heading "Beg
Your Pardon," it blamed the misunderstanding on "a linotyper's error."
"Mr. Alsop is not a Communist," the *Trib* acknowledged. "He has a long
record of opposition to communism and he has been a registered member of the Republican party all his adult life." Alsop sent McCormick a
brief note of thanks.[23]

But the damage done to other reputations was not so easily repaired.
On November 5, 1954, the long ordeal of John Paton Davies finally came
to an end, when Foster Dulles called Davies into his office and dismissed
him from the Foreign Service. Davies had been hurriedly summoned back
from Lima and was staying with the Nitzes. (Paul Nitze was stunned the
following day when his houseguest received a telephone call from Dulles,
the man who had just fired him, offering to write a character reference
for his victim, should Davies need it for a future job. Dulles subsequently
withdrew the offer when a partner in his old law firm pointed out that he
would face public criticism for the obvious contradiction.) That evening,
Davies wrote to his wife, Patricia, in Lima, "Keep your chin up, darling.
I know how hard this is for you. But we're beginning a new and, I trust,
happier and freer life. That is the side I look on."[24]

The former diplomat's friends were prompt to decry his firing. The
CBS newsman Eric Sevareid—one of those whom Davies had helped
out of the crippled airplane a dozen years earlier and led to safety through
the Burmese jungle—noted in his weekly late-night radio broadcast
that Davies had been dismissed for lacking "sufficient judgment, discretion, and reliability." "Sufficient . . . unto *what*?" the exasperated Sevareid asked. Joe Alsop's column the next morning was equally scathing,

incredulous that "the only senior American official who has ever officially advocated preventive war with the Soviet Union has been ruled a
'security risk.'"[25]

Davies's dismissal, coming after twenty-three years of service in the
diplomatic corps, also meant that he would be denied a government pen-
sion. With sky-high legal bills and a growing family, the self-described
"unfrocked diplomat" returned to Peru, where—after an abortive start
as a journalist and subsequent jobs in a soup factory and as an accountant
with a lumber-exporting firm—Davies started his own business, making
custom-designed furniture. His company, Estilo—"Style"—drew upon
pre-Columbian motifs for its inspiration and was soon winning international design awards. Although Paul Nitze was one of Davies's first
and biggest financial backers, Nitze never publicized his role.[26]

For the Alsops, the Davies verdict was the last straw. From their early
guarded optimism, the brothers had grown increasingly critical of Eisenhower. Joe blamed the men around Ike—particularly Bobbie Cutler,
Lewis Strauss, and C. D. Jackson—for turning Operation Candor into
a cynical, Madison Avenue–style public relations ploy. (At the White
House, Jackson had relabeled it "Operation Wheaties.") "From that
moment onwards," the brothers wrote, "there was a lie in the Eisenhower
administration's soul."[27] Instead of an honest accounting to the American people of the real dangers of a nuclear war, the new centerpiece of
"Candor-Wheaties" became the so-called Atoms for Peace program, a
Strauss-backed initiative to build nuclear reactors for power generation
in the Third World. The Alsops lamented the transformation of Candor into a "mush of platitudes" and joined with other critics in deriding
Atoms for Peace as "Watts for Hottentots."[28]

Similarly, the brothers' hopes that Project Lincoln might eventually
lead to a defense against Soviet bombers were dashed when John Foster Dulles announced, early in the year, that the administration's "New
Look" military policy would focus almost exclusively on the threat of
massive retaliation with nuclear weapons to deter Communist aggression. Under the slogan "more bang for the buck," the New Look's reliance on the bomb was also behind Eisenhower's plan to reduce defense
spending by almost five billion dollars in 1955 and shrink the size of the
army. Just as they had previously criticized Truman for cutting the Pentagon budget, the brothers blamed Ike for being "overly prudent" and
criticized the New Look as "really a decision to have almost no defense
at all." Thus, as Joe and Stewart were quick to point out, any threat to

respond to Soviet provocations with nuclear weapons was less credible once the enemy, too, had the same weapons in quantity. The test of the Russians' first hydrogen bomb six months earlier underscored their point.[29]

The brothers were equally dismissive of Eisenhower's foreign policy, describing the 1953 armistice in Korea as "a concealed surrender" and branding "a new Munich" the peace settlement for Indochina agreed upon at Geneva the following year. Not surprisingly, Joe and Stewart's standing with the president and others at the White House had sunk, correspondingly, to a new low.[30]

Shortly after Bohlen was confirmed, but before he headed for Moscow to replace Kennan, Joe attended a reception at the home of his friend the ambassador-to-be. Robert Cutler had also been invited to the party, in an apparent effort by Bohlen to bury the hatchet with his administration critics. Instead, Ike's national security adviser praised John Foster Dulles for remaining "steadfast" in support of Bohlen. (In reality, Dulles had all but demanded that Bohlen withdraw his name from consideration by the Senate. And, even after Bohlen had been confirmed, Dulles refused to be photographed alongside his new ambassador.) Alsop watched in fascination as Chip silently seethed while Cutler spoke, a muscle in Bohlen's cheek "bouncing detectably." Sensing violence about to erupt, Avis Bohlen preempted it with the same tactic that Kay Graham had used to put an end to the disastrous Georgetown anniversary party—by deliberately elbowing the tea service onto the floor. "Amid the broken tea cups and general need for tidying up, the conversation mercifully changed and the meeting ended amicably enough," Alsop remembered. Another telling incident occurred some months later, just before Christmas, as Cutler stopped by Alsop's house on a walk through Georgetown. When Joe offered to refill his guest's cup of holiday cheer, Cutler politely declined. "I suppose you think that, if you took another, you'd tell me some of those top secrets?" Joe asked snidely. "During the seven years after I went down the circular outer stairs, the Alsop column had no good word for me," Cutler would write in his memoirs. When Ike's national security adviser retired, in 1955, Joe penned an acidulous column about Cutler, titling it "Security vs. Democracy."[31]

While merely critical of the administration's defense and foreign policies, the Alsops were openly contemptuous of Eisenhower's failure to confront McCarthy. As Joe warned Foster Dulles in a letter, "You and the President will be the next victims if the administration continues to build up McCarthy by surrenders and seeming surrenders to him." In fact, when the brothers learned that the senator's next target would be the U.S. Army, they concluded that McCarthy was setting a trap for the president. Thus, as Joe Alsop knew, Eisenhower himself was vulnerable to the charge of being soft on Communism. Unable or unwilling to contact Ike directly, Joe decided that he would force the White House to act—by blackmailing the president to take on McCarthy, if necessary.[32]

Joe was personally conflicted about the issue, since he himself had engaged in a McCarthy-like attack against Ike some eight years earlier. In September 1946, Alsop wrote a Matter of Fact column arguing that war-weary Europeans had been attracted to Communism as a result of the misguided "pastoralization" policy being followed in U.S.-occupied Germany. The attempt to reduce the proud German people to glorified sharecroppers had inevitably alienated them, Alsop argued. In the column, Joe claimed the ill-conceived policy stemmed from the fact that "considerable numbers of American Communists and fellow travelers [had] infiltrated the military government"—a charge, ironically, that anticipated McCarthy's Red-baiting, guilt-by-association campaign. This Communist fifth column, Joe wrote, had subsequently facilitated the takeover of some major West German newspapers and labor unions. While Eisenhower was never explicitly named in Alsop's column, the future president had been, at that time, the military governor of the U.S.-occupied zone. Joe had even collected the names of alleged Communist Party members who had been on Ike's military staff during the occupation, but he refrained from publishing them.[33]

On February 19, 1954, Alsop met with Eisenhower's chief of staff, the former New Hampshire governor Sherman Adams. Joe told Adams that this time he had come not seeking information but offering it. Balancing a pad of paper on his knee, Alsop proceeded to read the list of names of suspected Communists who had served under Eisenhower's command in occupied Germany. Silent at first, Adams finally asked, "Why do you think I need to know this, Mr. Alsop?"

Joe described the subsequent scene in his memoirs:

I replied that with the army now under attack, my brother and I were convinced that McCarthy was planning to make the president his next victim and we had reason to believe that the president might be able to use the material I had just read.

I added that I had only one question. My brother and I, I said, were sure that all this material would be spread upon the record by McCarthy unless the White House stood up and fought for the U.S. Army. We were equally sure, I said, that if the White House stood and fought, McCarthy would be beaten and sink back into insignificance. We had considered, therefore, publishing the material in our column because if it were to appear so publicly and in such a straightforward way, it would not cause the kind of sensation that McCarthy was reaching for. We might still publish it, but before we did so we thought it best to seek some kind of signal from the White House as to whether the president was, indeed, going to fight.[34]

Adams—"looking still like a frost-bitten quince," Joe recalled—responded to this implicit blackmail threat with a firm "Alsop, we'll fight," according to the columnist. Leaving his notes behind with the shaken Adams, Joe assured Ike's chief of staff that he had forgotten their conversation already.

It was, accordingly, with some anticipation that Alsop attended the president's press conference two weeks later, on March 3, where a record number of reporters had gathered because of a rumor that Eisenhower was finally going on the offensive against the Wisconsin senator. But when Ike concluded the news conference without ever once mentioning McCarthy, a stunned silence ensued. The stillness in the room was finally broken by Joe Alsop's disbelieving whisper, uttered sotto voce: "Why, the yellow son of a bitch!"[35]

Although Eisenhower's press conference convinced Joe that his intercession with Sherman Adams had had little impact on the White House, in reality it gave impetus to a train of events already in motion—one that would culminate in McCarthy's downfall. Some weeks earlier, the president's chief of staff had urged the army's chief legal counsel to begin documenting in a chronology the various threats that McCarthy's aide Roy Cohn had made in an effort to get special favors for Cohn's friend Private David Schine. Subsequently tipped off by a White House source to the existence of the chronology—which, by that spring, ran to nearly forty pages—Alsop had quickly read the document in the army lawyer's office but was denied permission to quote from it in his column. Nonetheless, on March 11, 1954, a redacted version of the chronology was leaked to *The Washington Post,* also appearing that same day on the front page of *The New York Times.*[36]

Joe Alsop immediately noticed that the published version was only about a third the length of the document he had seen in the army counsel's office and was missing the most damaging portions—including the many expletives and obscenities that Cohn had used when threatening Secretary of the Army Robert Stevens. In a March 15 column, "The Tale Half Told," Joe and Stewart included a detailed description of the passages that had been "censored" by the army, citing them as evidence of the "unbounded arrogance, the inflated egotism, the Nazi-like sense of power that Cohn displayed." (The Alsop column also hinted at what was widely suspected but never talked about in Washington—namely, that Cohn and Schine were lovers and that the senator's aide exerted a "peculiar power" over McCarthy which allowed him to blackmail his boss.) A political cartoon appearing next to the Alsop column that day in the *Post,* titled "McCarthy's Last Stand," showed the Wisconsin senator defiantly standing amid the ruins of a shattered hobbyhorse, hefting one last brick.[37]

Until the publication of "The Tale Half Told," the Alsops' attacks on McCarthy had been part of the brothers' general disdain for what they regarded as the irrational security mania that had gripped the country in the wake of Joe-1, the invasion of South Korea, and subsequent revelations concerning so-called Russian atom-spies. "The nation," Joe later wrote, "had simply taken leave of all sense of proportion."[38]

But the latest Alsop column, with its implication regarding Cohn's homosexuality, was a risky move, for Joe especially. Their continued criticism of McCarthy had caused the brothers to lose subscribers every month since the election. And, since the Alsops split the cost of their column with the *Herald Tribune,* they were beginning to feel the financial pinch. Nonetheless, when an irate reader wrote to Joe, demanding that he retract his description of a recent McCarthy speech as "a farrago of inaccuracies," Alsop was defiantly unapologetic: "In short, what Senator McCarthy said on the Senate floor was a tissue of gross untruths, and when a man lies as flagrantly as this, I see no purpose in mincing words in describing what he has done."[39]

For the brothers, McCarthyism was also hitting closer to home. The firing of John Davies, the forced retirement of Charlie Thayer, and Chip Bohlen's own close call were all reminders that seemingly no one in public life was safe. The fact that McCarthy and Cohn had taken on the U.S. Army and were threatening the CIA with an investigation was likewise proof that even institutions once considered sacrosanct were being swept up in the Wisconsin senator's dragnet. (The agency's Sheffield Edwards had earlier advised the FBI "that Allen Dulles was becoming greatly concerned about attacks which Senator McCarthy might direct against the CIA . . . [Dulles] was particularly concerned about the possibility of McCarthy's questioning the [wartime] activities of Frank Wisner.") "Of course, except in the cases of the few personal friends who have been badly hurt in the State Department, we don't live it day to day as you do," a sympathetic Susan Mary wrote to Marietta from Paris, "but the poison blows across the Atlantic like some horrible prevailing wind."[40]

The poison was also indiscriminate in choosing its victims. That winter, Joe received a letter from William Taylor, who had been a fellow inmate at the Japanese internment camp in Hong Kong. Since that time, Taylor wrote, he had become a federal employee and was now under investigation by a loyalty board for "communist and subversive tactics in the prison camp at Stanley." Alsop promptly sent the board an affidavit, attesting that Taylor not only had been the leader of the Americans in the camp but was "a general all-around handyman" who had volunteered to chop wood for the community kitchen.[41]

As Joe hoped, publication of the detailed chronology documenting Cohn's threats "to ruin" the army had made the long-deferred showdown with McCarthy inevitable. Meanwhile, pressure on the Wisconsin senator was increasing from all sides. On March 9, McCarthy had been the focus of the journalist Edward R. Murrow's television program, *See It Now,* which used the popular new medium to expose McCarthy's Red-baiting. Joe Alsop sent Murrow a telegram two days later, offering "heartfelt congratulations on one of the great acts of political courage of our time." The army-McCarthy hearings were convened in April, with much of the thirty-eight days of testimony being watched on live television by a rapt national audience.[42]

By then, the war between the Alsops and McCarthy had become personal—on both sides. Roy Cohn threatened to sue Joe for the insinuations contained in the "Tale Half Told" column. In the midst of the hearings, on May 6, McCarthy implied that Joe Alsop had actually helped the army prepare the damning chronology. Summoned to a closed meeting of McCarthy's subcommittee the following day, Joe vehemently denied the charge in Cohn's presence.[43]

Although the army-McCarthy hearings did not officially conclude until mid-June 1954, the dramatic denouement occurred more than a week earlier—when Joseph Welch, the army's special counsel, responding to McCarthy's charge that Welch harbored a Communist on the staff of his Boston law firm, confronted McCarthy with a verbal challenge that rang through the packed gallery: "Have you no sense of decency, sir, at long last? *Have you left no sense of decency?*" The applause that followed Welch's outburst—by senators and spectators, with several reporters joining in—effectively marked the end of McCarthy's political career.[44]

Ironically, even with the demagogue defanged, Joe Alsop recognized that his own efforts to undo McCarthy had left behind a dangerous land mine, which the latter's supporters might yet use to their advantage. Two days before the hearings concluded, the chair of the Senate's Internal Security Subcommittee, William Jenner, a McCarthy ally, sent Alsop a letter, quoting at length from Joe's 1946 column on Communist infiltration of the U.S. occupation zone in Germany. He and his colleagues, Jenner wrote to Joe, were "extremely interested in obtaining the full facts" behind the column. Since the sole purpose of dredging up the issue in the first place had been to blackmail Ike into acting against McCarthy—action that was no longer necessary, given the outcome of the army-McCarthy hearings—Alsop recognized the danger inherent in Jenner's request: with the names that Joe had collected, McCarthy might yet rise again, phoenixlike, by focusing on a new target, President Eisenhower. Joe wrote back that "the time is gone by when any very useful purpose is served by digging up the follies of the dead and buried past"—pointedly reminding Jenner, in the process, that the 1946 column proved Joe and his brother "were anti-Communist then, long before a lot of other people who make a business of being anti-Communist now." Jenner decided not to press the issue, and less than six months later, when the Senate censured McCarthy, his spell on the country was broken.[45]

While Joe and Stewart would continue to warn against the danger of McCarthyism, the Wisconsin senator's moment in history had indeed passed. The Alsops deserved some credit for the outcome, having been among the first to take on McCarthy, well before Ed Murrow. When McCarthy died, on May 2, 1957, the two brothers silently, and guiltily, raised champagne glasses in a toast.[46]

CHAPTER THIRTEEN

"An Act of Very Great Folly"

WITH MCCARTHY VANQUISHED, Joe Alsop began looking for new dragons to slay. He took his first trip to Vietnam late in 1953, drawn to the country out of concern that the inconclusive armistice in Korea meant the front lines of the Cold War were shifting from Europe to Indochina, where French forces were fighting a determined insurgency led by the Communist Vietminh. On his way home, Alsop stopped in Paris, where he spent a preoccupied Christmas with the Joyces and the Pattens. "Joe was interesting about Indochina," Susan Mary wrote to Marietta of the visit. "Our people in Paris do not agree, but he considers a place called Dien Bien Phu crucially important. I had not heard the name of the fortress or seen it in the press—French or American. Joe says that it is considered impregnable by the chief French planners, but he has his doubts and for the first time I began to wonder if we are going to run the risk of becoming involved."[1]

American involvement in Vietnam was, in fact, exactly what Alsop hoped for. While in Paris, Joe had talked with both France's foreign minister, Georges Bidault, and Marc Jacquet, the lead French expert on Indochina. Bidault told Alsop that France's position in Vietnam could only be salvaged if the Eisenhower administration was willing to commit U.S. troops to fight alongside the French. As he had on numerous other occasions, Joe decided to use his column to influence rather than just inform. "I intend to force the hand of the American government in this matter as the only means of saving the situation," Alsop had promised Jacquet. On January 4, 1954, in a news article that ran on the front page of the *Herald Tribune* and was picked up by other papers the following day, Joe announced that a French request for military aid was likely imminent. The "loss of Indo-China," Alsop warned for the first time in print, "will be the prelude to the loss of Asia."[2] Reaction in the United States was so determinedly hostile to the idea of intervention, however, that Bidault and Jacquet immediately distanced themselves from the proposal, claiming that Joe had misinterpreted their remarks, since the conversation had been in French.[3]

A few weeks later, Joe and Stewart published a column titled "Where Is Dien Bien Phu?" The piece described the beleaguered French garrison at a strategic crossroads in northwestern Vietnam, near the Laotian border. Likening the "incredibly remote" jungle outpost to Yorktown—the site of the decisive battle of America's Revolutionary War—the Alsops urged that the United States send the aircraft parts and mechanics that the French government had requested, in order to maintain the vital flow of supplies to the encircled garrison. "The future of Asia may well be at stake in this remote and obscure engagement," Joe again warned.

As intended, the Alsop column focused attention at home and abroad on the escalating conflict in Southeast Asia. While in Vietnam, Joe had accompanied a platoon of Moroccan soldiers when the troops came under fire from an unseen enemy, suffering several casualties. "It's always like that," their French commander told Alsop afterward. "The enemy in front, on both sides and in the rear too. That's our war here."[4]

This time, Joe's pessimism was not only justified but prophetic: the French garrison at Dien Bien Phu surrendered a few months later, in early May 1954.

In addition to the setback in Indochina, a concatenation of ominous events that spring—including Soviet progress in the nuclear arms race, and signs that the NATO alliance might be on the verge of collapse—cast the elder Alsop into a pensive mood that was bleak even by his standards. And, while McCarthyism was on the wane, the domestic political scene did little to cheer Joe up. Returning from a trip to the Middle East in June, he wrote to Arthur Schlesinger Jr.: "Although it did not seem possible, my gorge has risen, my bile has increased, and bitterness has grown within me, since my return to this dreadful city. It is bad enough to prepare the destruction of the United States, but it really does seem outrageous that the Country should be disgraced first. I have no other news of politics except that Phil Graham feels almost exactly as I do, which I take as an interesting symptom."[5]

This grim forecast of the future prompted Joe to return to an idea he had first entertained after the shock of the Russian atomic bomb. In a confidential letter sent only to trusted friends—Nitze, Schlesinger, and Isaiah Berlin among them—Joe Alsop once again made the case for a surprise nuclear attack on Russia.[6]

Berlin showed the letter to some of his Oxford colleagues but did not respond directly to Alsop. Schlesinger, in his reply, confessed to Joe that he was "increasingly disturbed by the 'preventive showdown' view which you have sometimes considered in conversation and which is appearing more and more often in the column." Nitze's reaction was even more blunt—but, as ever, eminently logical. "It seems to me the arguments don't meet," he wrote to Alsop. When drafting his response to the Soviet bomb, Nitze himself had considered and dismissed the idea of preventive war. Nitze's NSC 68 had identified 1954 as the so-called year of maximum danger, when the Soviet Union's nuclear capability would be such that "the Kremlin might be tempted to strike swiftly and with stealth." But his rejection of preventive war was, once again, based more on practicality than morality: the United States lacked the number of bombs, and bombers, to ensure that a first strike would indeed be a knockout blow.[*7]

Over that summer and into the fall, Joe continued to explore the notion of preventive war at private dinner meetings of the Harvard Corporation with his fellow overseers: Nitze, Schlesinger, and the former air force secretary Thomas Finletter. By late September, however, Alsop had become alarmed that word of his interest in the topic was spreading beyond his close circle of friends. For a third—and final—time, he quietly shelved the idea.[8]

IN CONTRAST TO Joe's habitual angst, American fear of a Soviet invasion of Western Europe had seemingly receded in the wake of the "spirit of Geneva"—the name that Eisenhower gave to his July 1955 meeting with the new Soviet leader, Nikita Khrushchev. Their face-to-face encounter at the summit had included discussion of German unification and so-called confidence-building measures aimed at reducing the

---

* In a 1989 visit to the Soviet Union in the company of other academics, the author asked Georgi Arbatov, longtime director of the U.S.S.R.'s Institute for U.S. and Canadian Studies, if he knew whether Stalin had ever expressed fear of an American surprise nuclear attack. Arbatov said that Stalin worried such an attack might come in 1954.

danger of a surprise nuclear attack. As a result, the focus of the Alsops' column shifted to other, emerging concerns.[9]

First on their list was the resumption of a guerrilla insurgency in Vietnam with the pending departure of the French. Joe saw Communist China as the only power likely to gain from a Southeast Asian war in the long term. While in Vietnam again at the end of 1954, he had inadvertently strayed into enemy-occupied territory and been briefly detained by the Vietminh. Put on a boat headed back to Saigon, Joe made small talk with his fellow passengers, who, not understanding his English, nonetheless marveled at the American's hairy legs. At one stop, when he was about to be rearrested by an overzealous policeman, Alsop's newfound friends interceded to rescue him. "So I was saved, quite literally, by the hair on my knees, and my adventure with the Viet Minh ended."[10]

Another worry, for both brothers, was the Soviets' apparent progress on a new offensive weapons technology: the intercontinental ballistic missile, or ICBM.

As the Alsops had noted previously in their column, U.S. defense experts believed that the Soviet Union would have "a decided superiority" in the ocean-spanning, nuclear-tipped missiles, possibly as early as 1960. The world that the brothers had forecast a decade earlier in their *Saturday Evening Post* article seemed suddenly imminent. With Joe away in Asia, it fell to Stewart to sound the alarm about the developing missile race between the United States and the U.S.S.R. In a March 9, 1955, column, Stew pointed out that the Russians' advanced rocket technology would also give them a potentially decisive advantage in another strategic arena: the exploration of outer space. When reporting the recent boast of a Soviet scientist that the U.S.S.R. intended to launch an Earth-orbiting satellite in the near future, Stewart added a prediction of his own: "The Russians would gain enormous prestige in the scientific world, as well as registering a huge propaganda victory, if they were the first to break the bonds of gravity."[11]

Like the fate of a dishonored prophet, Stewart's clairvoyance gave rise to a farcical turn of events. In hopes of creating some anxiety in the Eisenhower administration over the prospect of being second into space, Stew concocted two imaginary headlines in a subsequent column to drive his point home: "Soviets Claim Successful Launching of Earth Satellite" and "U.S. Radar Confirms Existence of Soviet Satellite."

In the days that followed, Stewart's warning that the Soviets might be about to beat the United States in a space race would be the topic of animated discussions at half a dozen Georgetown dinner parties attended by high-ranking administration officials. Coincidentally, Stew's column with the fake headlines was included in a classified NSC report on the nascent U.S. satellite program that wound up on Eisenhower's desk shortly thereafter. Believing—wrongly—that the Alsop column was based on the top secret NSC report, a furious Ike ordered an immediate investigation to find the leaker. [12]

While the FBI inquiry once again came to naught, its fallout spoiled the welcome-home party that Stewart, Frank, Polly, and the Bissells were planning at the Wisners' Maryland farm for Joe Alsop, who was returning from his monthlong trip to Asia. Summoned to Allen Dulles's office, Wisner and Bissell were told that under the circumstances it would be unwise for the CIA's top officials—including the head of the agency's ultrasecret overhead reconnaissance program—to be seen in the company of the Alsops. Because of security restrictions, however, the reason for the party's cancellation could not be divulged to either Stewart or the would-be guest of honor. As a result, Joe recalled, "Stew, Tish and I spent a somewhat bewildered and solitary weekend together." [13]

SINCE MCCARTHY'S ECLIPSE, the Alsop column had regained some of its earlier popularity, boasting twenty-five million readers in nearly two hundred newspapers by late 1955. The previous spring, the brothers had once again been on the pages of *Pravda,* which denounced them as "preachers of atomic war." But perhaps the surest indication that the Alsops were back was the clue that appeared in *The New York Times's* crossword puzzle for a six-letter word, 32 across: "Writers Joseph and Stewart." And a cartoon in *The New Yorker* paid a backhanded homage to the pundits. Sitting at a bar, one tipsy patron challenges another: "Just who do you think *you* are, Mac? One of the Alsops, or something?" [14]

Still, their notoriety did little to lift the brothers' spirits. "I feel very bored and depressed here," Joe wrote to Isaiah Berlin in mid-July 1956, shortly after returning from a trip to Egypt. "About ten people I am fond of and my own house and garden are all that attach me to Washington [and] the American people will re-elect Eisenhower if they have to send him to a taxidermist first." A letter that Joe sent to Chip Bohlen in Moscow sounded the same theme: "There is something rancid about the city now, and I am always longing to get away from it." [15]

For his part, Stewart was growing increasingly resentful of his junior standing in the partnership with his brother. During the decade that the two had collaborated on Matter of Fact, the younger Alsop had always been on the bottom end of the 55–45 split of what their column earned. (When Stewart questioned whether Joe really needed to belong to two expensive Washington, D.C., clubs, the latter helpfully suggested that Stew cancel his own club membership and use Joe's guest privileges.) Since the *Herald Tribune*'s censorship of the columns on McCarthy, the brothers had also been chafing to end their relationship with the conservative newspaper. But Stewart's "family situation" made that financially impossible, as Joe explained to the head of the syndicate that published their column: "The Tribune represents a certainty of sort. With a wife and four children, it's hard to make a break with certainty."[16]

After the birth of their third son, in 1952, Stew and Tish had begun looking to expand beyond the cramped quarters of 3139 Dumbarton. (The new baby, Stewart junior, slept nights in a bassinet in the bathtub.) The couple located a rambling, eight-bedroom manse with an acre-sized lot on Springland Lane in nearby Cleveland Park—the place, it was said, "where Georgetowners go when they begin to reproduce." Although Stew complained that the house had no "theme," its spacious dining room proved ideal for entertaining.[17]

Stewart had also grown tired of the "foot-stomping row" that Joe initiated, seemingly weekly, in some dispute over a journalistic point of pride. The storms usually began with the older brother's patronizing "Oh, *Stoooo* . . ." Family weekends at Polecat Park were, the younger brother wrote, increasingly "a necessary refuge."[18]

As well, the strain of writing a four-days-a-week political column was itself taking a toll. Stewart compared the task to climbing a ladder without end—where the climber could only see a rung or two ahead. He found the challenge especially daunting during the Eisenhower years, since "there were many long placid stretches when hardly anything at all was going on. There was therefore hardly anything at all to write about, and thus no rungs on the ladder to grasp." A monthlong trip in June 1955 to Europe and the U.S.S.R.—where Stewart scored an exclusive interview with the Soviet premier, Nikita Khrushchev—had been a welcome break from the routine.[19]

But even the prospect of covering the upcoming presidential election failed to stir much excitement in the Alsops. A rematch between Eisenhower and Stevenson promised to be anticlimactic, given Ike's unquestioned popularity and Adlai's continued dithering. While Joe still regarded Stevenson as "a great man," he had concluded that the Democratic favorite was simply unsuited for politics. Stewart, who had voted for Adlai in 1952, likewise realized, after watching the reaction of listeners to a Stevenson campaign speech, that the candidate failed the all-important "cookout test": he was not someone you would invite to a barbecue. When Stevenson received his party's nomination a second time, Joe wrote that it was "like a man marrying his mistress, long after flames of passion have flickered and gone out, because he is used to her and badly needs someone to darn his socks."[20]

Nevertheless, at Stewart's prodding, the brothers embarked on another of their unscientific polling exercises in the American hinterland. Sensitive to the effect that Joe's gentlemen's-quarterly wardrobe had had on past respondents, Stewart asked that his brother don more conventional attire this time and at least *try* to blend in with the natives. The result, Joe grumbled, made him look "like a senior sewer inspector." When *Time* magazine suggested that the brothers' canvassing was actually restricted to promoting Stevenson at Georgetown cocktail parties, Joe indignantly fired back a letter to its publisher, Luce: "It is both grossly offensive and frivolously false to imply, as *Time* did, that our opinions are as it were the by products of our social life."[21]

As predicted, Eisenhower breezed to reelection. The brothers despaired that the status quo would endure, with no significant changes in either the city's politics or its personalities. "About Washington I can give you no good news whatever," Joe wrote to Susan Mary. "We have no policy. Indeed we hardly have any policy-makers. In my private opinion, nothing but God or dynamite can separate Foster Dulles from the State Department, and God has tried and failed. So I am inclined to think that the two years ahead . . . are going to be very nearly catastrophic." Joe announced in the same letter that he had decided to move to Paris, before embarking on a tour of Russia.

As he packed for the trip, Joe began saying his good-byes. He sent a note to Walter Lippmann, lamenting that he would miss their competitive banter about the Washington scene "while I'm wandering about the world hunting political crises, rather in the manner of an aging fireman hunting fires." Joe had originally hoped to rent his house on Dumbarton Avenue to a recently reelected senator, Jack Kennedy, and his young bride, Jacqueline. But Jackie's plans for remodeling had spooked the help, and at the last minute Alsop felt compelled to wire the couple, vacationing in Jamaica, that the deal was off: "José and Maria greatly like you and willing stay on but greatly upset all the same by what they obstinately regard as basic change in manner of life." Instead, the house went to Joe's longtime friend and fellow Georgetown denizen Oatsie Leiter, along with three single-spaced pages of suggested dinner party menus. (Joe warned that José habitually made the black bean soup too thick and failed to put enough brandy on the deep-dish apple pie *mont blanc.*) The disappointed Kennedys instead leased a town house on P Street, only a block down from the Wisners.[22]

Joe was particularly looking forward to visiting the Kremlin and entering the belly of the beast that he and his brother had been writing about for more than a decade. But the Soviet authorities were ominously unwelcoming. Chip Bohlen, writing from the U.S. embassy in Moscow, reminded Joe that *Pravda* had most recently described the journalistic pair as "the atom-happy brothers and as troubadours of the most aggressive circles of the USA." After several months of waiting, Stewart had obtained a visa to visit Russia only by appealing directly to Khrushchev. Hoping to avoid a similar delay, Joe addressed his appeal to Moscow's ambassador to Washington, Georgi Zarubin: "You and your government may well hold that my political viewpoint is unsound, to put it rather mildly. But I think I can claim to be a reporter above all." (To make doubly sure of the visa, Joe invited Zarubin and a gaggle of diplomats from the Soviet embassy to his house for drinks, where they promptly emptied the entire liquor cabinet. Watching from outside, FBI agents dutifully advised Hoover of the Russians' visit to the Alsop residence.)[23]

Joe's visa arrived in due course. He left for Paris in late December 1956 and spent a relaxing Christmas with Bill and Susan Mary Patten before moving into long-term quarters at the Hôtel St. James et d'Albany, near the city center. He was, Alsop acknowledged, "nearly intoxicated" by the chance to become a "world-wandering columnist"—while Stewart, on the other hand, "was patently glad to be rid of me."[24]

A COUPLE OF WEEKS LATER, in mid-January 1957, Joe arrived in Moscow during the depths of the Russian winter and checked into the city's Hotel National. *Pravda* greeted the news of his visit with a terse announcement. "Assassins, robbers, pirates and rapists of all flags and nations have been put to shame by the Alsops," the paper pointedly reminded Muscovites. That fraught welcome aside, Joe, this time as much a tourist as a reporter, admitted to being pleasantly surprised to discover that the outer walls of the Kremlin were not, as he had supposed, battleship gray "but a rich, dark strawberry red." Similarly, the fortress's imposing guard towers were "pure, medieval fantasy," with nearby St. Basil's Cathedral's "happy riots of colored and gilded domes," and the Kremlin palace itself "a bright butter-yellow picked out with white."[25]

Before leaving Georgetown, Alsop had submitted a request to Ambassador Zarubin that he, like Stewart, be given an opportunity to interview Nikita Khrushchev. While he waited for a response, Joe documented a chilly three-week detour through Siberia in *Matter of Fact*. Although the local cuisine did not fail to disappoint—in one town he encountered "an undefinable substance known as 'cutlette' . . . a nameless piece of meat, heavily fried in what appeared to be leftover machine oil"—Alsop was impressed by the friendliness of the people he met, with the notable exception of "my little, pasty-faced interpreter," whom he suspected of working for the KGB.

Back in Moscow, permission for the interview finally granted, Joe talked to Khrushchev for more than an hour at the city's Communist Party headquarters. The Soviet premier, "short, round, and well scrubbed . . . seemed for all the world like a jovial clown at a party," exuding "an almost playful energy," Alsop wrote. But the Russian leader also impressed Alsop as "an immensely bold gambler." Although Joe was put off by Khrushchev's boilerplate defense of Soviet foreign policy, their interview appeared on the front pages of the *Herald Tribune* and *The Washington Post*. In the days that followed, Alsop filed more than a dozen dispatches with his syndicate describing life in the U.S.S.R. "Your columns have been very successful indeed. George Kennan called up to congratulate you on them," cabled Stewart, adding that Chip Bohlen had been similarly "complimentary—though with the inevitable faint note of condescension."[26]

Alsop elected to stay in the Soviet capital for another fateful week, dining with diplomats at the American embassy and meeting new friends. Subsequently, Joe would describe his ensnarement by the KGB in a homosexual so-called honey trap with a detailed, nine-page mea culpa that eventually reached the highest levels of the U.S. government. What would become known there as Alsop's secret "confession" began, "This is the history of an act of very great folly, unpleasant in itself but not without interest for the light its [*sic*] casts upon our adversaries in the struggle for the world."[27]

According to Joe's account, on Sunday evening, February 17, during a dinner at Moscow's Grand Hotel with embassy officials, Alsop and his entourage were approached by a reporter for TASS, the Soviet news service, and the reporter's companion, a younger man whom Joe described as "an athletic blonde, pleasant-faced, pleasant-mannered fellow." Joining the party, the reporter's friend—who introduced himself as Boris Nikolaievich—conversed with Joe in French about literature and the arts. After the meal, Boris suggested that Joe come to his room at the Grand Hotel the following day. On Monday afternoon, immediately after the two had had sex, "the door burst open and a militia officer, the English-speaking vice director of the hotel and another unidentified man entered the room," wrote Alsop in his account. A knock at the door announced the arrival of two more men, whom Joe described with journalistic detail:

> The senior, who was plainly in command, was a man in his late forties, or early fifties, moderately corpulent, of middle height with a most striking face—the skin olive-brown, the nose rather hooked, the eyes, deep-set in the rather plump cheeks, flashing sharply through the steel rimmed spectacles unless he was considering his next move, when he would half close his eyes and drum on the table. He wore a muskrat *chapka* and smoked the imitation-Turkish Russian cigarettes almost continuously. The junior must have been in his early thirties, was perhaps 5'10", fattish, blondish, with a long nose and a loose-looking, rather [unreadable] pig face. Except that his suit was rather lighter blue than most Russians wear, there was nothing else to distinguish him.

In an episode worthy of a Graham Greene spy novel, the two KGB agents, promising Alsop "absolute secrecy," confronted him with photographic evidence of what they ominously called "the 'act,'" which they extracted from a scarlet dossier. Seeing its immediate effect on Joe, they warranted "that I must help them a little if they were going to help me," Alsop wrote. After three hours of "a most curious political discussion, about Soviet-American relations, in which, in effect I was asked to explain my viewpoint at great length," Alsop broke away, pleading a dinner engagement at the American embassy. The KGB men and Joe agreed to meet the following evening at Moscow's Praga restaurant.

In the detailed account he wrote after the incident, Joe claimed that he initially considered suicide the only possible response to the KGB's blackmail threat. But he ultimately resolved instead "to play the game out a bit further, to see where it would lead." Meeting the KGB men on Tuesday night at the restaurant—"a luxurious and enormous dinner had been prepared in a private room"—Joe, refusing to eat or drink anything, was offered a solution to his "problem." The senior Soviet agent said "he would like to be able to talk to me from time to time in 'order to get advice that would assist the cause of peace.'" After "pretending to agree to his proposal in principle," Joe was offered a special private tour of the Hermitage Museum when he traveled on to Leningrad, as previously planned, the next day.

On Wednesday morning, Joe wrote out a brief account of the incident and placed it in an envelope bearing Chip Bohlen's name. He gave the communiqué to a "reliable" intermediary with instructions that it should be opened in two weeks if Bohlen had not heard from Alsop in the interim. Taking the overnight train to Leningrad, Joe, finding the Hermitage closed the next morning, spent an anxious few hours "writing a fake column which would, I hoped, prevent my new friends from questioning me too closely about who had told me what concerning the current campaign here against dissident students and intellectuals." Checking into a hotel, Alsop was handed a telegram from Bohlen, instructing him to return to Moscow as soon as possible. (Chip, upon seeing the mysterious letter from Alsop, had opened it at once.) At the Leningrad airport, Joe was told that there was no room for him on the plane, so he returned to his hotel to find the two KGB blackmailers waiting. When Alsop explained that the urgent telegram from the ambassador concerned his ailing mother, the pair relented and allowed him to fly back to Moscow.

Alsop concluded his apologia: "The rest of the story is known to the American Minister, whose kindness and wise advice have placed me in his debt to an extent that can never be repaid."

In fact, before putting Joe on the next flight out of Moscow, to Paris via Prague, Bohlen had notified Frank Wisner of the incident at the Grand Hotel. It was Wisner who had recommended that Alsop write his lengthy account, in order to draw the sting from the KGB's blackmail threat.[28] Wisner subsequently passed Bohlen's communiqué—along with Alsop's account—to Allen Dulles, who, in late March 1957, forwarded both to his brother at the State Department as well as to the FBI director, Hoover, requesting that the latter keep the documents locked in a special file at the bureau.[29] In his memo and in two subsequent, top secret, eyes only letters to Hoover, Allen Dulles acknowledged that he harbored doubts about where the truth lay in Alsop's account—doubts shared by Hoover—and thus intended "to follow Subject's movement abroad to the extent feasible." The CIA subsequently interviewed Joe about the Moscow incident, advising him not to make any public statements and never to travel to the U.S.S.R. or its satellites again. Sheffield Edwards, the agency's head of security, helpfully sent Hoover the CIA's own list of names of "former associates of [Alsop]" who were suspected of being homosexual, along with the news that Joe "has said that he was subject to blackmail 20 odd years ago."*[30]

The FBI director lost no time before he, too, sent Alsop's "confession" on to Eisenhower's attorney general, Herbert Brownell, along with a request that the president also be informed. To make doubly sure that Ike knew about Alsop's affair, Hoover personally briefed Sherman Adams on the Moscow incident two weeks later.[31]

Word of Joe Alsop's sexual transgression doubtless occasioned joy among some in the Eisenhower White House, where the columnist was blamed for creating almost single-handedly the popular image of the president as a doddering, golf-playing fool. (In letters to friends, Joe had described the U.S. government under Ike as like "a dead whale on a beach.") Nonetheless, Eisenhower, after being apprised of the incident, instructed Allen Dulles to keep Alsop's self-incriminating account "securely." The CIA director put the document in his personal safe and refused others access to it without the president's express permission.[32]

Not all those around Eisenhower were so high-minded, however.

More than a year after the Moscow incident, in October 1958, an internal FBI memo recorded that "considerable personal discussion regarding this incident took place" between Hoover, Allen Dulles, Sherman Adams, and William Rogers, who had meanwhile replaced Brownell as attorney general. Evidently, the hope was that where the KGB had failed to coerce Alsop, the White House might yet succeed—or at least frighten Joe sufficiently that he would moderate his criticism of Eisenhower. If so, that hope proved futile, for Alsop continued to attack the administration on a variety of fronts. (The bureau, for its part, had already abandoned

---

* The agency might have later covered for Joe, however. According to the author David Wise, Yuri Nosenko, a Soviet defector, told a CIA operative in 1962 that the KGB "had the goods on [Alsop] . . . and if he gets out of line they can blackmail him if he doesn't write what they want." Wise claimed that the agency cut the incriminating portion of the interview out of the tape—since Alsop "was a good friend of . . . President [Kennedy's]."

any expectation that Joe would reform or come clean voluntarily about what had happened in Moscow. "It is believed that in the interim he has shed any remorse which he may have had and, if anything, he very likely has developed a confidence to face any interrogations or interviews in the United States," an aide wrote to Hoover.)[33]

But efforts to blackmail Joe Alsop did not end there. And reminders of the Moscow incident would periodically return to haunt the reporter for the rest of his life.

BACK IN WASHINGTON, Phil Graham was struggling with his own demons, even as his company prospered. With McCarthy gone, Graham had returned to a cause that was both near to home and close to his heart—the racial integration of the District of Columbia. Having grown up in the Deep South, he had firsthand experience of the Jim Crow laws that mandated the segregation of public facilities. Indeed, some reporters at *The Washington Post* complained that Phil not only favored news which emphasized racial harmony but also either spiked or buried in the paper stories showing evidence to the contrary. In 1949, when the federal government's desegregation of a District swimming pool prompted a race riot involving several hundred people, Graham had insisted that it be labeled an "incident" and given only a few paragraphs in the local news section of the *Post*. Phil defended the decision as part of his strategy to force the integration of all the city's pools, which was ultimately successful. In 1954, Graham had been a moving force in creating the Federal City Council, which he described in a *Post* editorial as an organization "to mobilize community opinion and to interest private capital in rebuilding some of the areas to be cleared of existing slums."[34]

But Phil Graham's sympathy for the poor and downtrodden was actually rooted in a larger concern—namely, that it would be impossible for America to win the Cold War if the country were seen as indifferent to the plight of its minorities.[35]

Since the war in Korea, both Phil and his paper had become demonstrably more hawkish. Shortly after that conflict began, Graham had approved a proposal from the Library of Congress for a why-we-fight book by the *Post*'s political cartoonist, to be titled *Herblock Looks at Communism*. A few days before the French surrender at Dien Bien Phu, Phil, siding with Joe Alsop, had written a *Post* editorial that declaimed, "We cannot stand aside and abandon the French." Early in 1956, when

Nikita Khrushchev announced the doctrine of peaceful coexistence with the West—prompting the *Post* editor Bob Estabrook to wonder rhetorically in a draft editorial whether the time had not come to call an end to the Cold War—Graham had fired off a two-page memo protesting the "rush" to embrace Khrushchev's idea. "'Co-existence,' I submit, is every ounce a bastard idea, sired by Wish, and mothered by Cold-war weariness," Phil wrote. Estabrook spiked the editorial.[36]

Foreign news coverage had never been *The Washington Post*'s strong suit. During the twin crises in Hungary and Suez, in 1956, Graham's newspaper did not have a single full-time reporter stationed in Europe or the Middle East; *The New York Times,* by contrast, had more than a dozen foreign correspondents in the field. (The *Post*'s diplomatic correspondent, Ferdinand Kuhn, once joked that his paper would "cover any international conference there is, as long as it is in the first taxi zone." The liberal commentator I. F. Stone claimed that it was always exciting to read the *Post* because you never knew where in the paper you'd find a page-one story.)[37]

Yet, for both the domestic scene and overseas, Phil was determined—as he told a *Post* reporter—that his newspaper would become a vehicle for positive change.[38]

By mid-decade, the *Post* was unquestionably in a strong position to carry out Graham's wishes. Early in 1954, Phil had scored a coup with the purchase of the *Post*'s morning rival, the Washington *Times Herald.* A few months later, he launched the start of a media empire by acquiring a controlling interest in WTOP, a D.C. television and radio station. In 1955, the *Post* finally surpassed its longtime competition, Washington's *Evening Star,* in both circulation and revenue. It was no real surprise, therefore, when the April 16, 1956, issue of *Time* magazine featured a grinning Phil Graham on its cover, describing the *Post* publisher in a feature article as "an energetic charmer whose facial furrows and tall, angular frame (6 ft. 1 in., 160 lbs.) give him a Lincolnesque look." While the magazine gave Graham credit for taking on McCarthy, it went on to note that the *Post*'s managing editor, Al Friendly, was a member of the liberal Americans for Democratic Action. *Time* also claimed that the paper's reporters—and, by implication, its publisher—"have political reflexes that respond favorably to Democrats, unfavorably to Republicans."[39]

In mid-1956, shortly after he decided that the *Post* would not endorse Eisenhower for reelection, Graham received a sarcastic note on White

House stationery from Ike's press secretary, James Hagerty, in response to a recent Herblock drawing: "It's sure nice to know that the Post cartoons are in such impartial, non-political hands. But maybe it's good to get it on the record." When the editor of *Editor and Publisher* magazine similarly complained that the *Post*'s society page only covered Democratic fund-raisers, Phil good-naturedly suggested that the Republicans have more parties.[40]

Phil Graham was, in fact, sensitive to the claim that his paper had a liberal bias. A continuing sore point was his periodical battles with Herblock over the latter's depiction of Richard Nixon. Since 1948, the cartoonist, who loathed Nixon, had drawn the subject with a heavy five o'clock shadow, giving the future senator and president-in-waiting the same thuggish appearance as another notorious Herblock target: Joe McCarthy. Phil and others on the paper had repeatedly remonstrated with the *Post* cartoonist, but to little avail. A truce of sorts held for a while, following Nixon's Checkers speech in the fall of 1952, when the vice presidential candidate had narrowly escaped being booted from the Republican ticket for allegedly misusing campaign funds. In an editorial that Graham wrote, the *Post* praised Nixon for "eloquently and movingly" responding to the charges against him. But Herblock resumed the feud shortly thereafter, with a cartoon portraying Nixon as a rat escaping the sewer. To avoid future trouble, Phil had finally taken the drastic step just before the election of banishing Herblock cartoons from the editorial page.*[41]

Whereas *Time*'s cover story on Phil Graham had described his life as "like a quick montage of the American dream," the reality was not nearly so rosy. The couple's friends noticed that Phil continued to tease and otherwise mistreat his wife. Katharine Graham would later write that she was "totally dependent" on her husband in those days. (A psychiatrist would perhaps find that dependency unremarkable, since Kay had received little affection from her parents growing up. Katharine's father, Eugene Meyer, was a remote presence, often away on business; her mother, Agnes, was a tall, opinionated beauty in her youth—Kay

---

* The *Post*'s managing editor, Russ Wiggins, once left a razor on Herblock's desk along with a poem that read, "Join the good and kind and true / The faithful, just and brave / And grasp this razor in your hand / And give that man a shave." The cartoonist wrote back, "He's shaved with new Gillettes 'n' Shicks 'n' / Still he is the same old Nix'n." When he finally drew a clean-shaven Nixon, in 1969, Herblock remembered, Kay Graham "let out a whoop and threw her arms around me. All hands seemed to be relieved and happy."

called her "the Valkyrie"—who, as she aged, became ever more vindictive and dismissive of her daughter. Agnes had her secretary inform Kay in a letter that neither parent would attend her graduation from the University of Chicago. The secretary misspelled Katharine's name.)[42]

Ironically, Phil was no less dependent on Kay, who had to lie about the reason for her husband's frequent absences from the paper—claiming that it was hepatitis, and not depression, that had laid Phil low. In order to bolster Kay's spirits, Polly Wisner organized a surprise party and dance at the P Street house for her friend's thirty-ninth birthday that June.

Another likely cause of Phil Graham's depression was his disappointment with Washington's political scene. Like the Alsops, Phil had finally become impatient with Adlai Stevenson's coy indecision. ("Harassed father tardily reports birth of nine pounds thirteen ounces boy Saturday evening. Name undetermined but have decided against Adlai," wrote Phil in a telegram announcing the birth of another son.) Graham had meanwhile shifted his allegiances to another prominent Democratic politician who seemingly shared his concerns with the country's racial problems—the Texan Lyndon Johnson, who had become the Senate majority leader in 1955. As he had earlier with Eisenhower, Phil assumed the role of Johnson's unofficial patron and promoter, helping to draft the senator's speeches and using *Post* editorials to champion the compromise civil rights legislation that Johnson helped get through Congress in the summer of 1957.[43]

In early September that year, just days before Ike signed Johnson's bill into law, Phil Graham found himself on the front lines of an even more contentious civil rights battle, when nine African-American students attempted to enroll at segregated Central High School in Little Rock, Arkansas. The state's governor, Orval Faubus, had called out the Arkansas National Guard to prevent the school's integration. Becoming personally involved in the crisis, Phil spent hours on the telephone to the two main antagonists, Faubus and Roy Wilkins, executive secretary of the National Association for the Advancement of Colored People, trying to mediate the standoff. At one point, Graham even proposed to Eisenhower that he and the president accompany the first black child through the throngs of jeering demonstrators and into the classroom—each man holding one of the student's hands. Ike ignored Phil's suggestion. Instead, when Eisenhower, publicly counseling "patience," left Washington for a golf vacation in the midst of the crisis, Graham telephoned congratulations to the editor of *The Arkansas Gazette* for publishing, on that newspaper's front page, a photograph of the president lining up a shot on the green. The caption read "A Study in Patience."[44]

Although the students were finally allowed to go to class after Eisenhower sent in the 101st Airborne Division and federalized the state's National Guard, the crisis left Graham—already drained because of his work on the Civil Rights Act with Johnson—even more physically and emotionally exhausted. In a letter to Joe Alsop that he marked "personal," Phil described his role at Little Rock as that of a "sort of self-appointed, quite unwanted, needler of White House and Justice Department," and the outcome as "frustrating and sad beyond even your belief."[45]

By the end of October, shortly after Phil arranged a luncheon meeting between *Post* reporters and the CIA's Allen Dulles—who wished, he said, "to discuss press coverage of the forthcoming Philippine election"—Graham was back in seclusion at Glen Welby, alternately fishing from a rowboat on the little pond that he and Kay called Lake Katharine or lying prostrate in bed with the curtains drawn. Once more, Kay covered for her husband's sudden and unexplained absence with a concocted story. The man whom *Time* magazine had called "the pillar of the *Post*" would not return to full-time work at the newspaper for another six months.[46]

CHAPTER FOURTEEN

"A Chap of Great Promise"

A T THE CIA, the ignominious collapse of WIN and the continued setbacks for Project Fiend had finally rattled even Frank Wisner, making the formerly trigger-happy deputy director of Plans suddenly gun-shy. In mid-June 1953, when more than a quarter-million disaffected workers and students rioted in Communist East Berlin, Wisner over-ruled the local chief of station's recommendation that the CIA arm the protesters. Frank ordered that the agency "do nothing at this time to incite East Germans to further action." The Berlin uprising was brutally suppressed.[1]

Wisner's uncharacteristic caution stemmed from the fact that he and his colleagues were no longer convinced that the Eisenhower adminis-tration would support their efforts to "roll back" the Iron Curtain, and hence to assist the agency, if there were to be an indigenous revolt in the Soviet satellites. In a memo to the CIA director, Allen Dulles, Frank noted that the only guidance he had thus far received on that score was to "keep the pot simmering—but to avoid boiling it over."[2]

Fiend had meanwhile been "completely reoriented," Wisner informed Dulles, to focus on sending "high level agents" into Albania, where they would attempt to contact and recruit specific individuals in Hoxha's gov-ernment and the military. If recruitment proved impossible, then the same teams would carry out so-called coup de main missions: assas-sinations. One such operation was already planned to kill an Albanian traitor—a villager who had initially welcomed the CIA team into his house but then sent for the security forces, which had set fire to the dwelling and not allowed those inside to withdraw or surrender. "Identity (5)'s great sacrifice of his house for the cause of the People's Democracy was widely broadcast" by Radio Tirana, an agency briefer noted, adding that "the mission if successfully carried out should have great propaganda value."[3]

Yet Fiend remained beset by the same flaws that had always dogged the project. There was still "an appalling lack of security" on the part of the Albanians familiar with Fiend's operational plans, one of their handlers reported to Director Dulles. Another case officer complained that a pixie team leader who remained in Albania "seems bent on conducting an international correspondence club." After two members of Fiend team FRIDAY, which had been tasked with poisoning Radio Tirana's celebrated hero, thought better of their assignment, another pair of "enthusiastic" volunteers was found who planned to kill the target "outright."[4]

The mystery surrounding the fate of the Fiend team that had included the suddenly left-handed wireless operator was finally resolved in late December 1953, when Radio Tirana triumphantly announced that the Sigurimi had captured eight CIA-trained "diversionists." Their trial, held the following April, resulted in the conviction of all eight. Six were shot by firing squad a few days later, one was hanged, and the sole survivor was sentenced to ten years in prison. In the wake of this latest disaster, Allen Dulles ordered future Fiend operations "put on ice" pending consultations with the British. A subsequent, eleven-page CIA damage assessment of what had gone wrong criticized the recruitment and training of the pixies, as well as Fiend's communication and security protocols.[5]

By that summer, even the Great White Case Officer was fed up with Fiend. A CIA Project Status Report in late June 1955 noted that the Albanian operation was "to be terminated" at the end of the fiscal year. The headquarters of the National Committee for a Free Albania in Rome was also to be promptly—and unceremoniously—shut down. Most of the agency's fractious pixies were allowed to immigrate to the United States or given financial support by the agency to settle in other countries. "We have begun destroying 'dead agent' files," a CIA case officer subsequently informed Allen Dulles.[6]

EVEN BEFORE ALLEN DULLES pulled the plug on Fiend, Frank Wisner had already moved on to other ventures.

While the CIA's paramilitary operations in Eastern Europe careened from disaster to disaster, with mounting casualties, a recent agency initiative had scored a virtually bloodless triumph in another region of the world. Dubbed, fittingly enough, Project Success, the CIA's gambit in Central America, approved by Dulles and orchestrated by Wisner, had just overthrown the democratically elected government of Guatemala.

The spread of Communism beyond Europe had long been one of the Dulles brothers' greatest fears. A particular bugaboo was the possibility that the Kremlin would establish a foothold in "America's backyard"—the Western Hemisphere. As early as August 1950, CIA analysts had warned about "the rapid growth of Communist activity in Guatemala," the banana-rich republic where Allen and his wife, Clover, had spent numerous vacations and where United Fruit was a major client of John Foster's law firm.[7]

The agency's lingering concern turned to acute apprehension two years later, when the Guatemalan president, Jacobo Árbenz Guzmán, began expropriating private holdings as part of a promised land reform. "We are on notice of the fact that in the upper echelons of the Administration it is expected that something will be done—of a drastic nature—to remove the menace of communist-controlled Guatemala," Frank Wisner informed the State Department. Wisner considered it "the $64 question." Frank and Tracy Barnes reportedly proposed simply assassinating Árbenz and members of his government but later rejected the idea—apparently fearful of making a martyr of the president.[8] A subsequent CIA plot, Project Fortune, sought to use the leader of neighboring Nicaragua, Anastasio Somoza, as a proxy to overthrow Árbenz. But Fortune foundered when Somoza's indiscriminate bragging to confederates blew the operation's cover. On November 16, 1953, Frank Wisner had approved the general outline of Project Success, which planned to use a locally raised guerrilla army of four hundred anti-Communist insurgents to oust Árbenz. Three weeks later, Allen Dulles allocated three million dollars to Success.[9]

The recent conclusion of another audacious CIA project, code-named Ajax, in overthrowing the elected government of Iran, doubtless played a role in emboldening Wisner and the agency to take on Guatemala. The mastermind of Ajax had been the Alsops' distant relative Kermit "Kim" Roosevelt Jr., Teddy Roosevelt's grandson, whom Joe had introduced to Wild Bill Donovan and to espionage back in 1941 and who had subsequently become head of the Plans Directorate's Middle East division. Kim Roosevelt had also participated in the Albanian operation, as acting head of Programs and Planning for Fiend. In August 1953, with the cooperation of Britain's MI6, Roosevelt helped engineer a coup that unseated the Iranian prime minister, Mohammad Mosaddegh, who had incurred the displeasure of the West by nationalizing the Anglo-Iranian oil company. At one point in Ajax, when it appeared that the coup had failed, Wisner ordered the operation called off—only to discover that the juggernaut could not be stopped. It was a lesson about persistence that he and his colleagues at the agency took to heart.[10]

Like Ajax, Success was a near thing. The Guatemalan coup was the culmination of a cascade of implausible events worthy of a comic opera. During a CIA-organized air raid on Árbenz's presidential palace, when the attackers ran low on bombs, they discovered that half-filled Coke bottles made the same whistling sound. The raid "did extraordinarily little damage to the city but dealt a powerful psychological blow," Dick Bissell remembered. Although the positive outcome was arguably due more to blind luck and Árbenz's missteps than to Bissell's cunning or Wisner's planning, the hapless Guatemalan president was compelled to flee, seeking asylum in the Mexican embassy on June 27, 1954. Three days later, an ebullient Frank Wisner called off the operation, announcing that the time had come "for the surgeons to step back and the nurses to take over the patient"—the "surgeons" in this case being the CIA's operatives, and the "nurses" the State Department's diplomats. Success had "surpassed even our greatest expectations," Wisner gleefully cabled the agency chief of station in Guatemala City. As it had in Iran, the CIA promptly installed its own man, Castillo Armas, to replace the deposed Guatemalan president.[11]

Wisner exploited his triumph with a follow-on project, code-named History, which he colorfully described as a "snatch job on documents while the melon was freshly burst open." The agents Frank sent to Guatemala City hoped to find a treasure trove of papers showing Árbenz to have been a cat's-paw of the Soviet Union. Instead, they were disappointed to discover that government buildings "had already been plundered systematically by the army and unsystematically by looters and street urchins." (One spy was reportedly able to purchase secret police files from a small boy.) Wisner nonetheless persevered, picking the best of the 150,000 documents his team had gathered for an illustrated booklet that was later distributed to the National Security Council and sympathetic senators.[12]

Like the CIA's Italian job in 1948, Success and Ajax became the model for future agency planners and case officers to emulate. Fiend's failures were already becoming a distant memory. The overthrow of hostile foreign governments was a task for which the CIA seemed "peculiarly qualified," Wisner now boasted. The Guatemalan project had also been the first introduction of Tracy Barnes and Dick Bissell to large-scale covert ops. The fact that both coups had been cliff-hangers—at one point, Allen Dulles was forced to go to a wealthy Democratic Party donor to get the money to pay for bombing the Guatemalan army—and had been achieved with relatively little bloodshed on a shoestring budget was a lesson not lost on those in the Plans Directorate.[13]

Finally, Ajax and the Guatemala coup also marked a long-deferred triumph of the mighty Wurlitzer—but at home, not overseas. As a classified history of the Iranian operation later noted, the CIA was able to "plant" one of the agency's own studies in the pages of *Newsweek*—via the State Department and "using the normal channel of desk officer to journalist." In the case of Project Success, most reporters had likewise accepted uncritically "the official view of the Communist nature of the Guatemalan regime"—including the producers of an NBC television documentary, aired shortly before the coup, titled *Red Rule in Guatemala*.[14]

Just two months after overthrowing Árbenz, Wisner was already on the lookout for the next trouble spot. To that end, he notified the head of the Plans Directorate's Western Hemisphere division that he had recently "spoken to Mr. Joseph Alsop briefly with a view to interesting him in doing some columns high-lighting the developing crisis in Honduras and focusing U.S. public attention on it."[15]

At the same time, Wisner was highly critical of Phil Graham for some recent stories in *The Washington Post*. In December 1954, he wrote to Phil to register "quite frankly my concern about the muck-raking quality of the then-current reports of a particular correspondent on the subject of Thailand . . . A better balanced job of reporting would have been more in order, in my opinion, in this time of exceptional danger and stress in Southeast Asia."[16]

While Wisner and the CIA eagerly facilitated the reporting of friendly journalists like the Alsops, in another standard practice they happily threw sand in the face of hostile reporters and the agency's critics in the press. After the *New York Times* reporter Sydney Gruson filed several reports from Guatemala suggesting that Árbenz was less a Marxist than a patriot and a nationalist, Gruson was taken off his beat by the *Times* and subsequently expelled from the country—at the instigation of Wisner and Allen Dulles. (Stewart Alsop had earlier confided to Frank that Gruson was a "fellow wanderer," or Communist sympathizer.) Wisner "was absolutely paranoid about the Grusons," the *Times*'s Harrison Salisbury later wrote. Frank evidently suspected Gruson and his wife, Flora Lewis—another journalist and a frequent contributor to *The New York Times Magazine*—of being Soviet agents.[17]

Yet at what should have been the height of his influence in the agency, Wisner found himself under renewed attack. Warned by a CIA whistleblower that the agency was "in a rotten state," Eisenhower had recently ordered a review of Allen Dulles's entire enterprise. Ike put at its head the retired air force general Jimmy Doolittle, hero of the daring daylight bomber raid on Tokyo just months after Pearl Harbor. On October 19, 1954, Doolittle and members of his panel—including the donor who had bankrolled the Guatemalan air raids—briefed the president at the White House on their findings. While critical of the agency at all levels, including the ill-fated ethnic agent teams—"information we have obtained by this method of acquisition has been negligible and the cost in effort, dollars and human lives prohibitive"—the report was particularly hard on what it called Wisner's "Cold War Shop" and on the CIA's Plans Directorate, which, Doolittle wrote, was "filled with people having little or no training for their jobs." The problems, Doolittle told Eisenhower, started at the very top: Allen Dulles was "highly emotional" and overprotective of those below him. "Frank Wisner is a chap of great promise but not a good organizer." ("Someone in room said Bissell was not a good man," scribbled the White House note taker.) The Doolittle Report urged "a complete reorganization" of the Plans Directorate. While Dulles withheld the bad news from Wisner, word of the report's findings undoubtedly filtered down to Frank.[18]

Allen Dulles was also being constantly reminded of Wisner's troubles by J. Edgar Hoover. The FBI continued to send the CIA periodic reports from unnamed sources, alleging that Frank was being blackmailed by the KGB for his wartime actions in Romania. Although the CIA security chief, Sheffield Edwards, dutifully ran down each of the FBI leads—Edwards wrote back to Hoover that his own investigation "indicates that the allegations are based on fabrication, distortion of fact and Rumanian refugee gossip"—the bureau's campaign to discredit Wisner remained relentless, determined, and wearing.[19]

In addition to having enemies without, Wisner felt he was being undermined as well from within. His paranoia was justified, in this case. As the CIA's liaison to the FBI, the counterintelligence chief, Jim Angleton, had become, in effect, the bureau's mole within the agency. "He has been very cooperative and, as you know, has volunteered considerable information which has been of assistance to us," an aide informed Hoover regarding Angleton. Nor was the gaunt, almost sepulchral counterspy Frank's only nemesis at the agency. Informed of the existence of OPC's stay-behind army in Europe shortly after he joined the CIA full-time, Dulles's apprentice, Dick Bissell, dismissed Wisner and Lindsay's pet project as "the most unpromising activity I've never [sic] seen in government, almost ridiculous." Bissell likewise judged the broadcasts of Radio Free Europe to the captive peoples of the Soviet bloc "of marginal value to the U.S. government." Briefed on the activities and objectives of AMCOMLIB, Bissell sarcastically wrote to Wisner that he was "delighted to see that the committee is going to be in favor of good and against evil."[20]

Bissell was, to be sure, from a different mold and mind-set from Wisner: an academic turned intelligence officer rather than a grizzled man of action. (Although he would later describe himself to John Kennedy as "a man-eating shark," the frenetic, ever-moving Bissell was nicknamed the Mad Stork by his CIA colleagues. But all agreed that Dickie was good at details. It was a point of pride with Bissell that of the millions of tons of matériel he had sent to Europe under the Marshall Plan, he had lost track of only one thing—a single shipment of South African coal.)[21]

The differences between Wisner and Bissell became evident in late November 1954, when Allen Dulles put the latter in charge of a hush-hush CIA project that arose out of a classified study of new defense technologies from a panel headed by the president of MIT, James Killian. A major focus of the Killian Report had been on technologies that could be used to guard against the danger of surprise attack. So sensitive was the annex dealing with intelligence that it was withheld even from the National Security Council and briefed only to Eisenhower and a handful of others. (That did not prevent the Alsops from dedicating a column to the top secret Killian Report a few months later. What the attorney general's office called a "serious leak" triggered another investigation of the brothers' sources by Hoover's FBI. As before, the leaker was not found.)[22]

Killian's Intelligence Panel, chaired by the Polaroid Corporation's president, Edwin Land, had recommended building an ultra-high-altitude spy plane—in effect, a jet-powered glider—that could fly with impunity over the Soviet Union, photographing suspected military targets below. Recognizing that any such aircraft would eventually become vulnerable to improved Soviet defenses, Land's panel also proposed two follow-on programs: a faster, second-generation spy plane, and an Earth-orbiting reconnaissance satellite. To hide its real mission, the first-generation spy plane was dubbed the Utility-2, or U-2. The satellite program would be carried out by the agency under the code name Corona. Dulles put Bissell in charge of both.[23]

Subtly, without fanfare or even acknowledgment, the CIA was changing from an organization of cloak-and-dagger back-alley operatives—and "scrabby old hideouts, with the plaster peeling and stopped-up toilets," as one remembered—to an antiseptic warren of faceless technicians shepherding mechanical spies soaring silently and efficiently overhead in the vacuum of space. What Frank Wisner had known as espionage would soon become "hum-int," human intelligence, in agency-speak, to be compared—often derisively—with "technical collection," the realm of the unbiased, emotionless, never-blinking machine: Bissell's realm.[24]

In that brave new world, Wisner represented the CIA's past. Bissell was its future.

IN SPITE OF FRANK WISNER's personal and professional travails, the CIA's successes in Iran and Guatemala had given him fresh hope that the agency could begin rolling back Communism elsewhere in the world. In an eyes only briefing paper that he and Bissell prepared on South Vietnam, Wisner described the situation there as "deteriorating." But Frank noted that the CIA's man on the ground in Saigon, Colonel Edward Lansdale—"an exceptionally able, energetic and imaginative officer"—felt "the situation is far from hopeless and that with vigorous US action and with strong leadership it should be possible . . . to check the downward spiral and very possibly reverse the trend of developments." At the same time, as Wisner counseled Joe Alsop in a letter, "it should be emphasized that the South Vietnamese themselves and especially Diem [South Vietnam's president] are in a very real sense the parties responsible for their own salvation."[25]

The attacks on him had also reawakened Wisner's legendary combative spirit. In a pep talk that he gave to senior figures in the Plans Directorate on July 18, 1955, Frank congratulated his subordinates for surviving the onslaught—"just about every 'dead cat' that could be thrown was, in fact, cut loose at us"—and promised that he and the CIA would not always be playing defense: "The time has now arrived when this Agency can and should go over onto the attack against its irresponsible critics. This is, of course, a matter which must be handled with the greatest of care . . . We should let it be understood that the 'open season' on CIA is closed, and that it is no longer a fashionable or profitable pursuit to sling mud at our people."[26]

Dulles and Helms sent the text of Frank's speech around the building. Wisner's planned offensive against the agency's critics would be deferred when it was subsequently overtaken by events—including the discovery of a new and unanticipated chink in the Iron Curtain. On June 5, 1956, *The New York Times* published the text of a recent speech by Nikita Khrushchev denouncing the earlier excesses of Stalin. Khrushchev's secret speech had been obtained by Jim Angleton through intelligence contacts in Israel. The speech was also broadcast repeatedly by Radio Free Europe and Radio Liberty, as well as distributed throughout the Eastern bloc by the CIA's leaflet-dropping balloons. The agency would credit Khrushchev's speech for a workers' uprising just a few weeks later in Poznan, a city in northwestern Poland. Wisner thought it encouraging that Khrushchev had not sent tanks to crush what seemed to be the first tentative stirrings of Polish independence.[27]

But the agency was caught off guard in late October, when a much larger and more violent insurrection broke out in Hungary. Early reports from Budapest by Geza Katona, the CIA's sole Hungarian-speaking operative at the U.S. embassy—who hastily filed his dispatches while lying prone on the floor of the communications room, as bullets whined outside—had suddenly exposed a gaping hole in the agency's own preparations: namely, a critical lack of intelligence on Hungary and a resulting inability to affect events there. "At no time in the period . . . did we have anything that could or should have been mistaken for an intelligence operation [in Hungary]," a classified CIA history would subsequently conclude.[28]

The emphasis that OPC, and the CIA, had put on covert operations at the expense of intelligence gathering had finally come back to haunt their founders—Frank Wisner most of all. (Nor was the CIA's man in Budapest exactly a figure out of a James Bond spy novel. According to a dossier later found in the files of the AVH, Hungary's secret police, Geza Katona was "a second-generation Hungarian-American, of medium build and with a Hungarian-style handlebar mustache he grew when he arrived here. He speaks pretty good Hungarian and loves to sing Hungarian folk songs and dance the *czardas*.")[29]

As he operated at the embassy under State Department cover, Katona's routine duties involved purchasing stamps and stationery and mailing letters for the diplomats. The unlikely spy used walks in city parks with his small dog as a cover for supposedly clandestine meetings with Hungarian contacts—many of whom, however, did not fail to notice a car full of AVH agents idling at the end of the block. (The CIA succeeded in fooling the KGB at least. A Soviet intelligence assessment done five days after the start of the uprising concluded, "The American Secret Services are more active in Hungary than Comrades Suslov and Mikoyan are"—a reference to the Communist Party leaders that Moscow had sent to Budapest to negotiate with the head of the anti-Soviet insurrection there.)[30]

Wisner had just embarked on a tour of CIA stations overseas when he received word of the revolt in Hungary—a country that, unlike Albania, had barely been on the Plans Directorate's radar screen. In London, Frank became furious after being stood up by the senior MI6 officer he was supposed to meet for dinner; he then flew on to Paris, where those at a NATO briefing remembered him as subdued and unusually quiet. The snub by the British spy was not the only reason. That same day, October 29, Israel's army invaded Egypt, the opening act in a joint Anglo-French-Israeli response to the Egyptian leader Gamal Nasser's nationalization of the Suez Canal. Since America's allies had not notified the United States of their plans, the Suez crisis, like the Hungarian uprising, took the CIA by surprise—and was evidence of yet another intelligence failure. (Dick Bissell, at least, could boast that his U-2s had managed to photograph British and French warships moving through the eastern Mediterranean. A CIA spy plane also documented the aftermath of an Anglo-French bombing raid on an Egyptian military airfield outside Cairo.)[31]

Arriving in Frankfurt on November 5, 1956, Wisner stayed at the home of Tracy Barnes, another Project Success veteran, who observed firsthand Frank's progressive psychological disintegration. Barnes's wife, Janet, likewise remembered Wisner as being in "awful shape." In an effort to calm himself, Frank went upstairs to play with their son's electric trains. The previous day, the Red Army had invaded Hungary with nearly a quarter-million troops and more than two thousand armored vehicles.

In Budapest, workers and college students had begun hurling Molotov cocktails at the Soviet tanks. Geza Katona, desperate for instructions from Washington, was advised by CIA headquarters that he should limit his efforts "to information collection only [and] not get involved in anything that would reveal U.S. interest or give cause to claim intervention." Fearful that its first message had not been clear enough, the agency sent Katona a second cable the following day, reiterating "that it is not permitted to send U.S. weapons in."[32]

On November 7, Wisner continued on with his star-crossed inspection tour, proceeding to the U.S. embassy in Vienna, where his host was his friend and former Georgetown neighbor Ambassador Tommy Thompson. As Frank drew physically closer to Hungary, his desperation seemed to grow. After the agency rejected Wisner's plea that it mobilize any defectors recruited by Red Cap and Red Sox to assist the Hungarian rebels, he became manic. (At CIA headquarters, too, frustration and feelings of impotence had given rise to some wild ideas. Following a few quick calculations, the head of the Intelligence Directorate pointed out how nuclear weapons might be used to close mountain passes in western Romania and Russian Ruthenia, making it impossible for the Soviets to resupply their forces in Hungary. His suggestion went no further.)[33]

On November 8, the question of American intervention became moot when resistance collapsed in Budapest and the surviving freedom fighters surrendered. At least twenty-five thousand Hungarian civilians and seven hundred Soviet soldiers had died in the revolt. Borrowing an embassy car, Wisner drove at breakneck speed the thirty miles from Vienna to the Austrian border, where hundreds of Hungarians were attempting to flee their country. The scene he encountered there was a bizarre and incredible tableau, punctuated by the sound of Russian gunfire in the distance. Frank personally witnessed a poignant incident, where a young resistance fighter who had crossed the border asked for a few liters of gasoline so that he might return to his country and battle the Russian tanks.[34]

Whether to show support for the Hungarian people or simply to gawk at the unfolding disaster, other Americans had also gathered at the crossing point. They included seventy-three-year-old Wild Bill Donovan, whom Eisenhower had appointed head of a hurriedly thrown-together refugee relief program, and Vice President Richard Nixon, who had been personally briefed on the Hungarian situation by Dick Helms just a few days earlier. Wisner also encountered two longtime friends, Walter and Marie Ridder, co-owners of the Knight-Ridder news service.[35]

At a restaurant in Vienna for dinner with the Ridders a few nights later, Wisner launched into a loud and emotional diatribe about the American government's responsibility for the tragedy in Hungary. Frank said that he felt personally betrayed and disgraced, since Hungary had been a case of déjà vu: it was reminiscent of the time in Romania, more than a decade earlier, when he had seen boxcars filled with people being shipped to an uncertain fate in the east.

Everything that Wisner had done since the war, first at OPC, then at the CIA, had been focused on encouraging exactly the kind of popular revolt that had just taken place in Hungary—only to see his own country sit idly on the sidelines when it finally occurred. Out of bitterness, he cabled Allen Dulles that some of the fleeing refugees he had talked to at the border blamed Radio Free Europe's broadcasts for stirring up false hopes that the United States would help them win their freedom.[36]

Pressing on doggedly with his inspection tour nonetheless, Wisner traveled next to Rome, where the CIA station chief, William Colby, recalled Frank "rambling and raving all through dinner, totally out of control." In a meeting with Ambassador Clare Boothe Luce, Wisner was finally overcome with emotion and wept. He and Luce—wife of the conservative Time-Life publisher and a prominent journalist in her own right—pledged that Soviet atrocities in Hungary "shall not be *permitted* to be shoved under the rug." (Luce showed Wisner an eyes only letter that she had drafted to send to Eisenhower. It read, in part, "Let us now ask for whom the bell tolls in Hungary today. It tolls for us if Freedom's holy light is extinguished in blood and iron there.")[37] In Athens, the last stop on his tour, Frank insisted on sending cables to CIA stations around the world with detailed directives on what needed to be done in the wake of the debacle in Hungary. The clerk in charge remembered Wisner pacing back and forth in the embassy's operations center, "dictating telegrams that did not make *any* goddamn sense."[38]

When he was finally back home in Georgetown, Frank's mood seemed to stabilize briefly. But Wisner's CIA colleagues noted that his manic moods would erupt at strange and unpredictable times; during one after-action briefing on the Hungarian disaster, he repeatedly interrupted the briefer to tell a long, rambling, and scatological story involving Russians, toilet paper, and a mix-up between the men's and the women's bathrooms.[39] A couple of weeks later, viral hepatitis, evidently brought on by the plate of raw clams that he had eaten in Greece, put Frank in the hospital just before Christmas with a 106-degree fever. "Do what your doctors and Polly tell you and you will be supporting your constitution against all its enemies foreign and domestic," Dean Acheson wrote to Frank in a get-well note. Joe Alsop sent Wisner three books on Chinese history to read during his hospital stay. Even when he was confined to a sickbed, however, Wisner's restless energy could not be restrained. At two o'clock in the morning, Frank bullied a nurse—he purportedly threatened to unleash the agency's "goons" on her—into letting him telephone Phil Graham with an idea for a series of Herblock cartoons, explaining to the sleepy publisher in minute detail exactly how they should be drawn.*[40]

During the time that Wisner remained hospitalized, his deputy, Dick Helms, took over the day-to-day running of the Plans Directorate. Perhaps to protect Frank, Helms also began cleaning up after his boss: he asked Angleton to pull together all the cables that Wisner had sent at the time of the Hungarian revolt, which were purged from the CIA's files.[41]

Even after he returned to work at the agency, Wisner noticed, from sidelong glances and conversations broken off mid-sentence in the hall, that he was no longer viewed as the larger-than-life figure he had been before his breakdown. When Frank sent the CIA's general counsel, Larry Houston, on a mission to describe some new psychological warfare scheme to Gordon Gray, both men soon realized that they had no idea what it was that Wisner wanted done. Gray, who had been Wisner's friend since adolescence, told Houston, "I think Frank is in real trouble."[42]

Although the CIA's post hoc assessment of the Hungarian uprising ultimately concluded that Radio Free Europe's broadcasts were not to blame for inciting the failed revolt, the agency nonetheless shut down

---

* While in the hospital, Wisner learned that Imre Nagy, the leader of the doomed Hungarian uprising, had been summarily executed by the Russians following a secret trial. Nagy's murder was the inspiration for the cartoons, as Frank later explained in a letter to Graham: "I cherished in particular the idea of representing Khrushchev with his arms drenched in blood up to the elbows, looking in vain for another Suez Canal in which to wash away his sins; and also a representation of Khrushchev as a baby duckling being nudged into a pool of Hungarian blood by a *large* Chinese-appearing mother-duck wearing a hat trimmed with wilted flowers (the hundred flowers that bloomed and died for Mao)."

several psy-war programs in its aftermath, including one of Frank Wisner's favorites—the propaganda leaflets being dropped over Eastern Europe. The brand-new aircraft that the CIA had recently acquired for Albania were mothballed when the State Department ordered leafleting suspended, "because of the belief that increased leaflet raids are interpreted by the populace as meaning the United States is preparing to liberate Albania." That winter, a magazine article written by Wisner's old friend and former colleague Franklin Lindsay opened a new wound. Lindsay's essay, "What Might Have Happened in Hungary," argued that the Hungarian revolt could have succeeded, and bloodshed been avoided, had the United Nations sent an observer team to Budapest when the fighting broke out—a notion that would surely have been anathema to Lindsay and the Wiz in OPC's enthusiastic early days.[43]

Causing further damage to Wisner's reputation was a fresh assessment of the agency's covert operations, undertaken as the disaster in Hungary was unfolding and given to Eisenhower just before Christmas 1956. The latest report was devastating not only for its conclusion but because of the source: the authors were the former defense secretary Robert Lovett and Wisner's longtime friend and Georgetown neighbor David Bruce, whom Truman had briefly considered for the post of CIA director. Not only was the Lovett-Bruce Report damning of the CIA in general—which Bruce described as "busy, monied and privileged"—but some of its arrows seemed aimed personally at Wisner: "The supporters of the 1948 decision to launch this government on a positive program [of psychological and political warfare] could not possibly have foreseen the ramifications of the operations which have resulted from it. No one, other than those in the CIA immediately concerned with their day-to-day operation, has any detailed knowledge of what is going on."[44]

For Wisner, however, perhaps the deepest cut was the dawning realization that after devoting his life to the secret world, he was being gently pushed out of it. "That was what bothered him the most," remembered Frank's son Ellis, "the feeling that people at the agency were starting to go around him."[45]

CURED OF THE HEPATITIS that put him in the hospital, Frank Wisner had yet to recover from the shock of the failed Hungarian uprising, and his eccentricities had become more pronounced once he was back at the CIA in 1957. Frank had always had a fetish about secrecy, but his concern with negative portrayals of the agency in the press, and leaks of classified operations, became obsessive. Wisner even objected to Allen Dulles's plans to celebrate the agency's tenth anniversary in a public ceremony. Talk of moving CIA headquarters from the ramshackle but familiar "tempos" on the National Mall to a gleaming new building in the Virginia countryside occasioned yet more anxiety. Polly recalled her husband spending "interminable hours" in animated conversation with the reporter Scotty Reston, trying to keep seemingly insignificant details out of stories in *The New York Times*. Wisner had no such worries with Joe Alsop, who had recently written to an inquiring university professor that he had "a rooted objection to any public discussion of our covert operations, past, present, or possibly prospective."[46]

With future, ambitious covert operations put on hold in the wake of the debacle in Hungary, Wisner returned to his earlier notion of taking the offensive against the agency's critics. To that end, he believed that it might be possible to enforce "good" journalistic ethics by legislative fiat, giving behind-the-scenes support to a bill proposed by the Massachusetts congressman Richard Wigglesworth that would have imposed legal sanctions on editors and publishers for allowing their reporters to publish state secrets or, prospectively, even articles that cast the U.S. government in a bad light. "So long as publishers tolerate unethical conduct on the part of employees (to say nothing of encouraging, rewarding and even requiring such conduct), unethical men will get and keep jobs and reap rich rewards in terms of salaries and advancement, and there's precious little that ethical, responsible working newspapermen can do about it," Wisner wrote to his friend Wig in July 1958.[47]

In letters that he marked "personal" and "confidential," Wisner also tried out the idea of such a ban on several of his friends in the press and the government. While some of the latter responded positively—"I am no expert, but I do not know why it should be inconceivable that the press be subject to some restraint approved in law by the Congress," replied Secretary of the Navy Tom Gates—members of the fourth estate were understandably less than enthusiastic. "I do not think it is possible to ask the press—at any level—to censure itself or to ask one newspaper not to print information another newspaper might get," wrote the *New York Times* columnist Cy Sulzberger. Addressing Wisner as "Dear Procrustes" in his own letter, Stewart Alsop argued that "reportorial ethical standards are to a considerable extent self-enforcing. A reporter who consistently betrays confidences rather soon has nothing of importance to report." Wisner and Wigglesworth eventually dropped their plans to nullify the First Amendment.[48]

Despite his recent hospitalization, there was no letup in Wisner's self-imposed work schedule or his frantic social calendar. He kept a tuxedo in his office so that he could go directly from the CIA to formal evening events and cultivate his contacts; "I work all day and all night," he told a colleague, in a rare admission of fatigue. Once again, the strain had begun to show. The annual fitness report that Allen Dulles wrote for Wisner still gave Frank high marks for his performance. But Dulles also observed that Wisner's "principal weakness is an oversensitiveness to criticism." There was, to be sure, an abundance of the latter—as well as further setbacks for Frank. Depressed by funding cuts imposed on the Plans Directorate in the wake of the Doolittle and Lovett-Bruce reports, Wisner tried—but failed—to negotiate a "treaty" between the CIA and the Bureau of the Budget that would have ensured continuing support for covert operations. Worried that President Achmed Sukarno of Indonesia might be flirting with Communism, Frank endorsed a Success-like op to overthrow Sukarno, even while cautioning his superiors that this time it might be impossible to hide the agency's hand in the plot. Indeed, when a CIA-supplied bomber was shot down and the pilot captured, exposing the operation, Wisner and the Plans Directorate received the blame, while Sukarno remained in power.[49]

By the late summer of 1958, Frank's mental state and mood seesawed wildly. Skeptical one day of creeping U.S. involvement in Southeast Asia, Wisner would astonish agency colleagues the next by suggesting that Czechoslovakia might be ripe for a popular anti-Communist uprising. But, overall, Wisner's legendary enthusiasm for dirty tricks had clearly waned. Even that shining symbol of the agency's covert prowess—Project Success—had lost its luster in the cold light of day. As Frank was forced to concede, the overthrow of Árbenz had resulted in a marked rise of anti-American sentiment in the region. The previous May, during what was meant to be a goodwill visit by Nixon to Caracas, Venezuela, the vice president's car had been surrounded and nearly overturned by demonstrators protesting U.S. interference in Latin America. Barely months after the CIA's client Castillo Armas had assumed power in Guatemala, both Wisner and Allen Dulles were complaining that Armas's government was corrupt, inept, and insolvent.[50]

Likewise hurtful for Wisner was the realization that his pride and joy, the mighty Wurlitzer, was being played with more skill by others at the agency. Allen Dulles had been the barely disguised source for a *Saturday Evening Post* article, "The Mysterious Doings of CIA," that gave a highly sanitized and uncritical account of Project Success. Even Frank's subordinates at the agency boasted of planting stories in the press. Desmond FitzGerald's new wife, Barbara, claimed that her husband scanned Matter of Fact in *The Washington Post* at breakfast every morning "to see if Alsop had taken the bait."[51]

By that fall, Wisner's mania and paranoia had returned with renewed force. Frank reportedly put forward a theory that the careless comment which had gotten George Kennan kicked out of the Soviet Union was evidence the Soviets had succeeded in an area where the CIA's own scientists had failed: mind control. Some agency hands alleged that Wisner attributed his own increasingly bizarre behavior to the Kremlin's sly manipulation. Sitting poolside at Paul Nitze's farm during the annual Fourth of July party, Frank unsettled his host by complaining that *The New York Times* was harboring traitors. Nitze realized with a start that one of those whom Wisner accused of being a "traitor" was his Woodley Park neighbor Scotty Reston.[52]

Like Stewart Alsop's Polecat Park and Phil Graham's Glen Welby, Wisner's Locust Hill Farm became an increasingly frequent refuge. Frank had spent much of the summer at the farm with his teenage son Ellis, harvesting hay, planting vegetables, and weeding the garden plot. It proved, however, only a temporary respite. Shortly after Wisner's arrival back in Washington, the demons, too, returned. Chip Bohlen, on leave from the Moscow embassy, found Wisner "very tense" during a Georgetown visit. (Joe Alsop had warned Chip bluntly beforehand that Wisner was "off his rocker.") Another of Frank's old friends, Franklin Lindsay, attending a party at the P Street house, found his former OPC colleague so wound up as to be virtually incoherent, Wisner was talking so fast. Worried about what was coming next, Polly turned for help to those who had long been close to her husband—Gordon Gray, Henry Sears, and the AEC commissioner John Graham, who had known Frank since college.[53]

The crisis came that fall. On September 12, 1958, after Frank's manic episode at work caused Desmond FitzGerald to summon the CIA's doctors, Wisner's friends persuaded him to enter Baltimore's Sheppard Pratt clinic, a private psychiatric hospital affiliated with Johns Hopkins University. (Later that same day, Jim Angleton, the FBI's mole at the agency, informed the bureau "on a strictly confidential basis" of Frank Wisner's breakdown. "Angleton personally contributes [*sic*] Wisner's troubles to the fact that Wisner was too deeply involved in matters outside of his official business, namely State Department affairs," wrote an aide to Hoover. "[Angleton] also feels that Wisner's wife, who is extremely socially ambitious, may have placed her husband under too much pressure to keep up with social commitments with the Georgetown set.") Frank Wisner would spend the next six months at the clinic, where his depression was treated with conventional psychoanalysis and electro-convulsive shock therapy.[54]

By early December, when it became clear that Wisner was not going to return to his previous job anytime soon, Allen Dulles appointed Dick Bissell the new deputy director of Plans. Richard Helms, who had expected to get the post, was instead made the Plans Directorate's chief of operations. ("My disappointment and surprise were indeed genuine," Helms later wrote in a memoir. He thought Bissell "a peculiar choice for the job.") Bissell in turn picked Tracy Barnes, his aide in helping to plan the Guatemala coup, as his deputy. To Helms, the elevation of Bissell and Barnes signaled Dulles's intention to give top priority at the agency to covert operations, not intelligence and analysis. Dick Bissell would assume his new post at the CIA on January 1, 1959—coincidentally, the same day that Fidel Castro came to power in Cuba.[55]

CHAPTER FIFTEEN

"The Prophet of the Missile Gap"

STEWART ALSOP'S WARNING in a spring 1955 Matter of Fact column that the U.S.S.R. might be the first nation in space, and the imaginary headline that Stew concocted to go with it—"Soviets Claim Successful Launching of Earth Satellite"—became suddenly, frighteningly real on October 4, 1957, when *Sputnik* was lofted into orbit. The Soviet achievement undercut the complacent and unquestioned faith of most Americans in their country's technological supremacy. Asked by a reporter what he expected U.S. astronauts would find when they got to the moon, the physicist Edward Teller's deadpan answer was "Russians."[1]

But while the Eisenhower administration tried, unsuccessfully, to dismiss the Soviet satellite as a "silly bauble," the Alsop brothers pointed out the real strategic significance of *Sputnik*—namely, that the Russians had succeeded in building a missile capable of carrying a hydrogen-bomb warhead to targets an ocean away: it was the advent of the intercontinental ballistic missile, or ICBM, which the Alsops had predicted back in early 1946. Behind *Sputnik,* the brothers argued, was a military threat no less fundamental than that of the first Soviet atomic bomb. And, like Joe-1, the Soviet challenge called for an American response commensurate with NSC 68 and the crash program that had resulted in the H-bomb.[2]

Ironically, it was not the deteriorating international situation so much as simple boredom that had finally compelled George Kennan and Paul Nitze to end their long and, in Kennan's case, largely self-imposed exile. Both men had found early retirement too much of a chore and were eager to reenter the fray. Each had volunteered to work on Adlai Stevenson's 1956 presidential campaign, but both would eventually join the troupe of disillusioned supporters. Nitze complained to Kennan that although he had helped write the Democrats' defense policy platform, hardly "more than two words of it survived" the party's convention in Chicago. Kennan, who had drafted a major foreign policy speech for Stevenson, sympathized with Nitze: "I found myself disgusted by everything about the Democratic convention except Stevenson himself . . . In these circumstances it seems obvious that the party has no need for anyone like myself at this juncture."[3]

The abortive Hungarian revolt had briefly awakened hopes in Kennan that the collapse of the Soviet empire might actually be at hand. For a fleeting few weeks, Kennan's dour pessimism lifted, and the interview that he gave to Joe Alsop for a *Saturday Evening Post* article, "The Soviet Will Never Recover," had sounded like Kennan channeling the early Frank Wisner. As a declaration of victory in the Cold War, however, it was premature. Soviet tanks were in the streets of Budapest by the time the issue hit the newsstands in late November—prompting the conservative *National Review* to bitingly observe in the aftermath of the revolt's failure, "It seems clear the Kennan of six months past had not the vaguest idea of what he was talking about."[4]

Kennan and Nitze had joined forces again early in 1957, when the pair testified in tandem before Congress on the future direction of American foreign policy. George and Annelise stayed at Paul and Phyllis's house in Woodley Park while the hearings lasted. In their testimony, the two men revived Plan A, urging the Eisenhower administration to explore the possibility of a joint Soviet-American agreement on withdrawing NATO and Warsaw Pact forces from Germany. For Kennan and Nitze, this reprise of the so-called disengagement doctrine represented a rare—and temporary—meeting of the minds.

But *Sputnik* brought the differences between the two men once again to the fore.

The previous summer, Nitze had been invited to join in another Pentagon-sponsored defense study. The original task assigned to the Gaither Committee—named for its chairman, the former Ford Foundation president and Rand Corporation trustee Rowan Gaither—was limited to assessing methods of protecting civilians against nuclear attack. In effect, Eisenhower had asked the experts, if there were to be a nuclear war, what should he do?

Shortly after the study began, however, Gaither, diagnosed with the cancer that would eventually kill him, agreed to hand the reins over to others on the panel. Gaither's surrogates included Nitze. The latter's Democratic affiliation, and well-known hawkishness, kept him off the steering committee. But, partly due to Nitze's persistent importuning, the Gaither panel subsequently extended its charter to include a whole-sale reassessment of the Eisenhower administration's New Look military strategy.[5]

Since his work on the wartime Strategic Bombing Survey, Nitze had been a vocal advocate of civil defense, even telling New York City's legendary planner, Robert Moses, that all new buildings going up after the war should be equipped with air raid shelters. (Moses had responded, "Paul, you're mad, absolutely mad. Nobody will pay any attention to that," Nitze remembered.) So it was hardly surprising that the Gaither Report would recommend building a nationwide program of deep underground shelters, at a projected cost of twenty-five billion dollars.[6]

But equally attention getting was the report's recommendation that Eisenhower spend another twenty billion dollars to dramatically accelerate plans for an arsenal of ocean-spanning missiles in order to counter the Soviet ICBM threat. Like Nitze's NSC 68, which had identified 1954 as the "year of maximum danger," the Gaither Report put a date on the prospective apocalypse, warning of "an increasing threat which may become critical in 1959 or 1960," when it was believed that the U.S.S.R. would have enough missiles to devastate the United States in a nuclear surprise attack.[7]

The launch of *Sputnik* had given not only seeming credibility but new urgency to the recommendations of the Gaither panel—as did the orbiting, on November 7, of a second and larger Soviet satellite, just three days before the Gaither Report was briefed to Eisenhower and Foster Dulles at the White House. Nonetheless, the president and his secretary of state refused to be cowed by the experts' proffered solution to the dilemmas of the nuclear age. At the briefing's end, Ike, after thanking the panel members for their work, announced that he now realized he had asked them the wrong question. It would be impossible to have the kind of war they had just described, Eisenhower said; there simply were not enough bulldozers to scrape the bodies off the streets.[8]

Some on the Gaither panel were unwilling to accept the president's dismissive response—Nitze branded it a "preemptive surrender"—and decided, in effect, to go around Ike. Two weeks after the White House briefing, the substance of the top secret report was leaked to Stewart Alsop, who praised the "brilliant civilians" behind the Gaither study in a Matter of Fact column. More details were published a month later by *The Washington Post's* Chalmers Roberts, two days after Roberts and Nitze met for a private lunch.[9]

At least one member of the Gaither panel did not believe that even an alarmed public would be enough to awaken the country to its grave danger. A few days after Roberts's article in the *Post,* Gaither's deputy, the Boston industrialist Robert Sprague, showed up at Foster Dulles's door to urge that the administration consider a sneak attack on the Soviet Union before the Russians had enough missiles to destroy the United States. After upbraiding his visitor for the suggestion—"he had long felt that no men should arrogate the power to decide that the future of mankind would benefit by an action entailing the killing of tens of millions of people, and he believed that the President agreed with him," Dulles replied frostily—the secretary of state, in effect, threw Sprague out of his office.[10]

WHILE EISENHOWER was being briefed on the Gaither Report, George Kennan was in London, where he was about to deliver the third of half a dozen of the BBC's Reith radio lectures, titled "Russia, the Atom, and the West." Kennan had been invited to update his famous "X article," and his first two half-hour lectures, on the Kremlin's mind-set, had been noncontroversial. However, the third lecture—where Kennan once again raised the prospect of disengagement, proposing a reunited but neutralist and disarmed Germany—not only drew attention on the Continent but was roundly condemned by the foreign policy establishment at home. That hostile reaction was yet a prelude to Kennan's fourth lecture, on the nuclear arms race, where he posed a rhetorical question that went directly to the heart of the discussions then taking place behind closed doors in Washington: "Are we to flee like haunted creatures from one defensive device to another, each more costly and humiliating than the one before, cowering underground one day, breaking up our cities the next, attempting to surround ourselves with elaborate electronic shields on the third, concerned only to prolong the length of our lives while sacrificing all the values for which it might be worth while to live at all?"[11]

Kennan argued that the "suicidal nature" of nuclear weapons made them "unsuitable both as a sanction of diplomacy and as the basis of an alliance." Instead of the bomb, Kennan argued, the Western democracies might wish to rely for their defense on "a territorial-militia . . . somewhat on the Swiss example, rather than regular military units on the World War II pattern." It was a bold reprise of the "small, mobile forces" idea that Kennan had proposed back in 1947 as an alternative to massive re-armament. Perhaps even more remarkable, however, was Kennan's musing that the mere threat of a maquis-like resistance to Russian military occupation meant that Western Europe might have "little need of foreign garrisons to assure its immunity from Soviet attack." (Ironically, while the existence of the stay-behind units that Wisner and Franklin Lindsay had created for just such an eventuality would have strengthened Kennan's case, he made no mention of them, out of either prudence or a concern with secrecy.)[12]

Kennan's Reith Lectures prompted not merely criticism but hooting derision from his critics—and even some of his friends. ("Dear George sure has gone off the deep end," Avis Bohlen mused to Charlie Thayer.) The lectures contained "patches of plain silliness" and reflected the lecturer's "almost neurotic horror of military power in all its modern forms," wrote Joe Alsop in a column he pointedly titled "A Hunger for Cozy Self-Delusion."[13]

A broadside attack on the Kennan thesis in a press conference called by Dean Acheson left the Reith lecturer "amazed and depressed to find how many indignant pigeons I had flushed out of the underbrush by what I thought were moderate and innocuous and not very startling words," Kennan wrote that winter. ("He viewed me, I suspect, with a sort of amused personal affection, but I never commanded on his part the same sort of respect he accorded to the law," Kennan later wrote of his relationship with Acheson. For his part, Acheson once said that Kennan was like the horse that makes a lot of noise crossing a bridge and then stops in mid-span, puzzled by the source of the din.) At the news conference, the former secretary of state accused Kennan of having a "mystical attitude" toward power. In response to Kennan's claim that the Red Army represented no threat to Europe's democracies, Acheson had asked, incredulously, "On what does this guarantee rest, unless Divine revelation?"[14]

Even Joe Alsop thought Acheson's assault on Kennan "brutal." Nitze later claimed that Acheson had invited him to join in the attack, but Nitze demurred, possibly mindful of the fact that he, too, had been a champion of disengagement. Instead, Nitze promised Acheson that he would try to talk some sense into their wayward friend.[15]

A few weeks later, in March 1958, Nitze got the chance, when he and

Kennan attended a conference in Geneva at the invitation of a mutual friend, the American diplomat Louis Halle. Following lunch with Halle at La Perle du Lac, Nitze and Kennan took a walk along the shore of stormy Lake Geneva, their coat collars turned up against the wind, debating the questions that Kennan had raised in his Reith Lectures. While Kennan admitted that the lectures had been quickly and sloppily prepared, Nitze claimed, "he still defended the central ideas."[16]

In a reply to his critics that he later wrote for a British journal—but did not send—Kennan tried to set the record straight about what he had intended in the lectures:

> The purpose of "containment," as I envisioned it in 1947, was to restore such bargaining power on the western side as would make negotiations possible and promising, which in 1947 it was not. My complaint in the Reith lectures was that by 1957 the term "containment" had come to be interpreted solely in the military sense, and the effort to build military strength had become an end in itself, in the pursuit of which we had not only driven ourselves into the blind alley of the atomic weapons race but had lost completely the idea of negotiation at any point. We had forgotten, in other words, the very purpose for which, as I and many others had assumed, we had originally set out to arm.[17]

As before, the centerpiece of Nitze's differences with Kennan concerned the role of the bomb. Early in 1956, Nitze had published a *Foreign Affairs* article in which he likened nuclear weapons to chess pieces, making a pointed distinction between U.S. "declaratory policy"—those "statements of policy which we make for political effect"—and the country's "action policy," or "what we were actually prepared to do." It was because he had no intention of putting limits on the latter that Nitze opposed any restrictions on the former, including any declaration by the American government that it would never be the first to use nuclear weapons in a future conflict. Kennan, on the other hand, had explicitly promoted a no-first-use policy in his response to Joe-1, and in the draft speech he had written for Adlai Stevenson. Kennan also made no secret of his moral revulsion to the idea of using nuclear weapons, even if only as a bluff. Yet the hostile response to Kennan's Reith Lectures was another reminder that his views on nuclear weapons remained, within the U.S. government at least, very much in the minority.[18]

WHILE KENNAN WAS LECTURING in London, Joe Alsop had recently returned to Paris from a long reporting trip throughout the Middle East. At the Hôtel St. James et d'Albany, Joe found a pair of letters waiting, imploring him to come home. "The center of the world remains on the Potomac and the reporting of it is not being anything like completely done," cajoled Phil Graham, still convalescing at Glen Welby. The missive Joe received from his brother Stewart was more blunt: "I have, to tell you the truth, strong doubts about your plan to stay another year abroad . . . From a personal point of view, I cannot think that this wandering Jew performance, however stimulating and rewarding it may be for a time, can be satisfactory as a way of life. From a business point of view, I also have doubts."[19]

The *Herald Tribune,* in fact, had already complained about the cost of Joe's overseas cables when he filed his reports from the field. By mid-1957, the paper was losing money; the legendary *Trib* would have a new owner the following year. And, as more readers tired of the incessant and unrelieved pessimism in Joe's dispatches, the number of newspapers subscribing to Matter of Fact had correspondingly declined, for the first time since McCarthy's downfall.[20]

Even Joe's good friends complained of being worn down by his grim outlook. Marietta Peabody—who had since remarried, to Ronald Tree, a wealthy American-born British journalist and former member of the House of Commons—wrote to Susan Mary that she had returned from Paris and a recent Alsop visit "feeling triple doomed, his recent articles send icicle shivers down one's spine and leave no hope. Knowing his convictions and courage, I sometimes wonder if he thinks out the effect on his readers, which is enough to turn us all into isolationists."[21]

The Alsop column was now, as well, facing increasing competition from another outlet that delivered commentary and the news: television. Stewart had adapted better than his brother to the rival medium, appearing in 1957 with Tish and the children on Edward Murrow's program *Person to Person.* Joe, on the other hand, grumbled that if there were one modern technology he could "uninvent" it would be TV. Only under pressure did he relent for that year's New Year's Eve party, allowing an ancient set with a tiny screen to be wheeled into the living room so that guests could watch Guy Lombardo's orchestra play "Auld Lang Syne."[22]

Happily, Stewart was flourishing in Joe's absence, enjoying an unaccustomed independence. Stew and Tish had kept alive the tradition of the Georgetown salon while Joe was in Paris—hosting the annual "Alsop ball" that autumn at Springland Lane. The guest list of more than a hundred included senators, senior American diplomats, and the ambassadors of four European countries. The event, Stew wrote to Joe, had been an unqualified success: "Unlimited champagne and unlimited coffee is, I have concluded, the basic formula. It was costly, but a necessary showing of the flag, as well." More important, Stewart was finally emerging from Joe's shadow. Stew boasted to his brother that he had spent the previous weekend at the Texas ranch of a rising Washington star—the Senate majority leader, Lyndon Johnson.[23]

In his letter to Joe, the junior partner also broke the news that he had decided he wanted out. Like "a pair of middle aged cart horses, who had been in harness together for a long time," he had begun "to chafe a bit," Stew explained to his older brother. Although Joe offered a fifty-fifty share of the profits as an inducement to stay, Stewart announced in February that he had already signed a lucrative contract with *The Saturday Evening Post,* where he would be a full-time contributor. Joe cut short his Parisian sojourn and began packing for a return to Washington.*[24]

JOE AND STEWART ALSOP formally announced their breakup as a journalist team in a March 12, 1958, column, titled "Hail and Farewell." "Being a newspaper columnist is a little like being a Greek chorus," they wrote. "You report, you analyze, you comment and you describe the parts of the drama that do not take place on the open stage." While the brothers celebrated America's leadership in the postwar world, Joe—like the chorus of a Sophoclean tragedy—could not resist ending on an ominous note. A peaceful future, he wrote, "seems more doubtful today than one could have thought remotely possible twelve years ago."

While their parting was initially amicable, like a couple in a failed marriage the two soon fell to fighting over money and trifles. When Stewart complained about the books that his brother had ordered by the "carload" from a shop in England, Joe countered with the camera that Stew had lost in Russia. The two-hundred-dollar air conditioner

---

* It is likely that another reason for Stewart's ending the partnership was the possibility that Joe's homosexual affair in Moscow might be exposed, damaging both their careers. Joe wrote Stewart a letter about the affair while he was still in Russia, but it is unclear if the brother ever saw it.

that Stewart had bought for the Dumbarton study without Joe's permission was another sore point. And, as in a contentious divorce, the Alsops' feuding over incidentals masked some larger unresolved issues. Joe bristled at Stew's charge "You always want to rewrite everything that I write."[25]

The biggest strain in their relationship would be brought about by an anthology of the columns that the brothers had written over the years—intended, ironically, as a "memorial" to their partnership. Joe rejected Stewart's proposed title for the volume; Stew diligently pored over the manuscript, changing to "younger" each reference to him as the "junior" partner. (Joe told friends in confidence that he had been "carrying" Stewart for years and that it was actually *he* who wished to be independent.) When the book, *The Reporter's Trade,* appeared in bookstores in 1958 and failed to make a profit, Joe blamed Stewart for persuading him to leave out the columns that had been most critical of Eisenhower.[26]

Back home again that spring on Dumbarton Avenue, Joe felt the relief of the returned traveler, writing to a friend, "I am gradually settling down to life in Washington again . . . It is a great deal more bearable than it was when I left, precisely because the Administration is now very frightened . . . It is heavenly to be back in the house, too." With Stewart's departure, Matter of Fact became a thrice-weekly column. The famous Dumbarton Avenue salons had also resumed and with them the familiar burden of entertaining out-of-town visitors. "When you have guests here, and you ask them whom they want to see, they always say 'Nobody but you,'" Joe complained good-naturedly to his old Harvard roommate Bill Patten. " 'Nobody but you' really means all the ambassadors, senators, cabinet members and Supreme Court justices that you can lay your hands on." ("I did manage one evening of a generally zoo-ish sort—A. Dulles, [French ambassador] Alphands, Chip and such-like, and the Grahams produced a Kennedy or two, but on the whole it was very quiet," Joe wrote to Susan Mary after a dinner party.)[27]

In a letter to Isaiah Berlin, however, Alsop confided that all was not well in Georgetown: "Meanwhile, the brief news is that Phil Graham, probably the most successful man among all his contemporaries, with a wife he loves, and the four most promising children I know anywhere, is having a severe nervous breakdown which seems to involve a good deal of weeping."[28]

Stewart Alsop, on his own at last, was already reaping the rewards of

Carmel Offie at New York's famous El Morocco nightclub in 1956. Frank Wisner's notorious fixer, code-named Monk, was "a world-class sophisticate who could put a stiletto in an opponent and offer him a treatise on the cognac he was serving him at the same time," claimed CIA counterspy James Angleton.

During the 1950s, the CIA was headquartered in temporary buildings next to the Reflecting Pool on the Capitol Mall. The "tempos" were "cold in winter, wet in rain, soggy and stifling in summer," remembered Richard Helms. Frank Wisner's "cowboys" in Buildings I and J worked next door to Helms's intelligence analysts—the despised "washerwomen"—in Buildings K and L.

Project Fiend's team FRIDAY. In the early 1950s, the CIA's ethnic agents were training for so-called coup de main missions—assassinations—in Albania. "It is doubtful whether, in a year's time, the US will be able to control the Frankenstein monster which they are creating," warned a British spymaster.

CIA director Allen Dulles is left holding the bag for the failed Bay of Pigs invasion. The farewell dinner for the man known as "the Great White Case Officer" was held at Washington, D.C.'s Alibi Club, a favorite agency hangout, on November 27, 1961. Richard Bissell is on the far left, Richard Helms is to Dulles's left (with cigar, ducking), and James Angleton is in the foreground (glasses).

TOP, LEFT Walter Lippmann at Mount Desert Island, Maine, summer 1961. Widely considered the capital's premier political journalist, Lippmann was Joe Alsop's chief rival and antagonist on the editorial page during the Vietnam War. When Lippmann left Washington in 1966, Alsop told friends he himself was now "dean of the columnists."

TOP, RIGHT In 1947, George Kennan, director of the State Department's Policy Planning Staff, pronounced the "containment" doctrine that would guide American policy toward the Soviet Union and presidents from Harry Truman to Ronald Reagan.

RIGHT In January 1950, Paul Nitze, a former investment banker and self-professed "problem solver," replaced George Kennan as head of the Policy Planning Staff. Kennan would later blame Nitze for "militarizing" the containment doctrine.

Richard Bissell, the CIA's deputy director for Plans, at the Brandenburg Gate in Berlin. Although Joe Alsop's friend "Dickie" described himself as a "man-eating shark," agency colleagues dubbed him "the Mad Stork." Bissell pioneered the CIA's overhead reconnaissance program but was fired in 1962 for the failed Bay of Pigs invasion.

An American Lawrence of Arabia in the Balkans and Near East—he taught the Red Army how to play polo—Charles Thayer was known as "the court jester of the Foreign Service." Forced out of the diplomatic corps in 1953 by Joseph McCarthy, "Charlie" became a struggling novelist in exile on the island of Majorca.

Although awarded the Medal of Freedom for wartime heroism, the U.S. diplomat and China expert John Paton Davies Jr. would be another victim of McCarthy. In 1954, Davies was fired by Secretary of State John Foster Dulles for lacking "sufficient judgment, discretion, and reliability."

Averell Harriman, Joe Alsop, and McGeorge Bundy at Harriman's seventieth birthday party, in Georgetown, November 1961.

Washington Post cartoonist Herblock, left, with newspaper moguls Walter and Marie Ridder.

Katharine Graham and former U.S. ambassador to the U.S.S.R. Llewellyn "Tommy" Thompson. "Within Washington there's a nucleus of people who know each other and enjoy each other's company and see each other no matter what's happening politically or who is in or out of power," Graham wrote shortly before her death in 2001.

On the morning of October 16, 1962, President Kennedy informs his resident "demonologist," Soviet expert Charles Bohlen, of Russian offensive nuclear missiles in Cuba. JFK and "Chip" discussed options in the crisis later that evening at Joe Alsop's house.

Joe Alsop's admiration of John Kennedy was "just short of idolatry—and not much this side," brother Stewart observed. Kennedy's assassination "broke my life in half," Joe wrote to Jackie.

Jacqueline Kennedy, 1961. When Jackie voiced reservations about her husband's run for the presidency, Joe Alsop had assured her "'it's the only game that's worth the candle.' Because <u>you</u> told me that—I thought about it every day—and gradually came to agree with you—And that was when the happy time started," she wrote to Joe in gratitude.

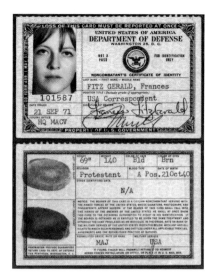

Frances "Frankie" FitzGerald's press credentials when reporting from Vietnam. After her 1967 article for *The Atlantic Monthly* magazine—"Truly, the United States has no talent for colonialism," she wrote—there would be no more dinner invitations to Joe Alsop's house.

In "Frank and His Friends," a September 1965 column, Joe Alsop paid tribute to the "promising young men" who the United States was sending to Southeast Asia. Left to right, in white shirts: Richard Holbrooke, Frank George Wisner, and *Washington Post* reporter Ward Just.

An unauthorized 1966 trip to the Cambodian border in a friend's sports car resulted in trouble for Frank George Wisner, nicknamed Metternich by his colleagues at Saigon's U.S. embassy. Left to right: Wisner, Ward Just, and Robin Pell.

By the end of the 1960s, Joe Alsop's defense of Richard Nixon's Vietnam policy was so anomalous among journalists as to be itself newsworthy.

"Joe Mayflower" (center) as Joe Alsop in Art Buchwald's 1970 Broadway play, *Sheep on the Runway*. "From being a much-feared columnist, warrior and prophet he has become a figure of fun. It was the war that did him in," observed Alsop critic John Kenneth Galbraith.

being freed from the influence of his headstrong older brother. Moving into a four-room suite of offices at *The Saturday Evening Post*'s Washington headquarters on Sixteenth Street, Stew published the first of several in-depth articles he planned for the magazine that summer. "The Mystery of Richard Nixon" focused on the man Stewart called "the second most important political figure in the country." Although some critics thought the portrait a "puff piece," others found it "illuminating" and "fair." Stewart's essay was, in any case, a contrast to Joe's more acidulous approach. (Nixon had promptly agreed to see Stewart, but the vice president waited a long time before responding to Joe's request for a "chatty lunch.") No longer compelled to daily climb the columnist's ladder rung by rung, Stewart had decided to write instead carefully researched profiles of major American political figures. He was already at work on a profile of Senator Lyndon Johnson. "Lyndon, besides being a man of immense ability, is also the vainest man I've ever met, even in our business," Stew confided to his brother.[29]

In Stewart's absence, Joe had begun casting about for fresh issues to focus on; by the summer of 1958, he had one.

Stewart had actually been first to warn that the United States was lagging behind the Soviets in the development of long-range missiles. He had correctly predicted, in a May 1954 column, that the Russians would test an ICBM capable of carrying a nuclear warhead as early as three years hence. Stew thus scored a journalistic coup when he reported the successful firing of a Russian ICBM in July 1957—only weeks after the United States had failed to get its own Atlas long-range missile off the ground. Although the administration initially challenged the claims in Stewart's scoop, a subsequent retraction by the Pentagon provided welcome vindication, as did *Sputnik* and the leaked Gaither Report a few months later. "You remember when missiles were a dreary little subject, and everybody wondered why we wrote so much about them?" Stew wrote to his brother in triumph. "The other night in the *Star,* every piece by every columnist was about missiles. Missiles, missiles, missiles. This obsession has its obvious dangers, but I think it is essentially a healthy thing."[30] (The Air Force Association's decision to award Joe and Stewart its 1957 Airpower Trophy—in recognition of their "outstanding contribution to airpower and national security in the field of arts and letters"—showed that the brothers had been forgiven their earlier enthusiasm for Project Lincoln.)[31]

In a column on August 1, 1958, titled "Untruth on Defense," Joe Alsop took on what he called "the missile gap"—and the Eisenhower administration. Joe's jeremiad charged that the government was "guilty of gross untruth concerning the national defense of the United States." Predicting that the Soviets would have a hundred operational ICBMs a year hence, when the United States had none, Alsop warned that the disparity in missile strength would only increase over time. By 1961, he wrote, the Russians were expected to have a thousand ICBMs versus America's seventy. Joe's conclusion was dire: "The effect of the present policy is indisputable. It will allow the Soviets to gain an overwhelming superiority in over-all nuclear striking power . . . At this instant, the last chance to save ourselves is slipping through our hands."[32]

It did not go unnoticed by the White House or the CIA that some of the numbers quoted in Alsop's column matched those of a top secret National Intelligence Estimate that had been briefed to Eisenhower only a few weeks earlier. Indeed, on the subject of missiles, Joe seemed unusually well informed. One source for his reporting was the Missouri senator Stuart Symington, a Democrat, former secretary of the air force under Truman, and member of the Senate's powerful Armed Services Committee. Another, probably indirect source was Symington's former aide Thomas Lanphier, a vice president of Convair, the company building the Atlas missile. Following *Sputnik* and the Gaither Report, Symington and other Democrats had seized upon "the gap" for partisan advantage. Lyndon Johnson worked the issue into contentious hearings that he convened on the Hill into how the Eisenhower administration had fallen down on defense preparedness. Senator John Kennedy read the text of Joe's August 1 column into the *Congressional Record*. At Alsop's urging, Kennedy also delivered a much-quoted speech on the Senate floor, warning that unless the missile gap was bridged, "the balance of power will gradually shift away from us." The figures that Kennedy cited for Russian missiles had come directly from Alsop's column. In return, Joe devoted a pair of his Matter of Fact columns to the Kennedy speech.[33]

Joe's fixation on the missile gap—a term he claimed to have coined—seemed obsessive, even for him. George Kistiakowsky, a Manhattan Project chemist who would shortly become Ike's science adviser, recalled being invited to breakfast at Alsop's house in the spring of 1959. As the two men sat amid the overgrown foliage in Joe's garden room, Alsop "spent the time painting a grim picture of a disastrous 'missile gap,' claiming that the Soviet Union already had 150 operational ICBMs which they were to launch against us in July 1959!" Another Alsop guest at this time, Ray Garthoff, a CIA analyst assigned to the Pentagon, remembered receiving similar treatment: "Not only did [Alsop] not try to 'pump' me for information, he seemed indifferent to what little I would say and much more interested in telling me his own ideas and conclusions."[34]

Joe's claims concerning the missile gap understandably infuriated Eisenhower. Although the president told aides, "I have no time to read them," after one particularly negative column Ike was heard to mutter that Joe Alsop was "about the lowest form of animal life on Earth." Yet Eisenhower was powerless to respond to Alsop without divulging the reason behind the administration's complacency regarding Soviet missile development—the fact that the ultrasecret U-2 spy plane had yet to locate a single operational ICBM in Russia. Without evidence to the contrary, Joe's word on the subject was widely taken as gospel. A subsequent, classified CIA internal history would dub Alsop "the prophet of the missile gap."[35]

Unable to blunt Alsop's attacks directly, the president's defenders sought to silence Joe by other means. Eisenhower's press secretary, James Hagerty, took out his frustrations the best way he knew how—by denying the columnist a press pass for Ike's upcoming visit to India. "He's a damn fairy," Hagerty sputtered to Robert Donovan, Joe's colleague at the *Herald Tribune*. "The FBI knows about him."[36]

Others in the administration resolved to try a different tack.

Since the incident involving Alsop and the KGB agent provocateur at Moscow's Grand Hotel, there had been—to Joe's immense relief—no further word from the Russians and no sign that the episode had caused him problems at home. That calm assurance ended on January 3, 1959, when an unattributed item appeared in the For the Record column of the *National Review*: "A prominent American journalist is a target of Soviet blackmail for homosexuality. U.S. authorities know it. His syndicate doesn't—yet. The feverish activities of Washington's internal security personnel suggest that a major scandal may be under an intelligence agency's rug. The complete nervous breakdown of a top intelligence officer sparked the furor." But there was no follow-up in the conservative journal, and Joe had every reason to believe that both his secret and Frank Wisner's remained safe.

Still, the issue would not go away. A few months later, in mid-April 1959, Attorney General William Rogers telephoned the FBI director, Hoover, to say that he had just told Secretary of Defense Neil McElroy of the Moscow incident and was "amazed" that McElroy did not already know of it. (In February, Alsop had written a column blaming McElroy for "the Eisenhower administration's decision to accept inferiority to the Soviets in ballistic missiles.") According to Hoover's memorandum of his conversation with Rogers, the attorney general had suggested that the two men "get together what we have on Alsop as he believed very few people knew of this . . . [Rogers] then commented that he was going to see that certain individuals were aware of Alsop's propensities . . . but he would not take the responsibility for such information going any further."[37]

In the days to come, Rogers spread the story of Joe Alsop's indiscretion to others in the government—including Lewis Strauss. The former AEC chairman, who was known to have a long-standing grudge against Alsop, had recently been denied confirmation by the Senate as Ike's new secretary of commerce—in large part because of his role in the Oppenheimer case. By August 1959, Hoover, too, had sent word of the Moscow incident to "other agencies, particularly those under the Department of Defense . . . on a need-to-know basis." Not surprisingly, the story continued to spread in Washington's corridors of power.[38]

Whatever Joe himself knew of the machinations going on behind his back, they had no discernible effect on his reporting. In January 1960, he wrote a series of five consecutive columns on the missile gap that appeared on the front page of newspapers around the country. "In order to save some hundreds of millions of dollars, the Eisenhower administration is literally playing a gigantic game of Russian roulette with the national future," Alsop charged. Quoting General Thomas Power, head of the U.S. Strategic Air Command, Joe claimed that Soviet ICBMs would be able to wipe out America's nuclear deterrent in only thirty minutes. By that calculus, Alsop predicted, "the Kremlin should be in a position to win the world about twelve months from now." Joe paid out of his own pocket to have the missile gap columns printed in a slick pamphlet that he sent to sympathetic senators, accompanied by a personal note.[39]

On February 9, a little more than a week after the last column in Joe's missile gap series appeared, an aide to J. Edgar Hoover wrote to the bureau director, recommending that an electronic bug be planted in Alsop's house: "It is believed that unless we establish some active coverage on Alsop we are leaving ourselves in a very vulnerable position. There are too many questions to which there are no answers unless he is watched. We can drift along and hope that nothing serious will ever take place, but this is not an objective approach to this problem. Well-established coverage of Alsop could develop information which eventually would save the Bureau valuable agent time and present answers to many questions." Fearful of the controversy that would result if Joe discovered the listening device, however, Hoover scrawled at the bottom of the memo, "No. Absolutely not."[40]

THE SUNDAY NIGHT SUPPERS continued uninterrupted at Dumbarton Avenue, despite the missile gap and Joe Alsop's grim prognosis for the future. To celebrate the start of the new year and decade, Joe hosted a dinner party at his house for his cousin Alice Roosevelt Longworth and the Grahams. The publisher of *The Washington Post* was finally back full-time at the paper, after a lengthy convalescence. "Phil Graham, who has spent a good part of the last year in tears, seems to be recovering at last," Alsop wrote to Isaiah Berlin, adding,

> Phil's crisis has, I think, quite largely resulted from an inner doubt about his own values. He was all out for the conventional sort of success. He achieved it on the largest scale. And then, somehow, it turned to dust and ashes in his mouth. I cannot understand this sort of upset myself. If I had Phil's success, and God knows I should have liked to have had, I should have been perfectly content to devote myself to making the Washington Post the great, pace-setting and genuinely influential newspaper which it ought to be and is not. But perhaps he did not know how to do this, and perhaps there was some other flaw in his makeup too. At any rate, he is vastly better.[41]

Frank Wisner, too, had recovered sufficiently to leave the Sheppard Pratt clinic and return to work at the CIA. "In general, the psychiatrists' former large revenues from our circle of friends are drying up fast," Joe optimistically informed Vangie Bruce in Bonn, where her husband, David, was serving as the U.S. ambassador to West Germany. Allen Dulles sent Wisner to what promised to be a less stressful post, as the CIA station chief at the American embassy in London. Frank and Polly promptly resumed their whirlwind social schedule, hosting a flock of diplomats and other notables in salons held at their leased Belgravia mansion.

But, in reality, neither Phil Graham nor Frank Wisner was free from the demons that haunted him. For both, the early years of the new decade would be a roller coaster of manic highs and seemingly bottomless lows.

For Joe Alsop, Georgetown had suddenly become a lonely place with Stewart gone, the Wisners packing for London, and the Joyces as well pulling up stakes; after a difficult year as acting director of the State Department's Bureau of Intelligence and Research, Bob Joyce had also been given a less stressful job, at the U.S. consulate in Genoa, Italy. As a result, Joe was suddenly feeling abandoned and alone. "Washington without the Joyces and with the Wisners about to leave reminds me of the Sahara in the penultimate stage of desiccation when the cattle-keeping people who painted those marvelous pictures the French found were dying off 'round drying water holes," Alsop wrote to Jane Joyce that summer.[42]

Fortunately for Joe, there were some new faces in the neighborhood.

Jack and Jackie Kennedy had recently vacated their P Street rental and moved around the corner to a redbrick town house at 3307 N Street, just a block down from Dumbarton and only a few doors away from the house occupied by *Newsweek*'s Washington bureau chief, Ben Bradlee, and his wife, Tony Pinchot. Joe Alsop had gotten to know the Kennedy clan through Jack's sister Kathleen, whom he had met and befriended during a 1946 trip to London. Joe's introduction to John Kennedy and the family's casual lifestyle had come the following year, at a Georgetown dinner with the newly elected congressman. Alsop would later tell the story of arriving at the Kennedy residence in formal attire and being "shown into a living room that appeared to have suffered recently from the ravages of a small, particularly unruly tornado." Two half-eaten hamburgers remained on the mantelpiece. "So I sat down to wait among the ruins, and one by one the occupants of the house, each more astonishingly good-looking than the last, strolled into the living room." Remarkably, the cocktail conversation that evening was dominated not by Joe but by the various Kennedys, while he "limped along behind as best as I could," Alsop remembered. Since then, Jack Kennedy had become a frequent presence at the Dumbarton Avenue salons, where the host was amused to see his usually jaded neighbors come to their windows and applaud when Kennedy appeared on the steps of Joe's circular staircase.[43]

Stewart had arguably been first to see the charismatic senator's potential as presidential timber. Attending a Kennedy campaign rally at a state college in Wisconsin, Stew was impressed when the candidate, in the course of a thirty-minute speech, quoted Aristotle, four U.S. presidents (Jefferson twice), the British playwright George Bernard Shaw, and Walter Lippmann. It was hardly surprising that Joe Alsop, too, would take an instant liking to John Kennedy, likewise born to a prominent New England family and another product of Harvard. In a July 1960 letter, Alsop paid Kennedy his highest compliment, calling him a candidate "with real Rooseveltian possibilities." ("A Stevenson with balls" was Joe's more earthy description.) Alsop told friends that Kennedy was "the perfect candidate."[44]

Indeed, Joe's admiration of Kennedy was "just short of idolatry—and not much this side," Stewart would observe. From the outset, the older Alsop made scant effort to hide his allegiances. "I still think Nixon, if elected, will make a strong if not a very nice President; but I also still think that another eight years of Republican Washington will be too tough to take . . . I think more of [Kennedy] every time I see him, but maybe this is partly because he likes and trusts me," Joe wrote to Susan Mary. Alsop would later admit that he had decided, early on, to help Kennedy "in any way possible to win the presidency." Describing his role as that of "a mostly ineffectual, advice-giving elder" to Jack and his brother Bobby, Joe volunteered to be "an informal member of the Kennedy preconvention team" in strategy meetings at Bobby's Hickory Hill estate.[45]

Meanwhile, Stewart, who was covering Nixon's presidential campaign for *The Saturday Evening Post,* joined Joe in another polling expedition during that unseasonably cold spring. Dressed in a huge fur-lined cloak that had belonged to his grandfather Robinson, and wearing an equally outsized fur hat specially made for him in Paris, Joe, according to his brother, "looked like an angry, large-nosed, bespectacled animal peering out from behind a bush." (As the Alsops were canvassing house to house outside Wausau, Wisconsin, one woman took a look at Joe, shrieked "Holy Mary Mother of God!" and slammed the door.) Stewart noted that his brother was "oddly unaware of his own oddity."[46]

As usual, Joe proved more interested in dispensing opinions than in acquiring them. When one respondent told Alsop that she could never vote for Kennedy because he was a Catholic, Joe brusquely fired back, "Thank you, madam. I think you're a GODDAM BIGOT." Visiting the grim mining town of Slab Fork, West Virginia, Alsop became convinced that religion might indeed play a major role in the coming election. Afterward, Joe wrote a column predicting that if John Kennedy lost the 1960 election, it would only be because of voter prejudice. The Alsops' family lawyer, a staunch Republican, was so outraged that he returned Joe's legal files along with a handwritten note: "I have no longer any desire to have any kind of association with you whatsoever."[47]

As it happened, both Joe Alsop and Phil Graham would play important roles in the events that proved decisive to Kennedy's election as president. In mid-July 1960, Alsop and the Grahams attended the Democratic convention in Los Angeles, staying at the Beverly Wilshire, which Joe called the "least unpleasant" of the convention hotels. Phil Graham had overcome his initial doubts and finally come around to supporting Kennedy. At a drunken dinner two years earlier, Phil, in a belligerent mood, had bluntly told the senator that he was too young and inexperienced to be president. Kay remembered Kennedy calmly replying that he was running nonetheless and methodically laying out the reasons why he thought he could win. After lunch at the Beverly Wilshire—where Joe bribed a waiter to get a table large enough to also accommodate the Grahams' children—Joe and Phil sat down to plot a strategy that would put John Kennedy in the White House.[48]

By the end of the convention's first day, it seemed likely that the only question yet to be settled was who would be Kennedy's running mate. Before coming to Los Angeles, Phil had held out hope that Lyndon Johnson might get the party's nomination. After Kennedy won on the convention's first ballot, however, Graham and Alsop decided to pitch Johnson as the best prospect for vice president. Cornering Kennedy in his suite at the Biltmore Hotel—what Joe, in a touch of drama, called "the antechambers of history"—Alsop began by making the case against the other odds-on favorites for the second slot on the ticket. As Joe remembered, Phil thereupon "made a most eloquent and intelligent presentation of the electoral advantages of a Johnson vice-presidency." Kennedy, after only a little hesitation, agreed to offer the job to Johnson—possibly in the expectation that the proud Texan would turn it down.[49]

Over the next forty-eight hours, Graham shuttled frenetically between Kennedy and Johnson, cajoling the latter into accepting a spot on the ticket and reportedly countering efforts by Bobby Kennedy to torpedo the deal. When Johnson, in a rare moment of indecision, told Graham that he was not sure he should announce that he had accepted Jack Kennedy's offer, Phil blurted out, "Of course you know what you're going to do. Throw your shoulders back and your chin out and go out and make that announcement. And then go on and win. Everything's wonderful." By the time of Kennedy's acceptance speech at the Los Angeles Coliseum early on the evening of July 15, freshly printed placards held high by a cheering audience of eighty thousand read, "Kennedy-Johnson."[50]

Following the convention, Joe was invited to the Kennedy compound at Hyannis Port on Cape Cod, where he was impressed anew with the energy and vitality of the close-knit clan. (When Bobby's five-year-old son, David, roughhousing with Joe, hit his head on a low porch beam, Alsop was amazed that no tears flowed. The Kennedy household was "an orphan asylum for junior Spartans," Joe marveled in a letter to Susan Mary.) Belatedly growing sensitive to reportorial colleagues' grousing that he had abandoned even the pretense of objectivity as a newsman, Alsop stayed at Eunice Shriver's house in the compound.[51]

As the November election drew nearer, Joe ingratiated himself with another, newer member of the Kennedy clan by marriage. "It is really rather moving, if you don't mind my seeming mushy, to see Jack going into the hardest campaign of the century with his rather special combination of a hard, realistic grasp of his problem and a high heart," Alsop wrote to Jackie that August.[52]

Along with Joan Braden, Joe had become a kind of confidant for John Kennedy's pregnant wife, even advising Jackie—in the same letter—on national politics and maternity fashions: "Normally, it wouldn't be known where you buy your maternity clothes. But even if you were plain Mrs. Kennedy of New York, London and the Riviera, it would be well known that you are a faithful and admiring customer of Givenchy. It will probably help, if there are some pieces in the paper about your buying your maternity clothes at Bloomingdale's."

Jackie, in turn, showed no reluctance about sharing confidences with Alsop. In a long, handwritten note on her light blue personal stationery, she replied, "You are very perceptive—to sense what was troubling me. A year or so ago—when I was wondering if it was really worth it to have Jack run for the Presidency—as you never saw your husband or child in the same place 2 days running—and were usually too tired to speak to each other—you said 'it's the only game that's worth the candle.' Because you told me that—I thought about it every day—and gradually came to agree with you—And that was when the happy time started."[53]

Jackie also unburdened herself on the frustrations of being the wife of a presidential candidate:

I have been appalled at some of the personal questions these women reporters ask me—and on the defensive about poor little Caroline, whom they want to chase around with flashbulbs and turn into a ghastly little Shirley Temple if I'd let them—and slightly irritated at the Kennedy girls who adore publicity!—I was being unreasonable. Now I will be reasonable—thank god you explained how—It makes everything so peaceful. I couldn't bear it if Jack should ever think I was at cross purposes with him . . . And there is one more thing you have taught me—to respect power. I never did—possibly because it came so suddenly without my having had to work for it—(power by marriage I mean). But if things turn out right—I will welcome it—and use it for the things I care about.

Following the first of the televised debates that fall between Kennedy and Nixon—the vice president "looked like a suspect who was being questioned . . . in connection with a statutory rape case," Joe wrote to a friend—Alsop had Jack and Jackie to dinner at his house, where he served the ubiquitous terrapin stew. The third and fourth debates had focused on foreign policy, an area where the Alsop brothers heartily endorsed Kennedy's promise to make sure that the country was "second to none" in military strength. Similarly, Joe was cheered by Kennedy's willingness to confront Khrushchev on a variety of outstanding issues: Cuba, Berlin, and nuclear testing among them.[54]

The shooting down of a U-2 spy plane over Russia a few months earlier—on May 1, 1960—had finally shed some light on Eisenhower's seeming complacency regarding the missile gap. (Ironically, Ike had actually suspended the overflights, fearing just such an outcome, and only recently resumed them, in response to pressure from others in his administration—who argued that they were necessary to counter critics like Joe Alsop.) Most commentators deplored the U-2 incident for damaging Soviet-American relations; George Kennan, for example, argued that it had undermined Khrushchev, who later walked out of a planned summit meeting in Paris with Ike. But Joe Alsop publicly rejoiced in Matter of Fact that the United States had developed the means to peer over the Iron Curtain and uncover Soviet secrets. In a column titled "The Wonderful News," Alsop celebrated that capability as "deeply reassuring." Although Joe raised the disturbing possibility that the Russians might yet be hiding their ICBMs out of sight of the U-2's cameras, he concluded that the "nightmare" of a missile-bristling Soviet Union "need not trouble the sleep of the West any longer."*[55]

ON TUESDAY EVENING, October 11, 1960, nearly a hundred people assembled at the stately home of Katharine Graham's parents to celebrate Joe Alsop's fiftieth birthday. The party, a gathering of Washington's elite, had been planned for months by Kay, Polly, and Stewart and was confirmation of Joe Alsop's drawing power—if not necessarily his popularity in the capital. The guest list included Arthur Schlesinger Jr., Dean Acheson, Chip Bohlen, and David Bruce. Most of the CIA's top spies—Allen Dulles, Richard Bissell, Des FitzGerald, and Tracy Barnes—also attended, as did Alsop's rivals among Washington reporters: Walter Lippmann, James Reston, and Arthur Krock. Since Jack and Jackie Kennedy were on the campaign trail in Illinois that night, the candidate's wife sent champagne and a personal note with the couple's regrets. "I cannot express—& become tearful when I try—in this supercharged emotional time—how we appreciate your friendship," Jackie wrote to Joe.[56]

Conversation at the party inevitably turned to the upcoming presidential election, only weeks away. Schlesinger told Acheson that he was surprised at how much Joe Alsop and the entire Washington press corps had become "emotionally engaged" in the Kennedy campaign: "They cannot stand the thought of a Nixon victory, and they have a confidence in Jack which none of them really had in Adlai." (The cranky Acheson was not impressed with either candidate: he thought both Nixon and Kennedy mere "school kids, bright sophomores, and couldn't see how anything either of them had said or done qualified them for the presidency.")[57]

---

* While it has been something of an enduring mystery why Joe Alsop continued to warn of a missile gap when his good friend Richard Bissell was head of the CIA's overhead reconnaissance program, the answer may not be all that difficult to divine: the U-2 had not photographed the entire U.S.S.R. by the time of the May 1 shoot-down, and the imagery from the Corona satellite, its replacement, would not definitively expose the missile gap as a myth until the late summer or early fall of 1961—when the United States discovered that Khrushchev's vaunted arsenal of ICBMs actually consisted of just four liquid-fueled R-7 missiles deployed at Plesetsk. But it is also true that Joe Alsop was keenly aware of the political utility of "the gap" to John Kennedy.

Phil Graham gave the birthday toast to the guest of honor, recalling the occasion when he had first met Joe, two decades earlier in Georgetown. Alsop had been wearing a wildly colored kimono and was having breakfast outside in his garden with Isaiah Berlin. Joe's laughter was audible throughout the neighborhood, Phil remembered. He had always been impressed, Graham said, not only by Joe's seemingly encyclopedic knowledge but equally by the passion and certainty with which he expressed his views—passion being one of Alsop's most obvious and endearing traits:

> He is a rasping geyser of bad temper, and he is a gentle fountain of friendship. He is constantly on the brink of fleeing to monasticism, and he is inexorably drawn to involvement in the noisy world. He is cuttingly cynical, and he is splendidly and sentimentally naive . . . When I knew him only little, his essence was easy to grasp. But the more I know of him I only know there is more of him to know. I hope and believe that is a loving thing to say of a man of fifty, for Kay and I love Joe as all of you do.[58]

A little more than two weeks later, on Election Day, Joe joined Kay and Phil in Graham's office at *The Washington Post* to listen to the early returns on the radio. The first results were encouraging: Joe and Phil both stood and cheered when Kennedy won Texas, mindful of their role in securing Lyndon Johnson's place on the ticket. But the trio retreated to Alsop's house when it became clear that the outcome would probably be a cliff-hanger. Joe wheeled in the ancient television on which he and his guests had previously watched Guy Lombardo. When Kay went home shortly after midnight, Joe and Phil stayed up, resolved to see the drama through to its end, drinking scotch and sodas on Alsop's couch. The two friends, Joe remembered, settled in for "a very long and very drunken evening."[59]

CHAPTER SIXTEEN

"A Breathless Time, Full of Promise and Energy"

"Hurrah for the New Frontier!" read the telegram that Susan Mary sent to Arthur Schlesinger Jr. and his wife, Marian, a week after John Kennedy was elected president. "It's *glorious* that you are to be in Washington," Soozle enthused. The rumor had already reached Paris that Schlesinger was to be the president's special adviser in the Kennedy administration. The Schlesingers would soon be moving to a redbrick town house at 3105 O Street.[1]

Indeed, the jubilation in Georgetown over Kennedy's election was widespread. Joe Alsop was particularly delighted, since it was he who had introduced Schlesinger to Kennedy at a dinner party more than a decade earlier. (The future president had impressed the Harvard historian as "very sincere and not unintelligent, but kind of on the conservative side," wrote Schlesinger in his journal.)[2]

The return of a Democrat to the White House marked not only the end of eight long years of political isolation for the likes of Joe Alsop but also a revival of the staid capital city's social life. It was, Joe would later recall wistfully, "a breathless time, full of promise and energy and, oddly enough, glamour, which is a not a quality usually associated with Washington."[3]

A sign and a symbol of how much had changed occurred in the early hours of January 21, 1961, when Alsop returned from the inaugural ball to discover a gaggle of inebriated guests outside his house, banging on the front door. (Joe had always told friends they could stop off for champagne anytime the lights were on.) Alsop was hurriedly retrieving bottles of Dom Pérignon and leftover turtle soup from the refrigerator when he was interrupted by another knock on the door. Filling the snow-covered street was a cortege of Secret Service cars and limousines and, in the doorway, a bareheaded John Kennedy. Inside, the president took Joe's proffered glass of champagne but passed on the odiferous terrapin stew. Jackie had chosen to go back to the White House after the ball. The president stayed at Alsop's party for more than two hours, not returning to the Executive Mansion until 3:40 a.m.[4]

A feature article in *Newsweek* later that year—"The Columnists JFK Reads Every Morning"—would be a frank acknowledgment of the influence that Joe and his colleagues in the Washington press corps had on the White House's new occupant. Alsop provided "warning," Walter Lippmann "reason," and Scotty Reston "information," the article proclaimed—making the journalistic trio "'must' reading on the New Frontier." A newly hired *Newsweek* reporter, twenty-six-year-old Ward Just, had interviewed Alsop for the piece. While impressed by Joe's erudition, Just also noted his subject's ever-present gloomy, foreboding mood: "Alsop blends into his writings deep convictions, hard-won facts, and pervading all, an air of imminent cataclysm."[5]

Joe bought a pair of ornate Augsburg candlesticks—"giltbronze, crystal and agate, formed of figures representing Hercules clad in the skin of the Nemaean Lion and holding up the globe for Atlas"—to celebrate Kennedy's victory. But even before he collected the case of 1949 claret that he had won betting on the election's outcome, Alsop was already counseling John Kennedy on important cabinet appointments. Joe called it "warwicking" the administration. "In my new role as a giver of unsolicited and probably unwanted advice," he began one letter to the president. Some of Joe's recommendations were plainly self-serving—like his request that Kennedy appoint the attorney Roswell Gilpatric to a high Pentagon position. Ros, who had been a frequent source of leaks to Alsop as undersecretary of the air force during the Truman years, became deputy secretary of defense.[6]

Joe Alsop and Phil Graham both championed Douglas Dillon, a Republican banker, for Treasury secretary. Schlesinger, who opposed the appointment, remembered Graham as "euphorically insistent" on Dillon. Not for the last time, the president overruled his special assistant to follow the advice of his Georgetown friends, asking Graham to personally pass the word to Dillon. That evening, Phil snuck into a downstairs cloakroom at Dillon's house, interrupting a dinner party for wealthy GOP fund-raisers, to give the secretary designate the good news.[7]

Alsop and Graham were less successful in efforts to make their mutual friend David Bruce secretary of state, but they were cheered when Kennedy instead offered Bruce an ambassadorship at his choice of European capitals. (Bruce chose London.) The president picked Dean Rusk—the Asia specialist who had learned of the Korean invasion at Joe's house—to head the State Department.

In a memo to the president, Schlesinger warned that John Foster Dulles had left State in need of a major shake-up: "Dulles's punitive action against the men, especially in the Russia and China Services (Chip Bohlen, George Kennan, Charles Thayer, John Davies, etc.) who had been most consistently independent and outspoken, indicated to the others what a great mistake it was ever to go out on a limb. The Department is still suffering from the hangover of the Dulles period." Averell Harriman, whom Kennedy made assistant secretary of state for Far Eastern affairs, was even more direct about the damage Dulles had done, describing State's China desk as "a disaster area filled with human wreckage . . ." The previous year, the Crocodile had hired Charlie Thayer to serve as his guide and interpreter during a tour of the Soviet Union. Thayer was still trying, thus far unsuccessfully, to make ends meet as a novelist after being forced out of the Foreign Service by Joe McCarthy.[*8]

The influence of Kennedy's Georgetown friends reached both high and low in the new administration. Hopeful that the president would share his interest in improving the D.C. government, Phil Graham promoted his personal candidate for District commissioner in a letter to Kennedy that he marked "personal." Phil also sent the president some suggestions for his inaugural address.[9]

The importuning of Alsop and Graham might even have helped rescue George Kennan from an unhappy and premature retirement: the temperamental diplomat secured the post of U.S. ambassador to Yugoslavia. Paul Nitze's preelection role as a defense adviser to the Kennedy campaign was rewarded by appointment as the assistant secretary of defense for international security affairs. Nitze had originally hoped to

---

[*] "Time and again [John Davies's] friends have tried to get action and promises have been made but nothing has taken place," Thayer had written to Harriman, who subsequently contacted Secretary of State Dean Rusk, imploring, "Dean: are you ready to have this case reviewed and injustice rectified?" Vindication of a sort finally arrived in January 1969, when the government restored Davies's security clearance but not his rank in the Foreign Service. Even then, the State Department leaked the news to *The New York Times* rather than announce it publicly.

be Kennedy's pick to run the Pentagon, but even his confirmation for the lesser post would run into trouble in the Senate over allegations of purported pacifist leanings. Months earlier, Nitze had given a speech at the Asilomar conference center in Pacific Grove, California. In the speech, he had unwisely played the part of intellectual gadfly, proposing that the U.S. Strategic Air Command be placed under the control of the United Nations. (His speech, Nitze later joked, was "pursuant to the definition of an economist—a man who lightly passes over the minor inconsistencies the better to press on to the grand fallacy.") But Nitze's efforts to demonstrate the "grand fallacy" of his own logic had backfired. The Asilomar speech would return to haunt him two years later, when he faced confirmation as secretary of the navy.[10]

Susan Mary's friend and longtime confidante, Marietta—a tireless fund-raiser at Georgetown parties for Kennedy's rival, Adlai Stevenson—received a diplomatic post in the new administration, as U.S. representative to the United Nations Commission on Human Rights. (Joe once wrote derisively to Soozle of Marietta: "beautiful bosums [sic] beating for beautiful causes.") Stevenson himself was named U.S. ambassador to the UN.[11]

During the weeks and months that followed the inauguration, Joe's house on Dumbarton Avenue became a kind of unofficial retreat and refuge for the young president. Alsop calculated that the presidential couple visited about every fortnight for supper, while John Kennedy himself sometimes arrived unannounced and alone, as he had on inaugural night.[*12]

Just a week after the new president was sworn in, Jack and Jackie reciprocated with a private dinner—their first in the White House—where Joe Alsop and the Grahams were the guests. Joe remembered a brass bucket the size of a milk pail filled to the brim with caviar—the gift of a Kennedy admirer—and "limitless Dom Perignon." Kennedy instructed his press secretary, Pierre Salinger, that only four newsmen—Joe Alsop,

---

* On one such evening, when Jackie was out of town, Alsop's other dinner guest was Mary Meyer, with whom the president was carrying on an affair. As Sally Bedell Smith noted, however, it is unlikely that Joe's house was the site for any of Kennedy's assignations—since the president knew of Alsop's affection for Jackie. Asked in 1979 about the president's "extremely complicated love life," Joe told an interviewer from the Kennedy presidential library: "You haven't even begun to scratch that surface. And not even scratch it. And I'm not going to talk about it, either, for this damn tape recorder. So there we are. Now I think we might have a drink and forget about it."

Phil Graham, Scotty Reston, and Walter Lippmann—were to be put through to him immediately when they telephoned the White House. Jackie later claimed that her husband regarded Reston as "awfully sanctimonious," whereas Lippmann, she felt, always remained at a distance from the president, in part because of Kennedy's Catholic faith. But the First Lady saw no such barriers for Alsop: "Well, Joe was his friend."[13]

ANOTHER BIG CHANGE in Joe Alsop's life came less than a month after the Kennedy inauguration, in mid-February 1961, when the fifty-year-old bachelor married Susan Mary Patten. Soozle's first husband, Joe's Harvard roommate, had succumbed the previous March to chronic emphysema. By late June 1960, Susan Mary wrote to a friend, she had already received three marriage proposals—two from married men with "nice but dull wives," while the third was "unexpected."[14]

Throughout that summer, Alsop steadily courted Susan Mary. An initial letter from Joe expressing interest, which he sent from the Democratic convention in Los Angeles—and reportedly wrote on airline stationery—met with a prompt rebuff. During an extended visit to Paris, however, Alsop pursued the object of his affection with fixed determination, even enlisting the aid of their mutual friend Arthur Schlesinger Jr. as a co-conspirator in his campaign. Susan Mary finally relented. "I am the luckiest man in the world," Alsop wrote to well-wishers.[15]

Because District of Columbia laws did not allow weddings on short notice, the couple exchanged vows at All Saints Episcopal Church in Chevy Chase, Maryland. Among those attending the private ceremony were the bride's mother and the groom's two brothers with their wives, while, outside the church, an FBI agent diligently recorded the license plate numbers of the guests' cars.

Indeed, J. Edgar Hoover and the bureau had continued to keep a close watch on the Alsops. In March 1961, the FBI director sent Attorney General Robert Kennedy a report on the dinner that Joe had recently attended at the French embassy: "During the course of the evening there was a discussion concerning the international political situation and Alsop did considerable talking. He allegedly made some statements critical of French foreign policy and at one point referred to France as a 'second rate power.' Immediately after Alsop made the statement, the French guest of honor excused himself and left the Embassy."[16]

During a pre-wedding dinner at Joe's house that Jack and Jackie Kennedy attended, Stewart advised Susan Mary never to let Joe behind the wheel of her new Jaguar. Susan Mary's goddaughter, twenty-one-year-old Frances FitzGerald, was more blunt, challenging the bride-to-be, "Can you cook?" The chef and the maid that Susan Mary brought with her from Paris would replace Joe's loyal retainers, for José had died shortly after Kennedy's inauguration.[17]

Accommodating to married life provoked surprisingly little complaint from the groom. A spacious separate bedroom for Susan Mary, decorated in blue and white, with an adjoining split-level wardrobe closet, was part of Joe's remodel of 2720 Dumbarton. Among the other necessary renovations was a garage for Susan Mary's car and a backyard swimming pool. The brothers' former office downstairs was converted into bedrooms for Anne, eleven, and Billy, twelve, Susan Mary's children from her previous marriage. But the garden room—Joe's favorite—remained untouched.[18]

Alsop also proved to be eagerly solicitous of the needs and wants of his instant family. He had long played the part of doting uncle to the children of his Georgetown friends and relatives, and he was known as "the dollar man" to Stewart's kids because of his reward for every A on their report cards. (The notable exception was for social studies, which Joe regarded as a poor substitute for history in the curriculum.) Joe likewise opened a charge account in his name at a neighborhood bookstore for his nephews and nieces. Although the children were allowed to buy any book they wished, Stewart's daughter, Elizabeth, recalled Joe's disapproving glare when the choice was modern fiction. Frank Wisner's son Frank II remembered being rewarded with "heaps of ice cream" upon successfully reciting verses of *The Rime of the Ancient Mariner*. After Marietta Peabody remarried, moving with Ronald Tree to Ditchley, an eighteenth-century manor house on a sprawling estate in the Devonshire countryside, Alsop had thoughtfully sent her then-seven-year-old daughter, Frances—"Frankie"—a new riding crop. Later, when Donald Graham, an English major at Harvard, sought Joe's advice on a topic for his undergraduate thesis, Alsop persuaded Donny to write about the British poet and novelist Dame Rose Macaulay. Informed that his stepdaughter, Anne, was encountering difficulties at school with Latin, Alsop tutored the child for a couple of hours each day before dinner. Joe made his stepson, Billy, the bartender for his Georgetown salons, where the twelve-year-old routinely met and conversed with cabinet secretaries, Supreme Court justices, and a constellation of Washington's other stars.[19]

At the outset, Alsop had made clear to his new bride that what he called their "partnership" would be platonic, given his own sexual preference. ("I thought I could change him," Susan Mary confided to Anne years later.)[20] There had been no further word of the Moscow incident since the oblique reference that appeared in the *National Review* more than two years earlier, but the timing of Joe's marriage hardly seemed coincidental. As Billy would observe, it gave Alsop much-needed "cover" as a family man, at a time when Joe was coming under increasing public scrutiny for being a Kennedy insider.[21]

Indeed, Joe himself would never know how close his secret had come to breaking out into the open. Shortly before Eisenhower left the White House, Lewis Strauss had again raised with the president the issue of Alsop's sexual indiscretion in Russia. "I remarked on the folly of protecting our enemies from the evil consequences of their own behavior," wrote Strauss in a memorandum of his conversation with Ike, "and referred to the fact that the report of Alsop's homosexual episode in Russia was in Allen Dulles' safe and that it might disappear in the course of time with a change of faces." Strauss noted a previous occasion when a confidential government report proving wrongdoing had vanished without a trace. Strauss's memo continued,

> The President said, "Well, we must see that that doesn't happen with the Alsop file and we will get it over here and take some notes about it." He called Mr. Dulles who was not available and then asked me to instruct General [Wilton] Persons to send for the report. I spoke to General Persons about it who, however, seemed reluctant to make the try and said that as Mr. Dulles was now signed up for the new Administration, he could probably in view of his friendship with Alsop find some excuse for not complying in any case. He said that he would try to get it.[22]

Two weeks later—on Christmas Eve 1960—Strauss had gone to the White House again, this time in response to a telephone call from General Persons, Eisenhower's chief of staff. In his office, Persons opened a desk drawer and withdrew a file folder, handing it to Strauss with the request that the latter read the contents in an adjoining room. The file contained a letter from Joe Alsop to Frank Wisner, as well as a typed description of Alsop's version of the incident, on paper bearing a stamp with Cyrillic writing.[23]

Strauss would also bring up the Moscow incident directly with Allen Dulles—whom Kennedy had reappointed as CIA director—when the two attended Washington's Gridiron dinner, in mid-March 1961. Dulles assured Strauss that he had indeed "communicated to the President the information concerning Mr. Alsop."[24]

Additionally, in a subsequent conversation with J. Edgar Hoover, Strauss learned that the FBI director had shown Robert Kennedy a copy of the same Alsop file, shortly after the president appointed his brother to the post of attorney general. "Mr. Hoover said that the Attorney General read the papers without any expression of the effect that they made upon him," wrote Strauss in another "memcon." Hoover told Strauss that he had likewise briefed the president on the Alsop affair—as an example of "the Communist tactics of blackmail"—in the company of the attorney general. But the FBI director was disappointed to learn, only a few days later, that Kennedy had recently been Joe's dinner guest "and that Alsop is at the White House frequently." As he had in the case of Frank Wisner, Hoover decided to bide his time.[25]

BEYOND SUGGESTING CANDIDATES for White House cabinet slots, Kennedy's Georgetown friends were soon besieging the new president with unsolicited advice on weighty matters of state. Even before the president moved into the Executive Mansion, Joe Alsop had written to Kennedy to ask if the president was yet "in really close touch with the developing crises in Laos and the Congo." He was, Joe confided, "shocked by the outlines of these two problems that I got from Dick Bissell today." Like Allen Dulles, Bissell remained in his old post at the agency, as head of the Plans Directorate.[26]

Following their European honeymoon, Joe had dropped Susan Mary off in Paris so that he could make a quick reporting visit to Vientiane, the Laotian capital. A recent military coup against that country's neutralist government had resulted in a nascent civil war between right-wing and Communist forces. Alsop had threatened to sabotage the confirmation of a senior State Department nominee unless the president took a hard-line stand against the Communist Pathet Lao guerrillas. (After a recent Lippmann column urging a negotiated settlement in Laos, Kennedy told an aide, "I agree much more with Walter than I do with Joe on this. But don't let Joe know that!") While Kennedy did not respond directly to Joe's threat, a few weeks later, in early March 1961, the president signed a secret directive sending helicopters and C-130 transports, but not U.S. troops, to Laos to help a new neutralist government fight the insurgency. Chip Bohlen, witnessing an encounter between Alsop and Kennedy at this time, thought the president "extremely masterful in his handling of Joe" on Laos. While Kennedy "didn't really say anything different than what had been in the papers or around, he did it in such a way that he gave Joe the impression that he was letting him in on [a scoop]."[27]

Alsop already enjoyed good relations with the president's national security adviser, McGeorge Bundy. As a longtime friend of the family, Mac boasted of his "tribal" connection with the Alsops. Bundy had also been among Joe's frequent dinner guests at Dumbarton Avenue.[28]

Joe was less familiar with the newly confirmed secretary of defense, Robert McNamara. The former Ford Motors president had a reputation as a "human computer" and had brought with him to the Pentagon a coterie of bright young men—the so-called whiz kids. But what had been meant as an introductory breakfast in the garden room went disastrously awry when Joe's toucan, perched behind McNamara's back, letting loose a loud shriek, spit a well-chewed banana on the defense secretary's bald spot. McNamara seemed unfazed, and their interview continued. (Shortly thereafter, however, Alsop traded the toucan for a pair of better-behaved and more sedate mourning doves.) McNamara, too, became another of the regulars at Joe's table.[29]

Alsop would later claim that he had known about the Kennedy administration's first major misstep—Project Zapata, the CIA's failed invasion of Cuba at the Bay of Pigs, in April 1961—for "some months" prior to the event and had even anticipated its tragic outcome, purposefully arranging to be on his honeymoon with Susan Mary when news of the debacle broke. Joe's longtime friend Dickie Bissell had been the "driving force" behind Zapata. Even so, the columns that Alsop wrote on the disaster were surprisingly uncritical of Kennedy and the CIA's top leaders. Instead, Joe pinned the blame on Eisenhower and the agency's overeager Cuban refugees. "From the outset, the new President had strong doubts about the scheme, and especially about the proposed American participation," Alsop wrote in Matter of Fact.[30]

Stewart Alsop was neither as circumspect nor as kind to the president as his brother. "I was pleased with our Mr. Kennedy too, but since Cuba not so much . . . He is falling flat on his handsome face—and so have we all," Stew wrote to a friend.[31] In late June 1961, he published a detailed anatomy of the abortive invasion in *The Saturday Evening Post.* "The Lessons of the Cuban Disaster" was most critical of the CIA masterminds of the plot, Allen Dulles and Richard Bissell. "They didn't just brief us on the Cuban operation, they sold us on it," an unidentified White House official had told Alsop of the agency's director and the head of the Plans Directorate. But Stewart's account faulted President Kennedy as well—for ruling out American military intervention in the event that the invasion ran into trouble. There were, Stew concluded, "astonishing errors in judgment" all the way around.[32]

The *Post* magazine article confronted Stewart with a tricky dilemma. As Stew acknowledged in the piece, Bissell, who lived on nearby Newark Street in Cleveland Park, was an "old friend" as well as his neighbor. (Stewart's children vividly remembered Bissell's ratty old station wagon coming up Springland Lane on sagging springs, swaying like a ship in heavy seas. Bissell's son Rich and Stewart's eldest son, Joe, carried on late-night conversations over a telephone wire that the boys surreptitiously strung between their two houses—a case of clandestine "bugging" that went undiscovered by the CIA's veteran spy.) But Bissell kept his counsel and never complained about the treatment he received in Stewart's magazine piece—at least not in the Alsop family's presence.[33]

Early in 1962, "Kennedy's Grand Strategy," another *Post* magazine article by Joe's younger brother, attracted international attention when it quoted the president as saying, in response to a question about nuclear war, "Khrushchev must *not* be certain that, where its vital interests are threatened, the United States will never strike first."[34] While Kennedy's comment was merely a reiteration of the long-standing position of previous U.S. presidents, who reserved the right to initiate the use of nuclear weapons in any conflict, the statement provoked a personal response from Khrushchev. Immediately after Stewart's *Post* article appeared, the Russian leader ordered Soviet military forces to heightened alert, in a tacit signal of his displeasure. Subsequently, *Pravda* editorialized, "It is incomprehensible what upside-down logic prompted [Kennedy] to make this rash and provocative statement about a possible preventive nuclear attack against the Soviet Union."[35]

Ironically, almost as an afterthought, the missile gap, an ongoing source of Soviet-American tensions, had been officially—and mysteriously—declared closed a few months earlier. In his column on September 25, 1961, Joe Alsop confidently announced the "cheerful" conclusion of the CIA's most recent National Intelligence Estimate, which showed "a sharp reduction in the number of inter-continental ballistic missiles with which the Soviets are credited." ("Everyone, of course, was flabbergasted at the speed with which Alsop had obtained the information contained in the estimate—within a matter of hours after it was published," noted the scribe at Allen Dulles's CIA staff meeting that morning. "Anything that's known to 15 or 20 people is certainly going to be known to the Alsop brothers," Dulles had noted, resignedly, upon becoming the CIA director.) On October 21, McNamara's deputy, Ros Gilpatric, quietly confirmed the good news in a speech before the Business Council of Hot Springs, Virginia. In the number of missiles, as well as in overall nuclear striking force, Gilpatric announced, the United States was—as Kennedy had promised it would be—"second to none." The missile gap—Joe Alsop's obsession and the campaign issue that many believed was responsible for Kennedy's election—had always been a chimera.[36]

The Washington Post reported the sudden and curious end of the missile gap without editorial comment by its publisher. By that fall, Phil Graham was once again back at work at his newspaper and, in another manic mood, had launched on a buying spree. With encouragement from Benjamin Bradlee, *Newsweek's* bureau chief in Washington and Phil's Georgetown neighbor, Graham had bought the magazine the previous March, for some nine million dollars—in what was described at the time as "one of the great steals of contemporary journalism." (For the two-million-dollar down payment, Phil pulled a crumpled personal check out of his own wallet, crossed out his name, and wrote, "The Washington Post Company." He later notified the *Post's* treasurer that he could cover the amount.) Phil's euphoria was doubtless fueled in part by the fact that the magazine purchase was *his* idea and that he, and not his father-in-law or his wife, was the broker of the deal this time. Graham's acquisition mania continued throughout a Canadian vacation the following year, when he bought a part interest in the Nova Scotia pulp mill that supplied paper to the *Post*. Other purchases included a second farm in Virginia, a turboprop airplane, and *ARTnews* magazine—the last an apparent nod to Kay's growing interest in the subject.[37]

Phil was no less eager to let the world know of his business and journalistic prowess. When a trade publication left Herblock out of its list of the country's best political cartoonists, Graham promptly wrote to the editor to complain: "We now have a screamingly successful prop-erty, *a la* profits. And we have a fairly good paper—I should think the second best in the U.S., a place horse in a not very fast race." It was not only things but people that Phil had begun collecting for his expanding empire. After much wooing, Graham lured Walter Lippmann away from the *New York Herald Tribune* and likewise acquired from the moribund *Trib* the syndicate that published Joe Alsop's column.[38]

In between his manic episodes and impulse purchases, however, Phil's depression always stubbornly returned. Shortly after the *Newsweek* pur-chase, Graham was once again back in seclusion at Glen Welby. Phil used the expression "going to my Far Country" to describe his depressed moods. The Grahams approached their friends Scotty and Sally Reston about becoming godparents to the children should something happen to them. Even though Katharine couched the request in hypothetical terms—the couple perishing in a plane crash, for example—Scotty privately suspected that Kay's real concern was her husband's perilous psychological condition. Scotty had previously confronted Phil about his abusive treatment of Kay. The *Times* reporter had wisely declined a lucrative offer from Graham to take over the *Post*'s editorial page, recog-nizing whose views would likely prevail in the end.[39]

The fact that Graham was known to be a close friend to the president of the United States was no small part of his enhanced status in Wash-ington, and he did not hesitate to exploit his access to the White House or to promote Kennedy's interests in return. Graham confessed to Isaiah Berlin that his attitude toward the president had, at an early stage, passed "beyond enthusiasm into passion." After *Newsweek* ran a fawning edito-rial titled "Presidential Wisdom," the magazine's new owner wrote to Kennedy, "Dear Mr. President: It is going to be hard to keep Newsweek to the right of the Chicago Tribune. But I shall try. Respectfully, Phil."[40]

In the eyes of some *Post* reporters, Graham's pro-Kennedy bias was increasingly evident in the Washington Post Company's publications. Phil had allegedly sat on the story of the Bay of Pigs until the fate of the invaders was sealed, subsequently spiked a *Post* editorial that would have criticized the president, and then wrote Kennedy a bracing "chin-up" let-ter in the wake of the fiasco. Two months later, Graham and Joe Alsop eagerly rallied to the administration's colors when the president asked for their support in mobilizing public opinion during the 1961 Berlin crisis. (In an article for *Saturday Review*—"The Most Important Decision in U.S. History"—Joe compared Kennedy's defiance of Khrushchev to the ancient Athenians standing up to the Persian king. But the magazine's editor, Norman Cousins, begged to differ—titling his editorial in the same issue "No Extermination Without Representation.") In a move widely seen as a reward for Graham's loyal service, Kennedy made Phil a member of the board of the federally funded Communications Satellite Corporation when COMSAT was created the following year.[41]

Yet, even as he approached the pinnacle of his fame and accomplishments, things became irredeemably unstuck for Phil Graham. By late 1962, the earlier pattern of oscillating moods had become a seemingly fixed mania, marked by increasingly aggressive outbursts and erratic behavior. From a misdirected telephone call just before Christmas, Kay discovered that Phil had been having an affair with a *Newsweek* stringer, Robin Webb, whom he had met the previous month during a trip to Paris. Two weeks later, Phil moved out of the house on R Street and into a suite at Washington's Carlyle Hotel. When Kay sent her husband a telegram, hinting at the possibility of reconciliation, she received what she described as "a pretty strange letter" from Phil in return: "I have now gone. Gone not to my Far Country but to my Destiny. It happens to be a beautiful Destiny and I shall be there while it is beautiful and while it is not."[42]

Phil Graham's relationship with the president was also becoming progressively more bizarre. In his megalomania, Phil offered to mediate a minor dispute between Jack Kennedy and the president's own brother. Graham was likewise counseling Robert McNamara on how to improve the Pentagon's relations with the press. ("I won't edit the Washington *Post* for you anymore if you'll give me back the Department of Defense," McNamara wrote back in jest.) Following another late-night phone call, in which Graham spewed a stream of salty invective at Kennedy, the president ordered the White House switchboard to accept no more calls from the *Post* publisher after 9:00 p.m.[43]

In retrospect, a warning of what was to come might have been seen in Graham's obsession with the president of France, Charles de Gaulle. The French leader's decision, early in 1963, to veto Britain's bid to join the European Common Market provoked a crisis in the Western alliance and was widely condemned on both sides of the Atlantic. But in a strident editorial that he wrote for the *Post,* Graham came to de Gaulle's defense. When the paper's managing editor, Al Friendly, and Russ Wiggins, in charge of the *Post's* editorial page, both threatened to resign if Phil went ahead with publishing the piece, Graham reluctantly relented, but then sent a rambling, three-page letter to President Kennedy under the heading "Some Thoughts About General de Gaulle." In the letter, Phil praised the stubborn French president for his courage. De Gaulle's critics, Graham wrote, seemed intent on "preventing any greatness in a man." Phil Graham evidently saw someone very much like himself in de Gaulle—a heroic figure beleaguered, defiant, and alone.[44]

AT THE CIA, the earnest hopes that Graham's friend Frank Wisner placed in the New Frontier had gradually yielded to disillusionment on both sides, following the dismal failure of Project Zapata. In a letter to his former boss, Richard Helms confessed to Wisner that the agency remained in "shell shock" since the debacle at the Bay of Pigs: "I do not have to paint a picture for you of the gloom and bitterness which have pervaded these halls. The former is the obvious reaction to a failure, the latter results from what many of us feel to be the high-handed manner with which the activity was mounted"—a veiled reference to Dick Bissell, Helms's nemesis and the Cuban invasion's chief architect. On May 1, 1961, Wisner replied to Helms's letter in a cryptic handwritten note:

> As upset and harassed as we have been in London over the develop-
> ments to which you have adverted, this must be nothing by com-
> parison to what is being experienced at your end of the line . . . You
> need have no doubt about my ability to read between the lines of
> your note and it goes without saying that you can depend upon
> my understanding with and sympathy for your position in all of
> this. I am gravely concerned about the future, and looking forward
> to discussing with you the longer range future repercussions and
> implication of this affair.[45]

Wisner would miss the farewell dinner for Allen Dulles that fall at Washington's Alibi Club, a favorite agency hangout. Along with Bissell, Dulles, the CIA's longtime spymaster, had been cashiered by Kennedy in the wake of the failed Cuban venture. Administration insiders, includ-ing Mac Bundy, believed that Bissell and Dulles had secretly counted on Kennedy sending in the marines if the invasion force ran into trouble.[46] After the president refused to order the navy to provide air cover for the invaders, Bissell had gone home to Cleveland Park and sat in his backyard garden, listening to opera blasting from the house at high volume. Bissell would subsequently become head of the Institute for Defense Analyses, a government-funded think tank. But, unhappy in the role, he soon quit that job to join an aerospace company based in Hartford, Connecticut. Nothing came of Bissell's idea of forming a business partnership with Frank Wisner to promote civilian nuclear power.[47]

Allen Dulles would dedicate his retirement years to writing a book, *The Craft of Intelligence,* which he meant to be a distillation of lessons learned in his long espionage career. But Dulles at the same time penned a more forthright—and unpublished—précis of what he believed had gone wrong in the operation which had ended that career. Dulles reworked "over and over" the conclusion, Bissell remembered, finishing the final draft with this passage: "Great actions require great determination. In these difficult types of operations . . . one never succeeds unless there is a determination to succeed, a willingness to risk some unpleasant political repercussions, and a willingness to provide the basic military necessities. At the decisive moment of the Bay of Pigs operation, all three of these were lacking."[48]

Among the other agency casualties of the Cuban debacle was Tracy Barnes. When Helms took over the Plans Directorate from Bissell, early in 1962, one of his first acts would be to remove Barnes—Bissell's acolyte and a veteran of Project Success—from his post on the Cuba desk of the directorate's Western Hemisphere division. Instead, Barnes was given oversight of the CIA's Domestic Contact Service, a branch within the agency that interviewed businessmen returning from Communist countries.

Wisner was sad to see so many of those he had worked with over the years at OPC and the CIA suddenly shown the door. But he was especially distraught at the firing of Dulles. "With the departure of our old Chief I should have thought that the demands of our critics would have been satisfied, and that there would be the opportunity for the restoration of confidence," he wrote to Helms wistfully.[49]

Although Frank and Polly continued their social whirl in the British capital—"they must have decided that everybody in Burke's Peerage was going to pass through their drawing room," observed a guest at one soiree—Wisner's heart was no longer in it. The realization had finally hit Frank that he was being permanently put out to pasture; while the CIA station at the London embassy was no backwater, it was still far from the Cold War's front lines. "The doctors feel as do I that he is fine and

I shall be very anxious to hear how you find him in June when he goes home to see you," Polly wrote to Helms that spring, expressing gratitude for the latter's concern about her "Old Man." On the verge of his second nervous breakdown, Wisner had let Helms know that he planned to retire from the CIA.[50]

The recurrence of Frank's depression prompted the Wisners' return to Georgetown. Shortly thereafter, Frank had been awarded the CIA's Distinguished Service Medal in a ceremony at the agency's new headquarters—the mammoth white marble edifice in the leafy Virginia countryside that had, despite Wisner's opposition, replaced the rickety wooden "tempos" on the Mall. It was yet another sign of how much the CIA had changed from the early days of OPC. John McCone, the former investment banker who had since replaced Allen Dulles as CIA director, offered Frank a new job—a sinecure—as his special assistant. Sharing space with a small D.C. law office in a commercial building on Eighteenth Street, Wisner found himself even further removed from the action. He spent his time reading books and writing reviews for the agency's internal publications. One of the volumes that he reviewed would be Dulles's *Craft of Intelligence;* his essay was less an academic critique of his former boss's book than an anguished cri de coeur: "Most thinking people have long since digested and, however reluctantly, accepted the necessity of combating the Communist threat by the expenditure of vast treasure and much blood. Why is it, then, that the occasional intelligence casualties which are incurred in the form of personnel losses and 'blown' operations are the subject of so much soul-searching self-criticism and anguished cries of *mea culpa,* to say nothing of having become the standard butt of deliberate distortions and sharp ridicule?" Wisner ended his review on what seemed, in retrospect, an uncharacteristically personal and self-reflective note: America and the West, he wrote, needed "to adopt a more sensible and realistic attitude toward what might be termed the *casualties* of intelligence operations in the cold war."[51]

CHAPTER SEVENTEEN

"We Will All Fry"

O N TUESDAY MORNING, October 16, 1962, the national security adviser, McGeorge Bundy, informed President Kennedy that U-2 photographs taken a couple of days earlier had given irrefutable proof that the Soviet Union, contrary to its recent assurances, was building bases in Cuba for offensive missiles capable of striking the United States with nuclear weapons. Two hours later, Chip Bohlen was the first person outside the president's inner circle to learn of the missiles when he paid a courtesy call at the White House. Bohlen was about to leave for Paris, to become the new U.S. ambassador to France.[1]

At lunchtime, President Kennedy brought together his brother, Vice President Johnson, the secretaries of state and defense, and a few other key advisers to be briefed on the situation and discuss possible responses to the Russian provocation. The meeting split up at 1:00 p.m. so that the president could attend a scheduled reception for the crown prince of Libya—and thus avoid giving reporters any inkling of the developing crisis.[2]

The principals reassembled in the early evening to continue their deliberations, where Kennedy commented on the need for another of his "great demonologists"—the Russian expert and ambassador at large Llewellyn "Tommy" Thompson—to join the discussion. The president remembered that Thompson had correctly predicted the Kremlin's moves during the previous year's Berlin crisis. While the consensus in the group was that Kennedy could not allow the Soviet move to go unchallenged, opinion was divided over whether military action or diplomacy was called for. At 8:00 p.m., the president left the meeting to attend a previously scheduled send-off dinner party for Bohlen at Joe Alsop's house.[3]

Joe and Susan Mary were first to notice the president's "deep brown study" during what was meant to be a festive occasion. The hostess fretted that the lamb roast in the oven would dry out while Kennedy and Bohlen carried on an animated conversation just out of earshot in Joe's garden. Usually voluble during dinner, the president barely said a word throughout all four courses—other than to ask the guests most knowledgeable about Russia, Bohlen and Isaiah Berlin, their opinion of how that country had reacted to crises in the past. Although his opinion had not been sought, Phil Graham also held forth at inebriated length on the subject. Joe thought it curious that Kennedy, who rarely repeated himself, posed the same question twice at the dinner table. (Earlier, the president had queried Bohlen alone on the same topic, as the two were conferring in the garden.) When the men retired to smoke cigars under the loggia, Kennedy stunned Alsop by casually musing that the odds of a nuclear conflagration within the next decade were probably fifty-fifty—a jarring prediction that prompted another guest, the French ambassador, "to turn the color of an uncooked biscuit," Joe recalled.[4]

After a final conversation with Bohlen in camera under the wisteria, Kennedy excused himself and left the party with Chip and Jackie in tow. Joe and Susan Mary remembered the two men still gesticulating and arguing as they descended the circular staircase to the street.

Twice more Kennedy would try, in vain, to persuade Bohlen to delay his departure for Paris until the missile crisis was resolved. Each time Chip had resisted, claiming that any change in his schedule might tip reporters off to the gathering storm. In a compromise, Bohlen promised Kennedy that he would leave behind a memorandum with his thoughts on how to handle Khrushchev. Chip also recommended Tommy Thompson as his surrogate on the subject of Russia. Thompson was the only one among Kennedy's advisers who knew Khrushchev personally, having stayed with the Soviet leader and his family at Khrushchev's dacha outside Moscow. After delivering a previously planned speech before New York's Franco-American Society on Thursday, October 18, Chip sailed to Europe with Avis on the SS *United States*.[5]

That same day, Kennedy called together the other fourteen members of what would become known as the Executive Committee of the National Security Council—the "ExComm"—to recommend options for dealing with the missile crisis. In addition to Thompson, the ExComm consisted of those who had met with Kennedy on the sixteenth, along with the CIA director, McCone, and the UN ambassador, Adlai Stevenson, who would occasionally attend meetings of the group. At Kennedy's initiative, Dean Acheson was among the few "outsiders" also invited to join, probably to defuse later criticism from the crusty former secretary of state. (Acheson had been sharply critical of Kennedy's actions in the Bay of Pigs invasion—observing, acidly, that it did not take "Price Waterhouse to discover that 1,500 Cubans weren't as good as 25,000 Cubans.")[6]

To Kennedy's amazement, the crisis in Cuba remained a secret hidden from the press even as deliberations continued at the White House. The president was not amused when Ted Sorensen, his special counsel, joked at one meeting that there had been no "leak at all other than your conversation with Joe Alsop." Kennedy shot back that he had told Alsop nothing.[7]

Coincidentally, Stewart Alsop had narrowly missed getting the scoop of a lifetime, when he interviewed Robert McNamara at the Pentagon on Friday, October 19. The subject was the defense secretary's "no-cities" speech in Ann Arbor, Michigan, a few months earlier, where McNamara had argued that hitting civilian targets should be avoided in a nuclear war. As McNamara told Alsop, "In a sense, nuclear war is irrational—all war is irrational. But being irrational doesn't make it inconceivable. You might be forced into nuclear war as a result of an irrational act on the other side, for example, or a misjudgment of our response to an attack on our vital interests." Although a nuclear holocaust caused by a miscalculation was doubtless on the defense secretary's mind that day, McNamara made no mention of the looming Cuban crisis.[8]

By Saturday evening, however, word had begun to spread in the capital city's newsrooms of an impending showdown with the Soviet Union. On Sunday morning, October 21, a front-page story by the *Washington Post* reporter Murrey Marder ran below the headline "Marine Moves in South Linked to Cuban Crisis." While Marder's article lacked specifics about the military mobilization that was already under way in Florida, there were, he wrote, "numerous indications . . . that a major international development was in the making."[9]

That same afternoon, Kennedy telephoned Phil Graham and Orvil Dryfoos, publisher of *The New York Times,* with an urgent request that their newspapers back away from the Cuba story. Both readily complied. Graham might actually have learned about the missiles during a visit to Attorney General Robert Kennedy's office the previous Wednesday.

Ironically, the president's phone call inadvertently tipped off Dryfoos and the *Times* to the story.[10]

On Monday morning, October 22, the *Post*'s banner headline read "Major U.S. Decision Is Awaited." The accompanying article began, "Official Washington yesterday wrapped itself in one of the tightest cloaks of secrecy ever seen in peace-time while key policy-makers worked out a major international decision they were forbidden to discuss." Kennedy's televised address to the nation that evening finally put an end to all speculation.[11]

During their tense meetings at the State Department and in the White House Cabinet Room, ExComm members had quickly concluded that, short of war or a diplomatic solution, there were three possible ways the crisis might end: a seaborne invasion of Cuba, a blockade to prevent more weapons from reaching the island, or air strikes aimed at destroying the missiles and their bases. But even air strikes would need to be followed up by a land invasion to ensure that all the missiles in Cuba had been destroyed.

The secret taping system that Kennedy had earlier installed in the White House recorded the sharp division within the ExComm. Acheson was the most hawkish among the president's counselors, having urged an immediate bombing raid on the missile bases, lest Khrushchev regard Kennedy as a weak and vacillating leader. The Pentagon's representative, Paul Nitze, similarly recommended that the president begin preparations to destroy the missiles in Cuba. Nitze had angered Kennedy during the ExComm meeting on the twenty-second. When the president asked him to make sure that the Joint Chiefs of Staff understood the Jupiter missiles in Turkey were not to be fired without a direct order from the White House, Nitze had protested that such a precaution was unnecessary. Kennedy replied: "I don't think we ought to accept the Chiefs' word on that one, Paul."[12]

Adlai Stevenson, on the other hand, had, early in the ExComm meetings, encouraged a diplomatic solution to the crisis and doggedly stuck to his position despite sharp criticism from the others. Kennedy rejected out of hand Stevenson's recommendation that the navy evacuate its base at Guantánamo, Cuba, as sending the wrong signal to Castro and Khrushchev. For the interim, the president decided on a naval "quarantine" of the island—a term of art chosen, in part, because a blockade was considered an act of war under international law. Joe Alsop praised

Kennedy's decision in his column on October 24, titled "The Strongest Argument." "The brave and necessary thing has been done," Joe wrote.[13]

Chip Bohlen's promised memo, portions of which Dean Rusk had read before the group on the eighteenth, counseled that any steps taken to remove the missiles by force would "inevitably lead to war." Bohlen recommended instead that Kennedy negotiate directly with Khrushchev in private and warn the Soviet leader with an ultimatum before undertaking military action. Like Bohlen, Tommy Thompson believed that Khrushchev's real goal was to put pressure on Kennedy elsewhere—perhaps forcing the United States to abandon Berlin in exchange for removing the missiles from Cuba. But whatever steps the president took, Thompson cautioned, he needed to "make it as easy as possible for [Khrushchev] to back down."[14]

Remarkably, Kennedy had not informed the U.S. ambassador to Moscow, Foy Kohler—who had assumed that post only a month earlier—of the Cuban crisis until just before the president's televised speech to the nation on October 22. One reason was doubtless a concern that word might get out prematurely of America's discovery of the missiles; but another was likely the fact that Kennedy trusted his "demonologists"— Bohlen and Thompson—to more accurately gauge how Khrushchev might react to any U.S. countermoves. Nonetheless, Kennedy rejected what became known as the Bohlen Plan—a stern letter to the Soviet leader, demanding immediate removal of the missiles in Cuba—after some ExComm members pointed out that Khrushchev might call the president's bluff by making his secret communiqué public.[15]

By Thursday, October 25, sentiment within the ExComm had turned to favor air strikes followed by an invasion—in the mistaken belief that Soviet nuclear warheads had not yet arrived on the island.*[16] Only Stevenson remained steadfast in his view that the crisis could still be resolved by negotiations, preferably through the UN. Adding to the anxiety in the ExComm meetings that day was the realization that Soviet soldiers on Cuba would almost certainly be killed by any U.S. bombing raids, raising the likelihood of a direct confrontation with the U.S.S.R. and

---

* In fact, there were at least 90 and perhaps more than 150 Soviet nuclear warheads already on the island, including a dozen mounted on short-range Luna rockets, which would almost certainly have been used against any invasion force. McNamara later mused that the odds that Kennedy had given Joe Alsop at Bohlen's farewell party were probably about right: there had been an even chance of nuclear war resulting from the missile crisis.

hence the prospect of nuclear war.[17] (In shorthand notes that he jotted down, Nitze recorded Undersecretary of State George Ball's ominous prediction: "Unless we return to political arrangement we will all fry.") Nonetheless, Nitze angrily dismissed as "total appeasement" Stevenson's plea for a negotiated settlement of the crisis.[18]

Shortly after becoming president, Kennedy had received a detailed briefing on American plans for a nuclear war and the likely outcome. While prospective U.S. casualties were not included in the estimate, the so-called Single Integrated Operational Plan posited a total of 285 million dead among the Russian, Chinese, and East European victims.[19]

Paul Nitze, too, had gazed into the abyss when he chaired a task force during the previous year's Berlin crisis. At the height of that confrontation, a few of those advising the president had suggested that the United States might wish to demonstrate its resolve by detonating one or more nuclear weapons high in the atmosphere above an uninhabited area in the U.S.S.R., such as the Soviet atomic test site on the remote Arctic island of Novaya Zemlya. Nitze had dismissed the notion of such a nuclear "warning shot" as "a mugs' game," which the United States might well lose. ("If we used three they might use six," he pointed out.) Additionally, some in the administration had raised the possibility of a so-called clever first strike—a limited nuclear attack on the U.S.S.R.'s military forces—as an alternative to invoking the history-ending SIOP, should the situation in Berlin escalate to violence. Nitze had opposed that desperate move as well.[20]

By the twenty-fifth, however, another option was receiving considerable attention in the ExComm: trading the Soviet missiles in Cuba for American missiles in Turkey. Stevenson had implicitly raised just such a possibility in a note he sent to Kennedy a week earlier, which emphasized that the president should remain open to negotiations on *"the existence of nuclear missile bases anywhere . . . before we start anything."*[21]

The intermediate-range Jupiter missiles that the United States began deploying overseas in mid-1960 had meanwhile been rendered obsolete by U.S.-based ICBMs and Polaris submarine-launched ballistic missiles at sea. The Jupiters in Italy and Turkey were already on a schedule to be scrapped. In a Today and Tomorrow column on October 25, Walter Lippmann had made the case for just such a swap, arguing that "an agreement of this sort may be doable and . . . there may exist a way out of the tyranny of automatic and uncontrollable events."[22]

Two unrelated incidents on the afternoon of Saturday, October 27, raised the tension in the ExComm still further. First was the news that a reconnaissance U-2 overflying Cuba had been shot down, killing the American pilot. Second was a stern and threatening message from Khrushchev that seemed to contradict an earlier and more conciliatory communication from the Soviet premier. Frustrated by the mixed signals emanating from the Kremlin, Kennedy speculated that the only course of action remaining open to him seemed a choice between the use of force to destroy the missiles and a concession to the Soviet leader. While he preferred the latter option, Kennedy said, the former seemed to be more likely, in light of Khrushchev's belligerent second message.[23]

Transcribers of the tape recording of the ExComm meeting that afternoon noted the "slow, dry" voice of Tommy Thompson breaking through the depressed silence that followed the president's glum observation. Kennedy's Russian expert was one of the few willing—or able—to contradict the president on the subject of Soviet behavior. The previous day, Thompson had correctly predicted that the Soviets would test the American blockade with a single ship, which would turn back if challenged. Thompson now interrupted to say that in his view a compromise with Khrushchev was still possible. In reality, Thompson's advice—like that of most of the president's advisers in the ExComm—had changed as the crisis unfolded, but he had never given up hope of a peaceful resolution.[24]

While ordering that preparations for military action against Cuba proceed, the president on the evening of October 27 instructed his brother to deliver a personal message to the Soviet ambassador, Anatoly Dobrynin. In it, the president pledged to end the blockade and guarantee that there would be no invasion of Cuba if Khrushchev agreed to remove his missiles. As part of the deal, the United States also promised to quietly withdraw its Jupiters from Turkey soon afterward. In order to prevent a split in the NATO alliance, however, Bobby Kennedy told Dobrynin that the missile swap needed to remain a secret between the American and the Soviet governments.

That same evening, Tommy Thompson was among the handful of ExComm members whom Kennedy called into the Oval Office for a special briefing. There were no dissenting voices when the president announced that he had offered Khrushchev a secret deal on the missiles, even though Thompson had, earlier that day, pronounced just such a trade "clearly unacceptable." "It was also agreed that knowledge of this [arrangement] would be held among those present and no one else," Bundy wrote of the meeting.[25]

On Sunday morning, October 28—exactly thirteen days after the crisis began and less than forty-eight hours before the first U.S. air strikes on Cuba were to be carried out—Khrushchev announced on Radio Moscow that the Soviet Union would dismantle its missile bases on Cuba and ship the weapons home.

PERHAPS BECAUSE OF LESSONS he learned in the Bay of Pigs fiasco, President Kennedy had overruled virtually all of his advisers—except Adlai Stevenson—in choosing to trade the missiles in Turkey for those in Cuba. Nonetheless, the president's trusted Soviet experts, Bohlen and Thompson, had played an important role during the crisis in two respects: by predicting, correctly, how Khrushchev would react to the naval blockade of Cuba, and in countering the more bellicose recommendations of ExComm hawks like Acheson and Nitze. As well, Bohlen had been perhaps the first to offer Kennedy advice on how to resolve the crisis, and Thompson would continue to counsel the president concerning details of the missiles' removal. Not surprising, both Dean Rusk and Robert McNamara regarded Thompson as the "unsung hero" in resolving the Cuban crisis.[26]

For Kennedy, a critical part of that resolution—in which Khrushchev was, in effect, his co-conspirator—meant keeping the missile swap a secret. With the vital midterm congressional elections little more than a week away, Kennedy calculated that the American people needed to believe that he had bested the Russian leader over Cuba. To that end, the president would have the help—albeit unwitting—of Joe and Stewart Alsop.

"Victory!" proclaimed the headline of Joe's column in *The Washington Post* on October 29, 1962. Finally disproven by Kennedy's actions, Alsop trumpeted, was the Kremlin's longtime belief "that the U.S. was too soft and weak-willed to stand up to a direct challenge." An unusually upbeat Joe went to see Averell Harriman at the State Department the following morning. "He wanted to talk about where we went from here," Harriman wrote in a memorandum of their conversation. "Alsop was in an amiable mood, said nothing unkind about anyone in the Administration."[27]

Within hours of its successful conclusion, the brothers were competing with other journalists to tell the "inside" story of the Cuban missile crisis. "The post-mortem season is in full swing," McGeorge Bundy observed on October 30, just a day after the president declared a policy at the White House of "keeping that book closed."[28]

It did not remain closed for long.

On November 5, in a column titled "The Soviet Deception Plan," Joe Alsop revealed that an unnamed "junior official of the Soviet Embassy" had been a key conduit for secret messages sent between Washington and Moscow during the crisis. That official was Georgi Bolshakov, a young Soviet military intelligence officer who worked at the embassy undercover as a TASS journalist. Prior to the Cuban crisis, Robert Kennedy had met with Bolshakov numerous times in an effort to gauge Soviet intentions. But the attorney general lost faith in his secret back channel when Bolshakov gave false assurances that the missiles in Cuba were defensive only. Joe's column outing the Russian was probably the Kennedys' revenge. Bolshakov was promptly recalled to Moscow. (The unfortunate spy joked about his fate during a farewell party at the Soviet embassy, which both Alsops and Robert Kennedy attended: "You asked us to remove our missiles from Cuba. And we did. You asked us to remove the Il-28s [bombers]. And we did. Finally, you asked us to remove Georgi Bolshakov. And we did. No more concessions!")[29]

Likewise looking for a scoop was Joe's brother Stewart, who had already contacted another friend, Charles Bartlett, a former Washington-based reporter for the *Chattanooga Times,* about a possible collaboration. Bartlett was a longtime friend of the Kennedys—he had reputedly introduced the young Jack to Jackie almost a decade earlier—who remained the president's confidant at the White House. Five days after the crisis began, Kennedy had shared with Bartlett some details of what was being discussed at the ExComm meetings. In a personal note to the president on October 29, Bartlett put his own spin on the article that he and Stewart Alsop proposed to write on the missile crisis: "It occurs to me that I could inject the warm feel that [Alsop] tends to lack and hopefully avert the little hookers that he intends to include. I feel strongly that it should be without involving you directly. I would exert my influence to keep the thing as close as possible to a historical context."[30]

The first "insider" account of the Cuban missile crisis appeared six weeks later, on December 8, 1962, as a feature article in *The Saturday Evening Post.* "In Time of Crisis" introduced some terms that would promptly enter the nation's political lexicon, including "hawks and doves." As Alsop and Bartlett explained, ExComm's hawks had favored an immediate invasion of Cuba and air strikes; the doves had counseled diplomacy.[31]

More than just a chronology of events, Alsop and Bartlett wrote that their article was "an attempt to extract from the high drama of the crisis its inner meaning," which was perhaps most clearly expressed in the quotation used as the article's opening epigraph, attributed to Dean Rusk at the climactic moment of the crisis: "We're eyeball to eyeball, and I think the other fellow just blinked." The lesson of the Cuban missile crisis was clear, Alsop and Bartlett proclaimed: "A President's nerve is the essential factor when the two great nuclear powers are 'eyeball to eyeball.'"

The magazine article went on to paint an unabashedly heroic portrait of the president, the attorney general, and the rest of the Kennedy team—with one notable exception: Adlai Stevenson. "Adlai wanted a Munich," an unidentified but "nonadmiring official" in the administration had told the authors—a reference to Britain's foredoomed efforts to appease Hitler before the outbreak of World War II. "He wanted to trade the Turkish, Italian and British missile bases for the Cuban bases." Opposite the quotation, a full-page photograph of a quizzical and perplexed-looking Stevenson, index finger to pursed lips, underscored the point.[32]

Even before the *Post* issue was on the newsstands, front-page stories around the country were citing the Alsop-Bartlett article as evidence of the president's unshakable resolve in dealing with the Russians—and Kennedy's deep unhappiness with Stevenson.[33]

There had been bad feelings between the two men going back at least to the 1960 Democratic convention. Stevenson had reportedly been miffed when those around Kennedy suggested that Adlai personally nominate his young rival, to avoid being "humiliated" by an unsuccessful draft-Stevenson movement. The Kennedy brothers, on the other hand, were furious when convention organizers had finally been forced to turn off the auditorium lights to put an end to the snake-dancing and cheering of enthusiastic Stevenson supporters, who quixotically hoped their candidate would make a third run for the presidency. Subsequently, Kennedy had, on various occasions, seemingly gone out of his way to humble the man who wished to be secretary of state but was instead appointed U.S. ambassador to the UN.[34]

Yet Stevenson's public characterization of the Alsop-Bartlett account as "inaccurate and untrue" and "fallacious in every detail" was rendered hollow by Stewart's subsequent disclosure that Kennedy himself had "proof-read" the draft article before publication and requested no changes. Pointedly, the president had let stand the anonymous remark about Stevenson wanting "a Munich." Challenged at a press conference to identify the "nonadmiring official" who was the source of the quotation, Kennedy dodged the question, saying only, "I think this matter should be left to historians."[35]

In fact, the "nonadmiring official" was Kennedy himself. The president had penciled in the "Munich" line when he annotated a typescript of the draft article submitted by Bartlett and Alsop. Although Clay Blair, editor of *The Saturday Evening Post,* urged Stew to respond to the article's critics by identifying the president as the source of the inflammatory quotation, Alsop held firm in a letter to Blair: "Alas, my lips are sealed. The whole business was strictly on a sealed-lips basis, as you know, and if I so much as hinted that JFK was in any way involved, I'd be run out of town. For good reason, too—there are certain rules of the game that you just can't break if you want to go on earning a living here. If anyone asked me if The Man was in any way personally involved in the episode, I would flatly and hotly deny it—for that matter, I've denied it already."[36]

Kennedy quickly quelled speculation by Joe Alsop that he intended to fire Stevenson—writing a letter in support of his embattled UN ambassador, and even sending Jackie on a personal mission to the United Nations to soothe Adlai's hurt feelings. Eventually, the contretemps over Stevenson and the "Munich" quotation died down.[37]

For an entire generation, however, the Alsop-Bartlett article would epitomize the standard heroic understanding of Kennedy's handling of the missile crisis. There had been no mention by the authors of the Turkey-for-Cuba trade that the president and Khrushchev had secretly arranged, since Bartlett and Alsop remained blissfully unaware of the deal and were kept in the dark by their informants. There was perhaps no better demonstration of the pitfalls to be encountered in the so-called access or elite form of journalism that the Alsops practiced.*[38]

---

* Adlai Stevenson would not be vindicated for another quarter century, when details of the secret missile trade became known. As a 1987 story in *The Washington Post* dryly observed, "It now appears that Stevenson was not the only 'dove' at the White House during the crisis." Russian documents released after the collapse of the Soviet Union in 1991 would show, as well, that Khrushchev had been willing to remove the missiles from Cuba even without a trade.

Moreover, while "In Time of Crisis" created something of a sensation, the Alsop brothers had missed the other real story behind the administration's war on Castro's Cuba. By late 1961, in the wake of the failed Bay of Pigs invasion, the president and his brother had set in motion a clandestine CIA operation aimed at overthrowing Castro's regime. The Kennedy brothers dedicated fifty million dollars and the full resources of the agency to a protracted but secret campaign of sabotage, subversion, and attempted assassination, energetically spearheaded by the attorney general himself. The expected culmination of Project Mongoose was to be the murder of the Cuban leader—accomplished, if necessary, by members of the American Mafia. To that end, the Alsops' good friend Richard Bissell had inquired in an eyes only memo to the CIA's Office of Security whether the latter "might assist in a sensitive mission requiring gangster-type action."[39]

So persistent, unrelenting, and ultimately quotidian were the CIA's covert efforts to kill Castro that fully a year after the missile crisis one of those who had survived the agency's post-Bay of Pigs bloodletting—Desmond FitzGerald—stopped off to celebrate a birthday lunch in Paris with his daughter, Frances, on his way to a meeting with a prospective Castro assassin at a CIA safe house—the agency's eighth unsuccessful plot to kill the Cuban dictator.[40]

Although the CIA's technical prowess had exploded the myth of the missile gap, and ultimately helped to expose the Soviet threat in Cuba, the presence of a Communist dictator less than a hundred miles from American shores would be a constant, nagging reminder of the failures of the "Bold Easterners." With Dulles and Bissell gone, Kennedy turned to McCone, the CIA's new director, for help with another clandestine mission. If unable to control events overseas, the president and those around him at least meant to influence how they were reported at home.

CHAPTER EIGHTEEN

"How Great Is One's Duty to Truth?"

IN ADDITION TO BRINGING HIM NOTORIETY, Stewart's article on the missile crisis had demonstrated that his ability to obtain a scoop was not dependent on the talent, or connections, of his older and better-known brother. An earlier *Saturday Evening Post* story by Stew was one of the first to warn that radioactive fallout from nuclear testing was being passed along to humans in the food chain. A subsequent magazine piece contained the revelation that President Kennedy had at one point considered the "nuclear sterilization" of Communist China with a surprise attack on that country's facilities for building and testing atomic weapons.[1]

Moreover, just as Stewart was achieving fame, Joe was encountering a new and surprising obstacle to his reporting on the Washington scene: the president himself. On October 27, 1962, at the height of the Cuban missile crisis, the Pentagon press office had issued an edict requiring that any Defense Department official meeting with a reporter either had to be accompanied by a public affairs representative or needed to submit a written report on what was discussed. The State Department announced a similar policy a short time later. While the missile crisis was used as the justification, the twin directives had actually been in the works for some time—in response to an earlier leak.[2]

The previous July, Hanson Baldwin, *The New York Times*'s military correspondent, had published a front-page story about the Soviets' efforts to protect their ICBMs from U.S. attack by means of hardened concrete shelters. Baldwin's story had included classified figures about Soviet missile strength taken from the CIA's latest secret National Intelligence

Estimate. But even more disturbing to the agency and the Kennedy administration was the fact that Baldwin's article contained details which could only have been obtained by satellite imagery—when even the existence of the CIA's Corona reconnaissance satellite remained top secret. The same day that the story appeared in the *Times,* President Kennedy instructed his brother, as attorney general, to order an FBI investigation of the leak. When the bureau, despite tapping Baldwin's office and home telephones, was unable to identify the leaker, the president ordered that further steps be taken to safeguard the nation's vital secrets. (The FBI wiretap did reveal, however, that the *Times* reporter had guessed, correctly, who was behind sending the bureau's gumshoes to his door. In an intercepted telephone call, Baldwin told a colleague, "I think the real answer to this is Bobby Kennedy and the president himself.")[3]

Outraged that his confidential sources were suddenly being denied to him by the president's edict, Joe Alsop appealed to his friends in the administration. "All responsible officials . . . seem to me to have the duty to be accessible, within reason, to reporters whom they judge to be responsible," Joe wrote in a November letter to Mac Bundy. When neither Bundy nor McNamara could be persuaded to rescind the press edict, Alsop appealed directly to the president, threatening Kennedy in both a letter and a telephone call with a forthcoming series of columns "criticizing this Administration very strongly." But Kennedy, too, proved unyielding.[4]

Joe's column on November 30, titled "Total News Control," left little doubt about where he stood on the issue of government efforts to manage the press: "No protest can be too vehement, for this is not just a profound political change; it is also a change in a viciously dangerous direction." Railing against what he called the "bun-faced minions of the Pentagon public relations branch," Alsop concluded his rant: "One of the essential safeguards of this republic—the safeguard provided by free ventilation and debate of facts of vital public interest—has thus been struck down."[5]

In fact, the directives issued by the Pentagon and the State Department were only the visible portion of a much larger secret government program—one that amounted to an ominous infringement by the Kennedy administration on the freedom of the press but remained hidden from the journalists who were its target.[6]

In August 1962, President Kennedy had asked his Foreign Intelligence Advisory Board, chaired by James Killian—the former MIT president who had headed the so-called surprise attack panel for Eisenhower—to assess the damage done by the Baldwin article and to recommend a remedy. (Although wiretaps were not specifically mentioned in Killian's subsequent briefing of Kennedy, one member of the board—the former Truman aide Clark Clifford—mused that "it would be mighty interesting to know who Alsop sees and who Chalmers Roberts sees and the rest of these fellows.")[7]

Not trusting Hoover and the FBI, the Kennedy brothers turned to the CIA to preempt future news leaks by spying on selected reporters. Under pressure from the attorney general, the director of the CIA, McCone, ordered the agency's Office of Security to wiretap the home and office telephones of Robert Allen and Paul Scott, two Washington-based journalists who, like Baldwin, had recently published classified information in their syndicated column. McCone even enthusiastically volunteered to organize an ongoing effort at the agency that would identify the source of news leaks with the aim of stopping them.[8]

Since the CIA's charter explicitly forbade it to engage in domestic spying, what the Kennedy brothers had asked McCone to do was certainly illicit and probably illegal. The CIA gave its renegade bugging operation the code name Mockingbird.[9]

Launched in mid-March 1963, Project Mockingbird was not long in obtaining results. The CIA's subsequent eyes only report on the wiretapping of Allen and Scott concluded, "The intercept activity was particularly productive in identifying contacts of the newsmen, their method of operation and many of their sources of information. For example, it was determined that during the period they received data from 13 newsmen, 12 of whom were identified; 12 senators and 6 members of Congress, all identified; 21 Congressional staff members, of whom 11 were identified; 16 government employees, including a staff member of the White House, members of the Vice-President's office, an Assistant Attorney General, and other well-placed individuals."[10]

Ironically, the Mockingbird report also noted that "the newsmen actually received more classified and official data than they could use, and passed some of the stories to other newsmen for release, establishing that many 'leaks' appearing under other by-lines were actually from the sources of the target newsmen." Although the agency suspended Mockingbird three months later, in mid-June 1963, the government's clandestine physical and electronic surveillance would continue and was apparently extended to include other reporters.[11]

No evidence has yet surfaced to suggest that Joe Alsop learned about Mockingbird and the CIA's clandestine surveillance of American newsmen. Many years later, however, Joe would tell an interviewer that he had long suspected he was the target of government eavesdropping—and that those who had ordered the bugging included the very men he considered his close friends: "I haven't any doubt, never doubted for an instant that [the Kennedys] tapped my wire. Not one instant. Why shouldn't they?"

STYMIED BY THE GOVERNMENT'S press edicts from reporting on the Washington scene, Joe Alsop returned to his old beat of covering news overseas. With the apparent resolution of the crisis in Laos, which a second Geneva conference had declared a neutral and independent state, Joe's attention turned to another Indochina tinderbox: South Vietnam.

During a previous trip to Saigon, in September 1961, Joe had observed that the government of President Ngo Dinh Diem seemed "overstrained" by the Communist insurgency there. In a column a few weeks later, Alsop wrote that "serious consideration is now being given to sending American troops to South Viet Nam . . . The choice is very ugly indeed . . . But even the potential, conditional engagement of American combat units in Southeast Asia is not an attractive prospect, to put it mildly."[12]

Alsop's friend John Kennedy plainly agreed. When two of the president's senior advisers, Maxwell Taylor and Walt Rostow, returned from a visit to South Vietnam later that month, they recommended that the United States dispatch up to eight thousand combat troops to support the counterinsurgency effort. But the president had balked at making such a commitment and instead sent Diem more military equipment and American advisers to train South Vietnam's army. With attention still focused on Berlin and Laos, Vietnam received little notice in the press—except from Alsop, who dubbed it "the hardly noticed crisis" in his column. "The Vietnamese problem is still as much underrated as ever," Joe told the *Newsweek* reporter Ward Just that December.[13]

Alsop's support for the diminutive Diem, a Catholic leader in a predominantly Buddhist country, had been early and continuous. In dispatches that he filed from Saigon, Joe described the embattled sixty-year-old president as "courageous" and the South Vietnamese army as "resilient." Early in 1962, Diem personally invited Alsop back to

Saigon. Returning the favor, Joe attempted to burnish the Vietnamese leader's reputation in subsequent columns, describing Diem as "an honest and true nationalist."[14]

In columns written later that year, Alsop seemed all but ready to declare victory in Vietnam. (Subsequently, in September 1965, he would coin the phrase that became the mantra of those urging escalation in the war—namely, that there was "light at the end of the tunnel."[15]) Vietnam even intruded into Alsop's springtime garden column—the one place where he previously had always avoided politics. On March 30, 1962, Matter of Fact declared, "Watching the new green cover a box bush is just as exciting as watching the progress of the anti-guerrilla effort in South Vietnam."[16]

Yet Alsop's prediction that the Saigon regime was on the verge of defeating the Vietcong sharply contradicted reports coming from younger and less-established journalists, like *The New York Times*'s David Halberstam and Neil Sheehan of United Press International wire service. Joe's sources for his Vietnam columns typically included Diem's own defense minister and the ever-optimistic U.S. commander in South Vietnam, the army general Paul Harkins. The stories filed by Halberstam and Sheehan, on the other hand, came from their own personal observation of Army of the Republic of Vietnam troops on the battlefield and from in-country interviews with district provincial chiefs—who gave a very different perspective on the war. Halberstam also reported on the corruption of the Saigon government and Diem's growing unpopularity.[17]

Like any true believer, Joe seemed impervious to negative views on how the conflict was going—even when they came from those fighting it. In October 1962, shortly after an Alsop column gave a glowing account of the strategic hamlet program—the latest American effort to subdue the Vietcong insurgents—a U.S. Army colonel who had just spent fourteen months in Vietnam wrote to Joe, "Can you imagine, Mr. Alsop, trying to sneak up on a native in his own habitat in a helicopter or in a tank? Those fellows are too smart to stand and fight. When they hear our mechanized equipment they simply fire and fade away. The majority of the claimed 'Vietcong casualties' are simply innocent villagers who didn't get out of the way soon enough." Joe was unmoved, reminding the colonel that he himself had been in Vietnam "something like ten times since 1954," adding, "I have also 'sneaked up on a native' in a helicopter in a quite violently successful operation. I shan't attempt to correct the obvious errors of fact in your letter. I must content myself with saying that I disagree with you."[18]

Alsop's positive assessment of progress in the war was eagerly welcomed, of course, not only by the Saigon regime but by President Kennedy, who was facing increasing criticism of his Vietnam policy as the number of American "advisers" in that country swelled to seventeen thousand by mid-1963. As always, Joe's reporting continued to rely mostly on official sources, including Frederick Nolting, the U.S. ambassador to South Vietnam. Nolting was also Joe's generous host during Alsop's visits to Saigon, where he stayed in a guesthouse at the embassy compound. (So familiar had the two men become by June 1963 that Joe did not hesitate to ask "Fritz" for a personal favor when Nolting left Saigon for a new assignment: "Please add to the furniture you're shipping back four pottery elephants, two white and two dark blue that your ex-CIA man found at the arts and crafts shop on rue Catinat." When the trinkets were late in arriving, prompting a complaint from Alsop, Nolting instructed his aide, "Tell Joe, God damn it, I'll bring the white elephants.") Nolting's replacement in Saigon, the Bostonian Henry Cabot Lodge Jr., was another longtime "tribal" friend of the Alsop family who did special favors for Joe.[19]

Diem's failure to achieve the promised victory, more disturbing reports from the battlefield, and growing protests against the regime—including self-immolations by Buddhist monks—persuaded Joe to make a return trip to South Vietnam that fall. The political and the military situation had deteriorated alarmingly since his previous visit. In an exclusive interview at the presidential palace, Ngo Dinh Nhu, Diem's brother, told Joe that he had decided to open secret negotiations with North Vietnam through French and Polish intermediaries—"behind the backs of the Americans"—aimed at ending the war. Nhu's shocking disclosure—made in the midst of what Joe took to be a drug-fueled mania—was almost certainly a bluff, meant to persuade Alsop to recommend more U.S. aid for Diem's government. But, if so, it backfired.[20]

Joe's column of September 18, 1963, titled "Ugly Stuff," inadvertently launched a comic-opera series of events that would nonetheless resonate in Washington, as well as throughout capitals in Asia and Europe. French diplomats denounced Alsop's article as "pure imagination" and "rubbish." Poland's representative on the international commission overseeing the Geneva Accords denied acting as a go-between for Hanoi.

A State Department official speculated that "some of Alsop's egotism appeared to have rubbed off on Nhu," whom he suspected of "'trying it on' through Alsop." Nonetheless, after Joe briefed Ambassador Lodge and the CIA's Saigon station chief on his meeting with Nhu—"Diem and Nhu have just about completely lost their minds and are operating in [an] unreal world"—a subsequent memo to the agency's director warned that Diem's government might be "exploring the possibilities of some kind of North-South rapprochement." Before the controversy faded, it had further undermined Lodge's faith that Diem and Nhu could be regarded as reliable partners in the war.[21]

Back home again, Joe reported to President Kennedy that South Vietnam's "harassed" leader was a "prisoner in [the] palace," in the grip of the "half-mad" Nhu, and no longer able to govern. Nevertheless, in the half-dozen columns that he wrote on Vietnam over the next several weeks, Alsop argued that the problems there were the fault of neither Diem nor Nhu—but of Joe's own colleagues' reporting on the war. In a column he titled "The Crusaders," Alsop compared the situation in Vietnam with that of China in 1944, when, as Joe claimed, criticism of Chiang had undermined the Nationalist cause and ultimately led to a Communist victory. Similarly, Alsop wrote, "the reportorial crusade against the [Saigon] government has also helped mightily to transform Diem from a courageous, quite viable national leader, into a man afflicted with a galloping persecution mania, seeing plots around every corner, and therefore misjudging everything." While Joe did not name those he branded the "local bleeding hearts" and the young, "high-minded crusaders," there was little doubt that he had in mind journalists like the twenty-nine-year-old Halberstam and the twenty-six-year-old Sheehan.[22]

One of Halberstam's colleagues at the *Times,* Scotty Reston, suspected that Joe's broadside against the war's critics had its origins in the Kennedy administration. "Why don't you call off Alsop?" Reston challenged McGeorge Bundy in a telephone call. "Don't you believe in freedom of the press?" Bundy sarcastically shot back.[23]

Yet Joe Alsop's spirited defense of the administration's policies in Vietnam presented its own difficulties for the president, as the U.S. ambassador to India, John Kenneth Galbraith, pointed out in a memo to Kennedy: "Any form of disentanglement is going to bring criticism from fighting Joe Alsop as it has in Laos. But the one thing that will cause worse damage and more penetrating attack will be increasing involvement."[24]

Alsop felt that his jeremiad against "crusaders" like Halberstam and Sheehan had been vindicated when Diem was deposed and assassinated, along with his brother Nhu, in a November 1963 military coup. The generals who plotted the coup, Joe believed, had been emboldened by the attacks on Diem in the American media. Just as galling, to Alsop, was the fact that the coup appeared to have the tacit approval of his friend Ambassador Henry Cabot Lodge—another of those who had been turned against Diem, in Joe's view, by *The New York Times*.[25]

ON FOREIGN POLICY, as with every other major issue that he confronted, President Kennedy continued to receive unbidden advice not only from Joe Alsop but also from Phil Graham. The previous October, Graham and Joe had urged Kennedy—again, unsuccessfully—to replace Secretary of State Dean Rusk with their friend David Bruce.[26]

Graham's irrational tirades and fits had steadily grown worse. In the course of one late-night telephone call to the president, when Phil yelled, "Do you have any idea who you're talking to?" Kennedy had gently responded, "I know I'm not talking to the Phil Graham I have so much admiration for." After Kennedy inadvertently left classified documents in Graham's suite at the Carlyle Hotel, Phil bragged to *Newsweek*'s Ben Bradlee that he had become a close adviser to the president on vital matters of state. Later, when a COMSAT attorney drafted an innocuous press release and presented it to Graham for his approval, Phil lunged across the table as if to strike the man. Phil wrote an insulting letter to the lawyer a few days later but then followed it with an abject apology.[27]

The crisis came during a January 1963 trip to Phoenix, Arizona, where Phil joined other prominent publishers at the annual meeting of the Associated Press. When the AP president rose to speak, Phil also stood, rudely elbowing the man out of the way. Standing at the lectern, Graham launched into a long, rambling, and obscenity-laced tirade attacking the news media in general and several of those present in the room by name. So drunk as to be almost incoherent, Phil accused the assembled journalists and publishers of cowardice for their failure to cover and print really important stories. (By some accounts, Graham said that prominent among those stories was the president's sexual dalliances at the White House and the Carlyle Hotel, regarding which, Phil claimed, he had personal knowledge.)[28]

In the stunned silence that followed, the *Los Angeles Times*'s publisher, Otis Chandler, and others, managed to get Phil off the dais and eventually back to Graham's hotel room. Chandler also notified *The Washington Post* of Phil's public breakdown. Learning of his friend's meltdown in Phoenix, President Kennedy dispatched a government jet to bring Phil back to Washington. When the plane landed at National Airport and Graham tried to walk away, he was placed in restraints and taken by ambulance to the psychiatric unit of the George Washington University Hospital. (Seeing an elderly woman terrified by the chaotic scene at the terminal, Phil sought to reassure her: "It's alright, miss, I'm only dying of cancer.")

Graham was transferred a few days later to Chestnut Lodge, a private sanitarium in nearby Rockville, Maryland, where his treatment included psychotherapy by a renowned psychiatrist, Dr. Leslie Farber, whose particular interest was existentialist philosophy. Although lithium was already being used in Europe to treat bipolar disorders, or manic depression, it had not yet been approved for use in the United States. In any case, Farber did not believe in drugs, and Phil Graham was said to have a particular aversion to taking pills. Graham was also aware of the effects that electroconvulsive shock "therapy" had had on his friend Frank Wisner. As Kay Graham eventually came to realize, however, it was Phil, and not Farber, who took over and ran the psychotherapy sessions through sheer force of personality.[29]

Although Kay had not been on the trip to Phoenix—Phil had taken Robin, his paramour, instead—she wrote the president a heartfelt note of thanks for sending the airplane to rescue her husband and for a follow-up phone call offering sympathy and understanding. While still at the hotel in Phoenix, Graham had begun telephoning his children as well as old friends and even distant acquaintances. One call had been to Kennedy, which the White House operator refused to put through to the president. From Chestnut Lodge, Graham wrote to Kennedy that he wished to resign his position on the board of COMSAT for "reasons of health."[30]

After barely two weeks at the clinic, Phil Graham persuaded Farber and the other psychiatrists that he was sufficiently recovered to leave Chestnut Lodge for a visit home. Flying instead to New York with Robin, Phil told his lawyer, Edward Bennett Williams, that he intended to divorce Katharine and take control of *The Washington Post* away from his wife and her family. The split between the Grahams divided Georgetown society along unfamiliar fault lines. Joe Alsop was one of those who sided with Kay, even supposedly writing a column denouncing Phil—which Joe decided, however, not to publish.[31]

Early in April 1963, Phil Graham wrote to Kennedy to say that he was planning to have lunch the following week in Washington with Robert McNamara, adding, "If there is any chance of seeing you late that afternoon I promise to be on my best behavior." The president did not respond. When Phil and Robin returned from a trip to Puerto Rico in mid-June, it was evident to all who saw him that Graham's demons were back. A few days later, Phil told both Farber and Ed Williams that the affair with Robin was over and that he hoped to reconcile with Kay. He temporarily moved back to the R Street house on June 19 but soon became so agitated that his wife persuaded him to return to Chestnut Lodge. There Phil resumed psychotherapy sessions, this time with a different psychiatrist.[32]

Before his relapse, Phil had been reaching out to friends like Scotty Reston. Graham turned to him, Reston later recalled, because he was seeking comfort in faith and believed, mistakenly, that Scotty was religious. But Reston, to his regret, was of little help: "I was not able to get through to him."[33]

That spring, Phil sent another journalist friend, Theodore "Teddy" White, a lengthy memorandum containing a detailed account of how he and Joe Alsop had persuaded John Kennedy to pick Lyndon Johnson as his running mate at the 1960 Democratic convention. White was the author of a recent best-selling book about the 1960 election, *The Making of the President*. Since Phil had a lifelong interest in how the past was portrayed—it was he, after all, who had coined the expression "Journalism is the first draft of history"—the memo was an apparent attempt to set the historical record straight before taking the next and final step.[34]

On Saturday morning, August 3, 1963, Phil persuaded the doctors at Chestnut Lodge to allow him a weekend visit to Glen Welby. To allay any suspicion, Graham made an appointment with a psychiatrist at the clinic for the following Tuesday. At the farmhouse, after having lunch on the back porch, he and Kay went upstairs for a nap. Still restless, Phil excused himself and went back downstairs. A short while later, Kay was awakened by the thunderous noise of a gun going off in the house. In a downstairs bathroom, Phil was bleeding from a self-inflicted head wound, the 28-gauge shotgun that he kept at Glen Welby lying next to the body.

Sorting through Phil's papers in the chaotic aftermath of his death, Kay came across a handwritten letter and an essay that her husband had written to Scotty Reston but neglected to send. The subject of the essay was the search for "balance" in one's life:

> "Balance" or "middle-of-the-road" are blinders and deceivers. That kind of language inevitably carries the suggestion that one can finesse the problem through a sort of vegetable neutrality. That is highly appropriate for turnips but not for men.
>
> Get right down to day-to-day living. How much should one pour into one's work? How much save for one's family? How much for solitary thought? How much for service to one's sovereign or one's God? How great is one's duty to truth? . . .
>
> How wrong it is to try to banish all this, to pretend it doesn't exist, by admonishing "balance" as an approach to life. Or the "middle-of-the-road." The man who leaves life by the most violent suicide is still at least more honest than those who choose suicide-while-living by defining away all that is human in life.[35]

THE ASSASSINATION OF President John Kennedy followed the suicide of Phil Graham by little more than three months. Susan Mary gave Joe the terrible news from Dallas as he sat in the garden room at Dumbarton, reading. Joe's secretary heard him sobbing uncontrollably in his office a short time later. Just the night before, Alsop and Ted Sorensen, the president's counselor, had watched a James Bond movie, *From Russia with Love,* in the White House theater.[36]

Stewart likewise learned of the assassination at home, where he had returned early from a European trip with a case of the flu. Katharine Graham was having lunch at *Newsweek* headquarters in New York with Arthur Schlesinger Jr., Ken Galbraith, and the magazine's senior editors. When a television bulletin confirmed that the president was dead, Kay joined the rush to the airport to fly back to Washington. Months before, Katharine had buried her husband at Oak Hill Cemetery, directly across R Street from the couple's home. Phil's grave was said to be visible from the second floor.[37]

As the shock of the assassination began to fade, Kennedy's Georgetown friends took stock of how fundamentally things had been altered by the president's death. Susan Mary and Tish Alsop volunteered to help

Jackie with the task of answering the hundreds of condolence letters that the former First Lady had begun to receive. But in the midst of mourning there were subtle signs of impending changes—including an abrupt end to the easy access that Kennedy's friends had long enjoyed to the corridors of power. Arriving at the White House in the company of Schlesinger and Galbraith, Kay Graham was among those asked to leave a planning meeting for the president's funeral by Sorensen, who told the owner of *The Washington Post* that he "did not think she belonged."[38]

Three days after the assassination, on November 25, Joe Alsop wrote a eulogy for Kennedy in a column titled "Go, Stranger!," comparing the martyred president to the Spartan dead at the Battle of Thermopylae. "Of all the men in public life in his time," Joe began the column, "John Fitzgerald Kennedy was the most ideally formed to lead the United States of America." While his cousin Alice Roosevelt Longworth, who accompanied Alsop to Arlington National Cemetery on the day of the president's funeral, thought Joe's column "too 'boy-stood-on-the-burning-deckish,'" others close to Kennedy felt that it was a proper tribute and captured the mood. "Your splendid letter has helped more than any one thing, except the funeral itself, to take me through my sorrow," McGeorge Bundy wrote to Joe. "Now we go on—and while it will not be the same, it will certainly not be dull; and if he is watching, I'll bet he's amused."[39]

In a letter to Isaiah Berlin, Alsop reflected candidly on what Kennedy's death meant to him: "For me, it is a very odd sensation indeed, to discover quite abruptly, without any prior realization, that I have lived the best years of my life between the ages of 48 and 53 . . . Furthermore—and this is another strange thing—I had never known I loved the President (for one does not think of this kind of relationship in those terms) until I felt the impact of his death."[40]

In his depression, Joe even briefly considered giving up his political column. Instead, years later, he chose to end his memoir with Kennedy's death.[41] Yet Alsop was not so blinded by grief that he was unable to see where his own interests lay as a journalist. During the traumatic weekend of Kennedy's funeral, Joe had written to Lyndon Johnson, promising support for the new president. Alsop followed up the letter with a phone call to the new occupant of the White House. Joe urged Johnson not to involve the attorney general in any board of inquiry tasked with looking into the assassination—lest Bobby Kennedy have the additional burden of reporting on the murder of his own brother. In an exchange recorded by the White House taping system, Joe also told Johnson that an editorial in the next morning's *Washington Post* would call for an independent investigation of the assassination. Alsop urged the president to "get ahead" of the *Post* editorial by announcing the appointment of a blue-ribbon commission—but one *not* headed by Hoover's FBI:

> ALSOP: Mind you, Mr. President . . . I am talking about a body which will take all the evidence the FBI has amassed . . .
> LBJ: No, but it's— . . .
> ALSOP: Wait a second, now. That is a way to transmit to the public . . . and in a way that will carry absolute conviction what the FBI has turned up.
> LBJ: Why can't the FBI transmit it?
> ALSOP: Because no one . . . on the left—they won't believe the FBI. And the FBI doesn't write very well.[42]

Before hanging up, Joe suggested that Johnson himself call the *Post*'s Kay Graham and Al Friendly about the pending editorial—"they'll be flattered"—and tell them of his plans to appoint the new commission, apologizing, "And I *hate* to interfere, sir. I only dare to do so because I care so much about you."

The old Joe was back.

PART III

DÉGRINGOLADE

The French have a fine word for collapse: *dégrin-golade*. It is impossible to translate precisely—it suggests a kind of slithery, sudden coming apart. It can be argued that the dégringolade of the United States is now occurring.

—STEWART ALSOP, *Newsweek,* April 1, 1974

CHAPTER NINETEEN

"The Other Side of the Coin"

A N UNHAPPY SECRET is worrying official Washington," Joe Alsop began his column on Wednesday, April 15, 1964. The "secret" was alleged Communist infiltration of the civil rights movement led by the Reverend Martin Luther King. "The King organization and King himself are clearly the prime Communist targets," Alsop wrote. He went on to argue that the "facts cited indeed constitute a strong argument for the earliest possible passage of a strong civil rights bill . . . to redress the Negro grievance." Just two weeks earlier, Alsop had written that the legislation recently introduced by President Johnson and being debated in Congress was likely "the last, best chance to avoid something very like a colonial war in America."[1]

King wondered whether Alsop's column linking him to Communists had not actually been "planted" by Johnson, in a face-saving attempt by the president to back away from the historic civil rights legislation that Johnson had proposed but that was currently stalled by a filibuster in Congress. Urged by his advisers to take the offensive and discredit the Alsop story, King had his lawyers threaten to sue if Joe did not issue a prompt retraction. But, as Alsop reassured his editor at the *Herald Tribune,* he felt "quite sure that King will take no further action in this matter; the source of my information was far too good to make it safe for him to do so." In fact, Joe's unacknowledged source was the FBI, where the director, J. Edgar Hoover, had initiated a protracted, and vicious, campaign to discredit the charismatic black leader.[2]

Joe's focus on the country's racial problems was a temporary diversion from his usual concern: the growing conflict in Vietnam. He was already at odds with Johnson over the prosecution of the war. Hoping instead to emphasize his domestic program, the Great Society, the president had thus far resisted calls to up the ante in Vietnam by committing more treasure and troops—a decision that Joe criticized relentlessly in *Matter of Fact*.[3]

In Alsop's view, a failure to confront—and defeat—the Communist insurgency in Vietnam would mean the end of American influence in Asia, with the result that "the United States world position will simply come apart at the seams." (Joe would later claim to have invented the so-called domino theory.) While Johnson humored Alsop whenever the two came face-to-face, the president vented to administration insiders. "He's crazy. He wrote me a two-page letter saying that we were already liquidating the United States' interest in the Pacific, and we'd move back to Hon-o-lu-la," Johnson complained to Secretary of Defense McNamara.[4]

Alsop's experience in wartime China had left him with a deep conviction that the United States had a moral obligation to help the downtrodden of the world and to stand firm against tyranny. But Joe's own recent personal history also gave him reason to believe that a U.S. defeat in Vietnam might have equally disastrous consequences at home—reviving a McCarthy-like witch hunt for those who had "lost" Indochina. "The disaster that threatens in Vietnam will make the so-called loss of China and the presence of Castro in Cuba seem like mere peanut-sized misfortunes," Alsop wrote to Richard Rovere of *The New Yorker*. "And I have not observed that the American people have grown vastly more philosophical about misfortune." If Vietnam were to be surrendered to the Communists, Joe predicted, "this new issue will be continuously inflamed over a long period of time . . . and will poison our national life for a generation."[5]

"I think he really wants to have a little old war out there," the national security adviser, McGeorge Bundy, told the president that spring. "I've never known him to go to any area where blood could be spilled that he didn't come back and say more blood. That is his posture toward the universe."[6]

After attending, in mid-June 1964, a White House dinner celebrating the Johnsons' wedding anniversary, Joe strolled around the grounds of the residence with the president. During their walk, Alsop confronted LBJ directly on Vietnam, predicting that Johnson would become the first president in American history to lose a war, unless he took more decisive steps to help the Saigon government. "I can't say the evening did anything to solve Lyndon's dilemma—or to smooth his path for the days ahead," Johnson's wife, Lady Bird, wrote in her diary that night.[7]

Johnson would later boast that he knew how to deal with reporters, including the Alsops. But even as his frustration with the brothers—especially Joe—grew, the president recognized that he needed their support. When an unflattering portrait of the president by Stewart appeared in *The Saturday Evening Post,* Johnson dismissed its author as "kind of a supercilious intellectual that thinks he's real smart," while admitting at the same time to a confidant, "Joe's pretty good to me . . . Did you see the Gallup [poll] this morning?"[8]

AS JOE CONTINUED to attack Johnson for "ducking the challenges in Viet Nam," the president might have taken solace in the fact that Alsop had his own secret vulnerabilities. In late November 1964, when Joe revealed that General Maxwell Taylor, the new ambassador to Saigon, had urged a greater U.S. military commitment to South Vietnam—provoking dissent within the administration over the war—Johnson heatedly ordered McNamara to discover who had leaked the Taylor memo. The White House taping system recorded the exchange:

> LBJ: Why don't you find out who [Joe] saw? . . . I have never seen the paper . . . I get most of my information from the government through the papers . . . I have to rely on Alsop to give it to me! That's a disgrace! And if you would read his FBI [file] on him—have you ever read it?
>
> MCNAMARA: No, sir, I haven't.
>
> LBJ: Well, you better read it. Because Walter Jenkins is just minor.[9]

A few weeks earlier, Jenkins, Johnson's longtime aide, had been arrested by District police in a YMCA restroom for "disorderly conduct"—a euphemism of the day for a homosexual assignation. Jenkins had been forced to resign from the administration when the story of the sex scandal appeared in local newspapers. Internal FBI memos indicate that on October 21, 1964, a week after Jenkins's arrest, the bureau's dossier on Joe Alsop was retrieved from the Special File Room—Hoover's private archive and the repository for the director's notorious "do-not-file" cases.*[10] On November 16, two weeks after Lyndon Johnson had been elected president in his own right, Hoover briefed LBJ on the contents of the Alsop file, including the Moscow incident. As intended, the information left its mark on the president. "[Alsop's] been involved in practically every capital of the world," Johnson had told McNamara.[11]

Despite his claims to the contrary, the president was increasingly bothered by Joe's criticisms of him over Vietnam. Alsop knew exactly how to get to the president; aware of Johnson's fragile ego, and his acute sensitivity to being compared unfavorably with the fabled Kennedys, Joe launched a campaign at year's end to, in effect, shame LBJ into escalating the war in Vietnam. In a column on December 30, 1964, Alsop compared the Vietnam War to the Cuban missile crisis, which was widely considered to be John Kennedy's finest hour. "If Johnson ducks the challenge, we shall learn by experience about what it would have been like if Kennedy had ducked the challenge in October, 1962," Joe wrote.[12]

Alsop would be back at the White House a few months later—this time with an altogether different complaint. He had long criticized the administration for managing the news coming out of Vietnam, in order to head off public criticism of the president's policies on the war. In March 1965, Joe accused LBJ of taking "press control" a step too far: wiretapping Alsop's telephone with blackmail on his mind. (He would never reveal who tipped him off or why he suspected the wiretap.) Joe had first gone to the president's press secretary, Bill Moyers, to protest that "certain people were using against him . . . scurrilously collected . . . information about his own personal life." Finding no satisfaction from Moyers, Joe returned to the White House at the end of the month—this time with Scotty Reston in tow—to confront Johnson directly. Immediately following that meeting, in a telephone call on March 29, the president told Moyers and the new attorney general, Nicholas Katzenbach, that Joe Alsop seemed "just short of the asylum now . . . with the same look in his eye and the same attitude . . . that Phil Graham had the last time I saw him." Nonetheless, Johnson asked

---

* Following Hoover's death in May 1972, his secret "Official and Confidential File" was found to contain 164 folders and nearly eighteen thousand pages, which had been deliberately kept separate from the main body of FBI records. The director's private file preserved derogatory information on various individuals—among them, Eleanor Roosevelt, Adlai Stevenson, and John Kennedy, as well as Joe Alsop—and also included documents confirming Hoover's authorization of "clearly illegal" break-ins, wiretaps, bugs, and the FBI's physical surveillance of so-called subversive activities.

Katzenbach to inquire of the FBI's director, Hoover, whether the bureau had ever tapped Alsop's telephone. Hoover promptly replied unequivocally that the FBI had not. Evidently, the CIA's director, McCone, was not asked whether the agency had bugged Alsop.[13]

The flap between Johnson and Alsop over wiretapping passed without further incident—or resolution. And the attention of both men was soon drawn instead to new developments in the war. Beyond sputtering to his subordinates, the president took no action to stop or attempt to restrain Joe Alsop's incessant hectoring on Vietnam. But a decided coolness had meanwhile replaced the earlier backslapping bonhomie.

JOE'S PREOCCUPATION with the country's racial problems, Vietnam, and his own personal troubles took a temporary backseat as the brothers turned to covering the 1964 presidential election. Joe won his bet with Johnson that the latter would receive at least 60 percent of the popular vote. "I am sure you will never find a happier debtor," Lady Bird wrote to Alsop. LBJ's lopsided victory over his conservative Republican challenger, the Arizona senator Barry Goldwater, had been amply forecast by public opinion polls and in Joe and Stewart's own reporting. ("If Goldwater is elected, let's emigrate together," Stew had joked to friends.) For Joe, the only glimmer of excitement that November had been Robert Kennedy's election as the junior senator from New York. Washington pundits speculated that the thirty-eight-year-old brother of the slain president meant to use his Senate seat as a stepping-stone to the Oval Office. If so, there was no doubt about where Joe Alsop stood on the issue. "Let me put it that if I can once again vote for a Kennedy for the Presidency, it will mean more to me than any other political development I can think of," Alsop wrote to the senator-elect.[14]

Joe still felt a powerful attraction to the Kennedy clan. A wistfully nostalgic documentary film on the life of the martyred president, shown at the Democratic convention in Atlantic City, combined with a lingering case of the flu cast Joe into a low-grade depression shortly after the election. Complaining to Walter Lippmann of a "sudden loss of all momentum," Alsop wrote that he felt like "an umbrella without any spokes." For the first time since the assassination of John Kennedy, Joe told his doctor, he had had to resort to pills to get to sleep. A visit to South Vietnam in December did nothing to raise Alsop's spirits. Buddhist protests and the chaos in Saigon created by another military coup convinced Joe that the

Vietcong might be in a position to win the war before the start of the New Year. When not even Joe's usual annual "cure"—a two-week stay at the Grand Hotel & La Pace Spa in Montecatini Terme, Italy—managed to shake his lethargy, Alsop turned for solace to his friends.[15]

Prominent among that number was Katharine Graham, whose own recent, grievous loss of Phil made her a sympathetic soul mate. After Kay and her son Donald had accompanied Joe to the Democratic convention that summer, Alsop sent both a heartfelt thank-you note, addressing it to "Whom It May Concern: The doubtfully valuable life of the undersigned was saved at Atlantic City by the kindness and good companionship of Katharine Meyer Graham. The next generation of Grahams also helped a lot. It is to be hoped that this life-saving will not be held against the life-savers at a later date."[16]

Most who knew her expected that Kay, in her mourning, would promptly liquidate her husband's publishing empire, including its flagship properties, *The Washington Post* and *Newsweek*. Instead, barely a month after her husband's suicide, Katharine Graham became president of the Washington Post Company. (To the amazement of one of her friends, Kay also kept up the tradition of the Georgetown salons: "I remember one dinner when she had to hold her head back to keep the tears from falling. She was grief-stricken.")[17]

Among those counseling Kay during this time of transition were her friends Walter Lippmann and Scotty Reston. When Kay confided that she felt entirely out of her depth taking Phil's place at the *Post,* Lippmann wrote to recommend that she summon to her office the reporter for any story she failed to understand: "In this way, you will kill two birds with one stone. You'll get informed on the news in a fairly painless way and you will get to know better than you probably would any other way the people who actually write the paper . . . I wouldn't try to worry out everything myself. Not everybody, by any means, understands everything, and nobody expects you to do that."[18]

Katharine took Reston's advice not to sell *Newsweek*—"My impression is that it would take a Svengali to change her mind," Stew Alsop mused—as well as Lippmann's suggestion that she bring the magazine's Washington bureau chief, Ben Bradlee, over to the *Post* as deputy managing editor and Al Friendly's eventual successor.[19]

Kay had initially been upset at Bradlee for not attending Phil's memorial service at the R Street house. ("I wasn't invited," Ben protested.) Bradlee had also sided more often with the husband when the Grahams feuded. The former *Washington Post* reporter had a reputation for outspokenness and impetuous behavior—"Humphrey Bogart in a button-down shirt" was one description of the handsome, blue-blooded, longtime newspaperman. Nonetheless, Bradlee promptly became an ally and unlikely confidant for the new and untested publisher, who was steadily gaining in both assurance and experience.[20]

From a woman once too shy to fire an incompetent laundress, Katharine Graham would undergo a personal transformation after Phil's death. When a *Post* reader called to protest a recent article describing him as "a left wing professor who married for money," Kay had cut the complainer short. "He says his wife is sensitive, shy, and feels guilty about it!" she wrote to Stewart Alsop. "But I added as one who obviously is in her position, that this accusation was one we all had to put up with and I had no sympathy with people who feel guilty about money. She should either get over it and enjoy it or give it away (I guess *he's* done that)." Another sign of Katharine's growing independence was the fact that she had begun using her own name in correspondence rather than signing letters, as before, "Mrs. Philip Graham."[21]

Under Katharine Graham's management, there would be no sudden change in the editorial policy of either *Newsweek* or *The Washington Post,* both of which remained resolutely pro-Johnson and supportive of the Vietnam War. (Although Kay had been something of a campus radical while at the University of Chicago in the late 1930s, she subsequently adopted her husband's politics.) "*Post* editorialists have often done a better job of explaining President Johnson's . . . policies than the president himself," gibed *Time* magazine. In February 1965, Kay had gone to South Vietnam in the company of the *Newsweek* editor Oz Elliott and a brace of the magazine's reporters. She returned more persuaded than ever of the necessity of American involvement there—a view that Kay shared with Russ Wiggins, the sixty-two-year-old World War II veteran who oversaw the *Post's* editorial page. Lyndon Johnson would boast that Wiggins and the *Post's* editorials were worth two marine divisions to him in Vietnam.[22]

Little more than a year later, however, Katharine Graham had a very personal stake in the war. Graduating magna cum laude from Harvard's class of 1966 with a degree in English history and literature, twenty-one-year-old Donald Graham, facing the imminent prospect of being drafted into the army, chose to enlist instead. Don had been elected president of the college newspaper, the *Crimson,* and authored some of the paper's unsigned editorials. (A Harvard grad described the election process as "a cross between a papal conclave and the anointing of a Mexican President . . . only more self-important.") After a *Crimson* editorial urged the United States to "get out of Vietnam," Graham received an eleven-page letter from an old family friend. "Both individual advisers and individual actions are fair targets for critical judgment," McGeorge Bundy wrote, "but no useful purpose is served by assuming that Dr. Strangelove is in charge down here." The eldest Graham son had occasionally stood out on campus for his political views—during the 1964 election, Don headed a group that had tried to persuade the *Crimson* to endorse Lyndon Johnson as a positive choice, rather than simply the lesser of two evils—and for his support of the Vietnam War. At the annual *Crimson* dinner, Don's colleagues presented him with a fitting going-away present: a live hawk.[23]

Per Don's request, Joe Alsop sent him a collection of books on Vietnam—including Bernard Fall's classic on the French defeat, *Street Without Joy*. In June 1967, Joe hosted his own farewell dinner at Dumbarton Avenue for Katharine Graham's son—the other guests, besides Kay, included Bob McNamara, Mac Bundy, and Dick Helms. Two weeks later, the army private Donald Graham arrived in Saigon as a battalion public information officer for the First Air Cavalry Division.[24]

BY THE LATE 1960S, a new generation was coming of age in Georgetown. Like their parents, the children of the Georgetown set would be drawn to—and marked by—the decisive conflict of their generation: Vietnam.

Frank George Wisner, after graduating from Princeton in 1961, had promptly joined the Foreign Service and been sent to Algiers for his initial posting. (The young Wisner remembered that his father discouraged him from following in his footsteps at the CIA. "If you join the Foreign Service, you're building something. We destroy things," the elder Frank told his son.) By mid-1964, Frank II was in South Vietnam's Mekong delta, assigned to the U.S. Agency for International Development as a senior adviser to the province leaders. An article titled "Princetonians in Vietnam" for the college's alumni magazine boasted that Frank was the youngest of that rank to serve in the country. Moving quickly up the ladder, he next became an aide to the deputy U.S. ambassador in Saigon, William Porter.[25] At the American embassy, Wisner's reputation for diplomatic savvy earned him the nickname Metternich. (He was quick to put an end to one ill-conceived public relations idea: a cockfight that would have pitted a northern bird against a southern one.) But Wisner would be scolded a few months later for making an unauthorized road trip near the Cambodian border in the Triumph sports car owned by his fellow Princetonian and AID colleague Robin Pell.[26]

Fortunately for the young Frank Wisner, there were other familiar faces in Saigon.

Richard Holbrooke, who had also worked alongside Frank for AID in the delta, joined him at the embassy, becoming an assistant to Porter and the U.S. ambassador. After two years in a boring job working for Nicolas Nabokov and the Congress for Cultural Freedom in Paris, Frances FitzGerald arrived in Saigon early in 1966 as a freelance journalist. Frankie, the daughter of Desmond FitzGerald and Marietta Peabody, had acquired the job at the CIA-funded CCF through her father's connections, not knowing of the organization's affiliation with the agency at the time. ("I had a desk and a blotter and pencils but nothing to do. I should have suspected, but people didn't suspect back then.") Having grown up in Georgetown—Frankie's godmother was Susan Mary Alsop—and at Ditchley, her stepfather's posh country estate in England, the twenty-five-year-old FitzGerald found the squalor and excitement of Saigon initially "overwhelming." From the rooftop vantage point of the Caravelle Hotel, she remembered thinking that tracer rounds looked more like fireworks than a portent of death. In a letter to his childhood friend, the young Frank Wisner had warned Frankie against coming to Vietnam: "I wish I could say you would not be consumed in this game as I am, but I fear I would be lying if I did. This is not your world—the guns, tanks and brutality all seem so pointless save in the very obvious point of it all, and the obvious is alive here." The headstrong Radcliffe graduate ignored him.[27]

Frank George Wisner had recently welcomed another Georgetown visitor to Saigon, a friend he had known since age four as Uncle Joe. In September 1965, Joe Alsop returned to Southeast Asia to assess the progress of the American effort there. Since the journalist's last visit, President Johnson had initiated large-scale bombing of North Vietnam and committed an additional fifty thousand troops to the war. ("There, *that* should keep Joe Alsop quiet for a while," LBJ told an aide.) In reports that he filed from the field, Joe professed to have discovered a "brand-new war"—one where the United States was "standing up and being counted once again." In a column on September 22, "Frank and His Friends," Alsop used the twenty-seven-year-old Wisner as an exemplar of what Joe called the "promising young men" that the United States was sending to Vietnam.[28]

Young Frank professed to be embarrassed by Alsop's praise in a letter to his father, who had previously warned his son to be wary of all journalists—Joe Alsop included. The son's most recent visit to his parents' P Street home had come shortly before he left for Vietnam, when the elder Frank was recovering from a second mental breakdown. The father had only recently been released from the hospital and remained "trapped in his own illness," the son remembered. The two men had gone for a drive in the Maryland countryside: "We talked about my going to Vietnam, and my father expressed his pride in where my career after Algiers had already taken me. He recognized that I was starting on a venture that he had embarked upon earlier. It was sort of passing the baton."[29]

BACK AT HIS LAW OFFICE on Eighteenth Street, Frank Gardiner Wisner continued to write book reviews and short articles for the CIA's internal publications. Even though he was no longer on the agency's active employment rolls, he still held out hope of reviving the once-mighty Wurlitzer. After a CIA-supported military coup in March 1964 overthrew the democratically elected president of Brazil, Wisner went to his usual press contacts—Stewart Alsop, Cy Sulzberger, and *The New York Times*'s Sam Brewer—with an appeal that they write something favorable to the new regime. "I continue to feel that it would be very useful for some reputable and unbiased observer such as yourself or perhaps Old Black Joe to drop in on Brazil for a brief visitation and look around," Frank wrote to Stewart.[30]

Wisner had reason to believe that his longtime friends would entertain his request. Frank not only had tried to recruit Stewart Alsop as his deputy at OPC years earlier but had recently done personal favors for both Sulzberger and Brewer. In Sulzberger's case, Frank had given him free legal advice when he was threatened with a defamation lawsuit by a Serbian Communist upset at the way he had been portrayed in Sulzberger's 1963 book, *Unconquered Souls*. Wisner also offered to help arrange the publication of Sulzberger's memoir, *A Long Row of Candles*. The previous December, the book publisher Frederick Praeger had discreetly contacted Frank about the idea of creating, with the CIA's financial support, an international publishing company engaged in " 'merchandising freedom' through high quality books concentrating on world affairs and education." "I intend to do all that I can to advise and assist Mr. Praeger and his associates, and in return I am inclined to believe that they will be even more amenable than heretofore to suggestions as to the selections of titles for publication both here and abroad," Wisner informed the State Department. Frank suggested to Sulzberger that the new, CIA-subsidized press might be a good fit for Cy's memoir.[31]

In Brewer's case, the distraught *New York Times* correspondent had quietly approached Wisner for help in resolving his own Cold War dilemma: Brewer's former wife, Eleanor, had run off to Moscow with the Soviet spy Kim Philby and was threatening to return to the United States to take custody of the couple's fifteen-year-old daughter, Ann. (Kim Philby's defection to the Soviet Union two years earlier had removed whatever doubt might still have existed about what lay behind the CIA's failure to penetrate the Iron Curtain. Regarding the agency's ethnic teams, Philby later wrote, "I do not know what happened to the parties concerned. But I can make an informed guess.")[32]

Finding the New York courts powerless to thwart Eleanor's plans, Brewer had written to Frank "to ask you whether it could do any good to call the attention of anybody in Washington to the situation." Wisner assured Brewer that he had indeed brought the matter to the attention of the proper "governmental authorities," ending the letter with an appeal of his own: "Have you given any further thought to my suggestion that you consider the writing of some articles, or possibly a book, on the Brazilian situation?" Eleanor Brewer's passport was lifted by the State Department upon her arrival in the United States six weeks later, and she returned to Moscow without Ann. When Brewer was subsequently awarded custody of the child by the courts, he thanked Wisner for his efforts.[33]

But this time Frank's pleas to his reporter friends went unanswered. "Old Black Joe" Alsop remained preoccupied with Vietnam. Stewart proved numb to the "gentle needle" that Frank hoped might "stimulate him [to write] a good and informative story on Brazilian developments." Likewise, Sam Brewer wrote back that his newspaper had no interest in doing the story that Wisner had outlined. Sulzberger—apologizing that he was about to decamp to his house on the island of Spetsai—similarly begged off. The mighty Wurlitzer would remain silent on Brazil.[34]

Instead, early in 1965, the fifty-five-year-old Wisner embraced a new cause—responding to the increasing number of attacks on the organization that had been his professional life. Unexpectedly, it proved to be a full-time job.

A book published the previous year, *The Invisible Government,* by the Washington journalists David Wise and Thomas Ross, had outraged the CIA by its portrayal of the agency as a renegade institution carrying out its own foreign policy, often in contravention of the nation's real interests. Even more disturbing, alleged Dick Helms—soon to become the CIA director—was the book's naming of active agency operatives. (When word got out that the CIA had tried, and failed, to buy up the entire print run of *The Invisible Government* from the publisher, sales naturally soared.) Within months of the book's appearance, moreover, an NBC television documentary had implicated the CIA in the assassination of Diem, comparing the agency to a rogue elephant. Wisner wrote to the CIA director, McCone, that the documentary contained "inaccuracies [and] distortions . . . many of which are of demonstrably Communist origin."[35]

Even the so-called Gray Lady of American journalism, *The New York Times*—which, a decade earlier, had ordered the reporter Sydney Gruson out of Guatemala at the urging of Wisner and Allen Dulles—began a series of exposés on the agency's misdeeds that fall.[36]

Until publication of *The Invisible Government,* the CIA's popular image had gone largely unsullied, the only real critics being McCarthy and the radical Right. By the mid-1960s, the assault was coming from the opposite end of the ideological spectrum. Wisner's ire increased when a 3,500-word article apearing in the London *Sunday Times* by the British historian Hugh Trevor-Roper, not only criticized the work of the Warren Commission but subtly suggested that the CIA might be complicit in the murder of President Kennedy. Frank asked his longtime friend and fellow OSS alumnus Arthur Schlesinger Jr. to respond to Trevor-Roper in the pages of *Encounter,* a British journal funded, in part, by the CIA. But Schlesinger excused himself on the grounds that the Kennedy assassination was simply too painful a subject for him to tackle.[37]

Not surprisingly, when Stewart Alsop proposed a brief piece in defense of the CIA for *The Saturday Evening Post,* Wisner jumped at the idea with alacrity. "In all fairness, it is time somebody had a kind word to say for the poor old Central Intelligence Agency," began Stew's February 1964 article, "Hogwash About the CIA." More than a year later, Stewart was still defending the agency, in a radio interview and with another *Saturday Evening Post* article. In 1966, Alsop wrote to his editor at the magazine, urging that the latter kill a forthcoming piece on the agency's covert operations in Africa, which Helms had told him was inaccurate: "I think this is the sort of thing we ought to leave to *Esquire*."[38]

Frank Gardiner Wisner had also become obsessed with how the CIA was portrayed in popular spy fiction. He sent the Scottish-American novelist Helen MacInnes some fourteen single-spaced pages of commentary and plot suggestions for her forthcoming mystery, *The Double Image,* and even arranged a special tour of FBI headquarters. At the same time, as Frank wrote to his former boss Allen Dulles, he was "very concerned" about *The Ambassador,* a 1965 novel written by the Australian Morris West, "not merely because of the egregiously unfair and inaccurate mauling which it gives to a certain organization, but even more so because of its attack upon the entire U.S. Government and our (attempted) leadership of the Free World in the struggle to contain and defeat Communist subversion and military aggression on a front as wide as the world."[39]

Frank sent equally prolix warnings about *The Ambassador* to his friends Dean Acheson and Joe Alsop, attaching his own twelve-page, single-spaced review that he hoped to publish as a rebuttal. Acheson wrote back that he actually rather liked the book: "There was no more evidence that I could see that the novel was written to harm the United States than that 'The Shoes of the Fisherman' was written to get a Russian made Pope." Alsop diplomatically suggested that he and Frank talk about the book over dinner.[40]

Wisner likewise took an inordinate—and ironic—interest in another book, *The Year of the Rat,* whose author, Mladin Zarubica, the son of a Yugoslav immigrant, claimed to have discovered Martin Bormann, a prominent Nazi who had been Hitler's private secretary, posing as a hunting guide in Latin America. In a memo he sent to his friend Desmond FitzGerald, Frank wrote: "I continue to feel that further attention should be paid by *someone* to the whereabouts and (probably sinister) activities of these big ones who got away."[41]

Wisner was doubtless crestfallen by Schlesinger's reluctance to refute Trevor-Roper and the other conspiracy theories growing up around the Kennedy assassination. Meanwhile, his lengthy response to the West novel went unpublished—yet more evidence that the once-mighty Wurlitzer had fallen silent and would likely not be heard again. By mid-1965, Wisner was once again suffering from deep depression.

In a visit home from college, Ellis, Frank's middle son, found his father emotionally distraught and "in a hole so deep that you couldn't imagine how he could climb out of it. It was the third time down, and it was pretty rough." One day the father took his youngest son, Graham, out in a rowboat on the lake near the Maryland farm, not returning with the boy until well after dark. Fearing the worst, Polly instructed the caretaker at the farm to hide the guns and turned again to those who had helped her husband in the past. Chip Bohlen took the news that Frank had canceled their plans to go bird hunting together in Spain—always one of Wisner's favorite activities—as an ominous sign. Dick Helms grew alarmed when Frank informed him in September that he meant to give up even his consultancy with the agency, breaking Wisner's last ties to the CIA.[42]

On Friday, October 29, 1965, less than an hour after his arrival at the Locust Hill farmhouse, Frank Wisner killed himself with a 20-gauge shotgun that the caretaker had overlooked. His death was eerily similar to Phil Graham's suicide two years earlier. While the CIA refused to release any details on the work that Frank had done at the agency, an obituary in *The Washington Post* quoted an anonymous colleague's description of him as "one of the founders of its covert operations."[43]

Following a memorial service in the Bethlehem Chapel on the grounds of Washington's National Cathedral, Frank Gardiner Wisner was buried at Arlington National Cemetery, his gravestone inscribed only with his wartime rank of navy commander. At the service, Frank's sister, Elizabeth, thanked those who had tried but failed to save her brother. In a subsequent letter to Dick Helms, who had also spoken at the service, she wrote, "From the many suggestions that came to him, from family as well as friends, as to finding an alternate way to live meaningfully—his consideration and definite rejection of any of them, I'd come to realize that he felt that where his ability to serve further in the organization ended, his life, in fact, was over. I never wanted to admit this to myself, but it was true—for him, the other side of the coin was blank."[44]

CHAPTER TWENTY

"I'm Afraid Joe Is a Cruel Man"

BY 1966, JOE ALSOP was increasingly isolated among the Washington press corps for his continued and stalwart defense of the Vietnam War. Joseph Kraft, Scotty Reston, and Walter Lippmann had all taken positions opposing, to various degrees, Johnson's deliberate escalation of the conflict. But Joe had further alienated his journalist colleagues by personally attacking them in print. In March, he savaged *The New York Times* for its coverage of an important battle in the Ia Drang valley, which, in Joe's view, had overemphasized U.S. casualties while downplaying an American victory. The *Times,* he charged, was "fighting a rearguard action against the facts."[1]

Alsop boasted to Isaiah Berlin that his attack on *The New York Times* had "fluttered the dovecotes rather sharply." Once again, Joe's real targets were the two reporters covering the war for the paper: David Halberstam and Neil Sheehan, who had recently joined the *Times.* In a heated exchange following martinis at his house, Joe told the *Times*'s Tom Wicker that Sheehan was "crooked" and "a liar." Halberstam—for whom Joe felt a particular enmity—was dismissed as "a young ass." John Oakes, editor of the *Times*'s editorial page, informed his associates that Alsop was accusing them and their venerable newspaper of "committing treason."[2]

Their colleagues at the *Times* quickly came to the defense of Sheehan and Halberstam. But, following a brief exchange of letters with Alsop, where he sought—in vain—an apology from Joe for the cocktail party outburst, Tom Wicker simply gave up trying. Scotty Reston, similarly unable to temper Alsop's bile, explained to a puzzled Halberstam, "I'm afraid Joe is a cruel man."[3]

Alsop was also engaged in a running battle with *The New Yorker*. When Richard Rovere opined in the magazine that the conflict in Vietnam might be unwinnable, Joe defiantly predicted that the war would actually be won in the next six to eight months. "What you never seem to take into account is that this war, no matter how just it is, no matter how unthinkable an American withdrawal may be, is doing terrible things to this country . . . No matter how much in the right Joe Alsop may be, the people do not like this war one bit," Rovere replied. Robert Shaplen, another *New Yorker* writer with long experience of Asia, blamed Joe's brand of reporting for his distorted view of the war: "You come in and out of the place, talk to Americans and your old friends, but believe me, talk to some Viets who know what's going on and you'll get a different picture."[4]

Alsop had likewise offended his few remaining friends in the Johnson administration by his continued criticism of the president for not doing more to win in Vietnam. "The President is still presenting the Vietnamese War to the country with techniques quite visibly borrowed from Madison Avenue," Joe wrote that winter. A dinner party at Polly Wisner's house for the new Israeli ambassador took an unexpectedly dark turn when the discussion suddenly veered to the conflict in Asia, as Averell Harriman recounted in a memo for his personal files:

> Joe Alsop interrupted to say that everything will be all right in the Middle East as soon as we have won in Vietnam. I mildly stated that the two were not connected. He said that was absurd. We cured Berlin by standing firm in Cuba. After some further arguments along this line, I exploded and told him he was a damn fool—he was like a trotting horse with blinders, could only see one situation; that he was doing his best to encourage the isolationists to forget about the rest of the world; if his advice was followed we would lose more there than we would ever gain in Vietnam . . . Seeing the futility of further discussion, I suggested we join the ladies. Incidentally, Stew Alsop was also there. He fully agreed with my statements.[5]

Lyndon Johnson responded to Joe's attacks by striking out not at the influential columnist but at those whom LBJ suspected of being Alsop's sources. Shortly after being appointed CIA director in June 1966, Dick Helms was called into the Oval Office by Johnson, who, "out of the blue," Helms remembered, "accused me of being entirely too close to Joseph Alsop and leaking information to him . . . President Johnson lapsed deeply into the vernacular in characterizing Alsop." In fact, the agency's new head was actually assisting the administration behind the scenes. After Helms gave Bill Moyers a confidential memorandum, disputing figures that Alsop had cited in a recent column on enemy troop strength, Johnson's press secretary sent the CIA director a note on White House stationery with a single word: "Thanks." On his own, Helms also commissioned a top secret, thirty-three page CIA study for Johnson—"Implications of an Unfavorable Outcome in Vietnam"— which he personally presented to the president. It concluded that the United States could lose the war without suffering a fatal blow to its power or international prestige. As it had everywhere in the country, the war was splitting the agency asunder. While analysts were issuing ever more pessimistic forecasts, the Plans Directorate urged its agents on to greater effort. "I felt like a circus rider standing astride two horses," Helms later wrote in his memoirs.[6]

Following an explosive confrontation outside National Airport, McGeorge Bundy simply refused to discuss the war with Alsop. Johnson's national security adviser had treated him "like a schoolboy," Joe protested. In a recent top secret memorandum to the president, Bundy had used words like "grim" and "deteriorating" to describe the situation in Vietnam, warning Johnson that "General Alsop" was wrong to predict imminent victory. Disillusioned on the war—and angry at Johnson, who accused him of also leaking secrets to Alsop—Bundy resigned from the administration in February 1966. Having already turned down an offer from Kay Graham to make him editor of *The Washington Post*'s editorial page, he instead became head of the Ford Foundation. Despite their differences over Vietnam, Joe held the farewell party at his house, and, as usual, wrote a glowing valedictory column dedicated to his friend Mac.[7]

Lyndon Johnson, too, was finding it increasingly difficult to hide his frustration with Alsop. But, while the president continued to be irritated by Joe's criticism of the bombing halts and so-called peace feelers that Johnson hoped might end the war, he was nonetheless grateful that Alsop at least still defended the struggle itself as worthwhile. The former CIA director John McCone jokingly wrote to Joe, following Washington's annual Gridiron dinner, "Be careful or [Johnson] will have you in a uniform. I am not sure that it will be the uniform of a four-star general or a prison garb! But he obviously has his eye on you." Joe's longtime friend and former collaborator at the *Trib,* Bob Kintner, who had meanwhile become a White House special assistant, negotiated a temporary truce between Alsop and the president that summer.[8]

The war was also creating tension between the two Alsop brothers. From his initial support of the conflict as a necessary if regrettable sacrifice, Stewart had gradually begun to entertain doubts. In a *Saturday Evening Post* article he wrote that fall, titled "Vietnam: Great Miscalculation?," Stew mused that the "other side may be totally unwilling to settle the war as long as they are convinced that *our* side can't win." "I admire Bob McNamara very much," Stewart wrote to Walt Rostow, a hawkish adviser to Johnson on the war, "but 'sometimes even Homer nods,' and I am increasingly convinced that his basic thesis about the Vietnamese war is both faultlessly logical, and wrong."[9]

Stewart's faith was further shaken during a November 1966 visit to Vietnam in the company of his good friend Tom Braden. Whereas Joe had criticized Operation Rolling Thunder, the U.S. bombing of North Vietnam, as too restrained—"It's like trying to knock a man out by biting his toe"—Stewart worried that the escalating raids would inevitably alienate the Vietnamese by causing civilian casualties without achieving militarily decisive results. "I've just returned from Viet Nam, more confused than ever," Stew wrote to a professor at George Washington University on November 30. Later that same day, however, he also told a journalist colleague, "So, as a practical matter, there is no way to sneak out by the back door, even if we wished to do so." On the flight home from Saigon, sitting next to Philip Geyelin, the young former *Wall Street Journal* reporter who would soon replace Russ Wiggins on *The Washington Post*'s editorial page, Stewart gave vent to the frustrations that Vietnam—and Joe—were causing in his life: "I can see I'm going to have to break openly with my brother on this war. I'm not looking forward to that."[10]

OUTWARDLY, JOE ALSOP seemed unfazed by the fact that he was now virtually alone among colleagues in his support for the war. Yet when the British journalist Henry Fairlie wrote in *Esquire* that Alsop's lonely stand showed him to be out of touch, Joe bristled in a letter to Fairlie: "I may be out of date, as I was in the McCarthy period, when my brother and

I fought a damned sight harder for a damned sight sooner than some of my colleagues whom you praise. But I don't think it's quite accurate to say that I am out of touch."[11]

Privately, Joe confided to Isaiah Berlin that his support for the war was beginning to take a toll: "I cannot tell you how isolated and suddenly out of fashion I feel. The old way of looking at the world in this country . . . is now increasingly outmoded among the intellectuals."[12]

The growing divide in the country over Vietnam was already evident weekly to the readers of American newspapers—in the dueling columns of Joe Alsop and Walter Lippmann. By late 1966, their debate on the war occupied the editorial pages of more than two hundred papers in the *Washington Post* syndicate. On Mondays, Wednesdays, and Fridays, Alsop's Matter of Fact column declared confidently that the war was being won and "standing fast is paying off." On Tuesdays and Thursdays, Lippmann's Today and Tomorrow urged the president to halt the bombing and seek a negotiated peace.[13]

In conversations with friends, Joe was disdainful and even dismissive of Lippmann's views, claiming that his rival lacked his own deep knowledge of the region. After one Lippmann column confused North Vietnam's landlocked capital, Hanoi, with Haiphong, a seaport, Alsop joked that Congress should pass a law forbidding Walter Lippmann to write about Southeast Asia. Lippmann, for his part, had been telling associates since 1964 that if Johnson escalated the war in Vietnam, at least half the blame would be Alsop's. When Joe sent Lippmann some books on Asian history, the latter returned the package unopened a few weeks later, apologizing, "Somehow I can't read about China." "It all but gave me a double hernia, straining not to reply: 'But if you cannot read about China, why in God's name write about it?'" Joe told the journalist Ward Just.[14]

Undeterred, Alsop next sent Lippmann a batch of the captured enemy documents that were routinely given to Joe by an intelligence officer at the American embassy in Saigon. ("We don't give these to anybody else," Alsop was told by his source, who recalled how "old Joe would squirrel them down his shirt.") Alsop assured Lippmann that the classified documents showed North Vietnam's army to be on its last legs. But Lippmann countered that Joe was only cherry-picking documents that supported his position while ignoring contrary evidence. A mutual friend summed up their feud: "Joe considered Lippmann an appeaser. Walter saw Joe as a warmonger."[15]

The jousting of the two rivals was nonetheless conducted in a surprisingly good-natured fashion. Walter signed his letters to Joe, "Affectionate as always." "Much as we disagree, I continue to respect and admire you," Alsop replied.[16]

No such mutual respect could be said to exist between Walter Lippmann and Lyndon Johnson. The president had taken to making disparaging comments about the revered columnist in public, including one verbal insult directed at Lippmann during a formal state dinner. In 1966, a leaked White House memo revealed the existence of a "Walter Lippmann project," aimed at discrediting the latter with "documentation illustrating the continuities and character of Walter Lippmann's opposition . . . to four Administrations on ten major issues." Lippmann's allies at the *Post* rallied to his defense. A Herblock cartoon, captioned "The War on Lippmann," depicted the columnist sitting serenely behind a typewriter while Johnson ineffectually hurled thunderbolts at his foe.[17]

By December, however, Lippmann had finally had enough—announcing that he and his wife were selling their house in Washington and returning to New York, where he intended to continue writing in opposition to the war, but in a friendlier atmosphere. While Lippmann's denunciation of "cronyism" in a parting speech at the National Press Club was widely interpreted as a backhanded swipe at Alsop, Joe hosted the inevitable farewell dinner for the couple at his home. Ironically, his adversary's departure from Washington only heightened Alsop's sense of isolation. "I miss you sadly, on Tuesday and Thursday, and the whole city will always miss both of you," Joe wrote to Walter and Helen.[18]

Subsequent to Lippmann's leaving, Alsop declared himself "dean of the columnists." Challenged by another reporter—and friend of Lippmann's—to justify that claim, Joe replied, defensively, of his longtime rival, "He's retired, and, anyway, I was here first."[19]

EVEN MORE PAINFUL for Joe Alsop than being ostracized by his fellow reporters was losing friends on account of the war. Many of those Joe had known for years, like McGeorge Bundy, simply stopped talking to him about Vietnam—as had Mac's brother William Bundy, whom LBJ had recently appointed assistant secretary of state for Far Eastern affairs. Following a column by Joe that attacked George Ball, a State Department official urging a negotiated peace in Vietnam, Bill Bundy sent Alsop a personal note: "You have made life harder for all of us, but particularly hard for those of us who would like to consider ourselves your friends in the responsible interchange of views between Government officials and journalists."[20]

Shortly after George Kennan told a televised Senate hearing early in 1966 that the war was "a hopeless effort" which left him with "a feeling of miserable helplessness," Kennan wrote to Alsop, "It is hard for me to discuss [Vietnam] with you, because you are—as you must well know—overbearing in argument in a manner that belies your own inner nature; I am shrinking and chicken-hearted in a manner that probably equally belies my own."[21]

Kennan had left his ambassadorial post in Belgrade after just two short years, putting an end to what he admitted to his friend John Davies had been "a disastrously unsuccessful tour of duty." In a typical display of political tone deafness, Kennan had upset Congress by lobbying to overturn a vote that revoked Yugoslavia's most-favored-nation trade status. As before, it was not so much Kennan's lobbying as his approach—"shrill and condescending," one congressman complained—that had most angered the legislators. His efforts at changing Washington having once more proved to be in vain, Kennan was glad to leave the diplomatic corps, and Secretary of State Dean Rusk was relieved to see him go.[22]

In January 1967, when Arthur Schlesinger Jr. published an anti-Vietnam War book titled *The Bitter Heritage,* Joe Alsop promptly responded with a scathing review in Matter of Fact: "Schlesinger's judgments on Vietnam are exclusively based upon secondary sources, many of them dubious, and all of them examined in the light of Schlesinger's strong and uninformed preconceptions." One reason for Alsop's scorn, unmentioned in the review, was his fear that Schlesinger would also turn Bobby Kennedy against the war. Joe had warned Schlesinger in advance that the attack was coming and "that the piece is not meant personally, although you will probably take it personally. It's simply a case of the cup running over, and your book causing the overflow." But being fore-warned did nothing to soften the blow. "Do you think we are all fools? Can you not admit the possibility that the problem is complex and that honorable men might differ?" Schlesinger replied in an emotional letter. When he encountered Alsop soon afterward at a Georgetown cocktail party, Schlesinger turned on his heel and walked away as Joe moved to shake his hand. The two men would eventually reconcile, but their friendship thereafter bore permanent scars.[23]

By criticizing Schlesinger, Alsop also managed to upset others in the

Kennedy clan. John Kenneth Galbraith, John Kennedy's ambassador to India, came to Schlesinger's defense by attacking Alsop. In a letter written on Harvard stationery, Galbraith demanded that Joe retract his column on *The Bitter Heritage*. The screed against Schlesinger's book, Galbraith claimed, was a sign of Alsop's "isolation from the general scholarly community." Joe promptly fired back: "I am sorry that you think that my piece on Arthur's book is long on polemics and short on facts . . . I do not feel isolated from the general academic community, since with most of the leading Asianists in the academic community I maintain fairly close relations. I do feel isolated, however, from the damn fools who constantly lecture about Asia without knowing anything about it. But I only feel isolated from them because I consider them to be damn fools."[24]

The Vietnam War had even intruded on Joe's home life. Dinner-table rows with Susan Mary had lately become both more frequent and more strident—partly on account of his wife's increasingly dovish views on the war. ("The heaven of not talking about Vietnam night after night," Susan Mary mused to Marietta in June 1967, when the six-day Arab-Israeli war brought a temporary truce to the feuding with Joe. "Now that the Middle East smoulders instead of flaming, I suppose we will be back floundering in that poisonous bog that seems to infect the healthiest conversation as dangerously as a tropical fever.") After one especially nasty exchange with his wife over Vietnam, Alsop delivered what was, for him, perhaps the ultimate put-down: "Jesus, Susan Mary, you sound just like a *New York Times* editorial."[25]

THE DEBATE OVER THE WAR in Vietnam was a reflection of differences not only of outlook but of age. The coming to maturity of children born after World War II—the baby boomers—had transformed the country, including, not least of all, staid and traditional Georgetown.

In December 1967, the music had finally stopped for that enduring symbol of the old order, the Dancing Class, which fell victim to declining interest and changing tastes. Emblematic of the change, missing from the so-called swan song dance were two of the best-known alumni of the class—Phil Graham and Frank Wisner. Shifting demographics were the cause of other, more visible changes. Owing to an influx of teenagers with cars in dubious mechanical repair, the Citizens Association of Georgetown had imposed parking restrictions on the enclave's crowded streets. Loud parties and blaring rock music likewise prompted the association to petition that the drinking age be raised in the District. At the Alsop home, it was no longer the soft-drink rings that friends of Anne and Billy carelessly left on his antique French furniture that upset Joe, but beer spills and wine stains on his rare Oriental carpets.[26]

As befitted their different personalities, the Alsop brothers had divergent reactions to the emerging generation gap. For Stewart, the phenomenon was a subject of interest and even some fascination. When his editor at *The Saturday Evening Post* proposed that he do a piece on the country's new rich, Stew suggested instead a feature article on the blossoming youth culture, which he had recently observed while out on a solitary nocturnal walk:

> One night, not feeling sleepy, I wandered lonely as a cloud through the streets of Chicago and came onto an area known as "Old Town." The streets were filled to the bursting point with Chicago's "with it" youth—ladies in stretch pants, with pressed hair, gentlemen in vaguely Edwardian costumes, long hair, and/or beards. Old Town is a city-wide mecca for such types, and especially on Saturday nights, I'm told, the joint really jumps. I noticed a hand-lettered sign in one of the honky tonks—"Everyone under 25 is welcome." The clear implication being that if you're an elderly 26, stay out.[27]

Joe, on the other hand, was repulsed by the music, the fashion, and the mores of the next generation. Following a speaking engagement at Yale, he ran into Billy, who was wearing a black turtleneck, skintight jeans, suede boots, and a sleeveless sheepskin jacket. Joe wrote to Don Graham of the encounter with his long-haired stepson, "As I am afraid I told him he looked like a very handsome minor actor in a minor play about the youth of Abe Lincoln."

Rebellious youth also put a strain on both Alsops' strong belief that their generation had an obligation to educate and instruct those who would follow them. For both brothers, moreover, the phenomenon was coming closer to home. Joe had been appalled when Billy announced that he and a female companion hoped to win the prize at a fancy costume ball by showing up stark naked. After protesting the Vietnam War while a student at Dartmouth, Stewart's son Ian, twenty-three, moved to Nepal, where he and his wife sold Tibetan woodcut prints to tourists in Katmandu. Stew's oldest son, Joe, had been kicked out of Groton a few years earlier for bugging the headmaster's study. Like many espionage capers gone awry, the plot was discovered when it became clear that the plotters knew too much about what went on behind closed doors.[28]

Joe tried, nonetheless, to introduce his friends' grown-up sons and daughters to the famous zoo parties. Often, the result was an unqualified disaster. If Alsop expected deference from his young guests, he had sorely misjudged his audience.

Those attending one particularly memorable dinner included Desmond FitzGerald, his daughter, Frankie, and Henry Breck, a young friend of Frankie's who was considering a career in the CIA. In the midst of what all remembered as "a high-decibel, gin-lubricated conversation," after Joe had gone on at length about the "Lords of the Delta" and the "new Lawrences of Arabia"—specifically, Frank George Wisner and Wisner's embassy colleague Richard Holbrooke—Frankie and Breck finally spoke out in protest, condemning the war as immoral. A spirited argument ensued, with Desie taking the side of Joe, who twice left the table in a rage, before returning to his guests. For Alsop, the fact that the children of his "high WASP" Georgetown friends opposed the war was almost a personal betrayal.[29]

Joe's efforts at bringing to his side a freshly minted war correspondent for *The Washington Post* fared little better. Late in 1965, Ben Bradlee had sent thirty-year-old Ward Just—the former *Newsweek* reporter who had interviewed Alsop for the magazine's piece on President Kennedy's favorite columnists—to Vietnam as the *Post*'s bureau chief. In Saigon, Just and Frankie FitzGerald became Joe Alsop's dutiful if somewhat reluctant hosts during the latter's visits to the city.[30] Like his other colleagues at the *Post,* Just had gradually grown dismissive of the "five o'clock follies"—the ritual briefings on the war by MACV, the U.S. Military Assistance Command, Vietnam—in which Joe Alsop always put such stock. ("Very early the word 'stalemate' came to mind," Just later said of his reporting.) Wounded in a grenade attack in the spring of 1966, Just returned to Washington to recuperate, becoming the guest of honor at one of Joe's dinners, where Alsop gave the final toast. "It was Joe at his most stentorian," Just remembered: "To the man who has felt the sting of battle and shed his own blood."[31]

Back in Vietnam, Just clashed with Joe over how to interpret a new phenomenon in the war: Vietcong and North Vietnamese troops were simply abandoning usable weapons after a battle. MACV and Joe Alsop saw it as a hopeful sign that enemy morale was finally cracking. The CIA and Just believed, however, that it was because so many new weapons were coming down the Ho Chi Minh Trail to the North Vietnamese that the enemy had a surplus. His dispute with Alsop "encapsulated the whole thing about the war," Just believed: "different interpretations of the same fact."[32]

Returning home again to Georgetown in December on holiday leave, Ward Just discovered a different reception awaited him at the dinner that Joe arranged at Robert McNamara's house, where the other guests included Bobby Kennedy, his wife, Ethel, and several senior Pentagon officials: "It was a really strange evening . . . It was evident it was staged so I would get on the team . . . They were pulling documents, captured enemy documents, out of their wallets—the latest stats and figures. They were not interested in anyone who had actually spent time there. They were like tourists . . . They had absolutely no interest in what I had to say."[33] Just left the supper early—and unconvinced. Several months later, in June 1967, when his Vietnam assignment ended, he would anger Alsop anew by titling his valedictory piece in the *Post* "This War May Be Unwinnable."[34]

As was becoming obvious to all sides, on the subject of Vietnam the children were at war with their parents. The two generations inhabited, in effect, different worlds. George Kennan's son, Christopher, a Grotonian, had meanwhile dropped out of Yale, transferring to the University of California's new, experimental campus above the beachside town of Santa Cruz. Three of Paul Nitze's four children accompanied other protesters in a march on the Pentagon—which their father, as deputy secretary of defense, had been given the job of protecting. Ben Bradlee's wife, Tony, Stewart Alsop's daughter, Elizabeth, and the sons of Dick Helms and Bob McNamara also engaged in demonstrations against the Vietnam War. In another sign of the times, a young *Post* photographer, whom Bradlee had sent to take pictures of a Vietnam protest, joined the protesters instead.[35]

ON NOVEMBER 28, 1966, the writer Truman Capote hosted a formal masked ball in Katharine Graham's honor at New York's Plaza hotel. Capote called it, immodestly, the "Party of the Century." The five hundred guests attending the Black and White Ball consumed a nearly equal number of bottles of Taittinger champagne, danced to music by the Peter Duchin Orchestra, and witnessed the novelist Norman Mailer, deep in his cups, come close to assaulting McGeorge Bundy over the war. Also at the ball was Frankie FitzGerald, who had returned days earlier from Vietnam. FitzGerald had spent what she called a "life-transforming" ten months traveling the country and had decided to write a book on the American experience in Vietnam. (In one adventure, Frankie and another female reporter had helicoptered into the village of My Tho and been driven the forty-five miles back to Saigon by a Sten-gun-toting ex-marine as hand grenades bounced around on the floor of his truck. "Dan Ellsberg was a little overdramatic with two girls in the car," Frankie recalled.) FitzGerald's article "The Tragedy of Saigon" had appeared that same week in *The Atlantic Monthly,* where she wrote, "Truly, the United States has no talent for colonialism." There would be no more dinner invitations to Joe Alsop's house.[36]

FitzGerald remembered the Black and White Ball as both fascinating and "horrifying . . . I'm completely out of place. I expected everyone to be totally involved in Vietnam like we were. We were kind of underwater in it. And they weren't . . . It was simply culture shock."

The contrast between the two worlds was no less stark in Vietnam. When not staying on the embassy grounds as a guest of the U.S. ambassador, Joe Alsop typically checked into Saigon's Majestic, shunning the Caravelle, the hotel of choice for most correspondents. Since he tipped the Majestic's ancient, diminutive majordomo—Mr. Ba—generously in advance, Joe was always assured that his favorite menu items would be available in the hotel restaurant, his taxi waiting by the entrance at the appointed hour, and his khaki suit freshly pressed. "Ba treated him like a nineteenth-century traveler, which he was," remembered Frank George Wisner, who occasionally served as Joe's in-country guide. Another embassy staffer marveled that Joe Alsop was accorded the status there of a virtual "independent government."[37]

Like an old-fashioned Oriental potentate, Alsop was able to summon to his side high-ranking State Department and CIA officials, seemingly on a whim. Joe addressed the architect of U.S. military strategy in Vietnam, General William Westmoreland, by the general's nickname, Westy. In the years of his biannual trips to Southeast Asia, Alsop had grown accustomed to being treated like royalty. ("Thanks for the tiger skins," begins one of his letters.) But, while he showered gifts on those who did him favors, he could also be a demanding guest. After Frank George Wisner arranged the shipment home of some rare *bleu de Hue* china that Joe had purchased, Alsop sent him twenty copies each of

Mary Chesnut's *Diary from Dixie* and Henry Adams's *Democracy,* asking that Wisner have them specially leather bound in Saigon as gifts. Like so many good intentions in Vietnam, the books—intended for villagers as part of AID's pacification program—disappeared en route.[38]

IN REALITY, JOE ALSOP was never as consistently hawkish on Vietnam as his later critics would claim. Since the war began, Alsop wrote to Ward Just, his views on the conflict had been on a dizzying roller-coaster ride between optimism and pessimism. Some of Joe's fellow reporters observed the same and even commented on the wild mood swings in Alsop's reporting. In January 1967, the *New York Post's* James Wechsler published an editorial titled "Alsop Archives." Having read more than a dozen of Joe's Matter of Fact columns on Vietnam between early 1964 and late 1966, Wechsler concluded, "What emerges is a remarkable portrait of manic-depressive journalism. We are winning, we are losing, victory is in sight, disaster is at hand. Obviously, there are fluctuations of fortune in any war. But a visit to the Alsop archives gives the reader an uneasy sense that each day's report was influenced by which side of the bed he left that morning and oddly underlined by his own lament of 'idiotically mercurial' public opinion." Wechsler drove home his point by contrasting Alsop's optimistic prognosticating with a recent wire service headline: "U.S. Fighting Men Suffered Their Heaviest Casualties of the War Last Week."[39]

By early 1967, however, Joe was no longer inclined to second-guess his earlier judgments on Vietnam; instead, his new fear was that his views on the war were simply being ignored. Like his earlier overtures to Lippmann, Joe's offer of captured enemy documents to other Washington correspondents—and his promise to introduce them to "my friends on Westmoreland's staff"—had been summarily rebuffed.

Powerless to alter the course of the war itself, Joe hoped instead to change the *reporting* on the conflict so that it might follow more in line with his own views. Alsop had already tried—and failed—to persuade Ben Bradlee to assign "an experienced older man as a colleague" for Ward Just on the Vietnam beat. Frustrated on that score, Joe began looking for a surrogate, an intellectual doppelgänger who might champion the war in his stead.[40]

Alsop believed he had found such a reporter in Peter Braestrup, a thirty-seven-year-old marine veteran of Korea, working then as a war correspondent for *The New York Times.* In a three-way exchange of letters among Alsop, Braestrup, and Bradlee, Joe played the role of eager matchmaker, urging Braestrup to desert the *Times* for the *Post:* "You will in fact be the first reporter assigned to Saigon to give the news that the war is not a stalemate, that the other side is in bad trouble, and so on and so on." Alsop even coached Braestrup on the right way to approach his prospective new boss: "Ben is a man who can perhaps be described as needing a bit of courting . . . *For now,* the best thing to say to Ben is that you have been excited by the way the 'Post' has come alive since he took over."[41]

By year's end, Alsop's campaign had paid off. Bradlee hired Braestrup in January 1968 to be *The Washington Post*'s Saigon bureau chief. To ease the new man's way, Joe wrote letters of introduction to Ellsworth Bunker, the new U.S. ambassador to South Vietnam, and to the army brigadier general Phillip Davidson, MACV's senior intelligence officer.

As far as Alsop was concerned, Braestrup arrived in Vietnam just in the nick of time. Russ Wiggins, the conservative editor of the *Post*'s editorial page, had recently left the paper to become the next U.S. ambassador to the United Nations—a move widely interpreted to be a reward for Wiggins's steadfast support of LBJ's policies in Vietnam. Under Phil Geyelin's stewardship, and with Kay Graham's tacit approval, *The Washington Post*'s editorial policy had gradually but decidedly turned against the war. (Geyelin once joked that if Wiggins was worth two divisions of marines, as LBJ averred, then he, Geyelin, was worth at least a company of Vietcong.) The change was, as a *Post* reporter later observed, a slow process—like an aircraft carrier altering course. But one decisive push in that direction was the growing disillusionment with the war of Kay's friend Secretary of Defense Robert McNamara, who would be fired by Johnson in February 1968.[42]

Another impetus, some believed, was the fact that Katharine Graham had a son in Vietnam. In the half a dozen or so letters that Uncle Joe and Donny exchanged between June 1967 and July 1968, when Donald Graham returned from Vietnam, Alsop found reason to be encouraged about the war. Early on, Joe had greeted with enthusiasm the news that his young friend was to serve in a frontline army unit: "I think you'll find [combat] an experience that gives a new proportion to a good many things. There's nothing quite like it." In another letter, Alsop sought to quell in Kay's son any lingering doubts: "Either we were wrong to meet the challenge in Korea, or we are right to be doing what we are doing today."[43]

That fall, during another visit to Vietnam, Joe had an opportunity to judge for himself how young Don was faring, when, at Alsop's request, the battalion public information officer was given permission to accompany Joe to a field briefing by General George Casey, the First Air Cavalry Division's chief of staff. As Graham recalled the incident, it quickly became unclear who was briefing whom:

> CASEY, POINTING TO A MAP: Well, Mister Alsop, here is Bien Dien
> province, and here is our army headquarters, and here is the
> headquarters of the Second North Vietnam Army Division . . .
> ALSOP, INTERRUPTING: GENERALLLL . . . , let me tell you
> about the Second NVA Division."

"I would estimate that for the rest of the briefing Joe talked *significantly* more than General Casey did, though Casey was a very assertive officer and a very smart guy," Graham remembered. "But when it came to Vietnam, Joe wasn't in a mood to listen."[44]

Not surprisingly, Graham maintained an upbeat tone in his own correspondence with Alsop. "About the state of his mind, I thought him a bit more hawkish than when he left this country," Joe wrote to Don's wife, Mary, upon returning home to Georgetown from Vietnam. But Graham's letters to others revealed a progressive disillusionment. While her husband was amazed at the troops' bravery, Mary wrote to Joe, he "seems to be getting very discouraged again (partly it must be the terrible weather), more about the infantrymen's feelings about 'the gooks' and about his own role than about anything else."[45] In late October 1967, Donald Graham wrote to his mother: "There really is too damned much self-deception going on among the US military in this country . . . It just seems goddamned awful that we are doing such immense damage to people who are truly innocent bystanders, who never wanted us to fight for them, or the North Vietnamese. And even if the outcome of the war is somehow positive, I think our treatment of these people will ensure that no government considered too friendly to the US will endure in South Vietnam."[46]

As he approached the end of his tour, Don's letters to Joe had begun to have a more reflective tone: "Perhaps our losses in this war are not too great compared to earlier ones, but the chances of an infantryman's being killed or badly wounded up here are still uncomfortably good. All of which is not, of course, to say that I intend to burn my draft card or return to campaign for Senator McCarthy. It just means that what benefits the end of the war will bring seem very remote from here. And I think you'll agree that when you see it from the ground up, war is damned depressing."[47]

On January 30, 1968, a few months before Donald Graham returned home, the fortunes of war in Vietnam took a dramatic turn. In a surprise offensive timed to coincide with Tet, the Lunar New Year's celebrations, Vietcong and North Vietnamese Army units launched a simultaneous attack on more than a hundred cities and villages throughout South Vietnam. For eight hours, enemy sappers occupied the grounds of the American embassy before being killed, captured, or driven off. The U.S. ambassador, Ellsworth Bunker, was photographed fleeing the official residence still dressed in his pajamas. Peter Braestrup had been filing reports from Saigon for barely two weeks when the Tet Offensive seemingly turned the prospects for a U.S. victory upside down.[48]

Joe Alsop, as usual, sought to put the best face he could on the debacle. Emphasizing the cost of the attack to the enemy—an estimated forty-five thousand Vietcong and NVA casualties—Joe wrote that like the Japanese kamikaze attacks at the end of World War II, Tet was a desperate last gasp by an all-but-defeated enemy. On February 12, he wrote to Donald: "Fortunately the attack was on balance a disastrous failure, despite the severe blow to the Saigon government's standing and prestige and the great disruption and destruction that it caused."[49]

Among the majority of Americans, however, Alsop's was decidedly a minority view. Writing in *The Washington Post*'s Outlook section, Ward Just declared that Tet—"audaciously conceived and executed with extraordinary ferocity—[had] as a practical matter killed dead the pacification program—and most of the assumptions that went with it." In a letter to Frankie FitzGerald from Dalat, South Vietnam, where he was serving with a pacification advisory team, Frank George Wisner reluctantly agreed: "The enemy is destroying our key villages in the southern part of the province . . . We don't have the forces to stop him, we cannot calm the people, effectively provide the amount of relief required or sustain the victims." Photographs that appeared on the front pages of newspapers around the world, showing the blackened U.S. chancellery building and dead soldiers on the embassy grounds, marked a turning point. Public opinion polls after Tet revealed that for the first time a solid majority of Americans wanted the United States out of the war.[50]

BY THAT SPRING, so did Lyndon Johnson.

In a nationally televised speech on March 31, 1968, the president announced that he did not plan to seek reelection. Listening to Armed Forces Radio in Vietnam, Joe Alsop thought the news "grim" and depressing. But, in a column he wrote just four days later, he argued that Johnson's actions had actually freed the president's hands to take more decisive action, including "what is needed, which is not much, to win the war in Vietnam."[51]

When Joe returned to Washington in May, the campaign to choose Johnson's successor was already well under way. For Alsop, the presidential race was a welcome diversion and a respite from reporting on Vietnam. Following a remarkable political resurrection, Richard Nixon was favored to be the Republican nominee. (Stewart Alsop found the return of Nixon "incredible." Weeks earlier, he had written, "The thought of covering a Johnson-Nixon campaign gives me the screaming collywobbles.") Among the Democrats, Vice President Hubert Humphrey vied with an antiwar candidate, the Minnesota senator Eugene McCarthy, for the party's nomination.[52]

Although he had once described Robert Kennedy as "an American Octavius Caesar," Joe Alsop sought to discourage Bobby from joining the Vietnam debate and running for president in 1968, believing that the time was not yet right and his young friend's political views still too "bohemian." Describing himself that winter as "an affectionate, admiring, and deeply concerned uncle," Joe warned Kennedy that "for practical reasons, you really must give more weight to the support of what people call the 'establishment' than I think you do now."[53]

Robert Kennedy ignored Alsop's advice on both counts. A week after Joe's letter, on February 8, 1968, Bobby came out strongly against the war during a luncheon speech in Chicago. Telling his audience that the Saigon regime's endemic corruption meant dispatching more American troops to fight in Vietnam would be "like sending a lion to halt an epidemic of jungle rot," Kennedy added that he deplored bombing such a "tiny country." In mid-March, from the same Senate Caucus Room where his older brother had declared his candidacy eight years earlier, Bobby announced that he would run for president.[54]

Alsop's response was quick in coming. The day after Bobby's speech on Vietnam, Joe called the senator's office three times. Unable to reach Kennedy in person, Alsop had finally resorted to telling the receptionist that her boss was a traitor to his country. In a column published shortly afterward, Joe wrote that, lamentably, Bobby had been seduced by the "peace-at-any-price counsel" of Vietnam defeatists like Arthur Schlesinger Jr. But even while disappointed by Kennedy's opposition to the war, Joe told Joan Braden that he held out hope that Bobby's natural combativeness might yet cause him to "tear into Vietnam like a tiger," if and when he became president, and not allow the United States to lose the war.[55]

Neither Robert Kennedy nor Joe Alsop considered their differences on the war reason enough to end a friendship. Following another attack in Matter of Fact on his antiwar stand, Bobby sent Joe a telegram—signing it with the name of the family's West Highland terrier: "Someone is writing parodies of your column and signing your name. This is no time for humor."[56]

Joe continued to offer Bobby political advice, even following the candidate to California for the all-important primary there. In a column that spring, Alsop judged Hubert Humphrey the "sole cloud left on Kennedy's horizon" before the summer's Democratic convention. In a nostalgic and plainly wistful column that he wrote on May 15, Joe compared Bobby—"this strange, impassioned man"—to the candidate's martyred brother: "He is supposed to be a ruthless and calculating politician, as well as a near-sympathizer of the New Left. He is in fact a romantic politician, far too given to taking dares, and much too willing to listen to the siren-songs that warmly responsive audiences always sing." The following day, Robert Kennedy sent Joe Alsop another telegram, this time signing it simply "Bobby": "You accomplished the once thought impossible—you made me lovable in Los Angeles."[57]

"ALTHOUGH I DISAGREED WITH HIM about Vietnam, losing Bobby Kennedy pretty well knocked me out—to the point, indeed, of my giving up sleep as a habit for a bit," Joe Alsop wrote to a friend in early July 1968. Robert Kennedy had been assassinated a month earlier at the

Ambassador Hotel in Los Angeles, following a rally to celebrate his victory in the California primary. In the wake of Bobby's murder, Alsop had resumed taking sleeping pills. There was once again an elegiac tone in his correspondence, as in the letter that he sent to Kennedy's widow, Ethel, following the senator's funeral at St. Patrick's Cathedral in New York: "It made me think, all over again, what a very lucky man I have been. At my age, all men I think begin to look backwards as much as forwards. But most look back a very long way, to the years when they were young and hungrily tasting this world's pleasures for the first time. Whereas my own best years, only just ended, were those in which the main figures were first the President and then Bobby; and they came to me when I had enough experience to appreciate my own good fortune."[58]

Like his brother Stewart, Joe would vote for Hubert Humphrey, but without enthusiasm, and neither man was surprised when Humphrey lost. Even though he had quarreled mightily with Lyndon Johnson over Vietnam, Joe bade a gracious farewell to the departing president in a Matter of Fact column.[59]

By the time he left the White House, Johnson felt little such affection for the Washington establishment. After Martin Luther King's assassination the previous April, when Johnson received word that an angry mob was marching on Georgetown with the intention of burning it down, the president was said to have smiled and responded, "Goddamn, I've waited thirty-five years for this day." Johnson had also developed a particular disdain for what he considered the semiofficial organ of that elitist enclave, *The Washington Post,* and its owner, Katharine Graham, whom he viewed, one observer wrote, as "the doyenne of the Georgetown-Kennedy crowd that makes him so anxious and angry." (Georgetown's denizens felt the same way toward Johnson. Dean Acheson wrote to his daughter at this time that LBJ was "a real centaur—part man, part horse's ass.")[60]

The friendship between the Grahams and Johnson had gradually soured as the paper's editorial policy, under Kay's direction, turned against the war. Ever since a 1965 Herblock drawing had depicted him as a whip-wielding plantation overseer, the president had held a grudge against the *Post's* political cartoonist. An embittered Johnson reportedly told Kay in frustration, "If Phil were running the paper it would have been a different presidency for me."[61]

For the *Post,* for the country, and particularly for Joe Alsop, the fixation on Vietnam had temporarily shifted that summer, when the Soviet

Union invaded Czechoslovakia. The August 1968 invasion put a violent end to the so-called Prague Spring, the fledgling political reform movement that had hoped to restore a semblance of democratic rule to the Russian satellite. The Czech invasion was just the latest reminder, argued Alsop in Matter of Fact, that the Cold War was still very much alive. Indeed, Polly Wisner confided to Joe that the Soviet attack had occasioned a sense of déjà vu: "I can't bear to think about the news, it reminds me all too much of twelve years ago and Hungary. So much of [Frank] died there . . . I am glad he is spared it all, so much he believed in has gone down the drain."[62]

The election of Richard Nixon that fall likewise drew attention away from Vietnam and roused in some a hope that the war might finally be brought to an end. Joe Alsop, on the other hand, counseling "patience and toughness," warned against "a barely concealed surrender." Stewart—declaring himself a "Nixonologist of long standing"—had made the case for the so-called new Nixon in the pages of *Newsweek* just before the election. But the discovery that "Vietnamization," which shifted the burden of battle to South Vietnam's soldiers, was the president's solution to the conflict left both brothers disappointed. Joe attacked the idea as a "recipe for murder" that would decimate and demoralize the ARVN troops and was almost certain to end in their defeat. On the other hand, Stew feared that it meant an intensification of the air war against North Vietnam, and hence more civilian casualties.[63]

The brothers soon came to believe that the real architect of the administration's strategy in Vietnam was not Nixon, however, but the president's national security adviser.[64]

"It Was the War That Did Him In"

Henry Kissinger had been a sophomore at Harvard in the fall of 1947 when he heard Joe Alsop debate the liberal commentator I. F. Stone on the topic "Must We Stop Russia?" More than twenty years later, Kissinger was one of Nixon's first rumored appointments when Joe came to call. The national security adviser later described the encounter in his memoirs: "Joe Alsop interviewed me with the attitude that his criteria for my suitability for high office would be more severe than Nixon's. He gave me to understand that his knowledge of the Indochina problem far exceeded that of any neophyte Presidential Assistant. I had the impression that he had suspended judgment about the wisdom of the President's choice and that I would remain on probation for some time to come."[1]

Kissinger need not have worried about being invited into Georgetown's salons, since the portly ex-academic quickly endeared himself to the capital's press corps. (Asked by reporters at a news conference whether he preferred to be addressed as "Doctor" or "Professor," Henry joked that "Excellency" would do.) As one of Kissinger's later critics wrote, grudgingly, "His wit, his apparently modest and self-deprecating irony, his exquisite charm, a willingness to discuss high matters of state after dinner, and the apparent confidences that he entrusted—all this made him irresistible. He was quickly recognized throughout Georgetown as the one oasis in this dour, rather hostile and boring administration of bond salesmen, advertising executives and zoning lawyers."[2]

Kissinger also proved adept at convincing journalists like Joe Alsop that he could be both a sympathetic ally and a willing confidant. ("He'd pour syrup all over the guy," observed a jealous rival reporter, after Kissinger interrupted their meeting to take a telephone call from Alsop.) Within weeks of Nixon's inauguration, the president's national security adviser had become, according to Kissinger's biographer, "the darling of the Georgetown set."[3]

In early February 1969, Joe telephoned Kissinger with a request to interview a Soviet expert on the staff of the National Security Council. Alsop got the interview—along with promised confidences that Kissinger said he could not reveal on the telephone. In March, Joe paired the bachelor national security adviser with the New York socialite Brooke Astor during a black-tie dinner at Alsop's home. ("She longs to meet you," Joe confided.) Alsop also promised to introduce him to Isaiah Berlin, "an extraordinarily interesting man."[4]

Anxious that the notorious five o'clock shadow not return to his visage in Herblock's cartoons for *The Washington Post*, Nixon was well aware of the need for an intermediary, a liaison to a world that the new president neither knew nor trusted. He encouraged Kissinger to take the initiative with the Georgetown set—even to the extent of leaking carefully selected secrets. Nixon's coaching of Kissinger in a conversation that winter was picked up and recorded by the ever-ready White House taping system:

> KISSINGER: One of these days you will face a crisis where someone is going to ram these facts of life home to us. We ought to prevent these crises from breaking out.
> NIXON: Very subtly you can let Alsop know that. He is already writing that. If you can convince Alsop—you know what I mean.[5]

For the Nixon administration, the preeminent crisis remained Vietnam. The morning after a dinner at Joe's house with Kay Graham, McGeorge Bundy telephoned Kissinger to warn that Alsop intended to "smoke [him] out" on whether the president planned to escalate the war. "Joe hasn't been put in charge of the war yet, but he is working at it," Kissinger joked. (In the same call, Bundy also let Kissinger know that he had already charmed the Georgetown crowd: "Kay mentioned that Henry had been absolutely brilliant in his discussion with the *Post* the other day.")[6]

In fact, Kissinger already enjoyed a close relationship with both Alsop brothers, especially Joe. When North Korea captured an American spy ship off its coast that April, Kissinger telephoned Joe to tell him, "The President wants to know what Alsop thinks we should do." Predictably, the flattery worked, and it went both ways. In May, Joe called Kissinger to request an advance copy of a televised speech that Nixon was about to make on Vietnam, confiding that "he wanted to support [the] Administration if he can." The resulting Alsop column—"Speech Shows Nixon Realizes Consequences of a Surrender"—indeed supported the president, praising what Joe called the latter's "very resolute" acknowledgment that an end to the war was not yet in sight. A few weeks later, Alsop allowed Kissinger to edit the interview he had given Joe on the war before it appeared in Matter of Fact. Joe's column at the end of June was helpfully headed "President's Views on Vietnam Are Misunderstood by Many."[7]

By the fall of 1969, Nixon and Kissinger were confident enough of Joe's allegiance to enlist his unwitting help in an elaborate diplomatic ploy. Hoping to pressure North Vietnam into accepting a peace settlement, Nixon had decided on a stratagem he dubbed the "madman theory." In essence, the president hoped to persuade America's enemies that his behavior was so unpredictable—and so inclined toward an irrational or at least disproportionate response—that reason dictated the other party should be the one to yield. In a conversation with the loyal aide who would become his chief of staff, Bob Haldeman, Nixon had confided, "I want the North Vietnamese to believe I've reached the point where I might do *anything* to stop the war. We'll just slip the word to them that, 'for God's sake, you know Nixon is obsessed about Communism. We can't restrain him when he's angry—and he has his hand on the nuclear button.'"[8]

On the night of October 20, 1969, Nixon coached Kissinger on how the latter should approach the Soviet ambassador, Anatoly Dobrynin, when the national security adviser and the Russian diplomat met the following day to discuss the ongoing Vietnam peace talks in Paris. The president told Kissinger he should "shake his head and say 'I am sorry, Mr. Ambassador, but he is out of control. Mr. Ambassador, as you know, I am very close to the President, but you don't know this man—he's been through more than any of the rest of us put together. He's made up his mind and unless there's some movement,' just shake your head and walk out." Lest Dobrynin fail to get the message, Kissinger volunteered that he would type up what Nixon had said and pass it along to the ambassador "on a plain slip of paper":

The P[resident] asked if K[issinger] could trust Joe Alsop enough to show him that . . . K[issinger] asked what he should do with it . . . The P[resident] said, he didn't know; he probably would have to print it. K[issinger] said yes, at the right moment he would have to print it . . . K[issinger] said he had looked over Alsop's notes after he left; his notes say our government is for the speediest conclusion of the peace negotiations. He says on the basis of giving the people free choice. In the next paragraph, he lists all the garbage they've been saying all along.[9]

Kissinger likewise counted on the Alsop brothers to advance the image that Henry hoped to project to the outside world. On the morning of April 30, 1970, the day that he announced the U.S. "incursion" into Cambodia, Nixon told Kissinger to "call in Alsop" and get the columnist's opinion of how the move would likely be received. Two days later, Matter of Fact pronounced the president's decision both "wise" and "brave"—even as demonstrations broke out on college campuses around the country, protesting the expansion of the war. In response, Nixon instructed Kissinger to contact his "friends" among Washington's opinion-making elite, adding, "I hope Jos. Alsop will take it up. He has influence in that community." Evidently, Joe's influence was not enough. After a speech where he declared the Cambodian invasion a success, Nixon asked Kissinger to find out how the speech had been received by the latter's "Georgetown friends." When Kissinger telephoned the Alsop home around midnight, Susan Mary answered. The couple had just returned from a dinner party attended by Senator Ted Kennedy and a few of the capital's other liberal lions. Kissinger asked Joe's wife about the "atmosphere" at the party. Susan Mary was blunt: "It was very bad. Everyone was in a rage." Kissinger relayed the bad news to Nixon: "She says it didn't go over very well."[10]

Kissinger could also count on Stewart Alsop for a sympathetic public portrait. A few days after the furor over the Cambodian invasion erupted, Kissinger invited Joe's younger brother into his office, presenting him with two sheets of yellow legal paper that contained Nixon's jottings. Kissinger told Stewart that the documents were proof that the president had made a "careful assessment" of all the options, and that the invasion "was not the act of a feckless fool" but, rather, had broad support within Nixon's cabinet. Stewart promised not to identify Kissinger as his source, and his *Newsweek* column, "On the President's Yellow

Pad," essentially repeated the national security adviser's version of events. In reality, Kissinger told an aide in confidence that Nixon had "flipped out," withheld details of the invasion from some on his own staff, and subsequently defended the plan against two of its most prominent critics in the administration: Secretary of State William Rogers and Secretary of Defense Melvin Laird.[11]

Secure in his role as Nixon's Machiavelli, Kissinger showed that he could punish as well as reward. When a *Newsweek* article accurately reported that he and Rogers were engaged in a struggle over which one spoke for Nixon's foreign policy, Kissinger told Rogers that he had talked to Kay Graham, who assured him that the article exaggerated their differences. In a phone call a few days later to *Newsweek*'s editor, Kermit Lansner, Kissinger accused the magazine of "amateurish dabblings." (Lansner promised to "be doubly careful in the future.") That summer, Kissinger angrily canceled plans for dinner at the R Street house with Kay Graham after the *Post* published an unflattering article about his dating habits. Shortly thereafter, Joe Alsop invited Henry to a "reconciliation" supper at his house with Kay, Stewart, Tish, and the Schlesingers.[12]

Subsequently, Kissinger would even enlist Joe's help in the famously vicious struggle for power within the administration, involving Alsop in a complex plot to undermine Rogers's standing with Nixon. Early in June 1970, Rogers met with the Soviet ambassador, Dobrynin, in an effort to head off a developing crisis in the Middle East. A tenuous cease-fire that had held since the end of the 1967 Arab-Israeli war was suddenly threatened by Russian efforts to bolster Egyptian air defenses against future attack. Kissinger had opposed Rogers's overture to Dobrynin—and even threatened to resign over the issue. Some months after Rogers's meeting with Dobrynin, on September 9, 1970, Alsop wrote a Matter of Fact column blaming "certain American officials" for having been "shamelessly bamboozled" by Dobrynin into believing that the Soviets would abide by the terms of the Middle East cease-fire. The obvious source for Joe's column, which had quoted from classified State Department papers prepared for the June meeting, was Kissinger. Alongside the indictment of Rogers, Alsop's column had also attacked Dobrynin, the long-serving Soviet ambassador, whom Joe accused of telling "black lies" and of "persuasive mendacity." Joe urged that Dobrynin be declared persona non grata by the State Department and recalled by Moscow.[13]

The episode was yet another skirmish in Kissinger's protracted campaign against Rogers, which continued into Nixon's second term. Anatoly Dobrynin would remain Moscow's ambassador to Washington for another sixteen years. But, for Joe Alsop, his September 9 column proved to have unforeseen—and fateful—consequences.

EVEN AS JOE'S ATTENTION turned to the Middle East, he remained focused on Russia. A series of recent clashes between Soviet and Chinese troops on their common border led to a new twist on an old obsession for Alsop: the prospect of the United States' being drawn into a Sino-Soviet nuclear war. ("Roots! We'll all be eating roots!" Ben Bradlee remembered Joe telling him at this time.) Only Alsop seemed to be fretting about the danger, which had arisen, he claimed, because the United States had carelessly allowed the Soviet Union to catch up with the West in nuclear weapons.[14]

As it had since the Russians had gotten the atomic bomb, the nuclear arms race remained a *Boléro*-like theme in Matter of Fact. The Nixon administration entered into the Strategic Arms Limitation Talks with the Soviets in the fall of 1969, and Kissinger was the top U.S. SALT negotiator. Hoping to defuse criticism from conservatives in advance of any agreement, he had made a well-known hawk, Paul Nitze, a member of the American negotiating team. (Nitze had once again hoped for a higher-level appointment, but Senator William Fulbright, chairman of the Senate Foreign Relations Committee, remained furious at Nitze for withholding documents that Fulbright had requested in 1966 for televised hearings on American involvement in Vietnam. Nitze had been secretary of the navy at the time.[15])

In their articles and columns, Joe and Stewart Alsop took Nitze's side in the ongoing SALT negotiations—championing deployment of a U.S. antiballistic missile system to shoot down Russian ICBMs, while opposing any limits on what amounted to a U.S. technological advantage in the arms race: multiple, independently targetable missile warheads.[16]

Predictably, Nitze's return to the nuclear strategy debate lured one of his foremost critics—George Kennan—out of retirement, at least temporarily. Except for periodic fulminations against student radicals and modern-day "revisionist" historians—who, he believed, wrongly put the blame for the Cold War on Truman rather than Stalin—Kennan had remained focused on his own scholarly writing since his retreat to bucolic Princeton; his latest book project was a diplomatic history of the

Franco-Russian alliance of 1894. History, as Kennan had observed, was "the common refuge of those who find themselves helpless in the face of the present."[17]

Joe Alsop's claim that Kremlin leaders could not be trusted to hold up their end of any SALT bargain—and would willingly sacrifice five million of their own citizens to achieve victory in a nuclear war—was a provocation that, to Kennan, simply cried out for a response. "Little as is my fondness for the present Soviet leaders, they are not simply sadistic madmen, thirsting for bloodshed," Kennan protested in a letter to Alsop. "Dear Joe: what bothers you is a real fixation. Of course, there is the possibility of a nuclear war so long as people go on with this mad weapons race. There is also the possibility of getting run over tomorrow by an automobile or suffering a heart attack . . . In the meantime, let us live, instead of just imagining and trembling."[18]

Alsop wrote to a friend that he considered Kennan's letter "pettish and non-responsive to my inquiry—no more than I expected, I must admit."[19]

BY THE END OF THE 1960s, Joe Alsop's indefatigable defense of Nixon's Vietnam policy was so anomalous among journalists as to be itself news-worthy. Only one other reporter, ABC's Howard K. Smith, who had a son serving in Vietnam, remained such a vocal hawk. Their loyalty was rewarded by the administration. "I always give them all the meetings," Kissinger told Nixon. "I don't say who said what, but I give them the sequence of the meetings."[20]

Even Stewart Alsop acknowledged that his "stubborn and courageous brother" had become part of "a tiny and beleaguered minority." In an October 1969 radio broadcast, CBS's Harry Reasoner identified Joe as the only reporter still "holding fast" to the notion that North Vietnam's army was near collapse. "This is presumably the same collapse they were near in 1966," Reasoner gibed. Following another public insult from Alsop, who accused liberals of "intellectual bankruptcy" on Vietnam, John Kenneth Galbraith responded in a press release: "Joe's case calls for deep sympathy. Second only to Lyndon Johnson, he is the leading non-combatant casualty of Vietnam. From being a much-feared colum-nist, warrior and prophet he has become a figure of fun. It was the war that did him in."[21] Others had already declared open season on Joe Alsop. In its May 1968 issue, *The New Republic*'s reporter in Saigon, Zalin Grant, had pilloried Alsop—"the super-hawk of American journalism"—for supposedly breaking an embargoed story on a recent U.S. military offensive, while Joe was sitting out the war in air-conditioned comfort at the ambassador's "pleasant villa" in Saigon. A few weeks later, Merle Miller of *Harper's* lampooned Alsop in that magazine for "telling us what he thinks and what we should think, if we are to survive. For Joseph Alsop, the world and the Republic are in dire and daily peril." Miller quoted an anonymous Alsop "ex-friend" who observed of the famous zoo parties at Joe's house, "A lot of people won't go there for dinner anymore. I'm afraid Joe's become what, if he were aware of it, he'd hate most of all, a b-o-r-e, on the subject of Vietnam, I mean."[22]

So unsparing were the attacks on Alsop that even some of his erstwhile critics felt compelled to come to his defense. "It is one thing to question Joe Alsop's views, quite another to question his tenacity and courage as a war correspondent," wrote Ward Just in a letter to Miller and the editor of *Harper's*. Just also wrote to Frances FitzGerald at this time about a telephone call he had recently gotten from Alsop—"the doyenne [*sic*] of the P Street mafia"—concerning the book Frankie was writing on Vietnam: "'She is making a terrible mistake,' [Alsop] said. 'A mistake from which her career may never recover.' He said that by the time your book was coming out, the war would be won—by us, of course, and your observations would be rendered—and here again I quote—'laughable.'"*[23]

Joe Alsop never apologized for the pampered treatment he received in Vietnam; he claimed that he "couldn't do a proper job any longer without being treated as an expensive package . . . shipped . . . from place to place as though I came from Cartiers instead of Avon, Connecticut." He still defied those who would pressure him into changing his mind on the war. But, privately, Joe let those close to him know that the attacks were having an effect. "I cannot tell you how much my old friends mean to me now-a-days, and I daily find myself missing Phil and the two others who used, so to say, to constitute the main furniture of my life in Washington," he wrote to Kay Graham. "Barring you and Polly there is hardly anyone I have left that gives the same kind of comfortable feeling."[24]

---

* FitzGerald's book, *Fire in the Lake: The Vietnamese and the Americans in Vietnam*, would win the Pulitzer Prize in 1973.

GALBRAITH'S OBSERVATION about Joe's having become a figure of fun became literally true as the 1970s began, with the premiere that January of a Broadway play, *Sheep on the Runway*. The playwright, the humorist Art Buchwald, wrote a syndicated column appearing in many papers on the same editorial page as Matter of Fact. Alsop's obsession with Vietnam had long been a target of Buchwald's satire. ("Joe commutes between the United States and Vietnam the way other people commute between Great Neck and New York.") But Joe Alsop had never before been the butt of the joke in an entire theatrical production, until *Sheep*.[25]

The play centered on a flamboyant American newspaper columnist, named Joe Mayflower, whose reporting trip to Nonomura—"a remote monarchy in the Himalayas"—inadvertently sparks a war in the mythical kingdom. Finding the capital of Nonomura too dull and peaceful, Mayflower travels to a northern province, where he claims to have discovered a Communist warlord plotting to overthrow the prince. ("God, I feel good," the fictional Joe exclaims upon his return. "There's nothing like a danger from the north to get the old juices flowing.") Mayflower subsequently convinces the Pentagon to launch an air strike, which ends up destroying the palace by mistake, whereupon the prince is overthrown by the warlord in a coup. All ends well, however, when it turns out that the warlord is actually working for the CIA.

Alsop simply hated *Sheep on the Runway*—probably because the depiction of him hit too close to home. When Joe forbade his friends to see the play, some reportedly went in disguise. Alsop also threatened to sue Buchwald for defamation. (In one scene, Mayflower declares, "My facts may sometimes be wrong, but my judgment is always right." Later, the construction is reversed.) Although Buchwald protested that Mayflower was never meant to be Alsop—he claimed, unconvincingly, that his model was really the liberal columnist Joseph Kraft—both Kay Graham and Ben Bradlee tried, unsuccessfully, to get the playwright to at least change the name of his main character.

Ironically, *Sheep on the Runway* received only mediocre reviews and might even have closed quickly had not Maxine Cheshire, *The Washington Post*'s gossip columnist, made Alsop's displeasure widely known to her readers. As a result, *Sheep* became a cause célèbre among the capital city's insiders. Buchwald's friend the Washington attorney Edward Bennett Williams offered to defend the playwright pro bono on behalf of "the Legal Aid Society of Georgetown." Joe's brother, writing as "Stewart Mayflower," protested in a *Washington Post* op-ed that the play "has about as much relationship to the political reality as McHale's navy has to the Navy." Stew's opinion piece would be included in the daily briefing packet given to the CIA's deputy directors.[26]

Joe Alsop eventually dropped his threat of a lawsuit, and *Sheep on the Runway* ended its Broadway run after little more than three months and 105 performances. But friends noticed that Alsop, in its aftermath, seemed even more sensitive than usual to slights—whether real or imagined.

THERE WAS, TO BE SURE, nothing imaginary about the photographs that started appearing in mailboxes around the capital later that year. The pictures showed a younger, and naked, Joe Alsop in an intimate embrace with Boris, the KGB agent provocateur who had ensnared him in a Moscow hotel room more than a decade earlier. Among those receiving the photographs—sent in unmarked envelopes, postmarked Hoboken, New Jersey—were Joe's friend Charley Bartlett and Alsop's supposed nemesis, Art Buchwald. "It scared the hell out of me. I'm not comfortable with getting photographs of people in compromising positions in the mail," Buchwald told a reporter years later.

Word of the photographs soon spread. Buchwald tore up the photos but not before he told the *Washington Post* editor Phil Geyelin of their existence. Both men agreed to remain silent on the subject. Bartlett, similarly nonplussed, confided the secret to a friend in the CIA, who, in turn, told Richard Helms. At the CIA director's suggestion, Bartlett sent the pictures on to Alsop anonymously, along with a note: "I thought you should have these. I'm not signing this because I don't want it to be an embarrassment to us when we meet." (Alsop, however, suspecting that the package had come from Bartlett, later confronted him. "Did you send me those pictures?" Joe asked. When Bartlett answered in the affirmative, the "conversation sort of dribbled off." A marked "coolness" in his relations with Alsop persisted after the incident.)[27]

Joe briefly considered coming out of the closet and making his homosexuality known. But Helms advised against it, reportedly reminding Alsop that he had his "wife and stepchildren to think about, as well as your brother and other close relatives. Consider the impact such a declaration would have on them." Instead, the CIA director proposed that he be the one to "quietly tell the KGB to knock it off." Shortly afterward, either Helms himself or an agency operative warned the Russians that unless they desisted, the CIA would respond in kind, releasing information that would compromise the careers of several KGB intelligence officers. Helms believed that no more photographs were sent.[28]

Joe never learned who had tried to blackmail him a second time or how many people had actually received the incriminating pictures. Enclosed with each package of photographs was a letter, unsigned and addressed simply to "Dear Sir":

> I consider it necessary to acquaint you with the following facts, which have been made known to me by close friends. Since their friendship means a great deal to me, I cannot mention their names, as you will understand after having read this letter.
>
> These facts pertain to the influential columnist, Mr. Alsop. During his visit to the Near East in 1957 he came in contact with Israelis, some of whom showed a very peculiar interest in him. It soon became evident that this interest was directed not so much to Mr. Alsop as such but to certain vices which ordinarily evoke disgust among normal people. This will be evident to you from the enclosed photographs.
>
> Confronted with these photographs Mr. Alsop's cowardice prompted him to agree to work for the Israeli intelligence service. The latter, taking advantage of his journalistic reputation, is using him in an attempt to influence public opinion in this country. Just before the six-day war in 1967 he was the first to mention in his column that the US government was supporting Israel and demonstrated his intimate knowledge of the Israelis plans as well as those of the US. Furthermore, the Israelis are taking advantage of his access to US government circles in order to carry out their intentions.
>
> I am sure you will agree that it is high time measures be taken to protect decent people from this filthy person.[29]

While Alsop would continue to routinely excoriate the Soviet Union in his column, there would be no more personal attacks in Matter of Fact on the Soviet ambassador, Anatoly Dobrynin. But the pictures had been an unsubtle reminder of Joe's vulnerability and graphic proof that his enemies were still out there, eager to do him harm.[30]

"Nobody Plays by the Rules Any More"

T HE ATTACKS ON HIM had made Joe Alsop more outspoken than ever—particularly on the subject of Vietnam. In March 1971, when the U.S. Army lieutenant William Calley was found guilty of order- ing the My Lai massacre—the murder of more than three hundred unarmed South Vietnamese civilians by American soldiers three years earlier—Joe's column protested that the enemy had committed atrocities much worse. Encountering Seymour Hersh, the reporter who had bro- ken the My Lai story, at a Georgetown cocktail party shortly afterward, Alsop loudly declaimed, "You, sir, are a traitor!" When a *Washington Post* editorial applauded the Calley verdict, in the process criticizing Alsop's "meandering search for extenuating circumstances," Joe demanded an apology from the editorial page's Phil Geyelin. When one was not imme- diately forthcoming, Alsop pressed Geyelin, who finally sent Joe a note that was almost plaintive: "I wish you would stop demanding an apol- ogy, in that formal way, as if we hadn't been old friends."[1]

Given his own views on the war, Arthur Schlesinger Jr. was surprised to be invited to Joe's sixtieth birthday party—hosted by Katharine Gra- ham at the R Street house—and pleased to find the crowd there "highly ecumenical so far as Vietnam is concerned." "We regard you and Averell as the furthest out we could go," Kay confided. Joe himself had made up the invitation list, frustrating Graham's efforts to limit the number of guests.[2]

Even as he grew more distant from friends and his colleagues in the press, Joe moved closer into the orbit of the Nixon administration. Early in 1971, Nixon tipped Alsop off to his plan for extending the conflict into Laos. Joe's next column—"Courage of a President"—not only praised the decision as long overdue but attacked its foremost congressional critic, Senator William Fulbright, as "downright eager to be proved right by an American defeat, and . . . loath [to be] proved wrong by U.S. success in Southeast Asia." Herbert Klein, the president's communications director, sent Joe's column to newspaper editors around the country. But for Washington reporters like Scotty Reston and Joe Kraft, the attack on Fulbright was a sign of Joe's overweening arrogance and a step too far. Kraft, who had meanwhile replaced Walter Lippmann on the *Post*'s editorial page—and as Joe's chief antagonist on the war—declared that Alsop had, in effect, become Nixon's spokesman: "It is the same ego trip—taken now by proxy." For his part, the *Times*'s own venerable columnist, eighty-four-year-old Arthur Krock, told Neil Sheehan that if there were ever to be a war crimes tribunal for Vietnam, then Joe Alsop would go to the dock for persuading John Kennedy to intervene in the first place.[3]

A decade into America's involvement in Vietnam, Nixon and Kissinger had come not only to expect but to rely on Joe's support for the war. In what many saw as a cynical—and doomed—effort to ingratiate himself with the Georgetown elite, the president annually hosted a birthday dinner at the White House for Washington's grande dame, Alice Roosevelt Longworth. As relatives of "Cousin Alice," Joe and Stewart Alsop were always invited. On the evening of February 10, 1971—the occasion of Alice's eighty-seventh birthday, two days after Alsop's "Courage" column appeared, and just as Operation Lam Son 719, the Laotian invasion, was getting under way—Joe and Susan Mary arrived at the White House. Among the other guests at their table that night was Admiral Thomas Moorer, chairman of the Joint Chiefs of Staff and one of the architects of the Laos invasion. The previous day, Nixon had told Kissinger that the Alsops would be attending the dinner and he wanted "Moorer there to brainwash them."[4]

So dependent had the president become on the support and approval of his favorite columnist that Nixon was also uncommonly solicitous of Joe Alsop's personal welfare. With the Laos operation encountering fierce resistance that spring, Nixon asked Kissinger, "Did you tell Joe Alsop I wanted him to go to Vietnam to get some honest reporting? . . . I do not want a white wash, just honest stories." A few weeks later, following intelligence reports that contained more bad news on the war, Nixon again queried his national security adviser about Alsop, anxiously asking, "Did you see him? How's his spirit? I hope he's not getting discouraged . . . Does he realize that there's no reason to be discouraged?" After rumors of marital strife between Joe and Susan Mary finally reached the White House that May, both Nixon and Kissinger expressed concern about the Alsops' "family trouble."[5]

Joe saw no reason to discontinue his twice-yearly pilgrimages to South Vietnam. Indeed, he found fresh cause for encouragement there from a new insider source. Alsop had first met John Paul Vann in 1967. A retired U.S. Army lieutenant colonel, Vann was, by that time, a civilian adviser to AID's pacification program. Although he initially balked at talking to Alsop, Vann was essentially ordered to the meeting by his superiors, and he continued to have reservations about Joe. "He gets everything wrong; he doesn't take notes; he screws up the works," Vann told another reporter.[6]

Initially pessimistic about the outcome in Vietnam, John Paul Vann had gradually become more hopeful of victory—or, at least, so he professed to willing listeners like Joe Alsop. Lacking neither ambition nor ego, Vann would become, in effect, the slender reed on which Joe hung his hopes for a successful conclusion to the war.

Fealty to the man whom Vann unself-consciously called "the president's journalist" was soon rewarded, and the gung-ho former paratrooper eventually became a regular item in Joe's column. Alsop took to calling South Vietnam's Mekong delta "John Vann's country," praising his friend in print as "an infinitely patriotic, intelligent, and courageous and magnificent leader." In his letters to Joe from Vietnam, Vann responded in kind. "Pacification continues to progress throughout the Corps at the rate I had expected," he wrote to Alsop in October 1970. "Obviously, the enemy still scores an occasional success by overrunning an outpost whose personnel are asleep, but overall, things look very good indeed." The following year, Vann became Joe's personal escort and cheerleader during Alsop's visits to Vietnam. "Going around the Provinces with you in your helicopter always damn near kills me, but is always the most enjoyable and profitable thing that I do on these trips of mine. And not least of the enjoyment is watching a great public servant at work," Joe wrote to Vann upon returning from one trip.[7]

Privately, Vann was far more circumspect about the prospects for victory and confessed to having mixed feelings about being a centerpiece for Joe's reporting. "Quite frankly, things are not nearly so rosy as Mr. Alsop paints them, and I personally am not too elated at him being so kind to me since his credibility is rather low," Vann wrote to an army confidant.[8]

When Vann returned home on leave in December 1970, he and his wife were invited to a dinner party at Dumbarton Avenue. Susan Mary, Katharine Graham, and the Bruces also attended. (Over cocktails, Joe and Susan Mary watched in wordless fascination as the guest of honor, evidently thinking that the brie hors d'oeuvre was cheesecake, cut a large slice and devoured it in several bites.) Throughout the evening, Vann regaled his hosts with tales of harrowing escapes and combat derring-do, to Alsop's obvious delight. When Vann returned to Vietnam early in the new year, his letter to Joe ended on an optimistic note: "I have great confidence in the fact that the enemy will suffer a significant defeat here in II Corps this spring."[9]

JOE'S COLUMN WAS SHOWING HIM to be increasingly out of step with the rest of the country and the times, and not just on Vietnam. Matter of Fact essentially ignored two of the phenomena that would define the 1960s generation: the civil rights revolution and the women's liberation movement. Joe had been reporting from the besieged marine base at Khe Sanh when Martin Luther King was assassinated in April 1968. His columns for the month made no mention of the black leader's murder or the ensuing urban riots, even as National Guard soldiers were called out to patrol the streets of Georgetown.

During an evening at Joe's house, late in the decade, Katharine Graham had finally decided to flout Georgetown's long-standing custom— where, following dinner, the women trooped upstairs, while the men retreated to the parlor to discuss politics over brandy and cigars. Alsop stubbornly refused to excuse the other diners from his table unless Kay gave in. But it was finally Joe who yielded, after Graham threatened to go home. (Joe thought it a "lavish compliment" when he called Katharine and her friend the *Washington Post* columnist Meg Greenfield "honorary men," Greenfield wrote.) During a dinner party at the California home of Otis Chandler, owner of the *Los Angeles Times,* Joe was approached by a young editor's wife, who explained that she found the quaint Washington custom "hilarious." "It's hard for me to believe this. I have never been to a party in my entire life where the men and women separated after dinner," she confided. Alsop stared at her a long moment and then sniffed, "Well, my dear, I have never been to a party where they did not."[10]

Increasingly, the elder Alsop seemed to relish his growing reputation as a mossbacked curmudgeon. When Joe received a letter from WETA, Washington's public broadcasting television station, inquiring how he liked its programming, Alsop wrote back that since he did not own a TV, "I am afraid I can be of no use to you." "I cannot understand what is happening to America any longer," Alsop admitted to Isaiah Berlin, "perhaps because I have finally become an old codger, frozen in the viewpoints of the past."[11]

IN CONTRAST TO JOE, STEWART ALSOP remained fascinated by the country's changing mood and mores and considered them a topic worth reporting. Like an archaeologist who had discovered a lost tribe living in unexplored jungle, the younger Alsop thought it important to attempt an understanding of the counterculture. Stew had invited his son Ian and daughter, Elizabeth, along on his reporting trip to the 1968 Democratic convention—where children and parent together were teargassed by the Chicago police in Lincoln Park. In the book that he called "a sort of memoir," Stewart would recount his attempt during the convention to interview Abbie Hoffman, the nominal leader of the so-called Youth International Party—the yippies—and an icon of the youth movement:

> STEWART: Mr. Hoffman, I wish you would explain to me the goals of your movement.
> ABBIE: ABOLISH PAY TOILETS, MAN! That's the goal of the revolution—eternal life and free toilets!

Stewart also interviewed David Dellinger, one of those later put on trial for disrupting the Chicago convention. Dellinger showed up at Washington's tony Sans Souci restaurant with one of the defendants, Jerry Rubin, and Paul Krassner, publisher of the satirical magazine *The Realist*. Rubin was shirtless and carrying a toy machine gun. For bodyguards, the trio had brought along a huge black man sporting a bandanna and pirate eye patch, as well as three young women dressed as witches.[12]

Stewart Alsop had long since come out of the shadow of his older brother. At the end of the 1960s, the younger Alsop's star was still on the ascent and threatening to eclipse Joe's. When *The Saturday Evening Post* finally folded in 1969—"foredoomed by efforts to appear 'with it,'" Stew thought—he had taken over Walter Lippmann's back-of-the-book commentary in *Newsweek*. The previous year, Stewart had published his own insider account of political life in the capital, *The Center: The Anatomy of Power in Washington*. A weekly radio program with CBS followed. Having finally outgrown Polecat Park, Stew and Tish purchased a seven-bedroom farmhouse on thirty acres in Frederick County, Maryland. The property came with a stocked fishpond and a clay tennis court. ("Buy it, Stew, and don't haggle," Joe advised his brother. "It will make Kay and Polly jealous.") Stew dubbed the family's new weekend retreat Needwood Forest.[13]

Along with Stewart's burgeoning fame came an offer from Harper and Row's president, Cass Canfield, who suggested that Stew and his friend Tom Braden write a political history of the tumultuous decade. "Limited enthusiasm" was Stewart's prompt reply to Canfield. Stew did briefly consider writing an inside-Washington novel, a literary genre just coming into vogue, but finally decided that "the mandatory sex scenes would embarrass me," he told the disappointed publisher.[14]

Instead, Stewart's journalistic interests turned to the changing political and social undercurrents roiling the country. Much of what he saw, he admitted, he did not like. What Stew called, disparagingly, the "children's crusade," campus demonstrations that ended in violence—like the one at Kent State University in May 1970, where the Ohio National Guard shot and killed four students—particularly disturbed him. Stewart sympathized with the Idaho senator Frank Church, who told of his recent visit to a Pittsburgh college where Vice President Spiro Agnew was to speak. Both men had been surrounded by security guards. It was, Church wrote, "the first time I have experienced this situation in my 14 years of public life . . . There is, as you say, a peculiar smell in the air; I don't like what it portends for the future." Stewart agreed with Church that "something has gone very wrong with our political life."[15]

FOR STEWART ALSOP, a prominent example of what had gone wrong were the ongoing, relentless attacks in the media against some of the traditional elite bastions of the establishment—foremost among them being the CIA. When a London *Times* article described him as "the unofficial public relations officer of the Central Intelligence Agency,"

Stewart Alsop had threatened to sue the paper for libel—"since it suggests that I am a creature of the CIA, and therefore, in effect, a dishonest journalist."[16]

The agency's troubles had flared up again in February 1967, when the left-leaning *Ramparts* magazine revealed that the CIA had, for years, secretly provided funds to the National Student Association. Public exposure of the agency's clandestine underwriting of Radio Free Europe and Radio Liberty, the Congress for Cultural Freedom, and the worldwide myriad of so-called freedom committees followed in short order. Stew's friend Tom Braden—who had meanwhile grown bored of Southern California, sold his newspaper, and, following a failed bid to become the state's lieutenant governor, moved back to Washington to become a political columnist—was one of the few willing to defend the agency in print. Braden titled a May 1967 article for the moribund *Saturday Evening Post* "I'm Glad the CIA Is 'Immoral.'" Did he and his CIA compatriots behave unethically during the Cold War? Tom asked rhetorically in the piece: "Only in the sense that war itself is immoral, wrong and disgraceful."[17]

Nonetheless, the CIA would not honor the memory of the man who initiated its first sustained covert operations until several years after his death. On January 29, 1971, CIA director Dick Helms dedicated a memorial at the agency to Frank Gardiner Wisner. In a closed ceremony at CIA headquarters, attended only by family members and close friends like the Alsop brothers—"very, very few non-Agency people have been invited," Joe assured Susan Mary—Helms spoke fondly of his seven years as Frank's deputy but also of Wisner's struggle with the "night of dark intent": "I can testify to the strength of Frank's character and the worthiness of his contribution. He was a strong, sensitive man who sought a perfection which, we all must acknowledge, is yet to be attained by any wise man in this world of ambiguity and imperfection."[18]

The CIA had originally considered awarding Frank Wisner a star on its Wall of Honor, rationalizing that his death had been "in the line of duty." When some agency veterans raised objections—since Wisner's death was a suicide—a bronze relief, commissioned by Frank's former OPC and CIA colleagues, became the compromise. Knowing how her husband loved tending his vegetable patch at Locust Hill Farm, Polly had already underwritten the cost of another, private memorial: a small plaque in the National Cathedral's Bishop's Garden notes that the sprinkler system is dedicated to Frank Gardiner Wisner.

ON A MONDAY MORNING in late July 1971, Stewart Alsop and his two young sons, Nick and Andrew, were disposing of the trash that had built up over a holiday weekend at Needwood Forest when Stew felt a sudden wave of profound weakness wash over him. Recovering somewhat on the drive back to Washington with Tish, he was persuaded to see his doctor later that afternoon. When a blood test revealed severe anemia, he was admitted that same day to Georgetown University Hospital. More tests over the next week produced a diagnosis: acute myeloblastic leukemia.

Stewart tried to make light of the situation in a phone call to Joe from the hospital. "My blood seems to have turned to water," he announced. Both men became too emotional to say much more.[19]

In fact, Stewart's prognosis was grim. While periodic remissions were possible, even likely, more than 90 percent of patients afflicted with AML died within two years. Transferred to the leukemia ward at the National Institutes of Health in nearby Bethesda, Stew soon began receiving concerned visitors, Joe and Susan Mary among them. The couple brought cucumber soup in a picnic basket as a respite from the hospital food and smuggled forbidden martinis in a thermos bottle. (When a nurse discovered their ruse and challenged them, Joe simply ignored her.) Alice Roosevelt Longworth sent the patient a single flower with a card attached: "Stew—what a nuisance—love from your aged coz." (The eighty-seven-year-old Alice, who had recently undergone a second mastectomy, signed her get-well card, "Washington's topless octogenarian.") In his own note to the afflicted, Ben Bradlee suggested that Stewart's problem was a lack of the right *kind* of blood: "Not that I want this bruited about, but I have a little extra, and it *is* blue." Stew wrote back: "Dear Ben. Coals to Newcastle. What cheek." While Stewart thanked Don and Mary Graham for their gift of a book—*The Greening of America,* by Charles Reich—he thought the author's thesis celebrating untrammeled personal freedom "profoundly anti-intellectual and fascist."[20]

Stewart found it ironic—but somehow appropriate—that his roommate at the NIH hospital was a nineteen-year-old Marshall Islander whose terminal cancer had likely been caused by exposure to radiation from the nuclear testing that the Alsop brothers had long supported in their column: "His was the world's first death from a hydrogen bomb, and the bomb was ours."[21]

In addition to chemotherapy, the standard treatment for those diagnosed with AML was platelet transfusions from a matched donor. Among the Alsop siblings, only Joe had the matching blood type. The transfusion process was frequent, time-consuming, and uncomfortable, with the donor required to sit upright in a chair at the hospital for up to four hours at a session while blood was collected. Wanting to be on call for the transfusions—and fearful of missing "un-recapturable time" with his ailing brother—Joe reluctantly agreed to curtail his travels. Stew's doctor also ordered the elder Alsop to give up his beloved martinis. "He hasn't a notion, of course, of the sort of sacrifice he is asking you to make," Stewart wrote to Joe. "As I told brother John this morning, a paraphrase of the Bible is in order: Greater love hath no man than this, that a man go on the wagon for his brother."[22]

Despite his illness, Stewart kept up both his weekly *Newsweek* column and his radio commentary. On the same day as his near collapse at Needwood Forest, he had written in the magazine of the latest assault on the establishment's underpinnings: the recent publication by *The New York Times* and *The Washington Post* of excerpts from the Pentagon Papers, a forty-seven-volume, top secret study of U.S. decision making in Vietnam that Robert McNamara had commissioned a few years before. Although the Alsop brothers had printed leaked secrets in their column for many years, the publication of the Pentagon Papers was, to Stewart, a step too far—and another unfortunate symbol of the country's decline. "The conclusion is obvious: nobody plays by the rules any more," he wrote in *Newsweek*: "One thing that has happened is that 'civil disobedience'—a euphemism for breaking those laws in which the law breaker does not believe—has become both respectable and relatively safe. The civil-rights movement of the early '60s began to make it respectable, and the increasing unpopularity of the Vietnam war has helped to make it safe as well as respectable."[23]

Months earlier, the Rand analyst Daniel Ellsberg had leaked the Pentagon Papers to the *Times*'s Neil Sheehan. When the *Times* began printing the excerpts, Nixon's attorney general had enjoined further publication on the grounds of national security. (Ironically, the newspaper's general counsel justified going ahead with the Pentagon Papers on the grounds that Stewart and Charley Bartlett had used supposedly classified information in their December 1962 article on the Cuban missile crisis. As the *Times*'s lawyer argued, "If Alsop could do it we could do it.")[24]

But just days after the *Times* complied with the attorney general's order, excerpts and articles based on the Pentagon Papers also began appearing in *The Washington Post,* whose national editor, Ben Bagdikian, had likewise received a copy of the documents from Ellsberg. Hoping to plug any further leaks, the Nixon administration took its case to the Supreme Court. By a 6–3 ruling on June 30, 1971, the justices sided with the newspapers. "Only a free and unfettered press can effectively expose deception in government," the Court declared in its majority opinion.[25]

Katharine Graham's decision to defy not only the Nixon administration but some of the *Post*'s own lawyers was a bold move that demonstrated, finally and decisively, her undisputed control of the newspaper she had inherited from her husband. Not incidentally, it also elevated the reputation of the *Post* to put it arguably on a par with that venerated newspaper of record, *The New York Times.*

For Kay's friend Stewart Alsop, on the other hand, the Pentagon Papers episode was further evidence of the corrupting effects of Vietnam, which had brought about a crisis in American liberalism. From his hospital bed, Stewart engaged in a private exchange of letters with the *New York Times* columnist Anthony Lewis, who had been urging him to come out publicly against the war. "I regard my function as an analyst, rather than advocate," Stew responded, adding, "I do think that we are in danger of a period of flag-waving political reaction. I think a chief reason for this danger is that the liberal movement of Franklin Roosevelt and Jack Kennedy has been twisted all out of shape by the Vietnam war, to the point where many ordinary Americans have come to think of liberals as being elitist, unsympathetic to the real concerns of the wage-earner, and basically anti-American." "As a matter of fact, I keep feeling myself inching over to the right—I try to pull myself back to the left, but it doesn't seem to work," Stewart had written to William Buckley, the editor of the conservative *National Review,* a few weeks earlier. "The fact that I find myself admiring almost all your pieces is a symptom."[26]

Although never as outspoken as his older brother on the war, Stewart agreed with Joe that the United States could not desert its ally South Vietnam—even while conceding that the original U.S. intervention had been a mistake. Stew branded *The Best and the Brightest,* a new book by David Halberstam about the architects of America's involvement in Vietnam, "a readable, inaccurate, and grossly unfair exercise in ideological hindsight." In private correspondence, however, Joe's brother came closer than ever to condemning the war. "The danger of defeat and humiliation in Vietnam is now clear and present, and unlike some of my colleagues, I find it an unpleasing prospect," Stewart wrote to the man he called "that inevitable future Secretary of State," Richard Holbrooke, who had recently left the diplomatic corps to become managing editor of the journal *Foreign Policy*. "But I'm quite convinced that we have no choice other than to get our ground forces out as quickly as we safely can."[27]

Facing the likelihood that his own end was possibly just months—or even weeks—away, Stewart considered writing a traditional memoir. (He told friends that his working title was *After Many a Summer Dies the Snob*.) Instead, Stew decided to share the story of his illness with the readers of *Newsweek*. On August 30, 1971, in a column inspired by a favorite proverb—"God tempers the wind to the shorn lamb"—Alsop wrote matter-of-factly of the death sentence he had been handed: "I have often wondered what it would be like to be told I had an inoperable cancer, and I suspect a lot of other people have asked themselves the same thing. This is my excuse for writing about a very personal experience, rather than the President's economic policies or some other topic in the news."[28] Looking to the future in spite of his dire prognosis, Stewart made arrangements to cover the Republican and Democratic conventions for the presidential election later that year—as usual, in the company of his brother Joe, Kay Graham, and the Bradens. Nonetheless, whether a result of his illness or simply a reflection of his growing pessimism about the country's prospects, Stewart's contributions to *Newsweek* began to take on an increasingly elegiac mood.

Just a few weeks after the Kent State shootings, a column titled "The Disintegration of the Elite" announced with some fanfare that the "old WASP elite . . . is dying and may be dead." Stew argued that the decline had begun with the Great Depression, was temporarily arrested when McCarthyism was beaten back, but accelerated with the eclipse of Great Britain in the 1956 Suez crisis and had become virtually complete with Vietnam. Yet it was not so much the loss of the East Coast, Ivy League–educated establishment that he mourned as the abandonment of establishment values, along with the public's declining confidence in the institutions that the elite had built up—not least of which was faith in the federal government. As Stewart believed, the rot that began from within had culminated in the war: "An elite that has lost its self-confidence soon ceases to be an elite. Vietnam completed the process of undermining the self-confidence of the WASP establishment." In a subsequent column, Stew even put a precise date on the end of the establishment: Tuesday, October 12, 1971, the day that seventy-eight-year-old Dean Acheson, the Groton-, Yale-, and Harvard-educated architect of Truman's foreign policy, slumped over his writing desk at home, dead of a heart attack.[29]

"There Is a Feeling of Doors Closing"

D R. HENRY A. KISSINGER'S SECRET FORAY into Communist China has even produced very major scholarly news," Joe Alsop began his column on Wednesday, July 21, 1971. Alsop's "scholarly news" was the fact that Kissinger's hosts in Beijing had shown Nixon's national security adviser a previously unknown Chinese archaeological treasure—a pair of "jade body-stockings" that completely covered the embalmed corpses of a second-century B.C. Han prince and his wife. "In addition, the corpse of the prince had what had best be called a jade jockstrap," wrote Joe.[1]

The "Jade Body-Stockings" column created an uproar in the White House—not for the story itself, but because of its source. As President Nixon instantly recognized, the details that Alsop reported of Kissinger's hush-hush trip to Beijing ten days earlier could only have come from the national security adviser himself. Yet Nixon, in his televised announcement of the secret initiative to China on July 15, had specified that nothing about Kissinger's historic twenty-hour meeting with the Chinese premier, Zhou Enlai, would be released to the press unless approved in advance by the White House. (Kissinger might have believed that he had been allowed an exception. "He has to quit seeing anyone from the *Times* or the *Post*, including columnists—except Joe Alsop," Nixon had instructed his chief of staff, Bob Haldeman, to tell Kissinger.)[2]

Kissinger plainly enjoyed the plaudits that had followed his triumphant, clandestine overture to America's longtime adversary. But he took no less pleasure in keeping reporters in the dark about the substance of what he had discussed with the Chinese. Even Alsop had been reduced to guessing. In Paris, where he was meeting with high-level Chinese diplomats to plan Nixon's upcoming visit to Beijing, Kissinger told Mao's ambassador to France, "The American press was beside itself at this moment, particularly Mr. Joseph Alsop who was writing endless speculation on what happened in Peking . . . Dr. Kissinger said that none of the U.S. side had talked to Mr. Alsop, and that's what makes him angry, that and the fact that Dr. Kissinger had gone to Peking without his permission."[3]

Joe's columns over the next several weeks were surprisingly upbeat about Nixon and Kissinger's new diplomatic initiative—if for no other reason than that it made even less likely what Alsop had long feared: a Soviet "preventive nuclear strike" against China. With the United States finally on talking terms with Russia's hated rival, such an attack seemed implausible. *The Washington Post*'s Moscow correspondent, Robert Kaiser, derided the notion of a pending Sino-Soviet war as "Joseph Alsop's hallucinations."[4]

But Joe continued to ride that particular hobbyhorse, nonetheless, ultimately drawing the attention—and concern—of Moscow as well as Beijing. Kissinger confessed to *Time* magazine reporters that Alsop's speculations had "infuriated" the Chinese. In a telephone call, Kissinger even felt the need to reassure the Soviet ambassador, Anatoly Dobrynin, that it remained a "pure, absolute total mystery" to him why Alsop believed a Russian attack on Chinese nuclear facilities was imminent. When Kissinger told Dobrynin that "it's like [Alsop] really knew something," the latter responded, "As if it were a special kind of connection [laughs]." But—as Kissinger also confided to Dobrynin—it was understood between them *why* Alsop might make such an irresponsible claim: "You know, Anatol, both you and I know he is violently anti-Soviet for a reason we both know and he is making the maximum amount of mischief."[5]

Although Kissinger had told Dobrynin that he intended "to cut off all contact" with Alsop because of the latter's irresponsible reporting, White House telephone transcripts and written memorandums showed that the national security adviser remained Joe's frequent, and favorite, source inside the Nixon administration. On one occasion, when a White House guard mistakenly shunted him to the White House pressroom—the despised "tank"—an outraged Joe personally complained to Kissinger and wrote a letter of protest to Nixon. "There's absolutely no question about the fact that the President will be mortified when he hears this," Kissinger had assured Alsop. "Because you are not a journalist as far as this building is concerned." Privately, however, Kissinger worried about how his special relationship with Alsop would be perceived by other reporters. In January 1972, when his China negotiations were once again in the headlines, Kissinger anxiously inquired of Nixon's press secretary, Ron Ziegler, about an upcoming news conference, "Are they likely to ask you about my leaking stuff to Alsop?"[6]

Nonetheless, Kissinger continued to socialize with Joe and others of the Georgetown set. When Katharine Graham agonized over whether to join a group of women picketing Washington's famed Gridiron Club—which refused to admit female correspondents to its annual dinner—Kissinger advised her, "It isn't worth it. If it were a great issue you should do it." Instead, the *Post* publisher joined Henry for supper at Joe's house the night of the Gridiron dinner.[7]

While Kay maintained her husband's usual policy of not interfering with the paper's editorials or Herblock's cartoons, that did not prevent Kissinger from expressing displeasure at the occasional criticism of him in the *Post*—or from subtly attempting to influence the newspaper's editorial policy through its publisher. After a *Post* editorial in early 1972 attacked the administration's peace plan for Vietnam, he was once again on the phone to Kay with a proposal: "But let's you and I have a deal that whenever there is a strain I go to you personally." Kay promised Kissinger that Phil Geyelin, who oversaw the *Post*'s editorial page, would call him later that day.[8]

Even as Kissinger's social life had become a stable of gossip columns in Washington's two dailies, the *Post* and the *Evening Star,* the national security adviser remained sensitive to how his liaison with Georgetown friends was viewed by his rivals in the Nixon administration—particularly the White House chief of staff, Bob Haldeman, and the president's domestic adviser, John Ehrlichman, the two so-called German shepherds who guarded access to Nixon. Ehrlichman had been behind the recent fall from grace of Secretary of Commerce Peter Peterson, who had gotten into trouble for attending dinners at Kay Graham's house and spending a weekend at Glen Welby. (Once, when she upbraided Kissinger for not returning her phone call, he joked, "Do you think I want to go the way of Pete?")[9]

By the end of Nixon's first term, Kissinger's attendance at Georgetown functions began to take on the air of a secret mission or a clandestine rendezvous. When he apologized to Graham for having to turn down her dinner invitation in order to attend a White House celebration of Pat

Nixon's birthday, Kissinger worried aloud about what would happen "if one of the Nixon courtiers points out that I was at your house." "We'd both be beheaded," Kay said. Nixon loyalists considered Kissinger's friendship with Graham and the Georgetown set almost tantamount to treason.[10]

ON MONDAY, JUNE 26, 1972, Katharine Graham telephoned Kissinger to make arrangements for lunch at Sans Souci later in the week. She also thanked him for a recent gift of Iranian caviar. The metro section in that morning's *Washington Post* contained a one-column article by the twenty-nine-year-old reporter Bob Woodward, who had been at the paper less than a year. Woodward's story concerned a request by the chairman of the Democratic National Committee that Nixon appoint a special prosecutor to investigate a break-in at the party's headquarters in the Watergate apartments nine days earlier. The hapless burglars had been apprehended while trying to plant electronic listening devices in the DNC offices. As Woodward reported, notebooks in the possession of two of the five suspects arrested for the break-in contained the name of Howard Hunt, the former OPC/CIA operative who had recently become a senior political consultant to the president's reelection campaign. Hunt's involvement linked the burglary to the White House.[11]

The first hint of what would become known as the Watergate scandal had come to Kay Graham on Saturday, June 17, when the *Post*'s managing editor, Howard Simons, telephoned her at Glen Welby. Simons had been tipped off by the DNC's general counsel to the break-in earlier that morning. Even as the Watergate story began to build over the next several weeks, Kissinger's cordial relations with his Georgetown friends remained unaffected by the scandal. A month after the break-in, he telephoned Kay Graham to discuss what could be done to end the "civil war" between Republicans and Democrats over Vietnam: "We can't go through four more years of tearing each other to pieces in this country."[12]

Shortly before the November election, however, the mood began to darken when Kissinger confronted Graham at a social gathering over the *Post*'s reporting on Watergate. "What's the matter? Don't you think we're going to be re-elected?" he challenged her. Kay remembered Kissinger as being "quite upset," complaining that the situation was "terribly, terribly unfair," and warning that the *Post* had gotten the Watergate story wrong.[13]

Henry Kissinger was not the only one among Kay Graham's friends to claim that her newspaper was following Watergate to a dead end. In his *Newsweek* column on September 25, 1972, Stewart Alsop dismissed the flap over what the president's spokesman had called "a third-rate burglary," concluding, "Mr. Nixon was a victim of overeager subordinates suffering from a Walter Mitty complex." Joe Alsop, too, was continually prodding Kay on whether Watergate was worth the attention it was getting in the *Post.* Almost another year would pass before Joe focused on the scandal, and then only to complain that, because of it, "the U.S. government is remarkably close to grinding to a halt." Both Alsop brothers lamented that the domestic scandal was drawing attention away from the subjects that really mattered: the SALT talks, the Middle East, China, and—of course—the war in Vietnam.[14]

JOE HAD BEEN IN South Vietnam the previous spring, when the enemy launched a major offensive—what Alsop in his column called "a last gasp." While the attack was ultimately beaten back, Joe conceded, in an admission rare for him, that "a final U.S. defeat in Vietnam is entirely possible." It would be his last visit to the war zone. Upon returning home, Joe sent a thank-you note to his host and guide in Vietnam, John Vann, who was still doggedly predicting victory in the war. "Good luck! Your luck is our luck!" Alsop wrote to Vann.[15]

That luck ran out on June 9, 1972, when Vann's helicopter slammed into a Vietnam hillside on a foggy night flight, leaving no survivors. A week later, Joe attended Vann's funeral at Arlington National Cemetery, where he was outraged to encounter Daniel Ellsberg, who had become an outspoken opponent of the war. Joe was also invited to an Oval Office ceremony honoring Vann, where President Nixon posthumously awarded the Vietnam War hero the country's highest civilian decoration, the Medal of Freedom. "He was the bravest man I've ever known," Joe would tell Neil Sheehan of Vann.[16]

All but ignoring Watergate in their reporting, the Alsop brothers turned instead to the upcoming presidential election. Neither man was impressed with the Democratic Party's front-runner, the South Dakota senator George McGovern, and both railed against him in their columns. In *Newsweek,* Stewart branded the liberal McGovern "a disastrously bad candidate." Joe went even further, claiming that McGovern—who ran on a platform promising to get the United States out of Vietnam—had espoused ideas that were "dangerous." Indeed, for the first time Joe declined an invitation to interview the Democratic nominee. The brothers considered their judgment vindicated when McGovern lost by a lopsided margin, with Nixon getting more than 60 percent of the popular vote.[17]

Despite his victory, the president promptly showed that he had no intention of showing magnanimity toward his enemies. On November 14, just a week after the election, Kissinger warned Kay Graham in a telephone call from the White House that "the depths of bitterness against the *Post* here is not to be described . . . I won't let my associates tell me who my friends can be but if at this period—If I want to resign, I can resign but I don't want a blowup." Thereafter, however, Nixon's national security adviser became even more careful about being sighted at Georgetown functions. Kissinger pointedly chose the Bradens' house in the Maryland countryside as the venue for his next dinner party with Washington's high rollers.[18]

THAT FALL, following a tennis game and dinner at Kay Graham's house—where the *Post*'s latest Watergate headline, "FBI Finds Nixon Aides Sabotaged Democrats," had dominated the evening's cocktail conversation—Stewart Alsop was again beset with a feeling of sudden weakness. Accompanying fever and chills signaled the onset of pneumonia. The remission that Stew enjoyed for nearly a year had abruptly ended.

The need to continue the blood transfusions for his brother had kept Joe tethered close to home throughout the fall. But the discovery of a new matching donor—an assistant to Stew's doctor at the NIH—meant that Joe was, at least temporarily, free to travel once again. Stewart's situation had stabilized enough after the November election that Joe and Susan Mary could embark on what was, for Joe at least, a sentimental journey: a return to China.[19]

The opening of the Communist giant to Western travelers had been one of the positive outcomes of Nixon's overture to Mao. After Joe and Susan Mary landed in Hong Kong, the couple made their way by train to Canton and Beijing, where they were received as honored guests and assigned four official guides. After a daylong excursion to the Great Wall, next on the Alsops' itinerary was a visit to the city of Kunming, where Joe had been General Chennault's wartime aide more than a quarter century earlier. Industrialization, Joe found, had since transformed the sleepy provincial capital into a manufacturing powerhouse. By contrast, he thought Beijing "an exceptionally cheerful city. Politeness, geniality and purposeful bustle are the main notes." The highlight of Alsop's visit would be his late-night meeting with the Chinese premier, Zhou Enlai, in Beijing's Great Hall of the People. Surrounded by a phalanx of Communist Party officials sitting silently around them, the two men conversed informally for nearly three hours through an interpreter while Susan Mary took notes.[20]

Alsop would subsequently devote more than half a dozen columns to the China visit and his interview with Zhou. Once back home, he wrote a lengthy, two-part *tour d'horizon* for *The New York Times Magazine* that contained a surprising, if grudging, paean of praise for his Communist hosts. In response to Zhou's repeated protestations that China had no interest in becoming a superpower, Alsop countered that "a truly successful China cannot help but be a super-power, even a super-giant power. The country is too large, the people are too numerous, to permit any other result." Joe persuaded Richard Helms—whom Nixon had recently fired from the post of CIA director—to type up his notes on the trip. (Seeing the writing on the wall, Helms had already been planning his retirement from the CIA, instructing his wife, Cynthia, to " 'find a small house for us anywhere but Georgetown . . .' It was because Nixon had always identified Georgetown as the source of his opposition," Cynthia remembered.)[21]

To some, Alsop's about-face on Communist China was no less remarkable than Nixon's. "You probably realize this, but you have completely seduced Joseph Alsop," Kissinger told Huang Hua, China's ambassador to the United Nations. Unmentioned by Alsop in his dispatches was a significant footnote to Nixon's opening to China—and another sign of how much the world had changed as a result.[22]

On Tuesday, January 30, 1973, shortly after Joe returned home, the State Department hosted a luncheon to honor those Foreign Service officers who had served in China and had—in the words of the official invitation—"demonstrated their professionalism and integrity by reporting events as they saw them." The dean of the surviving China hands, John Service, received a standing ovation from his peers. But Joe Alsop's old-time nemesis chose to pass up the State Department ceremony, instead sending regrets from his exile in Spain. "Washington would have been a long way to go for lunch," John Paton Davies explained.[23]

FROM A SMALL CLOUD ON THE HORIZON when Alsop left for China, the Watergate scandal had grown into a tempest that threatened to engulf the Nixon presidency by the time Joe returned to Washington that winter. In the interim, a pair of top officials in Nixon's reelection campaign had been found guilty of conspiracy in the bugging of Democratic headquarters, along with the five Watergate burglars. In response, the Senate had created a select committee to investigate White House involvement. Even so, Joe stubbornly continued to ignore Watergate in his column, focusing instead on growing Russian influence in the Middle East, what he saw as the perennial danger of a Sino-Soviet war, and the ever-dimming prospects for an American victory in Vietnam.[24]

The elder brother was also distracted by Stewart's deteriorating health. Joe had resumed donating blood platelets at NIH—he would sit for forty transfusions in all—and he was once again on the wagon for his ailing sibling. "I am now like a Siamese twin—needed to give blood once a week to my brother, and therefore unable to go abroad at all," Joe wrote a friend. But there were limits even to brotherly love and to Joe's forbearance. Compelled, in the sterile confines of the hospital, to give up his beloved Carlton cigarettes, Joe appealed to a higher authority. "Smokers, like myself, feel extreme discomfort if they have to go for two hours and a half without a cigarette," Alsop wrote to the man in charge of the NIH, Caspar Weinberger, secretary of the Department of Health, Education, and Welfare. Joe asked Weinberger if he might be granted an exception to the hospital's nonsmoking policy.[25]

That April, Stewart expressed his gratitude to Joe in a letter unusual both for its frankness and for its open expression of affection for his brother: "I am low. There is a feeling of doors closing, and I can't shake this damnable temperature . . . We Alsops are lousy about expressing such things. But I really do appreciate what you have done and are doing. Love, Stew."[26]

JOE ALSOP HAD RECENTLY COME to the realization that doors of a different kind might be closing for him as well.

Some months earlier, he had written a five-column screed decrying the busing of children to achieve racial balance in public schools. Katharine Graham told a friend that Joe's polemic against forced busing—which was becoming increasingly common throughout the country and which the *Post* owner herself likely supported—was typical Alsopian "overkill." When Kay's rather mild criticism reached Joe's ears, he responded with a three-page letter to his old friend. While defending the columns, Alsop conceded that they might have had a "cross, contentious tone."[27]

It was only the first of a mounting number of run-ins that Joe would have with his stalwart ally and erstwhile employer. "These last years have been a bad time for me," Alsop admitted to Kay. But no sooner had their contretemps over school busing faded than word came that Graham was also upset over what she called Joe's "China, China obsession"—his renewed jeremiads about a coming Sino-Soviet war. And, for Alsop, the bad news kept coming. "With a good deal of hesitation and embarrassment, I write you about the Paris *Herald Tribune*," he began another letter to Kay. The paper had finally dropped Alsop's column altogether, after a year of printing it only sporadically. Joe hoped that Graham might reverse the decision, since the newspaper popularly known as the *Paris Herald* was part of the *Post* syndicate.[28]

In fact, the whole future of Alsop's professional relationship with the *Post* newspaper had come into question. Joe's contract was due to expire at the end of 1974, and Otis Chandler's *Los Angeles Times* had expressed interest in picking up the syndicate contract. But Chandler considered Alsop's remuneration from the *Post* "overly generous," especially given the column's—and columnist's—declining popularity. Long accustomed to spending nearly as much as he made, Joe recognized that a reduction in his salary was likely, which would in turn require a change in his lifestyle.[29]

If this was not depressing enough, Susan Mary moved out of Joe's Dumbarton Avenue house and into her own apartment in September 1973. (In the separation agreement worked out between them, Joe promised to provide Soozle with fifteen hundred dollars a month until her mother died, or so long as the salary from his column continued.) The late-night drunken rows, the casual insults, and Alsop's sarcastic put-downs had finally taken their toll on what Joe, in happier times, had called his "beloved two yards of woman, whom I adore." The split came as no surprise to Susan Mary's children. "My mother's response was to look at the floor in a martyrlike pose, which . . . only enraged Joe more," remembered Billy.[30]

The rapid and unrelenting series of unfortunate events cast Alsop into a deep funk. Ben Bradlee noted that his friend's drinking, which had never been moderate, increased to the point where it verged on being out of control—with the gin in Joe's martini glass sometimes sloshing out onto the floor. Just as he believed that the country's luck had begun to run out with the murder of John Kennedy, Joe theorized that the decline of the Alsop family's fortunes coincided with the death of its larger-than-life matriarch, Corinne, in June 1971, just a month before Stewart's leukemia diagnosis. Joe spoke candidly to friends and relatives of having a "House of Usher feeling"—the sensation of impending doom prompted not only by the failure of his marriage but by Stew's worsening illness and the sword hanging over his own professional career. The brothers, meeting at the family home in Avon after Corinne's funeral to divide up the estate and sell the farmhouse, were "alternately excessively businesslike and oddly abstracted," Stewart remembered.[31]

For Joe, the loss of a pair of close friends exacerbated his sense of gathering gloom. Following a long and painful bout with stomach cancer, Chip Bohlen had died on the first day of 1974. Their mutual friend George Kennan, in Paris to research his latest book, scribbled in his diary the same day, "Grey and cold . . . I, in early morning, had one of the longest, most vivid, and most absurd of my 'futility' dreams: lost, confused, people waiting for me at places I couldn't find, time passing, it becoming later and later, and my plight—ever more hopeless and ridiculous. Let us hope this is not an omen for the new year." Learning of Chip's death two days later, Kennan wrote to Avis Bohlen that her husband had been, for him, "the nearest thing, I suppose, to a brother."[32]

Llewellyn "Tommy" Thompson—another of Joe's friends and the man to whom John Kennedy had turned for advice during both the Berlin and the Cuban crises—was also gone, likewise a victim of cancer. Even during his illness, emaciated and dying, Thompson had continued attending the cocktail hour and weekend bridge games at Needwood Forest. Thompson's passing occurred at the same NIH hospital where Stewart Alsop was receiving a blood transfusion in an adjacent ward. "I have begun to think that the '70s are the very worst vintage years since the history of life began on earth—with the possible exception of such intervals as the wanderings of Attila in Europe," Joe wrote to Vangie Bruce in despair.[33]

A few weeks earlier—in what might have been an act of preemptive bravado—Joe had sent Kay Graham what seemed like an ultimatum: "On the one hand, I do not think it possible or desirable for me to carry on the column after the end of next year without solid backing from the *Post*. On the other hand, I do *not* want the *Post*'s backing on the basis of friendship-cum-charity. If you do not conclude, after consideration, that giving me continued backing is the sensible, business-like thing to do at this juncture, I shall cheerfully pull down the shades as a columnist on January 1, 1975." Without committing herself or her newspaper to keeping Joe on, Kay reassured him in a letter at year's end, "Please don't think of things in terms of the Alsops' luck running out . . . I don't understand the tough series of blows you all have suffered. It's anguishing as hell . . . Don't worry about your situation. I'm sure it will work out."[34]

But Joe remained skeptical. "I'm in a sad state of uncertainty about my own future," he confessed."[35]

BY LATE SPRING 1973, it was no longer possible for even Joe Alsop to ignore Watergate. In mid-May, the Senate's select committee had begun televised hearings on the scandal. As with the army-McCarthy hearings a generation earlier, the nation remained spellbound as senior Nixon administration officials were hauled before the cameras and interrogated by the committee's folksy-seeming chairman, North Carolina's Democratic senator Sam Ervin. Joe Alsop monitored the proceedings on the same tiny black-and-white set that he had previously borrowed to watch the New Year's Eve celebrations in Times Square. In June, when Nixon's chief counsel, John Dean, implicated the president in efforts to cover up White House involvement in the break-in, Joe still took Nixon's side, denouncing Dean's testimony as "the self-serving allegations of a bottom-dwelling slug." Privately and to friends, however, Alsop conceded that Watergate "really has turned into a major horror," one that had cast the country and its people into a "tunnel of Stygian darkness, not quite knowing where the tunnel's next turning may bring us."[36]

As before, Joe's real concern was that the domestic scandal had proven "crippling" to the country by drawing attention away from foreign affairs. "I say we are now like a house with the roof on fire and the cellar flooding and the housewife constantly talks about the immorality of the chambermaid," he complained in a telephone call to Henry Kissinger. When the Yom Kippur War broke out between Israel and Egypt, a Soviet ally, in October 1973, Joe claimed that it proved his point: by weakening America, the Watergate scandal had emboldened the Russians. Reprising a term he had once used to describe the despised Eisenhower, Joe likened Nixon—"an impotent president" —to a beached whale. ("Beached whales do not last long, either," Joe observed pointedly in his column.) By encouraging Soviet adventurism, Watergate, Alsop warned the *Post* reporter Meg Greenfield, might yet bring about World War III.[37]

Battling the chronic weariness brought about by his disease and its treatment, Stewart continued his commentary for *Newsweek*. Unlike Joe, Stew was more concerned with Watergate's domestic repercussions. Despite his illness, Stewart offered to go to the D.C. lockup for a jail-house interview with G. Gordon Liddy, the flamboyant, ex-FBI soldier of fortune who had overseen the Watergate break-in. "It has long seemed to me that your powerful personality played an important part in the episode which has now generated a great constitutional crisis," Alsop wrote to Liddy. (Although Liddy politely declined the interview, his wife thanked Stew for describing her husband in a *Newsweek* column as "crazy-brave.") When other commentators compared Nixon's henchmen to common criminals and miscreants—"motivated by greed, an emotion effortlessly understood by almost all of us"—Stewart Alsop countered that the Watergate plotters were actually more dangerous, because they were different in kind: "They seem to have been motivated by more complex emotions—by a certain self-righteousness, by fear, by a special kind of political-ideological hatred . . . They were not practicing politics. They were making war, a special kind of war. The kind of war they were making has been made between nations for a long time now, and it is still being made. But this special kind of war has not before been made within a nation, certainly not within this nation." Stewart ended his *Newsweek* column of May 14, 1973, with a frank and surprising assertion: "Mr. Nixon, who has been a good president in many ways, must resign or be impeached."[38]

Both Alsop brothers believed that Nixon might yet "tough it out." But even Joe was beginning to tell friends that the president should consider stepping down for the good of the country. His reluctant change of heart was noticed by Joe's readers inside as well as outside Washington. In Beijing, where Kissinger had gone for discussions on Chinese-American relations, a puzzled chairman Mao asked why journalists like Alsop "are all now triggered against President Nixon." Kissinger's answer perhaps contained more hope than conviction: "Joseph Alsop—I think—that was a brief aberration, and he will return to his original position very soon."[39]

Having meanwhile replaced William Rogers as secretary of state, Kissinger worried that Watergate was undermining not only Nixon's authority but his own. Indeed, there was some evidence to that effect. When a speech Kissinger gave on a "new Atlantic Alliance," intended to attract attention away from the scandal, failed to receive the usual headlines in *The Washington Post,* Kissinger complained to Phil Geyelin and Joe Alsop. Geyelin's prompt and unapologetic reply confirmed Kissinger's worst fears. "With all due respect to you," the *Post* editor bluntly told Henry, "I don't think it's General Marshall at Harvard."[40]

Since he had always deliberately maintained a greater distance from Kissinger than his brother, Stewart probably felt he had more freedom to criticize the newly confirmed secretary of state. Even though Kissinger had asked Russian physicians, during a recent trip to Moscow, whether Soviet medicine had any advanced treatments for leukemia, Stewart upbraided Kissinger in his *Newsweek* column for the administration's attacks on its journalist critics.[41]

As Nixon's impeachment seemed to grow more likely that spring, even Joe finally felt compelled to report on the fallout of the Watergate story. To that end, he invited the Illinois congressman Thomas Railsback to lunch amid the lush foliage of his garden room. Joe regarded Railsback, a key Republican on the House Judiciary Committee, as a reliable "barometer" on whether the president would be removed from office. During the lunch—and on two subsequent occasions, when he was invited back to Joe's house—Railsback assured Alsop that he intended to vote against impeachment.[42]

However, when transcripts from the tape-recording system that Nixon had secretly installed in the White House were released, in late April 1974, they showed the president deeply involved in the Watergate cover-up. The Alsop brothers professed to be as appalled as the rest of the country at the cynical scheming, racial slurs, and deleted expletives emanating from the Oval Office. ("Sheer flesh-crawling repulsion," Joe wrote in Matter of Fact.) Yet, even as he branded Nixon "the armpit of humanity" and "ninety-nine percent nutty as a fruitcake," Joe argued that impeachment would be a "catastrophe" for the presidency as well as the nation.[43]

Stewart was less convinced. In a *Newsweek* column that month, he had used a French word, *dégringolade*—meaning "a kind of slithery, sudden coming apart"—to describe the state of the Union on account of Watergate. Stew's columns had begun appearing less frequently in the magazine, since he sometimes lacked the strength to meet a deadline. In his *Newsweek* commentary on May 6, 1974—" 'If They Get Us, We'll

Get Them'"—Stewart's title came from the recent utterance of a Nixon operative and summed up all that Stew felt had gone wrong with the American political process. It would be his last column.[44]

When writing *Stay of Execution,* the book about his illness, Stewart had given vent to an uncharacteristic pessimism: "For weeks now, I have been haunted and depressed by a sense that the American system, in which I have always believed in an unquestioning sort of way, the way a boy believes in his family, really is falling apart; by a sense that we are a failed nation, a failed people. And Watergate is surely a peculiarly depressing way to say farewell to all our greatness. It is a whimper—a sleazy little whimper, a grubby little whimper—rather than a bang."[45]

Stewart was doubtlessly aware that the specter he had begun to call, almost affectionately, "Uncle Thanatos," was drawing closer, as his body wasted away and his blood platelet count plummeted. He ended *Stay of Execution* with "There is a time to live, but there is also a time to die. That time has not yet come for me. But it will. It will come for all of us."

It came for Stewart Alsop on May 26, 1974, nine days after his sixtieth birthday. A memorial service at St. John's Episcopal Church, across Lafayette Square from the White House, drew more than seven hundred mourners. In addition to Joe and the rest of the Alsop clan, they included Kay Graham, Ben Bradlee, and senior figures from the Kennedy, Johnson, and Nixon administrations. At Stew's request, there was no eulogy. Instead, *Newsweek*'s Washington bureau chief, Mel Elfin, praised Stewart—in the back-of-the-book spot that had been Alsop's own—as "the very model of the Connecticut Yankee gentleman." A lengthy obituary in the London *Times,* noting Stew's service in the British army, described him as "one of the last members of the eastern, Anglophile establishments which led the United States into its Atlantic role after the Second World War."[46]

Joe Alsop wrote to Isaiah Berlin that Stewart's death was "like an amputation." In the column that he dedicated to Stewart, Joe praised his brother as "a brave and stoical man" who also possessed "quite exceptional gaiety and grace." But the encomium ended on an ominous note, with Joe remembering Stew's comment, as he lay ill, that they had been fortunate to live during the country's best days: "I look at the next generation, whom he cared for so intensely, and I hope against hope he was wrong."[47]

FOR JOE ALSOP, President Nixon's resignation some three months later seemed anticlimactic in the aftermath of Stewart's death. During the Watergate hearings, Alsop's home on Dumbarton Avenue had become a kind of last refuge for administration figures like Kissinger. (Hoping to inform Kissinger in advance of his plans to resign, Nixon had finally reached him by telephone at Joe's house, where the secretary of state was having dinner with Alsop.)

Looking back over the events of the previous year, Joe recognized, belatedly, that he had missed one of the biggest news stories of the decade in Watergate. Alsop also seemed to realize, too late, that it was his particular brand of reporting—his so-called elite or access journalism—that had caused him to underrate the importance of the scandal. Thus, Joe's principal sources at the White House—Kissinger and Nixon's chief of staff Alexander Haig—not only had a stake in the president's survival but were themselves shut out of the secretive Nixon's plans and thoughts. Even Congressman Railsback—Joe's impeachment "barometer"—had ultimately changed his mind and decided to vote for the president's removal. Alsop's friend and sometime rival Scotty Reston judged that Joe had been "professionally crippled" by his sources. Another *Times* reporter concluded, with McCarthy in mind, that Alsop "may have made more dragons than he slew."[48]

Joe had already apologized to Herblock for attacking the cartoonist over his unsympathetic portrayal of the disgraced president. "I get rather angry, when I see large numbers of people who actually elected Nixon in 1968, and also made his election a dead certainty in 1972, behaving rather like hyenas around a corpse," Alsop explained. He wrote a similar apologia to Kay Graham, acknowledging that his earlier doubts about the *Post*'s emphasis on Watergate had been misplaced:

> I tried to reach you yesterday, to say, "You're dead right, and I was nearly dead wrong" . . . I cannot tell you how much I admire the enormous courage that you have all shown, particularly you and Ben. Whether the final outcome will be happy, I cannot possibly say, and I sometimes have my doubts. But the fact is that a very dangerous system had grown up in the White House, which would have threatened this country if it had continued. It was destroyed by you and the other leaders of the Post and the Post reporters almost single-handed . . . So I send you my warmest congratulations, and also my apologies for giving our miserable President

the benefit of the doubt—which now turns out to be a completely wrong thing to do.[49]

Ironically, among those most surprised by Watergate's outcome was the *Post*'s own publisher. "My God, what have we done here? What's going to happen now?" Kay Graham had reportedly exclaimed when the Watergate tapes implicated Nixon in the cover-up. (Ben Bradlee, on the other hand, joyfully pinned the *Post*'s banner headline—"Nixon Resigns"—on his office wall.) Thanking him for what she called his "handsome and gracious" apology, Kay wrote to Joe, "I believe, as I have long believed, that the crew in the White House was an evil and dangerous lot—who sensing the danger from our reporting, were out to destroy us if they could."[50]

In another irony, Alsop would, after Watergate, rail against the modern trend toward what he called "advocacy journalism"—ignoring his own decades-long contribution to the practice. In his column, Joe noted that Kay Graham herself had recently warned that those in the newspaper business "'were all in danger of getting too big for our boots.'" "I fear that this danger is much worsened nowadays," Alsop wrote, "when too many people in my trade think the best way to make a big reputation is to convict a major public figure or institution of some sort of wrongdoing." For Joe, it was a tacit admission of how fundamentally his trade had changed, with a new generation of younger journalists—self-professed "investigative reporters" like Woodward and Carl Bernstein—promising to become the wave of the future.[51]

Joe's younger brother Stewart had always been closer to that wave. As early as a 1972 *Newsweek* column, Stew had quoted the "gonzo journalist" Hunter Thompson's description of the then presidential candidate Hubert Humphrey as "a treacherous, gutless old ward-heeler." Acknowledging that Thompson's language was "brutal," Stewart nonetheless "wound up his column by dismissing [Humphrey] in terms more polite than mine, but not less final," Thompson wrote approvingly.[52]

In the wake of Stew's death and Nixon's resignation, even Joe Alsop was willing to admit that the passion had gone out of his reportage. ("He wrote the same column for about three years," Kissinger told Senator William Fulbright, about Vietnam.) "I really hate this city," Alsop confided to Isaiah Berlin shortly after Stewart's passing. "I find the column a dreadful chore." He was, Joe told Kay Graham, only looking for "a reasonably satisfactory fin de carriere."[53]

In his column on September 25, 1974, Alsop announced that after more than four decades as a reporter he would retire at the end of the year. Barely a week later, Joe wrote to Scotty Reston, "Now . . . I have made a new rule that I don't care what anybody's political views are, and I am never going to ask about them. In fact, after January 1, I hope never to talk about politics again."[54]

It was a vow that Alsop would find impossible to keep. For a retirement project, however, he was already at work on a book dealing with an altogether different topic: the history of art collecting. Anticipating the need to do some belt-tightening in his changed financial circumstances, Joe reluctantly put 2720 Dumbarton Avenue on the market, obtaining a lifetime lease on a more modest town house around the corner at 2806 N Street from a friend, John Walker, the former director of the National Gallery of Art. He felt "like a hermit crab abandoning its shell," Joe confessed to readers.[55]

Having nonetheless decided "to pull down the shades as a columnist," Alsop wished to thank those who had been his stalwart friends. "I can't let the moment pass without sending you a line to say how very grateful I am for all your kindness I've experienced in so many, many years," Joe wrote to Katharine Graham. She replied in turn, "The thanks I owe you of friendship and pleasures enjoyed over the years is more than I can ever say—more I think than I even know. You have taught me so much about how to live and how to enjoy living—how much our friendships add and how great it is to give pleasure. I never give as much as I receive—a worry to me that I can compensate for in only this small way—by telling you so. It's always better to know how deeply one is loved."[56]

Joe also mended fences with some of his former enemies, including the *New York Times* reporter Neil Sheehan, who would be one of the last to have lunch in the garden room before the Dumbarton Avenue house was sold. Sheehan found Alsop disarmingly pleasant, although still angry about Vietnam. George Kennan, Joe's dinner guest the following day, found his host in a bleak mood. "[Alsop] was sad and subdued—plans to sell his beautiful house, which seems a great shame," Kennan wrote in his diary. "Retiring, I find, is just a bit like organizing your own funeral, then attending the service, and finally providing the wake," Joe complained to another longtime friend.[57]

Alsop's last columns were unapologetically emotional and nostalgic. In "A Return to One's Roots," Joe invoked the "long lost and long forgotten" stability of growing up in rural America and his fond boyhood memories of Stewart. "The Last 'Tribal Christmas'" was a farewell to the Dumbarton Avenue house and his generation-long custom of celebrating the holiday there with friends and family. Joe's final column—"'I Am Deeply Proud to Have Been a Reporter,'" appearing in newspapers on December 30, 1974—was the most personal. Alsop recollected that the "most pleasing moment" in his reporting career occurred when word reached him in Korea that Secretary of Defense Louis Johnson had been forced to resign. He and Stewart had brought about Johnson's fall by doing what they did best, Joe claimed: "calling attention to important facts that are being lied about or shoved under the rug." But Alsop also gave credit to those who had since taken up that task, praising Woodward and Bernstein's work as "the most magnificent recent case . . . quite unlike anything done by anyone else in my working lifetime."

Joe ended his last column:

> I am certain . . . that getting the significant facts and publishing them are still the great delights, the real tests, the main burdens and the true public functions of the reporter's trade . . . In my working lifetime, I have known a whole series of alleged American elites, definable as groups of people who inform themselves. I have never known any alleged American elite to be right about any subject whatever, except, arguably, subjects like the correct manufacture of soufflés.
>
> Meanwhile I have never known the American people to be really badly wrong, if only they were correctly and fully informed . . . In the reporter's trade, we have a serious job to do.[58]

Joe's retirement marked the end of an era—the disappearance of "the oldest surviving example of . . . the nationally syndicated political column," editorialized *The New York Times*. Alsop claimed to have no regrets about his decision and no desire to look back. "Everything that I would be writing about depresses me so that I can hardly bear to think about it, much less discuss it in print," he wrote to a friend.[59]

A short time after his last column, Joe sat down for an interview in the living room of his new N Street home with a reporter from a St. Paul, Minnesota, public radio station. Although the topic was ostensibly his forthcoming volume on art collecting, after a few perfunctory questions concerning Joe's research for the book, the young interviewer turned to a different subject altogether. "Your reputation underwent a certain . . . *change* . . . because of your position on Vietnam," he began nervously. Immediately, Joe interrupted with a response that was full-throated and unflinching: "As far as my reputation is concerned, we'll see about *that* later. Some people's reputation was rather low in 1938 and was rather higher in 1940." On that note, the interview abruptly ended.

But when the tape was broadcast, early in 1975, the radio announcer felt the need to add a postscript: "Joseph Alsop feels that his judgments, on art as well as on politics, will be borne out by history. And he apologizes for none of them."[60]

Epilogue
"We're All So Old or Dead":
The End of the Georgetown Set

JOE ALSOP'S LAST COLUMN appeared only four months before the end came in Vietnam—as American helicopters hurriedly evacuated dependents from the rooftop of the Saigon embassy and North Vietnamese tanks rolled into the city on April 30, 1975. A telephone call two weeks earlier from Neil Sheehan had found Joe in a low state: "[Alsop] is very depressed and says he is not reading the papers these days because of it." Joe told Sheehan about the letter he had recently received from an embittered South Vietnamese government official, who had refused a promised evacuation, explaining, "If I must die, I prefer to die in my own country among my own countrymen. I made the mistake of putting my faith in the United States."[1]

While Joe had reconciled with some of his former adversaries—Sheehan among them—that number, notably, did not include David Halberstam, the reporter who returned equal enmity toward the man who had tried to get him fired from *The New York Times*. In *The Powers That Be,* a book on the press and Vietnam published in 1975, Halberstam wrote, "If there was any disagreement over the progress of the war, it was not among resident correspondents, it was on the part of *visiting* journalists like Joe Alsop and Marguerite Higgins, who were there not so much to report on the war as to strengthen policy."[2]

Arthur Schlesinger Jr. claimed that Alsop fantasized about the day when those who had opposed him on the war would find themselves accused of losing Vietnam, the same way that John Davies and the State Department's experts had been blamed for losing China. When that day arrived, Schlesinger said, Joe planned to come to their defense, as he had with Davies, "arguing that Schlesinger may have been mistaken but he was never disloyal."[3]

But, of course, that day never came. Instead, it was the early and unwavering supporters of the war—like Alsop—who were pilloried by the public and in the press. Vietnam cost him "his health, his figure, and his reputation," Joe confided to a fellow journalist in a rare moment of candor.[*4]

As years passed, Joe's anger at those he blamed for the defeat in Vietnam did not abate. In October 1979, when Alsop received an invitation from the antiwar activist Joan Baez to a benefit for Vietnamese refugees, he responded with venom: "I must tell you frankly . . . that I can think of nothing more inappropriate than joining you and several others of those you list as participants in the party. In my eyes, you are all blood-guilty. You had a considerable role in causing this country quite needlessly to lose a war, with the most damaging consequences to American interests all over the world . . . I trust that you will sleep uncomfortably for many years to come because you are haunted by the consequences of your acts."[5]

Neither in his memoirs nor in any of his subsequent public statements did Joe Alsop ever explain or excuse his unyieldingly hawkish stand on Vietnam. When interviewers like Sheehan raised the issue, Alsop quickly changed the subject. Joe's former *Washington Post* colleague Ward Just speculated that Alsop's stubbornness had its roots in his psychological makeup: "Joe could not believe he was wrong about Vietnam because that would call into question all his views on other things. Maybe he just found that his heart was wrong."[6]

The Sunday night suppers continued at Joe's leased house on N Street, but with lower-wattage luminaries attending. Since Alsop had made no secret of his contempt for President Jimmy Carter—"the weakest President the U.S. has had since Buchanan"—it was hardly surprising that few faces from the new administration appeared around Joe's table. In a note to the author Lillian Hellman, Alsop lamented that Washington in the 1970s simply lacked the kind of larger-than-life figures that had made

---

* Joe would have been surprised to learn that one of his admirers was a Vietcong spy. Pham Xuan An—who had worked as a stringer for *Time* magazine during the war—confided to his biographer Larry Berman in a 2004 interview that he owed much to the Alsops' book *The Reporter's Trade:* "An told me that he learned 'the rule of the feet' from this book, meaning that a good reporter needed to get out from behind the desk and see at least four officials every day."

his Georgetown salons famous: "The hyenas laugh, the jackals whine, the vultures circle, and everyone waits for the lions and tigers that don't exist in our human zoo."[7]

Indeed, Washington, post-Vietnam and post-Watergate, had undergone a profound transformation.

Barely a week before Joe Alsop's final column appeared in the *Post,* a lengthy article in *The New York Times* by the investigative reporter Seymour Hersh revealed the CIA's involvement in years of illegal domestic spying. James Angleton, who had been in charge of counterintelligence at the agency since 1954, was a prompt casualty of Hersh's revelations. Angleton's resignation was announced by the CIA on Christmas Eve 1974. Over the years, Artifice had become increasingly convinced that a mole was operating at the heart of Western intelligence—not realizing, until it was too late, that the traitor was actually his old friend in Britain's MI6, Kim Philby. The *Times* exposé led, as well, to the creation, by January 1975, of three separate congressional committees to investigate the agency's alleged misdeeds. It was the beginning of what an official CIA history would call, justifiably, "the years of the gathering storm."[8]

Senate and House hearings over the next several months revealed, in turn, the agency's complicity in nearly a quarter century of foreign assassination plots, domestic surveillance, and human experimentation, much of it in violation of the CIA's 1947 charter. One of the principal victims—or villains—of the hearings was Frank Gardiner Wisner's longtime friend and former CIA director, Richard Helms. Having been fired by Nixon for refusing to have the agency interfere in the investigation of the Watergate break-in, Helms narrowly escaped a prison term in November 1977 for lying to Congress when he denied CIA involvement in the overthrow of Chile's democratically elected government four years earlier.[9]

Exactly how much had changed in the public's perception of the CIA became evident that fall, when the former *Washington Post* reporter Carl Bernstein published a lengthy article in *Rolling Stone* magazine on the longtime collusion between journalists and the agency. Bernstein listed Joe and Stewart Alsop among the dozen or so reporters whom the agency considered "known assets," who routinely carried out special undercover assignments for the CIA. When interviewed by Bernstein for the piece, Joe acknowledged that a 1952 visit to Laos had been at the behest of the CIA's Frank Wisner and likewise that a reporting trip to the Philippines the following year was at the bidding of Desmond FitzGerald. Alsop admitted, as well, to using his columns from Manila to promote the CIA-supported candidate in the upcoming elections. (Previously, Joe had told Neil Sheehan how he once used flattery to recruit a socialist in the Italian government for the CIA, having "cultivated the fellow and brought him to the point where money could be passed," although Alsop had declined to give the bribe himself: "I drew the line at that.") But Joe was unapologetic about having helped the agency. "I'm proud they asked me and proud to have done it," he told Bernstein. "The notion that a newspaperman doesn't have a duty to his country is perfect balls."[10]

Alsop's attitude toward the Soviet Union remained similarly unreconstructed, despite almost a decade of détente. In November 1979, when Islamic militants took over the American embassy in Tehran, Alsop attributed the Iranian hostage crisis not to the rise of religious fundamentalism but to Moscow's machinations aimed at gaining control of Middle Eastern oil. In contrast to George Kennan, Joe found little reason to believe that Mikhail Gorbachev's accession to power in the Kremlin augured a thaw in the Cold War. "My own grim Connecticut instincts tell me that your hopes can too easily be disappointed, but I pray you are right," Alsop wrote to Kennan.[11]

"Nothing, literally nothing, will induce me to go back into the political end of the newspaper business, or take a job in government, or do anything else that might benefit me if the men I believe in return to government," Joe wrote to Bob McNamara in late May 1980. Just two days later, however, Alsop was offering election advice to the presidential candidate Ronald Reagan, whose hard-line approach to the Soviets he both approved and admired. Joe's memo to Reagan was vintage Alsop: the nation was facing "the British choice of 1939—to fight like cornered rats, or passively accepting the kind of impairment of national independence that must always end, over time, in actual subjugation . . . In short, we are in the last quarter of the twelfth hour."[12]

Willingly, it seemed, Joe had taken to "wearing the mask—convincing in this case—of a sage in a city of yahoos," wrote the journalist Brendan Gill in a *New Yorker* profile of Alsop. Joe told his stepson, Billy, that he was the sole survivor of a world "dead as the auk." Describing himself to a C-SPAN interviewer in 1984 as an "extreme centrist," Alsop decried the partisan bickering among those he derisively called "the ideologists," who, he complained, had become an enduring feature of the Washington scene. "Either great American party that yields to its extreme group is doomed there and then," Joe predicted.[13]

In retirement, Alsop devoted much of his time to completing what he would describe as his only "major" book. *The Rare Art Traditions* addressed a topic seemingly as far removed from Cold War politics as possible. Joe actually began the book project shortly after John Kennedy's assassination but had worked on it only sporadically since. Within weeks of sending the manuscript to the publisher, Alsop was beset by severe back pains. A protracted hospital stay and double bypass heart surgery followed. Once home, he planned to start work on his memoir but found himself stymied by an unprecedented case of writer's block. Alsop eventually hired as his collaborator a young journalist who had come to interview him for a magazine article. Joe decided to begin the book with a nostalgic look back at his idyllic childhood on the Avon farm and to end it abruptly at John Kennedy's death. He borrowed the title—*"I've Seen the Best of It"*—from a remark Stewart had made when he lay dying. "You belong to the past much more than I do," Stew reminded his older brother in those last days.

Indeed, Joe's own personal correspondence showed him to be more comfortable looking back rather than ahead. Since his divorce from Susan Mary in 1978, Alsop had been spending more time in the company of his friend Katharine Graham—the two occasionally sharing a casual supper in front of the television at Glen Welby. (But Joe's affection for Kay did not prevent him from attacking a *Washington Post* story on terrorism as "illogical nonsense" and "radical chic" in a 1981 letter to Donald Graham, who had meanwhile succeeded his mother as publisher.) In 1986, Kay hosted a party at her R Street house for Joe's seventy-sixth birthday. Later, in a note to one of the guests, Dick Helms, Alsop reminisced about how much had been lost in the time gone by: "By now there are great gaps at the table I can never forget. They are not the sort one can be consoled for, either. But that is the nature of life . . . Instead of feeling sad when I thought of Stew and Avis, Chip and Tommy, Phil and all the others, I found myself considering how much they would have enjoyed the party—just the sort of party they all loved."[14]

The following year, Joe Alsop was diagnosed with terminal lung cancer. Within days of receiving the grim news from his doctor, he held a dinner party at the N Street house. Kay Graham, Meg Greenfield, and George Kennan attended, as did Chip's daughter Avis and Frank George Wisner. "Much like old times," Kennan wrote in his diary that evening. "Joe, whom even a cancer seems unable to subdue, presided grandly over the occasion, roaring, interrupting, shouting everyone down . . . We all knew Joe enough, and loved him enough, to take him in his stride; and the talk was animated in the old Georgetown fashion."[15]

Forced to concede, nonetheless, that his end was approaching, Joe began making preparations and saying good-bye. He appended a note to his will, explaining why he had decided to leave the bulk of his estate to his male relatives: "I care greatly, perhaps foolishly, about my name. As my father used to say, 'Our branch of the Alsop tribe has survived ten generations on this side of the Atlantic, always keeping their noses just above water.' This is now a vastly more difficult feat . . . To be specific, the very great advantages that were accorded certain groups of Americans have now quite properly been caused to vanish. And we are all, with some tragic exceptions, 'citizens with an equal share.' "[16]

In a final letter to Kay Graham, Joe wrote, "I find that you and your family have played an enormous role in everything that I truly enjoyed during a very crowded time. To be sure, that was already true when poor Phil was still alive. If it had not gone on being true, and in a bigger and bigger way, I hardly know what I should have done with the shank end of my long life."[17]

Alsop also began reaching out to those he felt he had wronged. Joe and Susan Mary had since reconciled—emotionally at least—and spent occasional evenings together, walking the familiar streets of Georgetown. (Alsop asked Paul Nitze to help Susan Mary look after her finances.) In a letter to Joe on their wedding anniversary, Soozle accounted the marriage "such a good show—it lasted a long time and gave great pleasure to many people—above all to me."[18]

Hoping, he wrote, to sort out the "desperately complicated" story of their relationship in wartime China, Joe exchanged a series of letters and long-distance telephone calls with John Paton Davies, who had since moved to Asheville, North Carolina. The eighty-year-old Davies thanked Alsop for his support at the various Senate and State Department investigations of the McCarthy era and offered this parting absolution of sorts: "So, cheer up, Joe!"[19]

In what he believed to be his final days, Alsop was ready to reveal the secret that had haunted his life and career for more than thirty years, writing to Tish in November 1988:

I have just arranged for Lew Ferguson to deliver to you a sealed letter, which he is now holding for me, when my time comes at last and the hampster [sic] cage is empty.

The sealed envelope contains a letter to Stew which I wrote from the Soviet Union. It is self-explanatory, and I send it to you in case various unpleasant persons use the Freedom of Information Act to get my government files after I am gone. In that event, I should like the letter to Stew to be published; for it deals with the only aspect of the affair that worries me.

I should add that I very much wanted to go public with the whole business but was dissuaded from doing so, indeed nearly ordered not to do so, by Chip Bohlen, who came to Paris for that purpose, among others.[*20]

A few months later, Alsop wrote to Marietta, "Unless my last and very depleting radiation treatment produces all sorts of miraculous results, my time is no longer very far away." In a three-page, handwritten codicil, Joe gave instructions on settling his estate. (The ornate candlesticks that he bought to celebrate John Kennedy's election Joe left to Susan Mary.) He also left instructions for his final hours: "People used to be allowed to die—indeed had to die—without being festooned with tubes for immeasurable purposes. I want *no tubes on any pretext.*" Among Joe's visitors at Georgetown University Hospital were Donald Graham—who brought the copy of Boswell's life of Johnson that Alsop had requested—and the *Post* reporter Walter Pincus, who smuggled in meals from Joe's favorite French restaurant after listening to the latter's incessant complaints about the hospital food. When radiation therapy failed to slow the disease, Alsop was sent home at his request, where he asked that his sickbed be moved into the study, closer to his books. Smoking his Carltons and drinking an occasional vodka toast with visitors, Joe said he had no fear of death—that he had recently read the end would be "like eating *foie gras* to the sound of trumpets." He again wrote to Marietta: "I seem to be an unconscionable time a-dying and, indeed, it begins to be doubtful whether the expected climax will occur at all."[21]

It came two months later, on August 28, 1989. Joe's body was found that morning next to his bed by Gemma Pozza, his longtime housekeeper. As Joe had requested, his memorial service was held, like Stewart's, at St. John's Episcopal Church without eulogies. The choir sang the same hymns as at Stewart's and their mother Corinne's funeral—ending

* Lew Ferguson, Joe's attorney, evidently delivered the letter to Tish after Joe's death, as instructed. Stewart's children believed their mother burned it.

with "God Be with You till We Meet Again," sung on the last Sunday evening of the long-ago summers at Henderson House. The wake at his brother John's house in Avon would be attended by Kay Graham, Polly Wisner, Tish Alsop, Susan Mary, and Gemma, who told Billy that in his final days Joe had been asking a question for which not even he pretended to have the answer: "Is there a God?"[22]

LESS THAN THREE MONTHS after Joe Alsop's death, the Berlin Wall came down—the beginning of the end for both the Soviet empire and the Cold War. The collapse of the U.S.S.R. late in 1991 also finally brought to a close what had been perhaps the longest continuous foreign policy debate in American history. For nearly fifty years, the protagonists in that debate, George Kennan and Paul Nitze, had engaged in a point-counterpoint exchange over whether it was Soviet capabilities or intentions that mattered more, and whether America's moral example or martial power was what kept the Russian bear at bay. Although the issues in contention were of obvious global importance, the debate itself was often surprisingly personal. Nitze and Kennan continued, each in his own way, to influence the administration in power—for good or ill.[23]

The two rivals even had dueling think tanks. Kennan's Institute for Advanced Russian Studies, headquartered at the Smithsonian castle on the Mall, was only blocks away from Nitze's School of Advanced International Studies on Washington's Massachusetts Avenue. But their namesakes remained seemingly worlds apart. As always, at the heart of their debate was the importance of military strength—and, specifically, the role of the bomb—in American diplomacy.

Paul Nitze had publicly resigned from the U.S. SALT delegation in mid-1974, complaining that Henry Kissinger was undermining the strategic arms negotiations through secret "back-channel" dealings with the Soviets. Although Nitze briefly held out hope, yet again, for a high-ranking Pentagon post following the 1976 election, it quickly became clear that President Jimmy Carter was more interested in reducing existing armaments than acquiring new ones. Within days of Carter's election, Nitze announced that he was joining with other conservatives in reviving the Committee on the Present Danger, a privately funded lobby for increased military spending whose original incarnation had been at the start of the Korean War. That fall, Nitze also joined Team B, a committee of like-minded scholars and defense experts who charged that the CIA had consistently underestimated the Soviet Union's military and economic strength. A memorandum that Nitze wrote for the hawkish group would give rise to the notion of a looming "window of vulnerability," during which time America's nuclear deterrent could be destroyed by a surprise Soviet first strike.[24]

Throughout the remainder of the 1970s and into the 1980s, Nitze and Kennan carried on their foreign policy feud through dueling essays, interviews, and newspaper op-eds, as well as with a brace of books. Shortly after Nitze announced creation of the new Committee on the Present Danger, Kennan began work on *The Cloud of Danger*, intended as a pointed rebuttal to those who, like Nitze, he accused of fearmongering. Likewise, "Advice to a Prophet," the poem by Richard Wilbur that Kennan chose as a preface to *The Nuclear Delusion*—an anthology of his writings, published in 1982—seemed aimed directly at Nitze: "Spare us all word of the weapons, their force and range, / The long numbers that rocket the mind."[25]

Continuing to decry what he called the "nuclear accountancy" and "military mathematics" of the Committee on the Present Danger and Team B, Kennan later that summer joined with three other elder statesmen of the atomic age—Robert McNamara, McGeorge Bundy, and the former SALT negotiator Gerard Smith—in calling for a U.S. policy of no first use of nuclear weapons. The idea that Kennan had originally put forward during the H-bomb debate of 1950 had been given fresh impetus by the nuclear-freeze movement of the early 1980s and by the endorsement it now received from the so-called gang of four.[26]

By then, however, there were signs that even Paul Nitze was beginning to come around to Kennan's way of thinking.

Returning, in July 1982, to the bargaining table with the Russians, this time as an arms control negotiator for the Reagan administration, Nitze undertook his own daring and out-of-channels initiative with his Soviet diplomatic counterpart, aimed specifically at ending a stalemate in the nuclear talks. But their so-called walk in the woods came to naught when Nitze and the Russian encountered opposition from both the Kremlin and the White House. It was not until four years later—during the 1986 summit meeting of Reagan and Gorbachev in Reykjavík, Iceland—that another opportunity arose to reduce the number and type of nuclear arms. At the summit, Nitze again discomfited his former political allies by proposing what he called "the grand bargain"—offering to trade the president's prized antimissile Strategic Defense Initiative, dubbed Star Wars by its critics, in exchange for radical reductions in land-based ICBMs, where the Soviets held an advantage. Ironically, Nitze's efforts were fatally undercut by his own earlier acolytes—eager young neocons who had since risen to positions of power in the Reagan administration.[27]

By the time the Soviet Union imploded, Nitze's views on the nuclear arms race had seemingly traveled full circle, returning to the same kind of controversial logic that had inspired his Asilomar speech more than a generation earlier. In a remarkable about-face, the man who invented the year of maximum danger and the window of vulnerability finally threw down his rhetorical weapons and disarmed. In a *Washington Post* op-ed on January 16, 1994, titled "Is It Time to Junk Our Nukes?," Nitze argued that since technology was making nuclear weapons obsolete, the United States should put greater reliance instead on precision-guided conventional munitions.

Shortly after Nitze's op-ed appeared, Kennan sent his perennial antagonist and ideological rival a personal note:

> Dear Paul: In the light of our long-standing friendship and mutual respect, it is a source of deep satisfaction to me to find the two of us, at our advanced ages, in complete accord on questions that have meant so much to each of us, even when we did not fully agree, in times gone by.[28]

But Kennan's disgust with the evolving U.S. domestic scene out-weighed any satisfaction that he might justifiably have felt about the long-awaited vindication of containment. The disaffected former dip-lomat denounced American triumphalism at the end of the Cold War as "intrinsically silly and childish." In what should have been a joyous occasion—a February 1994 valedictory dinner at the Council on Foreign Relations, celebrating Kennan's ninetieth birthday and the anniversary of the speech that led to his famous "X article"—the guest of honor glumly lectured his audience on the missed opportunities that might have short-ened or even averted the nearly half-century-long Soviet-American con-frontation.[29]

Like the modern-day equivalents of two other famous rivals, John Adams and Thomas Jefferson, George Kennan and Paul Nitze lived on into the new century that they had helped to shape. Kennan made his last diary entry in June 2000, concerning his plans for an authorized biography. Late in 2002, as the United States contemplated an invasion of Iraq, the ninety-eight-year-old Kennan warned of the unforeseen consequences likely to result from even a quick military victory over Saddam Hussein.[30]

Paul Nitze died on October 19, 2004, at age ninety-seven. In his memoirs, the logician and self-professed problem solver summed up his long life with a surprisingly emotional coda: "I have traveled, climbed mountains, caught fish, shot quail, played bridge, danced, loved, been loved in return, laughed, and cried." Kennan's death, at age 101, occurred just a few months later, in mid-March 2005. The man who had once criticized his fellow countrymen for making a "fetish of democracy" remained cranky and controversial to the end. In his final days, Kennan voiced support for a grassroots movement urging the citizens of Vermont to secede from the Union and declare the state an independent republic.[31]

THE DECLASSIFICATION IN 2007 of a treasure trove of former secrets—the CIA's so-called Family Jewels—shed a harsh and unforgiving light on some of the agency's Cold War activities. Among operations that the CIA itself deemed "questionable" in the 693 pages of previously top secret documents were multiple foreign assassination plots, Project Mockingbird's wiretapping of American journalists, and an abortive scheme by Frank Gardiner Wisner to "dispose of" some thirty-four Communists as part of Project Success, the 1954 overthrow of the Guatemalan government.[32]

Frank George Wisner followed in the family tradition of public service but, taking his father's advice, skirted the shadowy world of the CIA. Instead, he enjoyed a celebrated career in the diplomatic corps, eventually rising to the State Department's top ambassadorial rank. Between 1986 and 1994, Wisner would serve as the U.S. ambassador in a succession of diplomatic postings, including Zambia, Egypt, the Philippines, and India. Having been, in 1965, the youngest AID adviser in South Vietnam's Mekong delta, Frank witnessed the collapse of the Saigon regime a decade later from the vantage point of the State Department's Situation Room in Washington—helping to oversee the evacuation of Americans and their South Vietnamese allies as a member of the multiagency U.S.-Vietnam Task Force.[33]

In between his official diplomatic postings, the man who had been known as Metternich at the wartime Saigon embassy was chosen by the Pentagon and the State Department for some particularly sensitive missions, many having to do with preventing the global spread of weapons of mass destruction. In the early 1980s, Wisner was responsible for stopping a scheduled U.S. export of materials that could have assisted the apartheid regime of South Africa in adding a thermonuclear bomb to its existing arsenal of atomic weapons. More than a dozen years later, while ambassador to New Delhi, he slowed an escalating arms race in South Asia when he showed Indian officials a U.S. satellite photograph that revealed their preparations for a clandestine nuclear test.[34]

In another, nonlethal coup de main shortly after the collapse of the U.S.S.R., Frank presented Russian diplomats with irrefutable evidence proving that the Soviet Union, contrary to assurances, had continued to manufacture weaponized plague agents for offensive germ warfare. The Russians subsequently allowed Western inspectors to examine their secret bio-war facilities and agreed to destroy existing stockpiles. In his role as traveling troubleshooter for the American government, Wisner "believed in quiet diplomacy rather than open confrontation," wrote a reporter who chronicled the Russian "super-plague" story.[35]

Following his retirement from the Foreign Service in 1997, and after spending almost a decade in the private sector, Wisner would be chosen to represent the United States in negotiations aimed at securing the independent status of Kosovo.*[36] Since the new state would have a majority Albanian population, Frank, early in 2006, found himself in Tirana, an honored guest of the Albanian government at the dacha formerly occupied by Enver Hoxha, the Stalinist dictator whom Frank Gardiner Wisner had tried but failed to oust from power with Project Fiend. Sitting across Hoxha's antique desk from the elected president of a democratic, post-Soviet Albania, Frank George Wisner took a moment to savor the irony: "I just leaned back in my chair, looked up at the ceiling, and said to myself, 'Dad, I bet you won't believe where I am right now.'"[37]

---

* Wisner's career, in government and out, seems proof of the adage that timing is everything. Upon retiring from the Foreign Service, Wisner joined the board of directors for a subsidiary of the Houston-based Enron Corporation and also became vice-chairman for external affairs of the insurance giant American International Group, resigning in April 2009 after a liquidity crisis prompted the U.S. government to bail out AIG. Early in 2011, President Barack Obama made Wisner a special envoy to Egypt during the so-called Arab Spring. Part of Wisner's mission was reportedly to prod Hosni Mubarak, the Egyptian president, to undertake democratic reforms. If so, the effort came too late to prevent Mubarak's ouster in a popular revolt.

KATHARINE GRAHAM, the woman who would be dubbed, in Watergate's wake, the "Queen Bee of Washington," "Krusty Kay," "Our Lady of the Potomac," and the "Valkyrie of American Journalism," yielded control of her media empire only gradually—and, many thought, reluctantly—to the heir apparent, her son Donald. Following eighteen months spent as a beat cop on D.C.'s Metropolitan Police after he returned from Vietnam, Don Graham served a lengthy apprenticeship on his mother's newspaper. He officially took over as *Post* publisher early in 1979, becoming CEO of the Washington Post Company a dozen years later—just as the newspaper industry itself was starting to implode.[38]

During the time that she ran the *Post* empire, Katharine Graham had shown herself to be an able, no-nonsense manager: facing down the obstinate leader of a pressmen's union during a destructive strike in the 1970s, and guiding the Post company to unprecedented profits by the 1980s. Even when no longer at the helm of the *Post,* Kay Graham remained active in the role of roving reporter, traveling to various capitals to interview world leaders, often in the company of her friend and former *Newsweek* reporter Meg Greenfield, whom Graham made head of the *Post*'s editorial staff. In a journalistic coup of which Kay was particularly proud, during a 1988 trip to Moscow she and Greenfield interviewed Mikhail Gorbachev, who spoke candidly about the internal pressures building up inside the Soviet Union that would lead to its dissolution three years later.[39]

But Kay Graham's success came at some cost to her reputation, as she and her management style increasingly came under attack in her hometown—including from some within her own newspaper. *Post* veterans felt that Katharine's replacement of Al Friendly, the paper's managing editor since 1955, with Ben Bradlee, even if the right move, had been handled poorly—and showed Graham's insensitivity to the man who had been her family's longtime friend.

In November 1978, the rival Washington *Evening Star* published "The Katharine Graham Story," an unflattering five-part series that portrayed the *Post* publisher—in her view—"as a sort of Jekyll-Hyde." Several other major newspapers ran either the syndicated articles or news stories about the series, which irritated its subject even more by receiving generally good reviews from the critics. Katharine Graham found herself in an uncomfortable position when the author of the controversial *Star* series, Lynn Rosellini, married Graham Wisner, the youngest son of Kay's friend Polly. Katharine did not attend the wedding. (Kay got her revenge against the *Star* three years later, when the newspaper folded and the *Post* acquired its rival's building and printing presses, along with several of its top reporters.)[40]

Less than a year after Rosellini's negative portrait, the author Deborah Davis savaged Graham in a full-length biography, *Katharine the Great*. But Davis's book was withdrawn by the publisher, Harcourt Brace Jovanovich, shortly after it appeared, following veiled threats of a lawsuit by Ben Bradlee, who Davis claimed had actually been working for the CIA while a press officer at the U.S. embassy in Paris during the 1950s. At Katharine Graham's suggestion, Bradlee sent a sharply worded letter of protest to Kay's friend and the book's publisher, Billy Jovanovich, who reportedly ordered all twenty thousand copies of the offending volume shredded and pulped. ("I became a nonperson," Davis told a sympathetic interviewer. She later received a $100,000 breach-of-contract settlement from Harcourt, and a revised version of *Katharine the Great* would eventually be published by a boutique press.) There was an element of truth as well as humor behind Art Buchwald's toast to Kay at her seventieth birthday party in 1987: "If there is one thing that brings us all together here tonight, it is fear."[41]

Like Joe Alsop, Kay Graham discovered that the Georgetown dinner party had lost much of its drawing power and panache in the aftermath of Watergate. Since the *Post* endorsed the candidate Jimmy Carter over Gerald Ford in the 1976 presidential election, Kay was surprised, and then angered, when no one from the Carter White House showed up at the dinner she hosted for one of the president's fellow Georgians. An invitation sent to Carter's press secretary was not even acknowledged. Ironically, Kay's subsequent, unlikely friendship with Nancy Reagan—with whom Kay would admit to having "long gossipy lunches"—was viewed with suspicion and eventually condemned by Ronald Reagan's conservative allies, who feared their president was being co-opted by Washington's liberal insiders.[42]

For Kay, as for others in Georgetown, there was—as Graham observed to her friend Polly Wisner—the sense "that we had outlived our times." *Personal History*, her surprisingly sentimental and richly nostalgic memoir—published in 1997, and awarded the Pulitzer Prize for biography the following year—revealed that Kay, like her friend Joe Alsop a decade earlier, was looking more to the past than to the future. In *Katharine Graham's Washington*, an anthology of stories that she hoped would "bring to life her beloved city" but that remained uncompleted at the time of her death in 2001, Katharine wrote wistfully about the verbal jousting and "raging fights" that had taken place during Phil's day at the R Street house and around Joe Alsop's dining table: "They represented an important melding and fusion around social interaction, and helped to create a certain state of mind in Washington that no longer exists." It was a fitting, if unintended, valedictory for the era.[43]

"WE'RE ALL SO OLD OR DEAD," Susan Mary Alsop lamented in a 1996 *New Yorker* profile of Georgetown's famous personalities. After her divorce from Joe, Washington's feisty socialite had carried on, almost single-handedly, the tradition of the Georgetown salon. The *New York Times* reporter Maureen Dowd would describe Susan Mary as "a charming remnant of a patrician Washington that has largely disappeared" and the last representative of what Joe Alsop had once called "the ever-diminishing group of survivors of the WASP ascendancy." Since leaving Joe, Susan Mary had published four books of her own on the history of diplomatic life at the European courts, as well as a collection of the letters she sent to Marietta from postwar Paris. At seventy-five, Soozle became a contributing editor to *Architectural Digest*. (One of her articles in the *Digest,* "Social Graces in Georgetown," described the remodel of the Wisners' old P Street home by Polly and her second husband, the journalist Clayton Fritchey.) If, as the *New Yorker* profile observed, "Joe Alsop's career framed the natural life of the Georgetown set from its start to its real finish," then Susan Mary's passing in 2004 marked the end of a golden era in Washington's social life.[44]

Like Joe Alsop, the Georgetown set was a long time a-dying. A symbolic blow had fallen a decade earlier, when Joe's signature dish—terrapin soup—disappeared from Georgetown tables, its main ingredient having been declared a threatened species in Maryland and Virginia. Following Corinne Robinson's death, the ancestral Alsop homestead in Avon, Connecticut, would become part of a public golf course. At the fin de siècle, the *Washington Post* reporter Sally Quinn, Ben Bradlee's wife, wrote that power in the capital city had finally and decisively been supplanted by money, with the Sunday night suppers yielding to celebrity-studded fund-raisers. As if to prove Quinn's point, an attempt to revive the famous Georgetown salon—by the new, Harvard Business

School–educated publisher of *The Washington Post*, Katharine Weymouth, Kay Graham's granddaughter—faltered when it became known that prospective guests would pay up to $250,000 to attend a series of dinners with *Post* reporters.[45]

The traditional media empire that Phil Graham built and Kay Graham brought to international prominence with the Pentagon Papers and coverage of Watergate gradually unraveled in the first decade of the new century—the victim of competition from Internet Web sites and the digital preferences of a younger audience. *Newsweek* magazine, which Phil acquired in a celebrated journalistic coup for nine million dollars in 1961, would be sold for a single dollar in 2010. In 2013, following seven consecutive years of declining revenue, Donald Graham and Katharine Weymouth sold *The Washington Post* to the entrepreneur Jeff Bezos—a dot-com billionaire who, ironically, had made his fortune from the Web as an online bookseller—thereby putting an end to the Graham family's eight-decade-long dynasty and inaugurating an uncertain future for the *Post.*[46]

The transformation of political Washington, and of Georgetown, seemed irreversible. "The comedy had gone out of things," Ward Just observed during a visit to his old neighborhood. "The Republicans and Democrats were at each other's throats, and you had to be rich to live there. And we had all gotten older." Few elected representatives purchased homes in the capital anymore, preferring to live in rented apartments and fly home over the weekend to their families and constituents. Because of the enduring partisan divide in Congress, moreover, fewer still were eager to be seen fraternizing with colleagues from the other political party. Instead of spies, diplomats, and journalists, lobbyists and corporate moguls occupy the fancy houses of Kalorama and Georgetown.[47]

Social Washington had been similarly transformed. The cream-colored manse on P Street where Frank Gardiner Wisner had once traded cocktails and canapés for information was sold in 2002 to the failed presidential contender John Edwards—whose final political campaign became mired in a sex scandal—and later to the CEO of an investment firm specializing in hedge funds. Phil and Kay Graham's house on R Street was bought by a young venture capitalist, who spent much of his time elsewhere and reportedly disappointed neighbors by seldom entertaining at the historic Georgian mansion. What Joe Alsop called his Garage

Palladian house at 2720 Dumbarton Avenue changed hands in 2008 for over four million dollars. Although extensively remodeled inside by the new owner, a prominent D.C. real estate investor, the controversial ocher-colored stucco exterior remained untouched.[48]

IN APRIL 2012, a new play about Joe Alsop opened on Broadway. *The Columnist* was written by the Pulitzer Prize–winning playwright David Auburn and starred the Tony Award–winning actor John Lithgow in the lead role. Unlike with *Sheep on the Runway,* the previous Broadway play about Alsop, reviewers of *The Columnist* felt it necessary to explain to readers who the main character was and why he was important. "Nobody remembers Joseph Alsop now," wrote the theater critic for *The Wall Street Journal,* who described Alsop as "an all-but-forgotten writer." Other reviewers characterized Joe as "the most powerful journalist that everyone's forgotten," "a once-feared political pundit," and even "a defiant dinosaur." While the Alsop brothers' early attacks on McCarthy would be referenced in the play, along with the missile gap and Joe's friendship with John Kennedy, the opening scene was of Joe in a Moscow hotel room with his Russian lover in the late 1950s. And not surprisingly, the dramatic centerpiece of *The Columnist* would be Alsop's unwavering support for the war in Vietnam.[49]

During a fictional encounter on a Washington park bench in the late 1960s between Joe and his KGB lover, called Andrei in the play, it becomes clear just how out of touch Alsop has become: Joe dismisses the Beatles as "a silly fad" and has never heard of the movie *Dr. Strangelove.* ("I love my country," Alsop tells Andrei. "I just don't care very much for many of the people in it right now.") Later, when his judgment on Vietnam comes under fire, Joe's anguished outburst is a cri de coeur from an icon of the vanished WASP ascendancy: "For God's sake, don't expertise and authority mean anything anymore?" In the final scene, Joe—alone in his study, past deadline for his column—sits silently and dejected before his typewriter, without any idea of what to write.[50]

But *The Columnist* was also a period piece, a sometimes-nostalgic glimpse into a world unknown or largely forgotten by the contemporary audience: one devoid of celebrity-hosted talk shows and dueling Internet blogs; one where, while a cataclysmic war was always possible, it was of declining likelihood; where partisanship was no more muted, but civility generally prevailed; and where most Americans had not only faith in their institutions but also a collective belief in the country's ability—indeed, its obligation—to correct injustices in the world.

After three months and 109 performances, the final curtain closed on *The Columnist.*

ACKNOWLEDGMENTS

Several years of gratitude lie behind the researching and writing of this book. I would like to acknowledge, first, the contribution of my former student—and subsequent colleague—Dennis Hanks, who painstakingly located and scanned some three decades of the Alsops' newspaper column, Matter of Fact. Dennis is surely the world expert on the Alsops' writing at this time.

I would also like to thank the children of Frank Gardiner Wisner—Frank, Ellis, Graham, and Wendy—who graciously allowed me access to their father's personal papers and photographs, which they have since donated to the University of Virginia's Special Collections Library. Ellis was particularly generous with his time, guiding me on a tour of the historic houses of Georgetown, Locust Hill Farm, and other sites connected with Wisner family history and responding with patience to what probably seemed my endless series of questions. Likewise, Stewart Alsop's family—especially Joe and his wife, Christiane, and Elizabeth Winthrop Alsop—thoughtfully included me in their unforgettable "Alsopfest," the April 2012 family reunion that coincided with the opening of *The Columnist,* the Broadway play about their famous uncle and his "kinder, gentler" brother. The Alsop family also generously allowed me access to the private papers of Joe and Stewart. Bill Patten, Joe's stepson, donated several previously unpublished photographs from his mother's album for use in my book. The Wisners, the Alsops, and Donald Graham gave some fascinating details about the Georgetown set in personal interviews—as did Avis Bohlen, Ben Bradlee, Frances FitzGerald, and Ward Just. Tiki Davies, the daughter of John Paton Davies Jr., volunteered copies of the letters exchanged between her parents during her father's ordeal, a case of terror by tribunal.

I'm likewise grateful for the support, encouragement, and attention to detail of my new editor at Knopf, Andrew Miller, who, along with Mark Chiusano and Will Heyward, demonstrated his care for the manuscript in each of its several iterations. Andrew has already shown himself to be a worthy successor to legendary Knopf editor Ash Green. Emma Patterson of Brandt & Hochman gallantly took over the project following the untimely death of my longtime agent, Carl Brandt.

My thanks as well to those who read the manuscript, in whole or part, and thereby attempted to save me from errors of fact or interpretation: Kai Bird, David Brick, Bill Burr, Jim Hershberg, Barbara Maloney, Stan Norris, and Tom Powers. Several archivists—the unsung heroes of historians—contributed significantly to this work: Spencer Howard at the Herbert Hoover Presidential Library located memorandums and correspondence in the Lewis Strauss Papers relevant to the infamous "Moscow incident" involving Joe Alsop. Adriane Hanson at Princeton's Seeley Mudd Library helped solve a mystery about a meeting at Lake Geneva between George Kennan and Paul Nitze. Claryn Spies of Yale's Sterling Library located a rare photograph of Carmel Offie. Charlie Niles at the Howard Gotlieb Archival Research Center offered a helpful—and humorous—introduction to Stewart Alsop's papers at Boston University. Scott Taylor assisted in obtaining permission for my use of a photograph found in Richard Helms's papers at Georgetown University. Similarly, photo archivists at the Library of Congress pointed me to an "unprocessed" collection of Alsop photographs. The library's John Haynes tried valiantly—if unsuccessfully—to remove restrictions on the journalist Meg Greenfield's papers in time for them to be seen by me. Bob St. Francis, general manager of Washington's Sulgrave Club, gave me a memorable tour of the venue for D.C.'s famous Dancing Class.

Several other writers and researchers also selflessly assisted in my research. The CIA historian David Robarge and the scholar Hayden Peake helped identify historic personages in agency photographs—also offering sympathy and encouragement throughout my contest with the CIA's rigid and arcane declassification bureaucracy. David Coleman collegially shared documents he gathered for his excellent book on the Cuban missile crisis, *The Fourteenth Day. The Georgetown Set* could not have been written—or the project even begun—if not for some earlier books on Cold War–era journalism and espionage. Most notable among these are Robert Merry's authoritative biography of the Alsop brothers, *Taking On the World;* Burton Hersh's *Old Boys,* a work of truly prodigious research and gifted writing; and Evan Thomas's *Very Best Men,* one of the first books to peer into the CIA's world of secrets. Three forthcoming volumes promise to add much to our knowledge of that period: Avis

Bohlen is writing a highly anticipated biography of her father, Charles "Chip" Bohlen. Sherry Thompson Miller and Jenny Vujacic are at work on a similarly important biography of their father, Llewellyn "Tommy" Thompson. Martha Wyckoff and Jennifer Price are well along on a biography of Martha's relative the former CIA director John McCone. All of the above generously shared their research, answered my questions, and pointed out new documents and promising interview subjects.

I would also like to acknowledge the financial and emotional assistance of my colleagues at the University of California. The Humanities Institute at UC Merced provided additional funding for research, while the History Department at UC Santa Cruz welcomed me back to my undergraduate alma mater as a senior associate, and the UC Washington Center—UCDC—provided a familiar home away from home during numerous trips to the capital; all have graciously allowed me to maintain a multicampus faculty status.

A heartfelt thank-you to my friends Jean and Jim Poole of Alexandria, Virginia, as well as Sam and Barbara Dyer, residents of Washington, D.C. As my generous hosts during repeat trips to the nation's capital, they made what is by its nature a lonely enterprise—the writing of a book—a companionable experience. And, finally, a long-overdue acknowledgment to my soul mate and the love of my life, who encouraged me through this project with patience and good humor. Aven, it couldn't have been done without you. Thank you.

NOTES

Abbreviations Used in the Notes

CIA/CREST   CIA Records Search Tool, National Archives, College Park, Md.
DDRS   Declassified Documents Reference System, Library of Congress, Washington, D.C.
DNSA   Digital National Security Archive, nsarchive.chadwyck.com
Fiend Records   Nazi War Crimes and Japanese Imperial Government Disclosure Acts, 1936–2002, RG 263, National Archives and Records Administration, College Park, Md.
FRUS   U.S. Department of State, *Foreign Relations of the United States*
FRUS/EIE   *Foreign Relations of the United States, 1945–1950: Emergence of the Intelligence Establishment,* www.history.state.gov
FRUS/IC   *Foreign Relations of the United States, 1950–1955: The Intelligence Community,* www.history.state.gov
GFKP   George F. Kennan Papers, Seeley Mudd Library, Princeton University
HGARC/BU   Herbert Gotlieb Archival Research Center, Boston University
JFKL   John F. Kennedy Library, Boston
JWA   Joseph Wright Alsop
JWAP   Joseph Wright Alsop Papers, Library of Congress, Washington, D.C.
KTC/DNSA   Kissinger Telephone Conversations, Digital National Security Archive
NARA   National Archives and Records Administration, College Park, Md.
NYHT   *New York Herald Tribune*
NYT   *New York Times*
PPS/SD   Records of the Policy Planning Staff, 1947–1953, U.S. Department of State, RG 59, National Archives and Records Administration, College Park, Md.
SEP   *Saturday Evening Post*
WP   *Washington Post*

PROLOGUE "Salonisma": When Washington Worked

1. Merry, *Taking On the World*, 156; Beran, *Last Patrician*, 27; Blumenthal, "Ruins of Georgetown," 228.
2. Braudy, "Camelot's Second Lady," 158; Heymann, *Georgetown Ladies' Social Club*, 11.
3. Blumenthal, "Ruins of Georgetown," 221.
4. Greenfield, *Washington*, 57–58.

CHAPTER ONE "A Political Village"

1. Tuchman, *Stilwell and the American Experience in China*, 358.
2. Merry, *Taking On the World*, 63; Susan Mary Alsop, *To Marietta from Paris*, 43.
3. Stewart Alsop, *Stay of Execution*, 25.
4. Stewart Alsop to Sylvan Barnet, Sept. 6, "1957" folder, box 129, JWAP.
5. Merry, *Taking On the World*, 153.
6. Mark, "OSS in Romania," 321.
7. Hazard, *Cold War Crucible*, 72; Dobbs, *Six Months in 1945*, 111–13; Murphy, Kondrashev, and Bailey, *Battleground Berlin*, 456n.
8. Thomas, *Very Best Men*, 19–23; Burton Hersh, *Old Boys*, 189–94.
9. Graham, *Personal History*, 146; P. Graham to Commanding Officer, April 14, 1943, box 286, OSS Records, RG 226, NARA.
10. Halberstam, *Powers That Be*, 158–70; Graham, *Personal History*, 91–93, 138, 158.
11. Andrew Stephen, "Georgetown's Hidden History," *WP*, July 16, 2006. "Until 1945, Georgetown was a predominantly black, typical Southern village," noted Susan Mary. Spade and Archer Inc., *50 Maps of Washington, D.C.*, 3–4; Heymann, *Georgetown Ladies' Social Club*, 48.
12. Jay Franklin, "Main Street-on-Potomac," in Graham, *Katharine Graham's Washington*, 22–27.
13. Stewart Alsop, "The Drama of Conflict," in Graham, *Katharine Graham's Washington*, 56; Leibovich, *This Town*, 141.
14. Joseph Alsop, "Dining-Out Washington," in Graham, *Katharine Graham's Washington*, 136–46.
15. Katharine Graham, "Social Washington," in Graham, *Katharine Graham's Washington*, 109–15.
16. Ibid., 113–15, 122.
17. Years later, near the end of his life, Joe told Teeny "he had discovered that women were better company than men." Author interview with Corinne "Teeny" Zimmermann, Oct. 30, 2012, Washington, D.C.
18. The suppers, writes Evan Thomas, were "a mixture of trust, patriotism, and mutual manipulation." Sunday night suppers: Thomas, *Very Best Men*, 104; Holzman, *James Jesus Angleton*, 186; Merry, *Taking On the World*, 155, 158; Streitfeld, "The Hawk and the Vultures."
19. Joseph Alsop, *"I've Seen the Best of It,"* 94.
20. Author interviews: Ellis Wisner and Boyden Gray, Nov. 17, 2009, Washington, D.C.; and Elizabeth Winthrop Alsop, April 30, 2012, New York City; Patten, *My Three Fathers*, 232, 334; Joan Braden, *Just Enough Rope*, 99.
21. Joseph Alsop, "I'm Guilty!"; Braudy, "Camelot's Second Lady," 168; Collier, "Joe Alsop Story," 64.

22. Just, *In the City of Fear,* 35–36; Greenfield, *Washington,* 6.

23. As a CIA operative observed, the "Alsop method" was also what he and his spy colleagues used to pry secrets out of a source: "You ignite a spark and watch it build into a bonfire." Heymann, *Georgetown Ladies' Social Club,* 61; Blumenthal, "Ruins of Georgetown," 223; Isaacson and Thomas, *Wise Men,* 431–2; author interview with Elizabeth Winthrop Alsop, April 30, 2012, New York City.

24. JWA to Susan Mary Patten, Sept. 13, 1947, Joseph Alsop Private Papers.

25. "He was an odd man, sophisticated, talented, arrogant." Halberstam, *The Best and the Brightest,* 499; Halberstam, *Powers That Be,* 449.

26. JWA to Susan Mary Patten, Aug. 1947, Joseph Alsop Private Papers; Ritchie, *Reporting from Washington,* 64; Miller, "Washington, the World, and Joseph Alsop"; diary entry of Nov. 30, 1987, folder 2, box 326, GFKP. One Alsop relative had a simple explanation for Joe's unusual pronunciation: "It wasn't fake. It's Connecticut." Author interview with Tim Zimmermann, April 29, 2012, New York City.

27. Blumenthal, "Ruins of Georgetown," 226.

28. Collier, "Joe Alsop Story," 64; Joy Billington, "Joe Alsop, the Art of Being a Washington Mandarin," *Washington Star,* March 12, 1979.

CHAPTER TWO   "Some Higher Realm of Intellect and Power"

1. "The Case of Harry Truman," *NYHT,* Dec. 31, 1945; Almquist, *Joseph Alsop and American Foreign Policy,* 47–51.

2. Schlesinger, *Life in the 20th Century,* 378; Schlesinger and Schlesinger, *Letters of Arthur Schlesinger, Jr.,* 501–2. "This new social order was less preoccupied with the old snobberies of class and heritage than with one's level of accomplishment or, more specifically, one's proximity to power." Joseph Alsop, *"I've Seen the Best of It,"* 275.

3. Author interview with Corinne Zimmermann, Oct. 30, 2012, Washington, D.C.; de Margerie, *American Lady,* 42.

4. De Margerie, *American Lady,* 69, 73.

5. Joseph Alsop, *"I've Seen the Best of It,"* 438; Susan Mary Alsop, *To Marietta from Paris,* ix; Patten, *My Three Fathers,* 63; Seebohm, *No Regrets,* 14; Braudy, "Camelot's Second Lady," 156.

6. Herken, *Winning Weapon,* 53; JWA to Crossman, Nov. 22, "1946" folder, box 2, JWAP.

7. JWA to Chennault, Feb. 25, "1946" folder, box 2, JWAP.

8. "Moscow Talks Emphasize Lack of American Policy on Russia," *NYHT,* Jan. 4, 1946. "My feelings about our own people are just the other way around." JWA to Lippmann, Jan. 30, 1945, folder 38, box 50, Lippmann Papers, Library of Congress.

9. Susan Mary Alsop, *To Marietta from Paris,* 41.

10. "Washington, Jittery at Power of New Weapons, Keeps Silent," *NYHT,* Jan. 27, 1946.

11. Kluger, *Paper,* 414; Ridder, "Brothers Cassandra, Joseph and Stewart"; Merry, *Taking On the World,* 168; Ritchie, *Reporting from Washington,* 138.

12. "Acheson Atomic Control Report May Give Fresh Start to Congress," *NYHT,* March 24, 1946.

13. Isaacson and Thomas, *Wise Men,* 141–42; Weisbrode, *Atlantic Century,* 16–18; Merry, *Taking On the World,* 56.

14. Bohlen, *Witness to History,* 116; Isaacson and Thomas, *Wise Men,* 720; Susan Mary Alsop, *To Marietta from Paris,* 76.

15. "They found themselves returning again and again to the men who served as their most reliable and willing sources: Chip Bohlen and George Kennan." Merry, *Taking On the World,* 172; Nicholas Thompson, *The Hawk and the Dove,* 57–62; Bailey, *Marshall Plan Summer,* 10.

16. Gaddis, *George F. Kennan* (hereafter cited as *GFK*), 172–200.

17. Nicholas Thompson, *The Hawk and the Dove,* 7–8; Gaddis, *GFK,* 194.

18. Kennan, *Memoirs, 1925–1950,* 290–95; "Trip to Novosibirsk and Stalinsk," June 1945, folder 13, box 231, and Kennan to Bohlen, Jan. 26, 1945, folder 4, box 140, and Kennan to Freeman Matthews, Aug. 21, 1945, folder 6, box 28, GFKP.

19. Nicholas Thompson, *The Hawk and the Dove,* 51. Chip Bohlen's daughter Avis believed that Kennan was "more emotionally dependent" than her father: "My father was not much given to introspection." Author interview with Avis Bohlen, Nov. 16, 2009, Washington, D.C.

20. Kennan, *Memoirs, 1925–1950,* 293–95.

21. Joseph Alsop, *"I've Seen the Best of It,"* 272–73; Weisbrode, *Atlantic Century,* 80.

22. "Trip to Novosibirsk and Stalinsk"; Gaddis, *GFK,* 201–22.

23. Bailey, *Marshall Plan Summer,* 8–10; Lilienthal, *Journals,* 158.

24. Forrestal had already approached other Soviet experts about possible responses to the new threat, which he believed combined traditional Russian nationalism with "the additional missionary force of a religion." Hoopes and Brinkley, *Driven Patriot,* 266–69.

25. Millis, *Forrestal Diaries,* 135–40.

26. Kennan, *Memoirs, 1925–1950,* 326; Gaddis, *GFK,* 264–65.

27. Hixson, *George F. Kennan,* 97; Nitze, *From Hiroshima to Glasnost,* 85; Weisbrode, *Atlantic Century,* 97.

28. Weisbrode, *Atlantic Century,* 108; Behrman, *Most Noble Adventure,* 56.

29. "Planners don't talk," Marshall had reportedly advised members of his Policy Planning Staff. Isaacson and Thomas, *Wise Men,* 423.

30. "The Kennan Dispatch," *NYHT,* May 23, 1947; Barrett, *CIA and Congress,* 172.

31. As the historian David Mayers points out, it was not a hereditary aristocracy that Kennan favored so much as an "aristocracy of character and mind"—that is, a meritocracy. Mayers, *George Kennan and the Dilemmas of U.S. Foreign Policy,* 62.

32. Joseph Alsop, *"I've Seen the Best of It,"* 274; Isaacson and Thomas, *Wise Men,* 171. "He used to castigate people who talked openly about an 'American aristocracy,' " wrote Susan Mary's son, Bill, about his future stepfather. "Joe was obsessed with people's pedigrees. What made him squirm was when people talked about it openly." Patten, *My Three Fathers,* 169.

33. Diary entry of Oct. 5, 1992, folder 2, box 325, GFKP. Kennan "seemed to relish being unappreciated and misunderstood." Isaacson and Thomas, *Wise Men,* 24, 72–73.

34. Merry, *Taking On the World,* 74; Billington, "Joe Alsop, the Art of Being a Washington Mandarin"; Alterman, *Sound and Fury,* 48.

35. Merry, *Taking On the World,* 5–7, 74–75.

36. Alsop and Alsop, "Lament for a Long-Gone Past."

37. Gill, *New York Life,* 15–20; Merry, *Taking On the World,* 3–22; Joseph Alsop, *"I've Seen the Best of It,"* 40–53.

38. Patten, *My Three Fathers,* 232; Yoder, *Joe Alsop's Cold War,* 35; author interview with Corinne "Teeny" Zimmermann, Oct. 30, 2012, Washington, D.C.

39. Alsop and Alsop, "Lament for a Long-Gone Past."

40. Merry, *Taking On the World,* 44, 63–68.

41. But the two Kennans had very different views of prerevolutionary Russia. Frazier, *Travels in Siberia*, 58–60.

42. Gaddis, *GFK*, 47.

43. Kennan, *Memoirs, 1925–1950*, 11.

44. Nicholas Thompson, *The Hawk and the Dove*, 120.

45. Isaacson and Thomas, *Wise Men*, 229; Gaddis, *GFK*, 114–16.

46. Gaddis, *GFK*, 66.

47. "The Kennans seemed to have passed their neuroses along from generation to generation like the family bible. But I am not ashamed of them. They never lost their pride; they never begged; they never cheated. They were never mean, except to themselves." Kennan to his children, n.d. [1942], folder 9, box 140, GFKP; Gaddis, *GFK*, 13–14.

48. Kennan, *Sketches from a Life*, 114; Gaddis, *GFK*, 638.

49. Kennan to Acheson, May 23, 1947, folder 3, box 140, GFKP.

50. Reston, *Deadline*, 145; JWA to Acheson, Feb. 25, "1947" folder, box 2, JWAP; Reston, "The No. 1 No. 2 Man in Washington," *NYT*, Aug. 25, 1946; Isaacson and Thomas, *Wise Men*, 86.

51. Kennan, *Memoirs, 1925–1950*, 295.

52. "X" [George Kennan], "Sources of Soviet Conduct," 572–82. "The thesis of the X article . . . was that our main problem was a political one and that we had a good chance of coping with it by political means—(at least means short of a full-scale shooting war)—if we would stop moping, face up to the situation cheerfully and realistically, and conduct ourselves rationally, in terms of our own epoch." Kennan to Acheson, Jan. 3, 1949, folder 2, box 1, GFKP.

53. Joe Alsop claimed he had been given "a sort of précis" of the X article before its publication. Joseph Alsop, *"I've Seen the Best of It,"* 272; Kennan, *Memoirs, 1925–1950*, 354–57.

54. Behrman, *Most Noble Adventure*, 56.

55. Etzold and Gaddis, *Containment*, 102–6.

56. Bohlen, *Witness to History*, 263–65. Some phrases in Marshall's speech were lifted directly from Kennan's May 23, 1947, PPS paper. Jones, *Fifteen Weeks*, 250.

57. "Chip, for all his personal style, had a notorious tin ear and, as a rule, wrote very badly." Joseph Alsop, *"I've Seen the Best of It,"* 282. Bohlen's daughter Avis confirmed that her father's eloquence was not matched by his written prose, a fact also noted in Chip's State Department fitness report. Author interview with Avis Bohlen, Nov. 16, 2009, Washington, D.C.

58. During the winter and spring, Lippmann consulted regularly with Acheson and Kennan on the plans for European recovery, focusing on that issue in "Cassandra Speaking," his column for April 5, 1947. Jones, *Fifteen Weeks*, 144, 226–27, 237; Steel, *Walter Lippmann and the American Century*, 442–48; Kindleberger, *Marshall Plan Days*, 26.

59. Schlesinger, *Life in the 20th Century*, 382.

60. JWA to Lippmann, Jan. 30, [1945], folder 38, box 50, reel 40, Lippmann Papers, Yale University; author interview with Walter Pincus, Nov. 2, 2011, Washington, D.C. "In crisis situations, [Lippmann] urged negotiation and diplomatic discourse; Alsop wanted to send in the Marines." Wasniewski, "Walter Lippmann, Strategic Internationalism, the Cold War, and Vietnam," 122n.

61. On Arthur Krock, see American National Biography Online, www.anb.org.

62. "Byrnes Is Taking a Plan to Paris for Over-All Europe Settlement," *NYHT*, April 24, 1946; Kindleberger, *Marshall Plan Days*, 26.

CHAPTER THREE "Is War Inevitable?"

1. Elizabeth Winthrop Alsop, *Don't Knock Unless You're Bleeding*, 15, 19–23.
2. JWA to Susan Mary Patten, Sept. 1946, Joseph Alsop Private Papers; author interview with Elizabeth Winthrop Alsop and Joseph Alsop VI, April 30, 2012, New York City.
3. Stewart Alsop, "America Must Fish or Cut Bait," *NYHT,* Feb. 24, 1947; Joseph Alsop, "Panic and Paralysis in Face of World Crisis," *NYHT,* Feb. 26, 1947; Susan Mary Alsop, *To Marietta from Paris,* 89.
4. Acheson, *Present at the Creation,* 220–25.
5. Behrman, *Most Noble Adventure,* 101; Bailey, *Marshall Plan Summer,* 10.
6. "Will Taft Join Vandenberg?," *NYHT,* July 29, 1947; "Decide We Must," *NYHT,* Oct. 19, 1947; "Schism in the Republican Soul," *NYHT,* Jan. 12, 1948.
7. Graham, *Personal History,* 113–17; Halberstam, *Powers That Be,* 165–66; Felsenthal, *Power, Privilege, and the "Post,"* 117; Joseph Alsop, *"I've Seen the Best of It,"* 431.
8. Felsenthal, *Power, Privilege, and the "Post,"* 53; Roberts, *In the Shadow of Power,* 233; Lynn Rosellini, "The Katharine Graham Story," *Washington Star,* Nov. 15, 1978.
9. Roberts, *In the Shadow of Power,* 288. Eugene Meyer's testimony is in U.S. Congress, Senate, *Hearings Regarding the European Recovery Program,* 626–39. Kern, Levering, and Levering, *Kennedy Crises,* 18; Pusey, *Eugene Meyer,* 363.
10. Wala, "Selling the Marshall Plan at Home," 247–65.
11. "More than any other government document, the final report of the Harriman Committee converted the press to the cause of the true believers." Machado, "Selling the Marshall Plan," 17, 21; Abramson, *Spanning the Century,* 417; "Ex-Gov. Averell Harriman, Adviser to 4 Presidents, Dies," *NYT,* July 27, 1986.
12. Abramson, *Spanning the Century,* 603; Isaacson and Thomas, *Wise Men,* 618.
13. www.theardenhouse.com.
14. "Impatient, stubborn, and sometimes lacking diplomatic skills," Bissell was "the driving intellectual force in the Marshall Plan's eventual success." Abramson, *Spanning the Century,* 430.
15. Bissell, *Reflections of a Cold Warrior,* 1, 12–13.
16. Ibid., 6; Merry, *Taking On the World,* 26, 37–38; Thomas, *Very Best Men,* 90–91. "They had gone, by and large, to the same schools, Groton, again and again, Groton." Salisbury, *Without Fear or Favor,* 565.
17. Bissell, *Reflections of a Cold Warrior,* 15–18.
18. "Interview with Richard Bissell, June 16, 1966," box 867, Harriman Papers; Bissell, *Reflections of a Cold Warrior,* 35–37; "U.S. Report on Marshall Plan Is Said to Drop Ban on Socialism," *NYHT,* Nov. 2, 1947; "Pork Chops and the Marshall Plan," *NYHT,* Dec. 5, 1947.
19. "All the top *Post* reporters pitched in in what was a major effort to aid the Marshall Plan and Truman Doctrine." Roberts, *In the Shadow of Power,* 288. The insert was co-sponsored by the Foreign Policy Association. Graham, *Personal History,* 177; "Marshall Plan's Birth on Plane Told by Paper," *Los Angeles Times,* Nov. 23, 1947. The author thanks the Marshall Foundation for a copy of "This Generation's Chance for Peace."
20. Behrman, *Most Noble Adventure,* 149.
21. Diary entry of Jan. 23, 1948, folder 13, box 231, GFKP.
22. Herken, "Great Foreign Policy Fight," 66; Nicholas Thompson, *The Hawk and the Dove,* 42.

23. "Interview with Paul Nitze, April 20, 1984," "Alexander Calder, 1932–84" folder, box 20, Nitze Papers; Nicholas Thompson, *The Hawk and the Dove,* 30–31; "Interview with Paul Nitze, April 30, 1996," Archives of American Art, Smithsonian Institution, Washington, D.C., www.aaa.si.edu.

24. Nicholas Thompson, *The Hawk and the Dove,* 31; Kennan, *Sketches from a Life,* 8–9.

25. Kennan, *Sketches from a Life,* 4.

26. Nicholas Thompson, *The Hawk and the Dove,* 37; author interview with Paul Nitze, May 11, 1983, Washington, D.C.

27. Nitze to Oppenheimer, March 23, 1954, box 35, and Nitze to Berlin, Feb. 6, 1956, box 18, Nitze Papers. "Nitze was a polished, articulate man with a knack for convincing himself and others that he had knowledge of a subject when he, in fact, had little or none." Sheehan, *Fiery Peace in a Cold War,* 109.

28. Nitze, *From Hiroshima to Glasnost,* xvii–xxii; Herken, "Great Foreign Policy Fight," 67–68.

29. Nicholas Thompson, *The Hawk and the Dove,* 95.

30. Author interview with Paul Nitze, July 12, 1984, Washington, D.C.

31. U.S. Strategic Bombing Survey, *Japan's Struggle to End the War,* 13; Robert P. Newman, *Truman and the Hiroshima Cult* (Michigan State University Press, 1995), 42–45.

32. Nicholas Thompson, *The Hawk and the Dove,* 11–15; Nitze, *From Hiroshima to Glasnost,* 46–53.

33. Nitze, *Tension Between Opposites,* 118.

34. Susan Mary Alsop, *To Marietta from Paris,* 115.

35. Bissell, *Reflections of a Cold Warrior,* 37–38; Nitze, *From Hiroshima to Glasnost,* 58–60.

36. "European Recovery Program: Estimated Balance of Payments on Current Account of the Participating Countries, 1 April 1948–30 June 1949," "Brown Books, 1948–49" folder, box 96, Nitze Papers.

37. Nicholas Thompson, *The Hawk and the Dove,* 79–82; Kindleberger, *Marshall Plan Days,* 235; Behrman, *Most Noble Adventure,* 186, 303; Nitze, *From Hiroshima to Glasnost,* 66.

38. "What I consider is that you've got to argue very hard, and sometimes in a polemical manner." Author interview with Paul Nitze, June 1, 1981, Rosslyn, Va., Nitze, *From Hiroshima to Glasnost,* 64–65. There was evidently a personal element as well to Taber's attack. Fearful that Nitze might be picked to administer the Marshall program, Taber had sought "derogatory information" about the witness from the FBI in advance of the hearings. Nicholas Thompson, *The Hawk and the Dove,* 81.

39. Isaacson and Thomas, *Wise Men,* 419–38.

40. Susan Mary Alsop, *To Marietta from Paris,* 84–85.

41. JWA to Sheean, Aug. 5, "1947" folder, box 3, JWAP.

42. Steel, *Walter Lippmann and the American Century,* 444–46; Gaddis, *GFK,* 273.

43. Wasniewski, "Walter Lippmann, Strategic Internationalism, the Cold War, and Vietnam," 402; JWA to Lippmann, Feb. 16, "1950" folder, box 5, JWAP.

44. Halberstam, *Powers That Be,* 368–69; Schlesinger, *Life in the 20th Century,* 382; Wasniewski, "Walter Lippmann, Strategic Internationalism, the Cold War, and Vietnam," 296.

45. JWA to Lippmann, n.d. [1950], folder 38, box 50, Lippmann Papers, Library of Congress.

46. Joseph Alsop, *"I've Seen the Best of It,"* 274.

47. In his 1947 speech, Kennan noted that in addition to the "small mobile forces" made up of units from all three armed services, the United States would need to maintain the ability "to mobilize our strength rapidly if a clear threat of major war developed." Kennan, *Memoirs, 1925–1950,* 311; and *Memoirs, 1950–1963,* 248–49. Kennan's 1957 Reith Lectures presumed the prior withdrawal of Soviet and Western occupation forces from Germany. The dispute between Nitze and Kennan over the latter's alleged comment about marine divisions continued into the mid-1980s. Author interview with Paul Nitze, July 12, 1984, Washington, D.C.; Kennan to Herken, Nov. 5, 1985, folder 3, box 20, GFKP; Nicholas Thompson, *The Hawk and the Dove,* 300–302; Gaddis, *GFK,* 524; Isaacson and Thomas, *Wise Men,* 447, 496.

48. Berlin to Kennan, Feb. 13, 1951, folder 5, box 5, GFKP. Kennan had written, "American effort in aid to Europe should be directed not to the combating of communism as such but to the restoration of the economic health and vigor of European society." PPS-1, "Policy with Respect to American Aid to Western Europe," in Etzold and Gaddis, *Containment,* 102–7.

49. Alsop and Alsop, "If Russia Grabs Europe"; Buhite and Hamel, "War for Peace," 375; JWA to Sulzberger, April 13, "1948" folder, box 3, JWAP.

50. Nitze, *From Hiroshima to Glasnost,* 77–81.

51. Harvard Law Forum to JWA, Feb. 4, "1948" folder, box 3, JWAP.

CHAPTER FOUR "Would He Go into the Woods?"

1. Graham, *Personal History,* 166–67; "Remembering Katharine Graham," *WP,* July 18, 2001; Schroeder, *Snowball,* 384–86.

2. Heymann, *Georgetown Ladies' Social Club,* 10–11.

3. While Fitin "heartily welcomed" Donovan's initiative, the subsequent history of the OSS-KGB exchange showed it to be decidedly one-way. Bradley Smith, *Shadow Warriors,* 337–40.

4. The documents include the so-called Vassiliev Notebooks, brought to the United States by the former KGB agent Alexander Vassiliev in 2005 and available online at the Wilson Center's Cold War International History Project's Web site, www.wilsoncenter.org. White Notebook no. 1, 28, 85–87, 90–96, 102–5.

5. Lee had evidently been recruited by the Soviets in the 1930s and subsequently gave the KGB the names of other OSS operatives who he thought might be sympathetic to their cause. Costigliola, *Roosevelt's Lost Alliances,* 283. White Notebook no. 1, 93; Haynes, Klehr, and Vassiliev, *Spies,* 314–17.

6. "On 10 Jan. 1945 the material was passed along to Gromyko." White Notebook no. 1, 102.

7. Ibid., 105. In September 1944, Donovan informed President Roosevelt, "In order to prevent future misunderstandings, I am sending General Fitin lists of OSS personnel in Bulgaria and Romania as requested by him." Dunlop, *Donovan,* 456.

8. By the end of the year, Donovan had blown the cover of OSS agents in Bulgaria, Romania, and Yugoslavia and also revealed the identity of U.S. operatives about to be sent to Czechoslovakia. Bradley Smith, *Shadow Warriors,* 350–51.

9. Haynes, Klehr, and Vassiliev, *Spies,* 293–94; White Notebook no. 1, 105; Costigliola, *Roosevelt's Lost Alliances,* 284. The OSS station in Moscow was shut down on Au-

gust 30, 1945. Two weeks later, Truman abolished Donovan's organization. Bradley Smith, *Shadow Warriors,* 358.

10. White Notebook no. 1, 94.

11. Graham, *Personal History,* 134–35; Halberstam, *Powers That Be,* 170; Haynes, Klehr, and Vassiliev, *Spies,* 262–68; Ford, *Flying Tigers,* 54.

12. Graham, *Personal History,* 155–57; Nitze, *From Hiroshima to Glasnost,* 19–20; Haynes, Klehr, and Vassiliev, *Spies,* 17–31, 220–25.

13. Coincidentally, Price belonged to the same Washington, D.C.–based espionage ring as Duncan Lee, the OSS officer who spied on Donovan as the KGB agent Koch. Haynes, Klehr, and Vassiliev, *Spies,* 146–52, 173–76, 242–52.

14. The former CIA director William Colby claimed that when the OSS was under attack by J. Edgar Hoover in early 1945, Donovan called upon Alsop and Braden to wage a propaganda campaign promoting the spy agency's wartime exploits. Colby, *Honorable Men,* 59. Donovan also arranged for portions of the Alsop-Braden book to appear in major newspapers as feature articles. Merry, *Taking On the World,* 120, 151.

15. Alsop and Braden, *Sub Rosa,* 279–85.

16. "Draft of Narrative for Granting of Award to Captain Stewart J. O. Alsop . . . ," Dec. 30, 1944, "Alsop, Stewart" folder, box 12, OSS Records, RG 226, NARA; Stewart Alsop to "David," June 25, 1963, folder 10A, Stewart Alsop Papers, HGARC/BU.

17. Alsop and Braden, *Sub Rosa,* 7–8.

18. Joseph Alsop, *"I've Seen the Best of It,"* 365; Pisani, *CIA and the Marshall Plan,* 30. Kermit Roosevelt headed the CIA's Middle East desk in the 1950s.

19. Bradley Smith, *Shadow Warriors,* 340; "Foreign Secret Service Control May Fall into Hands of FBI," *NYHT,* April 30, 1946; Milton Ladd to Hoover, May 14, 1946, *FRUS/EIE,* 279.

20. "Battle Shaping Up over Proposal for Central Intelligence Agency," *NYHT,* Jan. 12, 1947; Burton Hersh, *Old Boys,* 184.

21. "Digest of Progress Report on the Central Intelligence Group," June 7, 1946, CIA/CREST; Weiner, *Legacy of Ashes,* 13; Richard Helms, *A Look over My Shoulder,* 70.

22. Weiner, *Legacy of Ashes,* 24–25; "Battle Shaping Up over Proposal for Central Intelligence Agency."

23. Richard Helms, *A Look over My Shoulder,* 73.

24. As the Truman aide Clark Clifford later explained, "The 'other' functions the CIA was to perform were purposely not specified but we understood that they would include covert activities. We did not mention them by name because we felt it would be injurious to our national interest to advertise the fact that we might engage in such activities." Rudgers, "Origins of Covert Action," 249.

25. Corson, *Armies of Ignorance,* 294–95; CIA, ORE 47/1, "The Current Situation in Italy," Feb. 16, 1948, in Warner, *CIA Under Harry Truman,* 181–89.

26. CIA History Staff, "The Office of Strategic Services: America's First Intelligence Agency" (Center for the Study of Intelligence, 2000), www.cia.gov/news; Robarge, "Moles, Defectors, and Deceptions, 23–47; and Robarge, "'Cunning Passages, Contrived Corridors,'": 43–55.

27. Winks, *Cloak and Gown,* 322–72; Burton Hersh, *Old Boys,* 178–83; Holzman, *James Jesus Angleton,* 79–87.

28. "Weekly Staff Meeting for Wed., 3 March 1948," www.cia.gov/foia; JWA to Angleton, April 9, "1948" folder, box 3, JWAP.

CHAPTER FIVE "To Fight Fire with Fire"

1. Author interview with Ellis Wisner, Nov. 17, 2009, Washington, D.C.; Thomas, *Very Best Men,* 17–19; Burton Hersh, *Old Boys,* 189–94.

2. A 1945 fitness report in Frank Wisner's OSS dossier described him as an "energetic, intelligent and confident young lawyer who is proud of his past work in the Balkans." "Theater Service Record," Feb. 5, 1945, "Wisner, Frank G." folder, box 847, OSS Records, RG 226, NARA; Tom Braden, "Birth of the CIA," 1–10.

3. Salisbury, *Without Fear or Favor,* 569.

4. Hazard, *Cold War Crucible,* 44, 89. Whatever covert cover Frank and his men had was blown within a month of their arrival in Bucharest, when Donovan sent Fitin a list of OSS agents in Romania.

5. "Citation for Legion of Merit," n.d., "Wisner, Frank G." folder, box 847, OSS Records, RG 226, NARA; Dobbs, *Six Months in 1945,* 114; Mark, "OSS in Romania," 324, 338n.

6. Tom Braden, "Birth of the CIA," 6; Murphy, Kondrashev, and Bailey, *Battleground Berlin,* 456n.

7. Wisner wrote to Dulles that he planned "to take up my duties" in Washington on or about October 9, 1947. Wisner to Dulles, Oct. 1, 1947, "Frank Wisner, 1947–1968" folder, box 59, Allen Dulles Papers; Thomas, *Very Best Men,* 24–25; Wisner, "Summary of Soviet-Communist Tactics Employed in Gaining Political and Economic Control of Rumania," n.d., "Rumanian Paper—Frank G. Wisner" folder, Wisner Papers.

8. Burton Hersh, *Old Boys,* 240.

9. Saunders, *Cultural Cold War,* 37–38.

10. Conant, *Irregulars,* 56, 120; Nichols, *Washington Despatches,* x.

11. Berlin and Hardy, *Letters,* 372.

12. Diary entry of Dec. 17, 1945, folder 13, box 231, GFKP. In early 1946, Isaiah Berlin wrote to a friend in England, "The State Department specialists, i.e., Chip and all his friends, take exactly the same view as George Kennan and all the people you know in Moscow, and there is no basic difference of view with us." Berlin and Hardy, *Letters,* 623.

13. Berlin and Hardy, *Letters,* 627. "I am as devoted to [Joe] as ever but I cannot deny that after six hours of black on black I begin to wilt and even show signs of wishing to go to bed." Berlin to Schlesinger, May 18, 1951, "Isaiah Berlin, 1949–1954" folder, box P-9, Schlesinger Papers.

14. Hazard, *Cold War Crucible,* 197; Weiner, *Legacy of Ashes,* 18–19.

15. Kennan to Robert Murphy, May 10, 1945, folder 5, box 140, GFKP; Nicholas Thompson, *The Hawk and the Dove,* 16–18; Gaddis, *GFK,* 139.

16. Kennan to Charles Cuningham, Feb. 1, 1951, folder 7, box 139, GFKP; Nicholas Thompson, *The Hawk and the Dove,* 84–85. Hilger was reportedly also implicated in an SS ruse that falsely reassured Italian Jews that they would not be shipped to concentration camps in the east. "It is thus beyond dispute that Hilger criminally assisted in the genocide of Italy's Jews," a National Archives researcher concluded. Wolfe, "Gustav Hilger," 1–6.

17. Richard Helms, *A Look over My Shoulder,* 83–91. Late in 1948, Rusty was taken over "lock, stock and barrel" by the CIA. "Minutes of Meeting of 27 Dec. 1948," "Gustav Hilger" folder, box 22, CIA Records, RG 263, NARA.

18. Simpson, *Blowback,* 116; Kennan to John Lewis Gaddis, Nov. 19, 1987, "Christopher

Simpson" folder, box 44, GFKP; Kennan to "Mr. Nicholson," July 14, 1950, and "Conversation with Mr. Kennan . . . ," Nov. 14, 1950, "Gustav Hilger" folder, box 22, CIA Records, RG 263, NARA. Following the German surrender, a U.S. Army intelligence officer expressed bemused wonderment at the fact that one branch of his government was hunting Ukrainian Nazis for prosecution while another—Wisner's—was busy recruiting them. Thomas, *Very Best Men,* 35–36; Loftus, *Belarus Secret,* 10–12, 54–56, 85.

19. "Among Kennan's many idiosyncrasies was a fascination . . . with the practice and product of intelligence as it was then understood—the clandestine collection of secret information." Grose, *Operation Rollback,* 7. Others have commented on Kennan's early interest in U.S. covert operations, and likewise his later reluctance to take responsibility for helping to initiate them. See Weiner, *Legacy of Ashes,* 533–34n; Nicholas Thompson, *The Hawk and the Dove,* 83; Corke, *U.S. Covert Operations and Cold War Strategy,* 81; Miscamble, *George F. Kennan and the Making of American Foreign Policy,* 110.

20. "There were so many spies that they completely obliterated each other," observed a British diplomat of wartime Lisbon. Gaddis, *GFK,* 159; Grose, *Operation Rollback,* 17.

21. Vandenberg to Secretary of State, June 27, 1946, folder 4, box 140, GFKP; U.S. Department of State, *Foreign Relations of the United States: 1947,* vol. 5, 466–69; Wright, "Mr. 'X' and Containment," 29. Kennan disavowed the notion of invading Taiwan the same day that he proposed it, probably in the face of withering criticism, and later attributed the idea to John Davies. Gaddis, *GFK,* 357, 402.

22. *FRUS/EIE,* 615–21; Weiner, *Legacy of Ashes,* 25–26.

23. Gaddis, *GFK,* 305; Holzman, *James Jesus Angleton,* 80; Burton Hersh, *Old Boys,* 222.

24. Simpson, *Blowback,* 90–92.

25. Houston to Hillenkoetter, Sept. 25, 1947, *FRUS/EIE,* 622–23. Houston's warning turned out to be prescient: "Taken out of context and without knowledge of history, these Sections could bear almost unlimited interpretation, provided the service performed could be shown to be of benefit to an intelligence agency or related to national intelligence." Rudgers, "Origins of Covert Action," 255. Corson, *Armies of Ignorance,* 294–98; Hoopes and Brinkley, *Driven Patriot,* 315.

26. Hilly and Souers both suspected a bait and switch: namely, an effort to take the job of intelligence away from the CIA and give it to another agency, which would also have responsibility for covert operations. Souers "said most of the effort now seemed to come from State, and specifically George Kennan." E. K. Wright, "Memorandum for the Record," May 6, 1948, CIA/CREST; Kennan to Lovett and Marshall, May 19, 1948, *FRUS/EIE,* 684–85.

27. "The Inauguration of Organized Political Warfare," April 30, 1948, "Political and Psych. Warfare, 1947–1950" folder, box 11A, PPS/SD; *FRUS/EIE,* 618, 685.

28. *FRUS/EIE,* 713–15. A declassified CIA history of OPC described NSC 10/2 as a "treaty between the Secretaries of State and Defense that gave the office two, competing masters." Subsequently, the CIA director Richard Helms wrote that the new organization was "*of* but not *in* the CIA" and a "lame compromise." Richard Helms, *A Look over My Shoulder,* 113; Warner, "CIA's Office of Policy Coordination," 211–19; Gerald Miller, "Office of Policy Coordination, 1948–1952," n.d., CIA/CREST.

29. *FRUS/EIE,* 702. A month later, according to Christopher Simpson, the U.S. Joint Chiefs of Staff extended OPC's clandestine mandate—in the event of war—to include "miscellaneous operations such as assassination, target capture and rescue of downed airmen." Simpson, *Blowback,* 101–2.

30. Kennan to Lovett, June 30, 1948, *FRUS/EIE*, 716.

31. Barrett, *CIA and Congress*, 50; Miller, "Office of Policy Coordination, 1948–1952," 9. As one intelligence historian has observed, in Wisner "the times and the man seem to have met . . . Under Wisner and his associates, covert action became a growth industry for the CIA." Rudgers, "Origins of Covert Action," 257; *FRUS/EIE*, 720–21, 728–29.

32. Project Umpire was to be followed by Project Ultimate, a plan to drop propaganda leaflets behind the Iron Curtain using weather balloons. Thomas Cassady to R. E. Dulin, March 11, 1948, *FRUS/EIE*, 653–54; Corke, *U.S. Covert Operations and Cold War Strategy*, 51; Gaddis, *GFK*, 318.

33. Davies, *China Hand*, 8–54.

34. "Well, if nobody else is going to jump, I'll jump. Somebody has to break the ice," Davies told the sixteen petrified passengers. Ibid., 109–11; Kahn, *China Hands*, 29–30; Hazard, *Cold War Crucible*, 193; Sevareid, *Not So Wild a Dream*, 245.

35. "Davies, with his brilliant, imaginative mind and his wide background of experience in China, was a rock of strength to us at that time in the Moscow embassy." Kennan, *Memoirs, 1925–1950*, 239; Davies to Kennan, Jan. 25, 1949, and Davies to "Mr. Krentz," Sept. 7, 1949, "John Paton Davies, 1947–1949" folder, box 45, U.S. State Department Records, RG 59, NARA.

36. Davies, *Dragon by the Tail*, 396. Although appointed by Kennan in August 1947, Davies did not officially become a member of the Policy Planning Staff until the summer of 1950. Corke, *U.S. Covert Operations and Cold War Strategy*, 74, 194n; Davies, *China Hand*, 261–2.

37. Joyce would later be John Davies's replacement on the State Department's oversight committee for OPC. Hazard, *Cold War Crucible*, 193–94, 227n; Miscamble, *George F. Kennan and the Making of American Foreign Policy*, 110; Reynolds, "Ernest Hemingway," 1–14; Haynes, Klehr, and Vassiliev, *Spies*, 152–55.

38. Looking back, years later, at the origins of U.S. covert operations, Paul Nitze was amused that America's so-called Department of Dirty Tricks had had its start with his friends in proper and staid Georgetown: "Kennan proposed it, Frank Wisner ran it, and Bob Joyce . . . was the State Department liaison."

39. Morgan, *Covert Life*, 218.

40. Stewart Alsop would later write to Wisner that he was glad he had turned down the job: "Dear me, do you suppose I would be in Dick Helms' shoes if you had succeeded in that recruiting attempt? The thought chills my blood." Wisner to Stewart Alsop, Jan. 22, 1964, and Stewart Alsop to Wisner, Jan. 27, 1964, "Stewart Alsop" folder, Wisner Papers. Lindsay background: Burton Hersh, *Old Boys*, 116–18, 236–37; Lindsay, *Beacons in the Night*; Corke, *U.S. Covert Operations and Cold War Strategy*, 85.

41. Kennan, *Memoirs, 1925–1950*, 59; Isaacson and Thomas, *Wise Men*, 159; Thayer, *Bears in the Caviar*, 106–14.

42. Unfortunately, both horse and falcon dropped dead before Thayer could realize his dream. Shortly thereafter, he was transferred to London for OSS training. Thayer, *Bears in the Caviar*, 280.

43. The OSS, Thayer later wrote, had an "inability to envisage conditions behind enemy lines where passions were strong, risks enormous, and the costs of failure supreme." Thayer, *Diplomat*, 170–71.

44. Weiner, *Legacy of Ashes*, 25–26. The study by Thayer and Lindsay "laid out in scholarly prose the human and organizational requirements for waging secret warfare against the Soviet Union." Hoopes and Brinkley, *Driven Patriot*, 310–14.

45. Wisner to Dulles, Oct. 1, 1947, folder 6, box 59, Dulles Papers; Burton Hersh, *Old Boys,* 173–76; Kinzer, *Brothers,* 73–75, 85–87.

46. Wisner to Dulles, March 10, 1948, folder 6, box 59, Dulles Papers. Later, Wisner commissioned a report on the subject: "Study of Russian Anti-Communist Forces in the German War," Feb. 17, 1949, www.cia.gov/foia.

47. Richard Helms, *A Look over My Shoulder,* 65.

48. Ibid., 56, 63–65; Schlesinger, *Life in the 20th Century,* 350.

49. Murphy, Kondrashev, and Bailey, *Battleground Berlin,* 105; Corson, *Armies of Ignorance,* 306–10; Srodes, *Allen Dulles,* 401.

50. Richard Helms, *A Look over My Shoulder,* 47–48.

CHAPTER SIX "Some Brave New Approach"

1. Alsop and Alsop, "Must America Save the World?," 71–77.

2. Almquist, *Joseph Alsop and American Foreign Policy,* 51; Sorensen, *Counselor,* 287; Merry, *Taking On the World,* 173; Millis, *Forrestal Diaries,* 487–88; Isaacson and Thomas, *Wise Men,* 431–32.

3. The author is grateful to Jim Sayler for drawing his attention to Krock's response to the Alsops' article.

4. Acheson, *Present at the Creation,* 223–25; Arnold Offner, *Another Such Victory: President Truman and the Cold War, 1945–1953* (Stanford University Press, 2002), 198–99.

5. Merry, *Taking On the World,* 175; "Big Easy 103," *NYHT,* Dec. 27, 1948. Divided Germany was likewise the inspiration for Joe Alsop's only work of fiction, a January 1948 story in *The New Yorker* magazine about murder in Soviet-occupied Berlin. Joseph Alsop, "Evening Among Ruins." The author thanks Elizabeth Winthrop Alsop for bringing Joe's story to my attention.

6. PPS-35, "The Attitude of This Government Toward Events in Yugoslavia," in Etzold and Gaddis, *Containment,* 169–72.

7. Merry, *Taking On the World,* 173; "The Tito Trouble; Subject: The Schism Between Tito and the Soviet Union," *NYHT,* July 2, 1948. A subsequent Alsop column, which leaked the fact that the United States had decided to covertly supply the Tito government with weapons and other aid, "deprived the Americans of any bargaining-counters in dealing with the Yugoslavia government." Heuser, *Western "Containment" Policies in the Cold War,* 119; "All Aid Short of War," *NYHT,* Oct. 5, 1949.

8. Merry, *Taking On the World,* 174–75; JWA to Clifford, Dec. 1, "1948" folder, box 4, JWAP.

9. Halberstam, *Coldest Winter,* 210.

10. Alterman, *Sound and Fury,* 12; "Notorious Joe: Behold here the Moscow comment on the 'ghoulish dream' of the panicky, cynical and bestially frank American warmongers and militarists—the brothers Alsop!" Sir John Balfour to JWA, Jan. 8, "1948" folder, box 3, JWAP.

11. Kluger, *Paper,* 414.

12. Isaacson, *Kissinger,* 584; Collier, "Joe Alsop Story"; "The News in the Garden," *WP,* March 18, 1974.

13. Merry, *Taking On the World,* 188, 239; Stewart Alsop, *Stay of Execution,* 85–89; JWA to "Judy darling," June 25, "1952" folder, box 8, JWAP.

14. Joseph Alsop, "I'm Guilty!," 31–38.

15. Merry, *Taking On the World*, 186; Yoder, *Joe Alsop's Cold War*, 34.

16. "Alsop House a Standout in Georgetown," *Washington Times*, March 11, 2005. The author would like to thank Sue Kohler, architectural historian for the U.S. Commission of Fine Arts, for information on the Alsop house.

17. Sarah Booth Conroy, "The House That Alsop Built: A Man and His Taste," *WP*, Sept. 29, 1974.

18. Schlesinger to JWA, Nov. 11, "1949" folder, box 5, JWAP.

19. Joe called the experience of remodeling the house an "almost indescribable horror." JWA to "Prich," Sept. 12, "1949" folder, box 5, JWAP.

20. Susan Mary Alsop, *To Marietta from Paris*, 139.

21. Nelson, *War of the Black Heavens*, 35–36; Walter Hixson, *Parting the Curtain: Propaganda, Culture, and the Cold War* (St. Martin's Press, 1997), 32; Kennan to Acheson, Jan. 3, 1949, folder 2, box 1, GFKP.

22. Kennan, *Memoirs, 1925–1950*, 437.

23. Ibid., 439–40.

24. Corke, *U.S. Covert Operations and Cold War Strategy*, 76–77; author interview with Paul Nitze, Oct. 18, 1979, Rosslyn, Va.; Nitze, *From Hiroshima to Glasnost*, 50; Mayers, *George Kennan and the Dilemmas of U.S. Foreign Policy*, 133–34.

25. Nicholas Thompson, *The Hawk and the Dove*, 91–93; Nitze, *From Hiroshima to Glasnost*, 70–71; Isaacson and Thomas, *Wise Men*, 530.

26. Nicholas Thompson, *The Hawk and the Dove*, 92; "Boldness at Last," *NYHT*, Sept. 2, 1949; Miscamble, *George F. Kennan and the Making of American Foreign Policy*, 288–89. Kennan told Acheson that Joe had admitted the leak came from "someone close to the White House." Kennan to Acheson, Sept. 2, 1949, folder 2, box 1, GFKP.

27. Miscamble, *George F. Kennan and the Making of American Foreign Policy*, 36; Kennan to Bohlen, Nov. 17, 1949, folder 2, box 140, GFKP; Joyce to Leonard Schapiro, Sept. 15, 1976, "Robert Joyce" folder, box 28, Nitze Papers.

28. Internet conspiracy theorists have suggested that Forrestal was actually murdered by Soviet spies, or possibly by Mossad agents, because of his opposition to creation of the state of Israel. While some of Forrestal's "paranoia" turns out to have been justified—he was right in believing that the U.S. government had been penetrated by Russian spies—his personal papers at Princeton leave little doubt that he was deeply depressed for some time prior to his death. Weiner, *Legacy of Ashes*, 38; Hoopes and Brinkley, *Driven Patriot*, 313–14; "The Fall of James Forrestal," *WP*, May 23, 1999; www.dcdave.com/article4/041120a.html.

29. Merry, *Taking On the World*, 209–11. The first Matter of Fact column on the "criminal folly" of the China hands appeared early in 1948. "I have already re-written the column three times to eliminate from it anything that might seem to point in John [Davies's] direction," Alsop wrote to Kennan. JWA to Kennan, Feb. 18, "1948" folder, box 3, JWAP.

30. Joseph Alsop, "Feud Between Stilwell and Chiang," "We Opened the Door for the Communists," and "Foredoomed Mission of General Marshall"; Davies, *China Hand*, 322–24.

31. "We were just like two elderly, once rival, now retired prostitutes, sitting in our rocking chairs and cackling about our respective triumphs," Alsop wrote of his meeting with Davies. Diary entry of Aug. 31, 1949, folder 17, box 231, GFKP; JWA to Martin Sommers, June 4, "1949" folder, box 26, JWAP.

32. "I shan't again talk to you about China," Joe promised Kennan. JWA to Kennan,

Sept. 21, "1949" folder, box 5, JWAP; Kennan to JWA, Sept. 27, 1949, folder 1, box 140, GFKP.

33. "Oh, What a Tangled Tale," *NYHT,* Jan. 23, 1950.

34. Oshinsky, *Conspiracy So Immense,* 108–10.

35. "Present Loyalty Program Seen Putting Premium on Ignorance," *NYHT,* Aug. 22, 1948; "The Mystery," *NYHT,* March 15, 1948; Schlesinger, *Life in the 20th Century,* 467–70.

36. "Lawyer's Analysis of Evidence Finds Hiss's Innocence Possible," *NYHT,* Jan. 9, 1949; Beisner, *Dean Acheson,* 289; Weinstein, *Perjury,* 159, 345n; Tanenhaus, *Whittaker Chambers,* 383n; Dean, *Imperial Brotherhood,* 75.

37. "Senator McCarthy and His 'Big Three,'" *NYHT,* March 5, 1950.

CHAPTER SEVEN "A Land of Conspiracy, Run by Conspirators"

1. Richard Helms, *A Look over My Shoulder,* 73–74. On the occasion of the CIA's fiftieth anniversary, Helms, in a speech to other agency veterans, waxed nostalgic: "Do you remember those hot summer days in Tempos K and L and others? On the second floor we learned the difference between perspiration and sweat." "50th Anniversary Address," Sept. 17, 1997, box 10, Helms Papers; Weiner, *Legacy of Ashes,* 32; author interview with Ellis Wisner, Nov. 17, 2009, Washington, D.C.

2. Colby, *Honorable Men,* 73; *FRUS/EIE,* 670–71; Wisner to CIA Director, "OPC Projects," Oct. 29, 1948, in Warner, *CIA Under Harry Truman,* 241–42; Lucas and Mistry, "Illusion of Coherence," 39–66.

3. Operation Bloodstone: Thomas, *Very Best Men,* 25; Burton Hersh, *Old Boys,* 226; Riebling, *Wedge,* 99. In 1947, a veteran of Wisner's wartime Romanian campaign published a satirical novel titled *Operation Bughouse,* about the Bloodstone operation.

4. Wisner to CIA Director, "OPC Projects," Oct. 29, 1948, in Warner, *CIA Under Harry Truman,* 241–42; *FRUS/EIE,* 653–54. One historian of Radio Free Europe writes that if Kennan was RFE's father, then Wisner was its uncle. Cummings, *Cold War Radio,* 101.

5. *FRUS/EIE,* 670, 719.

6. Wilford, *Mighty Wurlitzer,* 30–32; Richard Helms, *A Look over My Shoulder,* 354; Hazard, *Cold War Crucible,* 204; Burton Hersh, *Old Boys,* 256–60.

7. CIA History Staff, "A Look Back . . . the National Committee for a Free Europe, 1949" (Center for the Study of Intelligence, May 2007), www.cia.gov/news; Joseph Grew to Kennan, Oct. 28, 1954, folder 6, box 138, and Wisner to Kennan, Nov. 6, 1954, folder 8, box 52, GFKP; Johnson, *Radio Free Europe and Radio Liberty,* 36. Church Committee hearings: "Supplementary Detailed Staff Reports on Foreign and Military Intelligence," bk. 4, April 23, 1976 (U.S. Government Printing Office, 1976), 30; also www.maryferrell.org. Kennan told his authorized biographer in the 1980s, "I should never have accepted for the PPS the duty of giving political advice to Wisner's outfit." Gaddis, *GFK,* 319, 724n.

8. One OPC official recalled of the counterpart funds, "We couldn't spend it all . . . There were no limits and nobody had to account for it. It was amazing." Lucas and Mistry, "Illusion of Coherence," 59n.

9. Bissell, *Reflections of a Cold Warrior,* 68; Pisani, *CIA and the Marshall Plan,* 82; Wisner, "CIA Responsibility and Accountability for ECA Counterpart Funds Expended by OPC," Oct. 17, 1949, in Warner, *CIA Under Harry Truman,* 321–22.

10. Loftus, *Belarus Secret,* 72; Simpson, *Blowback,* 102, 311n; Weiner, *Legacy of Ashes,* 29.

11. Wilford, *Mighty Wurlitzer,* 32–35. "The prospect of blanketing Eastern Europe with timely propaganda material fascinated Frank, and it was balloons away!" Richard Helms, *A Look over My Shoulder,* 355; Hillenkoetter to Louis Denfeld, June 18, 1948, *FRUS/EIE,* 715.

12. Wilford, *Mighty Wurlitzer,* 226–27; Thomas, *Very Best Men,* 63; Stewart Alsop to June Bingham, April 28, 1961, folder 4A, box 5, Stewart Alsop Papers.

13. Gaddis *GFK,* 318. In an earlier meeting with Wisner, Kennan had emphasized that as the State Department's designated representative, "he would want to have specific knowledge of the objectives of every operation and also of the procedures and methods employed." *FRUS/EIE,* 720, 728–29; Corke, *U.S. Covert Operations and Cold War Strategy,* 62; Lucas and Mistry, "Illusions of Coherence," 59; Wilson Miscamble, "George Kennan: A Life in the Foreign Service," *Foreign Service Journal* 87, no. 5 (May 2004): 22–34.

14. *FRUS/EIE,* 724–25, 734. Pressed to come up with some ideas for "more aggressive" covert initiatives, Kennan suggested Poland as a possible future theater of operations for OPC. Gaddis, *GFK,* 354.

15. Kennan to Wisner, Oct. 19, 1948, "Gustav Hilger" folder, box 263, CIA Records, RG 263, NARA; Klaus Mehnert to Kennan, Dec. 15, 1948, folder 1, box 140, GFKP. Tish Alsop, after painting radiators while on her hands and knees at Kennan's farm one weekend, compared the experience to working on a prison press gang. Kennan, *Memoirs, 1925–1950,* 305; Isaacson and Thomas, *Wise Men,* 435.

16. Nelson, *War of the Black Heavens,* 49; Grose, *Gentleman Spy,* 328–29; Memorandum for file, "Operation Flattop," April 21, 1949, "Political and Psych. Warfare, 1947–1950" folder, box 11A, PPS/SD; *FRUS/EIE,* 734–35, 741–42.

17. Radio Free Europe: Nelson, *War of the Black Heavens,* 56; Thompson, *Radio Free Europe and Radio Liberty,* 26–28; Thomas, *Very Best Men,* 61. AMCOMLIB: F. Wisner, "History of Project," Aug. 21, 1951, doc. no. 16, Cold War International History Project, Woodrow Wilson International Center for Scholars, Washington, D.C., www.wilsoncenter.org.

18. CIA History Staff, "Origins of the Congress for Cultural Freedom, 1949–50" (Center for the Study of Intelligence, n.d.), www.cia.gov/news; Saunders, *Cultural Cold War,* 86–89.

19. Thomas, *Very Best Men,* 63.

20. William Bullitt's letter to a friend shows that the "royal dwarf" was already, in 1936, casting a magic spell: "You will be pleased to learn that last night Offie was the guest of honor at Maxim's at a dinner given the Marquis and Marquise de Polignac, who are the greatest snobs in France." Burton Hersh memorably wrote of Wisner's man, "Offie left the Foreign Service straining to maintain dignity, like somebody spotted pantsless emerging from a brush fire." Bullitt, *For the President,* 172, 273; Thomas, *Very Best Men,* 34–36; Burton Hersh, *Old Boys,* 245, 252, 295, 442, 446; Joseph J. Trento, *The Secret History of the CIA* (Random House, 2001), 48; Pisani, *CIA and the Marshall Plan,* 76–78.

21. Dallek, *Unfinished Life,* 57.

22. Morgan, *Covert Life,* 212, 232; Weiner, *Enemies,* 177, 479–80n.

23. Wilford, *Mighty Wurlitzer,* 60.

24. Prados, *Safe for Democracy,* 60–61.

25. A quarter century later, Hunt would help plan the infamous Watergate break-in. Hunt, *American Spy,* 34–40.

26. OPC was only a few weeks old when it came into conflict with the FBI. In a modus vivendi worked out between Wisner, Hoover, and the CIA's general counsel, Larry Houston, on September 22, 1948, Wisner reportedly agreed to recognize the "primary responsibility of the FBI in the field of United States domestic security." Riebling, *Wedge,* 100–101.

27. One theory held that Offie had bought up expensive apartments in Paris when they were being vacated by the retreating Germans and sold them to American expatriates after the war. Srodes, *On Dupont Circle,* 266–67; Burton Hersh, *Old Boys,* 444–45; Weisbrode, *Atlantic Century,* 107–8.

28. The FBI evidently began keeping a file on Offie in February 1950. Riebling, *Wedge,* 117; Srodes, *On Dupont Circle,* 267, 312n.

29. "Proposal to Overthrow Present Regime in Albania," Jan. 11, 1949, folder 1, vol. 13, box 48, ZZ-19, Fiend Records.

30. Bethell, *Betrayed,* 34–36. The official history of MI6 notes the British had earlier concluded that "two great powers cannot operate independently in small countries such as Greece and Albania." Jeffery, *Secret History of MI6,* 713.

31. PPS 59, "United States Policy Toward the Soviet Satellite States in Eastern Europe," Aug. 25, 1949, box 4, PPS/SD; Corke, *U.S. Covert Operations and Cold War Strategy,* 77; Schaller, *American Occupation of Japan,* 253–54. Joyce was reportedly "the most active supporter of the [Albanian] proposal." Aldrich, *Hidden Hand,* 161.

32. "Meeting on Albania," May 4, 1949, "Memo of Conversation with King Zog," May 5, 1949, and "Disagreement with COP's Reaction to [Redacted]," n.d., folder 1, vol. 13, box 48, Fiend Records.

33. Britain's recruits were "a motley crew of over 200 volunteers, mostly in a poor state of health, a proportion of whom were almost certainly working for Albanian state security." Aldrich, *Hidden Hand,* 162. The teams were to be recruited from so-called displaced persons camps located throughout Western Europe. Hazard, *Cold War Crucible,* 201.

34. Untitled transcript, June 10, 1949, Enver Hoxha file, box 57, CIA Records, RG 263, NARA. The author would like to thank Bill Burr of the National Security Archive for locating the transcripts of Wisner's oral briefings of Project Fiend.

35. "In this operation we have not considered employing directly any of the resources of the National Military Establishment. As events progress we may, however, have to ask for a limited amount of air power or naval assistance." Untitled transcript, June 10, 1949, Enver Hoxha file, box 57, CIA Records, RG 263, NARA.

36. Philby, *My Silent War,* 193–94; Thomas, *Very Best Men,* 66.

37. "Let us, therefore, be constantly on the lookout for ways in which to make our funds go further, not only in this project but in others," Wisner instructed Offie. "Project Outline for *Fiend,*" June 22, 1949, and Wisner to Offie, July 1, 1949, folder 1, vol. 2, box 46, Fiend Records.

38. Acheson to Italian embassy, Aug. 25, 1949, U.S. Department of State, *FRUS: 1949,* vol. 1, 318–19.

39. Prados, *Safe for Democracy,* 62.

40. Richard Helms, *A Look over My Shoulder,* 355–57; Burton Hersh, *Old Boys,* 271–72.

41. Stewart Alsop, *Center,* 235.

42. Bethell, *Betrayed,* 71–79, 95.

43. "The First British Operation, September 1949–October," n.d., folder 2, vol. 13, box 48, Fiend Records; Fiend File, "Sept.–Oct.–Nov. 1949 Notes" folder, box 8, Burke Papers.

44. C. L. Sulzberger, "West Held Easing Stand on Albania," *NYT,* March 27, 1950.

CHAPTER EIGHT "Why Has Washington Gone Crazy?"

1. Diary entry of Sept. 23, 1949, folder 17, box 231, GFKP.
2. "The Beria Bomb: I," *NYHT,* Sept. 26, 1949; "The Beria Bomb: II," *NYHT,* Sept. 28, 1949; "Dirty Words," *NYHT,* Sept. 30, 1949.
3. Diary entry of Oct. 5, 1949, folder 17, box 231, GFKP.
4. Diary entry of Sept. 30, 1949, folder 17, box 231, GFKP.
5. "I guess I'd overreacted to Moscow," Davies sheepishly explained to Joe. Joseph Alsop, *"I've Seen the Best of It,"* 271. Early in 1946, Joe had written of Davies, "A few months of Moscow have totally transformed him, and he is now compounding his former errors by even greater and no more judicious violence on the anti-Russian side." JWA to Chennault, Feb. 25, "1946" folder, box 2, JWAP; "In the Matter of John Paton Davies," *NYHT,* Nov. 10, 1954.
6. Diary entry of Sept. 30, 1949, folder 17, box 231, GFKP.
7. Nicholas Thompson, *The Hawk and the Dove,* 97.
8. Untitled notes, n.d., "Atomic Energy, 1948–1950" folder, box 50, PPS/SD.
9. Untitled draft, Nov. 18, 1949, "George Kennan" folder, box 43, Oppenheimer Papers; Herken, "Great Foreign Policy Fight," 72–73; Gaddis, *GFK,* 379.
10. Nitze would later credit Davies with providing "some of the more telling phrases" for NSC 68, including one that amounted to its *leitmotif:* "to frustrate the Kremlin's design." Nicholas Thompson, *The Hawk and the Dove,* 111–14; Nitze, *From Hiroshima to Glasnost,* 94. NSC 68: Etzold and Gaddis, *Containment,* 383–442; Gaddis, *GFK,* 380.
11. Bird and Sherwin, *American Prometheus,* 418–23; Herken, *Brotherhood of the Bomb,* 204, 206–10.
12. Arneson, "H-Bomb Decision."
13. Friendly had apparently learned about the H-bomb from an AEC commissioner at a cocktail party and wrote a little-noticed story about it in November 1949. After Senator Johnson's gaffe, the reporter and Phil Graham argued over whether Friendly should write about the superbomb debate. Graham decided not to publish Friendly's news article on the H-bomb but predicted—correctly—that both men would soon read the story in the Alsop column. Roberts, *In the Shadow of Power,* 290; Anders, *Forging the Atomic Shield,* 63.
14. Alsop and Alsop, *Reporter's Trade,* 69; Bundy, *Danger and Survival,* 212.
15. JWA to Nitze, Dec. 10, "1949" folder, box 5, JWAP; Isaacson and Thomas, *Wise Men,* 474.
16. In 1946, while at the National War College, Kennan had spoken of confronting the Soviet Union "firmly and politely with superior strength at every turn." Isaacson and Thomas, *Wise Men,* 375. Previously, Kennan's views on the atomic bomb had been surprisingly bloody-minded. But when a young scholar pointed out Kennan's changing views on the bomb in a 1976 journal article, using the diplomat's own words, his subject, a Pulitzer Prize–winning historian, demanded that the editor delete the incriminating quotations from the article on the grounds of national security. Nicholas Thompson, *The Hawk and the Dove,* 53, 254–57; Ben Wright, "Mr. 'X' and Containment," 1–31; "George F. Kennan Replies," *Slavic Review* 35, no. 1 (March 1976): 32–36.
17. Diary entries of Nov. 19 and 22, 1949, folder 17, box 231, GFKP; Gaddis, *GFK,* 362.
18. Memorandum, Aug. 2, 1949, U.S. Department of State, *FRUS: 1949,* vol. 1, 506–7.
19. Diary entry of Oct. 12, 1949, folder 17, box 231, GFKP.

20. Kennan meant his article to be a response to the clamor for preventive war that followed the surprise of Joe-1; it was written before Truman's H-bomb decision. Diary entry of Sept. 22, 1949, folder 17, box 231, GFKP; Miscamble, *George F. Kennan and the Making of American Foreign Policy,* 312–13.

21. "The Kennan Swan Song," *NYHT,* Feb. 24, 1950; Berlin to Schlesinger, March 2, 1950, "Isaiah Berlin" folder, box P-9, Schlesinger Papers.

22. Nicholas Thompson, *The Hawk and the Dove,* 107. Like Kennan, Bohlen believed that NSC 68 overemphasized the military dimension of Soviet expansionism, but neither was able to persuade Nitze or Acheson of the argument. Nitze, *From Hiroshima to Glasnost,* 98.

23. Transcript of *The H-Bomb Decision,* Video History Project, Alfred P. Sloan Foundation, New York City; author interview with Gordon Arneson, Oct. 19, 1979, Washington, D.C.; Isaacson and Thomas, *Wise Men,* 474.

24. Author interview with Paul Nitze, July 12, 1984, Washington, D.C.; Nicholas Thompson, *The Hawk and the Dove,* 113.

25. Kennan's pique was almost palpable in his memo. Kennan to Webb, March 30, 1950, *FRUS/IC,* 5–8. Part of Kennan's frustration sprang from the fact that the State Department's personnel section was not cleared to know about OPC's covert operations, and hence stymied all efforts to staff the oversight committee headed by Joyce. Aldrich, *Hidden Hand,* 172.

26. Diary entry of Jan. 10, 1950, folder 17, box 231, GFKP. Nonetheless, Kennan's efforts on Hilger's behalf continued. Kennan to Nicholson, July 14, 1950, "Gustav Hilger" folder, box 22, and "Hilger Report on the Stalin succession," March 13, 1950, "Gustav Hilger" folder 2, box 51, RG 263, CIA Records, NARA. The head of the CIA's Eastern Europe desk reported in late 1950, "Actually we have exhausted most all the topics on which Dr. Hilger is an authority over the past year and half." "Utilization of Dr. Hilger," Dec. 18, 1950, "Gustav Hilger" folder, box 22, RG 263, NARA.

27. Hilger's original job interviewing Soviet defectors for the army's Operation Rusty had meanwhile been taken over by the CIA. The German diplomat was living with his family in a Washington, D.C., suburb under an agency pseudonym: Stephen H. Holcomb. "Meeting of 17 Dec. 1948," "Gustav Hilger" folder, box 22, CIA Records, RG 263, NARA.

28. In later describing the situation of Eastern European exiles, the CIA's Tom Braden would quote from T. B. Macaulay's history of England: "A politician driven into banishment by a hostile faction generally sees the society which he has quitted through a false medium . . . Every little discontent appears to him to portend a revolution. Every riot is a rebellion." Nelson, *War of the Black Heavens,* 39.

29. The emphasis was also by Joyce. CIA History Staff, "Office of Policy Coordination, 1948–1952," www.cia.gov/foia. A few weeks later, on May 8, 1950, Wisner echoed Joyce's theme, advising his acolytes that the U.S. government, by adopting NSC 68, had resolved "to make a major effort in the field of covert operations." Memorandum, *FRUS/IC,* 12.

30. Jeffery, *Secret History of MI6,* 715. Tim Weiner estimates that as many as two hundred ethnic agent volunteers were killed before Project Fiend was finally abandoned in 1954. Weiner, *Legacy of Ashes,* 46; Fiend File entry for Oct. 27, 1949, "Sept.–Nov. Diary" folder, box 8, Burke Papers.

31. There were also problems coordinating Fiend with the British: "Anglo-American frictions plagued operations at all levels." Aldrich, *Hidden Hand,* 162. Given the rivalry between MI6 and the CIA, Kim Philby wrote candidly, "it is perhaps surpris-

ing that the [Albanian] operation ever got off the ground." Philby, *My Silent War*, 196–97. Telegram, Nov. 7, 1949, "Sept.-Nov. 1949 Diary" folder, box 8, Burke Papers; Bethell, *Betrayed*, 102–3. "The group was more a rallying point than a valid base for a political revolution. Nothing was done to discourage the expedient pretext that they were a kind of government-in-exile." Burke, *Outrageous Good Fortune*, 142.

32. The British had evidently worried from the start about Wisner's "grandiose" plans. Jeffery, *Secret History of MI6*, 714. "By 1951 Albania was a purely CIA operation." Aldrich, *Hidden Hand*, 164. "Albanian Operation—Fate of Valuable Teams in Albania," n.d., folder 2, vol. 14, box 48, and "Meeting on FIEND of 27 Feb. 1950," March 1, 1950, folder 1, vol. 15, box 49, Fiend Records.

33. "Reevaluation of Project BGFIEND," Nov. 29, 1949, folder 1, vol. 2, and "Operations Critique, Operation #1—BGFIEND," Nov. 20, 1950, folder 1, vol. 4, box 46, Fiend Records.

34. "Reevaluation of Project BGFIEND," May 15, 1950, "Enver Hoxha" folder, box 57, Fiend Records.

35. Oshinsky, *Conspiracy So Immense*, 119–29; Stewart Alsop, *Center*, 9.

36. Herblock's caption had the elephant asking, "You mean I'm supposed to stand on *that*?" *WP*, March 29, 1950.

37. Joseph Alsop, *"I've Seen the Best of It,"* 326–27; Yoder, *Joe Alsop's Cold War*, 65.

38. Yoder, *Joe Alsop's Cold War*, 83; JWA to Tydings, n.d., "1950" folder, box 5, JWAP.

39. Kennan, *Memoirs, 1950–1963*, 196–97; diary entry of April 15, 1951, folder 2, box 232, GFKP.

40. Susan Mary Alsop, *To Marietta from Paris*, 157.

41. Alsop and Alsop, "Why Has Washington Gone Crazy?," 20.

42. Diary entry of June 18, 1950, folder 1, box 232, GFKP.

43. Kennan, in his memo to Webb, took credit for OPC: "The idea of establishment of an organization of this sort for covert operations in the political field was largely my own, as was the initiative which led to the Department's prominent part in launching this venture." Kennan to Webb, March 30, 1950, *FRUS/IC*, 5–8. In his memoirs, Kennan glosses over his role in creating the U.S. capability for covert ops, however. Kennan, *Memoirs, 1950–1963*, 202–3.

44. Diary entry of Aug. 22, 1950, folder 1, box 232, GFKP.

45. "Having helped unleash the beast, the brothers fought to corral it." Ritchie, *Reporting from Washington*, 142; Joseph Alsop, *"I've Seen the Best of It,"* 307–8. "Were they fighting a fire that they themselves had helped to set?" Yoder, *Joe Alsop's Cold War*, 8. In his memoirs, Joe belatedly regretted that he had questioned the judgment of the China hands in his *Post* articles. Joseph Alsop, *"I've Seen the Best of It,"* 327; Gaddis, *GFK*, 397.

CHAPTER NINE "A Rather Serious Border Incident"

1. Joseph Alsop, *"I've Seen the Best of It,"* 306–7; Merry, *Taking On the World*, 193–94; JWA to H. L. Wolbers, July 27, 1972, "W" folder, box 138, JWAP.

2. Kennan to JWA, July 28, 1985, folder 8, box 1, GFKP; Nitze, *From Hiroshima to Glasnost*, 101–2.

3. Diary entry of June 25, 1950, folder 1, box 232, GFKP.

4. Gaddis, *GFK*, 397–98.

5. Diary entry of July 3, 1950, folder 1, box 232, GFKP.

6. "Possible Further Communist Initiative in the Light of the Korean Situation," June 26, 1950, folder 8, box 1, GFKP.

7. Almquist, *Joseph Alsop and American Foreign Policy,* 55; "Mr. Johnson's Untruth," *NYHT,* Feb. 15, 1950; "The Cost of Mr. Johnson," *NYHT,* Feb. 17, 1950; "Johnson and the Chiefs," *NYHT,* Feb. 20, 1950; "Mr. Johnson's Untruths," *NYHT,* March 3, 1950; Casey, *Selling the Korean War,* 66. Johnson delighted in showing visiting journalists a private phone behind a curtain in his Pentagon office, which he claimed had been Forrestal's direct line to the Alsops. Yoder, *Joe Alsop's Cold War,* 24.

8. "Interview with Paul Nitze, Oct. 20, 1990," American Academy of Achievement, www.achievement.org; Nitze, *From Hiroshima to Glasnost,* 93–96.

9. Wills, *Bomb Power,* 92–97; www.usfederalbudget.us/year_spending_1952; "The Lessons of Korea," *NYHT,* Oct. 22, 1950.

10. Crosswell, *Beetle,* 31.

11. Alsop claimed that Marshall had written "a secret letter" to the man who replaced him in China, blaming Joe personally for the failure of his mission. JWA to John Crosby, July 12, 1967, "C" folder, box 76, JWAP; JWA to Hillenkoetter, Nov. 9, 1949, and Hillenkoetter to JWA, Nov. 15, 1949, CIA/CREST.

12. JWA to Kennan, Dec. 31, 1949, and Kennan to JWA, Jan. 5, "1950" folder, box 5, JWAP; "An Unsung Hero's Exodus," *NYHT,* July 2, 1950.

13. Merry, *Taking On the World,* 186; Isaacson and Thomas, *Wise Men,* 545. That summer, Joe wrote to Acheson to remind him "that my request for the opportunity to talk things over with you is now a year and a half old." JWA to Acheson, July 12, "1950" folder, box 5, JWAP.

14. Justice Frankfurter, a friend to both Acheson and Alsop, tried to mediate their dispute, but without success. JWA to Nitze, Dec. 10, 1949, and JWA to Frankfurter, Jan. 6, "1950" folder, box 5, JWAP; Merry, *Taking On the World,* 185.

15. JWA to Bohlen, June 27, "1950" folder, box 5, JWAP; Merry, *Taking On the World,* 196.

16. Folder 1, box 232, GFKP.

17. Diary entry of July 26, 1950, folder 1, box 232, GFKP.

18. Diary entry of July 17, 1950, folder 1, box 232, GFKP; Nitze to Acheson, July 17, 1950, "Korea, 1947–50" folder, box 7, PPS/SD; Kennan to Marshall, Aug. 24, 1950, folder 10, box 29, GFKP.

19. Diary entry of July 17, 1950, folder 1, box 232; Kennan to Marshall, Aug. 24, 1950, folder 10, box 29, and C. B. Marshall, "Lines to George F. Kennan . . . ," Sept. 25, 1950, folder 8, box 139, GFKP; Nitze to Acheson, July 17, 1950, "Korea, 1947–50" folder, box 7, PPS/SD; Kennan, *Memoirs, 1925–1950,* 469–70.

20. Diary entry of July 25, 1950, folder 1, box 232, and Kennan to Nathan Leites, Nov. 23, 1950, folder 8, box 139, GFKP; Nitze, *From Hiroshima to Glasnost,* 86. In a letter to the author, Kennan claimed that he had no recollection of any such lunch or comment. Kennan to Herken, Nov. 5, 1985, folder 3, box 20, GFKP.

21. Diary entry of Nov. 16, 1950, folder 1, box 232, GFKP.

22. Kennan to JWA, Oct. 20, 1950, folder 8, box 1, GFKP; Joseph Alsop, *"I've Seen the Best of It,"* 310–25; "Baker Company," *NYHT,* Aug. 30, 1950, and "We Shall Cross," *NYHT,* Oct. 6, 1950.

23. Merry, *Taking On the World,* 238; Yoder, *Joe Alsop's Cold War,* 30.

24. Merry, *Taking On the World,* 197–201; "The Fight at Yongsan," *NYHT,* Sept. 4, 1950; "The Conquerors," *NYHT,* Sept. 27, 1950; "Homecoming Thoughts," *NYHT,* Oct. 16, 1950.

25. JWA to Slessor, Dec. 11, "1950" folder, box 6, JWAP.

26. JWA to Mike Handler, Jan. 18, "1951" folder, box 6, JWAP.
27. Kennan to Acheson, Nov. 24, 1950, folder 2, box 1, GFKP. One project, evidently suggested by Kennan, urged the Ford Foundation to fund the "long-range rehabilitation and placement" of Soviet defectors. Pisani, *CIA and the Marshall Plan,* 49–51. When Joe Alsop sent a five-dollar contribution to the Free Russia Fund, Kennan personally returned the check, explaining that "we are a subsidiary of the Ford Foundation and are not soliciting funds from any other source." Kennan to JWA, July 31, "1951" folder, box 6, JWAP.
28. Transcript of conversation, Dec. 1, 1950, folder 1, box 232, GFKP.
29. Kennan to Bohlen, Dec. 5, 1950, folder 8, box 139, GFKP. Nitze reportedly ordered the destruction of all copies of the planning staff report on the Russians' secret intervention, which he titled "Removing the Fig Leaf from the Hard Core of Soviet Responsibility." Nicholas Thompson, *The Hawk and the Dove,* 127–28; Walker, *Cold War,* 76–77; Nitze, *From Hiroshima to Glasnost,* 112.
30. Like OPC's freedom committees, the purpose of the Free Russia Fund "was to collect recent intelligence on the U.S.S.R., to ensure that defectors did not re-defect, and to build a community of exiles who might one day return to Russia to form the nucleus of a post-Soviet government." When the Ford Foundation subsequently balked at being a conduit, Kennan arranged for the CIA to provide money to the organization directly and later defended his actions when they became public. Gaddis, *GFK,* 419; Kennan to Smith, March 29, 1951, folder 2, box 1, GFKP.
31. During a visit to Chicago, where he would deliver a series of lectures on U.S. foreign policy, Kennan's morale hit a new low. Diary entry of April 17, 1951, folder 2, box 232, GFKP.
32. "More and more I feel myself becoming a receptacle for the confidence of other people," the diplomat mused later that day. "Am I not deceiving them all?" Diary entry of June 19, 1951, folder 2, box 232, GFKP.
33. Thomas, *Very Best Men,* 42; Powers, *Man Who Kept the Secrets,* 32–33.
34. Weiner, *Legacy of Ashes,* 53; Rudgers, "Origins of Covert Action," 258. As Smith noted in later testimony, while OPC "was actually in but not of the agency," it was "the place where the money was spent." CIA History Staff, "Office of Policy Coordination, 1948–1952," 40–41, CIA/CREST; Minutes, Oct. 20, 1950, *FRUS/IC,* 47–49. In his own memo to Smith, Wisner promised only to keep the CIA director "fully informed on all matters worthy of your attention." Wisner to CIA Director, Oct. 12, 1950, in Warner, *CIA Under Harry Truman,* 347; Thomas, *Very Best Men,* 43.
35. Burton Hersh, *Old Boys,* 301; Crosswell, *Beetle,* 36–37.
36. Aldrich, *Hidden Hand,* 163.
37. Regarding widely conflicting accounts of OPC's true size and budget, see Weiner, *Legacy of Ashes,* 53–55, 546n; Burton Hersh, *Old Boys,* 237; and Gaddis, *GFK,* 319. Evidently, as much as half of OPC's budget at this time came from Marshall Plan counterpart funds. Weiner, *Legacy of Ashes,* 28, 53; Treverton, *Covert Action,* 37–38.
38. Against Orwell's wishes, the script for *1984* was reportedly tweaked to make the connection with Communist authoritarianism even more obvious. Prados, *Safe for Democracy,* 89.
39. Tim Weiner claims that Wisner's organization sent more than fifteen hundred agents into North Korea during the spring and summer of 1952. Srodes, *Allen Dulles,* 402; Aldrich, *Hidden Hand,* 299–300; Weiner, *Legacy of Ashes,* 56–58; *FRUS/IC,* 161–63.
40. Perhaps foremost among them was the American Committee for Liberation, or AMCOMLIB, founded by Lindsay in 1951 and funded entirely by the CIA at the

time. *Time* magazine's publisher, Henry Luce, helped recruit the AMCOMLIB board of directors and chaired their first meeting. Nelson, *War of the Black Heavens,* 56–57.

41. Aldrich, *Hidden Hand,* 315.

42. Nelson, *War of the Black Heavens,* 46, 49; Thayer, *Diplomat,* 189; Richard Helms, *A Look over My Shoulder,* 356.

43. CIA History Staff, "Office of Policy Coordination, 1948–1952," 43–45; Burton Hersh, *Old Boys,* 237; Pisani, *CIA and the Marshall Plan,* 74.

44. Benson and Warner, *VENONA,* xxxii. Project Red Sox was a covert operation "involving the illegal return of defectors and emigres to [the] USSR as agents." "Research Aid," June 2007, RG 263, CIA Records, NARA. "These attempts . . . enjoyed very limited success," concluded a CIA historian. *FRUS/IC,* 203n.

45. "The foreign policy of the United States took shape at the Wisners' table." Weiner, *Legacy of Ashes,* 20. Wisner parties: Heymann, *Georgetown Ladies' Social Club,* 61; Thomas, *Very Best Men,* 104; author interview with Ellis Wisner, Nov. 17, 2009, Washington, D.C.

46. Bethell, *Betrayed,* 154–58. The official after-action report makes no mention of the Polish pilot buzzing the Albanian capital. "First Team Drop into HBPixie, 11–12 November 1950," Nov. 13, 1950, folder 2, vol. 5, box 46, Fiend Records.

47. Transcript, Jan. 4, 1951, folder 2, vol. 5, box 46, Fiend Records.

48. "Actions Designed to Organize a Third Force in South China," July 31, 1945, folder 2, vol. 17, box 49, Fiend Records.

49. Powers, *Man Who Kept the Secrets,* 41–43; Grose, *Operation Rollback,* 172–73; Hazard, *Cold War Crucible,* 208.

50. Thomas, *Very Best Men,* 187, 323, 330; "Eclectic Author Edgar Applewhite Dies," *WP,* Feb. 15, 2005.

51. Entries of Dec. 3, 1950, and Jan. 28, 1951, "Diaries and Datebooks" folder, box 8, Burke Papers.

52. Bethell, *Betrayed,* 161. Burke's cover in Frankfurt was as special assistant to the high commissioner for Germany, John McCloy. Concerning one OPC-sponsored project—creation of the "Free Europe Society"—Burke wrote that "McCloy no longer wanted to discuss the subject personally, implying it should be left to us." Entry of May 5, 1951, "Diaries and Datebooks" folder, box 8, Burke Papers. However, another account indicates that McCloy was well aware, and supportive, of OPC operations in Europe. Bird, *Chairman,* 355–56.

53. Burke's notes suggest that while the Russians might have been the adversary, OPC's longtime rival, the CIA's Office of Special Operations, remained the enemy: "OSO has beaten us to the punch again. Although we [OPC] are charged with building all air lift services, we, today, have no planes and no personnel. OSO has three C-47s . . . and we look bad again." Entry for May 11, 1951, "Diaries and Datebooks" folder, box 8, Burke Papers.

54. Sons of the Eagle to Burke, May 3, 1951, no folder, box 8, Burke Papers.

55. Richard Helms, *A Look over My Shoulder,* 100. In 1955, when Dulles, who had since become CIA director, tried to talk Wisner out of resuming the leafleting of China, Frank protested that "things are being accomplished," adding, "the [National Chinese] are doing it anyway. We can't stop it." Aldrich, *Hidden Hand,* 314.

56. Evidently, part of the problem concerned a recent *Post* editorial. Dulles noted in his diary that while Phil did not like the idea of having his reporters becoming CIA consultants—"because of the obvious difficulty"—Graham agreed with Dulles that

both men "might be well advised to have what amounted to a cleared list of such people, each of whom could be investigated in the normal course . . . [Graham] also suggested that in cases where we did not feel our position was adequately expressed in the press, we might be well advised to have some individual write a letter to the editor and this seemed to me to be a practical solution to some problems." Entries of Oct. 2 and 7, 1952, "Official Diary," CIA/CREST.

57. "Organization of CIA Clandestine Services," July 15, 1952, in Warner, *CIA Under Harry Truman,* 465–68; Richard Helms, *A Look over My Shoulder,* 359; CIA, "Report on the Covert Activities of the Central Intelligence Agency," n.d., www.cia.gov/foia.

58. Powers, *Man Who Kept the Secrets,* 50; Aldrich, *Hidden Hand,* 314.

59. Grose, *Operation Rollback,* 178–79; Powers, *Man Who Kept the Secrets,* 43.

60. "Identification of W/T Operators," Nov. 17, 1952, folder 1, vol. 6, box 47; "Valuable-Fiend Relations," May 28, 1951, folder 1, vol. 17, box 49; "Annihilation of Fiend Team OLIVE," Aug. 15, 1951, folder 1, vol. 18, box 49; "Disposal of Surplus Personnel," July 18, 1951, folder 1, vol. 4, box 46, Fiend Records.

61. "Secret Memorandum for the Record, dtd 21 Oct. 1952," Oct. 28, 1952, folder 2, vol. 2, and "Albanian Operations," Oct. 11, 1952, folder 1, vol. 2, box 46; handwritten note, Nov. 14, 1951, folder 1, vol. 19, box 50; "Annihilation of BGFIEND OLIVE Team," Aug. 14, 1951, folder 1, vol. 18, box 49, Fiend Records.

62. "[Since] this area, from the OSO standpoint, is relatively unimportant . . . we're not going to give it any more than the minimum," the OSO notified Wisner. "OSO Plan for Albania," n.d., folder 2, vol. 1, box 45, Fiend Records.

63. Dobbs, *Six Months in 1945,* 11–13; Mark, "OSS in Romania," 337n; C. H. Stanley to A. H. Belmont, May 21, 1952, Frank Gardiner Wisner FBI file. Following a yearlong inquiry by the CIA into the FBI's allegations, Smith wrote back to Hoover in an eyes only memo: "Our investigation discloses no association with Mr. Wisner since approximately 1945 nor any indication that he then had any knowledge of espionage activities on the part of Tanda Caragea [*sic*]." Smith to Hoover, Dec. 24, 1952, Frank Gardiner Wisner CIA file.

64. Crosswell, *Beetle,* 34.

65. Burton Hersh, *Old Boys,* 442. In 1953, Offie told the columnist Westbrook Pegler that he had been "framed" by his political enemies. Pegler, "Carmel Offie Sheds Cloak, Dagger," *Milwaukee Sentinel,* Jan. 28, 1953; Morgan, *Covert Life,* 210–12.

66. Burton Hersh, *Old Boys,* 295–96; Riebling, *Wedge,* 117.

67. "Minutes," Oct. 27, 1952, in Warner, *CIA Under Harry Truman,* 469–70.

68. Burton Hersh, *Old Boys,* 299.

CHAPTER TEN "Venomous, Exciting and Pretty Frightening"

1. In late April 1951, the administration's internal security program, begun in 1947, was expanded to authorize the firing of State Department employees "about whom there is a reasonable doubt as to their loyalty to the Government of the United States." Conrad Snow to Davies, June 27, 1951, and Kennan to Snow, June 21, 1951, folder 13, box 10, GFKP; Hixson, *George F. Kennan,* 164.

2. During the winter of 1949–1950, Acheson had spoken of Mao as a possible "Chinese Tito," and diplomatic recognition of China had been urged by Kennan and Davies, among others. However, "Who lost China?" had meanwhile become a kind of man-

tra for the China lobby and Joseph McCarthy. Xiang, "Recognition Controversy," 319–43; Isaacson and Thomas, *Wise Men,* 477; Chace, *Acheson,* 224.

3. Among the China experts whom Davies hoped to recruit were Edgar Snow, Agnes Smedley, and Anna Louise Strong, as well as John Fairbank and his wife. Snow to Davies, June 27, 1951, folder 13, box 10, GFKP. Tawny Pipit: Kahn, *China Hands,* 244–45; Corke, *U.S. Covert Operations and Cold War Strategy,* 78–79. The original idea for the operation evidently went back to an April 21, 1949, memo that Davies sent to the planning staff. Kennan to Acheson, Jan. 14, 1953, folder 1, box 139, GFKP; "Political Warfare Against the USSR," Oct. 10, 1949, "Political and Psych. Warfare, 1947–1950" folder, box 11A, PPS/SD.

4. Davies to Kennan, Dec. 30, 1953, folder 12, box 10, GFKP; Hixson, *George F. Kennan,* 164; "Reveal Secret Testimony in U.S. Far East Policy," *Connecticut Sun Herald,* Feb. 20, 1972, CIA/CREST.

5. Snow to Davies, June 27, 1951, folder 13, box 10, GFKP; Halberstam, *The Best and the Brightest,* 390.

6. Kennan to Snow, June 21, 1951, folder 13, box 10, GFKP.

7. JWA to Snow, July 18, "1951" folder, box 6, JWAP.

8. "Before the Loyalty Board," *NYHT,* July 25, 1951. The day that the Alsop column appeared, Kennan sent Joe a telegram, praising him as "a person of great distinction of mind and character and it makes me proud of your friendship." Yoder, *Joe Alsop's Cold War,* 61.

9. Joyce to Davies, July 22, 1952, folder 4, box 139, GFKP. Whereas McCarran tried to get the Justice Department to indict Davies for perjury, Kennan urged the CIA to fire Munson for unauthorized disclosure of classified information. Hixson, *George F. Kennan,* 164.

10. Kennan to Schlesinger, Jan. 11, 1952, "George Kennan" folder, box P-17, Schlesinger Papers; Gaddis, *GFK,* 429–30; J. E. Strunsky to Nitze, June 16, 1952, "George Kennan" folder, box 48, PPS/SD.

11. Kennan to Freeman Matthews, May 16, 1952, folder 4, box 139, GFKP; translation of TASS press release, Feb. 13, 1952, CIA/CREST.

12. Stewart Alsop to Taft, March 8, "1951" folder, box 20, JWAP.

13. Merry, *Taking On the World,* 216.

14. The subject matter of the two FBI memorandums, sent to Connelly on March 27, 1951, was redacted in Boardman's report, which was not declassified until 2008. L. V. Boardman to Belmont, April 1, 1957, Joseph Alsop FBI file. The bureau's reference might have been to an earlier incident in San Francisco, where Joe was picked up in a police sweep of a popular gay rendezvous spot. According to Alsop family lore, Stewart and Tom Braden had gone to the city, retrieved Joe, and subsequently tried to suppress the police report. Merry, *Taking On the World,* 361; author interview with Elizabeth Winthrop Alsop and Joseph Alsop VI, April 30, 2012, New York City.

15. Merry, *Taking On the World,* 217.

16. JWA to Wedemeyer, Sept. 23, "1951" folder, box 6, JWAP; Carol Cosden to Annelise Kennan, Jan. 22, 1953, folder 8, box 1, GFKP.

17. Campbell, *Getting It Wrong,* 59–61; JWA to Luce, Sept. 8, and Luce to JWA, Sept. 21, "1951" folder, box 6, JWAP.

18. "Russia's Atom Bombs," *NYHT,* Dec. 31, 1950. In the spring of 1952, the chairman of the Joint Committee on Atomic Energy asked the CIA director, Smith, whether a recent Alsop column on the H-bomb contained enough classified information to

justify another criminal investigation. Bourke Hickenlooper to Smith, June 19, 1952, CIA/CREST.

19. "The Young Gentlemen," *NYHT,* Feb. 19, 1951.
20. Boardman to Belmont, memo, March 29, 1957, Joseph Alsop FBI file; "A Complex and Dangerous Issue," *NYHT,* Aug. 15, 1947; Buell Weare to JWA, Sept. 4, 1947, Joseph Wright Alsop Private Papers. The author thanks the Alsop family for access to the Alsop-Hoover correspondence.
21. Alsop and Alsop, *Reporter's Trade,* 67; Yoder, *Joe Alsop's Cold War,* 21; JWA to Hoover, Aug. 27, 1947, Joseph Wright Alsop Private Papers.
22. Joe subsequently sent Nitze a handwritten note, conceding "that Stew and I have in fact been unwise in our handling of certain categories of information." JWA to Nitze, Feb. 7, 1951, "Joseph Alsop" folder, box 17, Nitze Papers; JWA to Jackson, Jan. 10, "1951" folder, box 6, JWAP.
23. Gray encountered opposition to his mission from the start. Paul Nitze reportedly told the PSB director, "Look, you just forget about policy, that is not your job; we'll make the policy and then you can put it on your damn radio." Prados, *Safe for Democracy,* 78–80; Pisani, *CIA and the Marshall Plan,* 130; Burton Hersh, *Old Boys,* 298; author interview with Boyden Gray, Nov. 17, 2009, Washington, D.C.
24. Merry, *Taking On the World,* 217.
25. JWA to McCarran, n.d., and McCarran to JWA, telegram, Oct. 12, "1951" folder, box 7, JWAP.
26. "The McCarran Investigations," *NYHT,* Sept. 15, 1951; Merry, *Taking On the World,* 221.
27. Schlesinger to JWA, with attachment, Sept. 18, "1951" folder, box 6, JWAP.
28. JWA to Stewart Alsop, Nov. 9, "1951" folder, box 7, and JWA to Schlesinger, Sept. 21, "1951" folder, box 6, JWAP.
29. Only a draft typescript could be found in the Alsop Papers, suggesting that Joe might not have sent the letter. JWA to Reid, n.d. [Nov.], "1951" folder, box 7, JWAP.
30. JWA to Stewart Alsop, Nov. 9, "1951" folder, box 7, JWAP.
31. Graham, *Personal History,* 75.
32. Ritchie, *Reporting from Washington,* 91; Graham, *Personal History,* 194–96.
33. Graham, *Personal History,* 199. "The only valid criticism I have on the cartoons, or have heard from other fans, has to do with the handling of Congress." Graham to Herblock, May 14, 1951, folder 6, box 29, Block Papers.
34. Graham, *Personal History,* 199; "A Career of Eloquence Reflects Philip Graham," 3, folder 6, box 29, Block Papers.
35. JWA to Schlesinger, Sept. 21, "1951" folder, box 6, JWAP; Graham, *Personal History,* 207; Heymann, *Georgetown Ladies' Social Club,* 51–52.
36. "In fact, the war between McCarthy and the *Post* was vicious and frightening," Kay Graham later wrote, adding, "We were helped to a certain extent by Joe Alsop and his brother Stewart, whose column had become important to the *Post,* and whose anti-communist themes helped soften the perception of the *Post* as somehow sympathetic to the communists." *Personal History,* 204.
37. JWA to Taft, March 8, "1951" folder, box 20, JWAP; "How Many Egg-Heads Are There?," *NYHT,* Sept. 26, 1952. The term had actually been coined by John Alsop but was first used by Stewart in his column. Merry, *Taking On the World,* 236.
38. Graham, *Personal History,* 200–202; Merry, *Taking On the World,* 232–34; Graham to Schlesinger, April 29, 1952, "Philip Graham, 1946–1960" folder, box P-15, Schlesinger Papers.

39. JWA to "Judy darling," June 25, "1952" folder, box 8, JWAP; author interview with Ben Bradlee, Nov. 18, 2009, Washington, D.C.

40. "I have no news whatever that would interest you, except that Phil Graham is both defiant and violent in his continued support of the Republicans. I would have thought he would have switched by now." JWA to Berlin, Oct. 4, "1952" folder, box 8, JWAP. Oshinsky, *Conspiracy So Immense,* 242–43; "McCarthy's Roorback," *WP,* Oct. 29, 1952. Phil defended the paper's front-page correction of McCarthy's charges in a letter he sent to Schlesinger's wife, Marian: "I did not notice any similar analysis in any of the four or five papers I read, but we got a tremendous response from our readers for doing it this way." Graham to Schlesinger, Oct. 30, 1952, "Philip Graham" folder, box P-15, Schlesinger Papers; Graham, *Personal History,* 203; Felsenthal, *Power, Privilege, and the "Post,"* 137.

41. Wisner to Kennan, Feb. 21, 1952, folder 13, box 10, GFKP; Kennan to Webb, March 30, 1950, *FRUS/IC,* 5–8. The CIA subsequently informed State "that not only was this particular project . . . classified, but . . . the very fact that the Government engaged in certain types of operations should not be acknowledged or given any discussion." Walter Pforzheimer memorandum to record, Aug. 3 and 15, 1951, and Feb. 27, 1952, CIA/CREST.

42. Kennan to Acheson, July 25, 1952, folder 3, box 139, GFKP.

43. Kennan, *Memoirs, 1950–1963,* 157–59; Nicholas Thompson, *The Hawk and the Dove,* 139–40. Kennan's expulsion might have been, in part, payback for his previous efforts on behalf of Gustav Hilger and his support of the so-called freedom committees. Thus, an internal Soviet Foreign Ministry document noted that Kennan "had shared the views of Nazi diplomats prior to World War II" and sponsored "reactionary organizations and political émigrés." Gaddis, *GFK,* 460.

44. Kennan was in Geneva when word reached him that he would not be able to return to the Soviet Union as the U.S. ambassador. Kennan, *Memoirs, 1950–1963,* 168–69; Gaddis, *GFK,* 473; Kennan to Elim O'Shaughnessy, Oct. 29, 1952, folder 5, box 139, GFKP.

45. Kennan, *Memoirs, 1950–1963,* 170.

CHAPTER ELEVEN "Stray and Gusty Winds"

1. JWA to Susan Mary Patten, Dec. 8, "1952" folder, box 8, JWAP.

2. Merry, *Taking On the World,* 242–43; Heymann, *Georgetown Ladies' Social Club,* 53.

3. Grose, *Gentleman Spy,* 325. "He was very good at giving you tidbits in order to draw what he wanted from you," remembered Chalmers Roberts, a *Washington Post* reporter and Dulles's friend. Srodes, *Allen Dulles,* 1–3.

4. Joseph Alsop and Stewart Alsop, "The Man Ike Trusts with the Cash," *SEP,* May 23, 1953; Joseph Alsop, *"I've Seen the Best of It,"* 347.

5. Merry, *Taking On the World,* 242–43. "It seems to be a law of nature that Republicans are more boring than Democrats." Stewart Alsop, "Just What Is Modern Republicanism?," *SEP;* July 27, 1957, Stewart Alsop to Friedrich Otto, Aug. 29, 1963, folder 10A, box 6, Stewart Alsop Papers; Joseph Alsop, *"I've Seen the Best of It,"* 341; "The Year Ahead," *NYHT,* Jan. 2, 1953.

6. Schlesinger and Schlesinger, *Letters of Arthur Schlesinger, Jr.* 61; Merry, *Taking On the World,* 242.

7. Cutler "had transformed the National Security Council into a virtual nest of Byzan-

tine ceremony, with a sacred agenda and other trappings that would have suited the Foreign Secretariat of a Byzantine emperor," Joe Alsop wrote. Joseph Alsop, *"I've Seen the Best of It,"* 349; Cutler, *No Time for Rest,* 317–18.

8. JWA to Cutler, Feb. 12, "1953" folder, box 8, JWAP; Cutler, *No Time for Rest,* 320; Almquist, *Joseph Alsop and American Foreign Policy,* 77.

9. "The Facts About the H-Bomb," *NYHT,* Jan. 5, 1953; "Mantis, Take Over," *NYHT,* Jan. 7, 1953. In fact, the Alsops had actually underestimated the power of Mike by half. The AEC commissioner Henry Smyth advised the brothers that while their column contained errors, secrecy prevented him from telling them what they were. Smyth to JWA, Jan. 2, "1953" folder, box 8, JWAP.

10. The proposal had its origins in the so-called Disarmament Panel on which Oppenheimer served at the end of the Truman administration. "Operation Candor": Herken, *Cardinal Choices,* 69–74.

11. "Eisenhower Warned of Danger of Atom Bomb Attack," *NYHT,* March 16, 1953; "Cost of Civil Defense," *NYHT,* March 18, 1953; "The Job to Be Done," *NYHT,* March 20, 1953.

12. Joe remembered his meeting with Finletter and Vandenberg as "one of the strangest experiences I've ever had." Joseph Alsop, *"I've Seen the Best of It,"* 353.

13. When Joe Alsop asked Teller whether he had been the source for a recent magazine article accusing Oppenheimer of deliberately impeding progress on the hydrogen bomb, Teller threatened to sue. Teller to JWA, Aug. 10, and JWA to Teller, Aug. 14, "1953" folder, box 9, JWAP; Oppenheimer, "Atomic Weapons and American Policy."

14. Another AEC commissioner told Alsop, regarding Strauss, "If you disagree with Lewis about anything, he assumes you're just a fool at first, but if you go on disagreeing with him, he concludes you must be a traitor." Halberstam, *Fifties,* 334. In his memoirs, Joe described Strauss as "short, natty and energetic in appearance and a very able and frighteningly ambitious man." Joseph Alsop, *"I've Seen the Best of It,"* 351. For examples of Strauss's behavior, see Herken, *Brotherhood of the Bomb,* 268–75.

15. Joseph Alsop, *"I've Seen the Best of It,"* 351; Bird and Sherwin, *American Prometheus,* 468–69; JWA to Crosby, July 12, 1967, "C" folder, box 77, JWAP.

16. Kennan to Acheson, Dec. 30, 1952, folder 1, box 1, and Kennan to Smith, Jan. 20, 1953, folder 2, box 139, GFKP.

17. In an earlier meeting, on January 22, Kennan told the secretary of state designate that he had decided "it would be better if I were to retire voluntarily . . . and retire to private life," possibly expecting Dulles to protest. This time, however, Dulles took Kennan at his word. Kennan, "Relations with the New Administration Concerning My Future Position," March 13, 1953, folder 1, box 233, and Kennan to Cutler, May 25, 1953, folder 1, box 139, GFKP; Kennan, *Sketches from a Life,* 159.

18. Kennan to Oppenheimer, March 15, 1953, "George Kennan" folder, box 43, Oppenheimer Papers; Hixson, *George F. Kennan,* 135; Graham to Kennan, May 4, 1953, and Friendly to Graham, May 25, 1953, folder 2, box 139, GFKP. Kennan's CIA contract was renewed for another year in 1955. Harrison Reynolds to Kennan, June 17, 1955, folder 14, box 7, GFKP; Gaddis, *GFK,* 518; U.S. Department of State, *FRUS, 1955–1957,* vol. 24, 96–98.

19. Kennan, *Memoirs, 1950–1963,* 182.

20. Nicholas Thompson, *The Hawk and the Dove,* 150–51; "Another Surrender," *NYHT,* June 24, 1953.

21. Nitze, *From Hiroshima to Glasnost,* 146–48.

22. Kennan to Acheson, Jan. 28, 1953, Kennan to Brownell, Sept. 6, 1953, Kennan to Davies, telegram, Nov. 25, 1953, folder 1, box 139, GFKP. "For more than two years I have been repeatedly on the verge of coming out publicly in this case, but have been restrained each time by the hope that the Government itself would take the necessary steps to protect Davies' reputation." Kennan to Murphy, Dec. 14, 1953, folder 2, box 139, GFKP; Isaacson and Thomas, *Wise Men,* 565.

23. Nitze also wrote a letter to *The New York Times* in support of Davies, arguing that the case was of "symbolic importance." Kennan to Nitze, Dec. 14, 1953, folder 6, box 34, GFKP; Nitze to Davies, Dec. 23, 1953, "J. P. Davies, McCarthy Hearings, 1953–1975" folder, box 22, Nitze Papers.

24. Kahn, *China Hands,* 258–59; Davies to Patricia Davies, Jan. 18, 1954, Davies Papers. The author thanks Tiki Davies for copies of her parents' correspondence.

25. Burton Hersh, *Old Boys,* 280–81; Powers, *Man Who Kept the Secrets,* 41–48; Grose, *Operation Rollback,* 176–79; Weiner, *Legacy of Ashes,* 66–68. When WIN's leaders asked that an American general be parachuted into Poland to show the CIA's seriousness and improve morale, the agency finally became suspicious. Prados, *Safe for Democracy,* 75.

26. On August 21, 1968, the day that Soviet troops invaded Czechoslovakia, the Soviets' Novosti news agency blamed the invasion on a "war of the black heavens" that had been launched a generation earlier by Radio Liberty and Radio Free Europe: "Historians have still to elucidate fully the vile role played by these Western radio stations." Nelson, *War of the Black Heavens,* epigram.

27. Weiner, *Legacy of Ashes,* 65–66; Murphy, Kondrashev, and Bailey, *Battleground Berlin,* 123–25; Thomas, *Very Best Men,* 66.

28. [Redacted], "Rome Monthly Survey Report," Jan. 6, 1953, and [Redacted], "The Possibility of an Appeal to Senator McCarthy for Investigation of the NCFA," May 15, 1953, vol. 3, box 46, Fiend Records.

29. Despite the ban, Wisner's operation had still managed to release more than three million anti-Communist pamphlets over Albania. Richard Helms, *A Look over My Shoulder,* 126; Wisner to Chief SE, "British Attitude Toward Possible Albanian Operation," Sept. 10, 1953, folder 1 of 2, vol. 26, box 52, Fiend Records.

30. Thomas, *Very Best Men,* 39; Hazard, *Cold War Crucible,* 234; Wisner, "Pros and Cons of Proposal to Detach Albania from the Soviet Orbit," June 4, 1952, folder 2, vol. 1, box 45, Fiend Records. Artichoke would lead in time to the CIA's infamous Project MKUltra, which tested LSD on prisoners and other unwitting subjects. Weiner, *Legacy of Ashes,* 65–66.

31. Emboldened anew by Jackson's support, Wisner reported to Dulles that there was, once again, support for steps "broad enough and strong enough to accomplish the objective of detaching Albania from the [Soviet] bloc." Memo, "Results of PSB Luncheon Meeting April 9," April 10, 1953, folder 2, vol. 24, box 51; Wisner, "Albania," Aug. 8, 1953, folder 2, vol. 25, box 52; and "Country Plan—Albania," Aug. 11, 1953, folder 1, vol. 1, box 45, Fiend Records.

32. Joyce to Matthews, Jan. 26, 1953, *FRUS/IC,* 400–405.

33. Burton Hersh, *Old Boys,* 318–20. A December 1949 MI6 report on the failure of Operation Valuable noted that Britain's Albanian volunteers had shown "a complete lack of discretion in their letters to political followers in Italy, Turkey, Syria, Egypt and France." Accordingly, the Sigurimi "was evidently aware of the imminent arrival of the parties some two months before they were actually infiltrated." Jeffery, *Secret History of MI6,* 716.

34. Interview with Franklin Lindsay, July 26, 2000, CIA/CREST; Grose, *Operation Rollback*, 188–89; Bower, *Red Web*, 165; Burton Hersh, *Old Boys*, 318–19. Lindsay's new job was at the Ford Foundation, which had become a pass-through for secret agency funding.

35. Grose, *Operation Rollback*, 213. Burke later went on to become an executive at the Columbia Broadcasting System and subsequently president of the CBS-owned New York Yankees, finishing his career as CEO of the company that ran New York's Madison Square Garden. He retired to Ireland, where he died in February 1987.

36. Tracy Barnes: Thomas, *Very Best Men*, 75–86. Phil Geyelin: Felsenthal, *Power, Privilege, and the "Post,"* 372. Desmond FitzGerald: *Very Best Men*, 44–50; Patten, *My Three Fathers*, 129.

37. Bissell, *Reflections of a Cold Warrior*, 1, 77–78.

38. Thomas, *Very Best Men*, 194.

39. Salisbury, *Without Fear or Favor*, 568–72, 576; Bernstein, "CIA and the Media," www.carlbernstein.com.

40. Diary entry of May 23, 1958, folder 8, box 15, Murphy Papers.

41. Heymann, *Georgetown Ladies' Social Club*, 51.

42. Carl Bernstein claimed that Alsop also visited Laos in 1952 at Wisner's behest. Joseph Alsop, *"I've Seen the Best of It,"* 379; Bernstein, "CIA and the Media"; "Official Diary," Dec. 22, 1952, CIA/CREST; "We Know Nothing," *NYHT,* Sept. 23, 1953; "The Philippine Stakes," *NYHT,* Sept. 25, 1953; Thomas, *Very Best Men*, 63.

43. "Dulles peddled this deception to Joseph and Stewart Alsop and others in Washington," Reston wrote. The Otto John affair "was exceedingly embarrassing for the CIA and for Allen Dulles personally." Reston, *Deadline*, 209. Salisbury, *Without Fear or Favor*, 485–86. The *Times* reporter Tad Szulc ultimately exposed the truth about John, who later returned to West Germany and was sentenced to four years in prison for treason.

44. Stewart subsequently sent a rough draft of his article to Wisner, asking for suggestions. Stewart Alsop to Bissell, June 26, and Stewart Alsop to Wisner, Sept. 10, "1956" folder, box 21, JWAP.

45. He was particularly interested, Joe added, in "those informed about Soviet preparations and purposes, who might be useful to talk to." JWA to Nabokov, Jan. 18, "1951" folder, box 6, JWAP.

46. Holzman, *James Jesus Angleton*, 123; Burton Hersh, *Old Boys*, 307. In 2010, the author was told by the CIA that the Edwards report on the Wisners could not be located in agency archives. Delores Nelson/CIA to Herken, April 28, 2010, personal correspondence.

47. Wise, *Molehunt*, 30–31. Braden was evidently not the only agency employee suspicious of being bugged by "No-Knock Angleton." Burton Hersh, *Old Boys*, 317.

48. Alsop and Braden, *Sub Rosa*, 6.

CHAPTER TWELVE "The Wild Pigs of Capitol Hill"

1. Weisbrode, *Atlantic Century*, 144.

2. Burton Hersh, *Old Boys*, 370.

3. Barrett, *CIA and Congress*, 185–86. Tim Weiner claims that Allen Dulles's resistance to McCarthy included a clandestine campaign, orchestrated by the agency's counterintelligence chief, James Angleton, to discredit the Wisconsin senator. The man

Angleton reportedly picked to run the operation, James McCargar, was an OSS veteran and one of Wisner's early hires at OPC. Weiner, *Legacy of Ashes,* 106.

4. Graham to Schlesinger, April 9, 1953, "Philip Graham, 1946–1960" folder, box P-15, Schlesinger Papers. Another reason for Graham's continued caution might have been the fact that he and his newspaper had almost been fooled by a con man, who falsely claimed to work for McCarthy. The *Post* had been planning an exposé based on the man's testimony. Oshinsky, *Conspiracy So Immense,* 311–13; Felsenthal, *Power, Privilege, and the "Post,"* 138; Halberstam, *Powers That Be,* 194.

5. Graham, *Personal History,* 208; Heymann, *Georgetown Ladies' Social Club,* 51–52.

6. Graham, *Personal History,* 209–10; Felsenthal, *Power, Privilege, and the "Post,"* 168–73.

7. Felsenthal, *Power, Privilege, and the "Post,"* 138–39.

8. Isaacson and Thomas, *Wise Men,* 569.

9. Dean, *Imperial Brotherhood,* 123; Morgan, *Covert Life,* 210–12; Srodes, *On Dupont Circle,* 266–67; author interview with Avis Bohlen, Nov. 16, 2009, Washington, D.C.; Barrett, *CIA and Congress,* 81.

10. "Yalta and All That," *NYHT,* Feb. 25, 1953; "Partnership Troubles," *NYHT,* March 13, 1953; "Jenkins' Ear," *NYHT,* March 23, 1953; "The Security Files," *NYHT,* March 27, 1953; Oshinsky, *Conspiracy So Immense,* 291; Dean, *Imperial Brotherhood,* 120–27.

11. Dean, *Imperial Brotherhood,* 140–45.

12. Oshinsky, *Conspiracy So Immense,* 266–78. Thayer had previously criticized the bureau for taking too long to complete background checks on VOA employees. Hoover scribbled on an FBI agent's report regarding the VOA, "Make a most thorough investigation of Thayer." Dean, *Imperial Brotherhood,* 97–110, 134; Nelson, *War of the Black Heavens,* 60; Weiner, *Enemies,* 479–80n; "All 118 Killed in Worst British Air Crash," *NYT,* June 19, 1972.

13. Dean, *Imperial Brotherhood,* 135, 143; Hixson, *George F. Kennan,* 162.

14. Stewart Alsop to Thayer, April 29, and JWA to Thayer, June 5, "1953" folder, box 9, and Thayer to JWA, May 28, "1953" folder, box 20, JWAP. That spring, Thayer noted in his diary that his bank balance was down to $19.64. "I'm really up against it," he wrote. Dean, *Imperial Brotherhood,* 142; Thayer, *Diplomat,* 264.

15. Wisner to Kennan, March 26, 1953, folder 8, box 34, GFKP.

16. Kennan, *Memoirs, 1950–1963,* 180.

17. Nitze's paper proposed an exchange of North Korean and Chinese POWs for American soldiers captured in the war: "Our position should contain an overtone of really significant military action in the event the negotiations were unsuccessful. This overtone should be no mere bluff." However, handwritten in the margin next to this paragraph was the notation: "*No.* W. B. Smith." Bedell Smith was undersecretary of state in the Eisenhower administration. "Exploitation of Stalin's Death," March 10, 1953, Korea, 1947–50 folder, box 7, PPS/SD. Bohlen's daughter remembered her father's regret that the United States did not respond to Soviet diplomatic overtures following Stalin's death. Author interview with Avis Bohlen.

18. Merry, *Taking On the World,* 156; Heymann, *Georgetown Ladies' Social Club,* 41–42.

19. Graham, *Personal History,* 210–11; "A History of the Sulgrave Club," 22, privately published. The author thanks the Sulgrave Club's manager, Robert St. Francis, for details on the Dancing Class.

20. Graham, *Personal History,* 213; Joan Braden, *Just Enough Rope,* 69–70; "Whirlaway," *WP,* May 10, 1954, CIA/CREST; Burton Hersh, *Old Boys,* 374.

21. Ignatieff, *Isaiah Berlin,* 192–93.

22. Schlesinger to JWA, July 5, "1953" folder, box 9, and Schlesinger to JWA, Dec. 9, "1949" folder, box 5, JWAP.

23. JWA to McCormick, June 8, and Donald Maxwell to JWA, June 29, "1954" folder, box 10, JWAP.

24. Nitze, *From Hiroshima to Glasnost,* 149–50. In his memoirs—published in 2012—Davies wrote that "for a man of prominent principles, [Foster Dulles] was less than dauntless in his relations with the political vigilantes." Davies, *China Hand,* 4, 7.

25. Kahn, *China Hands,* 30; "In the Matter of John Paton Davies," *NYHT,* Nov. 10, 1954.

26. Nitze's personal papers contain two thick folders detailing his business dealings with Davies's furniture company. "John Paton Davies, 1951–1980" folder, box 22, Nitze Papers; Halberstam, *The Best and the Brightest,* 379–81; Davies, *China Hand,* 333.

27. A confidential White House chronology of "Candor-Wheaties" noted that none of the drafts originally proposed for the speech were deemed "satisfactory because they either told too much or too little and were uniformly dull. During this time [there was] mounting columnist hue and cry, led by Alsops, referring to Candor . . . and disclosing much draft material." Ike's speech eventually became "a Strauss-Jackson act," the document concluded. "Chronology—Candor-Wheaties," Sept. 30, 1954, Nuclear Non-proliferation series, DNSA, www.gwu.edu/~nsarchiv; Alsop and Alsop, *Reporter's Trade,* 62–63.

28. "The Experiment in Truth," *NYHT,* Sept. 16, 1953; "Confusion Compounded," *NYHT,* Oct. 9, 1953. Ironically, one reason that Ike bowed to Strauss's wishes might have been the president's concern that leaks about his forthcoming Candor speech, published by the Alsops, "had taken the edge off the idea." "Chronology—Candor-Wheaties," Sept. 30, 1954, Nuclear Non-proliferation series, DNSA; Herken, *Cardinal Choices,* 75–76.

29. Joseph Alsop, *"I've Seen the Best of It,"* 390; Merry, *Taking On the World,* 249; "Old Loyalties Cloud 'New Look' at Defense," *NYHT,* Nov. 1, 1953.

30. "Mao's Good Fortune," *NYHT,* Oct. 2, 1953; "The New Munich," *NYHT,* July 23, 1954; Almquist, *Joseph Alsop and American Foreign Policy,* 78.

31. Joseph Alsop, *"I've Seen the Best of It,"* 350; Cutler, *No Time for Rest,* 320; "Security vs. Democracy," *NYHT,* June 15, 1955.

32. Joseph Alsop, *"I've Seen the Best of It,"* 354.

33. Alsop advised the editor of a CIA-funded German magazine, *Der Monat,* that he was collecting material on "the heavy communist infiltration in the Eisenhower and early Clay headquarters in Germany, which I want to have on hand for use if the occasion arises . . . If the thing goes too far, I want to be able to prove that bad judgment about world trends and a foolish tolerance of communists were not limited to our wholly a-political scientists. Under the present rules, Eisenhower himself would be a bad risk." JWA to Melvin Lasky, May 14, "1954" folder, box 10, JWAP; Yoder, *Joe Alsop's Cold War,* 110; Joseph Alsop, "U.S. Policy Errors in Germany Laid to 'Pastoralization' Theory," *NYHT,* Sept. 6, 1946; Joseph Alsop, *"I've Seen the Best of It,"* 358–59.

34. Joseph Alsop, *"I've Seen the Best of It,"* 359.

35. Merry, *Taking On the World,* 274.

36. Adams left little doubt in his memoirs about his intent in showing Joe the chronology: "I had given Alsop a target—to get that document busted loose from the Administration." Adams, *Without Precedent,* 123; "Army Charges McCarthy and Cohn Threatened It in Trying to Obtain Preferred Treatment for Schine," *NYT,* March 12, 1954.

37. Joe wrote that the "original document also contained certain suggestions as to the

nature of the McCarthy-Cohn-Schine relationship; here again, of course, there are clear hints in the published version." "The Tale Half Told," *NYHT,* March 15, 1954; Adams, *Without Precedent,* 147.

38. Joseph Alsop, *"I've Seen the Best of It,"* 356.

39. Rev. J. Brady to JWA, July 17, and JWA to Brady, July 21, "1953" folder, box 9, JWAP.

40. "Edwards stated that reports about Wisner's past activities are again circulating in Washington and Senator McCarthy has allegedly taken an interest in Wisner's past." V. P. Keary to A. H. Belmont, April 28, 1953, Frank Gardiner Wisner FBI file; Susan Mary Alsop, *To Marietta from Paris,* 204.

41. Taylor to JWA, Jan. 21, and JWA to Taylor, Jan. 25, "1954" folder, box 9, JWAP.

42. JWA to Murrow, March 11, "1954" folder, box 9, JWAP. While courageous and "substantial" in its public impact, Murrow's program was nonetheless, as Yoder writes, "belated"—since the Alsops "had made McCarthy a special project from the outset." Yoder, *Joe Alsop's Cold War,* 111.

43. Yoder, *Joe Alsop's Cold War,* 107–10.

44. Oshinsky, *Conspiracy So Immense,* 416–34.

45. Jenner to JWA, June 15, and JWA to Jenner, June 22, "1954" folder, box 10, JWAP.

46. "The Last of McCarthy?," *NYHT,* April 10, 1957. Like the Alsops, the journalist Drew Pearson had attacked McCarthy well before Murrow. Campbell, *Getting It Wrong,* 55.

CHAPTER THIRTEEN   "An Act of Very Great Folly"

1. Susan Mary Alsop, *To Marietta from Paris,* 230.

2. "Appeal for U.S. Troops for Indo-China Likely," *NYHT,* Jan. 4, 1954; Merry, *Taking On the World,* 251–52; "Joseph Alsop, Columnist, Dead at 78," *Los Angeles Times,* Aug. 29, 1989.

3. "The Day Joe Alsop Angered the French," *WP,* Aug. 22, 1982; "The First Domino: Joe Alsop's Indochina Crusade," *WP,* April 23, 1995.

4. Merry, *Taking On the World,* 250.

5. JWA to Schlesinger, June 25, 1954, "John, Joseph & Stewart Alsop, June 1954–1960" folder, box P-8, Schlesinger Papers.

6. "If my analysis is correct, as I believe it is, there is no alternative except to act *before* the final and decisive turn of the power balance. That means preventive action, preventive war if you like." JWA to Schlesinger, June 4, 1954, box P-8, Schlesinger Papers.

7. Schlesinger to JWA, June 1, 1954, box P-8, Schlesinger Papers; James Hershberg, "The End of the Cold War and the Transformation of Cold War History: A Tale of Two Conferences, 1988–89," unpublished manuscript; Nitze to JWA, July 1, 1954, "Joseph Alsop, 1952–85" folder, box 17, Nitze Papers.

8. After a subsequent discussion of preventive war with Joe "rather got under my skin," Nitze wrote to Finletter that he had sent Acheson, Bissell, and several others a copy of Joe's letter along with his reply. Nitze to Finletter, July 2, 1954, "Joseph Alsop, 1952–85" folder, box 17, Nitze Papers; Finletter to "all members of our group," Sept. 13, 1954, box 11, JWAP.

9. Eisenhower used the phrase in a speech before the American Bar Association's annual meeting, in Philadelphia, on August 24, 1955. *Public Papers of the Presidents: Dwight D. Eisenhower* (U.S. Government Printing Office, 1956), 802–9.

10. Joseph Alsop, *"I've Seen the Best of It,"* 385.
11. "U.S. Plans Earth's First Artificial Satellite in '57," *NYHT,* March 9, 1955.
12. "Perhaps rather naturally, [Eisenhower] did not suspect that this was a case of an NSC paper quoting the Alsops, rather than the reverse." Alsop and Alsop, *Reporter's Trade,* 67–68.
13. Joseph Alsop, *"I've Seen the Best of It,"* 391–93.
14. Merry, *Taking On the World,* 278; "Alsops Join Preachers of Atomic War," Foreign Broadcast Information Service, March 26, 1955, www.cia.gov/foia.
15. JWA to Berlin, July 12, and JWA to Bohlen, Aug. 8, "1956" folder, box 13, JWAP.
16. JWA to Ernest Cuneo, June 14, "1954" folder, box 10, JWAP; author interview with Joe Alsop VI, Sept. 17, 2013, Beverly Farms, Mass.
17. Collier, "Joe Alsop Story."
18. Stewart Alsop, *Stay of Execution,* 87.
19. Ibid., 86; Merry, *Taking On the World,* 287.
20. Joseph Alsop, *"I've Seen the Best of It,"* 393.
21. "Foxes and Lions," *Time,* Nov. 26, 1956. "Because of our lack of faith in the administration's foreign and defense policy, we both briefly considered voting for [Stevenson]. But we were so repelled by his performance that we could not, repeat not, bring ourselves to do so in the end." JWA to Luce, Nov. 23, "1956" folder, box 13, JWAP.
22. JWA to Leiter, Dec. 12, 1956, and JWA to Jacqueline Kennedy, telegram, Dec. 12, "1956" folder, box 13, JWAP.
23. Bohlen to JWA, March 26, "1955" folder, box 20, and JWA to Zarubin, Aug. 8, "1956" folder, box 13, JWAP; Boardman to Belmont, March 29, 1957, Joseph Alsop FBI file.
24. "One of my chief motives in asking permission to visit Russia is the fear that I may have misjudged the Soviet Union's present world role," Joe wrote, unconvincingly. JWA to Zarubin, Aug. 8, and JWA to Susan Mary Patten, Nov. 29, "1956" folder, box 13, JWAP; Joseph Alsop, *"I've Seen the Best of It,"* 396.
25. "Joseph Alsop Finds Kremlin a Surprise," *NYHT,* Jan. 16, 1957; Joseph Alsop, *"I've Seen the Best of It,"* 398–400.
26. Stewart Alsop to JWA, Jan. 24 and March 8, 1957, "W" folder, box 143, Stewart Alsop Papers.
27. Allen Dulles to Hoover, memorandum, April 1, 1957, www.cia.gov/foia; Yoder, *Joe Alsop's Cold War,* 154. Dulles's letter and Alsop's account of the Moscow incident were declassified by the CIA in May 1999.
28. Alsop evidently wrote his account of the Grand Hotel incident in Bohlen's presence at the Moscow embassy, addressing it to Frank Wisner. Strauss, "Memorandum for the Files," Jan. 3, 1961, "AEC Files—Alsop Brothers—Correspondence and Memos" folder, Strauss Papers. The author thanks the archivist Spencer Howard of the Herbert Hoover Library for locating files on Alsop and the Moscow incident in the Strauss Papers.
29. On March 28, 1957, a day after receiving Dulles's memo, Hoover ordered bureau agents to prepare a summary report on both Alsop brothers; an aide noted that the FBI files on the two journalists were already "voluminous." Bureau records indicate that the dossier on Alsop and the Moscow incident was retained in the FBI's Special File Room, and was pulled for review in 1964 and again in 1967. Hoover to Clyde Tolson et al., March 28, 1957, Belmont to Boardman, March 29, 1957, and Walter Short to Louis Nichols, April 4, 1957, Joseph Alsop FBI file; Allen Dulles to Hoover, March 27, 1957, www.cia.gov/foia.

30. Dulles to Hoover, April 5 and 16, 1957, www.cia.gov/foia; Dulles to Hoover, April 16, 1957, Edwards to Hoover, April 26, 1957; Susan Viscuso/CIA to Herken, May 23, 2011, personal correspondence; Wise, *Molehunt,* 76–77.

31. "The Attorney General was shocked to hear of this particular development." Hoover to Tolson et al., April 2, 1957, and Hoover to Tolson et al., April 17, 1957, Joseph Alsop FBI file.

32. JWA to Philippe Grumbach, April 11, "1958" folder, box 14, JWAP. David Halberstam credited Joe with being "unusually influential" in creating the image of Eisenhower as "an ill-informed figure who was out of touch with reality and whose defense policies were putting American security in jeopardy." Halberstam, *Fifties,* 704. Alsop told John and Jackie Kennedy that Ike was the worst president the country had ever seen—with the possible exception of James Buchanan. Kennedy and Beschloss, *Jacqueline Kennedy,* 134. Strauss, "Memorandum for the Files," May 21, 1959, "AEC Files—Alsop Brothers—Correspondence and Memos" folder, Strauss Papers.

33. G. H. Scatterday to Belmont, Oct. 28, 1958, and Belmont to R. R. Roach, March 4, 1958, Joseph Alsop FBI file.

34. Felsenthal, *Power, Privilege, and the "Post,"* 143–44; Graham, *Personal History,* 429; Heymann, *Georgetown Ladies' Social Club,* 63.

35. Felsenthal, *Power, Privilege, and the "Post,"* 164.

36. Block, *Herblock,* 140; Bray, *Pillars of the "Post,"* 30–31. Joe Alsop agreed with Graham about Khrushchev and peaceful coexistence: "I was not for one moment deluded by this promise." Joseph Alsop, *"I've Seen the Best of It,"* 397.

37. Halberstam, *Powers That Be,* 183, 177.

38. Felsenthal, *Power, Privilege, and the "Post,"* 142.

39. Graham, *Personal History,* 189, 194, 232; "Guest at Breakfast," *Time,* April 16, 1956.

40. Hagerty to Graham, May 16, 1956, and Graham to *Editor and Publisher,* Aug. 22, 1957, "Katharine Graham, 1980–1996" folder, box 29, Block Papers.

41. Block, *Herblock,* 224; Halberstam, *Powers That Be,* 193.

42. Graham, *Personal History,* 48, 93; Lynn Rosellini, "The Katharine Graham Story," *Washington Star,* Nov. 13, 1978.

43. Graham to Schlesinger, April 29, 1952, "Philip Graham, 1946–1960" folder, box P-15, Schlesinger Papers. A 1955 Herblock cartoon features an enigmatically smiling Stevenson seated at a nightclub table across from an obviously smitten suitor representing the Democratic Party. The caption reads, "Yes? You were going to say something?" Block, *Herblock,* 224.

44. Halberstam, *Powers That Be,* 309–11; Felsenthal, *Power, Privilege, and the "Post,"* 162–65; Graham to Herblock, Sept. 16, "Philip Graham, 1948–1963" folder, box 29, Block Papers.

45. Graham to JWA, Oct. 6, "1957" folder, box 129, JWAP.

46. "Deputies' Meeting," Oct. 11, 1957, CIA/CREST.

CHAPTER FOURTEEN "A Chap of Great Promise"

1. Hazard, *Cold War Crucible,* 233; Weiner, *Legacy of Ashes,* 76.

2. The memo that Wisner sent to Allen Dulles on January 8, 1954, was typically prolix: "I do not find that we have ever received definitive or authoritative policy guidance of the kind which would authorize us to proceed with the development of plans of a

general character to either whip up or exploit uprisings which may occur in the satellites." *FRUS/IC,* 469–71.

3. "BGFIEND Operational Plans for 1952," Feb. 19, 1952, folder 1, vol. 20, box 50, Fiend Records.

4. "Project Fiend Review for DCI," Nov. 8, 1951, folder 1, vol. 2, box 46; "Letter from Red Team," April 24, 1952, folder 1, vol. 5, box 46; "Operational Plan and Operational Clearance Request for Coup-de-Main Team Members—SHAM/BGFIEND," July 16, 1952, folder 1, vol. 22, box 51, Fiend Records.

5. "Tirana Trials of CIA Agents," April 20, 1954, folder 1, vol. 6, box 47; "Albanian Operations," Aug. 31, 1953, folder 2, vol. 25, box 52; "CE Review of APPLE Trial," May 18, 1954, folder 1, vol. 6, box 47, Fiend Records.

6. "Project Status Report," June 30, 1955, folder 2, vol. 29, box 52; "Project Status Report," Aug. 31 and Nov. 29, 1956, folder 1, vol. 30, box 52, Fiend Records.

7. Cullather, *Secret History,* 16–17; Grose, *Gentleman Spy,* 370–76.

8. Barrett, *CIA and Congress,* 170; Grose, *Gentleman Spy,* 373. According to a 1979 CIA investigation, in September 1952, the Plans Directorate had put together a list of fifty-eight Guatemalan Communists to be killed by local paramilitary forces in the event of a successful coup. But the CIA inquiry concluded that "not only was there no disposal of communist leaders during the operation, there was none after." "Report of Questionable Activity in Connection with Project PBSUCCESS," Oct. 11, 1979, CIA/CREST.

9. Cullather, *Secret History,* 129.

10. Weiner, *Legacy of Ashes,* 81–92. The CIA would not formally admit to its role in the Iranian coup until 2013, sixty years after Ajax. Wisner initially urged that agency personnel involved in Ajax receive a special letter of commendation but later grew "troubled about the security implications" and withdrew his suggestion. "CIA Confirms Role in 1953 Iran Coup," National Security Archive Electronic Briefing Book no. 435.

11. "Of all the factors that contributed to Arbenz's overthrow, I have always believed that the most decisive was the bombing." Bissell, *Reflections of a Cold Warrior,* 86. Cullather, *Secret History,* 103. "[Wisner] was very happy to be rid of this thing, the nightmare was over." Burton Hersh, *Old Boys,* 352.

12. The CIA was disappointed that the stolen documents showed "no traces of Soviet control and substantial evidence that Guatemalan Communists acted alone, without support or guidance from outside the country." Cullather, *Secret History,* 106–9; Weiner, *Legacy of Ashes,* 104.

13. Barnes and Bissell were brought into the planning of Success early in 1954. Immerman, *CIA in Guatemala,* 139; Bissell, *Reflections of a Cold Warrior,* 83. "The triumph showed what could be accomplished through covert action." Cullather, *Secret History,* 105.

14. Donald Wilbur, "Overthrow of Premier Mossadeq of Iran, November 1952–August 1953," 86, National Security Archive Briefing Book no. 28, "The Secret CIA History of the Iran Coup," www.gwu.edu/~nsarchiv; Cullather, *Secret History,* 56.

15. Joe told Wisner that he needed some more background before he could write about Honduras. Wisner to Chief, W.H. Division, Aug. 31, 1954, www.cia.gov/foia. In his memoirs, Joe Alsop hinted that he had been tipped off to the CIA's role in both the Iranian and the Guatemalan coups, but had deliberately chosen not to report on either: "This type of journalistic discretion—or complicity, if one prefers the word—was never fashionable and today would likely come under bitter attack." Joseph Alsop, *"I've Seen the Best of It,"* 443.

16. "I should appreciate your keeping this note as a confidential matter between us," Frank wrote to Phil Graham. Wisner to Graham, Dec. 20, 1954, "G" folder, Wisner Papers.

17. According to Salisbury, Allen Dulles confided to Julius Adler, his former Princeton classmate and the *Times*'s general manager, that the agency was concerned about "Gruson's leanings." Salisbury, *Without Fear or Favor*, 478–82; Burton Hersh, *Old Boys*, 349; Reston, *Deadline*, 209; Wisner to Dulles, June 2, 1954, http://www.cia.gov/foia.

18. "Report on the Covert Activities of the Central Intelligence Agency," n.d., www.cia.gov/foia; Weiner, *Legacy of Ashes*, 107–9. Memorandum of conversation, Oct. 19, 1954, *FRUS/IC*, 561–63.

19. Dulles to Hoover, April 19, 1954, and Edwards to Hoover, May 24, 1955, Frank Gardiner Wisner FBI file. Edwards's letter noted that some of the bureau's claims about Wisner came from "an investigator with a Senate investigating subcommittee, who has been attempting to build a case for Congressional hearings on CIA operations."

20. Burton Hersh, *Old Boys*, 320; Weiner, *Enemies*, 177; Johnson, *Radio Free Europe and Radio Liberty*, 128; Bissell to DDP, July 22, 1954, doc. no. 46, International Cold War History Project, www.wilsoncenter.org.

21. Thomas, *Very Best Men*, 188; Thomas, *Ike's Bluff*, 213, 405.

22. Bissell, *Reflections of a Cold Warrior*, 92–96; Damms, "James Killian, the Technological Capabilities Panel, and the Emergence of President Eisenhower's 'Scientific-Technological Elite,'" 57–78; "The Killian Report," *NYHT*, Sept. 19, 1955. One of the bureau's anonymous informants on the Alsops worked for the *New York Herald Tribune*. He told a Hoover aide that "he felt it was 'a damn shame' that the President cannot have a report without having it leaked to the Alsops." Hoover to SAC, Washington, D.C., Sept. 19, 1955, and Nichols to Tolson, Sept. 15, 1955, Joseph Alsop FBI file.

23. Pedlow and Welzenbach, *CIA and the U-2 Program;* Richelson, *America's Secret Eyes in Space*.

24. Stewart Alsop, *Center*, 250.

25. "Briefing Points on South Vietnam," Nov. 2, 1954, "Documents on U.S. Policy in the Vietnam War, 1954–68" series, DNSA; Wisner to JWA, March 30, 1956, "Stewart and Joe Alsop" folder, Wisner Papers.

26. Barrett, *CIA and Congress*, 214.

27. Richard Helms, *A Look over My Shoulder*, 364. Wisner had originally wanted to withhold the Khrushchev speech until Red Sox and Red Cap were "up to snuff" and then release it to spur popular uprisings in the Soviet bloc, but he was overruled by Angleton and Dulles. Corson, *Armies of Ignorance*, 313; Burton Hersh, *Old Boys*, 382; David Binder, "'56 East Europe Plan of CIA Is Described," *NYT*, Nov. 30, 1976. Binder claimed that the CIA's ethnic agent program was not abandoned until 1958.

28. Grose, *Gentleman Spy*, 437–38. The classified CIA history of the Hungarian uprising, written in 1958, concluded, "This breath-taking and undreamed-of state of affairs not only caught many Hungarians off-guard, it also caught us off-guard, for which we can hardly be blamed since we had no inside information, little outside information, and could not read the Russians' minds." "CIA and Hungary, 1956," National Security Archive Electronic Briefing Book no. 206. James McCargar, the former OSS operative whose experience in Hungary went back to 1946, had quit OPC a few years later, reportedly protesting to Wisner that his mission was being undermined by the corrupt dealings of Carmel Offie. Burton Hersh, *Old Boys*, 388–90. Peter

Grose describes McCargar as "the Scarlet Pimpernel of a renegade American intelligence service." Grose, *Operation Rollback*, 73–74. Using a pseudonym, McCargar later wrote an account of his time as an undercover agent in Hungary. Felix, *Short Course in the Secret War.*

29. Marton, *Enemies of the People*, 157. "In 1953, as indeed in all other years including 1956, 'all [CIA] efforts to obtain and maintain contact with reporting sources in Hungary were unsuccessful.'" Gati, *Failed Illusions*, 73.

30. "The 1956 Hungarian Revolution: A History in Documents," www.gwu.edu/~nsarchiv.

31. Thomas, *Very Best Men*, 144; Grose, *Gentleman Spy*, 438.

32. "CIA and Hungary, 1956." One of Frank's CIA colleagues later wrote that "there can be no doubt that Wisner and other top officials of his Directorate of Plans, especially those on the covert side, were fully prepared with arms, communication stocks and air resupply, to come to the aid of the freedom fighters. This was exactly the end for which the Agency's paramilitary capability was designed." Colby, *Honorable Men*, 134.

33. A partially declassified CIA document indicates that the agency, on October 31, 1956, approved a scheme "which proposed that certain defectors [deleted] who had volunteered to go back into Hungary be allowed to go." "CIA and Hungary, 1956." Hazard, *Cold War Crucible*, 236; Burton Hersh, *Old Boys*, 401.

34. JWA to Susan Mary Patten, Dec. 3, "1956" folder, box 13, JWAP.

35. According to his biographer, Donovan "was to be found night after night on the Austro-Hungarian frontier, physically helping refugees coming through the great frozen bulrush swamps as Soviet tanks clanked in the darkness and flares arched across the night sky." Brown, *Last Hero*, 830.

36. Thomas, *Very Best Men*, 147.

37. Wisner to Luce, June 25, 1958, "Clare Boothe Luce" folder, Wisner Papers.

38. Burton Hersh, *Old Boys*, 401.

39. Powers, *Man Who Kept the Secrets*, 75.

40. Acheson to Wisner, Dec. 28, 1956, "Frank Wisner" folder, box 34, Acheson Papers; Wisner to Graham, July 5, 1958, "G" folder, Wisner Papers.

41. Thomas, *Very Best Men*, 375n.

42. Burton Hersh, *Old Boys*, 383.

43. Richard Helms, *A Look over My Shoulder*, 366; "Project OBTUSE," n.d., folder 1, vol. 9, box 47, Fiend Records. Based on a study of Soviet documents, Charles Gati concluded that Lindsay's idea might actually have succeeded, since Khrushchev would have been reluctant to crush the revolt with UN representatives on the scene. Gati, *Failed Illusions*, 236.

44. Bruce might have also been angry at Wisner for planning Project Fortune without informing the State Department. Beisner, *Dean Acheson*, 628; Grose, *Operation Rollback*, 219. Invariably described as "aristocratic" and "a courtly Virginian," Bruce kept a personal diary in the 1950s that contains numerous entries regarding dinner parties, "drinking bouts," and "eating the black stuff"—caviar—with the Wisners and the Grahams. Burton Hersh, *Old Boys*, 499n. Bruce's criticism of the agency as rich and elitist is ironic, considering that he married into the Mellon fortune and left behind a four-thousand-bottle wine cellar and a multimillion-dollar estate in Georgetown when he died in 1977. Weisbrode, *Atlantic Century*, 103–4; Heymann, *Georgetown Ladies' Social Club*, 81–92.

45. Author interview with Ellis Wisner, Nov. 17, 2009, Washington, D.C.

46. Burton Hersh, *Old Boys,* 306; Merry, *Taking On the World,* 300.

47. Wisner to Wigglesworth, July 12, 1958, "W" folder, Wisner Papers. Wigglesworth served in Congress from 1928 to November 1958 and died in 1960.

48. Wisner to Sulzberger, July 23, 1958, Sulzberger to Wisner, Aug. 5, 1958, Stewart Alsop to Wisner, July 29, 1958, "W" folder, Wisner Papers.

49. Prados, *Safe for Democracy,* 174–79.

50. Wisner's estimate of U.S. prospects in Vietnam also varied widely, depending on the times and Frank's mood. "Briefing Points on South Vietnam," Nov. 2, 1954, "U.S. Policy in the Vietnam War, 1954–68," DNSA; Sheehan, *Bright Shining Lie,* 140. Cullather, *Secret History,* 112, 114.

51. Anonymous, "The Mysterious Doings of CIA," *SEP,* Oct. 30, 1954; Thomas, *Very Best Men,* 200.

52. Thomas, *Very Best Men,* 211–12; Burton Hersh, *Old Boys,* 404.

53. JWA to Bohlen, Sept. 6, and Bohlen to JWA, Sept. 12, "1958" folder, box 14, JWAP; author interview with Ellis Wisner, Nov. 17, 2009, Washington, D.C.

54. "Hospital Papers" folder, box "E–I," Wisner Papers; Belmont to Roach, Sept. 13, 1958, Frank Gardiner Wisner FBI file.

55. "After a great deal of soul-searching and after consultation with Frank himself and with his full understanding, I am appointing Dick Bissell as DD/P." Allen Dulles to W. H. Jackson, Dec. 7, 1958, CIA/CREST; Richard Helms, *A Look over My Shoulder,* 163–64.

CHAPTER FIFTEEN "The Prophet of the Missile Gap"

1. James Killian, *Sputnik, Scientists, and Eisenhower: A Memoir of the First Special Assistant to the President for Science and Technology* (MIT Press, 1977), 6–12.

2. Alsop and Alsop, *Reporter's Trade,* 67, 355–58.

3. Nitze to Kennan, Aug. 30, 1956, and Kennan to Nitze, Sept. 5, 1956, folder 6, box 34, and Kennan to Stevenson, Aug. 24, 1956, folder 4, box 46, GFKP; Nitze, *From Hiroshima to Glasnost,* 160; Gaddis, *GFK,* 516.

4. JWA to Kennan, Oct. 29, 1956, folder 8, box 1, GFKP; Hixson, *George F. Kennan,* 150; Joseph Alsop, "Soviet Will Never Recover."

5. By late August, the Alsops had written a column about the forthcoming top secret study. In a letter to Acheson, Nitze described the Gaither panel as "another committee to do an agonizing reappraisal of our budget and defense position." "Mr. Gaither's Job," *NYHT,* Aug. 26, 1957; Nitze to Acheson, Sept. 4, 1947, folder 295, box 23, Acheson Papers.

6. Kaplan, *Wizards of Armageddon,* 125–43; Nitze, *From Hiroshima to Glasnost,* 166–69; Herken, *Counsels of War,* 46, 112–16.

7. U.S. Congress, Joint Committee on Defense Production, *Deterrence and Survival in the Nuclear Age* (U.S. Goverment Printing Office, 1976), 12.

8. Kaplan, *Wizards of Armageddon,* 145–48; author interview with Jerome Wiesner, Feb. 9, 1982, Cambridge, Mass.

9. Eisenhower told Foster Dulles that his real concern was not the Gaither Report itself but the likelihood that it would not remain secret for long. Memorandum of conversation, Nov. 7, 1957, DDRS-1984-1630; "We Have Been Warned," *WP,* Nov. 25,

1957; "Enormous Arms Outlay Is Held Vital to Survival," *WP,* Dec. 20, 1957; entry of Dec. 18, "1957 Daybook" folder, box 1, Nitze Papers.

10. Memorandum of conversation, Jan. 3, 1958, DDRS-1984–1631.

11. Kennan, *Memoirs, 1950–1963,* 229–53.

12. Gaddis, *GFK,* 524.

13. Kennan, *Memoirs, 1950–1963,* 249–50; Isaacson and Thomas, *Wise Men,* 580; "A Hunger for Cozy Self-Delusion," *WP,* Jan. 19, 1958.

14. "Altogether, what between the distortions, the misunderstandings and the ridicule, I felt very much put upon," Kennan grumbled. Kennan, *Memoirs, 1950–1963,* 236, 252; diary entry of Oct. 5, 1992, folder 2, box 326, and Kennan to Stevenson, Feb. 19, 1958, folder 3, box 46, GFKP.

15. Nitze, *Tension Between Opposites,* 130–31. John Gaddis writes that it was actually Nitze who encouraged Acheson to reply to Kennan: "Acheson did not simply jump at this opportunity; he pounced on it." Gaddis, *GFK,* 528–29.

16. In a 1984 interview with the author, Nitze recounted his walk around the lake with Kennan in detail. But Kennan, the following year, wrote to the author that he had "no recollection of it and think it most improbable." Nitze's calendar and his correspondence with Halle show that the two men were in Geneva on March 25–26, 1958, and that Halle had previously "written to George Kennan in the hope he can make it too." Kennan's calendar confirms that he was in Geneva on the same days as Halle and Nitze. Halle to Nitze, Feb. 4, 1958, "Louis Halle" folder, box 26, and entries for March 25–27, "1958 Daybook" folder, box 1, Nitze Papers; author interview with Paul Nitze, July 12, 1984, Washington, D.C.; Kennan to Herken, Nov. 5, 1985, folder 3, box 20, GFKP. The author thanks the Princeton archivist Adriane Hanson for her sleuthing into Kennan's whereabouts on those dates.

17. Kennan to Editors, Sept. 15, 1958, "Unused Material Intended for Rebuttal of Criticism of 1957 Reith Lectures" folder, box 26, GFKP.

18. Nitze, "Atoms, Strategy, and Policy"; Kennan to Stevenson, Jan. 26, 1954, folder 3, box 46, GFKP. "I realize the momentum that is behind all this, and the imponderables involved. I understand how many people are committed, and how deeply, to playing with these toys," Kennan wrote to an atomic scientist in 1959. Hixson, *George F. Kennan,* 190–91.

19. Stewart Alsop to JWA, Nov. 25, 1957, "Corr. with Stewart Alsop, 1957–58" folder, box 143, JWAP.

20. The publisher of Pittsburgh's *Post-Gazette* notified Joe that "we dropped your column some years ago, because we thought it too full of gloom and doom." William Block to JWA, July 21, and Alsop to Block, Aug. 3, "1960" folder, box 16, JWAP.

21. Susan Mary Alsop, *To Marietta from Paris,* 311.

22. "Who the hell is Guy Lombardo?" Alsop asked his guests. Merry, *Taking On the World,* 334; Yoder, *Joe Alsop's Cold War,* 177. Joe later admitted that "avoiding television" had been a mistake for his career, since his audience became more limited over time. Joseph Alsop, *"I've Seen the Best of It,"* 402.

23. Stewart Alsop to JWA, Nov. 25, 1957, "W" folder, box 143, JWAP.

24. Author interview with Elizabeth Winthrop Alsop and Joseph Alsop VI, April 29, 2012, New York City.

25. Joseph Alsop to Stewart Alsop, July 30, "1958" folder, box 74, JWAP.

26. Hoover to Belmont et al., March 12, 1958, Joseph Alsop FBI file. Stewart Alsop to JWA, Oct. 3 and 16, "1958" folder, and JWA to Stewart Alsop, "Undated" folder, box 14, JWAP; Merry, *Taking On the World,* 335–37.

27. JWA to S. M. Patten, April 6, "1959" folder, box 15, JWAP; JWA to Susan Mary Patten, Sept. 13, 1960, Joseph Alsop Private Papers.

28. JWA to [Unknown], March 31, and JWA to Berlin, March 20, "1958" folder, box 13, JWAP.

29. Merry, *Taking On the World,* 329. Many of Joe's letters to prospective interview subjects, while typically fawning, nonetheless contained an undercurrent of threat, as in his letter to Nixon: "It may be impertinent for me to say so, but I judge from various comments that I have heard and read since returning to Washington that your present position is not without certain delicate aspects. And it is hard to know how not [sic] put the foot wrong unless we have had a frank talk." JWA to Nixon, March 27, "1958" folder, box 13, JWA to Nixon, April 2, "1958" folder, box 14, Stewart Alsop to JWA, Nov. 25, 1957, "Corr. with Stewart Alsop" folder, box 143, JWAP.

30. "Pentagon Studies All-Out Guided Missile Project," *WP,* May 25, 1954; Stewart Alsop to JWA, Dec. 27, 1957, "Corr. with Stewart Alsop" folder, box 143, JWAP.

31. Telegram, June 26, "1957" folder, box 21, JWAP.

32. "Untruth on Defense," *WP,* Aug. 1, 1958.

33. "Because Alsop and his brother and fellow columnist Stewart Alsop were known to be wired into the CIA through long-standing friendships with men like Bissell and Allen Dulles, the missile numbers they cited were accepted as gospel in many quarters in Washington." Taubman, *Secret Empire,* 274–75, 392n. Missile gap and intelligence estimates: NIE 11–5-58, "Soviet Capabilities in Guided Missiles and Space Vehicles," n.d., in Steury, *Intentions and Capabilities,* 65–70; Thomas, *Very Best Men,* 385n; Thomas, *Ike's Bluff,* 310–13; Sheehan, *Fiery Peace in a Cold War,* 254–59; Preble, *John F. Kennedy and the Missile Gap,* 55–58, 198n; Whittell, *Bridge of Spies,* 142–46.

34. Kistiakowsky, *Scientist at the White House,* 250–51. "Bill Bundy simply asked Alsop not to call me any more, and that did it." Garthoff, *Journey Through the Cold War,* 65.

35. Ambrose, *Eisenhower,* 563. "Unfortunately for the country and the world, Alsop's thesis proved to be more persuasive than President Eisenhower's calm." Fursenko and Naftali, *Khrushchev's Cold War,* 254; Preble, *John F. Kennedy and the Missile Gap,* 55.

36. Wise, *Molehunt,* 77n; Streitfeld, "The Hawk and the Vultures"; Merry, *Taking On the World,* 363.

37. Streitfeld, "The Hawk and the Vultures"; Yoder, *Joe Alsop's Cold War,* 155–56; "Commentary on McElroy Gospel," *WP,* Feb. 2, 1959.

38. Strauss, "Memorandum to the Files," April 6, 1959, "AEC Files—Alsop Brothers—Correspondence and Memos" folder, Strauss Papers; Yoder, *Joe Alsop's Cold War,* 156; Theoharis, *J. Edgar Hoover, Sex, and Crime,* 114. Although Alsop volunteered to tell his story to the FBI, Hoover demurred, writing on one memo, "The fact Alsop inquired re FBI views doesn't mean we have to give them to him." The FBI director justified his wider dissemination of Alsop's "confession" on the grounds that homosexual clerks in the White House mailroom had already seen the file and thus compromised the confidentiality of the case. Hoover to Tolson et al., April 17, 1957, and Belmont to Roach, April 26, 1957, and Scatterday to Roach, Aug. 4, 1959, Joseph Alsop FBI file.

39. "Conflicts on 'Missile Gap,'" *WP,* Jan. 25, 1960; "The Soviet Missile Arsenal," *WP,* Jan. 26, 1960; "The Missile Gap and Survival," *WP,* Jan. 27, 1960; "Estimate of Red Missiles," *WP,* Jan. 28, 1960; "The Bridge," *WP,* Jan. 29, 1960; pamphlet, *The Missile Gap,* n.d., box 157, JWAP.

40. Sam Papich to F. A. Frohbose, Feb. 9, 1960, Joseph Alsop FBI file.

41. JWA to Berlin, April 30, "1958" folder, box 14, JWAP.

42. JWA to Joyce, June 16, "1959" folder, box 15, JWAP.

43. Joseph Alsop, *"I've Seen the Best of It,"* 406, 410; JWA to Susan Mary Patten, Sept. 13, 1960, Joseph Alsop Private Papers.

44. Merry, *Taking On the World,* 345; JWA to Sir Anthony Rumbold, July 20, "1960" folder, box 16, JWAP.

45. Joseph Alsop, *"I've Seen the Best of It,"* 403, 419–20; JWA to Susan Mary Patten, n.d. [Summer 1960], Joseph Alsop Private Papers.

46. Stewart Alsop, *Stay of Execution,* 99.

47. Ibid., 101; Merry, *Taking On the World,* 347.

48. Graham, *Personal History,* 259.

49. Joseph Alsop, *"I've Seen the Best of It,"* 426–28. Joe later dismissed the notion that Kennedy had expected Johnson to reject the offer. JWA to Johnson, March 25, 1964, "J" folder, box 69, JWAP.

50. Alsop credited Graham with "keeping the thing glued together despite the bitterness and suspicions that divided the two camps." JWA to Philip Potter, "P" folder, box 70, JWAP. "What Really Happened," *WP,* July 18, 1960; Graham, *Personal History,* 261–67. Phil Graham's confidential 1963 memorandum of the episode is reprinted in White, *Making of the President, 1964,* 407–15.

51. De Margerie, *American Lady,* 111. "It was the bravest behavior by a child I've ever seen," Joe later wrote to Bobby. JWA to Kennedy, Aug. 4, "1960" folder, box 16, JWAP.

52. JWA to Jacqueline Kennedy, Aug. 4, 1960, "Notes, 1960–1966" folder, box 130, JWAP.

53. Jacqueline Kennedy to JWA, n.d. [Aug. 1960], "Notes, 1960–1966" folder, box 130, JWAP.

54. "Things have to turn out right for people like you and Jack or there is no justice," Jackie later wrote to Joe. Kennedy to JWA, n.d. [Sept. 1960], "Notes, 1960–1966" folder, box 130, JWAP.

55. "It is hard not to conclude that Bissell *wanted* Alsop to raise alarms about a [missile] gap." Thomas, *Ike's Bluff,* 316. "The 'missile gap' was finally dispelled between June and September 1961 by satellite reconnaissance photographs that confirmed the actual very small Soviet ICBM deployments." Garthoff, *Journey Through the Cold War,* 48. Alsop's view of the missile gap also became more nuanced over time. Joe waited until the winter of 1960–1961 before finally admitting that "the gap" had been a myth. "There was no certainty whatever in the conviction that the missile gap did not exist because of the findings of the U-2 . . . Public humility, after all, was a small price to pay for peace of mind," Alsop wrote in his memoirs. Whittell, *Bridge of Spies,* 145; Fursenko and Naftali, *Khrushchev's Cold War,* 250–60; Alsop to Editor/*Economist,* Feb. 17, "1960" folder, box 16, JWAP; "The Dulles Testimony," *WP,* Feb. 2, 1960; Joseph Alsop, *"I've Seen the Best of It,"* 414–15. Ironically, while Alsop claimed that he had not known about the U-2 until the shoot-down, a column that he wrote five months earlier contained the highly classified revelation that NASA's Project Discoverer, allegedly a scientific research mission, was actually a top secret satellite reconnaissance program in disguise. "Big Brother's Eye—and Ours," *WP,* Jan. 1, 1960.

56. Jacqueline Kennedy to JWA, n.d. [Oct. 1960], "Notes, 1960–1966" folder, box 130, JWAP.

57. Schlesinger, *Journals,* 88.

58. Merry, *Taking On the World,* 355–56.

59. Ibid., 356–57; Joseph Alsop, *"I've Seen the Best of It,"* 430–31.

CHAPTER SIXTEEN "A Breathless Time, Full of Promise and Energy"

1. Susan Mary Patten to Schlesinger, telegram, Jan. 11, 1961, "Alsop, June 1954–1960" folder, box P-8, Schlesinger Papers.
2. Schlesinger, *Life in the 20th Century,* 378.
3. Joseph Alsop, *"I've Seen the Best of It,"* 436.
4. Ibid., 433–34; Merry, *Taking On the World,* 358, White House Diary, Jan. 1961, www.jfklibrary.org.
5. Just remembered Alsop as "being thrilled to be included in the top tier." Author interview with Ward Just, July 24, 2012, Martha's Vineyard, Mass.; "The Columnists JFK Reads Every Morning," *Newsweek,* Dec. 18, 1961.
6. JWA to Kennedy, June 21, 1963, "J. Alsop, 3/60–9/63" folder, President's Office Files, Special Correspondence, box 27, JFKL; Almquist, *Joseph Alsop and American Foreign Policy,* 96.
7. Schlesinger, *Journals,* 93.
8. Davies, *China Hand,* 338; Thayer to Harriman, May 13, 1965, "Charles Thayer, 1961–1968" folder, box 514, Harriman Papers; Finney, "Long Trial of John Paton Davies."
9. Graham to Kennedy, Jan. 23, 1961, "Philip Graham" folder, President's Office Files, Special Correspondence, box 30, JFKL.
10. Nitze, *From Hiroshima to Glasnost,* 170–74, 179–81; author interview with Paul Nitze, May 11, 1983, Washington, D.C.
11. Joseph Alsop to Susan Mary Patten, n.d. [Dec. 1947], Joseph Alsop Private Papers.
12. Sally B. Smith, *Grace and Power,* 378; transcript of oral history interview with Joseph Alsop, Oct. 29, 1979, 59, JFKL.
13. Joseph Alsop, *"I've Seen the Best of It,"* 437–38; Kennedy and Beschloss, *Jacqueline Kennedy,* 324.
14. De Margerie, *American Lady,* 108.
15. JWA to Charles Whitehouse, Jan. 16, "1961" folder, box 17, JWAP.
16. Hoover to Kennedy, March 13, 1961, Joseph Alsop FBI file.
17. Patten, *My Three Fathers,* 190–91.
18. Elizabeth Winthrop Alsop, *Don't Knock Unless You're Bleeding,* 9–11.
19. Merry, *Taking On the World,* 281; author interview with Donald Graham, March 23, 2010, Washington, D.C. Uncle Joe also earned the gratitude of the Grahams' sixteen-year-old daughter, Elizabeth, for the roses that he sent before her coming-out party. Elizabeth Graham to JWA, n.d. [1959], "Undated" folder, box 15, JWAP. Even before the wedding, there were signs of strains in the relationship—including an argument between Joe and Susan Mary over whether one should serve champagne at Sunday brunch. Patten, *My Three Fathers,* 191, 199; Merry, *Taking On the World,* 363, 373.
20. Transcript of Doug Fabrizio interview with Anne Milliken and David Auburn, June 11, 2012, RadioWest, KUER.
21. Patten, *My Three Fathers,* 183.
22. "Memorandum for the Files of Lewis L. Strauss," Dec. 13, 1960, "AEC—Memoranda for the Record, 1959–1962" folder, box 488, Strauss Papers.
23. "Memorandum for the Files of Lewis L. Strauss," Jan. 3, 1961, "AEC—Memoranda for the Record, 1959–1962" folder, box 488, Strauss Papers. The memo has a hand-written notation at the top of the page, dated Nov. 12, 1975: "Material not to be used publicly while J. Alsop is alive."

24. "Memorandum for the Files of Lewis L. Strauss," March 13, 1961, box 488, Strauss Papers.
25. "Memorandum for the Files of Lewis L. Strauss," Feb. 16, 1962, box 488, Strauss Papers. Several months later, Roger Robb, the prosecutor in the Oppenheimer case, telephoned Strauss to say that he had learned from the former attorney general Rogers that the original of Alsop's so-called confession "was at the CIA but that the Department of Justice has a photostatic copy of it." Telephone log for Aug. 23, 1962, "AEC Files—Alsop Brothers—Correspondence and Memos" folder, box 488, Strauss Papers.
26. JWA to Kennedy, n.d., "J. Alsop, 3/60–9/63" folder, President's Office Files, Special Correspondence, box 27, JFKL.
27. Almquist, *Joseph Alsop and American Foreign Policy,* 99; transcript of Charles Bohlen oral history interview, May 21, 1964, 38, JFKL.
28. Bird, *Color of Truth,* 106, 179.
29. Joseph Alsop, *"I've Seen the Best of It,"* 441.
30. Weiner, *Legacy of Ashes,* 173–74; Joseph Alsop, *"I've Seen the Best of It,"* 443; "If You Strike at a King," *WP,* April 24, 1961.
31. Stewart Alsop to Sam Griffith, April 21, 1961, folder 4A, box 5, Stewart Alsop Papers.
32. Stewart Alsop, "Lessons of the Cuban Disaster."
33. Author interviews with Elizabeth Winthrop Alsop and Joe Alsop VI, April 30, 2012, New York City.
34. Stewart Alsop, "Kennedy's Grand Strategy." Stewart sent an advance copy of the article to Phil Graham with the comment "it seems to me to have a certain news value, especially the part about nuclear warfare." Alsop to Graham, March 22, 1962, folder 6A, box 6, Stewart Alsop Papers.
35. Beschloss, *Crisis Years,* 371. During a visit to Moscow in early May 1962, Kennedy's press secretary "spent a considerable amount of time at lunch telling [Khrushchev] that that was the wrong impression, that Kennedy was not in favor of preventative war." Transcript of Pierre Salinger oral history interview, Aug. 10, 1965, 195, JFKL. Rather than an "incautious interview," Kennedy's statement seemed more likely a deliberate warning to Khrushchev, following the recent Berlin crisis. Bundy, *Danger and Survival,* 481.
36. "Facts About the Missile Balance," *WP,* Sept. 25, 1961; "Diary Notes," Sept. 25, 1961, CIA/CREST; Bird, *Color of Truth,* 228.
37. Halberstam, *Powers That Be,* 364; Graham, *Personal History,* 276–80, 293–94.
38. Graham to Editor/*Editor and Publisher,* April 4, 1961, folder 3, box 29, Block Papers.
39. Graham, *Personal History,* 308; Reston, *Deadline,* 199. Phil next offered the editorial page job to Stewart Alsop, who turned it down for the same reason. Merry, *Taking On the World,* 383.
40. Stacks, *Scotty,* 185; Graham to Kennedy, March 20, 1961, "Philip Graham" folder, President's Office Files, Special Correspondence, box 30, JFKL.
41. Felsenthal, *Power, Privilege, and the "Post,"* 186.
42. Graham, *Personal History,* 308.
43. Felsenthal, *Power, Privilege, and the "Post,"* 201.
44. Graham to Kennedy, Feb. 9, 1963, "Philip Graham" folder, President's Office Files, Special Correspondence, box 30, JFKL.
45. Helms to Wisner, April 26, 1961, "H" folder, Wisner Papers; Wisner to Helms, May 1, 1961, "Correspondence" folder, box 4, Helms Papers.
46. Cullather, *Secret History,* 100. In a 1995 interview, Bundy claimed that Dulles and

Bissell "never really believed Kennedy when he said he wasn't going to put American forces in." Bird, *Color of Truth,* 198.

47. Thomas, *Very Best Men,* 315.
48. Three days after the failed invasion, Allen Dulles ordered the agency's inspector general, Lyman Kirkpatrick, to uncover the causes of the Cuban disaster. Kirkpatrick's report was so critical of Bissell that the latter was allowed a rebuttal, actually written by Tracy Barnes. Michael Warner, "The CIA's Internal Probe of the Bay of Pigs Affair," n.d., www.cia.gov/foia.
49. Wisner to Helms, Jan. 1, 1962, "Correspondence" folder, box 4, Helms Papers.
50. Burton Hersh, *Old Boys,* 424; Polly Wisner to Helms, n.d., "1961 Correspondence" folder, and Frank Wisner to Helms, Jan. 1, "1962 Correspondence" folder, box 4, Helms Papers.
51. "John McCone arranged to recruit Wisner . . . to take advantage of Frank's close ties to *The Washington Post* and the Alsop brothers," wrote the journalist Charles Murphy. Burton Hersh, *Old Boys,* 438. Draft review of *The Craft of Intelligence,* n.d., folder 6, box 59, Dulles Papers. Frank also agreed to read a draft novel by Charles Thayer, who was still struggling to eke out a living as a writer. The manuscript, titled "An Officer and a Gentleman," was a barely disguised autobiographical account of Thayer's ordeal at the hands of Joseph McCarthy. Wisner urged Thayer not to publish the novel, warning that "there are better and wiser ways of exposing and denouncing an oppressive tyranny than setting fire to one's own gasoline saturated garments." Dean, *Imperial Brotherhood,* 279n, 282n.

CHAPTER SEVENTEEN "We Will All Fry"

1. Appointment book, Oct. 16, 1962, www.jfklibrary.org; "Chronologies of the Crisis," in "Cuban Missile Crisis, 1962: The 40th Anniversary," National Security Archive Electronic Briefing Book.
2. Among the library of books written on the missile crisis, the following have been most helpful: Fursenko and Naftali, *"One Hell of a Gamble";* Dobbs, *One Minute to Midnight;* Stern, *Averting "the Final Failure";* Stern, *Cuban Missile Crisis in American Memory;* Zelikow and May, *Presidential Recordings.*
3. Coleman, *Fourteenth Day,* 38; May and Zelikow, *Kennedy Tapes,* 107. As Joe Alsop noted, all three of Kennedy's Kremlinologists—Kennan, Bohlen, and Thompson—had previously predicted that Berlin would most likely be the cause of the next crisis in Soviet-American relations. "Another Year of Decision," *WP,* Feb. 13, 1961.
4. Joseph Alsop, *"I've Seen the Best of It,"* 446–48.
5. Although the president was evidently persuaded by Bohlen's rationale, Robert Kennedy would later bitterly complain, "Chip ran out on us." Bohlen, *Witness to History,* 489–93; Sorensen, *Counselor,* 287.
6. Bird, *Color of Truth,* 198.
7. Sorensen, *Counselor,* 287.
8. Transcript, n.d. [Oct. 19, 1962], "Interviews with Robert McNamara, 1962 and 1966" folder, box 64, JWAP.
9. May and Zelikow, *Kennedy Tapes,* 204; Graham, *Personal History,* 297–98.
10. "Phil tried to throw Murray [*sic*] off the track." "Notes," n.d., "Phil Graham" folder, box 2, Montague Kern, Patricia Levering, and Ralph Levering Papers, JFKL.

11. "What [Graham] did was to insist to reporter Murray [*sic*] Marder that his story of imminent decisions and official silence should not point specifically at Cuba, and Marder revised his story in a way that took Cuba out of the lead without taking it out of the story." Bundy, *Danger and Survival,* 402.

12. Stern, *Cuban Missile Crisis in American Memory,* 24.

13. Ibid., 129–33; "The Strongest Argument," *WP,* Oct. 24, 1962.

14. "The Cuban Missile Crisis, 1962: The 40th Anniversary"; Stern, *Cuban Missile Crisis in American Memory,* 99–108.

15. Jason Mullins, "Embassy Moscow: A Diplomatic Perspective of the Cuban Missile Crisis," www.georgetown.edu/globalsecuritystudiesreview/2013/05/07.

16. R. Standish Norris, "The Cuban Missile Crisis: A Nuclear Order of Battle, October/November 1962," unpublished manuscript, 174–75; "The Cuban Missile Crisis, 1962: The 40th Anniversary."

17. Stern, *Averting "the Final Failure,"* 161, 271–76.

18. Nitze, *From Hiroshima to Glasnost,* 227; May and Zelikow, *Kennedy Tapes,* 548–49; Nicholas Thompson, "We Will All Fry," *News Desk* (blog), *New Yorker,* Oct. 16, 2012, www.newyorker.com.

19. Scott Sagan, "SIOP-62: The Nuclear War Plan Briefing to President Kennedy," *International Security* 12, no. 1 (Summer 1987): 22–52; Rhodes, *Arsenals of Folly,* 87.

20. Author interview with Paul Nitze, May 11, 1983, Washington, D.C.; "Minutes," July 30, 1962, in William Burr and Robert Wampler, eds., "'Master of the Game,'" National Security Archive Electronic Briefing Book no. 139, Oct. 27, 2004; Kaplan, "JFK's First-Strike Plan"; William Burr, ed., "First Strike Options and the Berlin Crisis, September 1961," National Security Archive Electronic Briefing Book no. 56, Sept. 25, 2001.

21. Stern, *Cuban Missile Crisis in American Memory,* 130.

22. "Blockade Proclaimed," *WP,* Oct. 25, 1962; Dobbs, *One Minute to Midnight,* 199; U.S. Department of Defense, *To Defend and Deter,* 259.

23. Zelikow and May, *Presidential Recordings,* 356–512.

24. Dobbs, *One Minute to Midnight,* 291. Although he might have been among the first to suggest it at an ExComm meeting, Tommy Thompson ultimately opposed a Turkey-for-Cuba missile trade, believing that it would fatally undermine faith in the NATO alliance, of which Turkey was a member. Nitze, *From Hiroshima to Glasnost,* 219; Stern, *Cuban Missile Crisis in American Memory,* 104–6; May and Zelikow, *Kennedy Tapes,* 40; Stern, *Averting "the Final Failure,"* 421n; Blight and Lang, *Fog of War,* 31–32.

25. Stern, *Cuban Missile Crisis and American Memory,* 30, 107.

26. Mayers, *Ambassadors and America's Soviet Policy,* 205–9.

27. Memorandum of conversation, Oct. 30, 1962, "Joseph Alsop, 1961–67" folder, box 430, Harriman Papers.

28. "Post-mortems, October 15–28," n.d., folder 2, "Cuban Crisis, 1962: Executive Committee, NSC," Robert F. Kennedy Papers, JFKL, www.jfklibrary.org.

29. In an ExComm meeting on November 2, Kennedy observed of press coverage of the crisis, "But I think if we can hold it as tight as possible, then we can put it out in our own way." Coleman, *Fourteenth Day,* 55, 157; Fursenko and Naftali, *"One Hell of a Gamble,"* 322–23.

30. Bartlett to JFK, Oct. 29, 1962, "Charles Bartlett" folder, JFKL, www.jfklibrary.

31. Rusk's famous remark summed up the "heroic" interpretation of the missile crisis. Ironically, neither Alsop nor Bartlett interviewed Rusk, and the source of the quotation is disputed. Michael Dobbs, "The Price of a 50-Year Myth," *WP,* Oct. 15, 2012.

32. Alsop and Bartlett, "In Time of Crisis." The quotation about trading the missiles came from Alsop's interview with the NSC aide Michael Forrestal. Typescript, "Mike Forrestal on Cuba," n.d., "Notes/Cuba/SJOA" folder, Stewart Alsop Private Papers. Fursenko and Naftali argue that the president had an underlying motive for co-operating on the Alsop-Bartlett article: "[Kennedy] wanted a little stir over Adlai Stevenson to distract people from asking whether there had been a trade." *"One Hell of a Gamble,"* 322.

33. In a personal message that Khrushchev sent to Kennedy on December 11, the Soviet leader expressed displeasure at the leaks which had led to stories like that by Alsop and Bartlett, but also indicated that he understood the president's motive: "Judging by the contents of these articles it is clear that their authors are well informed and we get the impression that this is not a result of an accidental leak of the confidential information . . . This evidently is done for the purpose of informing the public in a one-sided way." Fursenko and Naftali, *"One Hell of a Gamble,"* 322.

34. Dallek, *Unfinished Life,* 266. In a subsequent interview, McGeorge Bundy claimed that it was not Stevenson's advice during the missile crisis but the latter's "constant reluctance to do what the President wanted" that had most angered Kennedy. Transcript of McGeorge Bundy oral history interview, March 1964, 19, JFKL, www.jfklibrary.org.

35. In the press conference, Kennedy cleverly sidestepped his own role in the Alsop and Bartlett article: "It is my judgment that this statement or interpretation of Governor Stevenson's position did not come from a member of the National Security Council." The president is not a member of the NSC. Transcript of press conference, Dec. 12, 1962, JFKL, www.jfklibrary.org.

36. "Kennedy wanted the press to believe that any rumors about the [missile] trade had come from Stevenson and his supporters." Fursenko and Naftali, *"One Hell of a Gamble,"* 321. "Footnote for the Historians," *SEP,* Jan. 16, 1963; Blair to Stewart Alsop, March 10, 1964, and Stewart Alsop to Blair, March 12, 1964, "Notes/Cuba/SJOA" folder, Stewart Alsop Private Papers. The author thanks Stewart Alsop's family for allowing him access to their father's notes and personal correspondence concerning "In Time of Crisis."

37. Transcript of Charles Bartlett oral history interview, Feb. 20, 1965, 127–34, JFKL, www.jfklibrary.org.

38. "Transcript Confirms Kennedy Linked Removal of Missiles in Cuba, Turkey," *WP,* Oct. 22, 1987.

39. Richard Helms, *A Look over My Shoulder,* 196–207; Bissell, *Reflections of a Cold Warrior,* 199–200; Weiner, *Legacy of Ashes,* 156–57, 161. The CIA's efforts to assassinate Castro were detailed in the so-called Family Jewels, documents released by the agency in 2007 "as examples of activities exceeding CIA's charter." "Subject: Johnny Roselli," n.d., in "CIA's Family Jewels," National Security Archive Electronic Briefing Book no. 222, June 26, 2007.

40. Thomas, *Very Best Men,* 302.

CHAPTER EIGHTEEN "How Great Is One's Duty to Truth?"

1. Stewart Alsop to Tom Congdon, June 17, 1962, folder 10A, box 6, Stewart Alsop Papers; Stewart Alsop, "Madness of Mao Tse-tung"; Richelson, *Spying on the Bomb,* 156n.

2. JWA to Edward Schwenn, Oct. 15, "1963" folder, box 19, JWAP.

3. Hanson Baldwin, "Soviet Missiles Protected in 'Hardened' Positions," *NYT,* July 26, 1962. The leak to Baldwin might have been intended to counter talk at the Pentagon of a preventive nuclear attack on the Soviet Union—the "clever first strike" that had been proposed during the 1961 Berlin crisis. Naftali, *Presidential Recordings,* 187, 444n; Tim Weiner, "J.F.K. Turns to the CIA to Plug a Leak," *NYT,* July 1, 2007.

4. JWA to Bundy, Nov. 26, "1962" folder, box 18, JWAP; telephone log, n.d., "J. Alsop" folder, box 27, President's Office Files, Special Correspondence, JFKL, www .jfklibrary.org; Coleman, *Fourteenth Day,* 75.

5. "Total News Control," *WP,* Nov. 30, 1962.

6. Coleman, *Fourteenth Day,* 71–75.

7. Naftali, *Presidential Recordings,* 200, 597.

8. Coleman, *Fourteenth Day,* 76–77. McCone might have had a personal motive in creating the so-called leak task force. During the Cuban missile crisis, he had given a background briefing to a group of journalists, including Scott, who chided the CIA director for not finding the weapons sooner: "McCone, I guess we're going to have to blow you out of [the water] for not reorganizing your estimating processes." McCone, "Memorandum for the File," Oct. 23, 1962, in McAuliffe, *CIA Documents on the Cuban Missile Crisis,* 287–88.

9. Mockingbird was another of the CIA's "Family Jewels," activities outside the agency's charter, from assassination plots to illicit wiretaps. "CIA's Family Jewels"; Philip Taubman, "Project Mockingbird: Spying on Reporters," *NYT,* June 26, 2007; Weiner, "J.F.K. Turns to the C.I.A. to Plug a Leak"; Coleman, *Fourteenth Day,* 64–77.

10. "Project Mockingbird," n.d., and W. E. Colby, "Special Activities," June 1, 1973, "CIA's Family Jewels."

11. Transcript of oral history interview with Joseph Alsop, Oct. 29, 1979, 50, JFKL; Taubman, "Project Mockingbird;" Weiner, "J.F.K. Turns to the C.I.A. to Plug a Leak." Weiner writes that McCone's task force "kept watch on Baldwin, four other reporters, and their sources from 1962 to 1965."

12. Almquist, *Joseph Alsop and American Foreign Policy,* 100–102; "Cloud over South East Asia," *WP,* Oct. 6, 1961.

13. "The Hardly Noticed Crisis," *WP,* Oct. 11, 1961; "Columnists JFK Reads Every Morning."

14. Almquist, *Joseph Alsop and American Foreign Policy,* 101; Joseph Alsop, *"I've Seen the Best of It,"* 459.

15. Fred Shapiro, ed., *The Yale Book of Quotations* (Yale University Press, 2006), 547.

16. Bradlee, *Conversations with Kennedy,* 208; "On Missing the Spring," March 30, 1962.

17. "The War We May Be Winning," *WP,* Sept. 28, 1962; Prochnau, *Once upon a Distant War,* 360–61, 413–14.

18. F. W. Coykendal to JWA, Oct. 4, and JWA to Coykendal, Oct. 4, "1962" folder, box 18, JWAP.

19. JWA to Nolting, June 28, 1963, and Dixon Boggs to JWA, July 17, "1963" folder, box 19, JWAP. "Like John Milton, who sought to explain the ways of man to God, Lodge sought to explain the ways of Saigon to Washington." Just, *To What End?,* 34.

20. "Ugly Stuff," *WP,* Sept. 18, 1963; Joseph Alsop, *"I've Seen the Best of It,"* 460–62.

21. James Hershberg, "'Dickering with Communists' and Pushing the Spaghetti in 'That Snake Pit Called Saigon': New Evidence on the ICC and the 'Maneli Affair,' 1963." The author thanks Jim Hershberg for a copy of his unpublished paper and

related documents. Chester Cooper to CIA Director, Sept. 19, 1963, "U.S. Policy in the Vietnam War, 1954–1968," DNSA.

22. "The Command Post," *WP,* Sept. 16, 1963; "The Crusaders," *WP,* Sept. 23, 1963; "The War Can Be Won," *WP,* Sept. 25, 1963. In his memoirs, Joe still harbored bitterness toward "the aimlessly crusading American press [that] had the effect of an uncontrolled elephant in a French drawing room." Joseph Alsop, *"I've Seen the Best of It,"* 459.

23. Merry, *Taking On the World,* 406. Like Alsop, the Kennedy administration was suspicious of Halberstam's motives, and it tasked the CIA with analyzing the latter's dispatches from Vietnam. While the agency found that Halberstam's reports were "by and large accurate," it described them as "invariably pessimistic." Prochnau, *Once upon a Distant War,* 360.

24. Galbraith, *Life in Our Times,* 447.

25. Logevall, *Choosing War,* 48, 67; Joseph Alsop, *"I've Seen the Best of It,"* 462.

26. JWA to Kennedy, Oct. 3, "1962" folder, box 18, JWAP.

27. Graham, *Personal History,* 317.

28. Ibid., 310–11; Heymann, *Georgetown Ladies' Social Club,* 133–35.

29. Halberstam, *Powers That Be,* 382; Graham, *Personal History,* 329.

30. Graham to Kennedy, n.d., "Philip Graham" folder, President's Office Files, Special Correspondence, box 30, JFKL.

31. Heymann, *Georgetown Ladies' Social Club,* 137.

32. Graham to Kennedy, April 2, 1963, "Philip Graham" folder, President's Office Files, Special Correspondence, box 30, JFKL.

33. Stacks, *Scotty,* 219; Graham, *Personal History,* 318.

34. White, *Making of the President, 1964,* 407–15.

35. Graham, *Personal History,* 330.

36. Sorensen, *Counselor,* 360; Merry, *Taking On the World,* 406–7; Joseph Alsop, *"I've Seen the Best of It,"* 463.

37. Sorensen, *Counselor,* 360; Graham, *Personal History,* 353–55.

38. Sorensen, *Counselor,* 384; Merry, *Taking On the World,* 407. Katharine Graham remembered Sorensen's snub in a subsequent telephone conversation with the new president, Lyndon Johnson, and in her memoirs. Graham, *Personal History,* 353.

39. "Go, Stranger!," *WP,* Nov. 25, 1963; Patten, *My Three Fathers,* 211; Bundy to JWA, Dec. 6, "1963" folder, box 19, JWAP.

40. JWA to Berlin, Dec. 11, "1963" folder, box 19, JWAP.

41. "But, clearly, after that bright, blustery November day, nothing would be quite the same in my life again or, it hardly needs saying, in the life of this country." Joseph Alsop, *"I've Seen the Best of It,"* 464.

42. Beschloss, *Taking Charge,* 45–46.

CHAPTER NINETEEN "The Other Side of the Coin"

1. "The Last, Best Chance," *WP,* March 30, 1964; "An Unhappy Secret," *WP,* April 15, 1964.

2. JWA to John Whitney, May 4, 1964, "P" folder, box 70, JWAP; Branch, *Pillar of Fire,* 293–94; Garrow, "FBI and Martin Luther King."

3. "President Johnson's Choice," *WP,* May 22, 1964; "Upward or Downward?," *WP,* May 28, 1964.

4. "The First Domino: Joe Alsop's Indochina Crusade," *WP*, April 23, 1995; Beschloss, *Reaching for Glory*, 150.

5. JWA to Rovere, Jan. 15, 1965, "R" folder, box 72, JWAP; Yoder, *Joe Alsop's Cold War*, 15.

6. Branch, *Pillar of Fire*, 246.

7. Beschloss, *Taking Charge*, 262–63, 357, 410; Ritchie, *Reporting from Washington*, 148.

8. "Our Great Leader is the prima-est of prima donnas," Stewart wrote to his editor at the *Post*. Beschloss, *Taking Charge*, 289–90; Goodwin, *Lyndon Johnson and the American Dream*, 133; Stewart Alsop to Otto Friedrich, Feb. 27, 1964, folder 12A, box 7, Stewart Alsop Papers.

9. "The Deceptive Calm," *WP*, Nov. 23, 1964; Beschloss, *Reaching for Glory*, 149–50.

10. Athan Theoharis, ed., *The J. Edgar Hoover Official and Confidential File* (University Publications of America, 1990), ix–x, 7.

11. FBI records indicate that the Alsop dossier was moved into the "confidential room" on April 4, 1957, shortly after the bureau received Joe's account of the Moscow incident. Nichols to Short, April 4, 1957, Joseph Alsop FBI file.

12. "[Alsop] knew intuitively that the thing Johnson feared most was that history would write that he had been weak when he should have been strong . . . the Alsop columns on Johnson were part of a marvelous continuing psychodrama." Halberstam, *The Best and the Brightest*, 499; "Johnson's Cuba II," *WP*, Dec. 30, 1964.

13. In January, Alsop wrote Moyers that he had "stumbled" across the administration's campaign to control reporters' access to information quite by accident—and learned that "the new regulations were primarily and quite personally aimed at me." JWA to Moyers, Jan. 11, 1966, "M" folder, box 74, JWAP. "Now, who else—would the CIA ever tap anything?" Johnson mused. Katzenbach answered, "I don't think they ever tap in this country, Mr. President. But I can't say that absolutely authoritatively." Beschloss, *Reaching for Glory*, 252–54; Branch, *At Canaan's Edge*, 186–88, 820n; Hoover to Belmont et al., memorandum of conversation, March 30, 1965, Joseph Alsop FBI file.

14. Merry, *Taking On the World*, 414; Stewart Alsop to [Unknown], July 21, 1964, folder 13A, box 7, Stewart Alsop Papers; JWA to Kennedy, n.d. [Nov. 1964], "K" folder, box 70, JWAP.

15. JWA to Lippmann, n.d. [Oct. 1964], folder 38, box 50, Lippmann Papers, Yale University; JWA to Dr. Andre Varay, Aug. 31, 1964, "U–V" folder, box 70, JWAP; Bray, *Pillars of the "Post,"* 52.

16. JWA to Katharine and Donald Graham, Aug. 31, 1964, "G" folder, box 69, JWAP.

17. Lynn Rosellini, "The Katharine Graham Story," *Washington Star*, Nov. 15, 1978.

18. Lippmann to Graham, Oct. 3, 1964, folder 913, box 74, Lippmann Papers, Yale University.

19. Stewart Alsop to Blair, May 19, 1964, folder 13A, box 5, Stewart Alsop Papers; Graham, *Personal History*, 340–49, 379.

20. Lynn Rosellini, "The Katharine Graham Story," *Washington Star*, Nov. 16, 1978; Gerber, *Katharine Graham*, 35; Halberstam, *Powers That Be*, 521; Graham, *Personal History*, 380–84.

21. Bradlee remembered that he and his wife were on vacation in Provence when they were awakened by an early morning telephone call. He was actually not surprised by Phil Graham's suicide, already knowing of the *Post* publisher's psychological instability. Author interview with Ben Bradlee, Nov. 18, 2009, Washington, D.C.; Bradlee,

Good Life, 252; Halberstam, *Powers That Be,* 519; Graham to Stewart Alsop, n.d., "G" folder, box 75, Stewart Alsop Papers.

22. Graham, *Personal History,* 376; Halberstam, *Powers That Be,* 529; Felsenthal, *Power, Privilege, and the "Post,"* 240.

23. Hendrik Hertzberg, "Young Don Graham," *New Yorker,* Aug. 7, 2013; Bird, *Color of Truth,* 317. "The *Crimson*'s editorial policy on the war changed all the time, depending upon who woke up in time to get to the [editorial] meeting . . . The conventional position was 'get out right away.'" Author interview with Donald Graham, March 23, 2010, Washington, D.C.

24. Graham, *Personal History,* 395; Bray, *Pillars of the "Post,"* 50.

25. Author interview with Frank George Wisner, Oct. 20, 2010, Washington, D.C.; "Princetonians in Vietnam," *Princeton Alumni Weekly,* Nov. 19, 1965. Thanks are due to Ms. Leah Haynesworth, Princeton class of 2011, for a copy of the *PAW* article on Frank George Wisner.

26. Ward Just to Frances FitzGerald, "Corr., 1967" folder, box 24, Frances FitzGerald Papers, HGARC/BU.

27. Author interview with Frances FitzGerald, Nov. 19, 2009, New York City; Wisner to FitzGerald, Dec. 21, 1965, folder 12, box 23, FitzGerald Papers; Hoffmann, *On Their Own,* 151–52.

28. "One of the few consolations of prolonged bachelorhood is the ease with which bachelors are adopted as members of their friends' families. If you like children and remain a bachelor until fairly late in life, you thus become Everybody's Universal Uncle." "The Brand-New War," *WP,* Sept. 13, 1965; "Power's Long Arm," *WP,* Sept. 17, 1965; "Frank and His Friends," *WP,* Sept. 22, 1965; Eric Alterman, "A Newsmaker in Every Sense of the Word," *NYT,* April 19, 2012.

29. "Be careful of Joe," Frank Gardiner Wisner had reportedly warned his son. "He's a man of some emotion. And his views get the better of him." Author interview with Frank George Wisner, Oct. 20, 2010, Washington, D.C.

30. Wisner to Stewart Alsop, May 18, 1964, "Stewart Alsop" folder, "Personal Correspondence" box, Wisner Papers.

31. Sulzberger to Wisner, Aug. 28, 1962, and Wisner to Sulzberger, Dec. 3, 1962, "Cyrus Sulzberger" folder, "Personal Correspondence" box, Wisner Papers. While Sulzberger thanked Wisner for the offer, he ultimately found another press for his memoirs. Wisner to Praeger, Dec. 23, 1963, "Frederick Praeger" folder, and Praeger to Wisner, April 24, 1965, "Frederick A. Praeger, Inc." folder, "Personal Correspondence" box, Wisner Papers.

32. Wisner's suicide meant Frank would be spared Philby's subsequent, blunt assessment of him as "a youngish man for so responsible a job, balding and running self-importantly to fat." Philby, *My Silent War,* 193–94.

33. Brewer to Wisner, May 31, 1964, and Wisner to Brewer, June 3, 1964, "Personal Correspondence, 1964" folder, "Personal Correspondence" box, Wisner Papers; "U.S. Takes Passport from Mrs. Philby," *NYT,* July 18, 1964; "Reporter Granted Custody of Child," *NYT,* July 28, 1964.

34. Wisner to Stewart Alsop, May 20, 1964, "Stewart Alsop" folder, "Personal Correspondence" box, Wisner Papers.

35. Wisner to McCone, March 4, 1965, folder 6, box 59, Dulles Papers. Wisner cajoled Charles Thayer into sending a damning critique of *The Invisible Government* to book review editors at *The New York Times* and *The Washington Post,* but only the *Post* pub-

lished it. Frank also urged Charlie to write a book-length rebuttal to Wise, promising "some significant assistance . . . to the author by the persons whose interests would be served by such a book." Wisner to Thayer, Aug. 26, 1964, "T" folder, "Personal Correspondence" box, Wisner Papers.

36. Wisner to Dulles, Feb. 3 and Dec. 30, 1964, and Jan. 28, 1965, folder 6, box 59, Dulles Papers; Thomas, *Very Best Men,* 318–20; Helms to Alsop, May 22, 1965, and Wise to Stewart Alsop, May 14, 1965, "Correspondence, 1965" folder, box 4, Helms Papers.

37. Schlesinger did eventually write a critical review of "The Red Pawn," and Dulles sent Wisner a copy. Wisner to Acheson, April 9, 1965, and Acheson to Wisner, April 19, 1965, folder 439, box 34, Acheson Papers; Wisner to Dulles, Dec. 30, 1964, folder 6, box 59, Dulles Papers; Knight, *Kennedy Assassination,* 77; Bradley Smith, *Shadow Warriors,* 414.

38. Stewart Alsop, "Hogwash About the CIA," *SEP,* Feb. 15, 1964; Stewart Alsop to Johnson, May 31, 1966, folder 19A, box 8, Stewart Alsop Papers.

39. Wisner to Papich, Sept. 20, 1965, and Wisner to MacInnes, March 31, 1965, "Helen MacInnes, New Novel, 1965" folder, "Personal Correspondence" box, Wisner Papers. West's novel was a barely fictional account of the anti-Diem coup in Vietnam. In the novel, the CIA station chief and the U.S. ambassador are both complicit in the Diem character's murder. West, *Ambassador,* 229.

40. Acheson to Wisner, April 23, 1965, folder 439, box 34, Acheson Papers. Wisner's letters to Joe Alsop about the West novel were manic and rambling. Wisner to JWA, March 30 and April 19, 1965, "W" folder, box 73, JWAP.

41. "Memorandum for Desmond FitzGerald and Raeford Herbert," Jan. 8, 1965, "Personal Correspondence, 1965" folder, "Personal Correspondence" box, Wisner Papers.

42. Author interviews with Ellis Wisner and Avis Bohlen.

43. "Frank G. Wisner, Dead; U.S. Intelligence Figure," *WP,* Oct. 30, 1965.

44. Wisner to Helms, n.d., "Elizabeth Wisner" folder, box 3, Helms Papers.

CHAPTER TWENTY "I'm Afraid Joe Is a Cruel Man"

1. JWA to Reston, Nov. 30, 1965, "R" folder, box 72, and JWA to Rovere, Oct. 25, 1967, "R" folder, box 77, JWAP.

2. JWA to Berlin, March 18, 1966, "B" folder, and Wicker to JWA, March 1, 1966, and JWA to Wicker, March 11, 1966, "W" folder, box 70, JWAP.

3. Wicker to JWA, March 8, 1966, "W" folder, box 75, JWAP; Stacks, *Scotty,* 250.

4. Rovere to JWA, Jan. 13, 1967, "R" folder, and Shaplen to JWA, Feb. 8, 1967, "S" folder, box 77, JWAP.

5. "Memo for Personal Files," March 6, 1968, "Memcons, A" folder, box 586, Harriman Papers.

6. Moyers to Helms, March 7, 1966, CIA/CREST; Richard Helms, *A Look over My Shoulder,* 292–93, 309; Cynthia Helms, *Intriguing Life,* 117–18; CIA, "Implications of an Unfavorable Outcome in Vietnam," Sept. 11, 1967, www.cia.gov/foia.

7. "So I love you—and I meant no offense—and I still prefer not to talk about South East Asia right now—but I'm perfectly willing to have a fight about why if you think it worth while." Bundy to JWA, n.d. [1964], "B" folder, box 69, JWAP; JWA to Bundy, n.d. [1964], "Joseph Alsop" folder, box 84, Bundy Papers; McGeorge Bundy, "The Situation in Vietnam," Feb. 7, 1966, in *U.S. Policy in the Vietnam War, 1954–1968,* DNSA; Bird, *Color of Truth,* 342; "An Era Ends," *WP,* Dec. 10, 1965.

8. McCone to JWA, March 14, 1966, "M" folder, box 74, JWAP; Almquist, *Joseph Alsop and American Foreign Policy,* 120; Alterman, "Newsmaker in Every Sense of the Word."

9. Stewart Alsop to Rostow, Sept. 13, 1966, folder 20A, box 8, Stewart Alsop Papers; Merry, *Taking On the World,* 447–48.

10. Stewart Alsop to Vladimir Petrov, Nov. 30, 1966, Stewart Alsop to Clayton Fritchey, Nov. 30, 1966, folder 20A, box 8, Stewart Alsop Papers; Merry, *Taking On the World,* 451.

11. JWA to Fairlie, June 10, 1966, "F" folder, box 74, JWAP.

12. JWA to Berlin, March 18, 1966, "B" folder, box 73, JWAP.

13. A typical exchange occurred in early June 1966, when Lippmann's column "Limiting Our Vietnamese Effort Is the Way Out" appeared sandwiched between two of Alsop's columns, "Standing Fast Is Paying Off" and "There Are Grounds for Encouragement on War."

14. JWA to Just, Oct. 24, 1967, "J" folder, box 76, JWAP; Almquist, *Joseph Alsop and American Foreign Policy,* 119; Halberstam, *The Best and the Brightest,* 500; JWA to Lippmann, May 2, 1967, "L" folder, box 77, JWAP.

15. Ritchie, *Reporting from Washington,* 142.

16. "However much we may disagree—Tues. and Thurs. are always incomplete if one can't begin with you along with coffee," Joe wrote. JWA to Lippmann, "Oct. 1964," folder 38, box 50, Lippmann Papers, Yale University; JWA to Lippmann, May 2, 1967, and Lippmann to JWA, Jan. 14, 1967, "L" folder, box 77, JWAP.

17. Turner, *Lyndon Johnson's Dual War,* 160; "The War on Lippmann," *WP,* May 7, 1967.

18. "Cronyism is the curse of journalism. After many years, I have reached the firm conclusion that it is impossible for an objective newspaperman to be a friend of a President," Lippmann told his National Press Club audience. "Lippmann to Quit City After Nearly Three Decades Here," *WP,* Dec. 30, 1966; JWA to Lippmanns, June 1, 1967, folder 38, box 50, Lippmann Papers, Yale University.

19. Ritchie, *Reporting from Washington,* 155.

20. William Bundy to JWA, Nov. 24, 1964, "Joseph Alsop" folder, box 84, Bundy Papers.

21. Gaddis, *GFK,* 592–93; Kennan to JWA, May 21, 1967, folder 8, box 1, GFKP.

22. Gaddis, *GFK,* 568; Nicholas Thompson, *The Hawk and the Dove,* 182–83.

23. "Schlesinger's Silly Book," *WP,* Jan. 16, 1967; JWA to Schlesinger, Jan. 13, 1967, and Schlesinger to JWA, Feb. 8, 1967, "S" folder, box 77, JWAP; Bird, *Color of Truth,* 359.

24. Galbraith to JWA, Jan. 20, 1967, and JWA to Galbraith, Jan. 23, 1967, "G" folder, box 76, JWAP.

25. De Margerie, *American Lady,* 133; author interview with Avis Bohlen, Nov. 16, 2009, Washington, D.C.

26. Susan Mary Alsop, *To Marietta from Paris,* 351.

27. Stewart Alsop to Robert Johnson, Sept. 28, 1966, folder 20A, box 8, Stewart Alsop Papers. In 1965, Stewart had gone to riot-ravaged Watts in Los Angeles. Shortly afterward, he interviewed a Ku Klux Klan leader in North Carolina. Stewart Alsop, *Stay of Execution,* 243; Merry, *Taking On the World,* 443, 446.

28. Stewart Alsop, *Stay of Execution,* 9, 184; Elizabeth Winthrop Alsop, *Don't Knock Unless You're Bleeding,* 33–34. "I hope and believe that the 'stark' was an exaggeration, but God knows these days," Joe wrote to Susan Mary. JWA to Susan Mary Alsop, March 17, 1969, folder 9, box 128, and JWA to Graham, Dec. 21, 1967, "G" folder, box 130, JWAP.

29. Author interview with Frances FitzGerald, Nov. 9, 2009, New York City; Hoff-

mann, *On Their Own,* 151; Thomas, *Very Best Men,* 322; Heymann, *Georgetown Ladies' Social Club,* 191. A year later, Desmond FitzGerald was struggling with his own doubts about the war. "My father seems less and less confident about Vietnam," Frankie confided to a friend in June 1967, only weeks before her father's fatal heart attack while playing tennis. FitzGerald to Just, June 1, 1967, "Corr., 1967" folder, box 24, FitzGerald Papers.

30. Wisner reminded Ward and FitzGerald that Alsop was "a visiting dignitary . . . And must be met with all protocol." Just to FitzGerald, n.d., "Corr., 1967" folder, box 24, FitzGerald Papers.

31. "My reporting had grown increasingly bleak . . . My specialty in the war was a highly developed sense of ambiguity . . . My columns [at the end] just simply tended to trail off." Author interview with Ward Just, July 24, 2012, Martha's Vineyard, Mass.; "Post Correspondent, Ward Just, Wounded," *WP,* June 9, 1966.

32. Author interview with Just.

33. Blumenthal, "Ruins of Georgetown," 230; author interview with Just.

34. Ward Just, "This War May Be Unwinnable," *WP,* June 4, 1967. In his 1982 novel about Washington, D.C., *In the City of Fear,* Ward Just wrote about the atmosphere in Georgetown—the fictional Shakerville—in those earlier days: "Poor, poor Shakerville, tired of the war, exhausted with the war, fighting it all day in the office and then again at home, and even out at someone else's house. Stuffing ourselves on it, we're fat as geese with reports from the war."

35. Holzman, *James Jesus Angleton,* 260; Nitze, *From Hiroshima to Glasnost,* 269; Stewart Alsop to Braden, April 21, 1961, folder 3, box 74, Stewart Alsop Papers.

36. Davis, *Party of the Century.* Joe Alsop wired another guest, Joan Braden, a simple three-word telegram: "Darling, no pink." Joan Braden, *Just Enough Rope,* 4. Author interview with FitzGerald; Hoffmann, *On Their Own,* 152; FitzGerald, "Tragedy of Saigon," 65–66.

37. Author interview with Frank George Wisner, Oct. 20, 2010, Washington, D.C.; Merry, *Taking On the World,* 423–25; Almquist, *Joe Alsop and American Foreign Policy,* 118.

38. JWA to [Unknown], Feb. 16, 1965, "C" folder, box 71, and JWA to Wisner, Oct. 30, 1967, "W" folder, box 131, and JWA to Wisner, April 1, 1966, "W" folder, box 75, JWAP.

39. JWA to Just, n.d. [1966], "J" folder, box 74, JWAP; James Wechsler, "Alsop Archives," *New York Post,* Jan. 23, 1967.

40. JWA to Kraft, March 8, 1966, "K" folder, box 74, and JWA to Bradlee, March 9, 1966, "B" folder, box 73, JWAP.

41. JWA to Ellsworth Bunker, Dec. 20, 1967, and JWA to Braestrup, Nov. 16, 1972, and various, "B" folder, box 76, JWAP.

42. "It was Geyelin who changed the *Post's* editorial side to anti-Vietnam." Author interview with Ben Bradlee, Nov. 18, 2009, Washington D.C. Kay Graham later upbraided Johnson for getting "rid of McNamara in that really terrible way." Turner, *Lyndon Johnson's Dual War,* 206; Felsenthal, *Power, Privilege, and the "Post,"* 257; Halberstam, *Powers That Be,* 544.

43. JWA to Graham, May 1, 1967, and various, "G" folder, box 130, JWAP.

44. Author interview with Donald Graham, March 23, 2010, Washington, D.C.

45. JWA to Mary Wissler Graham, Oct. 19, 1967, and Mary Wissler Graham to JWA, Oct. 16, 1967, "G" folder, box 130, JWAP.

46. Graham, *Personal History,* 396.

47. Graham to JWA, Dec. 6, 1967, "G" folder, box 130, JWAP.
48. Braestrup would later write a two-volume account of the reporting on Tet, arguing, in effect, that the offensive was a military disaster but a psychological triumph for the enemy. Braestrup, *Big Story.*
49. "Red Raids on Cities Are Sign of Weakness, Not Strength," *WP,* Feb. 2, 1968; JWA to Graham, Feb. 12, 1968, "G" folder, box 130, JWAP.
50. Ward Just, "Guerrillas Wreck Pacification Plan," *WP,* Feb. 4, 1968; Wisner to FitzGerald, April 5, 1968, "Corr., 1968" folder, box 25, FitzGerald Papers.
51. Merry, *Taking On the World,* 459; "'My God, There's a Man . . . ,'" *WP,* April 3, 1968.
52. Stewart Alsop to Steve Allen, March 4, 1968, folder 1, box 74, Stewart Alsop Papers.
53. "The Uncles' Club, as I call it—Sorensen, Teddy, Bob McNamara, Doug Dillon, and one or two others—of which I am a minor member—will probably succeed in preventing [Bobby] from making a fool of himself this time." JWA to Donald Graham, Jan. 19, 1968, "G" folder, box 130, and JWA to Robert Kennedy, Feb. 1, 1967, "K" folder, box 76, and JWA to Berlin, June 30, 1966, "B" folder, box 73, JWAP.
54. "Kennedy Calls for End to 'Illusion' on Vietnam, *WP,* Feb. 9, 1968; Braestrup, *Big Story,* 484.
55. JWA to Graham, Jan. 19, 1968, "G" folder, box 130, JWAP; "RFK Is Unwise in Accepting Peace-at-Any-Price Counsel," *WP,* Feb. 12, 1968; Alterman, *Sound and Fury,* 49; Joan Braden, *Just Enough Rope,* 150.
56. Kennedy to JWA, Feb. 3, 1968, "K" folder, box 130, JWAP.
57. "Robert Kennedy on the Stump Projects Image of Brother," *WP,* May 15, 1968; Kennedy to JWA, May 16, 1968, "K" folder, box 130, JWAP.
58. JWA to Lee Lescaze, July 3, 1968, "L" folder, box 131, and JWA to Ethel Kennedy, n.d. [June 1968], "K" folder, box 130, JWAP.
59. Stewart was also kind to Johnson in his own column. "Well, Good-By, Lyndon," *Newsweek,* Sept. 2, 1968.
60. Graham, *Personal History,* 406; Beschloss, *Reaching for Glory,* 367; Isaacson and Thomas, *Wise Men,* 708.
61. Bradlee to Herblock, n.d. [1965], folder 5, box 7, Block Papers; Felsenthal, *Power, Privilege, and the "Post,"* 260; Graham, *Personal History,* 398–401.
62. Wisner to JWA, n.d. [Aug. 1968], "W" folder, box 131, JWAP.
63. "Nixon Told War Can Be Won If U.S. Maintains Pressure," *WP,* Dec. 30, 1968; Almquist, *Joseph Alsop and American Foreign Policy,* 139; Stewart Alsop to Anthony Lewis, Oct. 9, 1969, "K–L" folder, box 77, Stewart Alsop Papers; Stewart Alsop, "The Case for Nixon," *Newsweek,* Sept. 30, 1968; Stewart Alsop, "The Flaw in the Game Plan," *Newsweek,* Sept. 29, 1969.
64. Stewart Alsop, "The Powerful Dr. Kissinger," *Newsweek,* June 16, 1969.

CHAPTER TWENTY-ONE "It Was the War That Did Him In"

1. Kissinger, *White House Years,* 21.
2. Shawcross, *Sideshow,* 97.
3. Isaacson, *Kissinger,* 358, 576.
4. Telcon, JWA and Kissinger, Feb. 5, 1969, KTC/DNSA; Merry, *Taking On the World,* 474.
5. Telcon, Nixon and Kissinger, Feb. 14, 1969, KTC/DNSA.

6. Telcon, Bundy and Kissinger, March 26, 1969, KTC/DNSA.

7. "A[lsop] said if it will be fairly vigorous speech, which he believes it will, support may be desirable and A[lsop] wondered if K[issinger] would approve of his coming down and glancing at speech in quiet corner of office and then going to work." Telcons, JWA and Kissinger, April 21 and May 14, 1969, KTC/DNSA; "Speech Shows Nixon Realizes Consequences of a Surrender," *WP*, May 16, 1969.

8. Seymour Hersh, *Price of Power*, 53, 74; Isaacson, *Kissinger*, 163–64.

9. Telcon, Nixon and Kissinger, Oct. 20, 1969, KTC/DNSA.

10. Telcons, Nixon and Kissinger, April 30 and May 2, 1970, KTC/DNSA; Isaacson, *Kissinger*, 271.

11. The president evidently approved of Kissinger's deception, according to a telephone conversation recorded at the White House. Telcon, Nixon and Kissinger, May 22, 1970, KTC/DNSA; Merry, *Taking On the World*, 487–88; Shawcross, *Sideshow*, 140–42; Isaacson, *Kissinger*, 262, 264–67; Seymour Hersh, *Price of Power*, 192. "Henry Kissinger specialized in, above all else, telling very different people what they wanted to hear, which, in the case of the Georgetown axis, was always reassuring, since it was hearing its own opinions, again and again." Halberstam, *Powers That Be*, 605.

12. Telcons, Rogers and Kissinger, April 14, 1969, Lansner and Kissinger, April 17, 1969, JWA and Kissinger, Aug. 10, 1970, KTC/DNSA.

13. Seymour Hersh, *Price of Power*, 224–33; "Dobrynin on Mideast," *WP*, Sept. 9, 1970.

14. "Analysts Seem to Disbelieve Danger of Sino-Soviet War," *WP*, Jan. 30, 1970.

15. Fulbright had told Clark Clifford that he would oppose Nitze's appointment for a variety of reasons—including the latter's refusal to produce documents on the 1964 Gulf of Tonkin incident when Fulbright requested them for his 1966 Senate hearings. Notes, May 15, 1969, "Paul Nitze" folder, box 35, Clifford Papers.

16. "Failure to Accelerate ABM Will Embolden Soviet Leaders," *WP*, Jan. 14, 1970; "Wolf, Wolf," *Newsweek*, Dec. 8, 1969.

17. Gaddis, *GFK*, 617; Kennan to Bohlen, Oct. 14, 1969, folder 16, box 5, GFKP; Nicholas Thompson, *The Hawk and the Dove*, 158.

18. Kennan to JWA, May 25, 1971, folder 8, box 1, GFKP; JWA to Kennan, "K" folder, box 135, JWAP.

19. JWA to Meg Greenfield, June 2, 1971, "G" folder, box 135, JWAP.

20. Telcon, Nixon and Kissinger, May 22, 1971, KTC/DNSA.

21. Merry, *Taking On the World*, 459; Editor/*Accuracy in Media*, to JWA, Dec. 16, 1969, folder 9, box 10, and "Statement of John Kenneth Galbraith," Sept. 22, 1968, "G" folder, box 130, JWAP.

22. Zalin Grant, "Alsop Lets His Friends Down," *New Republic*, May 25, 1968. Joe explained in a subsequent letter to the editor that the embargoed story had been published by mistake. Miller, "Washington, the World, and Joseph Alsop."

23. JWA to Stewart Alsop with enclosure, June 11, 1968, folder 9, box 128, JWAP; Just to FitzGerald, Feb. 27, "1969 Corr." folder, box 24, FitzGerald Papers.

24. Almquist, *Joseph Alsop and American Foreign Policy*, 126; JWA to Graham, Nov. 21, 1967, "G" folder, box 130, JWAP.

25. Buchwald, *Counting Sheep*, 58.

26. Ibid., 58–59, 61–64, 180, 215; "Stewart Alsop Comes Across on the Mayflower Flap," *WP*, Feb. 15, 1970, CIA/CREST.

27. "Soviets Tried to Blackmail U.S. Journalist," *Los Angeles Times*, Nov. 3, 1994; Streitfeld, "The Hawk and the Vultures"; Merry, *Taking On the World*, 489–90.

28. Richard Helms, *A Look over My Shoulder,* 150–51; personal communication to author by Charles Bartlett, Feb. 2, 2013. Richard Helms claimed in his memoir that he approached the Soviets through a CIA agent intermediary. Helms's widow, in her memoir, writes that her husband warned the Russians directly. Cynthia Helms, *Intriguing Life,* 177.

29. The letter was included in a package that Joe arranged to be sent to Stewart's wife, Tish, after his death. See the epilogue. In 1995, four years after the collapse of the Soviet Union, the *Washington Post* reporter David Streitfeld inquired of the FSB— the KGB's successor—whether it had any files on Joseph Alsop. The FSB's spokesman claimed that he found nothing in the archives relating to Alsop. Streitfeld, "The Hawk and the Vultures."

30. Joe's September column on Dobrynin had also, of course, attacked Secretary of State William Rogers. As attorney general during Eisenhower's second term, Rogers had suggested that the 1957 Moscow incident might be used to blackmail Alsop.

CHAPTER TWENTY-TWO "Nobody Plays by the Rules Any More"

1. Alsop finally relented, writing to Geyelin, "But let's forget about it." JWA to Geyelin, April 6 and 8, 1971, and Geyelin to JWA, April 5 and 7, 1971, "G" folder, box 135, JWAP.

2. Schlesinger, *Journals,* 329.

3. "Courage of a President," *WP,* Feb. 8, 1971; "Klein Circulates Column by Alsop," *WP,* Feb. 10, 1971; Joe Kraft, "The Alsop Implications," *WP,* Feb. 14, 1971; Salisbury, *Without Fear or Favor,* 87.

4. Telcon, Nixon and Kissinger, Feb. 9, 1971, KTC/DNSA.

5. Telcons, Nixon and Kissinger, Feb. 18, March 21, and May 20, 1971, KTC/DNSA.

6. "I am not at all sure that we see the Vietnamese situation from the same angle of vision," Alsop had written to Vann. JWA to Vann, Oct. 4, 1967, "V" folder, box 77, JWAP; Sheehan, *Bright Shining Lie,* 733–35.

7. That spring, after his latest trip to Vietnam, Alsop wrote to Vann to thank him for "a really glorious experience." JWA to Vann, April 22, 1970, and Oct. 19, 1971, and Vann to JWA, Oct. 30, 1971, "Joseph Alsop, 1967–72" folder, box 25, Sheehan Papers.

8. Vann to John Forrest, Oct. 9, 1969, "Joseph Alsop, 1967–72" folder, box 25, Sheehan Papers.

9. "JPV-Rel/w Alsop, 1968–70," n.d., "Joseph Alsop, 1971–89, Notes" folder, box 58, and Vann to JWA, Jan. 27, 1972, "Joseph Alsop, 1967–72" folder, box 25, Sheehan Papers.

10. Graham, *Personal History,* 420; Bellows, *Last Editor,* 139.

11. JWA to WETA, Aug. 17, 1970, "W" folder, box 135, and JWA to Berlin, June 16, "1967" folder, box 130, JWAP.

12. Stewart Alsop, *Stay of Execution,* 229. In 2009, when the author asked Paul Krassner what was discussed at his meeting with Stewart Alsop, Krassner "could not remember a single detail." But it was, after all, the 1960s. Paul Krassner, personal communication, Sept. 16, 2009.

13. Stewart Alsop, *Stay of Execution,* 43, 88–90.

14. Canfield to Stewart Alsop, July 30, 1969, and Stewart Alsop to Canfield, Oct. 13, 1969, "C" folder, box 74, Stewart Alsop Papers.

15. Church to Stewart Alsop, Oct. 16, 1971, and Stewart Alsop to Church, Oct. 29, 1970, "C" folder, box 74, Stewart Alsop Papers.

16. Stewart Alsop to Editor/*Times* (London), Sept. 4, 1964, folder 11A, box 7, Stewart Alsop Papers.
17. Tom Braden, "I'm Glad the CIA Is 'Immoral.'"
18. "In Memoriam, Frank Gardiner Wisner, 1909–1965," 6. The author thanks the CIA historian David Robarge for a copy of the Wisner memorial pamphlet.
19. Merry, *Taking On the World,* 493–94.
20. Stewart Alsop, *Stay of Execution,* 150; Stewart Alsop to Grahams, Oct. 31, 1972, "G" folder, box 75, Stewart Alsop Papers.
21. Stewart Alsop, *Stay of Execution,* 269–70.
22. Stewart Alsop to Susan Mary Alsop, Sept. 2, 1971, folder 10, and Stewart Alsop to JWA, April 3, 1973, folder 9, box 128, JWAP.
23. The outcome Stewart feared most was "that the disintegration of the authority of the 'established government' could produce an authoritarian regime, if it were combined with a severe economic depression." "Could It Happen Here?," *Newsweek,* July 19, 1971.
24. In an editorial, the *Times* had condemned the missile crisis article when it first appeared. Stewart Alsop, "'Breach of Security,'" *Newsweek,* June 28, 1971; Salisbury, *Without Fear or Favor,* 122–23.
25. Graham, *Personal History,* 444–55.
26. Stewart Alsop, *Stay of Execution,* 80–81. Lewis and Alsop also argued over the *Times*'s publication of the Pentagon Papers, which Stewart condemned on the grounds "that any government has a right to certain secrets if it is to operate in delicate international affairs." Lewis to Stewart Alsop, July 14, 1971, and Dec. 28, 1972, Stewart Alsop to Lewis, Aug. 5, 1971, and Jan. 12, 1973, "K–L" folder, box 77, and Stewart Alsop to Buckley, March 18, 1971, "B" folder, box 74, Stewart Alsop Papers.
27. Stewart argued that it would be "a worse mistake if we are put in the position of a great power abandoning and betraying a small power we have made wholly dependent on us, however unadmirable the government of that small power may seem to many of us." Stewart Alsop to John Sherman, Nov. 10, 1971, Stewart Alsop to Sheffield Cowles, Jan. 5, 1972, Stewart Alsop to John Campbell, April 22, 1969, "C" folder, box 74, and Stewart Alsop to Holbrooke, April 22, 1972, "H" folder, box 76, Stewart Alsop Papers.
28. "God Tempers the Wind," *Newsweek,* Aug. 30, 1971.
29. "The Disintegration of the Elite," *Newsweek,* June 8, 1970; Stewart Alsop, *Stay of Execution,* 154–56.

CHAPTER TWENTY-THREE "There Is a Feeling of Doors Closing"

1. "Jade Body-Stockings," *WP,* July 21, 1971.
2. Isaacson, *Kissinger,* 349.
3. Memcon, July 26, 1971, "China and the U.S.," DNSA.
4. Joe was still warning about a Sino-Soviet war more than two years later. "Silver Cloud, Dark Lining," *WP,* July 19, 1971; JWA to Kaiser, Oct. 12, 1972, "K" folder, box 137, and JWA to Greenfield, Nov. 1, 1973, "G" folder, box 138, JWAP.
5. Joe speculated that a recent visit to Moscow by Nixon and Kissinger had been to head off "the nuclear castration of China." "Countering Russia," *WP,* June 23, 1972; Telcon, Kissinger and Dobrynin, June 24, 1972, KTC/DNSA.

6. Nixon later discovered that Kissinger, by that fall, had talked to some two dozen reporters about his secret trip. "My Talks with Chou En-lai," July 14, 1971, in "Beijing-Washington Back-Channel and Henry Kissinger's Secret Trip to China," National Security Archive Electronic Briefing Book no. 66, Feb. 27, 2002; Isaacson, *Kissinger,* 349; Seymour Hersh, *Price of Power,* 380n; Telcons, Kissinger and Graham, March 13, 1971, and Kissinger and Ziegler, Jan. 19, 1972, KTC/DNSA.

7. Katharine Graham attended her first Gridiron dinner in 1975, the year the club finally admitted women. Graham, *Personal History,* 428–29.

8. Telcon, Kissinger and Graham, Jan. 29, 1972, KTC/DNSA. When Herblock drew a cartoon that showed muddy footprints leading from the Watergate back to the White House, Kay asked him nervously, "You're not going to print that, are you?" The *Post* did. Graham, *Personal History,* 463.

9. Felsenthal, *Power, Privilege, and the "Post,"* 316–17; Graham, *Personal History,* 471–72; Telcon, Graham and Kissinger, Dec. 16, 1972, KTC/DNSA.

10. Telcon, Kissinger and Graham, March 15, 1971, KTC/DNSA.

11. Telcon, Graham and Kissinger, June 26, 1972, KTC/DNSA; "O'Brien Asks Nixon for Special Probe of Bugging Incident," *WP,* June 26, 1972.

12. Telcon, Kissinger and Graham, July 25, 1972, KTC/DNSA.

13. Ibid.; Graham, *Personal History,* 460–68; Bernstein and Woodward, *All the President's Men,* 235–37.

14. Graham, *Personal History,* 468; "Dirty Business," *Newsweek,* Sept. 25, 1972; "The Price of Paralysis in the Senate," *WP,* June 20, 1973.

15. "Nixon's Grimmest Crisis," *WP,* May 8, 1972; Sheehan, *Bright Shining Lie,* 759; JWA to Vann, "Joseph Alsop, 1967–72" folder, box 25, Sheehan Papers.

16. Sheehan, *Bright Shining Lie,* 9–10, 31; JWA to Whitehouse, June 22, 1972, "W" folder, box 138, JWAP; "Neil's Joe Alsop Notes," Nov. 8, 1974, "Joseph Alsop, 1971–89, Notes" folder, box 58, Sheehan Papers.

17. Alsop, "The Devil and George McGovern," *Newsweek,* Nov. 6, 1972; Alsop, "Political Hallucination," *WP,* Sept. 13, 1972; Merry, *Taking On the World,* 505.

18. Telcon, Graham and Kissinger, Nov. 14, 1972, KTC/DNSA. Joan Braden assured Kissinger, "I am your loyalist friend." Telcons, Braden and Kissinger, July 24, 1972, Graham and Kissinger, Dec. 16, 1972, Kissinger and Rowland Evans, April 5, 1973, KTC/DNSA; Joan Braden, *Just Enough Rope,* 174–75, 182. In 1972, Kissinger nonetheless spent Christmas at Joe and Susan Mary's house. Kissinger to JWA, Dec. 1, 1972, "K" folder, box 137, JWAP.

19. Merry, *Taking On the World,* 506–9.

20. "The Pleasure of Peking," *WP,* Nov. 29, 1972; "The Honesty of Chou," *WP,* Dec. 4, 1972; "A 'Characteristically Chinese' Revolution," *WP,* Jan. 12, 1973.

21. Helms to Kissinger, Dec. 20, 1973, "Henry Kissinger" folder, box 2, Helms Papers; Cynthia Helms to author, Feb. 8, 2013, personal communication.

22. Memcon, Jan. 3, 1973, "Kissinger Transcripts," DNSA.

23. Kahn, *China Hands,* 300; Finney, "Long Trial of John Paton Davies."

24. "Last Two Guilty in Watergate Plot," *WP,* Jan. 31, 1973; www.washingtonpost.com/wp-srv/politics/special/watergate/#chapters.

25. JWA to A. Knight, June 28, 1973, "K" folder, box 139, and JWA to Weinberger, May 8, 1974, "W" folder, box 154, JWAP. More than two weeks after Stewart's funeral, Weinberger wrote to Joe, "Agreeing to make a special exception in your case." Weinberger to JWA, June 18, 1974, "W" folder, box 143, JWAP.

26. Stewart Alsop to JWA, April 3, 1973, folder 9, box 128, JWAP.

27. JWA to Graham, Feb. 24, 1972, "G" folder, box 137, JWAP; Merry, *Taking On the World,* 502–3.

28. JWA to Graham, Nov. 12, 1973, "G" folder, box 138, JWAP.

29. JWA to Graham, Nov. 3, 1972, "G" folder, box 137, JWAP. Joe's column, which before Vietnam had more than 200 newspaper subscribers, was down to 175 near the end of the war. Merry, *Taking On the World,* 520–21.

30. Telcon, JWA and Kissinger, Dec. 2, 1971, KTC/DNSA; Patten, *My Three Fathers,* 256; "JWA Letters to SM, 1978" folder, Joseph Alsop Private Papers.

31. Author interview with Ben Bradlee, Nov. 18, 2009, Washington, D.C.; Merry, *Taking On the World,* 479, 518–20.

32. Diary entry of Jan. 1, 1974, folder 2, box 239, and Kennan to Avis Bohlen, Jan. 20, 1974, folder 16, box 5, GFKP.

33. Stewart Alsop, *Stay of Execution,* 59, 199, 201; Merry, *Taking On the World,* 525.

34. JWA to Graham, Nov. 12, 1973, "G" folder, box 138, JWAP.

35. Graham to JWA, Dec. 31, 1973, and JWA to Graham, Jan. 8, 1974, "G" folder, box 141, JWAP.

36. "Dealing with Dean and the Dollar," *WP,* June 6, 1973; JWA to J. Kearns, June 5, 1973, "K" folder, box 139, and JWA to Whitehouse, June 11, 1973, "W" folder, box 140, JWAP.

37. Telcon, JWA and Kissinger, April 24, 1973, KTC/DNSA; Almquist, *Joe Alsop and American Foreign Policy,* 149.

38. "War, Not Politics," *Newsweek,* May 14, 1973. When a reader accused him of "grotesque exaggerations" about Watergate, Stewart wrote back, "I think I rather understated the case." David Garth to Stewart Alsop, May 9, 1973, and Stewart Alsop to David Garth, June 14, 1973, "G" folder, box 75; Stewart Alsop to Liddy, July 30, 1973, and Liddy to Stewart Alsop, Aug. 4, 1973, "L" folder, box 77, Stewart Alsop Papers.

39. Alsop, "Toughing It Out," *Newsweek,* July 23, 1973; "The Case for Resignation," *WP,* Nov. 2, 1973; Memcon, Nov. 12, 1973, "Kissinger Transcripts," DNSA.

40. Telcon, Geyelin and Kissinger, April 25, 1973, KTC/DNSA; Dallek, *Nixon and Kissinger,* 475.

41. Some critics were also wiretapped. "I don't go around bugging people," Kissinger told the *Post*'s Phil Geyelin early in 1974. Kissinger formally admitted to and apologized for the wiretaps in 1992. Telcons, Stewart Alsop and Kissinger, June 2, 1973, and Geyelin and Kissinger, Feb. 2, 1974, KTC/DNSA; "Kissinger Details Role in Wiretaps," *WP,* July 24, 1974; "Kissinger Issues Wiretap Apology," *NYT,* Nov. 13, 1992.

42. Woodward and Bernstein, *Final Days,* 231.

43. Ibid.; Almquist, *Joseph Alsop and American Foreign Policy,* 150–51; Greenberg, *Nixon's Shadow,* 167.

44. *"Degringolade?," Newsweek,* April 1, 1974, and " 'If They Get Us, We'll Get Them,' " May 6, 1974.

45. Stewart Alsop, *Stay of Execution,* 298–300.

46. Merry, *Taking On the World,* 529–30.

47. Ibid., " 'A Brave and Stoical Man,' " *WP,* May 31, 1974.

48. Woodward and Bernstein, *Final Days,* 256–57; Almquist, *Joseph Alsop and American Foreign Policy,* 167; Patten, *My Three Fathers,* 227.

49. JWA to Herblock, April 19, 1974, folder 6, Block Papers; JWA to Graham, May 17, 1974, "G" folder, box 141, JWAP; Woodward and Bernstein, *Final Days,* 256–57.

50. Felsenthal, *Power, Privilege, and the "Post,"* 326–27; Graham to JWA, May 20, 1974, "G" folder, box 141, JWAP.

51. "The Reporter's Trade," *WP,* Dec. 27, 1974.

52. Hunter S. Thompson, *Fear and Loathing,* 141.

53. Telcon, Kissinger and Fulbright, Feb. 22, 1975, KTC/DNSA; Merry, *Taking On the World,* 531.

54. "After 42 Years, a Decision to Retire," *WP,* Sept. 25, 1974; JWA to Reston, Oct. 4, 1974, "R" folder, box 142, JWAP.

55. "On Taking a Lifetime Lease, and Making a New Beginning," *WP,* Feb. 1, 1976; Merry, *Taking On the World,* 533.

56. JWA to Graham, Dec. 12, 1973, "G" folder, box 138, and JWA to Graham, May 17, 1974, Graham to JWA, May 20, 1974, "G" folder, box 141, JWAP.

57. A few years earlier, Sheehan had written a piece for *The New York Review of Books,* in effect accusing the United States of war crimes in Vietnam. "Neil's Joe Alsop Notes," Nov. 8, 1974, "Notes" folder, Sheehan Papers; JWA to J. Keswick, Jan. 2, 1975, "K" folder, box 229, JWAP; diary entry of Nov. 9, 1974, box 239, GFKP.

58. "A Return to One's Roots," *WP,* Dec. 2, 1974; "The Last 'Tribal Christmas,'" *WP,* Dec. 25, 1974; "Reporter's Trade"; "'I Am Deeply Proud to Have Been a Reporter,'" *WP,* Dec. 30, 1974.

59. Merry, *Taking On the World,* 533; JWA to Whitehouse, Dec. 9, 1974, "W" folder, box 143, JWAP.

60. Transcript of interview with Joseph Alsop, Jan. 22, 1975, Minnesota Public Radio, St. Paul. The author thanks MPR's Amy Stephens for locating the Alsop interview tape.

EPILOGUE "We're All So Old or Dead": The End of the Georgetown Set

1. Notes on telcon, April 14, 1975, "Joseph Alsop" folder, box 58, Sheehan Papers.

2. Halberstam, *Powers That Be,* 449. In *The Making of a Quagmire,* his 1965 book on Vietnam, Halberstam wrote, "However, being criticized by Alsop is no small honor in our profession." Halberstam also slammed Alsop's 1950 articles on China as "on the borderline of respectability. They were not particularly thoughtful or deep, for that is not his style, and they did not charge conspiracy; they only implied it, as is also his style." Halberstam, *The Best and the Brightest,* 115–16.

3. Schlesinger, *Journals,* 310.

4. Berman, *Perfect Spy,* 167; Peter Osnos, "Reviving a Forgotten Journalism Icon on Stage," *Atlantic,* April 2012, www.theatlantic.com.

5. JWA to Baez, Oct. 23, 1979, "Joan Baez" folder, box 257, JWAP.

6. Author interview with Ward Just, July 24, 2012, Martha's Vineyard, Mass.

7. Joseph Alsop, *"I've Seen the Best of It,"* 479.

8. Seymour Hersh, "Huge CIA Operation Reported in U.S. Against Antiwar Forces, Other Dissidents in Nixon Years," *NYT,* Dec. 22, 1974; www.intelligence .senate.gov/churchcommittee.html.

9. Helms would be a hero to many in the agency for "keeping the secrets," in contrast to a subsequent director at the agency, William Colby. Powers, *Man Who Kept the Secrets,* 304–7; Richard Helms, *A Look over My Shoulder,* 414–15; Cynthia Helms, *Intriguing Life,* 155–63; "Helms Pleads 'No Contest' in Testimony Case," *WP,* Nov. 1, 1977; and various, "Richard Helms" folder, box 87, McGrory Papers.

10. Bernstein, "CIA and the Media,"; Alsop to Editor/*Rolling Stone,* Nov. 11, 1977, "Carl Bernstein" folder, box 257, JWAP; "Notes on Conversation," Aug. 25, 1976, "Joseph Alsop" folder, box 58, Sheehan Papers. In a 1988 interview—declassified in 2007—Helms told CIA historians that he had "no apologies for the fact that the agency used newspapermen. After all, we're all in the United States, we're all Americans; we all should be working for our country." "Reflections of DCIs Colby and Helms on the CIA's 'Time of Troubles,'" *Studies in Intelligence* 51, no. 3 (Sept. 2007): 24.

11. JWA to Kennan, Jan. 30, 1988, folder 8, box 1, GFKP. Joe took credit for getting his theory about the Soviet role in the Iranian revolution into a news story in *The Washington Post.* JWA to Nitze, Dec. 18, 1978, "Joseph Alsop" folder, box 17, Nitze Papers.

12. JWA to McNamara, May 20, 1980, and Alsop memo, May 22, 1980, "Joseph & Susan Mary Alsop, 1980–1985" folder, McNamara Papers.

13. Gill, *New York Life,* 18; Patten, *My Three Fathers,* 300; C-SPAN transcript of interview with Joseph Alsop, Nov. 19, 1984, www.c-spanvideo.org/program124869–1. The author thanks Elizabeth Winthrop Alsop for bringing the C-SPAN interview with her uncle to my attention.

14. Yoder, *Joe Alsop's Cold War,* 188; JWA to Donald Graham, April 20, 1981, "Katharine Graham" folder, Joseph Alsop Private Papers; JWA to Helms, Oct. 11, 1986, "Joseph Alsop" folder, Helms Papers.

15. Diary entry of Nov. 30, 1987, folder 2, box 326, GFKP.

16. Gill, *New York Life,* 21.

17. JWA to Graham, Jan. 2, 1989, folder 13, box 252, JWAP.

18. De Margerie, *American Lady,* 154; Susan Mary Alsop to Nitze, March 12, 1978, "Joseph Alsop, 1952–1985" folder, box 17, Nitze Papers.

19. JWA to Davies, Jan. 2, 1989, and Davies to JWA, Feb. 7, 1989, "D–F, 1989" folder, box 252, JWAP.

20. Unsigned letter, Nov. 14, 1988, in envelope marked "Personal and Confidential: Property of Joseph Wright Alsop," Joseph Alsop Private Papers.

21. JWA to Tree, June 7 and 22, 1989, "R–T, 1989 folder," box 253, JWAP; author interviews with Donald Graham, Walter Pincus, and Corinne Zimmermann. Joe instructed that he wanted "no invented prayers, nor any prayers adjusted to the occasion by the Rector—except insofar as the old Prayer Book authorizes." And, finally, "I wish to be buried in Middletown, cheaply." Last will and testament, n.d., Joseph Alsop Private Papers.

22. Merry, *Taking On the World,* 539; Patten, *My Three Fathers,* 301; "In Memoriam: Joseph Wright Alsop, Jr., October 11, 1910–August 28, 1989," Joseph Alsop Private Papers.

23. Herken, "Great Foreign Policy Fight"; Nicholas Thompson, *The Hawk and the Dove,* Callahan, *Dangerous Capabilities,* 76–77.

24. Nitze, *From Hiroshima to Glasnost,* 340–41, 351–61; Nitze and the Committee on the Present Danger: Gaddis, *GFK,* 635–40; Sanders, *Peddlers of Crisis.* Nitze and Team B: Nicholas Thompson, *The Hawk and the Dove,* 259–62; Cahn, *Killing Detente,* 155–63.

25. George Kennan, "Breaking the Spell," *New Yorker,* Oct. 3, 1983; Paul Nitze, "A Plea for Action," *NYT Magazine,* May 7, 1978; Lukacs, *George F. Kennan,* 150.

26. By 1986, the gang of four had six more recruits. "U.S. 'No-First-Use' Policy Urged for Nuclear Arms," July 12, 1986, *WP.*

27. Nitze, *From Hiroshima to Glasnost,* 376–89, 430–34.

28. Nicholas Thompson, "Worthy Opponents," *Boston Globe,* April 3, 2005.

29. Kennan had also argued, in vain, against the Clinton administration's decision to

extend the NATO alliance to include former Soviet republics, branding it "a fateful error." Leslie Gelb, "Foreign Affairs; Who Won the Cold War?," *NYT,* Aug. 20, 1992; Kennan to Gelb, Aug. 25, 1992, folder 10, box 43, Kennan to Strobe Talbott, April 22, 1997, folder 4, box 47, and copy of Kennan Council of Foreign Relations speech, Feb. 15, 1994, folder 11, box 25, GFKP.

30. Shortly thereafter, when that invasion seemed imminent, Kennan wrote to his nephew, "What is being done to our country today is surely something from which we will never be able to restore the sort of country you and I have known." Albert Eisele, "George Kennan Speaks Out About Iraq," Sept. 26, 2002, History News Network, http://hnn.us/articles/997.html.

31. Nitze, *From Hiroshima to Glasnost,* 465; Mayers, *George Kennan and the Dilemmas of U.S. Foreign Policy,* 54; Thomas Naylor, "George F. Kennan (1904–2005), Godfather of the Vermont Independence Movement," *Vermont Commons,* April 2005, 8. In a 1992 letter to Arthur Schlesinger Jr., Kennan had, as well, seemingly reverted to his earlier views on race. Kennan to Schlesinger, Feb. 18, 1992, folder 5, box 43, GFKP.

32. Wisner's proposed coup de main in Latin America was never carried out. The agency's investigators cleared Frank and the CIA of plotting the murder of Guatemalan Communists. "Report of Questionable Activity in Connection with Project PBSUCCESS," Oct. 11, 1979, CIA/CREST.

33. Author interview with Frank George Wisner, April 30, 2012, New York City.

34. India's nuclear scientists would wait another three years before exploding their next bomb, in 1998, having learned in the meantime to hide their work from prying overhead eyes. "Export of Helium-3 to South Africa," May 12, 1982, "Nuclear Proliferation Document Set," National Security Archive, George Washington University; Liberman, "Rise and Fall of South Africa's Bomb," 45–86; Richelson, *Spying on the Bomb,* 431–33.

35. David Hoffman, *Dead Hand,* 430–32.

36. "Frank Wisner, the Diplomat Sent to Prod Mubarak," *NYT,* Feb. 2, 2011; "Times Topics," *NYT,* May 8, 2013; David Sanger, *Confront and Conceal: Obama's Secret Wars and Surprising Use of American Power* (Crown, 2012), 298–300.

37. Author interview with Frank George Wisner, Oct. 20, 2010, Washington, D.C.; "U.S. Envoy Discusses Kosovo Independence Declaration," Feb. 18, 2008, www.pbs .org/newshour.

38. Himmelman, *Yours in Truth,* 442; Felsenthal, *Power, Privilege, and the "Post,"* 440–48; "Nice Guy, Finishing Last: How Don Graham Fumbled the Washington Post Co.," *Forbes,* Feb. 27, 2012.

39. Graham, *Personal History,* 608–9.

40. Halberstam, *Powers That Be,* 524–25; Felsenthal, *Power, Privilege, and the "Post,"* 364–67, 431–32; "'Katharine Graham Story' Heats Up Washington 'Media War,'" *Chicago Tribune,* Nov. 20, 1978.

41. Felsenthal, *Power, Privilege, and the "Post,"* 368–72; Davis, *Katharine the Great;* Graham, *Personal History,* 586; Heymann, *Georgetown Ladies' Social Club,* 342.

42. One of Carter's former aides, Hamilton Jordan, contritely admitted years later that the snub had probably been a politically costly mistake for the administration. Graham, *Personal History,* 610–12.

43. Heymann, *Georgetown Ladies' Social Club,* 345; Graham, *Katharine Graham's Washington,* 136.

44. Maureen Dowd, "The WASP Descendancy," *NYT,* Oct. 31, 1993.

45. Blumenthal, "Ruins of Georgetown"; "Sally Quinn Announces the End of Power in

Washington," *WP,* June 7, 2012; "A Publisher Stumbles Publicly at the *Post,*" *NYT,* July 4, 2009.

46. At the time it was sold, *Newsweek* was reportedly losing forty million dollars a year; the *Post*'s circulation had dropped by nearly half since its peak in 1993. "Newsweek to Cease Its Print Publication," *WP,* Oct. 19, 2012; "Washington Post to Be Sold to Jeff Bezos, the Founder of Amazon," *WP,* Aug. 5, 2013.

47. Members of today's Washington Club, "that spinning cabal of 'people in politics and media' [have] become part of a system that rewards, more than anything, self-perpetuation," writes the *New York Times Magazine* reporter Mark Leibovich. *This Town,* 7.

48. Author interview with Ward Just; "Alsop House a Standout in Georgetown," *Washington Times,* March 11, 2005. The author thanks Sue Kohler, architectural historian at the U.S. Commission of Fine Arts, and Boucie Addison of Washington Fine Properties for details on the Wisner and Alsop houses.

49. Terry Teachout, "Alsop's Foibles," *Wall Street Journal,* April 25, 2012; Terry Teachout, "A News Columnist with His Own Secret," *Wall Street Journal,* April 27, 2012; Osnos, "Reviving a Forgotten Journalism Icon on Stage"; Alterman, "Newsmaker in Every Sense of the Word."

50. Auburn, *Columnist.*

BIBLIOGRAPHY

Manuscript Collections

Acheson, Dean. Papers. Sterling Library, Yale University.
Alsop, Joseph Wright, V, and Stewart Alsop. Papers. Library of Congress, Washington, D.C.
Alsop, Joseph Wright, V, and Stewart Alsop. Papers. Private collection.
Alsop, Stewart. Papers. Howard Gotlieb Archival Research Center, Boston University.
Block, Herbert. Papers. Library of Congress, Washington, D.C.
Bohlen, Charles. Papers. Library of Congress, Washington, D.C.
Bundy, McGeorge. Papers. John F. Kennedy Presidential Library, Boston.
Burke, Michael. Papers. Howard Gotlieb Archival Research Center, Boston University.
Clifford, Clark. Papers. Library of Congress, Washington, D.C.
Davies, John Paton, Jr. Papers. Private collection.
Digital National Security Archive, nsarchive.chadwyck.com.
　"China and the U.S."
　"The Kissinger Telephone Conversations: A Verbatim Record of U.S. Diplomacy, 1969–1977"
　"Kissinger Transcripts"
　"U.S. Policy in the Vietnam War, 1954–1968"
Dulles, Allen. Papers. Seeley Mudd Library, Princeton University.
Harriman, W. Averell. Papers. Library of Congress, Washington, D.C.
Helms, Richard. Papers. Special Collections Library, Georgetown University.
Kennan, George Frost. Papers. Seeley Mudd Library, Princeton University.
Kennedy, John F. Papers. President's Office Files, John F. Kennedy Presidential Library, Boston.
Lippmann, Walter. Papers. Library of Congress, Washington, D.C.
Lippmann, Walter. Papers. Sterling Library, Yale University.
McGrory, Mary. Papers. Library of Congress, Washington, D.C.
McNamara, Robert. Papers. Library of Congress, Washington, D.C.
Murphy, Charles J. V. Papers. Howard Gotlieb Archival Research Center, Boston University.
National Security Archive, George Washington University, Briefing Books, www.gwu.edu/~nsarchiv.
　"The Beijing-Washington Back-Channel and Henry Kissinger's Secret Trip to China, September 1970–July 1971"
　"The CIA and Hungary, 1956"
　"The CIA's Family Jewels"
　"The Cuban Missile Crisis, 1962: The 40th Anniversary"
　"First Strike Options and the Berlin Crisis, September 1961"

"The Master of the Game: Paul Nitze and U.S. Cold War Strategy from Truman to Reagan"

"The 1956 Hungarian Revolution: A History in Documents"

"Nuclear Proliferation Document Set"

Nitze, Paul H. Papers. Library of Congress, Washington, D.C.

Oppenheimer, J. Robert. Papers. Library of Congress, Washington, D.C.

Schlesinger, Arthur, Jr. Papers. John F. Kennedy Presidential Library, Boston.

Sheehan, Neil. Papers. Library of Congress, Washington, D.C.

Strauss, Lewis L. Papers. Herbert Hoover Presidential Library, West Branch, Iowa.

U.S. Central Intelligence Agency

CIA Records Search Tool (CREST), National Archives and Records Administration, College Park, Md.

Nazi War Crimes and Japanese Imperial Government Disclosure Acts, 1936–2002, RG 263, National Archives and Records Administration, College Park, Md.

U.S. Department of State

Records of the Policy Planning Staff, 1947–1953, RG 59, National Archives and Records Administration, College Park, Md.

U.S. Federal Bureau of Investigation files

Alsop, Joseph Wright V. No. 100–354477.

Wisner, Frank Gardiner. Nos. 62–97311, 65–62278, 100–344488.

U.S. Office of Strategic Services, RG 226, National Archives and Records Administration, College Park, Md.

Vassiliev, Alexander. Papers. Woodrow Wilson International Center for Scholars, Washington, D.C., www.wilsoncenter.org.

Wisner, Frank Gardiner. Papers. Special Collections Library, University of Virginia (in process).

Books, Articles, and Unpublished Manuscripts

Abramson, Rudy. *Spanning the Century: The Life of W. Averell Harriman, 1891–1986.* William Morrow, 1992.

Acheson, Dean. *Present at the Creation: My Years in the State Department.* W. W. Norton, 1969.

Adams, John. *Without Precedent: The Story of the Death of McCarthyism.* W. W. Norton, 1983.

Aldrich, Richard. *The Hidden Hand: Britain, America, and Cold War Secret Intelligence.* John Murray, 2001.

Almquist, Leann G. *Joseph Alsop and American Foreign Policy: The Journalist as Advocate.* University Press of America, 1993.

Alsop, Elizabeth Winthrop. *Don't Knock Unless You're Bleeding: Growing Up in Cold War Washington.* Smashwords ebook, 2013.

Alsop, Joseph. "Evening Among Ruins." *New Yorker,* Jan. 31, 1948.

———. "The Feud Between Stilwell and Chiang." *Saturday Evening Post,* Jan. 7, 1950.

———. "The Foredoomed Mission of General Marshall." *Saturday Evening Post,* Jan. 21, 1950.

———. "I'm Guilty! I Built a Modern House." *Saturday Evening Post,* May 20, 1950.

———. *"I've Seen the Best of It:" Memoirs.* With Adam Platt. W. W. Norton, 1992.

———. "The Most Important Decision in U.S. History—and How the President Is Facing It." *Saturday Review,* Aug. 5, 1961.

———. "The Soviet Will Never Recover." *Saturday Evening Post,* Nov. 24, 1956.

———. "We Opened the Door for the Communists." *Saturday Evening Post,* Jan. 14, 1950.

———. "Why We Can Win in Vietnam." *Saturday Evening Post,* June 4, 1966.

Alsop, Joseph, and Stewart Alsop. "If Russia Grabs Europe." *Saturday Evening Post,* Dec. 20, 1947.

———. "If War Comes . . ." *Saturday Evening Post,* Sept. 11, 1948.

———. "Lament for a Long-Gone Past." *Saturday Evening Post,* Jan. 26, 1957.

———. "Must America Save the World?" *Saturday Evening Post,* Jan. 21, 1948.

———. "Our Own Inside Story." *Saturday Evening Post,* Nov. 8 and 15, 1958.

———. *The Reporter's Trade.* Reynal, 1958.

———. *We Accuse: The Story of Miscarriage of American Justice in the Case of J. Robert Oppenheimer.* Simon & Schuster, 1954.

———. "Why Has Washington Gone Crazy?" *Saturday Evening Post,* July 29, 1950.

———. "Your Flesh *Should* Creep." *Saturday Evening Post,* July 13, 1946.

Alsop, Stewart. *The Center: The Anatomy of Power in Washington.* Hodder and Stoughton, 1968.

———. "Kennedy's Grand Strategy." *Saturday Evening Post,* March 31, 1962.

———. "The Lessons of the Cuban Disaster." *Saturday Evening Post,* June 24, 1961.

———. "The Madness of Mao Tse-tung." *Saturday Evening Post,* Oct. 26, 1963.

———. *Stay of Execution: A Sort of Memoir.* J. B. Lippincott, 1973.

Alsop, Stewart, and Charles Bartlett. "In Time of Crisis." *Saturday Evening Post,* Dec. 8, 1962.

Alsop, Stewart, and Thomas Braden. *Sub Rosa: The OSS and American Espionage.* Harcourt, Brace, 1964.

Alsop, Susan Mary. *To Marietta from Paris, 1945–1960.* Doubleday, 1975.

Alterman, Eric. *Sound and Fury: The Making of the Punditocracy.* Cornell University Press, 1999.

Ambrose, Stephen. *Eisenhower: The President.* Simon & Schuster, 1984.

Anders, Roger, ed. *Forging the Atomic Shield: Excerpts from the Office Diary of Gordon E. Dean.* University of North Carolina Press, 1987.

Arneson, Gordon. "The H-Bomb Decision." *Foreign Service Journal* 46 (May–June 1969).

Auburn, David. *The Columnist.* Faber & Faber, 2012.

Bailey, Thomas. *The Marshall Plan Summer: An Eyewitness Report on Europe and Russians in 1947.* Hoover Institution Press, 1977.

Barrett, David. *The CIA and Congress: The Untold Story from Truman to Kennedy.* University Press of Kansas, 2005.

Behrman, Greg. *The Most Noble Adventure: The Marshall Plan and the Time When America Helped Save Europe.* Free Press, 2007.

Beisner, Robert. *Dean Acheson: A Life in the Cold War.* Oxford University Press, 2006.

Bellows, Jim. *The Last Editor: How I Saved "The New York Times," "The Washington Post," and the "Los Angeles Times" from Dullness and Complacency.* Andrews McMeel, 2002.

Benson, Robert L., and Michael Warner, eds. *VENONA: Soviet Espionage and the American Response.* Central Intelligence Agency, 1996.

Beran, Michael. *The Last Patrician: Bobby Kennedy and the End of American Innocence.* St. Martin's Press, 1998.

Berlin, Isaiah, and Henry Hardy, eds. *Letters, 1928–1946.* Cambridge University Press, 2004.

Berman, Larry. *Perfect Spy: The Incredible Double Life of Pham Xuan An, "Time" Magazine Reporter and Vietnamese Communist Agent.* Smithsonian Books, 2007.

Bernstein, Carl. "The CIA and the Media." *Rolling Stone,* Oct. 20, 1977.

Bernstein, Carl, and Bob Woodward. *All the President's Men.* Simon & Schuster, 1974.

Beschloss, Michael. *The Crisis Years: Kennedy and Khrushchev, 1960–1963.* HarperCollins, 1991.

———. ed. *Reaching for Glory: Lyndon Johnson's Secret White House Tapes, 1964–1965.* Simon & Schuster, 1998.

———. *Taking Charge: The Johnson White House Tapes, 1963–1964.* Simon & Schuster, 1997.

Bethell, Nicholas. *Betrayed.* Times Books, 1984.

Bird, Kai. *The Chairman: John J. McCloy and the Making of the American Establishment.* Simon & Schuster, 1992.

———. *The Color of Truth: McGeorge Bundy and William Bundy, Brothers in Arms.* Touchstone, 1998.

Bird, Kai, and Martin Sherwin. *American Prometheus: The Triumph and Tragedy of J. Robert Oppenheimer.* Knopf, 2005.

Bissell, Richard. *Reflections of a Cold Warrior: From Yalta to the Bay of Pigs.* Yale University Press, 1996.

Blight, J. G., and J. M. Lang. *The Fog of War: Lessons from the Life of Robert S. McNamara.* Rowman & Littlefield, 2005.

Block, Herbert. *Herblock: A Cartoonist's Life.* Macmillan, 1993.

Blumenthal, Sidney. "The Ruins of Georgetown." *New Yorker,* Oct. 21 and 29, 1996.

Bohlen, Charles. *Witness to History, 1929–1969.* W. W. Norton, 1973.

Bower, Tom. *The Red Web: MI6 and the KGB Master Coup.* Aurum Press, 1989.

Braden, Joan. *Just Enough Rope: An Intimate Memoir.* Villard Books, 1989.

Braden, Tom. "The Birth of the CIA." *American Heritage,* Feb. 1977.

———. "I'm Glad the CIA Is 'Immoral.'" *Saturday Evening Post,* May 20, 1967.

Bradlee, Benjamin. *Conversations with Kennedy.* W. W. Norton, 1975.

———. *A Good Life: Newspapering and Other Adventures.* Simon & Schuster, 1995.

Braestrup, Peter. *Big Story: How the American Press and Television Reported and Interpreted the Crisis of Tet in Vietnam and Washington.* Yale University Press, 1983.

Branch, Taylor. *At Canaan's Edge: America in the King Years, 1965–68.* Simon & Schuster, 2006.

———. *Pillar of Fire: America in the King Years, 1963–64.* Simon & Schuster, 1981.

Braudy, Susan. "Camelot's Second Lady." *Vanity Fair,* Feb. 2006.

Bray, Howard. *Pillars of the "Post": The Making of a News Empire in Washington.* W. W. Norton, 1980.

Brown, Anthony C. *The Last Hero: Wild Bill Donovan.* Vintage, 1984.

Buchwald, Art. *Counting Sheep: The Log and the Complete Play.* G. P. Putnam's Sons, 1970.

Buhite, R. D., and W. C. Hamel. "War for Peace: The Question of an American Preventive War Against the Soviet Union, 1945–1955." *Diplomatic History* 14, no. 3 (Summer 1990).

Bullitt, Orville, ed. *For the President: Personal and Secret: Correspondence Between Franklin D. Roosevelt and William C. Bullitt.* Houghton Mifflin, 1972.

Bundy, McGeorge. *Danger and Survival: Choices About the Bomb in the First Fifty Years.* Random House, 1988.

Burke, Michael. *Outrageous Good Fortune.* Little, Brown, 1984.

Cahn, Anne. *Killing Detente: The Right Attacks the CIA.* Pennsylvania State University Press, 1998.

Callahan, David. *Dangerous Capabilities: Paul Nitze and the Cold War.* HarperCollins, 1990.

Campbell, W. Joseph. *Getting It Wrong: Ten of the Greatest Misreported Stories in American Journalism.* University of California Press, 2010.

Casey, Steven. *Selling the Korean War: Propaganda, Politics, and Public Opinion, 1950–1953.* Oxford University Press, 2008.

Chace, James. *Acheson: The Secretary of State Who Created the American World.* Simon & Schuster, 1998.

Colby, William. *Honorable Men: My Life in the CIA.* Simon & Schuster, 1978.

Coleman, David. *The Fourteenth Day: JFK and the Aftermath of the Cuban Missile Crisis.* W. W. Norton, 2012.

Collier, Barnard Law. "The Joe Alsop Story." *New York Times Magazine,* May 23, 1971.

Conant, Jennet. *The Irregulars: Roald Dahl and the British Spy Ring in Wartime Washington.* Simon & Schuster, 2008.

Corke, Sarah-Jane. *U.S. Covert Operations and Cold War Strategy: Truman, Secret Warfare, and the CIA, 1945–53.* Routledge, 2008.

Corson, William. *The Armies of Ignorance: The Rise of the American Intelligence Empire.* Dial Press, 1977.

Costigliola, Frank. *Roosevelt's Lost Alliances: How Personal Politics Helped Start the Cold War.* Princeton University Press, 2012.

Crosswell, D. K. R. *Beetle: The Life of General Walter Bedell Smith.* University Press of Kentucky, 2010.

Cullather, Nick. *Secret History: The CIA's Classified Account of Its Operations in Guatemala, 1952–1954.* Stanford University Press, 2006.

Cummings, Richard. *Cold War Radio: The Dangerous History of American Broadcasting in Europe, 1950–1989.* McFarland, 2009.

Cutler, Robert. *No Time for Rest.* Atlantic Monthly Press, 1965.

Dallek, Robert. *Nixon and Kissinger: Partners in Power.* Harper, 2007.

———. *An Unfinished Life: John F. Kennedy, 1917–1963.* Little, Brown, 2003.

Damms, Richard. "James Killian, the Technological Capabilities Panel, and the Emergence of President Eisenhower's 'Scientific-Technological Elite.'" *Diplomatic History* 24, no. 1 (Winter 2000).

Davies, John Paton, Jr. *China Hand: An Autobiography.* University of Pennsylvania Press, 2012.

———. *Dragon by the Tail: American, British, Japanese, and Russian Encounters with China and One Another.* W. W. Norton, 1972.

Davis, Deborah. *Katharine the Great: Katharine Graham and "The Washington Post."* National Press, 1987.

———. *Party of the Century: The Fabulous Story of Truman Capote and His Black and White Ball.* John Wiley, 2006.

Dean, Robert. *Imperial Brotherhood: Gender and the Making of Cold War Foreign Policy.* University of Massachusetts Press, 2001.

de Margerie, Caroline. *American Lady: The Life of Susan Mary Alsop.* Viking, 2012.

Dobbs, Michael. *One Minute to Midnight: Kennedy, Khrushchev, and Castro on the Brink of Nuclear War.* Knopf, 2008.

———. *Six Months in 1945: FDR, Stalin, Churchill, and Truman—from World War to Cold War.* Knopf, 2012.

Dravis, Michael. "Storming Fortress Albania: American Covert Operations in Microcosm, 1949–1954." *Intelligence and National Security* 7, no. 4 (1992).

Dunlop, Richard. *Donovan: America's Master Spy.* Rand McNally, 1982.

Etzold, Thomas H., and John Lewis Gaddis, eds. *Containment: Documents on American Policy and Strategy, 1945–1950.* Columbia University Press, 1978.

Felix, Christopher [pseud.]. *A Short Course in the Secret War.* Dutton, 1963.

Felsenthal, Carol. *Power, Privilege, and the "Post": The Katharine Graham Story.* G. P. Putnam and Sons, 1993.

Finney, John. "The Long Trial of John Paton Davies." *New York Times Magazine,* Aug. 31, 1969.

FitzGerald, Frances. "The Tragedy of Saigon." *Atlantic Monthly,* Dec. 1966.

Ford, Daniel. *Flying Tigers: Claire Chennault and the American Volunteer Group.* Smithsonian Institution Press, 1991.

Frazier, Ian. *Travels in Siberia.* Farrar, Straus and Giroux, 2010.

Fursenko, Aleksandr, and Timothy Naftali. *Khrushchev's Cold War: The Inside Story of an American Adversary.* W. W. Norton, 2006.

———. *"One Hell of a Gamble": Khrushchev, Castro, and Kennedy, 1958–1964.* W. W. Norton, 1997.

Gaddis, John Lewis. *George F. Kennan: An American Life.* Penguin Press, 2011.

Galbraith, John K. *A Life in Our Times: Memoirs.* Houghton Mifflin, 1991.

Garrow, David. "The FBI and Martin Luther King." *Atlantic,* July/Aug. 2002.

Garthoff, Raymond. *A Journey Through the Cold War: A Memoir of Containment and Coexistence.* Brookings Institution Press, 2001.

Gati, Charles. *Failed Illusions: Moscow, Washington, and Budapest, and the 1956 Hungarian Revolt.* Stanford University Press, 2006.

Gerber, Robin. *Katharine Graham: The Leadership Journey of an American Icon.* Portfolio Press, 2005.

Gill, Brendan. *A New York Life: Of Friends and Others.* Poseidon Press, 1990.

Goodwin, Doris K. *Lyndon Johnson and the American Dream.* Signet Books, 1976.

Graham, Katharine. *Katharine Graham's Washington.* Knopf, 2002.

———. *Personal History.* Vintage, 1998.

Grant, Zalin. "Alsop Lets His Friends Down." *New Republic,* May 18, 1968.

Greenberg, David. *Nixon's Shadow: The History of an Image.* W. W. Norton, 2003.

Greenfield, Meg. *Washington.* Public Affairs, 2001.

Grose, Peter. *Gentleman Spy: The Life of Allen Dulles.* Houghton Mifflin, 1994.

———. *Operation Rollback: America's Secret War Behind the Iron Curtain.* Houghton Mifflin, 2000.

Halberstam, David. *The Best and the Brightest.* Random House, 1972.

———. *The Coldest Winter: America and the Korean War.* Hyperion Books, 2007.

———. *The Fifties.* Villard Books, 1993.

———. *The Powers That Be.* Knopf, 1979.

Haynes, John, Harvey Klehr, and Alexander Vassiliev. *Spies: The Rise and Fall of the KGB in America.* Yale University Press, 2009.

Hazard, Elizabeth. *Cold War Crucible: United States Foreign Policy and the Conflict in Romania, 1943–1953.* Columbia University Press, 1996.

Helms, Cynthia. *An Intriguing Life: A Memoir of War, Washington, and Marriage to an American Spymaster.* Rowman & Littlefield, 2013.

Helms, Richard. *A Look over My Shoulder: A Life in the Central Intelligence Agency.* Ballantine Books, 2003.

Herken, Gregg. *Brotherhood of the Bomb: The Tangled Lives and Loyalties of Robert Oppenheimer, Ernest Lawrence, and Edward Teller.* Henry Holt, 2002.

———. *Counsels of War.* Knopf, 1985.

———. "The Great Foreign Policy Fight." *American Heritage,* April/May 1986.

———. *The Winning Weapon: The Atomic Bomb in the Cold War, 1945–1950.* Knopf, 1981.

Hersh, Burton. *The Old Boys: The American Elite and the Origins of the CIA.* Charles Scribner's Sons, 1992.

Hersh, Seymour. *The Price of Power: Kissinger in the Nixon White House.* Summit Books, 1983.

Heuser, Beatrice. *Western "Containment" Policies in the Cold War: The Yugoslav Case, 1948–53.* Routledge, 1989.

Heymann, C. David. *The Georgetown Ladies' Social Club.* Atria Books, 2003.

Himmelman, Jeff. *Yours in Truth: A Personal Portrait of Ben Bradlee.* Random House, 2012.

Hixson, Walter. *George F. Kennan: Cold War Iconoclast.* Columbia University Press, 1989.

Hoffman, David. *The Dead Hand: The Untold Story of the Cold War Arms Race and Its Dangerous Legacy.* Random House, 2009.

Hoffmann, Joyce. *On Their Own: Women Journalists and the American Experience in Vietnam.* Da Capo Press, 2008.

Holzman, Michael. *James Jesus Angleton, the CIA, and the Craft of Intelligence.* University of Massachusetts Press, 2008.

Hoopes, Townsend, and Douglas Brinkley. *Driven Patriot: The Life and Times of James Forrestal.* Knopf, 1992.

Hunt, Howard. *American Spy: My Secret History in the CIA, Watergate, and Beyond.* John Wiley, 2007.

Ignatieff, Michael. *Isaiah Berlin: A Life.* Henry Holt, 1998.

Immerman, Richard. *The CIA in Guatemala: The Foreign Policy of Intervention.* University of Texas Press, 1982.

Isaacson, Walter. *Kissinger: A Biography.* Simon & Schuster, 1992.

Isaacson, Walter, and Evan Thomas. *The Wise Men: Six Friends and the World They Made.* Simon & Schuster, 1986.

Jeffery, Keith. *The Secret History of MI6, 1909–1949.* Penguin Press, 2010.

Johnson, Haynes, and Harry Katz. *Herblock: The Life and Work of the Great Political Cartoonist.* W. W. Norton, 2009.

Johnson, Ross A. *Radio Free Europe and Radio Liberty: The CIA Years and Beyond.* Stanford University Press, 2010.

Jones, Joseph M. *The Fifteen Weeks: An Insider Account of the Genesis of the Marshall Plan, February 21–June 5, 1947.* Harcourt, Brace, 1955.

Just, Ward. *In the City of Fear.* Viking Press, 1982.

———. *To What End? Report from Vietnam.* Houghton Mifflin, 1968.

Kahn, E. J., Jr. *The China Hands: America's Foreign Service Officers and What Befell Them.* Viking Press, 1975.

Kaplan, Fred. "JFK's First-Strike Plan." *Atlantic Monthly,* Oct. 2001.

———. *The Wizards of Armageddon.* Simon & Schuster, 1983.

Kennan, George Frost. *The Cloud of Danger: Current Realities of American Foreign Policy.* Atlantic Monthly Press, 1977.

———. *Memoirs, 1925–1950*. Pantheon Books, 1967.

———. *Memoirs, 1950–1963*. Little, Brown, 1972.

———. *The Nuclear Delusion: Soviet-American Relations in the Atomic Age*. Pantheon Books, 1983.

———. *Sketches from a Life*. W. W. Norton, 2000.

———. "The Sources of Soviet Conduct." *Foreign Affairs* 25, no. 1 (July 1947).

Kennedy, Caroline, and Michael Beschloss, eds. *Jacqueline Kennedy: Historic Conversations on Life with John F. Kennedy*. Hyperion, 2011.

Kern, Montague, Patricia Levering, and Ralph Levering. *The Kennedy Crises: The Press, the Presidency, and Foreign Policy*. University of North Carolina Press, 1983.

Kindleberger, Charles. *Marshall Plan Days*. Allen & Unwin, 1987.

Kinzer, Stephen. *The Brothers: John Foster Dulles, Allen Dulles, and Their Secret World War*. Times Books, 2013.

Kissinger, Henry. *The White House Years*. Little, Brown, 1979.

Kistiakowsky, George. *A Scientist at the White House: The Private Diary of President Eisenhower's Special Assistant for Science and Technology*. Harvard University Press, 1976.

Kluger, Richard. *The Paper: The Life and Death of the "New York Herald Tribune."* Knopf, 1986.

Knight, Peter. *The Kennedy Assassination*. University of Edinburgh Press, 2007.

Leibovich, Mark. *This Town: Two Parties and a Funeral—plus Plenty of Valet Parking!—in America's Gilded Capital*. Blue Rider Press, 2013.

Liberman, Peter. "The Rise and Fall of South Africa's Bomb." *International Security* 26, no. 2 (Fall 2001).

Lilienthal, David E. *Journals: The Atomic Energy Years, 1945–1950*. Harper & Row, 1964.

Lindsay, Franklin. *Beacons in the Night: With the OSS and Tito's Partisans in Wartime Yugoslavia*. Stanford University Press, 1993.

Loftus, John. *The Belarus Secret*. Knopf, 1982.

Logevall, Fredrik. *Choosing War: The Lost Chance for Peace and the Escalation of War in Vietnam*. University of California Press, 1999.

Lucas, Scott, and Kaeten Mistry. "Illusion of Coherence: George F. Kennan, U.S. Strategy and Political Warfare in the Early Cold War, 1946–1950." *Diplomatic History* 33, no. 1 (Jan. 2009).

Lukas, John. *George F. Kennan: A Study of Character*. Yale University Press, 2007.

Machado, Barry. "Selling the Marshall Plan." George C. Marshall Foundation, 1997.

Mark, Eduard. "The OSS in Romania, 1944–45: An Intelligence Operation of the Early Cold War." *Intelligence and National Security* 9, no. 2 (April 1994).

Marton, Kati. *Enemies of the People: My Family's Journey to America*. Simon & Schuster, 2009.

May, Ernest, and Philip Zelikow, eds. *The Kennedy Tapes: Inside the White House During the Cuban Missile Crisis*. Harvard University Press, 1997.

Mayers, David. *The Ambassadors and America's Soviet Policy*. Oxford University Press, 1995.

———. *George Kennan and the Dilemmas of U.S. Foreign Policy*. Oxford University Press, 1988.

McAuliffe, Mary, ed. *CIA Documents on the Cuban Missile Crisis, 1962*. Central Intelligence Agency, 1992.

Merry, Robert. *Taking On the World: Joseph and Stewart Alsop—Guardians of the American Century*. Viking, 1996.

Miller, Merle. "Washington, the World, and Joseph Alsop." *Harper's,* June 1968.

Millis, Walter, ed. *The Forrestal Diaries.* Viking, 1951.

Miscamble, Wilson. *George F. Kennan and the Making of American Foreign Policy, 1947–1950.* Princeton University Press, 1992.

Morgan, Ted. *A Covert Life: Jay Lovestone, Communist, Anti-Communist, and Spymaster.* Random House, 1999.

Murphy, David, Sergei Kondrashev, and George Bailey. *Battleground Berlin: CIA vs. KGB in the Cold War.* Yale University Press, 1997.

Naftali, Timothy, ed. *The Presidential Recordings: John F. Kennedy: The Great Crises.* Vol. 1. W. W. Norton, 2001.

Nelson, Michael. *War of the Black Heavens: The Battles of Western Broadcasting in the Cold War.* Syracuse University Press, 1997.

Nichols, H. G., ed. *Washington Despatches, 1941–1945: Weekly Political Reports from the British Embassy.* University of Chicago Press, 1981.

Nitze, Paul H. "Atoms, Strategy, and Policy." *Foreign Affairs* 34, no. 2 (Jan. 1956).

———. *From Hiroshima to Glasnost: At the Center of Decision: A Memoir.* Grove, Weidenfeld, 1989.

———. *Tension Between Opposites: Reflections on the Practice and Theory of Politics.* Charles Scribner's Sons, 1993.

Oppenheimer, J. Robert. "Atomic Weapons and American Policy." *Foreign Affairs* 31, no. 4 (July 1953).

Oshinsky, David. *A Conspiracy So Immense: The World of Joe McCarthy.* Oxford University Press, 2005.

Patten, William. *My Three Fathers—and the Elegant Deceptions of My Mother, Susan Mary Alsop.* PublicAffairs, 2008.

Pedlow, Gregory, and Donald Welzenbach. *The CIA and the U-2 Program, 1954–1974.* Center for the Study of Intelligence, 1998.

Philby, Kim. *My Silent War: The Soviet Master Agent Tells His Own Story.* Grove Press, 1968.

Pisani, Sallie. *The CIA and the Marshall Plan.* University Press of Kansas, 1991.

Powers, Thomas. *The Man Who Kept the Secrets: Richard Helms and the CIA.* Knopf, 1979.

Prados, John. *Safe for Democracy: The Secret Wars of the CIA.* Ivan Dee, 2006.

Preble, Christopher. *John F. Kennedy and the Missile Gap.* Northern Illinois University Press, 2004.

Prochnau, William. *Once upon a Distant War: David Halberstam, Neil Sheehan, Peter Arnett—Young War Correspondents and Their Early Vietnam Battles.* Vintage, 1996.

Pusey, Merlo. *Eugene Meyer.* Knopf, 1974.

Reston, James. *Deadline: A Memoir.* Random House, 1991.

Reynolds, Nicholas. "Ernest Hemingway: Wartime Spy." *Studies in Intelligence* 56, no. 2 (June 2012).

Rhodes, Richard. *Arsenals of Folly: The Making of the Nuclear Arms Race.* Knopf, 2007.

Richelson, Jeffrey. *America's Secret Eyes in Space: The U.S. Keyhole Spy Satellite Program.* Harper Business, 1990.

———. *Spying on the Bomb: American Nuclear Intelligence from Nazi Germany to Iran and North Korea.* W. W. Norton, 2006.

Ridder, Walter. "The Brothers Cassandra, Joseph and Stewart." *Reporter,* Oct. 21, 1954.

Riebling, Mark. *Wedge: The Secret War Between the FBI and CIA.* Knopf, 1994.

Ritchie, Donald. *Reporting from Washington: The History of the Washington Press Corps.* Oxford University Press, 2005.

Robarge, David. "'Cunning Passages, Contrived Corridors': Wandering in the Angletonian Wilderness." *Studies in Intelligence* 53, no. 2 (Dec. 2009).

———. "Moles, Defectors, and Deceptions: James Angleton and CIA Counterintelligence." *Journal of Intelligence History* 3, no. 2 (Winter 2003).

Roberts, Chalmers. *In the Shadow of Power: The Story of "The Washington Post."* Seven Locks Press, 1989.

Rudgers, David. "The Origins of Covert Action." *Journal of Contemporary History* 35, no. 2 (2000).

Salisbury, Harrison. *Without Fear or Favor: "The New York Times" and Its Times.* Times Books, 1980.

Sanders, Jerry. *Peddlers of Crisis: The Committee on the Present Danger and the Politics of Containment.* South End Press, 1983.

Saunders, Frances. *The Cultural Cold War: The CIA and the World of Arts and Letters.* New Press, 1999.

Schaller, Michael. *The American Occupation of Japan: The Origins of the Cold War in Asia.* Oxford University Press, 1985.

Schlesinger, Andrew, and Stephen Schlesinger, eds. *The Letters of Arthur Schlesinger, Jr.* Random House, 2013.

Schlesinger, Arthur, Jr. *Journals, 1952–2000.* Penguin Press, 2007.

———. *A Life in the 20th Century: Innocent Beginnings, 1917–1950.* Houghton Mifflin, 2000.

Schroeder, Alice. *The Snowball: Warren Buffett and the Business of Life.* Bantam, 2008.

Seebohm, Caroline. *No Regrets: The Life of Marietta Tree.* Simon & Schuster, 1997.

Sevareid, Eric. *Not So Wild a Dream.* Knopf, 1965.

Shawcross, William. *Sideshow: Kissinger, Nixon, and the Destruction of Cambodia.* Simon & Schuster, 1979.

Sheehan, Neil. *A Bright Shining Lie: John Paul Vann and America in Vietnam.* Vintage, 1988.

———. *A Fiery Peace in a Cold War: Bernard Schriever and the Ultimate Weapon.* Random House, 2009.

Simpson, Christopher. *Blowback: America's Recruitment of Nazis and Its Effects on the Cold War.* Collier Books, 1988.

Smith, Bradley. *The Shadow Warriors: OSS and the Origins of the CIA.* Basic Books 1983.

Smith, Sally B. *Grace and Power: The Private World of the Kennedy White House.* Random House, 2004.

Sorensen, Ted. *Counselor: A Life at the Edge of History.* HarperCollins, 2008.

Spade and Archer Inc. *50 Maps of Washington, D.C.* Simon & Schuster, 1991.

Srodes, James. *Allen Dulles: Master of Spies.* Regnery, 1999.

———. *On Dupont Circle: Franklin and Eleanor Roosevelt and the Progressives Who Shaped Our World.* Counterpoint Books, 2012.

Stacks, John F. *Scotty: James B. Reston and the Rise and Fall of American Journalism.* Little, Brown, 2003.

Steel, Ronald. *Walter Lippmann and the American Century.* Vintage, 1981.

Stern, Sheldon. *Averting "the Final Failure": John F. Kennedy and the Secret Cuban Missile Crisis.* Stanford University Press, 2003.

———. *The Cuban Missile Crisis in American Memory: Myths Versus Reality.* Stanford University Press, 2012.

Steury, Donald, ed. *Intentions and Capabilities: Estimates on Soviet Strategic Forces, 1950–1983.* Center for the Study of Intelligence, 1996.

Streitfeld, David. "The Hawk and the Vultures." *Washington Post,* April 13, 1995.

Tanenhaus, Sam. *Whittaker Chambers: A Biography.* Random House, 1997.

Taubman, Philip. *Secret Empire: Eisenhower, the CIA, and the Hidden Story of America's Space Espionage.* Simon & Schuster, 2003.

Thayer, Charles. *Bears in the Caviar.* J. B. Lippincott, 1951.

———. *Diplomat.* Harper & Row, 1959.

Theoharis, Athan. *J. Edgar Hoover, Sex, and Crime.* Ivan Dee, 1995.

Thomas, Evan. *Ike's Bluff: President Eisenhower's Secret Battle to Save the World.* Little, Brown, 2012.

———. *The Very Best Men: Four Who Dared: The Early Years of the CIA.* Simon & Schuster, 1995.

Thompson, Hunter S. *Fear and Loathing: On the Campaign Trail '72.* Grand Central, 1973.

Thompson, Nicholas. *The Hawk and the Dove: Paul Nitze, George Kennan, and the History of the Cold War.* Henry Holt, 2009.

Treverton, Gregory. *Covert Action: The Limits of Intervention in the Postwar World.* Basic Books, 1987.

Tuchman, Barbara. *Stilwell and the American Experience in China, 1911–1945.* Macmillan, 1971.

Turner, Kathleen. *Lyndon Johnson's Dual War: Vietnam and the Press.* University of Chicago Press, 1985.

U.S. Congress. Senate. Committee on Foreign Relations. *Hearings Regarding the European Recovery Program.* Pt. 2, 80th Cong., 2nd sess. U.S. Government Printing Office, 1948.

———. Senate. Select Committee to Study Governmental Operations with Respect to Intelligence Activities (Church Committee). *Supplementary Detailed Staff Reports on Intelligence Activities and the Rights of Americans,* Bk. 3. 94th Congress, 2nd sess. U.S. Government Printing Office, 1976.

U.S. Department of Defense. *To Defend and Deter: The Legacy of the United States Cold War Missile Program.* U.S. Government Printing Office, 1996.

U.S. Department of State. *Foreign Relations of the United States, 1950–1955: The Intelligence Community.* www.history.state.gov.

———. *Foreign Relations of the United States, 1955–1957.* Vol. 24. U.S. Government Printing Office, 1978.

———. *Foreign Relations of the United States, 1945–1950: Emergence of the Intelligence Establishment.* U.S. Government Printing Office, 1996.

———. *Foreign Relations of the United States, 1949.* Vol. 1. U.S. Government Printing Office, 1976.

———. *Foreign Relations of the United States, 1947.* Vol. 5. U.S. Government Printing Office, 1969.

U.S. Strategic Bombing Survey. *Japan's Struggle to End the War.* U.S. Government Printing Office, 1946.

Wala, Michael. "Selling the Marshall Plan at Home: The Committee for the Marshall Plan to Aid European Recovery." *Diplomatic History* 10, no. 3 (Summer 1986).

Walker, Martin. *The Cold War: A History.* Henry Holt, 1995.

Warner, Michael. "The CIA's Office of Policy Coordination: From NSC 10/2 to NSC 68." *Intelligence and Counterintelligence* 11, no. 2 (Summer 1998).

———, ed. *The CIA Under Harry Truman.* Center for the Study of Intelligence, 1994.

Wasniewski, Matthew. "Walter Lippmann, Strategic Internationalism, the Cold War, and Vietnam, 1943–1967." University Microfilms, 2004.

Weiner, Tim. *Enemies: A History of the FBI.* Random House, 2012.

———. *Legacy of Ashes: The History of the CIA.* Doubleday, 2007.

Weinstein, Allen. *Perjury: The Hiss-Chambers Case.* Random House, 1997.

Weisbrode, Kenneth. *The Atlantic Century: Four Generations of Extraordinary Diplomats Who Forged America's Vital Alliance with Europe.* Da Capo Press, 2009.

West, Morris. *The Ambassador.* William Morrow, 1965.

White, Theodore. *The Making of the President, 1964.* Atheneum, 1965.

Whittell, Giles. *Bridge of Spies.* Broadway, 2010.

Wilford, Hugh. *The Mighty Wurlitzer: How the CIA Played America.* Harvard University Press, 2008.

Wills, Gary. *Bomb Power: The Modern Presidency and the National Security State.* Penguin Press, 2010.

Winks, Robin. *Cloak and Gown: Scholars in the Secret War, 1939–1961.* Quill Press, 1987.

Wise, David. *Molehunt: The Secret Search for Traitors That Shattered the CIA.* Random House, 1992.

Wolfe, Robert. "Gustav Hilger: From Hitler's Foreign Office to CIA Consultant." www.fas.org/sgp/eprint/wolfe.pdf.

Woodward, Bob, and Carl Bernstein. *The Final Days.* Simon & Schuster, 1976.

Wright, C. Ben. "Mr. 'X' and Containment." *Slavic Review* 35, no. 1 (March 1976).

Xiang, Lanxin. "The Recognition Controversy: Anglo-American Relations in China, 1949." *Journal of Contemporary History* 27 (April 1992).

Yoder, Edwin. *Joe Alsop's Cold War: A Study of Journalistic Influence and Intrigue.* University of North Carolina Press, 1995.

Zelikow, Philip, and Ernest May, eds. *The Presidential Recordings: John F. Kennedy: The Great Crises.* Vol. 3. W. W. Norton, 2001.

INDEX

Georgetown houses: Shutterstock
Joe and Stewart Alsop: Bettmann, Corbis
Frank Wisner: Courtesy of the Wisner family
Charles Bohlen, Frank Wisner, Llewellyn Thompson, Philip Graham, Joseph Alsop:
    Courtesy of Elizabeth Wisner Hazard
Philip Graham: Getty Images
Katharine Graham: Bettmann, Corbis
2720 Dumbarton: Courtesy of Susan Mary Alsop and William Patten
Joe Alsop in garden room: Courtesy of Susan Mary Alsop and William Patten
Joseph Wright Alsop, the columnist's namesake: Courtesy of the Joseph Alsop family
Joe Alsop, peering over the top of tortoiseshell glasses: Courtesy of the Joseph Alsop
    family
Susan Mary Alsop at Heron Bay, Marietta Tree's estate in Barbados, 1965: Courtesy of
    Susan Mary Alsop and William Patten
February 1957, U.S. Ambassador to the Soviet Union Charles Bohlen's telegram: Author's
    photo, Library of Congress
Frank Wisner, University of Virginia track team: Courtesy of the Wisner family
Frank Wisner, Romania, 1944–45: Courtesy of the Wisner family
Frank Wisner's Locust Hill farm: Courtesy of the Wisner family
The Wisners and Joyces at the Alhambra fortress: Courtesy of Susan Mary Alsop and
    William Patten
The National Cathedral's Bishop Garden: Author's photo
Bronze plaque in honor of Frank Gardiner Wisner: Courtesy of the CIA History Staff
Carmel Offie at the El Morocco: Special Collections, Yale University Library
CIA headquarters, 1950s: Courtesy of the CIA History Staff
Project Fiend's Team FRIDAY: Courtesy of the National Archives and Records
    Administration
CIA Director Allen Dulles holding the bag: Courtesy of the CIA History Staff
Walter Lippmann, 1961: Courtesy of Susan Mary Alsop and William Patten
George Kennan, 1947: Bettmann, Corbis
Paul Nitze: Getty Images
Richard Bissell: Courtesy of the CIA History Staff
Charles Thayer: Harry S. Truman Library
John Paton Davies: Courtesy of the Davies family
Harriman's 70th birthday: Courtesy of Susan Mary Alsop and William Patten
Herblock with Walter and Marie Ridder: Courtesy of Susan Mary Alsop and
    William Patten

Katharine Graham and Llewellyn "Tommy" Thompson: Courtesy of Susan Mary Alsop and William Patten
Bohlen and JFK: Bettmann, Corbis
JFK: Courtesy of Susan Mary Alsop and William Patten
Jackie: Courtesy of Susan Mary Alsop and William Patten
Richard Holbrooke, Frank George Wisner, and Ward Just: Courtesy of Ward Just
Cambodian border in sports car: Courtesy of Ward Just
Frances "Frankie" FitzGerald's press credentials: Howard Gotlieb Archival Research Center, Boston University
Vietnam: U.S. Army/Library of Congress
Art Buchwald's 1970 Broadway play, *Sheep on the Runway*: Leo Friedman/New York Public Library

A NOTE ABOUT THE AUTHOR

Gregg Herken is professor emeritus of American diplomatic history at the University of California. He is the author of *The Winning Weapon, Counsels of War, Cardinal Choices,* and *Brotherhood of the Bomb.* He and his family live in Santa Cruz, California.

A NOTE ON THE TYPE

This book was set in Adobe Garamond. Designed for the Adobe Corporation by Robert Slimbach, the fonts are based on types first cut by Claude Garamond (c. 1480–1561). It is to him that we owe the letter we now know as "old style."

Composed by North Market Street Graphics, Lancaster, Pennsylvania

Printed and bound by Berryville Graphics, Berryville, Virginia

Designed by Maggie Hinders